R O D A L E ' S
ILLUSTRATED
ENCYCLOPEDIA *of*
HERBS

RODALE'S
ILLUSTRATED ENCYCLOPEDIA

To Rebecca With love, Claire

Hot Pepper & Rosemary Oil

# of HERBS

CLAIRE KOWALCHIK & WILLIAM H. HYLTON, Editors

Writers:

ANNA CARR
CATHERINE CASSIDY
ELLEN COHEN
ALICE DECENZO
MARJORIE HUNT

JUDITH BENN HURLEY
WILLIAM H. HYLTON
CLAIRE KOWALCHIK
SUSAN MILIUS
KIM WILSON

LINDA JACOPETTI, Book Designer
FRANK FRETZ, Illustrator
ALISON MIKSCH, Photographer
KAY LICHTHARDT, Photo Stylist

 Rodale Press, Emmaus, Pennsylvania

The editors would like to thank Holly Harmar Shimizu, curator of the National Herb Garden in Washington, D.C., for her assistance in researching this book.

Printed in the United States of America.
Distributed in the book trade by St. Martin's Press
ISBN 0-87857-699-1 hardcover

28   30   29   27   hardcover

Notice

This book is intended as a reference volume only, not as a medical manual or a guide to self-treatment. We caution you not to attempt diagnosis or embark upon self-treatment of serious illness without competent professional assistance. The information presented here is not intended to substitute for any treatment that may have been prescribed by your physician.

CONTENTS

CONTENTS—continued

ACONITE

Aconitum Napellus   **Ranunculaceae**

The violet-blue, hooded flower of aconite holds great beauty for the garden, but too, that hood shrouds a poison of great power.

HISTORY

Greek legend tells that aconite grew on the hill of Aconitus where Hercules fought with Cerberus, the three-headed dog that guards the entrance to Hades, and from this raging dog's mouths fell foam and saliva onto aconite, giving this plant its deadly poison.

Hecate, a Greek goddess of magic arts and spells, poisoned her father with aconite, and Medea is said to have killed Theseus with it. Aconite has been called love poison. According to legend, women who were fed aconite daily from infancy could poison others through sexual contact.

Outside of legend, men did find use for this plant as a poison. In ancient times, on the island of Ceos in the Aegean sea, poisons made from aconite were given to the old men when they became ill and were no longer useful to the state. Hunters painted arrow tips with aconite and mixed it into bait for use in hunting wolves; hence the plant's common names, wolf's bane or wolfbane. In Europe and Asia, soldiers dropped it into the water supplies along the route of their enemies.

During the Middle Ages, witches had an interesting use for this herb. They mixed it with belladonna in ointments that they rubbed on their bodies for flying. These two herbs are indeed good "flying" herbs. In combination, the irregular heart action produced by aconite and the delirium produced by belladonna surely produced a sensation of flying. Of course, the witches needed to be very careful with such a powerful ointment, or they would have been flying forever.

As evidenced by these stories, aconite certainly produces a physiological effect on the body. However, aconite was not only used as a poison. As a medicinal herb, aconite was introduced to modern medicine in 1763 in Vienna. In 1788, it was added to the *London Pharmacopoeia* and also the first *U.S. Pharmacopoeia.*

USES

So what good is this plant if it is so poisonous? Well, homeopaths and Chinese herbalists still use it medicinally, prescribing infinitesimal dosages. This is perilous work at best. At *your* home, keep this plant in the garden.

Medicinal: Aconite slows the heart, decreases blood pressure, induces sweating, and reduces inflammation. Applied locally, it is

VERY TOXIC

DESCRIPTION

Aconite is a perennial herbaceous plant with a smooth, round, and leafy stem.

Flowers: Violet-blue (white and mauve varieties); "petals" actually 5 sepals, uppermost one in shape of helmet, 2 lateral, 2 lower oblong-oval; in terminal racemes about 6 in. long.

Leaves: Alternate, smooth, dark green on upper surface, light green underneath, palmately lobed; leaves on upper stem 3–5 lobes, those on lower stem 5–7 lobes; lobes are jaggedly toothed.

Fruit: 3, 4, or 5 podlike capsules.

Height: 2–4 ft.

FLOWERING

Late summer and fall.

RANGE

The mountains of France, Switzerland, and Germany; widely cultivated in Europe and North America.

ACONITE POISONING

So acrid is the poison, that the juice applied to a wounded finger affects the whole system, not only causing pains in the limbs, but a sense of suffocation and syncope.

M. Grieve
A Modern Herbal

1

ACONITE—continued

GROWING CONDITIONS

- Plant hardiness zones 2–7.
- Soil pH 5–6.
- Rich, deep, moist soil.
- Partial shade to full sun.

absorbed into the skin and produces a warm, tingling sensation followed by numbness. Liniments containing aconite have been used to relieve rheumatic and neuralgic pains.

Homeopaths use aconite in their remedies, and the Chinese make a drug from the roots of several species of this herb, but because the therapeutic dose is so close to the toxic dose, aconite was long ago deleted from the *U.S. Pharmacopoeia* and the *British Pharmacopoeia*.

Toxicity: Due to the extreme toxicity of this herb, it should never be used for any type of treatment. The entire plant, but especially the root, contains several toxic alkaloids. Aconitine is the most abundant alkaloid; others include picratonitine, aconine, benzoylamine, and neopelline. These alkaloids first stimulate and then depress the central and peripheral nerves. A dose of as little as 5 milliliters of a tincture of aconite may cause death. Cases of poisoning have been reported when the leaves have been mistaken for wild parsley or the roots for horseradish. Even used externally, it may be absorbed in sufficient quantities to cause poisoning.

Ornamental: What gardener could resist planting this intriguing herb? Its curiously shaped flowers, which earned it the nickname monkshood during the Middle Ages, are quite pretty both in the garden and in cut flower arrangements.

Aconite is an excellent addition to perennial flower beds. Because of its height, it can be attractively set in a large group of flowers behind lower growing plants. It blooms late in the summer and fall and can be grown in a lightly shaded area or in direct sun. If you add this plant to your garden, keep children away from it!

CULTIVATION

Aconite can be grown from seed sown in April ½ inch deep. It will flower in two or three years. The easiest and most practical form of propagation is root division. In the autumn of every third or fourth year, dig up the plant and separate and replant the "daughter roots" that have developed at the side of the old roots. The plants should be placed about 18 inches apart.

The tops of aconite should be cut after the plants have been killed by frost. In areas where winters are harsh, cover the beds with branches of evergreens or some other loose, insulating material.

Aconite does not like its roots disturbed and should not be transplanted.

Pests and diseases: Aconite is susceptible to crown rot, powdery mildew, mosaic, verticillium wilt, and cyclamen mite. (See the entry Growing Herbs for information on controlling pests and diseases.)

AGRIMONY

Agrimonia Eupatoria   **Rosaceae**

"Ten minutes 'til showtime!"

The singer uncorks her green bottle and pours half a glass of agrimony water, gargles, then spits in the sink. She pats her mouth dry with the hand towel, paints her lips crimson, then combs her hair one last time. She is ready to sing.

Singers and speakers have been known to gargle with agrimony to clear and refresh their throats before performances. You, too, can use such a gargle to relieve a sore throat from a cold or the flu.

HISTORY

Agrimony's throat-soothing activity is only one of its properties. This herb has been used for many other purposes, and historically, some of those uses are . . . well, a little unusual.

The strangest use of agrimony was in an old remedy for internal hemorrhages. Herbalists mixed it with pounded frogs and a little human blood. This sounds more like a witch's potion than a medicinal remedy.

In ancient Greece, this herb was prescribed for eye complaints. The Anglo-Saxons called agrimony garclive and used it primarily to treat wounds. In Chaucer's time herbalists still prescribed it for wounds. They also mixed it with mugwort and vinegar to treat patients with back pain.

An old English medical manuscript reported:

> If [agrimony] be leyd under mann's heed,
> He shal sleepyn as he were deed;
> He shal never drede ne wakyn
> Till fro under his heed it be takyn.

Currently, no sedative properties have been found in agrimony, but should you want to place a sprig of this herb on your pillow rather than swallow some sleeping pills, well, it's worth a try—at least it is probably safer. Unless, of course, it convinces your spouse that more is wrong with you than insomnia.

At the end of the sixteenth century, herbalists prescribed agrimony remedies for rheumatism, gout, and fevers. In the United States and Canada, up through the late 1800s, agrimony was used to treat digestive problems, bowel complaints, asthma, coughs, and sore throats.

USES

The French drink agrimony tea merely for pleasure, but it also may offer some health benefits.

DESCRIPTION

Agrimony is a hairy, deep green perennial herb with a cylindrical, slightly rough stem bearing a few branches. The whole plant is slightly aromatic, while the flowers themselves have a spicy odor. (See photo on page 169.)

Flowers: Yellow, ⅜ in. across; 5 egg-shaped petals slightly notched at end; 5–12 stamens, grow close and profusely on spike.

Leaves: Alternate, odd pinnate, toothed, and downy; lower leaves 7–8 in. long and have more leaflets; upper leaves 3 in. long with fewer leaflets; leaflets vary in size with small ones alternating between much larger ones; largest leaflets measure 1–1½ in. long.

Fruit: A bristly burr.

Height: To 5 ft.

FLOWERING

July and August.

RANGE

Originally native to Europe, now common in the United States and in parts of Asia. In the western part of the United States, it is found in the middle mountains of southern California and in the north central sections of Arizona.

HABITAT

Woods, sides of fields, waste places, along roadsides and fences.

3

GROWING CONDITIONS

- Plant hardiness zone 7.
- Soil pH: tolerant of wide range of pH.
- Average, dry soil.
- Light shade.

AGRIMONY—continued

Medicinal: Agrimony does have astringent properties, and the tea has been prescribed for internal bleeding and loose bowels. Chinese herbalists have recommended it to stop bleeding of the intestines, of the uterus between menstrual periods, and they have prescribed it for patients with blood cells in their urine. Even the British herbalist Culpeper said that agrimony "helps them that make foul, troubled or bloody water, and makes them part with clear urine speedily." Agrimony is also reputed to help cure problems of the kidney, liver, spleen, and gallbladder. The Zulu use it in cases of tapeworm.

For any of these kinds of problems, you should see your physician rather than just treat yourself at home. However, for minor ailments, teas and poultices made with agrimony can be tried and may be beneficial.

To relieve a sore throat or mouth, try gargling with an infusion of agrimony. Agrimony tea has been drunk to alleviate coughs and to clear skin eruptions. John Lust, author of *The Herb Book,* recommends that you make an infusion from 2 to 4 teaspoons of the dried leaves with 1 cup of water and drink a cup a day.

To heal external sores, you might try a poultice made from the fresh leaves. However, the plant contains certain compounds that react with sunlight, and if a treated area is exposed to the sun, a rash might develop.

In general, though, agrimony appears to be safe to use. James Duke, Ph.D., a botanist with the U.S. Department of Agriculture, rates this herb as safe as coffee, stating that he wouldn't be afraid to drink 2 cups a day.

Ornamental: Agrimony may not produce showy blossoms, but with its high-reaching spikes of small yellow flowers, it can be used attractively in a rock garden or a wildflower border, and of course, the herb garden.

Cosmetic: Because of its astringent properties, agrimony makes a fine lotion for the skin. Reportedly, an agrimony bath soothes aching muscles and joints.

Dye: Agrimony is perhaps best known for the yellow dye that can be made from the leaves and stems. The best yellows are obtained from plants harvested late in the fall. Those harvested earlier produce a yellowish buff color. (See the entry Dyes from Herbs for specific information.)

CULTIVATION

Agrimony is easily started from seed and will self-seed once it is established. Plant seedlings in groups of six or eight with 6 inches between each plant. Agrimony is susceptible to powdery mildew.

ALOE

Aloe spp.   Liliaceae

In the African Congo, the Slukari hunters rub the gel of aloe over their bodies to remove the human scent before they stalk their prey. In many countries, women rub the gel of aloe on their faces to keep their skin fresh and supple. All over the world, men and women rub the gel of aloe on burns to heal the skin.

HISTORY

Aloe reaches far back into time. The Greek historian Dioscorides recorded the use of aloe as a healing herb 2,000 years ago. The gel was applied externally to wounds. It was used to clear blemishes and to maintain healthy skin. People believed it prevented hair loss and so they rubbed it into their scalps. Internally, herbalists prescribed it for stomach disorders, constipation, insomnia, hemorrhoids, headaches, mouth and gum disease, and kidney ailments.

Word of aloe's value as a healing herb spread everywhere. It is said that Alexander the Great conquered Madagascar so that his army had a good supply of the herb for healing wounds.

USES

More and more households these days have a pot of aloe on the kitchen windowsill. This queer little plant from Africa is becoming, deservedly, the number one home remedy for burns and poison ivy.

Medicinal: The skin-saving properties of aloe have both folk-loric and scientific backing. Reports of its healing effects on burns, sores, and poison ivy abound. Such enthusiasm for this herb inspired numerous clinical studies into its efficacy, and scientists have found that aloe has anesthetic, antibacterial, and tissue restorative properties. Aloe gel does indeed heal burns from flame, sun, and radiation. The gel soothes itching and burning. Depending upon the severity of the burn, the tissue regenerates with no scar, and normal pigmentation of the skin returns.

In folk medicine, aloe has been used quite often to treat skin cancer. James Duke, Ph.D., head of a U.S. Department of Agriculture search for plants with cancer-fighting potential, reports, "I have received more letters about this as a folk remedy for skin cancer than any other species."

For its skin-healing properties, aloe has been added to various creams and lotions. It is an ingredient in ointments used to relieve sunburn and burns from X-ray treatment of cancer. Aloe is also added to a benzoin tincture that is used as an antiseptic and a protective coating on abraded, blistered skin and cold sores.

EXTERNAL USE ONLY

DESCRIPTION

Characterized by its rosette of long, tapering, fleshy leaves that exude a mucilaginous sap when broken, aloe comprises more than 300 species. All are perennial and range in size from plants with very short stems to some with stems 20 ft. tall. *Aloe barbadensis* (also known as *A. vera*) is the most common species.

Flowers: Tubular, yellow to orange-red, to 1 in. long; in a raceme atop a 3–4 ft. flower stalk.

Leaves: Pale green or grayish green, narrow, fleshy, spiny, taper to a point; thick, smooth, rubbery epidermis; form main body of plant.

Height: Up to 2 ft.

RANGE

Native to Africa and Mediterranean region; widely cultivated in Egypt, the Near East, Bermuda, the Bahamas, the West Indies, South America, and in southern Florida and Texas. Common domestic houseplant.

ALOE—continued

PATIENT ALOE

In a region of Saudi Arabia around Mecca, the name of aloe, *saber,* means patient. Aloes are considered "patient" plants because they are evergreen and require very little water. Men and women plant them at the edges of graves on a spot facing the epitaph to signify patience during the wait between burial and resurrection.

However, in the case of aloe, it is the natural home remedy that prevails over modern medicine. Fresh aloe gel produces the best results. Studies show that aloe's healing properties dissipate in storage. Stabilizers are added to commercial creams and lotions in order to preserve the efficacy of the gel, but there is good reason to suspect that stabilizers don't work as advertised.

The best way to use this herb is to break off a leaf, slice it down the middle, and apply the gel to the skin. For a burn or sore that needs more than just very minor attention, make a simple poultice by placing the cut leaf on the area and wrapping it with gauze.

Internally, an extract of aloe works effectively as a laxative, but it may cause severe intestinal pain; therefore, it is not used for this purpose very often. Aloe laxative is largely restricted to veterinary use these days. This herb has also been recommended for many other ailments including amenorrhea, asthma, colds, convulsions, hemorrhages, and ulcers. However, no scientific evidence supports the use of aloe for these problems.

Ornamental: The fleshy, spiky leaves give aloe an unusual but attractive appearance. In warm arid or semiarid regions, aloe can be planted outdoors. Place it singly or in groups. An aloe can look stunning set against a building where the wall presents a plain background to show off the stout, pointed leaves. The smaller species are well-suited to rock gardens. Decorate patios, terraces, and windows with aloes, and, of course, aloes make great houseplants.

Cosmetic: Legend tells that Cleopatra massaged fresh aloe gel into her skin every day to preserve her beauty. Josephine, wife of the emperor Napoleon, used a lotion prepared from milk and aloe gel for her complexion.

Aloe reportedly helps to clear acne, and dermatologists have successfully treated oily skin and dandruff with it. Aloe has been added to all sorts of commercial creams and lotions for softening and moisturizing the skin. The gel applied alone may cause some drying of the skin. If this occurs, try mixing a little vitamin E with the gel, or use a moisturizer.

CULTIVATION

Since aloes require a minimum temperature of about 41°F to survive, most people grow them in containers to bring indoors for the winter, or to keep indoors all year-round.

Aloes are easily propagated from suckers or offshoots that grow around the base of the plant. These offshoots can be removed from the main plant when they have grown to 1 to 2 inches for an indoor plant and 6 to 8 inches for an outdoor plant. The easiest way to remove them is to take the plant out of the soil, separate the suckers, and then repot them.

A fertile soil containing some limestone is best, but aloes will also prosper in soil low in nutrients. Drainage is very important, so the soil should not contain large quantities of organic matter. Coarse material added to the soil allows air and water to pass through easily.

Aloes prefer full sun but tolerate some shade. They do not require frequent watering; however, plants that are fully exposed to the sun require a little more water than those in partial shade, or they will become thin and stunted. During the spring and summer, water when the soil has become moderately dry. In the winter, allow the soil to dry completely between waterings.

An aloe will thrive for years in the same pot if it has good soil. The plants seem to grow best when the roots are fairly crowded. Repotting—if you must—is best done in late winter or spring.

When you harvest, cut the outermost leaves first, as these are the oldest. The plant produces new leaves from its center.

Pests and diseases: If you find little white tufts of waxy wool on your aloe, it's a sign that mealy bugs have infested your plant. Root mealy bugs also sometimes attack aloes. (See the entry Growing Herbs for information on controlling pests and diseases.)

ALOE EYE DROPS

Aren't those sunglasses doing a good job protecting your eyes?

Soon you may be using aloe eye drops instead of sunglasses. Neville Baron, M.D., an ophthalmologist in Secaucus, New Jersey, has found evidence that an aloe extract absorbs damaging ultraviolet rays, and he suggests aloe may be the source of the "miracle eye drop of the twentieth century." People with cataracts, degeneration of the retina, or abnormalities of the lens may be helped by aloe eye drops, and those with normal eyes may be protected from ultraviolet damage by using them.

The experience of another physician, Derry Lawrence, M.D., of Corpus Christi, Texas, seems to support Dr. Baron's enthusiasm. Dr. Lawrence, an amateur welder, uses aloe to heal his eyes from occasional flash burns of the conjunctiva. In a letter to the *New England Journal of Medicine,* he reported that "the clear gel from freshly broken or cut aloe vera leaf is sterile and soothing; in one or two direct instillations into the affected eye or eyes, it brings rapid, total symptomatic relief and seems to speed healing."

GROWING CONDITIONS

- Plant hardiness zone 10.
- Soil pH: neutral.
- Average, well-drained soil.
- Full sun to light shade.

AMERICAN HELLEBORE

Veratrum viride   **Liliaceae**

If you come stumbling across this plant in the woods, just recover your footing and move on, unless you are looking for a stout, leafy herb for a shady portion of your garden. Actually, you are more likely to bump into this plant than stumble over it as it can reach 8 feet in height. The history of American hellebore is rich with medicinal importance, but that is exactly where its medicinal use should remain—in history—at least for the home herbalist. *Veratrum viride* will make you quite ill if you ingest any part of it.

HISTORY

The American Indians and early colonists found medicinal uses for it, using the rhizome primarily. They dried it and ground it to a powder. To treat a wound, the Indians would spread animal fat on the injury, then sprinkle powdered hellebore on top of that. The powder was put on cavities to relieve toothaches—a possibly deadly treatment. American settlers sliced the rhizome, boiled it with vinegar, and applied the resulting fluid to external rashes and sores. To remove lice, they made a strong decoction, which was combed through the hair.

The medicinal use of American hellebore became more important during the eighteenth and nineteenth centuries when it was classified as an analgesic and prescribed for such ailments as epilepsy, convulsions, pneumonia, and peritonitis. It was also recommended by herbalists as a cardiac sedative and occasionally as an appetite stimulant.

In 1862, American hellebore became known in England where doctors prescribed it for respiratory problems, convulsions, neuralgia, and headaches.

USES

American hellebore does have some use in modern medicine, but that is limited because of its toxicity.

Medicinal: According to James Duke, Ph.D., author of *The CRC Handbook of Medicinal Herbs,* the Soviets steep American hellebore in vodka and drink it to alleviate the pain of rheumatism and sciatica. Whether it is the hellebore or the vodka that relieves the pain is uncertain. Sounds like a good excuse to drink vodka.

American hellebore does have more "official" medicinal uses. The herb contains several ester alkaloids that affect physiology by lowering both systolic and diastolic blood pressure, slowing the heart rate, and stimulating blood flow in the kidneys, liver, and

VERY TOXIC

DESCRIPTION

American hellebore is a stout, unbranched perennial with a leafy, hairy, cylindrical stem. The flowers are borne at the top of the plant.

Flowers: Develop on terminal panicle, up to 2 ft. long; downy; greenish-yellow; 3 sepals; 3 petals; 1 in. wide; 6 stamens; accompanied by a downy, pointed bract.

Leaves: Alternate, bright green, oval or elliptical, pointed, downy, gradually decrease in size as they ascend, 6–12 in. long, 3–6 in. wide, bases of leaves overlap and surround stem.

Fruit: 3-celled, 1 in. long, split open when ripe, seeds are flat and winged.

Height: 2–8 ft.

FLOWERING

Midsummer.

RANGE

Indigenous from Canada to the Carolinas. It is more abundant in the northern regions, found in Alaska and the mountains of Idaho, Oregon, and Washington, but has been spotted as far south as Georgia.

HABITAT

Swamps, woods, wet meadows, stream edges.

extremities. Because of these properties, extracts of American hellebore are mixed with other chemicals in drugs used to treat hypertensive toxemia during pregnancy and pulmonary edema in serious cases of acute hypertension.

Toxicity remains a problem, however. The effective medicinal dose comes close to the toxic dose, so the herb has drifted in and out of favor with the medical establishment. It was out of favor until the 1950s, when new techniques allowed the drug derived from this herb to be used more safely. In addition, scientists discovered properties in American hellebore that lowered blood pressure, and it became quite popular for such applications. Today, it still is used occasionally for lowering blood pressure in emergency situations, but once again, other, safer treatments are favored.

Homeopaths still make use of American hellebore. They prepare tinctures from the fresh root and prescribe it for many illnesses and ailments including amenorrhea, fever, flu, headache, measles, and pneumonia.

Toxicity: This herb should *never* be used at home. Ingestion of American hellebore can cause burning in the throat, impaired vision, abdominal pain, nausea, diarrhea, faintness, shallow breathing, spasms, loss of consciousness, paralysis, and sometimes death. Since American hellebore is not quickly absorbed but does quickly cause vomiting, death rarely occurs. *Don't* take this as encouragement to experiment with it as medicine. Even if you don't die from ingesting the plant, the effects will make you think you are.

Ornamental: As frightening as American hellebore sounds, it offers a striking appearance in the garden. The flowers, although they don't blast color from the top of the stem, do form attractive panicles, and the bright green foliage is quite handsome. According to herb folklorist Cyrus Hyde, American hellebore was a traditional part of the Pennsylvania Dutch herb garden, and it was often placed in the center of a formal plot.

American hellebore likes the shade, so if you are looking for a plant for a shady spot (and it is difficult to find many), try growing American hellebore. It is well-suited to wildflower gardens, woodland settings, and, of course, the herb garden. Remember its height, and place it in back of shorter herbs and flowers.

CULTIVATION

You can propagate American hellebore by division or seed. Be sure to plant it in a moist, shady location where it grows easily, requiring little care. Full sun can burn the foliage.

GROWING CONDITIONS

- Plant hardiness zone 4.
- Moist soil.
- Light shade.

9

SUSPECTED CARCINOGEN

DESCRIPTION

Angelica resembles celery somewhat and has a similar fragrance. Hence, it has been called wild celery. Its stem is stout, round, hollow, and purplish in color, and it divides into many branches. (See photo on page 444.)

Flowers: Tiny white or greenish flowers in globe-shaped compound umbel; umbel 2–6 in. across; honeylike fragrance.

Leaves: Pinnate with coarsely toothed oval leaflets, 1–3 in., terminal leaflet 3-lobed; long leafstalks.

Fruit: Oblong, contains two yellow, winged seeds.

Height: 5–8 ft.

FLOWERING

June and July.

RANGE

Native of Europe and Asia; widely cultivated in other countries including the United States.

HABITAT

By the sea and streams; in marshes, swamps, and moist meadows; and by mountain brooks.

ANGELICA

Angelica Archangelica   Umbelliferae

Angelica is a storied herb, in more ways than one. Many tales surround it, tales both of its angelic nature and of its pagan associations, of its healing powers and its wonderful taste, as well as those of its potential hazards. Many of these stories, of course, are merely gossip, fun to listen to and to tell.

But there's also the tall tale of angelica, or rather the tale of tall angelica. It's about a plant that towers as high as 8 feet—a full residential story—at maturity. For an herb—we're not talking tree here—angelica is a remarkably tall plant, one that stands out in any herb garden.

HISTORY

Throughout history, angelica has been a standout herb. Consider the gossipy story surrounding its name. The plant allegedly blooms every year on May 8, the feast day of St. Michael the Archangel. Well, the Latin name of angelica is *Angelica Archangelica,* and you can see the connection. The connection was probably the beginning of its reputation as an angelic plant with magical powers of healing and protection, too.

Another tale is set in early summer in the lake region of what used to be Latvia. Peasants march into the towns, their arms laden with angelica for sale. They are chanting ancient songs *whose words they do not understand.* Is this a holy ritual gone pagan? Is it a tradition maintained since pre-Christian times? If they know the words to the songs, why don't they know what they mean? What's the significance of the angelica? Why not some other plant? Mysterious it is, but such is the history of angelica.

Angelica was supposed to ward off evil spirits and witches. Peasants would make necklaces of the leaves for their children to wear to protect them. The juice of the roots was used to make Carmelite water, considered a "sovereign remedy," and drunk to ensure a long life and to protect against the poisons and spells of witches.

Legend has it that in 1665, the year of the great plague, a monk met an angel in his dreams. The angel told him that angelica could cure the plague. Appropriately angelica water became an ingredient in an official remedy published by the College of Physicians in London and called "the King's Majesty's Excellent Recipe for the Plague." The recipe called for nutmeg, treacle, and angelica water to be beaten together and heated over a fire. Those suffering from the plague were to drink this twice a day.

Angelica remedies were taken for rabies, colic, to induce urination, and for pleurisy, coughs, and other diseases of the lungs. Prepared in a syrup, it was considered a digestive aid, and to "help dimness of sight and deafness," the juice of angelica was poured into the ears.

By the end of the seventeenth century, the use of angelica as a medicinal plant had declined considerably, but it was still prescribed for a few problems such as flatulence. The decline didn't stop the British from adding it to their pharmacopoeia in 1934.

The American Indians used angelica for many medicinal problems: to discharge mucus from the respiratory tract, to induce vomiting, and to cure consumption and tuberculosis. They mixed poultices from angelica and the leaves of *Artemisia canadensis,* a sagebrush, to place on the side of the body opposite a pain in order to relieve that pain. These poultices were also applied to swellings. The Indians of the Rocky Mountains made decoctions and teas from angelica root and drank them as tonics and to build up strength after an illness.

USES

While magical qualities clearly have been associated with this herb for a long time, its many properties and uses are very real. The stem can be steamed and eaten like asparagus; the leaves brewed into a fine tea; the oil of the root added to the bathwater for a relaxing soak; and these are only a few of its uses.

Medicinal: The medicinal use of angelica today centers on the treatment of digestive and bronchial problems. A decoction of the root or the seeds is used to treat indigestion, gastritis, inflammation of the intestines, and flatulence. A simple infusion of the leaves is reported to aid digestion. Try a cup of angelica tea after dinner.

Perhaps the Indians were right to have used angelica to treat a congested respiratory tract; it is used today to cure bronchial colds. The root reportedly has expectorant and diaphoretic properties.

A decoction of the root or an infusion of the leaves was also drunk as a tonic and to relieve insomnia, and it was recommended for promoting menstrual flow and to induce abortions. The plant has been used to treat nervous headaches, fevers, skin rashes, wounds, rheumatism, and toothaches. At one time the seeds were even thought to contain antimalarial properties.

Michael Moore, author of *Medicinal Plants of the Mountain West,* recommends a teaspoon of the root or seeds boiled or steeped in a cup of water.

CHEF TIPS

- When stewing rhubarb, substitute one-quarter of the amount with peeled, chopped, fresh angelica stem.

- Peel and chop fresh angelica stems and roast with onions and pork.

- When simmering pumpkin, squash, or sweet potato, add a bouquet garni of fresh or dried angelica leaf and bay leaf to the cooking water.

A POISONOUS LOOK-ALIKE

Unless you like to live dangerously and are willing to risk poisoning, you are better off not gathering angelica in the wild. Water hemlock, *Cicuta maculata,* can and has been mistaken for *Angelica atropurpurea.* Both grow in the same type of habitat. If you do find a group of plants that resemble angelica, contact a botanist through a local university who could help you to identify it.

ANGELICA—continued

While all these decoctions and infusions are being recommended by herbalists, the effectiveness of angelica in any of them has yet to be scientifically proven, and its safety is being debated.

Toxicity: Generally, angelica has been considered safe in small doses, but differences of opinion do exist. Botanist James Duke, Ph.D., author of the *CRC Handbook of Medicinal Herbs,* considers angelica as dangerous as coffee (but no more so), while pharmacognosist Varro Tyler, Ph.D., author of *The Honest Herbal,* cites evidence of angelica's carcinogenicity and emphatically recommends *not* using angelica as a drug. The U.S. Food and Drug Administration still considers it safe for food use.

Culinary: Licorice lovers enjoy angelica. Its sweet and hardy flavor permeates the fresh or dried leaves, stem, root, and seeds of the plant.

Add the fresh leaves to green salads, fruit soups, savory soups, hearty meat stews, or garnish a dish with them. When dried and ground, the leaves zip up the flavor in desserts and pastries. Gently press them in before glazing and baking.

The dried, ground root has a taste similar to the leaves but is bolder and earthier. This flavor works well in yeast breads, quick breads, cakes, muffins, and cookies.

However, the most celebrated part of angelica is its stem. Candy the stem and savor it alone, or use it to decorate cakes, tarts, and puddings. It may be unique to your neighbors, but candied angelica stems have been enjoyed for years.

In Iceland, the stems and roots are eaten raw with butter. Cut them and prepare them like asparagus.

And in the middle of the afternoon, during that long, slow hour between two and three, make tea from the dried leaves. Enjoy the tea, have a couple of angelica cookies, and relax.

Many uses exist for angelica in the home, but this herb has important commercial culinary value as well. The root and seeds are used to flavor herb liqueurs such as Benedictine and Chartreuse, and the root is a flavoring ingredient in gin and vermouth.

Available commercially: Candied stem, but difficult to find.

Substitute: For flavor, use ground anise seed. For decorative candied stems, use candied violets.

Aromatic: Angelica has a pleasant fragrance. To freshen a musty room, you can make a sort of incense from angelica: Burn the seeds or pieces of the dried root over a low flame. Add the dried leaves to potpourris or herb pillows.

For the bath, this herb adds a pleasant scent, and it is said to calm the nerves. So if you've had a particularly stressful day, try soaking in angelica waters. Maybe you will feel a little angelic yourself.

Commercially, the essential oil of angelica is added to perfumes, creams, soaps, ointments, shampoos, and oils.

Ornamental: Angelica does make a striking border plant, due to its remarkable height and its globe-shaped umbels, but keep that height in mind. You don't want to hide any herbs behind it.

Dye: Angelica produces a dark green in wool mordanted with iron.

Other: Oils from the roots of *A. Archangelica* have been added to tobacco to give flavor to cigarettes. Arkansas Indians also mixed the root of *A. atropurpurea* with tobacco.

CULTIVATION

The best way to propagate angelica is by seed. Division and propagation with offshoots do not work as well. Do not cover the seeds when sowing; they need light to germinate. The conventional wisdom is that you must sow the seeds as soon as they ripen, for their viability is short-term. Tom De Baggio of Earthworks Herb Garden Nursery reports, however, that he has been able to maintain the viability of seeds for more than a year by storing them in an airtight container in the refrigerator. Make sure the seeds are thoroughly dry before storing; they develop mold easily.

Angelica may be sown in a seed bed, then transplanted the next year to a nursery bed or a permanent site. Plants should be 1½ feet apart in a nursery bed and 3 feet apart in the garden.

Angelica is listed in *Hortus Third* as both a biennial and a perennial herb, but it isn't really either. It dies after flowering and producing one crop of seeds (which is why it isn't strictly a perennial). Flowering and seed production usually—but not always—occur in the second or third year, but its cycle is easily disrupted by cutting the flower stalks every year before the seeds form. The plant will continue to grow for many years. This effectively makes the plant a perennial biennial, doesn't it?

Pests and diseases: This herb may grow pest-free and disease-free, but then again it may not. Check your plants periodically for spider mites, leaf miners, earwigs, and aphids. If the summer has been particularly wet, crown rot may develop. (See the entry Growing Herbs for information on controlling pests and diseases.)

Harvesting and storage: The time for harvesting depends on what is to be gathered. Harvest roots in the fall of the first year; stems and leaves in the spring of the second year; and seeds when ripe.

**BETTER THAN
A COLD SHOWER?**

At one time, it was thought that taking a glass of wine containing a small quantity of powdered dried angelica root would cool sexual desire. Perhaps simply the wine subdued the passion.

OTHER SPECIES

Angelica atropurpurea grows wild in swampy areas in North America from Newfoundland to Delaware and Minnesota. It resembles *A. Archangelica* but is a little smaller, produces fewer branches, and is a little paler in color.

It is used medicinally in the same ways as *A. Archangelica*. However, *A. Archangelica* is the species most widely cultivated in herb gardens in the United States.

GROWING CONDITIONS

- Plant hardiness zone 3.
- Soil pH 6.3.
- Rich, moist, well-drained soil.
- Partial shade.

ANISE

Pimpinella Anisum   **Umbelliferae**

If a better mousetrap is ever developed, it just may use anise as the bait. Most people don't think of anise in terms of its popularity with mice, but in the sixteenth century, anise found wide application as mousetrap bait. According to several old herbals, the mice found it irresistible. Of course, many humans find anise irresistible, too, for it has a wide variety of applications in cooking and medicine.

HISTORY

Anise has been fascinating humans for much of recorded history. In the sixth century B.C., Pythagoras, the mathematician and philosopher, apparently spent some time contemplating the use of anise. He believed that simply holding this herb could prevent seizures in epileptics. (No wonder he is best known as a mathematician.) One century later, Hippocrates prescribed a more reasonable use for anise. He recommended it for coughs.

The Roman scholar Pliny stated that anise "removed all bad odors from the mouth, if chewed in the morning," a use that is still recommended today. Pliny also believed that the herb helped to maintain a youthful appearance, and he may have been the source of the idea that anise could prevent bad dreams if kept near the bed at night.

The Romans widely cultivated anise for its fragrance, flavor, and medicinal properties. They mixed the seeds with other savory spices and with meal to make a cake called *mustaceum*. The practical Romans got two benefits from this *mustaceum:* it was a digestive aid and a flavorful dessert, and anise contributed to both uses. *Mustaceum* was often served after heavy meals, including wedding feasts. Some believe that the tradition of the modern wedding cake is an outgrowth of this early Roman custom.

Because of the value of anise, it became one of the spices used by the Romans to pay taxes. In England, in 1305, King Edward I did the Romans one better and levied an import tax on the herb itself. Despite its popularity, it was not cultivated in England until the middle of the sixteenth century.

USES

Anise has remained irresistible to this day as a medicinal, culinary, and aromatic herb.

Medicinal: If the Romans didn't start the tradition of the wedding cake, they may at least have begun anise's long reputation as a digestive aid. Anise is still widely recommended for improving di-

DESCRIPTION

Anise is an annual herb that somewhat resembles Queen Anne's lace. The flowering umbels bloom at the top of a round, grooved stem.

Note that the leaves of seedlings are rounded and toothed, but develop a feathery appearance in the mature plant.

Flowers: In compound umbels, small, yellowish white, five petals, five stamens, two styles.

Leaves: Long stalks; lower leaves roundish, heart-shaped, coarsely toothed; upper leaves feathery, divided pinnately or have three narrow lobes; leaflets may be toothed or toothless.

Fruit: Flattened, oval, downy, gray-brown seeds; ⅛ in. long; lengthwise ribs.

Height: 2 ft.

FLOWERING

Summer.

RANGE

Native to Egypt and the Mediterranean region. Cultivated in Europe, India, Mexico, Russia, and the United States.

gestion and preventing flatulence. However, if you don't feel like making *mustaceum,* a simple tea will do. Crush the seeds and steep a teaspoon in a cup of boiled water for about ten minutes. Drink the tea a sip at a time. This is a pleasant and relaxing way to finish a large meal, and the benefits of preventing indigestion and flatulence certainly make it worthwhile.

Hippocrates' recommendation to take anise for coughs is also heeded today. The essential oil of the seed is said to work as a mild expectorant, which may be due to the direct effects of the oil on the secretory cells of the respiratory tract. Anise also has a mild antimicrobial action, which is another reason why it has been used as an ingredient in cough syrups and lozenges. However, the primary reason for adding anise to cough medications is for its flavor, which cough sufferers enjoy and which masks the bitter tastes of other ingredients.

A long list of medicinal properties has been ascribed to anise, and it has been used in folk medicine for a similarly long list of ailments. None of these properties or uses has been examined scientifically, however.

Culinary: As the loftiest of licorices, anise imparts a refined and consistent flavor to foods. The seed can be used whole or ground as needed. It mingles well with eggs, stewed fruit, cheese, spinach, and carrots. Scandinavian, Greek, East Indian, Moroccan, and Arabic cuisines have all made good use of anise. It is also popular in Hispanic cookery, especially in soups and stews, and it intensifies the sweetness in pastries, cakes, and cookies. Cinnamon and bay complement anise, and together they make duck, pork, fish, and game irresistible.

The leaves also can be used. Chop them and add them to salads, or use them whole as a garnish. Dry them to make tea.

One of the most noted uses of anise is as a flavoring in various liqueurs. Combine equal parts of anise, coriander, and fennel seed in sugared vodka, and you have anisette. Farrel's Rosehip and Anise Liqueur mixes anise, rosehips, sugar water, and vodka. Anesone is a liqueur similar to anisette, but stronger and sweeter. Several other anise liqueurs are made in countries all over the world. The French make *pastis;* the Spaniards, *ojen;* the Puerto Ricans, *tres castillos;* the Turks, *raki;* the Latin Americans, *aguardiente;* and, of course, *ouzo* is made in Greece.

Available commercially: Whole seed and ground, but whole seed is preferable.

Substitute: Fennel seed and leaf.

Aromatic: To enjoy the fragrance of anise oil, crush the seeds and add them to a sachet. Commercially, the oil is used to scent

CHEF TIPS

- Create a wonderful cheese by combining 1 cup creamed cottage cheese with 1 tablespoon minced fresh anise leaf, ½ teaspoon ground anise seed, and ½ teaspoon Dijon mustard.

- Substitute anise seed for caraway seed in bread and cracker recipes.

- When making court bouillon or fish stock, add anise seed to taste.

STAR ANISE

This evergreen grows as a bush or small tree and is native to China. The star-shaped fruit contains an essential oil with very similar properties and uses as those of anise oil. Commercially, it is often used as a substitute for anise.

GROWING CONDITIONS

- Soil pH 6.0.

- Poor, light, dry, well-drained soil.

- Full sun.

15

ANISE—continued

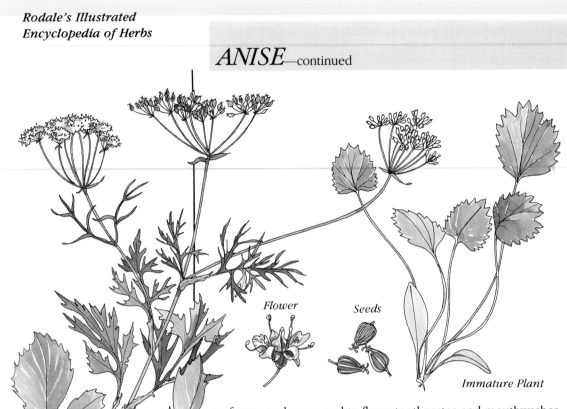

Flower   *Seeds*

Immature Plant

perfumes and soaps and to flavor toothpastes and mouthwashes.

Companion planting: Anise reportedly enhances the growth of coriander when planted nearby.

Other: What catnip is to cats, anise is to dogs; they love the scent of this herb. For drag hunting, a sack saturated with oil and dragged across the countryside provides a scent for foxhounds to follow. In greyhound racing, the artificial hare is scented with anise.

CULTIVATION

Anise has a long taproot, which makes transplanting difficult, so it is best to grow the plants from seed. Seeds should be sown in the spring in rows that are spaced 2½ to 3 feet apart. The seeds require a temperature of 70°F to germinate. Thin the seedlings to a distance of 1½ feet. Easy to care for, anise demands only a weed-free home in a sheltered location. Its growth is spindly; it is easily wind damaged.

Harvesting and storage: Harvest the seeds by cutting the whole seed heads after they have ripened, but before they have broken open. Clip them into a bag or container so the seeds do not scatter.

To store anise seeds, first dry them on a piece of paper or cloth laid in the sun or placed indoors in a dry area near moderate heat. Once they have dried, place them in tightly sealed containers. If you distill the oil for storage, keep it also in a tightly sealed container away from excessive heat.

ARNICA

Arnica montana   Compositae

Suppose you spent the whole day yesterday helping your best friend move into a new apartment—on the third floor. Today, every muscle in your body aches. Well, gather some arnica flowers, and cook them with oil or lard. Soon you'll have a soothing ointment that will help those aches and pains to fade away.

The soothing qualities of arnica have been known for quite some time both in Europe and North America. While European herbalists concocted remedies from *Arnica montana,* American Indians made healing ointments and tinctures with native species. A salve made from arnica helped to relax stiff muscles, and a tincture was used to treat wounds. In 1820, arnica was officially added to the *U.S. Pharmacopoeia* and is still listed in the *U.S. Dispensatory.*

USES

Recipes for healing liniments and salves continue to be passed on, for they really do work. In Germany, more than 100 drug preparations contain arnica. It is also an important homeopathic remedy.

Medicinal: An arnica ointment relieves the pain and reduces the inflammation of sprains and bruises. A 1981 German study found two substances in this herb, helenalin and dihydrohelenalin, that produce anti-inflammatory and analgesic effects.

To make a liniment, heat 1 ounce of flowers in 1 ounce of lard or oil for several hours. Strain and let the ointment cool before applying it to bruises or sore muscles.

Toxicity: The helenalin in arnica may cause dermatitis in some individuals. If this occurs, it is advised that you discontinue use. Otherwise, arnica is perfectly safe to use externally.

The internal use of this herb, however, is another matter. Taken internally, arnica can be quite poisonous. Varro Tyler, Ph.D., reports in *The Honest Herbal:* "Scientific studies of the effects of alcoholic extracts of arnica on the heart and circulatory system of small animals have verified the folly of using the drug internally for self-medication. Not only did it exhibit a toxic action on the heart, but in addition, it caused very large increases in blood pressure. More recent studies have confirmed arnica's cardiac toxicity."

CULTIVATION

Arnica may be propagated from division, cuttings, or seeds. It prefers an acid soil but will grow in most soils, as long as they are well drained. *A. montana* needs full sun. Other species of arnica prefer full sun but will tolerate light shade. *A. cordifolia* and *A. latifolia* are two that grow best under a little shade.

EXTERNAL USE ONLY

DESCRIPTION

Arnica is a true perennial herb. Its stem is round and hairy and ends in one to three flower stalks, each bearing a daisylike blossom.

Flowers: Yellow-orange ray flowers surrounding a disk of tubular flowers in the center, 2–3 in. across.

Leaves: Entire, bright green, toothed, somewhat hairy on upper surface; lower leaves ovate with rounded tips, ciliated, up to 5 in. long; upper leaves smaller and lance-shaped, opposite and attached directly to stem.

Fruit: Bristly achenes.

Height: 1–2 ft.

FLOWERING

Midsummer.

RANGE

Indigenous to the mountains of Europe and Siberia; naturalized in cultivation in North America; *Arnica fulgens* and *A. sororia* native to southwestern Canada and the western United States; *A. cordifolia* grows from Alaska to New Mexico and Arizona and southern California.

GROWING CONDITIONS

- Soil pH 4.0.
- Sandy, humusy, dry soil.
- Full sun.

17

AUTUMN CROCUS

Colchicum autumnale   **Liliaceae**

The autumn crocus . . . it grows only about 12 inches high. The flowers bloom in September, showing simple lavender or light pink segments. A plant gentle in appearance, it is powerful in action, deadly powerful.

Autumn crocus contains colchicine, a strong gout-healing drug and, more significantly, one of the most powerful poisons known to man. As the English herbalist William Turner described it in 1563, "much of it is stercke poyson, and will strongell a man and kill him in the space of one day." Autumn crocus produces a "fire in the throat and mouth," "a terrible unquenchable thirst," and "anguishing colic and bloody diarrhoea."

HISTORY

The ancient Greeks and Romans knew the powers of this plant. They prepared medicinal remedies to treat gout and other illnesses. Actually, the Egyptians may have used the autumn crocus to treat gout 4,000 years ago. However, medicinal use declined once people found out how poisonous this plant was. Then instead of using autumn crocus to heal, they used it to kill.

The corm would be ground into a powder and used to poison targets of enmity. Wine was often the vehicle. The Greek naturalist Theophrastus wrote that when slaves became angry with their owners, they ingested tiny bits of the corm to make themselves ill and thus unable to work.

Off and on over the centuries, autumn crocus has been a medicine. From 1618 to 1639 the corm was listed in the *London Pharmacopoeia.* After being out of established use for nearly 150 years, it was put back in the pharmacopoeia in 1788.

USES

Autumn crocus has proven itself a great healing herb, but a potentially dangerous one. Don't experiment; keep it in the garden.

Medicinal: The oldest use of autumn crocus prevails today. The alkaloid colchicine is extracted from the corm and the seeds of this plant and prescribed either in tablet form or intravenously for patients with gout, a form of arthritis. Colchicine aborts an oncoming attack and prevents a recurrence. No other forms of arthritis are treated with this drug.

In Egypt and Israel doctors have had great success treating familial Mediterranean fever with colchicine. This disease occurs quite frequently in these two countries and is characterized by fever and pains in the abdomen, joints, and chest.

Scientists once hoped that colchicine would provide a cure for

---

VERY TOXIC

DESCRIPTION

The autumn crocus is a perennial herb that grows from a corm. The corm is conical or ovate, 1¼–2 in. long when mature; membranous dark brown outer layer, light brown inner layer; interior white, firm, fleshy; contains a bitter, milky juice.

Although the autumn crocus looks very much like a true crocus, it can be distinguished by its six stamens, which classify it as a member of the lily family, not the iris family to which true crocuses belong. The wider leaves of *Colchicum autumnale* also distinguish it.

Flowers: Tubular with tube growing directly from corm; no stem; six light pink to lavender segments called tepals, each 1¼–1¾ in. long.

Leaves: Appear in April; three to four; dark green, smooth, glossy, oblong-lanceolate; 6–10 in. long, 1–1½ in. wide.

Fruit: One to three oblong, pointed seed capsules, 1½ in. long, ¾ in. wide, three lobes and three cells.

Height: Up to 1 ft.

FLOWERING

September.

RANGE

Native to Europe and North Africa, but becoming scarce there as a wildflower; widely cultivated.

cancer. In 1938 scientists discovered that colchicine inhibits cell division, and research continued into the drug's potential as a cancer treatment. Contemporary researchers, however, regard colchicine as too toxic for such use.

Toxicity: Colchicine can be deadly. As little as 7 milligrams have been fatal, although the usual lethal dose is 65 milligrams. Even therapeutic use of colchicine can be harmful, for the doses required may be close to toxic quantities. All parts of the plant are poisonous. Reports tell of people mistaking the corm for an onion, eating it and dying. An elderly couple died after eating autumn crocus leaves prescribed by an herbalist. Autumn crocus should *never* be used as a medicinal herb.

An overdose of the drug causes nausea, vomiting, abdominal pains, purging, extreme thirst, weak pulse, and coldness and pain in the extremities. Damage occurs to the kidneys and blood vessels.

Ornamental: Instead of using this plant to make medicines, plant it in the garden strictly for its beauty. The autumn crocus blooms in . . . autumn, of course, poking up its pretty blossom amid the vestiges of summer flowers.

Set autumn crocuses at the front of a perennial garden, or use them in borders along shrubbery. They need to be planted in locations that are sheltered from the wind. For a natural look, plant them in an irregular fashion rather than in strict rows. At the New York Botanical Garden, they are planted among azaleas to provide continuous ground cover.

Other: Since 1937 scientists have used colchicine in plant breeding to develop new strains of crops that are more disease resistant or that produce larger fruits and vegetables. For example, varieties of garden flowers with especially large blossoms have been developed. In addition, scientists have used colchicine in research on embryonic growth and wound healing in animals.

CULTIVATION

Autumn crocuses are usually grown from corms planted in August or as early in the fall as possible. The ground should be spaded deeply and enriched with compost, leaf mold, peat moss, or other organic material. Place the corms 2 to 3 inches deep in the soil and space them 6 to 9 inches apart.

If you are using seeds, sow as soon as they are ripe, covering with only ⅛ inch of soil. Seedlings can be transplanted when they are two years old. They will not bloom for three to six years.

Pests and diseases: Leaf smut can infest autumn crocuses. (See the entry Growing Herbs for information on controlling diseases.)

GROWING CONDITIONS

- Plant hardiness zone 5.
- Loamy, moist soil.
- Full sun to partial shade.

BARBERRY

Berberis vulgaris   **Berberidaceae**

What can you do with barberry? Make barberry jam. Build the knot of your knot garden. Dye your wool yellow with the dried roots and bark. Soothe your sore throat. You can find many uses for this stout but pretty shrub.

DESCRIPTION

Barberry is a perennial shrub. It is covered with a smooth, gray bark, and at the joint of each branch are three sharp spines, ½–1 in. long. (See photo on page 273.)

Flowers: Bloom at ends of branches in 2½ in. long hanging racemes; six concave, rounded, bright yellow petals; six stamens; six yellow-green ovate sepals compose calyx.

Leaves: Four or five leaves on each branch, grouped closely together, ovate to elliptical, spiny teeth around edges, green above and gray below, to 2⅜ in. long.

Fruit: Ovoid to ellipsoid orange-red berries, each containing two seeds.

Height: To 8 ft.

FLOWERING

Spring.

RANGE

Europe, temperate Asia, northern Africa, and North America from Nova Scotia to Delaware and Pennsylvania, west to Minnesota, Iowa, and Missouri.

GROWING CONDITIONS

- Plant hardiness zone 4.
- Moist, fertile, well-drained soil.
- Full sun to partial shade.

HISTORY

As with most herbs, barberry's history is medicinal. While today we might make a barberry preserve to spread on toast or an English muffin, in ancient Egypt a barberry syrup mixed with fennel seed was taken to prevent the plague. In Europe during the Middle Ages, medicines made from barberry were prescribed as antiseptics, purgatives, and tonics. In North America, the Indians prepared decoctions from the root bark and drank them to restore the body from general debility and to improve the appetite.

USES

Medicinal: Barberry's reputation as a medicinal herb is heralded more by practitioners of folk medicine than by modern scientists, but since the herb generally is considered safe, you might want to try some of the remedies.

The next time you have a sore throat, make a gargle by crushing some berries and mixing in water. One of the main constituents of barberry, berberine, is reported to be astringent, anesthetic, and antibacterial, properties that help heal sore throats.

Barberry's astringent properties also work on the bowel to help control diarrhea, and the herb is said to be an effective purgative. To prepare a remedy, boil the dried root in water and then let it cool. Twentieth-century herbalist Michael Weiner recommends 1 teaspoon of root to 1½ pints of water, boiled slowly for 30 minutes. John Lust, author of *The Herb Book,* suggests briefly boiling ½ to 1 teaspoon of root in 1 cup of water and letting the mixture steep for 5 minutes.

Laboratory studies with berberine have shown it to have stimulant effects on the heart in low doses and depressant effects in high doses. High doses also were shown to depress respiration, stimulate the smooth muscle of the intestine, and decrease bronchial constriction. Berberine also has sedative, anticonvulsant, and uterine stimulant properties.

Ornamental: If you are planning a knot garden, think about using barberry. It works wonderfully. You can easily train it and prune it to twist and turn through your design. The foliage is quite lovely, and you can choose from several varieties.

Barberry lends itself well to hedges of any kind. Trim it for a formal look or just let it go in an informal setting. Hedges only a few inches high can be planted around flower beds using dwarf species such as *Berberis Thunbergii* var. *minor*.

You can choose from either evergreen or deciduous varieties. The evergreens have lovely foliage, and some species produce very attractive flowers. Their fruits, however, are generally less brilliantly colored than the deciduous barberries. Plant the deciduous varieties for their good form and the beautiful colors of their foliage in autumn. Some produce pretty blossoms, and most bear brightly colored berries.

Culinary: When autumn arrives with that bit of bite in the air, harvest the fruit of the barberry to use in your cooking. It will add a bite and color to match the season. Barberry tastes like cranberry with a dash more citrus. Make jellies, jams, preserves, and chutneys with the red berries. They add allure when simmered in syrups, soups, and stews and can be removed before serving, if you prefer. For a unique cake or pastry decoration, the berries can be candied.

Substitute: Cranberries or rosehips for the berries.

Dye: While you are harvesting berries for jams, pull out some roots for making yellow dye. The roots should be harvested in late summer or fall for this purpose. Fresh or dried, the roots or bark will create a nice yellow dye for wool, linen, and cotton. No mordant is required, and the color fastness will be fair to good. To get a lighter yellow in wools, use an alum mordant.

CULTIVATION

Barberries are easy to grow in a fertile, moist, well-drained soil. They prefer a sunny location but will tolerate shade during part of the day. They are easily propagated from seeds sown in greenhouses, in cold frames, or outdoors. Seeds planted in the fall will germinate the following spring. Barberries do hybridize readily, so plants grown from seed may not be true to the seed parent. If you want to produce an exact replica, use cuttings. Some plants may produce rooted suckers, which can be separated.

Prune and thin the branches immediately after the shrub flowers or in late winter. If you neglect your bushes and they become overgrown, they can be rejuvenated by cutting them to within a foot of the ground in late winter, then fertilizing them and watering substantially during summertime dry spells.

In areas where winters are cold and harsh, shelter barberries from the winds to keep them from dying back.

BASIL

Ocimum Basilicum   **Lamiaceae**

DESCRIPTION

Basil is an annual with leafy stems that give it a bushy appearance. The leaves are very fragrant. (See photos on pages 100, 101, 102, and 238.)

Flowers: White, ½ in. long, two-lipped; upper lip has four lobes; four stamens; in racemes at tops of stems.

Leaves: Opposite, oval, toothed; curl inward along midrib; 2–3 in. long, sometimes longer; yellow-green to dark green depending on fertility of soil.

Fruit: Tiny, dark brown seeds.

Height: 1–2 ft.

FLOWERING

July and August.

RANGE

Native to India, Africa, and Asia; cultivated extensively for commercial use in France, Egypt, Hungary, Indonesia, Morocco, Greece, Bulgaria, Yugoslavia, and Italy, and to some extent in the other temperate countries of the world; much cultivated in the United States, particularly in California.

The French call basil *herbe royale*. In Italy, basil has been and still is a sign of love. According to tradition, when a woman puts a pot of basil on the balcony outside her room, it means that she is ready to receive her suitor. Given the popularity of growing basil on windowsills today, a man would no longer be advised to consider this a sign of romance. Another tradition holds that when a man gives a woman a sprig of basil, she will fall in love with him and never leave him. Today, he'd probably have better luck if he made her pesto and served it over pasta with salad, bread, and a little wine.

HISTORY

Basil hasn't always been associated with romance and fine dining. In fact, there was a time when people feared this herb.

According to an anecdote attributed to Tournefort, a seventeenth-century botanist, "A certain Gentleman of *Siena* being wonderfully taken and delighted with the Smell of *Basil,* was wont very frequently to take the Powder of the dry Herb, and snuff it up his Nose; but in a short Time he turn'd mad and died; and his Head being opened by Surgeons, there was found a Nest of Scorpions in his Brain." In keeping with this view of the herb, some believe its name was derived from that of the legendary basilisk, a reptile who could kill with a glance or a breath.

A contrary theory claims the name is a derivative of *basileus,* Greek for king. In India, the people worship basil more highly than kings. It is a sacred herb dedicated to the gods Vishnu and Krishna. Sprigs of the species *Ocimum sanctum* at one time were laid on the breasts of the dead to protect them from evil in the next world and to offer them entrance to paradise.

USES

Men and women certainly love basil today. At home, it has become one of the most popular herbs in the garden and in the kitchen, but there exists a host of other possibilities for it.

Medicinal: Given that basil is a member of the mint family, it isn't surprising that, medicinally, it is recommended for digestive complaints. Instead of an afterdinner mint, try an afterdinner cup of basil tea to aid digestion and expel gas. Steep a teaspoon of the dried leaves in a cup of boiled water. Herbalists recommend it for stomach cramps, vomiting, and constipation. Basil has been described as having a slight sedative action, which would explain why it is sometimes recommended for nervous headaches and anxiety.

James Duke, Ph.D., reports in the *CRC Handbook of Medicinal Herbs* that a poultice made of the seeds has been used externally on

Bush
Basil

Purple
Ruffles Basil

Dark
Opal
Basil

Holy
Basil

Sweet
Basil

23

BASIL—continued

CHEF TIPS

- Add several large basil leaves to the liquid when poaching fish, shellfish, or chicken.

- Cut a 10×10-in. square of aluminum foil and set it shiny-side-down. Arrange slices of zucchini, onion, and tomato in the middle of the square and toss in several basil leaves. Fold the square around the vegetables to make a tight packet, then bake in a 350°F oven (or grill) for 20 minutes.

- Add a handful of basil when making beef stock. When making tomato or pizza sauce, substitute basil for oregano.

- Basil's flavor intensifies during cooking.

PESTO

Create an easy pesto sauce by combining 1 cup of fresh basil leaves, 3 tablespoons of pine nuts or walnuts, 3 tablespoons of grated Parmesan cheese, and 2 or 3 cloves of garlic. Puree in a food processor, adding enough olive oil to make a smooth paste. Use with pasta, rice, fish, vegetables, or in soup.

sores, and in fact clinical studies show that extracts from the seeds do indeed exhibit an antibacterial effect.

Modern medicine currently has no use for basil, and no studies have been done to confirm any of its supposed effects. However, a basil infusion is safe to drink and can certainly be tried as a tonic for the digestive system.

Culinary: Tomato sauce and pesto have made basil famous, but don't stop with these two dishes. This herb's wonderful taste and aroma will enliven so many other foods.

Basil has a rich and spicy, mildly peppery flavor with a trace of mint and clove. For the best flavor use fresh leaves, but frozen and dried leaves are acceptable. Use them cooked or raw. Crush, chop, or mince them and add to recipes, or throw whole leaves in salads. Sprigs of basil make a wonderfully aromatic garnish. The flowers are edible and can be used as a garnish, too.

Traditional in Italian, Mediterranean, and Thai cookery, basil is superb with veal, lamb, fish, poultry, white beans, pasta, rice, tomatoes, cheese, and eggs. It blends well with garlic, thyme, and lemon. Basil adds snap to mild vegetables like zucchini, summer squash, eggplant, potatoes, cabbage, carrots, cauliflower, parsnips, spinach, and to the soups, stews, and sauces in which these vegetables appear. Make a basil vinegar using white vinegar; dark opal basil makes a particularly attractive and tasty vinegar.

Storage note: Basil is best stored in an oil, vinegar, or frozen paste. Note that if you're freezing pesto, omit the garlic until you're ready to use the sauce because the garlic may become bitter after three months. Basil can also be dried and stored in tightly sealed containers.

Available commercially: Dried, frozen, and canned in pesto sauces and fresh; some markets offer fresh in the summer.

Aromatic: Bring that wonderful fragrance indoors from your garden by adding the dried leaves of basil to potpourris and sachets. The fragrance is sweet and strong but not overpowering. The heavily scented opal basil and the sweet-scented thyrsiflora basil are particularly good. For a lemony fragrance, use lemon basil.

Ornamental: An herb garden just isn't an herb garden without basil, but you'd be hard pressed to find it in the flower garden. But why not plant it there? The lovely green foliage can offset brilliantly colored flowers, and certainly the fragrance will be welcome.

There are many varieties of basil, each having a little something to add to a garden: dark opal basil offers stunning purple foliage and mauve flowers; the ruffled varieties offer a little texture. For attractive borders, miniature basil is a superb choice. And there are diverse other basils available, too, as the accompanying table reveals.

BASIL SPECIES AND VARIETIES

Name	Flower Color	Leaves	Comments
Ocimum americanum (TP) Lemon basil	White	Pale dull green	Strong lemon fragrance; excellent in vinegar
O. Basilicum 'Anise' Anise basil	White	Purplish	Sweet anise flavor and fragrance
O. Basilicum 'Cinnamon' Cinnamon basil	White	Like sweet basil	Cinnamon flavor and fragrance
O. Basilicum 'Crispum' Lettuce-leaf basil	White	Very large, crinkled	Excellent in salads
O. Basilicum 'Green Ruffles' Green ruffles basil	White	Lime green, serrated, ruffled, much longer than sweet basil	Excellent ornamental
O. Basilicum 'Minimum' (TP) Bush basil	White	1–1½ in.	Dwarf, compact form; good for pot culture
O. Basilicum 'Nano Compatto Vero' (TP) Nano Compatto Vero basil	White	Light green, ¼–½ in. wide	Described as having excellent flavor and form
O. Basilicum 'Piccolo Verde Fino' Piccolo Verde Fino basil	White	2-in. leaves	Between sweet fine basil and sweet basil in size
O. Basilicum 'Purple Ruffles' Purple ruffles basil	Lavender	Dark maroon, shiny	Striking ornamental; excellent in vinegar and as garnish
O. Basilicum 'Purpurascens' Dark opal basil	Lavender	Deep purple, shiny	Striking ornamental; excellent in vinegar and as garnish
O. Basilicum 'Thyrsiflora' (TP) Thyrsiflora basil	White and deep lavender	Bright green, smooth	Very sweet fragrance; used in Thai cooking
O. gratissimum (TP)	White, yellow anthers	Gray-green, hairy	Strong clove scent, spicy flavor
O. kilimandscharicum (TP) Camphor basil	White, red anthers	Green	Camphor scented; tea taken for stomachaches and colds; not used in cooking
O. sanctum (TP) Holy basil	Lavender	Gray-green, coarse	Sweet fragrance; excellent ornamental; not used in cooking

NOTE: TP denotes tender perennial.

Cosmetic: Basil reputedly brings luster to hair. Brunettes can add it to a rosemary rinse and blondes to a chamomile rinse. Combine the oil of basil with other herb oils in perfumes and toilet waters. Use it in herbal bath mixtures. The fragrance alone is invigorating.

The cosmetic industry doesn't consider it strange to use basil in lotions, shampoos, perfumes, and soaps. Basil is widely cultivated for such use.

BASIL BOUQUETS

If you can spare them from the kitchen, cut sprigs of either sweet or purple basil to add to fresh flower bouquets and arrangements both for their attractive leaves and sweet, anise-clove scent.

GARDEN IDEAS

- Plant opal basil with marigolds for a striking contrast.
- Grow sweet basil and opal basil together in a window box.
- Plant the varieties Green Ruffles or Purple Ruffles for their lovely ruffly texture.

GROWING CONDITIONS

- Soil pH 6.0.
- Rich, moist, well-drained soil.
- Full sun.

BASIL—continued

Companion planting: Gardeners have long recommended planting basil near peppers and tomatoes to enhance their growth.

Other: Basil is one of the ingredients in the liqueur Chartreuse.

CULTIVATION

Early Greek and Roman physicians believed that to grow a good crop of basil, one had to shout and curse when sowing the seeds. From this custom was born the French idiom *semer le basilic,* "sowing the basil," for "raving."

Fortunately you don't have to shout and scream at this herb to get it to grow. Basil cooperates quite readily. It grows easily from seed. Since it is quite sensitive to the cold, sow it outdoors in the spring when you are certain the danger of frost has passed and when the soil has warmed to a temperature of about 50°F. The seeds should be planted ⅛ inch deep. When the seedlings appear, thin the plants to leave 1 foot of space between them.

Basil may be started indoors and the seedlings transplanted after the last frost. It germinates readily in soil temperatures of from 75° to 85°F. Use a moist medium. Marilyn Hampstead, herb grower and owner of Fox Hill Farm in Parma, Michigan, uses a mixture of fine-grade vermiculite and perlite. Plant the seeds ⅛ inch deep, pressing the soil gently over the seeds. Hampstead recommends covering the containers with clear plastic to prevent the loss of moisture. When germination occurs (about three days for most varieties), loosen the plastic to allow some ventilation. Remove it completely once the seedling leaves have completely opened (a couple of days after germination). Ventilation is important in preventing damping off, a fungal disease.

About seven days after germination, the seedlings can be transplanted to 2-inch pots or into flats. When the weather has warmed up, plant them outside.

Basil likes well-drained, rich soil. It will grow best if well-rotted manure or manure compost is mixed with the soil before planting. Mulching the area after seedlings have shot up helps to keep the ground moist and warm and discourages weeds. It is beneficial to mulch basil when you expect a drought. Don't mulch until the soil has warmed up; basil roots need heat.

To encourage a bushy plant, keep pruning basil. Before it flowers, cut the main stem from the top, leaving at least one node with two young shoots. Thereafter, cut the branches every two or three weeks. Use the leaves fresh or store them.

Harvesting and storage: Cut sprigs when flower buds form and before they have opened. Basil can be harvested until the first frost.

BATHING WITH HERBS

Imagine that you have an important presentation coming up at work, and you've been preparing for it day and night for the past week. Your mind is busy to exhaustion with all the details of your presentation. Or perhaps the kids are sick. Your sleep was interrupted and your day disrupted by their coughs and cries. They are all better, but you are ready for the funny farm. Or you are training for a marathon or some other physical competition, and your legs ache from an especially hard workout.

Do yourself a favor. Take some time off; just an hour will do. Go into the bathroom and lock the door. Tune in a radio station that plays the kind of music that relaxes you. Light some candles—herb-scented ones are great!—and sink into a hot herbal bath. Rest your head and neck on a towel. Your body feels so much lighter in the water. Let your arms float. The rising steam lifts the fragrances of chamomile and lavender around your face. Ahhhhh . . . just what you needed.

Baths can be soothing and soporific. They can also stimulate and refresh. They help to heal the body and the mind, and, of course, they are cleansing and leave your skin pleasantly fragrant.

As early as the third century B.C., people were enjoying the pleasures and benefits of bathing. Bathhouses, public as well as private, could be found everywhere in ancient Greece and Rome. Given the sanitary conditions of the time, frequent bathing was certainly essential, and the fragrances of the bath were most likely a relief from the aromas of the home. But baths were enjoyed for their healing and beautifying properties as well. At the Roman Baths of Caracalla, considered the most beautiful of ancient bathhouses, an individual could choose from any one of 20 types of baths, including mineral or oil, steam, massage, or friction baths.

In today's fast-paced world, showers seem more practical than baths, but quite the opposite is true. Exactly because of the hectic, high-pressured pace, a hot herbal bath can be practical: Its soothing, healing, or refreshing qualities can offer vital relief. And with the great availability of herbs and herb oils, anyone can enjoy a wonderful herbal bath.

PREPARING AN HERBAL BATH

The notion of merely tossing a handful of herbs into the bath and then soaking in the water amid fragrant flowers and leaves may seem rather romantic, but it won't be very romantic when you step out of the tub and have to pick leaves and flowers off your body.

One of the easiest and, some say, most effective ways to prepare

27

STIMULATING HERBS

basil
bay
calendula flowers
citronella
fennel
horseradish roots
lavender flowers
lemon verbena
lovage roots
marjoram
mint
nettle
pine needles
queen of the meadow
rosemary
sage
savory
thyme
vetiver roots

SOOTHING HERBS

catnip
chamomile flowers
comfrey
elder (whole plant)
evening primrose flowers
hyssop
jasmine flowers
juniper berries
lemon balm
linden flowers
marsh mallow roots
melilot
mullein
passionflower flowers
rose flowers
slippery elm inner bark
tansy flowers
valerian roots
vervain (whole plant)
violet

BATHING WITH HERBS—continued

an herbal bath is to wrap dried herbs in some cheesecloth and hang the bundle from the spout while running the water. When you've filled the tub, let the bundle steep for a while before removing it—squeeze all the moisture from it to capture everything you can from the herbs—and climbing in. For something a little nicer, make a drawstring bag from a piece of colored or printed muslin. An even easier method is to use a large round or oval tea infuser that has a chain and can be hung beneath the tap. Use a generous handful of herbs or about ½ cup. To soften the water and the skin, add some oatmeal to the herbs.

Another method for preparing an herbal bath is to make a strong infusion from the herb or herbs you choose, then adding it to the water. Pour boiling water over ½ cup of dried herbs; let the mixture steep for 10 to 20 minutes. Strain the liquid and add it to the bath.

Some recipes call for the addition of an herbal decoction to a tubful of water. A decoction is prepared by adding herbs to cold water, then bringing the mixture to a boil. A decoction is invariably stronger than an infusion, even though the two may be prepared with equal proportions of herb material to water.

Temperature: To get the most benefit from your bath, pay close attention to the temperature of the water. Warm baths relax muscles, while cool baths stimulate the body. Most physicians and researchers agree that a water temperature equivalent to your internal body temperature (96° to 98°F) is ideal for a relaxing bath. Higher temperatures are likely to make you feel very sleepy. A water temperature around 92°F is still relaxing but also refreshes the body. And if you need some pep and zip, try something in the range of 70° to 85°F.

Be careful of *hot* baths. Water temperatures above 104°F dehydrate the body, dry the skin, and can be exhausting. A bath that is too hot can lower blood pressure and lead to fainting. If you have diabetes, a nerve disorder, or high blood pressure, or if you are pregnant, don't let that water temperature get too high.

TYPES OF HERBAL BATHS

You can create a bath to perk you up for a fun evening on the town, or one to calm you down for a good night's sleep. Some baths help to relieve aches and pains, others moisturize the skin, and some simply leave you wonderfully fragrant. It just depends on which herbs you use.

Herbal baths are simple to prepare. Experiment with your own bath formulas. Prepare baths from different concentrations to see what works best for you. You can choose from many herbs to create a bath that will either refresh, soothe, heal, beautify, or simply smell good. Here are some ideas to get you started.

Healing baths: Hippocrates, the father of medicine, prescribed baths for patients suffering from certain muscle and joint diseases. Because of its calming effect, bathing was one of the early treatments for mental problems. Today, hydrotherapy still is used in the treatment of arthritis and certain muscle problems.

Water alone heals and soothes, but add herbs to the bath, and the benefits increase.

Baths for stiff muscles and aching joints: A combination of sage and strawberry leaves or sage and mugwort in the bath relieves aching muscles and joints. The same is true of a combination of equal parts of agrimony, chamomile, and mugwort. In the book *Growing and Using the Healing Herbs,* Gaea and Shandor Weiss recommend an infusion made from 1 ounce each of burdock root, mugwort, comfrey leaf, and sage, and 1 quart of water.

Tonic baths: Blackberry leaves are reputed to refresh and brighten the skin during a long, cold winter. Collect the young shoots and leaves, dry them, make an infusion (6 to 8 ounces of plant matter is recommended), and add it to the bathwater.

Some combinations of herbs that have a tonic effect on the skin include: equal parts of comfrey, alfalfa, parsley, and orange peel; three parts of jasmine flowers to one part orange blossoms; equal parts of rose petals, orange blossoms, and lavender; and equal parts of comfrey, nettle, dandelion, and daisy.

To receive the most benefit from tonic baths, take one every evening, several days in a row.

Baths that aid circulation: One English recipe that is said to get the blood moving calls for a decoction of equal parts of marigold, nettle, and bladder wrack added to the bathwater. Ginger has been used in oriental medicine to promote circulation in the treatment of arthritis, bursitis, and gout. The Weisses recommend heating 2 pounds of grated ginger in 1 gallon of water for ten minutes. Strain the mixture to remove the ginger before adding to the bath.

Baths that relieve tension: Recent studies have indicated that stress, especially internal tension, can increase the risk of heart problems. If you are under particular stress, an herbal bath can help heal the mind and the body. Try any of the soothing herbs listed on page 28. Valerian and sweet flag have been specifically recommended for tension relief. Add a decoction made from 1 pound of the leaves of valerian or ½ pound of the leaves and roots of calamus to the bathwater. A decoction of equal parts of hops and queen of the meadow used as a rinse after a regular bath is also said to be healing.

TONIC HERBS

blackberry leaves
comfrey
dandelion
ginseng root
jasmine flowers
nettle
orange
patchouli
raspberry leaves

FRAGRANT HERBS

angelica roots
bay
clove
geranium
jasmine flowers
lavender flowers
lemon flowers and peel
lovage root
mint
myrtle leaves and flowers
orange leaves, flowers, and peel
patchouli
pennyroyal
queen of the meadow
rose flowers
rosemary
sandalwood
southernwood

HERBS FOR FOOTBATHS

agrimony
alder bark
burdock
goat's rue
lavender flowers
mustard seed
sage
witch hazel bark and leaves
wormwood

HERBS FOR ACHING MUSCLES AND JOINTS

agrimony
bay
juniper berries
mugwort
oregano
poplar buds and bark
sage
strawberry leaves

ANTISEPTIC HERBS

dock
eucalyptus
sandalwood

ASTRINGENT HERBS

agrimony
alum root
bay
bayberry bark
clary
comfrey leaves and root
dock
frankincense resin
lady's mantle
lemongrass
mullein
myrrh resin
nasturtium flowers
periwinkle
potentilla root
queen of the meadow
raspberry leaves
rose flowers
rosemary
strawberry
white willow bark
wintergreen
witch hazel bark and leaves
yarrow flowers

BATHING WITH HERBS—continued

Baths for inflammations of the skin: Alder, dandelion leaves, elecampane, lady's mantle, mint, and plantain are all said to help heal inflammations and generally cleanse the skin. Marigold leaves are reputed to heal body scars and soothe varicose veins.

Other herbs: Burdock root and hyssop are both reported to be diaphoretic (induce sweating) when added to the bath. For a cold or the flu, add eucalyptus to the hot bathwater. The fragrant oils that rise up with the steam will help clear congestion.

Beautifying baths: A French beauty who remained attractive into her seventies, Ninon de Lenclos, was perhaps the one person who most exemplified the beautifying powers of the herbal bath. If you'd like to try her herbal bath, mix together a handful each of dried lavender flowers, dried rosemary leaves, dried mint, chopped comfrey roots, and thyme. Make an infusion in a quart of water, then add it to the bath. "Rest 15 minutes in the 'magic water' and think virtuous thoughts," advised *la belle* de Lenclos.

BATH OILS

To moisturize and scent the skin, add oils to the bath. They are easy to make at home. Simply combine three parts of a vegetable or nut oil to one part of herbal oil, or mix vegetable and nut oils and add the herbal oil. Almond and avocado oils are often recommended. Herbal oils can be bought commercially, or you can extract them yourself (see the entry Scents from Herbs). Collect several vials of herb oil; when it comes time to prepare your bath, you can choose according to your fancy.

Most oils do not mix with water; instead, they lie on the surface. When you step out of the bath, they coat your skin. If you want one that disperses, replace the vegetable or nut oils with castor oil.

Of course, you can also add aromatic oils directly to the water if you are simply interested in the fragrance. Start with a few drops at a time—pure plant oils are powerful.

When to add the oil: Many people add oils while they run the bathwater, but it is best to wait until after you have soaked for about ten minutes. This allows your skin to absorb moisture before the oil coats it. Oil acts as a barrier and just as it can trap moisture in your skin, it can prevent water from penetrating it.

To benefit most from the moisturizing effects of the bath, first wash your body to remove any dirt and oils that may have accumulated. A cup of salt added to the water is said to draw water up from the lower layers of the skin to the drier surface. Then after soaking for about 10 minutes, add a bath oil. Don't spend more than 20 minutes in the bath altogether, or the process will be reversed, and the bath will dry your skin.

Wormwood

Garlic Chives

Rue

Hops

Hidcote Lavender

Globe
Thistle

Tansy

Rosemary

Quaking Grass

Wormwood

Feverfew

Globe
Amaranth

Cockscomb

Poppy
Seed
Capsule

Bayberry

Wild
Marjoram

Sweet
Wormwood

Lunaria

Bay

BAY

Laurus nobilis   **Lauraceae**

Even its name suggests greatness. *Laurus* is the Latin word for bay tree and *nobilis* means "renowned." From the leaves are woven wreaths of victory. Use this herb in any way and you will reap great success and victory. Add it to shellfish boils, soups, and stews. Infuse the leaves and pour into bathwater for a soothing soak. Create your own herbal victory wreath to give or to hang in your home.

HISTORY

Bay—this symbol of glory and reward—is a romantic herb, and indeed it had very romantic beginnings.

Apollo, the Greek god of the sun, smitten with love for the fair nymph Daphne, pursued her relentlessly. Daphne, though, wanted nothing to do with Apollo. (This was all Cupid's doing. He shot an arrow into Daphne that made her hate Apollo.) To help her escape this pursuit, Daphne's father, Peneus, changed her into a laurel tree. Apollo fell upon his knees before this tree and declared it eternally sacred. From then on he wore a wreath of laurel leaves upon his head in remembrance of and dedication to his beloved Daphne.

Thus the tree became a sign of glory, honor, and greatness. Throughout Greece and Rome, men and women wove wreaths to crown the heads of kings, priests, prophets, poets, and the victors of battles and athletic or scholarly contests. Scholars wore wreaths of bay when they achieved academic honors. At the first Olympics in 776 B.C., laurel garlands were presented to the champions.

The reputation of this plant has never dwindled. Great powers of protection were attributed to it. Bay could keep you safe from thunder and lightning, for example. During storms, the fearless Roman emperor Tiberius (42 B.C.–A.D. 37) could always be found under his bed, a laurel wreath upon his head. In 1575 Thomas Lupton, in his *Book of Notable Things,* wrote that "neyther falling sickness, neyther devyll, wyll infest or hurt one in that place where a bay tree is." The British herbalist Culpeper reiterated this, proclaiming that a man standing near a bay tree could not be hurt by witches, the devil, thunder, or lightning.

Of course, any plant with such power had to be a good medicinal herb. In the Middle Ages herbalists prescribed it to promote menstruation and induce abortions. Culpeper recommended it for snakebites, wasp and bee stings, for colds, rheumatism, urinary problems, pains of the ears, bruises, scrapes, and all sorts of ills.

Perhaps it is because bay was revered so highly as a protector and as a symbol of greatness and honor that the death of this tree was considered an evil omen. In fact, in 1629 pestilence broke out in

DESCRIPTION

Bay is an aromatic, evergreen tree of medium size, with shiny gray bark. (See photo on page 33.)

Flowers: Inconspicuous, no petals, composed of four-lobed calyxes, greenish yellow, in small umbels from the leaf axils.

Leaves: Alternate, shiny, dark green, thick and leathery with wavy edges, elliptical, 1½–3½ in. long, ½–1½ in. wide, short stalks.

Fruit: Dark purple or black one-seeded berries, about the size of a small grape (½ in. long).

Height: Up to 10 ft. (5 ft. in pot culture); in the southern United States and in Mediterranean regions, where the plant grows indigenously, it has reached more than 60 ft.

FLOWERING

Spring.

RANGE

Indigenous to the Mediterranean region and Asia Minor; commercial cultivation in Turkey, Algeria, Belgium, France, Greece, Mexico, Morocco, Portugal, Spain, the Canary Islands, Central America, and the southern United States.

BAY—continued

Padua, Italy, after the bay trees of the city had died. Shakespeare wrote in *Richard II:*

> 'Tis thought the king is dead; we will not stay.
> The bay trees in our country are all wither'd.

If your bay trees wither, are they warning you of impending evil or death? More likely they are telling you that they caught a bit of frost.

USES

The bay has a myriad of divergent uses to this day.

Medicinal: You may find use for this herb if your stomach isn't feeling quite right, or if you have a little gas. Bay has a reputation for soothing the stomach and relieving flatulence. Whether or not this reputation is deserved hasn't been determined scientifically, but you can try an infusion of the dried or fresh leaves and decide for yourself how well it works.

Perhaps a more renowned medicinal use of bay has been as a healing agent for rheumatism. So when the damp weather starts to bring on aches and pains in your muscles and joints, rub a little bay oil into them for relief. Bay oil is also said to benefit sprains, bruises, and skin rashes. The oil can be pressed from the berries, distilled from the leaves, or if you don't want to do any of the work, buy the oil commercially. Again, the efficacy of this remedy hasn't been proven.

In addition to these two uses, bay has been described as an astringent, diaphoretic, diuretic, emetic, emmenagogue, narcotic, nervine, and stimulant. Studies of the essential oil show that it has bactericidal and fungicidal properties. It contains eugenol, which has been found to have narcotic and sedative effects in mice. Perhaps with some continued study, researchers will find some promising medicinal uses for the oil.

Toxicity: As an external ointment, the essential oil may cause dermatitis in some persons. Taking the infusion internally appears to be safe.

Culinary: Bay may not be used very often medicinally, but in the kitchen nearly every soup, stew, or tomato sauce is visited by this herb. Cooks instinctively add bay leaves to Spanish, Creole, and French soups, stews, marinades, and sauces. They're great in shellfish boils, pickling brines, and with game. Use them in combination with peppercorns, saffron, garlic, allspice, citrus, and prepared and dried mustards. Just remember to take the leaf out of the soup before you serve it. Many painful stories have been told of sharp bay leaves stuck in the throats of those who have dined on stew.

Commercially, the essential oil of bay is extracted and used to flavor baked goods, meats, sausages, and canned soups.

Available commercially: Dried whole, crumbled and ground, but whole is preferable.

Ornamental: The bay is a lovely tree, and anyone can grow it for its beauty. If you live in an area with mild winters and warm summers, such as California, you can grow it outdoors as a landscape tree. In locations that suffer harsh winters, the bay must be grown in tubs or large containers that can be brought indoors for the winter. The advantages are that they can be used to decorate patios, steps, and terraces, and that they can be easily rearranged.

Bays are easily pruned into formal shapes; they lend themselves well to standards.

Craft: Branches of bay leaves dry beautifully. The color becomes much lighter, but the shape of the leaves remains. Place a sprig in a tussie-mussie. Add them to an herb wreath. They work well in a live wreath, too. The shiny, dark green leaves create a nice background for other herbs, and the stoutness of the leaves and branches provides good support and form to a wreath.

Cosmetic: The fragrant oil of bay soothes the skin when added to the bathwater. Simply make an infusion of a handful of leaves in boiling water. Let it steep and then add to the bath, or use it as a skin lotion.

Other: You've always wondered why your grandmother put bay leaves in her canisters of flour. You thought maybe old age—or her grandchildren—made her a little crazy. Well, lots of grandmothers do the same thing. Bay leaves have a reputation as an insect repellent. Whether or not they really work in your flour canisters or boxes of cereal is debatable, but it can't hurt to try.

CULTIVATION

Bay has *earned* a reputation for being difficult to propagate. Many writers say that the bay tree can be started from seed or cuttings. Maintained at a temperature of 75°F, the seeds are supposed to germinate within four weeks. Most gardeners, however, say that the seeds always turn moldy.

Cuttings taken in the fall from fresh, green shoots seem to yield a higher percentage of success; they may take from six to nine months to root, however. Purchasing a young tree from a nursery just could be the easiest way to start a bay.

Harvesting and storage: Bay leaves may be harvested and dried throughout the year. Cut off individual older leaves to use as needed or to dry. Pick them early in the day. When drying, place boards or some other object on top of the leaves to prevent them from curling. They should be dry after about 15 days. Store them in tightly sealed containers.

CHEF TIPS

- Add a rubbed bay leaf to the water when cooking beans, lentils, rice, or other grains.
- Include a rubbed bay leaf in spiced fruit punches.
- Rub the skin and cavity of a chicken with prepared mustard, then tuck two bay leaves into the cavity before roasting.

BAYS GO TO D.C.

In January of 1986, Phyllis and Thomas Bryan of Allentown, Pennsylvania, gave President Reagan five bay trees to be used as ornamentals at the White House. The trees are quite rare, having originated from cuttings taken from trees that were brought to the United States from Belgium by Mr. Bryan's grandparents. The original bay trees now grow in Longwood Gardens in Kennett Square, Pennsylvania.

GROWING CONDITIONS

- Plant hardiness zone 8.
- Soil pH 6.2.
- Moderately rich, well-drained soil.
- Full sun to partial shade.

BAYBERRY

Myrica cerifera   Myricaceae

Its fragrance suits bayberry. Plain in appearance, bayberry survives in poor, sandy soils and withstands whipping ocean winds and salty air. Fittingly, its fragrance doesn't assault our noses, insisting on being recognized, but fills the air slowly and pleasantly.

SUSPECTED CARCINOGEN

DESCRIPTION

Bayberry is a perennial evergreen shrub with grayish bark and waxy branchlets. (See photos on pages 33 and 446.)
Flowers: Insignificant, yellowish, no petals or sepals, grow on catkins; male and female flowers on separate plants; female catkins globular in shape, male elongated.
Leaves: Long, narrow, taper at both ends, 1–4 in. long, delicately toothed, dark green, dotted with resin glands, when crushed emit pleasant fragrance.
Fruit: Nutlet, thickly coated with whitish gray wax.
Height: To 35 ft.

FLOWERING

March and April.

RANGE

Along coast from New Jersey to Florida, west to Alabama and Mississippi, and along the St. Lawrence River to the start of the Great Lakes.

HABITAT

Sandy soil by the water, open fields, and along streams.

GROWING CONDITIONS

- Plant hardiness zone 7.
- Soil pH 5.0–6.0.
- Moist, peaty soil.
- Full sun.

USES

Historically, bayberry has been used in folk medicine for its tonic, stimulant, and astringent properties, but the safest and probably most enjoyable use of this herb is in making candles.

Medicinal: Bayberry tea has been recommended for sore throats, spongy gums, jaundice, and uterine hemorrhages. Snuffing the powder is supposed to relieve nasal congestion and cure nasal polyps. Poultices made with the root bark are said to heal ulcers, cuts, bruises, and insect bites.

Given the rave reviews herbalists have proclaimed over the years, you might be moved to try a bayberry infusion, but consider this pharmacological review. In his book, *The Honest Herbal,* pharmacognosist Varro Tyler, Ph.D., points out that even present-day herbalists are drawing on chemical analyses made of bayberry in the 1860s using procedures "now thought extremely primitive." In a study in the 1970s, scientists injected bark extracts into rats, and after 78 weeks the animals developed malignant tumors. Tyler concludes that "even if bayberry were a useful drug for any particular condition—a hypothesis which remains unproven—its safety, at least in large doses, is still in doubt . . . ."

Aromatic: American settlers made candles from the fragrant wax of bayberries. You can, too, but you'd better know a spot where a lot of bayberry bushes grow. It takes 1 bushel of these tiny fruits to make 4 pounds of wax. You can also add the wax to soaps and ointments. To remove it from the fruit, boil the berries in water. The wax will float to the surface and can be skimmed off when it hardens.

Cosmetic: An infusion of bayberry bark is said to be astringent and is recommended as a lotion for the skin or in the bath.

Other: The berries of bayberry dry nicely. Incorporate a few branches into a dried arrangement.

CULTIVATION

Bayberries can be started from seeds as soon as they are ripe. They will grow in poor, sandy soil, but moist, peaty earth provides the best medium.

Plant them in the spring or early fall. They should be cut back severely after planting, but thereafter, they require little care.

BEEBALM

Monarda didyma   **Lamiaceae**

Wherever you need a little zip, a little color, throw some beebalm flowers. Beebalm adds a brilliant splash of color to the flower bed. It can add the same colorburst to foods and beverages. Toss some blossoms into a salad, or float them in a bowl of punch. Beebalm's flavor has a bright tang, too.

HISTORY

Native to North America and discovered by the Indians, beebalm's history is briefer than many other herbs. It was discovered in an area of New York now named Otsego after the tribe that lived there. It is the same rural county where author James Fenimore Cooper wrote his novels, tales of the Indians and the region's first white men. (The name Otsego is often reported as Oswego.)

The Indians brewed beebalm tea to drink for pleasure and for medicinal purposes. When the white settlers came to the area, they learned of the tea and began brewing it themselves. It became quite popular and during the period of the Boston Tea Party, was drunk in place of black tea.

The colonists also admired the beauty of the flower and grew beebalm in their gardens for its ornamental value.

In the late 1700s, the Shakers founded a settlement near Oswego. They learned of beebalm and valued it highly for tea and other culinary uses and for its medicinal properties.

Although native to North America, beebalm is cultivated widely in Europe. It crossed the ocean in the mid-1700s when John Bartram of Philadelphia sent seeds to England. From England, beebalm traveled to the European continent, where it is generally cultivated under the names golden melissa or Indian nettle.

USES

Beebalm is still widely enjoyed for its beauty and its use.

Medicinal: With castor oil and cough syrup . . . you pinch your nose shut when you swallow them. Or you buy a variety laden with the spoonful of sugar that helps the medicine go down. You won't have to do either of these with beebalm. This remedy goes down easily all by itself.

Herbalists recommend an infusion of beebalm for coughs, sore throats, nausea, flatulence, and menstrual cramps. No scientific studies have been done to confirm any of these uses, but if a remedy has been around since before the United States was settled, it might be worth a try. If it doesn't work, at least you will have a pleasant tea to sip.

DESCRIPTION

Beebalm can be annual, biennial, or perennial. A member of the mint family, it grows on square stems. Beebalm effuses a citruslike fragrance. (See photo on page 378.)

Flowers: Brilliant scarlet flowers bloom clustered in whorls at top of stem; grow in two or more tiers; whole head rests on a collar of red-tinged bracts; individual blossoms asymmetrical, with narrow tubular corolla 2 in. long that broadens toward mouth; formed from an upper and lower lip—upper lip is erect or arching; lower lip has three lobes, the middle one longer than the others; two stamens.

Leaves: Opposite, dark green, ovate, toothed margins, 3–6 in. long.

Fruit: Four nutlets that resemble seeds.

Height: 3–4 ft.

FLOWERING

July and August.

RANGE

Native to North America from Maine south to Georgia and west to Michigan and Ontario.

HABITAT

Grows in moist soils of thickets, woodlands, and stream banks.

Modern medicine has not entirely ignored this plant. Scientists have found that the oil extracted from *Monarda didyma* and *M. punctata* contains thymol, which is antiseptic against fungi, bacteria, and some parasites. Pharmacologists add thymol to ointments and powders applied externally to fungal infections. Internally thymol has been used as an antiseptic for the stomach and intestines and as a vermifuge to get rid of hookworms, but in its pure form and in the doses required for a therapeutic effect, thymol can cause vomiting, diarrhea, and other symptoms, so its use has declined. Today, thymol is produced synthetically.

Culinary: Few people consider it a culinary herb, but why not use it as such? The taste of beebalm is reminiscent of citrus with a soft mingling of orange and lemon. Use the leaves fresh in cooking or dried in tea blends. Add fresh flowers to salads or use them as garnishes, both for their flavor and their brilliant color.

Include fresh whole or chopped leaves in recipes for duck, pork, meat sausages, and curries. The citrusy flavor of beebalm naturally complements many fruits: strawberries, apples, oranges, tangerines, and melons, and it works well in combination with mint.

Available commercially: Dried as tea.

A western species, *M. menthifolia,* known as wild oregano or oregano de la sierra, can also be used to flavor foods. Wild indeed—the flowers are hot. Michael Moore, author of *Medicinal Plants of the Mountain West,* suggests adding them to salsa or chili dishes. The leaves can be used in the same ways as Mexican or Greek oregano.

Aromatic: While the citrusy flavor of beebalm adds a tang to the taste of foods, the citrusy fragrance brightens the scent of potpourris. The entire plant emits a strong and pleasant fragrance, very similar to that of bergamot oil, which is extracted from a tropical tree—the orange bergamot, *Citrus aurantium.* (This is how beebalm acquired another of its common names, bergamot.) Add the leaves and flowers to sachets and potpourris. Not only will you enjoy the fragrance but the dried petals of beebalm will add color to the potpourri.

Commercially, the oil of beebalm is sometimes used in the perfume industry.

Ornamental: The brilliant flowers of beebalm seem to burst forth from their stems in crimson glory. Who could resist planting this stunning herb in the garden? You can choose from among many colors: pink, white, violet, salmon, a mahogany shade, and several shades of red. *M. didyma* and *M. fistulosa* are the two primary species from which most of the horticultural varieties have been derived. Choose whatever colors you like, but remember that the scarlet-blooming beebalm is special for its ability to attract hummingbirds.

GROWING CONDITIONS

- Plant hardiness zones 4–9.
- Soil pH 6.5.
- Rich, moist, humusy soil.
- Full sun to shade.

Cosmetic: In lotions and baths, infusions of beebalm stimulate the skin.

Craft: The dried flowers lose some brilliance of form and color, but they still look quite lovely and can be used in herb wreaths or any dried herb arrangement.

Companion planting: Beebalm is said to enhance the growth of tomatoes.

CULTIVATION

One of the advantages of growing beebalm is that it will thrive in a variety of soils and light conditions. However, it does best in a sunny location or in part-day shade in a fertile soil that holds moisture well.

Beebalm can be propagated from seeds; however, because this herb cross-pollinates so readily, the plants are unlikely to be uniform in color and form. Furthermore, the seedlings do not establish themselves for at least a year, so harvesting cannot be started until the second year. If you use seeds, plant them within the first two years; thereafter their viability declines considerably. Germination should occur in about two weeks. If you want plants that are true to their parent, increase beebalm by division done in autumn or spring.

Leave a distance of 2 feet between clumps of beebalm. Beebalm spreads rapidly. The hills surrounding the Shaker settlement near Pittsfield, Massachusetts, are rife with beebalm, successors to plants that escaped the Shakers' herb gardens.

Cyrus Hyde of Well-Sweep Herb Farm in New Jersey suggests that you rejuvenate beebalm that has grown in one spot for more than three years. Dig up the clump and discard the center, replanting only the sucker shoots from the outside of the clump. The plants should be mulched if a cold winter fails to protect them with a layer of snow.

Harvesting and storage: When harvesting beebalm, cut it down to within 1 inch of the ground as soon as the lower leaves begin to yellow. Cutting the plant back immediately after it blooms will usually promote a second flowering in early autumn.

Leaves for tea may be cut as needed or during two major harvesting periods: once just before the herb flowers, and again after it flowers. The teas will differ in taste. To obtain the best flavor from the herb, strip the leaves from the stems and lay them to dry for two or three days in a warm, shady place. If the leaves have not dried in this time, place them in the oven under low heat to complete the process. A drying period longer than three days may discolor the leaves and produce a less flavorful tea.

CHEF TIPS

- Mince fresh leaves and toss with plain yogurt, a bit of honey, and fresh fruit.

- Add a handful of fresh leaves when making apple jelly. Strain before boiling down to the gel stage. Add a beebalm flower to each jar before sealing.

- Use sprigs to garnish fruit punches and iced teas.

BEEBALM SPECIES AND VARIETIES

Monarda citriodora: pink-purple blossom; strong lemon scent; excellent in tea.

M. didyma 'Adam': moderate red blossom.

M. didyma 'Alba': ivory blossom.

M. didyma 'Blue Stocking': violet-purple blossom.

M. didyma 'Cambridge Scarlet': bright red blossom.

M. didyma 'Croftway Pink': clear rosy pink blossom.

M. didyma 'Mahogany': deep red blossom.

M. didyma 'Melissa': pale pink blossom.

M. didyma 'Pale Ponticum': lavender blossom.

M. didyma 'Pillar Box': bright red blossom.

M. didyma 'Snow maiden': white blossom.

M. fistulosa: lavender blossom; strong fragrance.

BETONY

DESCRIPTION

Betony is a perennial herb with a hairy square stem that is often unbranched. A characteristic that distinguishes betony from other plants in the same family is that its flowers are displayed in what is called an interrupted spike—the flowers bloom in a short spike at the top, beneath which is a stretch of stem-bearing leaves, and farther down more flowers. (See photo on page 309.)

Flowers: ¾ in., red-violet, tubular, formed by an upper and lower lip; two pairs of stamens; five sepals make up calyx; flowers are borne in whorls at top of stem; whorls of flowers bloom from leaf axils at other places along stem.

Leaves: Deep green, hairy, coarsely toothed, opposite; grow in pairs at relatively wide intervals along the stem; those on lower part of stem oblong, heart-shaped, long stalked; upper leaves fewer, narrower, very short stalks; those beneath flowers may be sessile.

Fruit: Four brown, seed-like nutlets can be found in the bottom of the calyx after the flower has died.

Height: Up to 3 ft.

FLOWERING

July and August.

RANGE

Europe, northern Africa, and western Siberia; widely cultivated.

HABITAT

Grows wild in shady areas in woods and meadows.

Stachys officinalis   **Labiatae**

You wake up on a cold winter day and peer outside. It snowed last night, and inches of powder cover the ground, branches of trees, the birdbath. It's caught in the ridges of tree bark. A good day to snuggle up under the afghan with a good book, a cup of hot tea, and maybe some chocolate chip cookies.

In the kitchen, you set the kettle on the burner, open the cupboard, and take down a teacup and the glass jar of dried betony leaves. You crumble some leaves into the tea infuser, then sigh contentedly, waiting for the water to boil.

Betony has great virtue. This tea is going to be *good.*

HISTORY

The Egyptians didn't make tea with betony, but they did regard it as a magical herb. Given the powers that people attributed to this plant through the ages, it seems that this reputation stayed with betony for a long, long time.

The Spanish saying "He has as many virtues as betony" illustrates the regard people had for this plant. Indeed, if a person had as many virtues as betony had medicinal uses, he or she must have been a saint. The Romans listed betony as a cure for 47 different illnesses. In the latter half of the seventeenth century, a physician recorded 30 medicinal uses for it. Even wild beasts were said to value betony as a medicine and to seek it out when they were wounded.

Perhaps the greatest virtue of betony was as a guard against harm. Men and women believed that betony warded off evil spirits. During the Middle Ages, they planted it in churchyards and wore amulets made from it. The British book *Demonology and Witchcraft* advised readers that "the house where *Herba Betonica* is sown is free from all mischief."

USES

Times change. Today, if you are as virtuous as betony, you'd better consider some self-improvement classes. Though herbalists still value betony, modern medicine definitely attributes only one property to the herb: astringency.

Medicinal: Herbalist John Lust, author of *The Herb Book,* describes betony's uses for asthma and bronchitis, heartburn, kidney problems, "spitting blood and excessive sweating," and even worms. "The juice of the plant can be used to heal cuts, external ulcers, and old sores," Lust continues. "If you have a sprain, don't throw away the leaves boiled to make a decoction: Make them into a poultice to put on the injured part."

But Purdue University pharmacognosist Varro Tyler, Ph.D., says that what betony *can* help to cure are throat irritations and diarrhea. Betony contains tannins, Tyler points out, which make it astringent and thus useful in these ailments. Other healing virtues are unsubstantiated, he says. For a sore throat make an infusion from the leaves and gargle with it. For diarrhea drink the infusion as a cup of tea.

A study done by scientists in the Soviet Union found that betony contains a mixture of glycosides, which showed some effect in lowering blood pressure. This might explain why infusions of betony have been recommended for headaches and mild anxiety attacks. But Tyler maintains that more work needs to be done in this area before any conclusions can be drawn.

Toxicity: Betony is generally considered safe to use medicinally. Overdosing may irritate the stomach.

Culinary: If you don't need to take the tea for medicinal purposes, try an occasional cup simply for pleasure—the next time it snows, for example. Betony makes a fine substitute for regular black tea. Try blending it with other dried herbs.

Ornamental: Beauty is another of betony's virtues. The tall, purple-flowered spikes look stunning in the garden. Plant them in flower beds and borders. The lower ones are well-suited to rock gardens. The variety *Stachys officinalis* var. *alba* grows to a height of 9 inches and produces pure white flowers.

CULTIVATION

Naturally occurring species of betony easily grow from seed, cuttings, or division. However, with garden varieties, you are better off propagating plants by division or cuttings.

Betony plants require little care except for occasional weeding. They grow best in a deep, fertile, well-drained soil that is kept moderately moist. They prefer a sunny location but will grow in an area that is shaded during part of the day.

As a general rule, betony plants should be divided and replanted every three or four years. However, if the plants are doing well, this can be postponed until crowding starts to cause them to decline.

Harvesting and storage: Leaves can be harvested at any time, but they are best when taken before the plant is about to flower. Dry them and store in a tightly sealed container.

GROWING CONDITIONS

- Plant hardiness zone 4.
- Average, well-drained, moderately moist soil.
- Full sun to partial shade.

BIRCH

DESCRIPTION

Elegance and grace describe the birch tree. It is a slender tree distinguished by attractive, papery bark. It grows fast but does not live long, having an average life span of 50 years. Birches can generally be divided into the white and black birches, according to the color of their bark. The best known are the white birches, whose bark is easily peeled off the trunk in strips.

Flowers: Tiny, no petals, borne on male and female catkins; male catkins pendulous and develop from buds at the tips of the twigs; female catkins cone-shaped and produced further back along twigs; a single birch produces both male and female catkins.

Leaves: Alternate, ovate, serrated edges, undersides slightly hairy, resemble beech leaves although smaller.

Fruit: Tiny winged nuts ripen on the female catkins.

Height: 40–90 ft.

RANGE

White, paper, or canoe birch, *Betula papyrifera,* in northern forests of North America from Pennsylvania and Nebraska to the Great Lakes region, in northern areas of the Pacific Northwest, and north throughout Canada.

Black or sweet birch, *B. lenta,* from Maine to Tennessee and west to Iowa.

River or black birch, *B. nigra,* in the South and as far north as Massachusetts.

Betula spp.　　**Betulaceae**

The birch, an elegant tree with a slender trunk, light branches, and a smooth, thin bark, graces any landscape. The English poet Coleridge refers to the birch as the "Lady of the Woods," and indeed this tree would beautify any landscape with her grace and elegance.

HISTORY

The American Indians knew that birch tea helped to relieve headaches. They gathered the leaves of the black birch, steeped them in hot water, and drank the tea to relieve headaches and ease rheumatism. Some tribes brewed a medicinal tea from the leaves and dried bark for fevers, kidney stones, and abdominal cramps caused by gas in the digestive system. Poultices of boiled bark helped to heal burns, wounds, and bruises.

The Indians passed on this knowledge to the white frontiersmen, who then used birch medicinally. They gargled with it to freshen their mouths and drank it to stimulate urination, to expel intestinal worms, and to treat gout.

Some tribes of Indians gathered the conelike fruiting structures of *Betula pumila* and boiled them to make a tea for women to take during painful menstruation. They also roasted these cones over the coals of a campfire and inhaled the smoke to cure nasal infections.

Besides medicinal remedies, the American Indians found a number of other uses for this lovely tree. They constructed canoes and wigwams from the bark of *B. papyrifera.* The bark, although papery and flexible, is quite strong and durable and impervious to water. The largest and smoothest trunks were selected in the spring, and cut sections were pried off with a wooden wedge; they measured from 10 to 12 feet long and 2 feet 9 inches broad. The sheets were stuck together with the fibrous roots of the white spruce, rendered supple by soaking in water. The seams were waterproofed by coating them with the resin of the balsam fir. The canoes weighed little—a four-passenger model ranged from 40 to 50 pounds.

For the white man, the birch offered medicine, paper, and whipping rods. Imagine cutting the branches of such a graceful, gentle tree to beat the backsides of disobedient children. Better to use the branches to make a medicinal extract or birch beer.

USES

Birch trees are enormously useful. You can make canoes from the bark, birch beer from the branches, or maybe a medicinal infusion from the leaves. But if you have the room, surely you'll want to grow this elegant tree simply for the pleasure of its beauty.

Medicinal: Birch contains methyl salicylate, which has counterirritant and analgesic properties. Thus, there may be some validity to the folk medicine use of birch to relieve the ache of rheumatism. Try making a tea from the leaves or a decoction from the bark. Or make a hot poultice from the leaves, bark, and catkins to apply externally. The skin absorbs methyl salicylate. A poultice can also be used on skin irritations and minor wounds.

Modern medicine has not tested these remedies, so you'll have to try them yourself to find out if they work. Pharmacists do combine synthetic methyl salicylate with menthol in creams and liniments used to relieve the pain of musculoskeletal conditions such as rheumatism, osteoarthritis, and low back pain.

Culinary: A more enjoyable way to use your sweet birches, *B. lenta,* is to make birch beer with them. To make this refreshing soda, try this recipe suggested by Gaea and Shandor Weiss in their book *Growing and Using the Healing Herbs:*

Place 4 quarts of finely cut twigs or inner bark into a 5-gallon crock. Add 4 gallons of water or birch sap and bring to a boil. Stir in 1 gallon of honey, and remove the mixture from the heat. When it has cooled, strain the mixture to remove the bark and twigs. Keep the liquid in the crock, and place one yeast cake on a piece of toast and float it on the liquid. Cover the pot, and let the mixture ferment for about one week, until it begins to settle. Bottle the birch beer, and store it in a cool, dry place. It can be kept for several months up to a year, depending on storage conditions.

Ornamental: When the birch beer is ready, pour yourself a big mug of it over ice, go sit in the swing on the front porch, and gaze out

LANDSCAPE IDEA

When deciding which birch to plant, consider the soil type. Most will grow well in an average soil. In poorer, sandy soils, the gray birch and European white birch will do well, while river, cherry, and yellow birches prosper in wetter locations. Those birches with light-colored barks look striking when set against a background of evergreens such as hemlocks.

GROWING CONDITIONS

- Soil pH 5.0–6.0.
- Moderately fertile, moist but well-drained soil.
- Partial to full sun.

over the land. Watch the breeze rustle the leaves and lift the branches on the white birches.

The birch effuses grace and elegance with its slender form and light bark. It makes a lovely landscape tree and can look especially beautiful placed near a rocky pool or pond where in autumn the water reflects the golden leaves.

With its delicate, airy form, the birch offers a dappled shade that usually will not interfere with the plants that grow beneath it. In fact, rhododendrons and other evergreens that need some protection from the sun benefit from being planted under birch trees.

Birches complement rock gardens when planted near them. Their appearance suggests a mountain terrain—usually the desired effect in these gardens. They offer a practical purpose, too, diffusing sunlight, which benefits many rock garden plants.

Cosmetic: An infusion of birch reportedly acts as a tonic and refreshes the skin when added to the bath. Try an infusion of the leaves or a decoction of the bark as a skin-freshening lotion. You can also extract the oil for either of these purposes.

Other: In some areas of the southeastern United States, particularly in Appalachia and the Ozarks, people chew the twigs of *B. lenta* to clean their teeth. People who want to quit smoking should consider chewing on a birch branch to relieve the oral fixation.

CULTIVATION

Generally, birches thrive in an area with a moderately fertile, well-drained soil that has an average moisture content. They do not require regular pruning, but should some storm damage occur, cut the branches in the early summer after the leaves have developed and the rise of sap has slowed down, so that the wounds will not bleed heavily.

Birches can be propagated from seeds. Pick the ripe, brown, woody catkins and put them into a bag to prevent loss of seed. Spread out the seed to dry for several weeks. Sow birch seed in late summer or fall soon after they have been collected (or in the spring after stratifying for four to eight weeks).

To start them indoors, sow them in soil that is fine, sandy, and peaty, covering them lightly or merely pressing them into the surface of the soil. Place polyethylene or glass over them until the seedlings begin to shoot forth. When sowing the seeds outdoors, rake them lightly into the soil. Then spread a cover such as brushwood over the bed to provide some shade and protection through the first two or three months of their first summer. When planting seeds, sow them thickly, as it is likely that a large percentage of them will not germinate.

BLACK HELLEBORE

Helleborus niger   Ranunculaceae

By blooming in the winter, black hellebore has cheered many hearts. Because of its season, it was named Christmas rose. And because of its astonishing ability to defy the cruel elements of winter, it signified to men and women that this herb must have great power.

In the Middle Ages, people strewed the flowers on the floors of their homes to drive out evil influences. They blessed their animals with it and used it to ward off the power of witches. These same people believed, however, that witches employed the herb in their spells and that sorcerers tossed the powdered herb into the air around them to make themselves invisible.

USES

That black hellebore is a powerful plant cannot be disputed. However, its power does not heal and protect as legend tells—it poisons.

Medicinal: Although the British herbalist Culpeper recommended it for leprosy, jaundice, gout, sciatica, and convulsions, and more recent herbalists have prescribed it for amenorrhea, tumors, warts, and various other ailments, black hellebore poisons rather than heals. It is not currently used in modern medicine except by homeopaths, who use it in carefully controlled, infinitesimal doses. Don't you try it.

Toxicity: Black hellebore contains two highly toxic glucosides, helleborin and helleborein, which are violently irritant both internally and externally.

Ornamental: The dark side of this herb is offset by the beauty of its flower and especially by the delight of discovering it in winter. You must be cautious of this herb even as an ornamental, however. Bruised leaves have caused severe dermatitis in some individuals. When handling the plant, wear gloves. And be sure to keep children away from it.

Black hellebore is well-suited to shrub borders, foundation plantings, and rock gardens. Since it tolerates partial shade, it can be used in open woodland settings. Grow it alone or in groups.

CULTIVATION

Propagate black hellebores from seed or division. Divide in the spring once flowering has subsided. If you start them from seed, you will have to wait a few years to see the flowers.

These hellebores like a rich soil; give them a generous organic mulch in the fall and fertilize again in the spring. A covering of pine branches will help the plants through a severe winter.

VERY TOXIC

DESCRIPTION

This small perennial herb actually produces its true stem underground. What appears aboveground is a flower stalk bearing two or three beautiful roselike blossoms. The root is black, hence the name.

Flowers: Two or three, terminal, slightly nodding; white or tinged with pink; five sepals form flower, roundish, concave, five inconspicuous tubular petals in center, numerous yellow stamens longer than the true petals, 10 pistils; 1½ –2½ in. in diameter.

Leaves: Deep green, leathery, hairless, evergreen; divided into seven to nine oblong, toothed leaflets; basal but with long stalks.

Fruit: Podlike follicles.

Height: 1 ft.

FLOWERING

January through March.

RANGE

Native to the southern and central mountainous regions of Europe; naturalized in parts of North America.

GROWING CONDITIONS

- Plant hardiness zones 4–8.
- Soil pH 6.5–7.0.
- Rich, moist, well-drained soil.
- Partial shade to full sun.

47

BLOODROOT

Sanguinaria canadensis   **Papaveraceae**

The American Indians discovered this herb. What a surprise it must have been to cut the root or pluck a leaf from this plain and simple plant and to see red-orange sap ooze out, like blood from a wound. No wonder this herb was named bloodroot.

UNSAFE

DESCRIPTION

Bloodroot is an herbaceous perennial. A naked stem rises from a bud at the end of the thick horizontal rhizome. Orange sap flows through the entire plant but shows the deepest color in the root. (See photo on page 168.)

Flowers: Solitary, 1–2 in. across, 7 to 16 white petals, arranged in whorls; corolla slightly cup-shaped.

Leaves: Heart-shaped but deeply lobed in palmate manner, edges toothed or wavy, upper surfaces smooth and yellowish green, underneath paler and showing orange veins; 8 in. across at maturity but only partly developed at bloom time; long channeled petiole that grows up from buds on the rhizome.

Fruit: Oblong, two-valved capsule, 1 in. long, holds several reddish brown oval seeds.

Height: 6–14 in.

FLOWERING

Very early spring.

RANGE

Native to North America; common in New England, Long Island, Pennsylvania, and New Jersey; also grows in Kentucky, Ohio, Indiana, Wisconsin, Illinois, Kansas, and from Florida to Texas.

HABITAT

Cool, moist, deciduous woods and woodland slopes.

HISTORY

The sap dripping onto their fingers may have given the Indians the idea that they could use it to color their skins. They painted their bodies with it to frighten away enemies. Perhaps this was the meaning intended when Indian women stained their bodies with bloodroot before being forced to spend the night with Captain John Smith.

In addition to dyeing their bodies with bloodroot, the Indians dyed cloth with it—a purpose for which bloodroot can still be used today.

Of course, Indians found medicinal uses for this herb as well. A tea made from the roots was drunk to treat sore throats, fevers, and rheumatism. Certain tribes chewed the root and spat the juice on burns to heal them. Indians living on the shores of Lake Superior applied the sap to skin cancers to cure them.

The white man also found medicinal purposes for it. Bloodroot was an official botanical drug listed in the *U.S. Pharmacopoeia* from 1820 to 1926.

USES

Medicinal: Bloodroot exhibits real pharmacological action produced by the alkaloid sanguinarine. Sanguinarine stimulates respiration, increases blood pressure, excites the flow of saliva, and increases peristalsis in the intestines. In small doses, preparations of bloodroot act as an expectorant, stimulant, and diaphoretic. It has often been used for its expectorant properties, and preparations from bloodroot were once prescribed to clear mucus from the respiratory system in cases of chronic bronchitis, bleeding lungs, pneumonia, whooping cough, colds, and similar ailments.

One of the more interesting medicinal claims for bloodroot lies in its therapeutic effects on cancers, particularly skin cancers. The Indians who lived along the shores of Lake Superior were the first to use the sap of bloodroot on cancerous growths. Wilson and Wilson in *Medical Botany* report on the successful efforts of various people in treating cancers (particularly breast cancers and superficial tumors) with bloodroot.

Toxicity: Although bloodroot may have some positive actions on the body, it could have some negative ones, too. No cases of poisoning have been reported, but incidences of persons experiencing nausea, headaches, and vomiting have occurred. James Duke, Ph.D., author of the *CRC Handbook of Medicinal Herbs,* experienced tunnel vision after nibbling a small piece of the rhizome. Any medical treatment with bloodroot should be done by a physician.

Ornamental: You're used to seeing bloodroot growing wild in the woods, but it can be cultivated in the garden. It may look rather insignificant to some, but the simple white blossom really is lovely, and the leaves offer a unique and attractive texture and shape. Because it is a wildflower, it suits native gardens and rock gardens perfectly, but plant it anywhere you like. It can be grown among shrubs and beneath trees that do not cast a heavy shade, and it looks most attractive when planted in a natural-looking grouping rather than any formal pattern.

A beautiful double-flowered cultivar, *Sanguinaria canadensis* 'Multiplex' (also known as *S. canadensis* var. *plena*) produces additional petals instead of stamens, creating a fuller, almost roselike corolla. It blooms a few days later than *S. canadensis,* and the flowers last much longer.

Dye: The Indians dyed fabrics with bloodroot, and so can you. Shades the color of the root can be stained in wool and silk. To dye these fabrics orange, use no mordant. With a mordant of alum and cream of tartar, the wool and silk will take a rust color; use tin to create a reddish pink shade. The root should be used fresh and is best when harvested in autumn, according to Betty E. M. Jacobs, author of *Growing Herbs and Plants for Dyeing.*

Jacobs states that only 8 ounces of chopped root with 4¼ gallons of water are required. She recommends using the simultaneous dyeing method with bloodroot (see the entry Dyes from Herbs).

CULTIVATION

Bloodroot can be propagated from seeds, but division of the rhizome is easier and should be done in early autumn. Leave 6 to 8 inches of space between plants. If you need to move them for any reason, the best time is late August or September. Add decayed organic matter to the soil, and bloodroots will be healthier.

The double-flowered variety, *S. canadensis* 'Multiplex', should only be propagated by division, according to Thomas H. Everett, author of the *New York Botanical Garden Illustrated Encyclopedia of Horticulture.*

GROWING CONDITIONS

- Plant hardiness zone 3.
- Acid soil.
- Rich, moist, humusy soil.
- Full sun to partial shade.

BLUE COHOSH

Caulophyllum thalictroides   Berberidaceae

UNSAFE

DESCRIPTION

Blue cohosh is a deciduous, perennial plant with a round, erect stem. The mature plant is bluish green in color, hence the name blue cohosh.

Flowers: ⅓ in. wide, yellow-green, bloom in cluster at top of stem; six petals, much smaller than the sepals, resemble glands; six sepals, six stamens, one pistil.

Leaves: Only one large leaf, divided into two or three leaflets, may be further divided into three segments; very short stalk; borne near the top of the plant.

Fruit: Dark blue, spherical, berrylike, pea sized.

Height: 1–3 ft.

FLOWERING

April.

RANGE

From New Brunswick to Manitoba south to South Carolina, Alabama, Tennessee, and Missouri.

HABITAT

Deciduous woods and moist banks along streams.

GROWING CONDITIONS

- Soil pH: neutral.
- Rich, moist, humusy soil.
- Shade.

If ever there was a woman's herb, blue cohosh is it. *Caulophyllum thalictroides* has been touted widely as a healer of female ailments. One of the oldest native American drug plants, it was, for the American Indians, the herb of choice when it came to problems of the uterus.

The white medicine men learned of blue cohosh from the Indian medicine men, and it was listed for a brief time during the late 1800s in the *U.S. Pharmacopoeia.*

USES

Again and again, books on folk medicine report how effective this herb is, yet nowhere can you find a scientific report that recommends using blue cohosh.

Medicinal: Homeopaths and practitioners of folk medicine prescribe blue cohosh for a number of ailments, including bronchitis, cramps, sore throat, nervousness, rheumatism, and, of course, uterine cramps and delayed menstruation.

The alkaloid methylcytisine and the glycoside caulosaponin are primarily responsible for the herb's effects. Methylcytisine stimulates respiration and the motion of the intestines, and it raises blood pressure. Caulosaponin seems responsible for stimulating the uterus.

Toxicity: The inadvisability of using this herb stems from the fact that caulosaponin constricts the blood vessels of the heart, which has a toxic effect on the cardiac muscle. Thus, it is not good for anyone with high blood pressure. In studies with small animals, it has caused intestinal spasms. The plant is clearly potent, but it isn't advisable to use it for self-medication.

Ornamental: Although not a showy plant, the foliage of blue cohosh is decorative in its reddish purple youth and its blue-green maturity. The blue fruits appear in autumn to enhance the attractiveness of the herb, and they last a long time. Plant blue cohosh in a woodland setting or a native garden. It looks best grown in clumps.

CULTIVATION

Blue cohosh can be propagated by division or from seeds. To divide the plant, make cuttings from the rhizome. This should be done in early fall or spring. Seeds should be sown as soon as they are ripe and can be planted in a cold frame or a protected bed outdoors. From seeds sown in the fall, some will germinate the following spring; others will not germinate for a year.

BONESET

Eupatorium perfoliatum   Compositae

One of early America's foremost medicinal plants, a popular panacea of extraordinary powers, boneset today is chiefly regarded as a weed with an interesting past.

From the name, you might think its powers included—somehow—the ability to mend broken bones. Well, boneset traditionally was a cough-and-fever remedy. But in the old days, a flu that caused severe body aches was called a breakbone fever. So the name makes some sense. What doesn't make sense, say contemporary scientists, is how boneset got its high reputation. It simply doesn't work.

Used extensively by American Indians, relied upon heavily by early American settlers, boneset's reputation spread beyond this country to Europe. It had no equal as a cough, cold, and fever remedy during the eighteenth and nineteenth centuries. Civil War troops received boneset infusions not only as remedies when they fell victim to fevers but also as tonics to keep them healthy. Although its popularity with the medical profession waned well before the turn of the century, it was regularly listed in the *U.S. Dispensatory* from 1820 through 1950.

In the tradition of the Indians, the herb's leaves and flowers were steeped in a pot of boiling water to create an infusion normally administered in spoonfuls or half-cup doses. Drunk as hot as possible, boneset infusions were also used as emetics (to induce vomiting) and cathartics and to relieve indigestion, dyspepsia, catarrh, rheumatism, snakebite, pneumonia, malaria, typhoid, female disorders, and bladder ailments.

Boneset's heyday has passed. Current information—no tales, just the facts—makes clear it is no panacea, only a weed.

Varro Tyler, Ph.D., of the Purdue University School of Pharmacy, Nursing, and Health Sciences points out that chemical studies of boneset have revealed that "compounds with pronounced therapeutic virtues are apparently absent." He calls it an "outdated, bad-tasting, worthless fraud."

David Spoerke of the University of Utah School of Pharmacy indicates that boneset may cause kidney and liver damage as well as internal hemorrhaging and severe intestinal problems. These are reasons enough to stick with aspirin when you have a fever.

Boneset can be used in a natural landscape or a wild garden, since it is a reasonably attractive—though not first rank—plant. It is comfortable in any fairly decent soil, which is why it grows wild in so many areas. A hardy perennial, it is easily grown and easily increased by division in the spring or early fall and by seed.

DESCRIPTION

Common boneset, *Eupatorium perfoliatum,* is one of the hardiest members of the *Eupatorium* genus, and it is a large genus. It grows from a crooked rootstock and hollow, hairy stems. Its species name refers to the way in which the stem seems to perforate the center of the joined leaf pairs.

Flowers: Dense terminal compound heads comprised of clusters of 10–16 tiny, tubular florets; white to bluish purple.

Leaves: Long, tapering, pointed, remotely toothed; stalkless, oppositely joined, encircle the stems; dark green, shiny on top, pubescent beneath; to 8 in. long.

Fruit: Achenes with a full crown of white bristles.

Height: 2–5 ft.

RANGE

Indigenous to Mexico, the West Indies, and tropical South America; naturalized from New Brunswick south to Florida and Texas and west to the Dakotas.

GROWING CONDITIONS

- Plant hardiness zones 5–9.
- Soil pH: very tolerant.
- Rich, moist soil.
- Full sun.

BORAGE

Borago officinalis   **Boraginaceae**

"What makes the Hottentot so hot? What put the ape in apricot? What have they got that I ain't got?" Borage?

Had the Cowardly Lion known that borage brought courage to those who ate it or drank borage-flavored wine, he wouldn't have had to make that journey to the Emerald City. As a matter of fact, he wouldn't have had to look any farther than his own backyard, where he could have grown bunches of borage to make him brave.

DESCRIPTION

Borage is an annual, self-seeding plant that bears many leafy, branched, hollow stems covered with stiff, white hairs. The sprawling habit of the branches creates a handsome, rounded shape to the whole plant. (See photos on pages 377 and 513.)

Flowers: Blue, star-shaped corolla, ¾ in. in diameter, five segments, five protruding stamens with black anthers, in terminal drooping racemes, on long peduncles, five-segmented calyx.

Leaves: Basal form a rosette, upper ones alternate, wrinkled, hairy, up to 6 in. long, ovate to oblong-lanceolate, grayish green.

Fruit: Four nutlets.

Height: 2–3 ft.

FLOWERING

Midsummer (depends on seeding time).

RANGE

Native to Europe, Asia Minor, northern Europe, and Africa; naturalized in Great Britain; widely cultivated in North America.

HABITAT

Sunny locations including waste places and along roadsides.

HISTORY

Borage's reputation for invoking courage goes back a long way. With such a reputation, it naturally was a favorite among soldiers during war. Ancient Celtic warriors preparing for battle drank wine flavored with borage to give them courage. Their fears would vanish, and they would feel elated. (It was probably the wine.) According to the sixteenth-century British herbalist John Gerard, Roman soldiers used to say, *"Ego borago gaudia semper ago."* Gerard translated this as "Borage always brings me courage," but this is a pretty loose translation; *gaudia* means delight, not bravery.

Very much related to the feeling of courage is the sense of elation and well-being that borage was said to produce. Several of history's most noted herbalists and scholars spoke of this. The early Roman scholar Pliny, believing the herb to be an anti-depressant, called it *euphrosinum*. The Greek Dioscorides wrote in his *De Materia Medica* that one should take borage to "cheer the heart and lift the depressed spirits." John Gerard reported that " . . . those of our time do use the floures in sallads to exhilarate and make the minde glad . . . for the comfort of the heart, to drive away sorrow, and increase the joy of the minde." The Welsh called borage *llanwenlys,* meaning herb of gladness, and Sir Francis Bacon wrote, "The leaf of Burrage hath an excellent spirit to repress the fuliginous vapour of dusky melancholie."

USES

It would be nice to think that anytime you needed to allay a little fear or muster up a little courage, maybe before an important meeting at work or before going out on stage for a performance, you could drink a little borage-flavored wine. But it's likely that if bold you were to become, it would be the wine, not the borage, doing the talking. Such a disappointment notwithstanding, borage can bring you joy and gladness both in the garden and in the home.

Medicinal: In addition to prescribing borage to relieve depression, the early herbalists believed it to be a diuretic, demulcent, and emollient, and these same beliefs are held by herbalists today. Infusions and decoctions of borage flowers are taken to relieve fevers, bronchitis, and diarrhea among other ailments. Poultices made from the leaves are reported to be cooling and soothing and so are applied to external inflammations and swellings.

According to Varro Tyler, Ph.D., pharmacognosist and author of *The Honest Herbal,* borage's properties can be linked to some of its constituents. Its tannin content makes it slightly astringent and slightly constipating. Its mucilage is responsible for its mild expectorant actions, which explains the use of borage in treating bronchitis, and its malic acid and potassium nitrate might produce some diuretic action. Herbalists, it seems, have not been too far off track. However, Tyler also points out that in laboratory tests with small animals, the only action borage produced was slight constipation. "It has no significant value as a medicine," he said.

Toxicity: Some herbalists warn that borage may be toxic to the liver. However, these claims have not been verified in any way. Tyler and James Duke, Ph.D., author of *CRC Handbook of Medicinal Herbs,* agree that borage is safe to eat.

Culinary: One of the ways in which borage brings joy is as a flavoring in foods. It has a crisp cucumber flavor. The leaves are used raw, steamed, or sautéed like spinach. You can eat the stems, too; peel, chop, and use them like celery. Toss fresh borage flowers in salads or garnish foods with them. In candied form, they make splendid decorations for pastries and dessert trays.

The leaves and stems enhance cheese, fish, poultry, most vegetables, green salads, iced beverages, pickles, and salad dressings. They blend well with dill, mint, and garlic. If you object to the fuzziness of borage leaves, use them for flavor only and remove them from food before serving.

Substitute: Fresh salad burnet.

Storage note: Borage is unacceptable when dried and frozen. The only way to store it for the long-term is in a flavored vinegar.

Ornamental: For the gladness borage brings, you don't have to look any farther than your own backyard. There you can grow this herb and delight in its blue, star-shaped blossoms. The rough, somewhat sprawling habit of borage makes it a little too unrefined in appearance to be planted in formal garden settings. Of course, it suits an herb garden well, and it blends nicely with other plants in a wildflower garden. Add it to your vegetable patch.

Companion planting: Borage is said to strengthen the resistance to insects and disease of any plants neighboring it. It is an especially

CHEF TIPS

- Heighten the flavor of iced cucumber (or other chilled vegetable soups) by adding 2 tablespoons of minced fresh borage to 4 cups of soup. Use borage flowers for garnish.

- Add a handful (amount for 2 quarts of stock) of leaves and stems when making chicken or fish stock.

- Make a strong tea by boiling leaves and stems in water. Use the tea in place of water in a recipe for lemon or strawberry fruit ice.

MARRY ME?

According to old wives' tales, borage was sometimes smuggled into the drink of prospective husbands to give them the courage to propose marriage.
Mary Campbell
A Basket of Herbs

BORAGE—continued

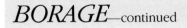

GROWING CONDITIONS

- Soil pH 6.6.
- Fairly rich, moist, light soil.
- Full sun.

good companion for strawberries, the two plants being mutually beneficial. Just make sure the borage remains the junior partner.

Other: If you need to attract bees to your garden, plant some borage. Bees love the flowers.

CULTIVATION

Borage is easily grown from seed. You can sow the seed as soon as the danger of frost has passed. When seedlings appear, thin them to a distance of about 2 feet. Borage occupies a lot of room once it matures. After the initial planting, the herb readily reseeds itself.

Borage will do well in just about any garden soil, but for optimum growth maintain a fairly rich medium. A manure compost is the best fertilizer. The soil should be loose, well aerated, and hoed regularly to eliminate weedy competition. Keep the soil moist, too. This is easily done by using mulch. If you need to transplant borage, move plants when they are quite young; be gentle with the roots.

Don't be disappointed if the flowers don't appear on your new plant the first year. Sometimes borage can be a biennial.

Container gardening: Borage grows easily indoors in pots. Just provide it with a sunny spot, moisture, and a fertile potting medium, and give the roots plenty of space in which to spread.

BROOM

Cytisus spp.   **Leguminosae**

Broom is a colorful, near-hardy shrub that looks very much like its household namesake. At one time, the tall, thick mass of upright branches at the base of the plant were cut and deftly tied to the end of a stick to produce a crude, yet serviceable, broom.

USES

Nowadays, broom is used primarily as an ornamental that thrives where many plants barely survive.

Medicinal: Though broom continues to be used in folk medicine in Europe, many American herbalists consider it too dangerous to use. Heed the words of American herbalist John Lust: "Large doses of Scotch broom can cause fatal poisoning."

Toxicity: The flowering stem tops, when collected before blooming, contain sparteine, a volatile compound that causes diuretic, cathartic and, in large doses, emetic (vomiting) reactions. Scientific research has demonstrated that sparteine both slows down the heart and stimulates uterine contractions. Because of this, it was used therapeutically to slow the pulse in cardiac disturbances and to induce labor. Both uses have been discontinued, however, because they were found to be unsafe.

Ornamental: Beautiful to the eye, these profusely flowering shrubs are grown for their delicate, yet brilliant flowers. The flowers bloom continuously throughout the spring and summer and dazzle the looker with their bright yellow hue. The lush, yellowish green leaves retain their color until the first frost, catching the attention of the unsuspecting nature lover.

Dye: The flowering tops produce yellow dyes for wool.

CULTIVATION

Typically known as a dry-soil plant, broom is easy to grow. It requires only sun and well-drained soil. The soil can be sandy or gravelly, more acid than alkaline, but it should not be too rich.

All the broom varieties may be cultivated by seed, grafting, or cuttings, the last being, perhaps, the easiest. The best time to take cuttings is during the month of August. Hardwood and softwood cuttings root equally well.

The care required for broom is minimal. You won't need to worry about insect infestation and disease, but do take care when you transplant or prune, because the roots are scant. Pruning protects the plants from becoming spindly at the base, and it should be done as soon as the flowers have faded.

UNSAFE

DESCRIPTION

Broom is a low, deciduous shrub with many slender branches. (See photo on page 169.)

Flowers: Pea-shaped, two-lipped, yellow, ¾ in. long; ten stamens; solitary or paired, from axils.

Leaves: Sparse on leggy branches; alternate; lower leaves stalked with three obovate or oblong-lanceolate leaflets; upper leaves stalkless, one lanceolate leaflet; leaflets ¼–½ in. long.

Fruit: Brownish black, shaggy pod, containing 12 to 18 seeds; ¾ in. long.

Height: 3–6 ft.; can grow as tall as 10 ft. under perfect conditions.

FLOWERING

As early as April, but usually in May and June.

RANGE

Native to Europe; naturalized throughout North America.

GROWING CONDITIONS

• Soil pH: more acid than alkaline.

• Poor, ordinary, well-drained soil.

• Full sun.

BURDOCK

Arctium Lappa   Compositae

It's a vegetable; it's an ancient healing herb; it's an unspeakable pest. Love it or loathe it, burdock is a plant that demands to be noticed.

DESCRIPTION

Burdock is a coarse but dramatic plant. Stout and much branched, each stem is topped by a bristly "flower," which is actually an armored clump of many flowers. Picked out of the clump, the individual flowers are surprisingly small and frail looking. The flower clumps turn into burrs that cling to anything that brushes by. Although it is a biennial, in cultivation it can be treated as an annual by sowing seeds in spring and harvesting the stout taproot in fall.

Flowers: In solitary burr-like heads, to 1¾ in. across; individual purplish red blossoms tubular.

Leaves: Alternate, mostly ovate-cordate, to 20 in. long, white, wooly beneath, with long leaf stalks.

Fruit: Oblong, wrinkled achenes with a tuft of stout bristles.

Height: 1½–6 ft.

FLOWERING

Summer.

RANGE

Eurasia; naturalized in North America.

HISTORY

A centuries-old medicinal plant, burdock appears in the writings of both the great London herbalist John Gerard and a man who for a time was his neighbor, William Shakespeare. The former valued it more highly than the latter, who used it as an image of a persistent annoyance or sign of humble fortune. "How full of briers is this working-day world!" exclaims Rosalind in *As You Like It.* And Celia responds: "They are but burs, cousin, thrown upon thee in holiday foolery. If we walk not in the trodden paths, our very petticoats will catch them." (The annoyance persists to this day for Shakespearean scholars, as they exchange daintily reasoned opinions over the question of a misprint in *King Lear:* Was the word "harlocks," sometimes interpreted as "hordocks," intended to be burdocks? No one knows, but it *is* something to ruminate about.)

Two species came to the New World where they quickly escaped to become hardy, widely dispersed weeds. A fast-growing biennial with large, wavy, egg-shaped leaves, burdock has been distinguished throughout history by the burrs it sets after flowering, but it is burdock's long, thick taproot that has made it a boon to herbalists and an implacable enemy to other gardeners. Yanking a misplaced mint out of the garden is one thing, but burdock roots just don't yank.

In spite of burdock's reputation as a pest, it was part of the drug-plant shortage list issued by the British Board of Agriculture and Fisheries in 1914. The war had cut off European supplies of drug plants, and procuring homegrown plants became a patriotic effort. A shortage of the weedy burdock, however, may sound more like a blessing than a crisis to anyone but an ardent herbalist.

USES

Medicinal: The first question here is safety, and the information is a bit confusing. Before 1978, there seemed to be no cause for concern. However, that year the *Journal of the American Medical Association* published an account of a 26-year-old woman who bought burdock root tea at a health food store and prepared cups for herself and her husband. Later, she remembered that both of them had dry mouths and blurred vision shortly after that first cup, but she forgot about the symptoms at the time. Some time after that, she drank a cup of the tea which had been steeping for 1½ days, and in about five minutes her vision blurred, her mouth felt dry, and according to her husband, she seemed to be hallucinating. She was taken to the emergency room, where doctors treated her for poisoning from an atropinelike alkaloid, and she recovered. The doctors were puzzled. Atropine, a poisonous alkaloid found in belladonna and related plants, had never before been associated with burdock. The lab analyzed tea from the package and found an atropine concentration of 300 milligrams per gram. The incident was not conclusive, suggests Dr. Varro Tyler, who studies medicines from natural sources at Purdue University. No one ever showed that the material in the tea package was indeed burdock root. Perhaps belladonna root itself had been substituted. Whatever you decide about burdock's safety, get your herbs from a reliable source.

Herbalists use the root, leaves, and seeds of the plant.

Dried burdock root has been administered mainly as a blood purifier. Herbalists consider it a diuretic and diaphoretic. Its use as a laxative sounds complicated to the point of uselessness. As twentieth-century American herbalist John Lust says, "The decoction or infusion of burdock root is aperient [laxative], but not for all individuals; for some it may even be constipative." Burdock root has been used in treating psoriasis and acne, among other skin conditions.

Recipes vary somewhat. Twentieth-century herbalist Michael Weiner, author of *Weiner's Herbal*, steeps a teaspoon of the root in 1½ pints of boiling water for 30 minutes and recommends drinking it at room temperature once or twice daily. Another modern-day herbalist, Michael Moore, puts about a teaspoon of the root in a cup of cold water, brings it to a boil, then lets it simmer for 20 minutes; he recommends drinking a cup of this tea once in the morning and once in the evening. Lust puts a teaspoon of the root in a cup of cold water, lets it stand for five hours, and *then* brings it to a boil. He recommends drinking this tea only once a day. Lust also recommends that the seeds be used only with medical supervision.

One colorful use may not need supervision, however, and the treatment may look so unexpected that women may not want anything but privacy for an experiment. It's an old treatment, described by London herbalist Nicholas Culpeper in the seventeenth century: "By its [burdock's] leaf or seed you may draw the womb which way you please, either upward by applying it to the crown of the head in case it falls out; or downwards in fits of the mother, by applying it to

BURDOCK, A.K.A . . .

beggar's buttons
gypsy's rhubarb
pig's rhubarb
snake rhubarb
clotbur
bardana
hardock
hareburr
hurr-burr
turkey burrseed

CONFUSION

Don't confuse burdock (*Arctium*) with cocklebur (*Xanthium*). Their common names are used interchangeably, but the burdock burrs are loose, hairy bunches of many seeds, while the cockleburs are spiky capsules containing two seeds.

Likewise, don't confuse the burdock discussed here, *A. Lappa*, which is often called great burdock, with *A. minus*, which is usually called common burdock. The common burdock is a generally smaller plant, if anything with a 5-foot stalk can be called small. Its leaf stalks are hollow (the great burdock's are solid), and the flower heads are stalkless or on short stalks (the great burdock's have distinct stalks).

the soles of the feet: or if you would stay it in its place, apply it to the navel, and that is one good way to stay the child in it.''

Herbalists have made poultices of the leaves that were used on bruises, burns, and knee swellings. Weiner records a recipe for a poultice to treat gout: "Boil the leaves in urine and bran until the liquid almost is gone; apply the sodden remains to the affected area.''

No chemical studies of the root have shown any evidence that it is diuretic, diaphoretic, or helpful in skin diseases, says Dr. Tyler. However, two polyacetylene compounds in the root do inhibit the growth of bacteria and fungi. These compounds were found in the fresh root, but only traces of them appeared in dried roots.

Culinary: Burdock fuses the flavors of potato and celery. The root is used fresh in cooking and most commonly is scrubbed or peeled, chopped, and steamed for about 30 minutes or sautéed for about 15 minutes. It can also be peeled, chopped, and soaked for about 30 minutes in several changes of cold water before cooking. This will help keep its whole color. The dried root is used in teas.

As for the rest of the plant, there seems to be somebody somewhere who eats each part. The tender spring leaves of first-year plants become a raw salad green or, steamed or sautéed like spinach,

BURDOCK—continued

a cooked vegetable. The young stalks can be picked, peeled, and chopped and used raw or, like asparagus, steamed for about 10 minutes. Even the young second-year stalks, reportedly, can be edible if peeled to reveal the pith and cooked.

Frequently used in Japanese cooking, burdock's taste is mild and appropriate in simple soups, stews, salads, pickles, and relishes.

Available commercially: Dried in tea blends.

Substitute for the root: Celeriac or celery root.

CULTIVATION

Burdock is a very tough plant—no pest problems, says Holly Shimizu, curator of the National Herb Garden in Washington, D.C. It grows easily from seed, and she recommends buying seed from one of the horticulturally selected varieties, because its flavor would be better. She treats burdock as an annual and starts seeds indoors in early spring "just to get a head start." (In Washington, that's March.) The seeds can also be sown outside once the soil has warmed up. Seedlings cope with transplanting, but older plants don't because of their long taproots.

Shimizu grows burdock in rich, friable, moist soil. At the end of its first year, the root is ready for digging, which is potentially quite a project. Roots often go down 3 feet, says Shimizu. Some gardeners simplify the process by planting burdock on mounds of soft soil so the digging will be easier.

Harvesting and storage: For digging the root, just when is the end of the first year? Fall? The following spring? The answer seems to be all of the above. Gaea and Shandor Weiss, authors of *Growing and Using the Healing Herbs,* dig roots in the fall. Michael Moore, a West Coast resident, prefers the spring of the following year when the roots are just sprouting, in part because spring harvesters don't have to contend with the burrs. Holly Shimizu remembers digging burdock roots in winter even though the ground was covered with frost. It was hardly easy, but it was the custom at the botanical garden in Belgium where she worked. Other growers suggest using a posthole digger to make a deep hole beside the root to simplify the process.

According to some herb books, the first-year plants will have only basal rosettes of leaves. This is an error, says Shimizu. First-year plants certainly do have a stalk.

When the root is finally out of the ground, use it fresh or dry it. To speed up drying, slice the root and put the pieces in a food dehydrator.

CHEF TIPS

- Shred soaked raw burdock root and toss with shredded carrot, minced fresh ginger, and lemon juice. Serve in lettuce cups as a first course or salad.

- Add dried burdock root to hot lemony beverages, and strain before serving.

GROWING CONDITIONS

- Plant hardiness zones: all.

- Deep, loose, well-drained soil.

- Full sun.

CALENDULA

Calendula officinalis   Compositae

> What flower is that which bears the Virgin's name,
> The richest metal joined to the same?

If you answered calendula, you would be correct. Calendula, you wonder, not marigold? Well, not the modern marigold that we think of first. When John Gay, a poet and dramatist of the late 1600s, wrote this riddle, he was referring to the first marigold, the pot marigold, also called calendula.

HISTORY

It was the ancient Romans who gave this plant its name calendula. They observed that the flowers were in bloom on the first day, or *calends,* of every month, and so named them. The Romans grew the flowers simply because they were pretty, and the fact that they bloomed almost continuously surely was an added joy. They also cultivated calendulas to treat scorpion bites.

Calendula never became a major medicinal herb, although it was used to treat headaches, toothaches, red eyes, and fevers. Herbalists often assigned medicinal properties to herbs as suggested by some physical feature of the herb itself such as color or shape. (This method became known as the Doctrine of Signatures.) Thus calendula's yellow color suggested that it would be good in treating jaundice. The renowned seventeenth-century herbalist Nicholas Culpeper claimed that calendula strengthened the heart.

While calendula wasn't considered a highly effective medicine, it was believed to possess a powerful magic. For instance, a sixteenth-century concoction that was thought to enable one to see fairies required that one:

> Take a pint of sallet oyle and put it into a vial glasse; and first wash it with rose-water and marygolde water; the flowers to be gathered toward the east. Wash it till the oyle becomes white, then put into the glasse, and then put thereto the budds of young hazle, and the thyme must be gathered neare the side of a hill where fairies use to be; and take the grasse of a fairy throne; then all these put into the oyle in the glasse and sette it to dissolve three dayes in the sunne and then keep it for thy use.

A woman who could not choose between two suitors was advised to take dried calendula flowers, marjoram, thyme, and wormwood; grind them to a fine powder; and simmer them in honey and white wine. Then she should rub the mixture over her body, lie

DESCRIPTION

Calendula is an erect, coarse, many-branched annual. The entire plant is covered with fine hairs and seems slightly clammy. When bruised, it gives off a distinctive odor. (See photos on pages 100, 168, and 378.)

Flowers: Ray flowers in solitary, terminal heads, 1½–4 in. across, pale yellow to deep orange; close at night.

Leaves: Oblong to oblong-obovate, edges smooth to faintly toothed; middle and upper leaves clasp the stalk, lower leaves short-stemmed; to 2¾ in. long.

Fruit: Achenes, mostly boat-shaped, rough-skinned; light yellow seeds unusual in shape and formation, ranging from winged to curled.

Height: 18 in.

FLOWERING

Spring through fall.

RANGE

Native from the Canary Islands through southern and central Europe and North Africa to Iran.

GROWING CONDITIONS

- Soil pH 6.6.
- Average, well-drained soil.
- Full sun.

down, and repeat three times: "St. Luke, St. Luke, be kind to me; In dreams let me my true love see!" And in dreams she would see the man she was to marry. If he was going to be a loving husband, he would be kind to her, but if he was going to be disloyal, he would be unkind. Such a method, if it worked, could prevent a lot of divorces.

Well, the true magic of calendula must have been in its flavor and color, for the most common use of this plant was in cooking. Calendulas were tossed into food at every opportunity. They were practically a vegetable. In England, they were sown with spinach—and often were cooked in the same pot with it. They were just the thing to flavor a stewed lark or sparrow, advised an Elizabethan cookbook. John Gerard, an herbalist of the time, reported that no serious soup in the Netherlands was without calendula petals, and in the eighteenth century, one cook described making oatmeal with calendula flowers. Cooks made calendula puddings, calendula dumplings, even calendula wine.

Such a useful plant came to the Americas with European settlers. They joined the army in the nineteenth century and were used during the Civil War to help stop bleeding and to promote the healing of wounds. By this time, though, their heyday was past.

USES

It doesn't appear that calendula will reach such heights of glory again, but the flowers can add a touch of surprise when added to foods, and they certainly brighten any flower garden.

Medicinal: Tinctures of calendula flowers have been recommended in the treatment of a wide variety of ailments including amenorrhea, cramps, toothaches, fever, flu, stomachaches, even tuberculosis and syphilis. The plant is supposed to induce sweating in a fever, increase urination, aid digestion, and act as a general tonic.

Some people have hoped that a cure for cancer might be found in calendula, and decoctions and poultices made from the leaves or the whole plant have been tried. Actually, a report issued in 1969 noted that extracts in water showed some activity against sarcomas in mice, but this seems to have been an isolated finding and thus not particularly meaningful.

Others apply calendula remedies to external sores, cuts, bruises, burns, and rashes. An easy ointment can be made by crushing fresh flowers and mixing them with olive oil. For a powder, dry and grind the flowers and mix them with arrowroot powder, cornstarch, or talc. Calendula flowers rubbed into beestings are said to relieve the pain.

Scientific research says little about any of these remedies. Pharmacognosist Varro Tyler, Ph.D., does not believe anyone should

I STOOD TIPTOE UPON A LITTLE HILL

Open fresh your round of
    starry folds,
Ye ardent marigolds!
Dry up the moisture from your
    golden lids,
For great Apollo bids
That in these days your praises
    should be sung
On many harps which he has
    lately strung:
And when again your
    dewiness he kisses
Tell him I have you in my
    world of blisses!
So haply when I rove in some
    far vale
His mighty voice may come
    upon gale.

        John Keats

CALENDULA—continued

PLANETARY HARVESTING

Should a gardener wish to pick calendulas in the traditional way, the twelfth-century *Macer's Herbal* advises waiting until the moon is in the sign of the Virgin but not when Jupiter is in the ascendant.

But figuring out just what "in the ascendant" meant to a twelfth-century herbalist can start a lively discussion among modern astronomers and astrologers. The former might suggest that Jupiter could be said to be in the ascendant when its plane of rotation intersected the earth's and it by-passed the earth going "up" toward the sun. Thus calendula picking would be interrupted every 11 years. An astrologer might suggest that Jupiter in the ascendant meant basically Jupiter as the morning star. Thus calendula picking would be less productive during part of the year, often during the spring and early summer.

Once one has solved the problem of Jupiter, the flowers should be picked by someone fasting, recently cleansed of deadly sin, who recites three Our Fathers and three Hail Marys.

have high hopes for discovering calendula cures.

Culinary: In her book *Jeanne Rose's Herbal Guide to Inner Health,* Jeanne Rose refers to calendula sandwiches. These are made from a mixture of calendula flowers, sesame seed, mayonnaise, cheese, and liverwurst—more appealing than stewed sparrow with calendula but still a bit unusual. For something a little more commonplace, like soups, stews, and poultry, calendula flowers can be dried and ground into a powder that substitutes for saffron. The flowers yield yellows and oranges as well as flavor and can be used to color butter, custards, and liqueurs.

Ornamental: Calendula's popularity today results from the beauty of its bloom more than its flavor. The plant is a feature of many ornamental gardens. Plant breeders have developed many improved varieties with long flower stalks, flower heads of increased size—most of them fully double, and a range of colors from creamy yellow to brilliant orange.

Craft: The flowers of calendula dry nicely and add a nice burst of color to herb and flower arrangements.

Dye: Calendula adds color to fabric, also. Use the flowers to make a yellow dye for wool mordanted with alum.

Cosmetic: According to Jeanne Rose, a calendula rinse brings out highlights in brunette and blond hair. Used in herbal bath mixtures, it can stimulate the body.

CULTIVATION

Calendulas can easily be grown from seeds. Their viability lasts but a year, so fresh seed is essential. Sometime in April or May, when the sun is shining and the soil temperature is at least 60°F, sow the seeds directly in the garden. Although the plants need to be kept free of weeds and thinned to 9 or 10 inches apart, there is not much more care necessary. Calendula is a hardy plant and will survive frosts and even early snows. As a matter of fact, in warmer climates, it does best during the cooler seasons. A temperature of 25°F will damage it.

Pests and diseases: Calendulas can be destroyed by leaf spot. They may also be affected by stem rot, leaf blight, powdery mildew, and smut. Pests include slugs and snails, aphids, whiteflies, caterpillars, leafhoppers, thrips, blister beetles, and nematodes.

Harvesting and storage: To harvest your own, pinch the flower head off the stem. Pull each petal. Dry them in the shade on paper (the dried petals tend to cling to screening). The petals should be kept from touching one another since this can lead to discoloration. Because the petals are so hygroscopic, they should be stored in a moisture-proof container to preserve the color and flavor ordinarily lost in humid conditions.

CARAWAY

Carum Carvi   Umbelliferae

For many years caraway has been a household staple for both culinary and medicinal purposes. Evidence of the seed has been found among Mesolithic food remnants, suggesting it has been used for more than 5,000 years. It is mentioned in the Ebers Papyrus, a medicinal manuscript dating to 1500 B.C., and a twelfth-century German medical work. It appeared in Roman cookery and flavored that of the English as well, according to the *Form of Cury,* a cookbook prepared by Richard II's cook in 1390. On a mundane level, caraway has been used to relieve flatulence, indigestion, and colic in babies.

USES

Caraway is still used today in cooking and may be best known as an ingredient in rye bread. In addition, herbalists continue to prescribe it for a few minor ailments.

Medicinal: Caraway is thought to be relatively safe if taken as a seed, rather than as an oil. The seeds can be crushed and steeped in water or milk to make a tonic for digestive upset. The oil is volatile and is said to be a mucous membrane irritant with carminative properties.

Culinary: Every part of the plant is edible. Austrians use the seeds in beef dishes, while Germans use them to season pork. Goulash, the Hungarian herdsman stew, is often made with caraway seeds. The rural people of Norway and Sweden eat a black, polentalike caraway bread. The leaves, which are used less frequently, can be added to salads, soups, and stews. The root is eaten as a winter vegetable in certain parts of the world. The oil is used to flavor Kummel, a liqueur produced in Germany and Russia, and the aquavit of Scandinavia.

Caraway's characteristics seem to combine anise and dill, with a tang and a surprising nuttiness. The seeds are used whole or are ground as needed. The fresh leaves are minced for green or fruit salads or used whole as a garnish. Treat the root like a parsnip: it can be steamed, pureed, chopped into soups and stews, or sliced thinly and enjoyed raw.

Try caraway with eggs, cheese, creamy soups and sauces, cabbage, beets, spinach, potatoes, snap beans, peas, cauliflower, turnips, zucchini, rye, barley, oats, pork, and fish. It is common to the cuisines of Germany, India, Scandinavia, and Indonesia and is best known for its use in pickled vegetables, sauerkraut, split pea soup, bread, cakes, and applesauce.

Available commercially: Whole dried seeds or ground seeds (whole seeds are preferable).

DESCRIPTION

Caraway is usually termed a biennial. Some varieties display an annual habit, flowering and going to seed in their first year of growth.

In its first year of growth, the biennial plant produces a long taproot that looks like a parsnip, from which the hollow, grooved stems grow.

Flowers: Minute, white, in compound umbels.

Leaves: Finely cut, bipinnate, 6–10 in. long; some plants stay green throughout a mild winter.

Fruit: Oblong seeds; pointed on either end; bearing five distinct, pale ridges.

Height: To 2 ft.

FLOWERING

Spring.

RANGE

Native to the Middle East, Asia, and central Europe; naturalized in North America.

CHEF TIPS

- Caraway seed can become bitter during long cooking. When preparing soups and stews, add the crushed or whole seed only 15 minutes before you take the pot off the stove.

- Add crushed seed to waffle batter (¼ teaspoon for a recipe that serves four).

- Sprinkle crushed seeds over popcorn.

63

Seed Head

Seeds

*Flowering
Stem*

Flowers

GROWING CONDITIONS

- Plant hardiness zones 3–4.
- Soil pH 6.4.
- Light, dry soil.
- Full sun to light shade.

Substitute: Anise seeds ground with a bit of toasted sesame seeds.

Storage note: Caraway leaf does not dry or freeze well.

CULTIVATION

You can take cuttings to produce new plants, but there is really no need to since caraway is easily cultivated from seed. Once you plant it in your garden, you're almost guaranteed to have a recurring supply of the herb. Set the seeds outside in early spring, 6 to 8 inches apart, in ½-inch-deep drills about 12 to 18 inches apart. You can also plant an autumn crop that will produce the following summer. For some reason, caraway does not like to grow near fennel, but it makes a good companion for peas, using garden space efficiently and helping to keep the weeds down. The long taproot makes transplanting difficult. If you decide to try, nip off the end of the taproot to promote a stronger, healthier root structure. Give your caraway fertile, well-drained soil in full sun, but don't let the earth dry out; the best specimens are grown with continuous watering.

Harvesting and storage: When harvesting caraway seeds, your timing must be precise to catch them before they fall. They are ripe when they turn brown. Snip the stalk before the seeds fall, then tie the stalks in bundles and hang them, upside down, in a warm but airy place. Let the seeds drop onto a paper-lined tray. After a few weeks, when the fallen seeds are thoroughly dry, store them in an airtight jar for future use.

CARDAMOM

Elettaria Cardamomum   **Zingiberaceae**

Cardamom is one of those distinctive spices that have been adopted by some very different cuisines. It's native to East India, so, not surprisingly, it's a key ingredient in curry powder. It's also widely used in Scandinavian pastries. A tropical shrub, it is a lovely, aromatic specimen plant for the greenhouse.

USES

Today, cardamom is primarily a culinary herb and an important one at that. In the past, however, it also enjoyed a minor reputation as a medicinal and aromatic herb.

Medicinal: The seeds contain an essential oil rich in terpenes, terpineol, and cineol. These ingredients make cardamom a stimulant, like cinnamon, ginger, or other stronger volatile oils.

Chewing on the seeds is said to relieve flatulence and indigestion, even as it sweetens the breath. A few drops of cardamom oil will work even better, but the oil is expensive and hard to come by.

Culinary: Cardamom tastes like an airy, gentle ginger with a pinch of pine. The pods of the plant, which can be white, green, or black, are opened, and the tiny seeds inside are used whole or ground as needed. One medium-sized pod contains 10 to 12 seeds that when ground will make about ⅛ teaspoon.

Cuisines famous for cardamom include East Indian, Scandinavian, Arabic, and central African. Cardamom enhances squash, sweet potatoes, duck, pork, pastries, pickling brines, sweet and sour meatballs, coffee, and sweet pastries. Its flavor combines well with cumin and coriander seed.

Available commercially: Dried in pods or ground. The pods are preferable since cardamom seeds keep best if they remain in their pods until just before you are ready to use them. Once the pods open, the seeds lose much of their flavor and aroma.

Aromatic: Place a few cardamom leaves in blanket chests and drawers. They will give your woolens a lovely spicy scent. The seeds can be included in potpourris and sachets.

Chew on the seeds to cleanse your breath after a spicy meal.

Add a tablespoon of seeds or leaves to the tub for an especially invigorating bath.

CULTIVATION

Elettarias are difficult to grow, which is why cardamom is one of the more expensive spices. They need constant moisture—as much as 150 inches of annual rainfall—and as jungle plants, partial shade.

DESCRIPTION

True cardamom is a perennial with tall, simple canes or stems that grow out of a thick rhizome.

Flowers: Small, white, with blue and yellow lips, occur in long trailing racemes.

Leaves: Dark green, alternate, lance-shaped, about 1 ft. long.

Fruit: Ribbed capsules with three cells, each containing 4–6 tiny tan seeds.

Height: 6–12 ft.

RANGE

Native to the shady forests of India, Ceylon, and Malaysia; cultivated mainly in Guatemala and India.

CHEF TIPS

- Add ground seeds to orange marmalade (about ⅛ teaspoon per pint).

- Add whole seeds to fruit punches or marinades.

- Create a dressing for fruit salads by combining ½ cup of plain or vanilla yogurt, 1 or 2 teaspoons of honey, ⅛ teaspoon of ground cardamom, and 2 teaspoons of finely shredded coconut.

CASCARA SAGRADA

Rhamnus Purshiana   Rhamnaceae

Back in the days before laxatives were available as ready-to-use liquids, tablets, and powders, the bark stripped from this member of the buckthorn family performed a necessary function for millions of people. And it performed this function very effectively, judging from its name: *Cascara sagrada,* in Spanish, means "sacred bark."

DESCRIPTION

Also known by the nicknames "shittim" and "wahoo," cascara sagrada is a deciduous shrub or small tree with a distinctive reddish gray bark, which produces one of the most widely used herbal laxatives on earth.

Flowers: Tiny, greenish yellow; in umbellate clusters from leaf axils; tubular corolla consists of five ¼-in. lobes.

Leaves: Thin, elliptical; finely serrated edges, conspicuously veined; short point at tip; underside covered with fine hairs; 2–6 in. long.

Fruit: Small, globular berries about ½ in. in diameter; turn from scarlet to black when ripe; juicy flesh encloses two or three pea-sized seeds or stones.

Height: 5–25 ft.

FLOWERING

Spring.

RANGE

A native of the Pacific northwestern states and provinces.

HABITAT

Chaparral thickets, canyon walls, and moist, evergreen forests above 5,000 ft.

HISTORY

The name "sacred bark" dates back to the seventeenth century, when it was bestowed on this tree by Spanish and Mexican explorers. Apparently, they were intrigued by the American Indians' use of the bark for a wide variety of medicinal purposes. Its most important use, however, was as a remedy for constipation and upset stomach.

Word of its effectiveness spread quickly over the years, and soon settlers of the American West began to use cascara bark for their ills. A popular remedy was a "tea" made by soaking a piece of dried bark in cold water overnight; the next morning the liquid was drunk as a tonic. A more potent laxative was manufactured by boiling fresh bark for several hours or by pouring boiling water over pulverized bark and letting it cool. Cascara was first identified by a scientist named Pursh (hence its botanical name) in 1814, and during the nineteenth century was widely used by herbalists throughout the United States.

The bark was first used by the medical community in 1877, when the pharmaceutical company of Parke-Davis first marketed it. A year later, a bitter, emetic fluid extract of cascara bark was introduced by the same company for the treatment of chronic constipation. The extract found its way to Europe, and soon after European pharmaceutical companies and herbalists began importing the bark itself. In 1890, the plant finally earned an official listing in the *U.S. Pharmacopoeia.*

USES

Even today, the bark as well as other parts of the cascara sagrada tree are harvested in abundance from the forests of Oregon, Washington, and British Columbia.

Medicinal: To this day, no synthetic medicinal preparation can equal the mild and speedy action of this "sacred bark"; and unlike the old days, cascara is now marketed in the form of pills, powders, and liquids made palatable with licorice, anise, and other flavorings.

In the right doses, it can also be administered to constipated dogs.

The active ingredients that make cascara such an effective laxative are two types of a substance called anthraquinone. The first type, free anthraquinone, causes an increased peristalsis, or movement, in the large intestine. The other type, sugar derivative, is absorbed in the digestive tract and circulated through the bloodstream. These sugar derivatives eventually reach a nerve center in the large intestine and trigger a laxative effect.

Preparations derived from fresh (newly stripped) bark can cause nausea and a terrific griping effect on the intestinal system—which is why most preparations are manufactured from bark that has been aged for at least a year. According to Julia Morton, D.Sc., F.L.S., in her book *Major Medicinal Plants,* chemical changes that occur within the bark during storage seem to render it more acceptable to the digestive system. (The *International Pharmacopoeia* suggests that the bark may also be dried artificially at 100°C for one hour to achieve the same effects of 12 months' storage time.)

COMMERCIAL CULTIVATION

Rhamnus Purshiana, though a native of the Pacific northwestern states and provinces, can be cultivated in the eastern states and elsewhere, under the right conditions. The laxative properties of its bark, however, vary greatly from region to region. Trial commercial cultivation of the trees in various parts of the United States proved largely unsuccessful, as the quality of the bark produced was substantially lower than bark from wild trees.

GROWING CONDITIONS

- Plant hardiness zone 7.
- Moist, fertile soil.
- Full sun to partial shade.

CASCARA SAGRADA—continued

RHAMNUS SPECIES

The members of the *Rhamnus* genus are surprisingly diverse. Noteworthy relatives of cascara sagrada include:

Rhamnus californica: A rounded shrub, grows 6–8 ft. Dark green leaves with lighter green undersides, 1–4½ in. long. Bisexual flowers. Two-stoned berries; edible but not particularly tasty. An evergreen, the coffee berry or pigeon berry is quite variable in appearance. Native to North America, it ranges from Oregon and Nevada to Mexico.

R. cathartica: Tall shrub, rarely more than a small tree; grows to 20 ft. Many branches tipped with a short, stiff spine. 1½–2½-in., broad-ovate, toothed leaves. Male and female flowers usually on separate plants. The common buckthorn is deciduous and extremely hardy. Naturalized in eastern North America.

R. frangula: Dense shrub or small tree; grows to 20 ft. Lustrous, dark green, usually toothless leaves, 1½–3 in. long. Bisexual flowers in clusters of 8–10. Alder buckthorn, a deciduous plant, is valued for its extreme hardiness, rapid growth, and attractiveness. Naturalized to eastern North America.

R. pumila: Beautiful, ground-hugging shrub; grows only a few inches high. Finely toothed, elliptic to roundish leaves, ¾–2½ in. long. Fruits, ¼ in. in diameter, black. *R. pumila* is an excellent and attractive rock garden plant.

Dr. Morton points out, however, that unusually large doses or the habitual use of preparations made from dried bark can also cause intestinal distress, including inflammation of the colon, nausea and vomiting, and chronic diarrhea. People who suffer from such conditions as irritable bowel syndrome or ulcers should not use this herb at all. Nursing mothers should also refrain from using cascara sagrada, since the laxative effect will be transmitted to their infants.

Morton suggests that a reasonable dosage of the powdered bark extract is 10 to 30 grains, dissolved in water; for fluid extract, 0.6 to 2 cc. (usually 1 cc.) is appropriate. If you are in possession of properly cured cascara sagrada bark, *Weiner's Herbal* offers this laxative recipe: Slowly boil 1 teaspoon of bark in 1½ pints of water in a covered container for about 30 minutes. Allow the liquid to cool in the covered container; drink 1 tablespoon of the *cold* solution per day, as needed.

Culinary: Cascara sagrada is not generally known for its culinary uses, but it does have a few. Cascara extract is used by the food industry to flavor liqueurs, soft drinks, ice cream, and some baked goods. The fruit of the cascara tree may be eaten cooked or raw, and in some parts of California, the flowers are a source of honey, which—as you might guess—has a mild laxative effect.

Ornamental: Many of the buckthorns are used as ornamentals, though cascara sagrada does not immediately leap to mind as one of them. It is found most frequently in the wild but is a reasonable choice within its range wherever a deciduous tree is needed.

Shrubby buckthorn varieties, such as *Rhamnus frangula* and *R. cathartica*, make appropriate additions to a rock garden and can be used as hedges. Shearing the sides and top helps to maintain these species, but otherwise they need minimal special care.

Dyeing: The bark of cascara sagrada can be used to impart a variety of gray, brown, and yellow shades to wool. (See the entry Dyes from Herbs for more information.)

CULTIVATION

As with most other buckthorn varieties, cascara sagrada fairs best in a moist, fertile soil. It can prosper in direct sunlight or partly shaded areas. Propagation can be achieved by seed, layering, or cutting. Rare varieties of *Rhamnus* often may be grafted onto cascara sagrada seedlings.

Harvesting and storage: Trees cultivated for pharmaceutical purposes should be stripped of their bark in the spring and fall. The bark should be aged at least a year before it is used.

CASTOR BEAN

Ricinus communis   Euphorbiaceae

The castor bean or castor oil plant is not only an important medicinal plant but a great ornamental one as well. It's of particular commercial importance for its oil, that foul-smelling, worse-tasting stuff once forced down the throats of any children who happened to look a bit pale. In the garden it's a dramatic accent plant and, some say, a deterrent to moles and rabbits.

HISTORY

The castor bean has been known to man for thousands of years. Ancient Indians called it *eranda,* a Sanskrit name that is still used in some parts of Asia. We know that Egyptians valued the plant highly since seeds have been found in some 4,000-year-old tombs. The ancient Greeks were equally familiar with castor bean and knew how to extract the oil. However, they believed castor oil should only be used externally. In the Middle Ages, European herbalists continued to use the oil as a kind of liniment and lubricant. Not until the eighteenth century did it gain its reputation as a laxative extraordinaire.

USES

Some terrific medicines, insecticides, and lubricants are derived from the castor bean, but this is not a plant for home remedies.

Medicinal: Because it is fairly mild, castor oil is still widely prescribed as a laxative for children and elderly patients. Too much can bring on nausea and vomiting, so follow a doctor's advice on dosage. The oil is also used as an ingredient in contraceptive creams and eye medications.

Toxicity: The seeds are poisonous, and other parts are irritating to sensitive individuals. The culprit is ricin, a blood-coagulating protein that is found in all parts of the plant. The seed pods are generally identified as poisonous because these are the most likely to be swallowed by a curious youngster. And just one seed can kill a child. But ricin is found throughout the plant, and some people break out in a rash when they simply touch the leaves. Consumed, ricin causes vomiting, diarrhea, thirst, and blurred vision.

The oil is quite safe when extracted commercially. The poisons aren't soluble in oil, so they stay in the pomace as the seed pods are pressed. It would seem fairly easy to press one's own pods to make castor oil, but the danger of poisoning is too great. Why look for trouble? Use manufactured products only.

DESCRIPTION

Castor bean has a distinctively tropical look about it. Gardeners cultivate dozens of varieties that vary considerably in leaf shape and size, color, and growth habit. Depending on the climate, some are perennial trees, and others are fast-growing annual herbs.

Flowers: Male and female on same plant in clusters on terminal spikes; female flowers uppermost, petal-less, three- to five-part calyx, greenish, red stigma; male beneath, petalless, four- to five-part calyx, red or green, several yellow stamens.

Leaves: Alternate; palmate with five to nine, toothed, pointed lobes; long leaf stalks; to 1–2 ft. wide; young leaves purplish; mature leaves gray-green or dark purplish red.

Fruit: Capsules, spiny, ½–1 in. long, contain seeds (the castor beans).

Height: 8–10 ft.

FLOWERING

Midsummer.

RANGE

Native to tropical Africa and the East Indies, naturalized throughout the tropics and in some cooler regions. In southern Florida, it is a noxious weed.

CASTOR BEAN—continued

GROWING CONDITIONS

- Plant hardiness zones 8–10.
- Fertile, moist, well-drained soil.
- Full sun to partial shade.

Ornamental: Castor bean is one of those foolproof plants that can't be beat in the right setting. For new homes in southern regions, it's a quick solution to first-season foundation planting. In established beds, clumps of *Ricinus* are effective as a background for more subtle flowering annuals such as white petunias or phlox. Planted in large pots, they nicely decorate a veranda or terrace.

Other: Old-timers call *R. communis* "mole plant" and claim that it keeps all sorts of rodents and rabbits away from the vegetable patch. They recommend planting a living fence of castor bean around the entire garden. There's no scientific evidence that castor bean really repels animals and, since some varieties are quite invasive, you should be careful where you plant it. We do know, however, that ricin, the poisonous chemical throughout the plant, is a potent insecticide. In the past, folks believed its "smell" deterred mosquitoes. Again, there's no proof that the plants really harm insects.

CULTIVATION

Plant castor bean seeds about 1 inch deep in rich, well-drained soil. Where the growing season is short, start them indoors or under glass, then transplant to the fertile garden after the danger of frost is past. Choose a spot in full sun, and water the plants well.

CATNIP

Nepeta Cataria   Labiatae

An ancient remedy, these plants went wherever Europeans tried to settle. Though colonies of people did not always take root, the catnip usually did.

HISTORY

It would be difficult to guess how long cats have known about catnip, but people have appreciated it for at least 2,000 years. The plant was familiar to Roman cooks and doctors. When so many classical preoccupations disappeared during the Middle Ages, catnip remained in people's minds, gardens, and medicine repertoires. It was used, more bravely than effectively perhaps, against some of the great terrors of those days, like leprosy. But some of its uses were timeless. *Agnus castus,* a Middle English herbal known by the first two words of the manuscript, recommends catnip tea for "evils that a man has about his throat." That cup of something warm, pungent, and minty brings comfort to the coughing, congested cold-sufferer of any era.

The struggle between catnip grower and cat has been going on in yards and kitchen gardens for centuries. In 1754, the British horticulturist Philip Miller wrote a thoroughly exasperated description of cats rolling on a patch until it was absolutely flat, a serious loss in days when catnip could be sold for tea or medicine. His answer: sowing, instead of transplanting, and thorn hedges.

Catnip came to America along with other necessities for pioneer living. America's first geographer listed it in 1796 as a commercial crop. It escaped cultivation and invaded the landscape. It even worked its way into American literature, appearing in the writings of Washington Irving, Nathaniel Hawthorne, and Harriet Beecher Stowe.

Today it is touted as a remedy not for physical ailments, but for economic ones. In the Northwest particularly, farmers are being encouraged to save their farms by growing catnip and other herbs. However, it may be no more protection against bankruptcy than it was against leprosy. "It's a minuscule market," warns Lon Johnson from Washington's Trout Lake Farms. The major buyers are in the pet industry, and they can get catnip collected from the wild for less than half of the cost of cultivated catnip. Even high-quality cultivated catnip that has been de-stemmed and stored carefully can have trouble in the marketplace. Pet industry buyers respond more to price than to quality. As long as they find some kind of catnip, as

DESCRIPTION

A coarse-leaved, gray-green perennial, catnip reveals its minthood by its stem, which is perfectly square in cross section, a sign of the mint family. Soft, white fuzz covers the stem and leaves.

Flowers: Tubular, ¼–½ in. long, white with purple-pink spots; two-lipped corollas; deep red anthers; tubular calyx, ribbed, five-parted; occur massed in spikes.

Leaves: Opposite, ovate with heart-shaped bases, coarsely toothed, 2–3 in. long; gray-green above, whitish beneath; downy, especially on undersides.

Fruit: Four smooth, tiny nutlets.

Height: 1–3 ft.

FLOWERING

July through September.

RANGE

Eurasia; naturalized throughout North America.

A PROVERB

If you set it,
    the cats will eat it,
If you sow it,
    the cats don't know it.
Philip Miller
The Gardener's Dictionary
1754

CATNIP—continued

long as a cat toy can be labeled "catnip filled," a human will buy it, and the cat can't comment on the quality of the thrill.

USES

Medicinal: A tea made from the dried leaves and flowering heads has been used to treat just about everything from colds to cancer. Most commonly, it has been used as a carminative (digestive aid), tonic, and sleeping aid, a mild nightcap. Varro Tyler, Ph.D., author of *The Honest Herbal,* has evaluated the modern medical evidence supporting or denying folk cures and found a bit of evidence that catnip tea may be sedative. *Cis-trans*-nepetalactone, the major component of the volatile oil, has a chemical structure similar to the valepotriates, proven sedatives found in valerian. So modern medicine might agree about catnip's benefits. "Besides, it's relatively inexpensive," says Dr. Tyler. "It tastes good, and no harmful effects from using it have been reported. What more can one ask of a beverage?"

Earlier doctors agreed with him. The dried leaves and flowering tops of catnip were listed in the *U.S. Pharmacopoeia* from 1842 to 1882.

One mild caution comes from contemporary herbalist Michael Moore. In general, catnip "may act to increase menstrual flow to varying degrees," so he advises pregnant women not to use it. However, he feels that "the chances of stimulating spotting are remote."

To make catnip tea, simply pour boiling water over the dried catnip and let it steep. One of the more detailed tea recipes came from Euell Gibbons. He advised using a little more catnip per cup than you would ordinary tea. He cautioned that catnip's flavor and aroma are very volatile, so he protected his tea while it steeped by setting a saucer on the cup.

A less common but more colorful use of catnip was as a sort of fumigant. Catnip was used by women, who sat over the fumes of catnip tea, to take away barrenness and wind, wrote the controversial seventeenth-century herbalist Nicholas Culpeper. (Reportedly, he grew herbs in London and criticized the practices of other great herbalists for their love of rare imported medicinal plants that only the rich could afford.)

The question of catnip fumes and whether someone can get high from smoking the herb has been much discussed, even in the *Journal of the American Medical Association,* where an article published in the late sixties caused a terrific flap. In the article, physicians reported that catnip was indeed mildly psychoactive; however, the article appeared with a picture of a marijuana plant labeled as catnip and vice versa. The editors were bombarded with letters, some of them explaining the effects of the "catnip" as the result of botanical incompetence. Dr. Tyler took a dim view of the whole controversy: "Any drug whose mind-altering effects are as questionable as this one is scarcely worth considering for that purpose."

Culinary: Perhaps catnip will make a comeback as a salad ingredient now that trendy recipes call for such exotic greens and sharp flavors. Cooks could simply borrow Roman recipes for salads, one of which called for catnip and 11 other herbs and greens (including green fleabane).

Catnip tea also has suffered a decline in culinary popularity. It was a standard beverage in England, where it was grown commercially, before trade with China and new-fangled imports crowded it out.

Other: For a use that is both a little culinary and a little medicinal, Euell Gibbons made candied catnip leaves to serve at the end of a meal, as a digestive aid or an after-dinner mint, depending on your attitude. His recipe calls for dipping catnip leaves into a mixture of beaten egg white and lemon juice. Then he sprinkled each side with sugar and let them dry for a day or so. He stored them in a tightly closed container in the refrigerator.

Cat toys: Catnip is a feline aphrodisiac, observed Dr. Charles Millspaugh. (A homeopathic doctor, Dr. Millspaugh gave up his practice to study botany and, in the mid-nineteenth century, wrote America's answer to the great European herbals.) It's certainly a feline pleasure, although the response to it seems to be a genetic trait that some cats have and others simply don't.

A house cat wallowing in the herb is a familiar sight, but what about bigger animals? An admirer of the big cats at the Philadelphia Zoo brought in several fistfuls, and the director of animal health, Dr. Keith Hinshaw, gave permission for the keepers to leave some of the plants in the cages of a 110-pound leopard and a 480-pound lion. (This was a special occasion, Hinshaw adds hastily. He can't accommodate catnip owners in general.) Both cats loved it, sniffing and rolling around on the herb and generally seeming to be in ecstasy. The lion may just be a cat who knows how to enjoy life; it responds to the smell of a particular cage-cleaning chemical in the same way.

It is smelling, not eating, the catnip that does the trick, say animal physiologists. A happy cat may chew on the plant, but that's mostly to bruise it and release more of the airborne magic. Nepetalactone triggers something in cat brains. Human brains, physiologically different, can only feel envy at all the feline fun.

CATNIP—continued

CATNIP RELATIVES IN THE GARDEN

Nepeta faassenii: Produces masses of bluish ½-in. blooms; grows 1–1½ ft. high.

N. siberica: Produces 1-in. lavender violet flowers in whorls; grows 1½–3 ft. high.

N. nervosa: Produces spikes of flowers in blue or yellow; leaves have prominent veins; grows 1–2 ft. high.

N. grandiflora: Interrupted spikes of blue flowers, each ¾ in. long; grows 1½–3 ft. high.

CATMINT TEA

Before the use of tea from China, our English peasantry were in the habit of brewing Catmint Tea, which they said was quite pleasant and a good deal more wholesome.

Miss Bardswell
The Herb Garden

GROWING CONDITIONS

- Plant hardiness zones 3–4.
- Soil pH 6.6.
- Average, sandy, well-drained soil.
- Full sun to partial shade.

From a cat's point of view, responding to catnip can be dangerous. An oil extracted from the plant has been used as a lure in trapping bobcats, lynx, cougars, pumas, and mountain lions. The oil is no longer a common lure; a synthetic attractant, which is cheaper, has replaced it.

CULTIVATION

Squinting and fumbling at those practically invisible seeds may not be the easiest way to start a catnip patch. Cuttings are far easier to handle, say the Huffmans, who grow catnip commercially at the edge of the Everglades. In spring, they find that stem sections 4 inches long stuck into a moist medium will root in about a week. Midsummer and fall cuttings take longer, if they root at all. Of course, the easiest way to start a catnip patch is with a whole plant. The Huffmans have dug wild plants and successfully settled them into a garden. However, even that effort may not be necessary. A gardening friend with any catnip plants soon has extra catnip plants.

Once started, the plants are sturdy. They must be, to have established themselves as weeds so widely. The Huffmans have seen catnip growing wild at 6,500 feet in Colombia, and plant guides to North America dismiss its range as "throughout." Just provide well-drained soil; standing water will drown the plants.

Catnip will be most fragrant in good sunlight, advises Rosetta Clarkson. (In her herb books *Herbs and Savory Seeds* and *Magic Gardens,* she mentions catnip here and there, mindful of her tiger-striped cat who endured the name Orphie Whiffendorfer, weighed 20 pounds, and demanded considerable catnip.)

Pests on catnip have not been a problem for Trout Lake Farms. Johnson, an organic grower, reports that his 10 acres of the herb are basically pest-free. He doesn't even see cats prowling around the fields. His crops are direct-seeded, halfway proving an old adage that direct-seeded plants will not interest cats, while transplants will be sniffed and batted and worried to pieces. (However, no one has volunteered to transplant 10 acres of catnip for comparison.)

Harvesting and storage: Gather the leaves and tops in late summer when the plant is in full bloom, and dry them carefully in the shade, advised Dr. John Gathercoal, who studied drugs from natural sources at the University of Illinois in the forties. He advised sorting out the tough stalks. The official standards for the drug, back when there were official standards, allowed no more than 5 percent of stems over 4 millimeters in diameter. Store away from moisture.

CAYENNE PEPPER

Capsicum annuum   Solanaceae

If you've ever sprinkled just a bit too much of this exotic condiment on your supper and wound up breathing fire for a few minutes, you'll no doubt agree that cayenne should be treated with delicacy and respect. And while most people don't think of the hot red pepper—which is what cayenne is—as a medicinal herb, herbalists love cayenne. They don't limit their enjoyment to putting it on hoagies and steak sandwiches, either.

HISTORY

The hot, biting taste of the fruit from the cayenne pepper plant was first introduced to Europe with the return of Christopher Columbus from the New World. Although cayenne was probably cultivated for hundreds, even thousands, of years in the tropical Americas, Africa, India, and other tropical areas of the world, Columbus seems to have been the first Westerner to take conscious note of food flavored with this pungent herb. Certainly it eluded literary reference; there is no name for cayenne in ancient Chinese, Latin, Sanskrit, Greek, or Hebrew. The name cayenne is derived, quite aptly, from the Greek word meaning to bite.

The first appearance of cayenne in history books was in 1493, when Peter Martyn wrote of its arrival in Italy after Columbus's voyage. With the growing European interest in and market for herbs and spices, the discovery of cayenne was important. Later in the sixteenth century, the great London herbalist John Gerard reported its cultivation in Great Britain. Since that time, cayenne pepper has adopted many names—red bird pepper, Africa pepper, cockspur pepper, and goat's pepper, to name a few—and has become important with herbalists the world over.

USES

Though it shares a name, the plants of the genus *Capsicum,* like cayenne, are not related to the black condiment you normally find on dining tables and in kitchens. But they do share some of the same qualities: Both make you sneeze, and both have some interesting uses of which most people are unaware.

Medicinal: You'd hardly guess that a spice so hot to the tongue could have any soothing medicinal properties. Yet herbalists for many years have used cayenne in the treatment of a variety of symptoms—from gas and diarrhea to asthma and toothaches.

DESCRIPTION

With its oddly shaped fruit and its colorful presence, the cayenne plant looks as unusual as it is biting to the tongue. In its native form, cayenne is a shrubby, tropical perennial with angular hardwood branches and stems that often have a slight purple cast at the nodes.

Flowers: Drooping, bloom in pairs or clusters on long stems from leaf axils; corolla star-shaped with five pointed segments, greenish or yellowish white, often with reddish or golden veinlike markings, ⅜–½ in. across; five bluish stamens.

Leaves: Broad, elliptical, puffy and wrinkled looking; can be either hairless or downy; 3–6 in. long.

Fruit: Technically berries; pendulous, podlike; shiny, leathery covering of varying shades of red, orange, and yellow when ripe; distinctively pungent odor; contain small, kidney-shaped whitish seeds in several rows.

Height: To 1 ft.

FLOWERING

Summer.

RANGE

Subtropical and tropical zones of Europe, Asia, Africa, and North America.

CAYENNE PEPPER—continued

CAPSICUM TAXONOMY

When Carolus Linnaeus named the genus *Capsicum* in the mid-1700s, he identified only two species. The number of species identified by botanists slowly increased. By the early 1900s, more than 100 cultivated species of *Capsicums* had been described and named.

But a complete reevaluation of the genus by H. C. Irish of the Missouri Botanical Garden yielded a dramatic change. "Where previous botanists had treated almost every pepper whose pod had a different shape or color as a separate species," Charles Heiser, Jr., wrote in his book *Nightshades, The Paradoxical Plants,* "Irish recognized that many such differences represented only minor variations within a species, and concluded that there are only two species, which brought things right back to where Linnaeus had them in the beginning."

Today, *Hortus Third,* a respected horticultural reference book, lists two species of *Capsicum*: *C. annuum,* which includes cayenne peppers and chilies, as well as bell peppers, and *C. frutescens,* which is the pepper from which Tabasco sauce is made. All the many peppers cultivated in the United States—hot or not; red, green, yellow, or brown—are considered variations of these two species.

Cayenne from Sierra Leone in Africa is said to be the most pungent and medicinal. Common paprika is the mildest form of cayenne but is also the highest in vitamin C content.

Mature hot red peppers are bursting not only with heat but with nutrition as well. Ounce per ounce, they have more vitamin C than anything else you can probably grow in your garden: 369 milligrams per 3.5 ounces. The same goes for vitamin A content: a whopping 21,600 I.U. In tropical areas, where people eat goodly amounts of hot peppers every day, they're also getting important amounts of iron, potassium, and niacin from these spicy pods. (Sweet green peppers, when they turn red, are also highly nutritious but are inferior to the hot variety on every count.)

The active ingredient in cayenne pepper is a substance called capsaicin, which, when taken internally or applied externally, acts as a powerful stimulant. All *Capsicum* varieties contain some amount of capsaicin—some more than others; cayenne has one of the highest concentrations. It is the capsaicin that makes your eyes water and your mouth burn when you've sprinkled a bit too much Tabasco sauce on your huevos rancheros.

Oddly enough, this fiery substance has been valued by herbalists throughout the ages for its soothing and restorative effects on the digestive system. Folk medicine recommends it highly, as Maude Grieve, author of *A Modern Herbal,* put it, "for purging the system of bad humors."

The twentieth-century American herbalist Jethro Kloss called cayenne "one of the most wonderful herb medicines that we have," and he termed it a "specific" for fevers. Take some in capsules, he said, followed by a glass of water.

Juliette de Bairacli Levy, author of the *Herbal Handbook for Farm and Stable,* calls cayenne "a supreme and harmless internal disinfectant."

Herbalist R. C. Wren called it "the purest and most certain stimulant in herbal *materia medica* . . . . A cold may generally be removed by one or two doses of the powder taken in warm water."

Other authorities highly recommend cayenne as a gargle for a sore throat and as a remedy for a hangover. West Indians soak the pods in hot water, add sugar and the juice of sour oranges, and drink freely when feverish. This seems to make a lot of sense, as the cayenne would induce cooling perspiration, the sugar would supply energy, and the oranges would add lots of vitamin C and bioflavonoids. A digestive remedy and appetite stimulant known as "mandram," also from the West Indies, calls for a blend of cayenne, thinly sliced cucumbers, shallots, chives or onions, lemon or lime juice, and Madeira wine.

Folk medicine aside, cayenne pepper can aid the digestive system by stimulating the production of saliva and gastric juices. A pinch in food has often been thought to prevent stomach trouble; some people ingest cayenne in the form of capsules. However, consumption of cayenne can be dangerous for those people with intestinal disorders such as duodenal ulcers or chronic bowel diseases. Even in individuals with healthy digestive systems, cayenne in excessive amounts can cause severe stomach upset and even kidney damage. Those who suffer from these conditions should consult with a physician before using cayenne. (In normal culinary uses, however, cayenne should not cause problems.)

Cayenne can also be applied externally in poultices as a stimulant for chilled skin or as a remedy for painful joints. It slightly irritates the skin and stimulates blood flow to the area, which reduces inflammation. Cayenne does not cause skin redness because it affects the sensory nerves and not the capillaries. But excessive contact with the skin may result in severe dermatitis and blistering.

To make a powerful liniment for sprains and congestion, gently boil 1 tablespoon of cayenne pepper in 1 pint of cider vinegar. Bottle the unstrained liquid while it's hot.

One authority says that to relieve the pain of a toothache, first clean out the cavity of the tooth, then make a small plug of absorbent cotton, saturated with oil of capsicum. Press this into the cavity. It will probably burn like the devil at first, but it's said to be a good remedy, and the effect long lasting.

PEPPER SNEEZES

If the ripe pods of *Capsicum* are thrown into the fire, they will raise strong and noisome vapours, which occasion vehement sneezing and coughing and often vomiting, in those who are near the place, or in the room where they are burnt. Some persons have mixed the powder of the pods with snuff, to give to others for diversion; but where it is in quantity, there may be danger in using it, for it will occasion such violent fits of sneezing, as to break the blood-vessels of the head, as I have observed in some to whom it has been given.

Phillip Miller
The Gardener's Dictionary
1754

CAYENNE PEPPER—continued

In all medicinal applications, moderation—and respect for its powerful nature—is the key to using cayenne effectively.

Culinary: Cayenne adds a hot flash whenever it's used. It isn't to be confused with chili powder, which is also hot and has a similar appearance in its dried, ground form. Chili powder is actually a combination of various chilies, herbs, and spices.

Add half a pinch of cayenne to native American, Cajun, Creole, Spanish, Mexican, Southeast Asian, Szechuan, and East Indian recipes, or to egg dishes, cheeses, creamy soups and sauces, curries, and chili blends.

Available commercially: Dried or ground.

Substitute: Hot chili powder.

Storage note: Omit cayenne from recipes that will be frozen because the flavor could become too intense. Instead, add cayenne when ready to serve.

CULTIVATION

Although cayenne is native to the tropics, you can grow it with good results in temperate latitudes. In fact, it should do as well as tomatoes or eggplant would in your garden, reaching a height of 2 feet or more by late summer and bearing long, podlike fruit. Cayenne grows best in soil that is quite rich. But even if you have average garden soil, you can get satisfactory results by fertilizing with compost, rock phosphate, greensand, or wood ashes.

The hot red peppers have a long growing season (14 to 18 weeks), so it's best to start them indoors from seed. Get the Long Red Cayenne variety. About two weeks or more after the last frost—when the soil has warmed up some—you should set the young plants out in the garden 12 to 18 inches apart, allowing 3 feet between rows. The plants will need plenty of water during the early stages of growth, but a thorough straw mulching will protect them against drought later in the season.

Harvesting and storage: Cayenne peppers are ready to be harvested when the fruit has turned uniformly bright red. Don't pull the peppers off; cut the stems ½ inch from the pepper cap. Hot peppers keep best if they are dried immediately and then stored in a cool, dry place. So string them up on a line to dry. Or you can pull the entire plant and hang them upside down in a well-ventilated place until the peppers dry.

When perfectly dry, the peppers can be ground into a fine powder in a food processor. (Be careful not to inhale the powder, or you'll be in for a surprise!)

CHAMOMILE

Chamaemelum nobile, Matricaria recutita   **Compositae**

Chamomile is one of the most well-known herbs that grows. Even nursery rhymes and fairy tales include mentions of this revered herbal brew—remember Peter Rabbit whose mother soothed his aching head with a cup of chamomile tea?

While most people are more than familiar with its name, few are aware that chamomile is *two* different plants. The chamomiles (often spelled "camomile"; either spelling is correct) do have enough common qualities, however, that the confusion between them is justified. Both have daisylike blossoms, feathery foliage, and a pretty apple fragrance and flavor. Though neither plant bears any resemblance to an apple or apple tree, the applelike qualities are what earned the chamomiles their collective name: chamomile in Greek means "ground apple."

But though they share a name and a fragrance, they are different. *Matricaria recutita,* known as German chamomile, wild chamomile, sweet false chamomile, or mayweed—and often mistakenly called *Matricaria chamomilla*—is a tall, erect annual reaching a height of 2 to 3 feet. *Chamaemelum nobile,* formerly named *Anthemis nobilis* and often called Roman chamomile, is a perennial that seldom grows more than 9 inches high; this chamomile normally carries a stronger fragrance than its German counterpart.

HISTORY

For centuries both kinds of chamomile have been reputed to have gentle healing properties. In early Egyptian times, chamomile was used to cure agues, malarial chills that plagued the ancient civilization. The great herbalists Dioscorides and Pliny recommended baths or poultices of chamomile to relieve headaches and disorders of the kidneys, liver, and bladder. The tea Peter Rabbit's mother gave him has been a popular remedy throughout the ages. Brewed from the dried flowers, chamomile tea is still used to calm nerves and to relieve a number of ailments.

The chamomiles have served other useful purposes. Their fresh, delicate fragrance made them a popular "strewing" herb in medieval England. Strewing herbs was common as a way to freshen the air in homes where bathing was uncommon. In Spain, where the herb is called *manzanilla,* or "little apple," chamomiles were used to flavor a very fine sherry. Women used chamomile tea as a hair rinse to accentuate natural blond highlights. In the days before refrigeration, immersing meat in chamomile tea was supposed to help eliminate the rancid odor of spoilage. Chamomile was also reputed to make an excellent insect repellent.

DESCRIPTION

Though they share a name and a fragrance, Roman chamomile and German chamomile are different. *Chamaemelum nobile* is a low-growing perennial. *Matricaria recutita* is a tall, erect annual. (See photos on pages 100 and 273.)

Flowers: Remarkably like daisies; fresh apple scent. *C. nobile:* solid, solitary central disk, deep yellow color; rays silver-white to cream color; appear at the end of downy stems, often in pairs. *M. recutita:* Hollow, solitary central disk, deep yellow color; rays silver-white to cream color; appear at the end of downy stems; less fragrant than *C. nobile.*

Leaves: Alternate, divided into threadlike segments that give featherlike appearance; covered with downy fuzz. *M. recutita* a bit coarser than *C. nobile.*

Fruit: M. recutita: five-ribbed achene. *C. nobile:* three-angled achene.

Height: C. nobile: To 9 in. *M. recutita:* 2–3 ft.

FLOWERING

Late spring through late summer.

RANGE

Both chamomiles native to Europe, Africa, and Asia; naturalized in North America. Both widely cultivated.

CHAMOMILE—continued

GROWING CONDITIONS

Chamaemelum nobile:
- Plant hardiness zones 3–4.
- Soil pH 7.0.
- Light, dry soil.
- Full sun to partial shade.

Matricaria recutita:
- Soil pH 6.7.
- Sandy, well-drained soil.
- Full sun to partial shade.

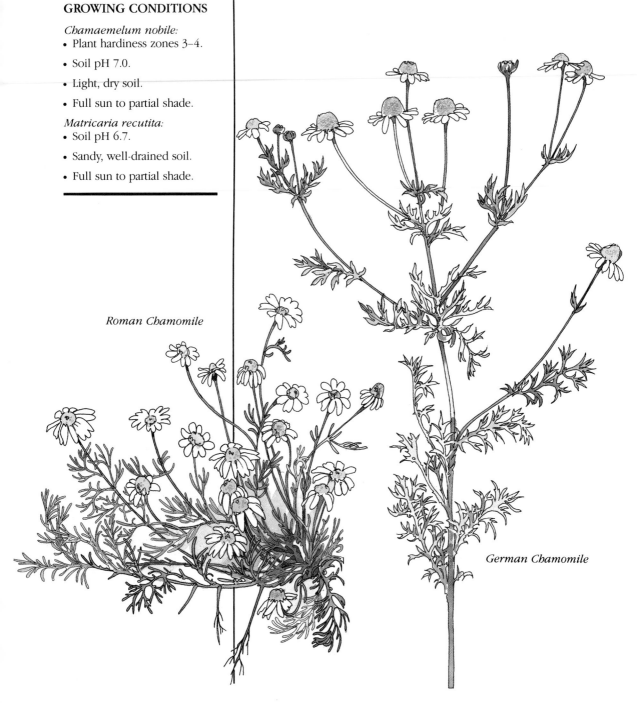

Roman Chamomile

German Chamomile

USES

Chamomile has remained one of the world's best-loved herbs. Many believe it can cure almost anything—like a European counterpart of ginseng. In fact, the Germans have a phrase to describe it: *Alles zutraut,* meaning "capable of anything."

Medicinal: The secret to the chamomiles' medicinal wizardry lies in a volatile oil derived from the flowers. Extracts of the plant or the oil itself have three primary uses: as anti-inflammatories for various afflictions of the skin and mucous membranes; as antispasmodics for treating ailments like indigestion and menstrual cramps; and as anti-infectives for numerous minor illnesses. Ointments, lotions, vapor baths, inhalations, and the like can also be made with chamomile extract.

While numerous scientific studies have proven the effectiveness of chamomile in other applications, its highly touted tea does not measure up as wondrously in research as its reputation would suggest. Pharmacognosist Varro Tyler, Ph.D., writing in *The Honest Herbal,* stated that most of the beneficial effects of chamomile are derived from its oil; even a strong tea, steeped a long time in a covered pot, contains only a small percentage of the vital oil. Nevertheless, he says, many herbalists staunchly believe that if the tea is used over a long period of time, beneficial effects may accumulate.

The chamomiles are not without some slightly unfavorable characteristics. Because the flowers contain pollen, tea made from either type of plant may cause contact dermatitis or other allergic reactions. People who have known sensitivities to ragweed, chrysanthemums, or other members of the Compositae family should be cautious about drinking the tea.

Aromatic: Its apple fragrance makes chamomiles a wonderful addition to potpourris and aromatic dried flower arrangements.

Ornamental: Because of their applelike scent, easy care routines, and endurance in the garden, chamomiles make lovely additions to any landscape.

Most plants don't fancy being squashed underfoot, but chamomiles don't seem to mind. In Great Britain, it is not unusual to find entire lawns of the sweet-scented herbs, which when stepped on fill the air with fragrance. The American climate is not always conducive to this use, but in particularly moist regions it may work.

The plants should be set about 6 inches apart and watered regularly until the gaps among them are filled. The first two cuttings should be done with hand shears, but thereafter, the chamomile

TRUE CHAMOMILE

Throughout history, the two chamomiles have been confused.

In general, the Germanic peoples have considered *Matricaria recutita* to be *the* chamomile, hence the name German chamomile, while the English-speaking peoples have considered *Chamaemelum nobile* to be *the* chamomile. The uses are so similar that confusion is bound to develop.

Herbal dogmatism and calumny add to the confusion. In English herbals *M. recutita* is oftentimes labeled a weed. A gardening book of Germanic orientation notes, "The more commonly found chamomile called mayweed, and others of the genus *Anthemis* [the genus in which Roman chamomile formerly was classified], often become obnoxious weeds; they are not cultivated as a rule."

Which plant is the true chamomile? One might speculate that *C. nobile* is the true chamomile and that Linnaeus, who first classified and named both plants, chose the specific name *chamomilla* for German chamomile simply because it closely resembled the plant commonly called chamomile, *A. nobilis.* (Modern taxonomists have renamed German chamomile from Linnaeus's *M. chamomilla* to *M. recutita.*)

CHAMOMILE—continued

CHAMOMILE LOOK-ALIKES

Several members of the *Anthemis* genus (which used to embrace Roman chamomile as a member) have the appearance and some of the characteristics of the chamomiles.

A. arvensis is a wild plant generally called corn chamomile. In France it was considered an excellent febrifuge.

A. cotula and *Matricaria inodora* are wild chamomiles, also known as mayweed. *A. coluta* is known as stinking chamomile, foetid chamomile, stinking mayweed, dog fennel, and a wide variety of other names, all of which indicate in one or another way that it is not a plant you love to have around. It has an unpleasant smell, and it has a reputation of blistering the hand that touches it. But it shares the medicinal properties of the more well-known chamomiles. *M. inodora* is known as the scentless mayweed and corn feverfew. Although it shares the medicinal properties of the chamomiles, it is almost totally scentless, hence the name.

A. tinctoria is the yellow or ox-eye chamomile, which also is a wild plant. As its specific name implies, it yields a yellow dye.

lawn may be mowed with a lawn mower, the blades being set fairly high. Mow regularly to prevent blooming.

Cosmetic: Infusions of chamomile make wonderfully soothing baths. Just steep a large amount of the herb in water for 15 minutes, let cool, and pour into bathwater, or use it as a skin lotion. One Beverly Hills skin-care specialist uses chamomile regularly in her facials because it is penetrating. To achieve this effect, pour boiling water over dried chamomile flowers in a large bowl, then let the steam waft over your face.

Chamomile is still used to bring golden highlights to brown hair; combined with neutral henna, it adds highlights to very dark hair.

Companion planting: Herbalists of old looked upon chamomile as "the plant's physician," believing that nothing contributed more to the overall health of a garden. It is said to benefit cucumber and onions especially, as well as most herbs.

CULTIVATION

Roman chamomile will grow in nearly any type of soil. The single-flowered type, which grows in the wild, favors rather dry, sandy soil. The cultivated type with double flowers prefers a richer soil and gives the heaviest crop of blossoms when planted in moist, slightly heavy, black loam. (Double flowers are considered more desirable for healing uses.)

The seed of Roman chamomile is very fine and requires a well-prepared soil; it will drop deep into an ill-prepared bed and disappear, never to sprout. Spring sowing is recommended.

It is easier and quicker to propagate Roman chamomile from the little offshoots or sets that the mother plant produces. They can be divided in the early spring and set into well-manured soil, spaced about 18 inches apart. Roman chamomile is extremely hardy, but if your winters are very severe and you don't want to risk losing the plants, mulch them heavily to protect them.

The annual German chamomile can be seeded in either the fall or spring. Planting it in the fall helps because viability is increased when the seeds are subjected to freezing and thawing. Once established, the German chamomile plant will reseed itself if some flower heads are allowed to remain unharvested.

Both Roman and German chamomile like lots of sun. Keep the soil evenly moist for optimum growth and flower production.

Harvesting and storage: If you are using the herb for teas, carefully harvest the flowers for drying when the petals begin to turn back on the disk.

CHERVIL

Anthriscus Cerefolium   **Umbelliferae**

That subtle, tender flavor—part anise, part parsley—that you've been trying to identify in the fish sauce, will almost certainly turn out to be chervil, the most retiring of the sister spices that make up the fines herbes of French cuisine, but one that's good company and not to be overlooked.

Chervil is a warm herb. Its taste and fragrance fill the senses the way warmth does, slowly, subtly. You notice chervil in the background, and you are glad to find it there because its flavor and fragrance are themselves warm and cheering.

HISTORY

Its flavor and fragrance resemble the myrrh brought by the wise men to the baby Jesus. Because of this and because chervil symbolized new life, it became traditional to serve chervil soup on Holy Thursday.

The warmth of this herb suggested medicinal uses to many of history's herbalists. The first-century Roman scholar Pliny and the seventeenth-century herbalist Nicholas Culpeper believed that chervil, as Culpeper put it, "does much please and warm old and cold stomachs . . . ."

During the Middle Ages, chervil was used for a variety of ailments. Eating a whole plant reportedly relieved hiccups, a practice still tried by some people today.

USES

Chervil works better in foods than it does in remedies.

Medicinal: Those who use chervil as a remedy drink an infusion of the leaves and flowers. Chervil has been considered a diuretic, an expectorant, a stimulant, a dissolver of congealed blood, a healer of eczema, a digestive, and a cure for high blood pressure, gout, kidney stones, pleurisy, dropsy, and menstrual problems. Of these properties, the most persistently recognized up to this day has been the ability to lower blood pressure, but no clinical studies support this or any of the other claims.

Culinary: It might not be an effective remedy, but chervil certainly is an effective seasoning in foods. Both the leaves and the stems can be used in cooking, and whole sprigs make a delicate and decorative garnish. If you come across *pluches de cerfeuille* in a French cookbook, it means "blanched sprigs of chervil," which are occasionally used in soup.

Chervil accompanies parsley, thyme, and tarragon in the fines herbes of French cooking and should be added at the last moment to

DESCRIPTION

There are two main varieties of chervil, one plain and one curly. Hardy annuals, they have a fernlike leaf structure as delicate and dainty as their flavor is subtle. The stems are branched and finely grooved, and the root is thin and white.

Flowers: Small, white, in compound umbels.

Leaves: Opposite, light green, compound, leaflets subdivided into opposite deeply cut leaflets. Only lower leaves have stalks.

Fruit: Oblong, segmented, beaked, ¼ in. long.

Height: 2 ft.

FLOWERING

May through July.

RANGE

Native to Europe and Asia; naturalized in North America.

CHEF TIPS

- Steam, peel, and slice about a pound of fresh beets. Combine ½ cup of sour cream or plain yogurt with 1 teaspoon Dijon mustard, 2 teaspoons minced fresh chives, and 2 teaspoons minced fresh chervil. Toss with the beets and serve.

- Toss about ½ pound of steamed green beans with ½ teaspoon of ground anise seed and 2 teaspoons of minced fresh chervil. Serve warm.

CHERVIL—continued

soups, stews, and sautés. Actually, anytime you use chervil in cooking, add it at the end. Lengthy heating turns the flavor bitter. Chervil enhances carrots, eggs, spinach, sorrel, fish (especially oysters), veal, cream, cheese, corn, and peas. It complements tarragon, shallots, freshly ground black pepper, marjoram, and lemon. Béarnaise sauce and classic French vinaigrette taste best with a little fresh chervil added.

Available commercially: Dried.

Substitute: Flat-leaf parsley.

Storage note: Much of chervil's gentle flavor fades with drying. To preserve maximum flavor, dry the leaves rapidly in a commercial dryer or oven. A better way to store chervil is by making butters, which can be kept in the refrigerator or freezer (see the entry Cooking with Herbs).

Aromatic: The leaves bring a subtle scent to potpourris.

Ornamental: Chervil flowers make an attractive addition to fresh or dried bouquets, including tussie-mussies.

CULTIVATION

Since it transplants poorly, it is best to grow chervil from seed in a permanent location. If light is present, seed will germinate in approximately 10 days. To be sure the seed is moist but exposed to the sun, sow it in furrows an inch deep, but do not cover it. Either water the seed with a misting hose, or cover the furrow with cheesecloth and keep the cloth damp. When the seedlings reach 2 inches in height, thin them to 9 to 12 inches apart.

The most difficult part of growing chervil is to keep your plants from setting seed and bolting. Sowing seeds every two weeks from March or early April until mid-July, or until the weather is hot, will give you a constant supply of leaves, even if you plant only a few seeds at a time. Leaves are ready to cut in six to eight weeks. Begin sowing again in late summer for a fall crop that will last until frost. Some plants will winter over and self-sow for early spring growth.

If a few seedlings are carefully transplanted to a cold frame in late summer, they may survive the winter there. Chervil is often planted in the shade under the protection of stockier plants, or mulched, if it is to go into cold winters or hot summers.

Seeds kept over winter do not germinate well. If you want to keep your patch of chervil going, sow seeds in the fall. They will germinate the following spring.

Container gardening: Chervil can be started from seed and easily grown in pots indoors, especially since it does not require a lot of sun (an east window suffices). A moderately rich soil with good drainage works well.

GROWING CONDITIONS

- Soil pH 6.5.
- Moist, humusy soil.
- Partial shade.

CHICORY

Cichorium Intybus   Compositae

Chicory has fallen on hard times. It's just another roadside herb these days, at best a coffee flavoring. But for thousands of years, these plants have been cultivated, and almost all the great sages of Western medicine have used them in one remedy or another. It was both a humble home remedy and a drug of choice for royalty; Queen Elizabeth I of England took chicory broth. But chicory may be taking its revenge. Many of the people who wouldn't think of tramping around on the dusty shoulder of a highway to look at the flowers on some scraggly weed are paying premium prices for trendy Italian greens like radicchio or Treviso, which are nothing more than the forced leaves of special varieties of chicory.

HISTORY

Growing chicory is a very old activity. The plant was in cultivation in Egypt, irrigated by the flooding of the Nile, about 5,000 years ago. Its name may have been derived from its Egyptian name.

The oldest complete herbal we have, from the first century A.D. and written by the Greek physician Dioscorides, mentions chicory, as do most herbals written since. Charlemagne respected it and listed it among the 75 herbs to be grown in his garden. In sixteenth- and seventeenth-century herbals, it was recommended for a motley collection of ailments, which show the theory of the Doctrine of Signatures in action. According to this doctrine, a plant's appearance should give some clue to its medicinal value. For example, chicory will ooze a white milk when scratched; thus British herbalist Nicholas Culpeper in the mid-seventeenth century recommended chicory extract "for nurses' breasts that are pained by the abundance of milk." Chicory flowers are a lovely sky blue, the color of the most beautiful of blue eyes, and the flowers close as if in sleep at night. Thus Culpeper and other herbalists recommended chicory water for "sore eyes that are inflamed."

In the United States, chicory is so common on roadsides that it's hard to realize it's not native, but all those miles of blue flowers we see today came from chicory imported by colonists. Thomas Jefferson had some planted at Monticello in 1774, the seeds probably coming from Italy. He used it as a ground cover in his fields and as cattle fodder, not to mention "a tolerable sallad for the table . . . ." It must have been a success. In 1795, he wrote to George Washington, describing chicory as "one of the greatest acquisitions a farmer can have." His fondness for chicory didn't exactly cause one of the public relations tempests of his presidency, but the plant certainly figured in

DESCRIPTION

Chicory is familiar to most people as a blue-flowered, roadside weed. A deep-rooted perennial, its stem is bristly and bears rigid branches.

Flowers: Dandelion-like, sky blue, 1–1½ in. wide; composed of ray flowers, toothed at outer edge; flower head closes by midday.

Leaves: Broadly oblong or lanceolate with ragged indentations, hairy; large at bottom of plant, diminishing rapidly in size toward the top, resulting in a naked-stem appearance.

Fruit: Hard, brownish, oval seeds, perhaps a tenth of an inch long.

Height: 3–5 ft.

FLOWERING

As early as March in the South and Pacific Northwest; elsewhere June to October.

RANGE

Native to Europe; naturalized throughout North America.

CHICORY—continued

the flap: In 1809, President Jefferson was revealed to be in contact with the duplicitous British (the War of 1812 was just around the corner). He defended his behavior, protesting that he was dealing with the International Board of Agriculture in London, performing such apolitical tasks as arranging for George Washington to receive some chicory seed.

Chicory could grow in a wide range of American climates. In 1785, Governor James Bowdoin of Massachusetts had it planted in his fields to feed sheep. And by 1818, it was "abundant" around Philadelphia, according to one of the pioneers of American medicinal botany, Dr. William Barton from the University of Pennsylvania.

Chicory advanced human health in ways totally unforeseen by the great classical herbalists; it caused such a scandal in the nineteenth century that it inspired pure food legislation. Although chicory/coffee blends are prized and praised today, chicory-labeled-as-coffee annoyed nineteenth-century consumers. One writer of the day explained: "The coffee-dealer adulterates his coffee with chicory, to increase his profits; the chicory-dealer adulterates his chicory with Venetian-red, to please the eye of the coffee-dealer; the Venetian-red dealer grinds up his color with brick-dust, that by his greater cheapness, and the variety of shades he offers, he may secure the patronage of the trade in chicory." Coffee dealers were required to state the amount of chicory on the package.

But labeling didn't stop the chicory dealers for long. A Liverpool company roasted chicory roots until they were quite brown, ground them to a powder, and then re-formed them into little bean-shaped pellets that they sold as coffee beans. Fortunately, later pure food legislation has been more successful.

USES

There's a popular belief that chicory smooths out coffee, counteracting its harsh stimulant effect, and there may be something to this belief. A 1940 research project determined that two of the bitter substances in chicory, lactucin and lactucoprin, acted as a sedative on the central nervous systems of rabbits and mice. Conceivably, these substances could counteract caffeine stimulation. It was just a hint; but apparently no further research has been done to find out whether there's enough of the compounds to have any effect on a human.

But there's still a good reason for adding chicory to coffee. Varro Tyler, Ph.D., a Purdue University pharmacognosist, points out that "chicory is certainly as safe and has much less effect on the nervous system and the heart than the caffeine-rich coffee with which it is usually mixed."

Medicinal: A decoction of chicory root is considered by herbalists to be a mild tonic, diuretic, and laxative. Bruised chicory leaves are used as a dressing for swellings, and the plant is associated with the liver.

Culinary: Chicory's flavor is strong and green and similar to dandelion. The leaves are used fresh or cooked like spinach, and the root is used dried in hot beverages, particularly coffee.

Include whole or shredded leaves in salads, stir fries, or sautés.

Available commercially: Greens and dried root.

Substitute: Dandelion greens for the leaf.

Storage note: Chicory leaves are unacceptable when dried or frozen.

CULTIVATION

Part of the secret of growing chicory is finding a good spot in the garden with deep, rich, friable soil, the sort of place where carrots thrive. Dig in some choice compost before seeding.

Direct seed in early spring and thin seedlings to about a foot apart. Pamper the plants throughout the season by pulling weeds when they first peep out of the ground, and water attentively if the weather turns dry. By midsummer, the plants may need a side dressing of compost. Don't give them too much nitrogen, or they'll be all leaf and not enough root.

To produce these forced greens, called Whitloof chicory or Belgian endive, dig the roots without nicking them; lop off the leafy tops; and store the roots in a cool, dry place. Some gardeners arrange them in a big box, alternating layers of roots with layers of dry sand, and then putting the box in an unheated garage.

Let the roots stay dormant for at least three months, and then select the first batch for forcing. Plant them in a container at least 18 inches deep filled with decent soil, perhaps a mixture of one part soil, one part sand, and one part peat moss. Put the box where there is some heat; 55°F will do. Keep light away from the plants. Covering each root with an inverted flowerpot will work if the drainage hole is blocked. In about three weeks, the pale yellow-green leaves should have formed cone-shaped buds, 6 to 8 inches long. Slice off the buds, discard the spent roots, and start the next batch.

By fall, you should have a respectable root to dig. You can harvest it now or leave it to develop next year. But fall is the time to think about another option, forcing the roots for winter greens.

GROWING CONDITIONS

- Plant hardiness zone 3.
- Soil pH 6.4.
- Average to poor, well-drained soil.
- Full sun.

CHIVES

Allium Schoenoprasum   Liliaceae

Did you ever wonder why recipes don't ever call for using *a* chive? Why no one ever talks about eating just *one* chive? Perhaps it is because they multiply so quickly and grow so closely together that when you go out to the garden to pick them, you can never pick just one. Or perhaps it is because chives taste so good that no one can eat just one.

HISTORY

Chives have been added to foods for nearly 5,000 years. Native to the Orient, they were probably first used by the Chinese and then the ancient Greeks. By the sixteenth century, they had earned a place in European herb gardens. When the colonists came to America, they brought chives along with other kitchen and medicinal herbs.

Although medicinal virtues were found in most herbs, herbalists did not find much use for chives, unlike their relative, the garlic. Chives were thought to have some magical power. Men and women believed that chives could drive away diseases and evil influences and so hung bunches of them in their home. Chives dry beautifully, so if they didn't protect a home, at least they were decorative.

USES

Although historically men and women didn't have much use for this plant other than in cooking, today we have discovered many virtues—another reason why you can't just pick *one* chive.

Medicinal: Chives do send up hot vapors from a sulfur-rich oil found in all members of the onion genus. This oil is also responsible for the flavor and medicinal properties of *Allium*. Sulfur oil is antiseptic and helps lower blood pressure, but only in fairly large quantities. Since chives have less of this oil than larger alliums, they have fewer medicinal applications.

Culinary: Best known for their use in cooking, chives taste like sweet, mild onions. Mince the fresh, slender leaves and use them in recipes or as a garnish. Whole leaves can be tied decoratively around small bundles of sliced carrots or asparagus.

French cooking combines chives with shallots, marjoram, and tarragon. Chives also complement onions, potatoes, artichokes, asparagus, cauliflower, corn, tomatoes, peas, carrots, spinach, poultry, fish and shellfish, veal, creamy sauces, cheese, and eggs. In fact, chives suit about every flavor except sweet. For texture and zip, add chives at the very last moment when cooking soups, stews, and sautés.

Don't overlook the flowers, either. Toss them in salads, or gar-

DESCRIPTION

Like all onions, chives are bulb plants, although the bulbs are so tiny you may not realize they are there. The hollow, green leaves and the flowering stems shoot up from the bulbs. (See photos on pages 31, 101, and 376.)

Flowers: Small; pale purple; form dense, globular umbel at top of stem; petals to ½ in. long, bluish purple anthers.

Leaves: Dark green, very slender, cylindrical, hollow, 6–10 in. high, surround stem at base of plant, taper to a point at top.

Fruit: Seed capsule.

Height: To 18 in.

FLOWERING

June.

RANGE

Native to Greece, Sweden, the Alps, and parts of northern Britain; widely cultivated.

HABITAT

Moist pastures and along stream banks.

GROWING CONDITIONS

- Plant hardiness zone 3.
- Soil pH 6.0.
- Moderately rich, well-drained soil.
- Full sun.

nish dishes with them. They look and taste good in herb vinegars, too.

Available commercially: Freeze-dried, frozen, and fresh.

Substitute: Green part of scallion.

Storage note: Home-dried chives are unacceptable.

Ornamental: Chives work nicely into a variety of garden settings. They are rarely bothered by pests, and whether clipped or blooming, keep their neat appearance throughout the spring, summer, and fall. Plant any species as a border for the flower, herb, or vegetable garden.

Craft: Both common and garlic chives dry beautifully and make splendid additions to dried herb and flower arrangements.

Companion planting: Some growers recommend chives as a companion plant especially for carrots, grapes, roses, and tomatoes. They supposedly deter Japanese beetles and black spot on roses, scab on apples, and mildew on cucurbits.

CULTIVATION

You can start chives from seed, which germinate very slowly and require darkness, constant moisture, and a temperature of 60° to 70°F for best results. Sow them ½ inch deep in pots or flats of soil mix. In two to three weeks, you'll begin to see green sprouts appearing. When seedlings are four weeks old, they can be moved to the garden.

For faster results, purchase spring plants or "borrow" some from a neighbor. Chives need to be divided every three years anyway, and most gardeners are eager to share. Plant clumps of up to six bulbs 5 to 8 inches apart in a sunny, well-drained location.

If you leave the plants to bloom, cut them back after they have flowered. They will send up leaves again in the spring.

Container gardening: Chives can be brought indoors for fresh harvests all winter long. Dig up a clump in late summer and plant them in a pot. Leave the container outside for several months to insure that the tops die back and the roots freeze. The bulbs need a cold dormant period in order to send out leaves again. Then, bring it indoors and place on a sunny windowsill. Plants will sprout within a few weeks, and you'll soon be enjoying freshly snipped chives again.

Harvesting and storage: The leaves can be snipped any time after established plants are 6 inches tall. In harvesting, cut several blades low to the ground (leaving about 2 inches), but don't mow down the entire clump; the plants need some leaves in order to keep growing.

The flowers and leaves are most often eaten fresh, and most attempts at storage produce disappointing results.

CHEF TIPS

- Sauté 1 or 2 cloves of minced garlic in a bit of olive oil, then add 1 pint of cherry tomatoes, and continue to sauté for about two minutes more. Add 2 tablespoons of minced fresh chives and toss to combine. Remove from heat and serve.

- Combine chunks of cucumber, ripe tomato, and feta cheese with minced fresh chives. Add a splash of olive oil and serve with crusty bread.

CINNAMON

Cinnamomum zeylanicum   **Lauraceae**

Cinnamon has a long history. Thousands of years ago, Egyptians included cinnamon in their embalming mixtures. Romans were used to paying dearly for it. Cinnamon was one of the spices that spurred world exploration.

DESCRIPTION

Cinnamon is a small, tender evergreen tree.

Flowers: Inconspicuous, yellowish, arise in long pannicles.

Leaves: Bright red, turning green with maturity, glossy; opposite, ovate to ovate-lanceolate, about 7 in. long.

Fruit: Pointed, ½ to ¾ in. long.

Height: To 40 ft.

RANGE

Native to Sri Lanka and southwest India; cultivated in other tropical areas.

USES

Medicinal: Herbalists recommend cinnamon as an astringent, stimulant, and carminative to aid digestion and relieve vomiting. Recent studies by Japanese researchers show that cinnamon contains a substance that kills fungi, bacteria, and other microorganisms, including *Clostridium botulinum,* which causes botulism, and *Staphylococcus aureus,* a source of staph infections. It also devastates *Aspergillus parasiticus* and *A. flavus,* fungi that produce aflatoxin, a potent carcinogen and poison. The findings suggest all sorts of possible medicinal uses for cinammon.

Culinary: Cinnamon's flavor is pungent and slightly sweet. The part of the plant used is the inner bark. As it dries, it curls into sticks or quills. These sticks are used whole or ground.

Cinnamon is as at home with savory meats as it is in desserts. It's vital to East Indian, Moroccan, Indonesian, Arabic, Iranian, Scandinavian, Mexican, Hungarian, Chinese, and Greek cookery and stimulates the flavors of carrots, spinach, onions, apricots, cherries, apples, blueberries, and oranges. It complements vanilla, nutmeg, fennel, freshly ground black pepper, ginger, clove, and cardamom. Its versatility extends from fruit pies to meat pies.

Available commercially: Whole or ground.

Substitute: Ground sweet flag at one-third of the amount.

Aromatic: Used sparingly, cinnamon oil or bark nicely complements rose blossoms for a simple potpourri. Simply sprinkle a bit of the cinnamon on the petals as they dry. For a kitchen air freshener, simmer pieces of cinnamon, cloves, broken nutmeg, and perhaps some ginger root in an open pot of water. The smell is delightful and welcoming. Weave some cinnamon bark into a wreath or rope to hang in the closet or place in your drawers. Renew the scent occasionally with a few drops of cinnamon oil.

CHEF TIPS

• Make a marinade for 1 pound of pork by combining 2 tablespoons of soy sauce, 1 teaspoon of minced fresh ginger, 2 cloves of minced garlic, and ¼ teaspoon ground cinnamon. Allow the pork to marinate for about an hour, then stir-fry.

• Add a bit of ground cinnamon to tomato sauce. It brings out the natural sweetness of the tomatoes.

• Add a cinnamon stick to apple or orange juice while it sits in the refrigerator. A stick is also wonderful in spicy punches, ciders, mulled beverages, and fruit soups.

CULTIVATION

Varieties of cinnamon can survive in the South, where they are grown as ornamentals or specimens in collections.

Plant in well-drained, sandy loam and provide plenty of nutrients because they are fast-growing trees. Propagation is by seed or cuttings of half-ripened wood, started in the spring in a hotbed.

CLARY

Salvia Sclarea   Lamiaceae (Labiatae)

Strolling along a dirt road through the country, a sudden gust of wind whips a speck of dirt into your eye. Ouch!

At home, your eye still red and teary, you skim through an herbal for a natural remedy. Clary is recommended for vision problems and eye irritations. You read more closely for specific instructions. Ouch! again. It says you must put a seed *into* your eye in order to remove debris *from* your eye.

HISTORY

If you accept what old herbals say, people have been putting clary seeds into their eyes for ages to clear sight and relieve eye irritations. The English name of this herb, clary, comes from the Latin species name, *Sclarea,* which in turn was derived from *clarus,* meaning clear. Because the decoction of the seeds is mucilaginous, it was thought that when used as an eyewash, any foreign matter would adhere to it and thus be cleaned from the eyes, improving vision and relieving a source of irritation.

As an ingredient in wine and beer, clary at one time probably did more to blur the vision than to clear it. During the sixteenth century in Europe, German wine merchants infused clary with elder flowers and added the liquid to Rhine wines. This converted them to Muscatel (hence another common name for this plant—muscatel sage) and made the wine more potent. Clary was also substituted for hops in beer.

USES

Most of the traditional uses of clary—flavoring alcoholic beverages and clearing the eyes—have declined in popularity. There are other valuable, and certainly more practical, uses for it.

Medicinal: Some herbalists still recommend using a clary eyewash to remove foreign particles from the eye. A typical approach is to soak six or seven seeds in boiled water until they swell and become mucilaginous. Using a cotton swab, one is gently placed in the corner of the eye. Any foreign matter should adhere to the mucilage and be cleared from the eye when the seed is removed. Whether or not any modern medical person would recommend such a practice is questionable.

Clary is also reputed to have antispasmodic, astringent, and carminative properties. Its antispasmodic properties are thought to

DESCRIPTION

Clary is an erect biennial with a square, hairy, light green or brownish stem and few branches. The entire plant releases a strong, pleasant balsamlike fragrance. (See photo on page 100.)

Flowers: Two-lipped corolla similar to garden sage but smaller; ½–1 in. long; upper lip, three toothed; pale blue, lilac, or white; in whorls of about six on long, loose terminal spikes; large bracts among flowers are purple or pale pink.

Leaves: Broad, oblong, heart-shaped, 6–9 in. long, dull green, downy, wrinkled, toothed, short stalk, opposite.

Fruit: Tiny seeds, dark brown to black.

Height: 3–5 ft.

FLOWERING

June and July.

RANGE

Native to southern Europe and the Mediterranean region; widely cultivated.

GROWING CONDITIONS

- Soil pH 4.8–7.5.
- Average to sandy, dry, well-drained soil.
- Full sun.

CLARY—continued

be caused by nerol, one of the constituents of the plant's essential oil. Herbalists recommend an infusion of clary for digestive upsets and as a kidney tonic. It is considered safe to use internally, so if your digestive system is upset, have a cup of clary tea. You might also try making a cup from a mixture of clary leaves and chamomile flowers.

Culinary: The fresh or dried leaves can be used in the same ways as garden sage (see the entry Sage). The flowers may also be used; they make a lovely garnish.

Tea can be made from the dried leaves or the flowers.

Commercially, food manufacturers extract the oil from clary to use as a flavoring in beverages, baked goods, puddings, candies, liqueurs, and more.

Aromatic: Clary has a strong fragrance resembling that of balsam. Try mixing the flowers with other herbs in sachets or potpourris. Its aroma reportedly blends well with lavender, beebalm, and jasmine.

If you grow a lot of clary, you can extract the oil from the flowers to scent baths, lotions, soaps, candles, and . . . whatever. Clary is cultivated commercially for its essential oil, which is used as a fixative in perfumes. It also scents colognes, creams, detergents, lotions, perfumes, and soaps.

Ornamental: Clary's white, blue, or purple spikes look pretty in an herb garden or formal garden, where you will enjoy its fragrance.

Cosmetic: Because of the herb's astringent properties, an infusion of clary makes a good skin-freshening lotion. Add an infusion to the bath, too.

CULTIVATION

You can propagate clary easily from seed sown in the spring. Once the seedlings are established, thin them, leaving about 9 inches around each plant. The plants will flower in their second year and will self-sow. Clary can also be propagated by division done in the early fall or spring. They will probably need to be divided every three years.

Clary does well in a dry area and, in fact, can develop root rot if the soil becomes too wet from lack of drainage. Clary does not require a rich earth. Most soils are suitable. If your soil is poor, fertilize occasionally, but don't be overzealous. Excessive fertilization results in leggy growth and fewer flowers.

To prepare the plants for winter, cut the tops after the first fall frost. In areas that experience especially harsh winters, cover the ground around clary with hay or evergreen branches when the soil has frozen to about an inch deep.

CLOVES

Syzygium aromaticum   **Myrtaceae**

Prowl around a darkened spice warehouse in an exotic harbor and sniff deeply. One especially heady, nostril-clearing, appetite-massaging odor will usually predominate—cloves. The aromatic oils of cloves are far from subtle, yet the familiar fragrance always carries with it an air of mystery and romance.

USES

Medicinal: The mild anesthetic property of cloves has been known for a long time. A home-style, temporary toothache anesthetic of some effectiveness is whole bruised cloves held in the mouth. Dentists to this day sometimes use clove oil mixed with zinc oxide for temporary fillings.

Dentists also sometimes use it to disinfect disturbed root canals, since cloves have moderately strong germicidal properties. Some people use powdered cloves or the oil as an ingredient in mouthwash or sore throat gargles.

The oil, usually diluted with other less flavorful oils, may be purchased at pharmacies. Pure clove oil may irritate the skin or cause allergic reactions. A less concentrated oil can be made at home by soaking whole cloves in olive oil.

Culinary: Cloves have a sharp, distinctive, wintergreen-like flavor. The small dried buds are used ground or whole. Generally the whole buds are removed from food before serving. Strongly flavored, clear clove oil can be substituted for ground cloves where the ground cloves would discolor the food.

Cloves have rapport with beets, green beans, carrots, squash, split pea soup, mixed winter fruit salads, fruit compotes, rhubarb, prunes, cranberries, pickling brines, strong meat stews, cakes, puddings, mincemeat, marinades, spiced teas, and mulled beverages. They are prominent in the cuisines of Russia, Scandinavia, Greece, India, and China.

Available commercially: Whole or ground and oil.

Aromatic: The fierce, oily fragrance of cloves has in scent making as well as in cooking a peculiar affinity for fruit. The clove-studded pomander is the traditional air freshener for stale rooms and is also used to repel moths and to ward off diseases. (See Scents from Herbs for details on making a pomander.)

CULTIVATION

Cloves must have a warm, wet, steamy climate. Since tropical conditions are hard to approximate and maintain in this country, even in greenhouses, the cultivation of clove trees is something you would do only as a challenging experiment or as a hobby.

DESCRIPTION

Botanically, the clove is a nonhardy, evergreen, woody tree. The whole tree is highly aromatic, though the commercially useful part is the unopened flower bud. The tree has a pyramidal habit, with the trunk dividing into large branches covered with smooth gray bark.

Flowers: Solitary racemes in terminal clusters or cymes; white through peach pink to red-tinged color; four petals, four-segment calyx; petal tips form hood shrouding rows of many stamens; astringent aroma.

Leaves: Undivided, oblong or lance-shaped, opposite, 5 in. or more long, glossy green, veined and sometimes hairy; paired on short petioles; fragrant.

Fruit: Long berry.

Height: 15–30 ft.

RANGE

Native to the Moluccas; widely cultivated in Madagascar, India, Malaysia, Brazil, Sumatra, the Philippines, Jamaica, and other warm regions.

GROWING CONDITIONS

- Plant hardiness zone 10.
- Ordinary soil.
- Full sun or partial shade.

COFFEE

Coffea arabica   **Rubiaceae**

With the popularity these days of many different kinds of herbal teas, it may come as a surprise to many long-time coffee drinkers that their favorite beverage is actually an herbal concoction as well (to be specific, it's a decoction). If not one of the best known, coffee is certainly one of the best-loved herbal brews. Many hundreds of years before Maxwell House and Mr. Coffee, people the world over were savoring the wonderful aroma and the uniquely refreshing properties of the fruit of the coffee tree.

DESCRIPTION

During fruit-bearing season, the coffee shrub or tree is a remarkably pretty sight. Because coffee fruit ripens in succession over long periods of time, there are times when each branch is strung with bright green and red berries and dotted with bunches of little white flowers. Coffees are evergreens and under optimum circumstances may live 100 years or more.

Flowers: Delicate, star-shaped, slightly tubular, four to seven spreading lobes twice as long as wide; bloom in small, abundant clusters; fragrance reminiscent of sweet-smelling jasmine; remain just two days after opening.

Leaves: Opposite, pointed, elliptical; smooth, shiny, and bright green on upper side, pale on underside; 2½ in. wide, 6 in. long; evergreen.

Fruit: Referred to as berry or cherry; almost round, smooth, glossy, ½–¾ in. long, deep red when ripe; soft, sticky, yellowish flesh; two flat, oval seeds with a groove running lengthwise down one side, enclosed in silvery parchmentlike skin (this skin is removed before roasting, after which the coffee seed takes on its characteristic rich brown color).

Height: 15–40 ft.

RANGE

Native of Africa; naturalized in Asia, South and Central America, and the East and West Indies.

HISTORY

Although the botanical name for the most well-known of coffee varieties is *Coffea arabica,* the plant hails not from Arabia but from what is now Ethiopia, where it still flourishes at elevations between 4,500 and 6,000 feet. Even primitive African tribes had discovered the remarkable stimulant qualities of coffee. They would prepare it as a food: Using mortars, they crushed the ripe berries (called cherries), mixed them with animal fat, and shaped the mixture into balls. These delicacies were consumed before tribal warfare. Coffee as a drink emerged later, not in the steaming hot form that we savor, but as a wine derived from the fermented juice of the ripe cherries. It wasn't until A.D. 1000 that the Arabs learned to boil coffee and serve it hot.

Italy was probably the first European country to become acquainted with coffee. Italian fleets toured the world and established a huge trade in silks, spices, perfumes, and dyes from the East; coffee most likely entered Europe in this way.

Coffee did not reach England until nearly a century later, where it immediately became popular at Oxford. After a fight to keep it at the level of a rare medicine, coffee's popularity won out in France as well. As travels to and trade with the East continued to increase, the drink's fame spread throughout Europe and became the inspiration of a whole new breed of tradesmen: coffee peddlers.

Until late in the seventeenth century, almost all coffee came from Arabia. But the increasing popularity of the beverage made it impossible for the Arabs to maintain their domination over its cultivation. Smugglers went into action, stealing precious beans from the Arabs and introducing them to other favorable climates: the West Indies, Java, India, and Brazil—now the world's biggest producer of coffee. (As the story goes, the fruit of one tree in the botanical gardens of Holland spawned Latin America's coffee industry.)

As the wars over cultivation ceased and supplies of coffee increased, a new "golden age" of coffee was ushered in. Coffeehouses flourished throughout Europe and to some extent in North America as well as the Middle East. In London and Paris, coffee was the drink of choice among intellectuals and scholars, artists and politicians, and other great thinkers. As America spread west, coffee became firmly entrenched in the lives of the settlers here.

The coffee production business has experienced ups and downs over the years, but the worldwide market has continued to grow and maintain the industry's profitability. Coffee's many varieties keep a number of Third World economies going, and the many roasting methods used today help to satisfy a wide range of palates.

USES

Its role as the quintessential "safe" stimulant has popularized coffee. It is the perfect morning pick-me-up, a common companion at business and social gatherings, a pause that revives. Yet even before coffee became the world's most important beverage, it was revered by old world herbalists and medics for its versatility.

Medicinal: Besides waking people up, coffee has been touted at one time or another in folk medicine to cure many other ills: snakebite, narcotic poisoning, heart disease, pleuritic effusion, asthma, atropine poisoning, flu, fevers, headaches, jaundice, malaria, vertigo, and assorted other ills. Coffee enemas have been prescribed for asthma and cancer.

The principal active constituent of coffee, of course, is caffeine. While caffeine may not cure all the ills listed above, in appropriate doses it is employed in many prescription and over-the-counter pharmaceuticals. Caffeine is a common ingredient in aspirin and other modern analgesics used to battle migraine headaches and other pains of a vascular origin. Combined with sodium benzoate, it

COFFEE—continued

BREW UP SOME ASTHMA RELIEF

A cup of coffee may help asthmatics catch their breath, according to a study from the University of California at Los Angeles Center for Health Sciences. Researchers compared the effect of caffeine from coffee with that of a common asthma medication in patients with asthma. They found that caffeine effectively widens the air passages in the lungs, allowing asthmatics to breathe easier and more deeply. "Even a single cup of strongly caffeinated coffee may quickly produce as much as a 15 percent increase in FEV1 [a measure of breathing capacity]," say the researchers.

If an asthma sufferer felt trouble brewing and didn't have his medication on hand, coffee could be a lifesaver.

Because it's only 40 percent as potent as theophylline (an asthma drug), a person would have to drink excessive amounts of coffee to get the same effects. Coffee shouldn't be used in place of medication on a regular basis.

GROWING CONDITIONS

• Plant hardiness zone 10.

• Moist, rich, well-drained soil.

• Full sun.

can be injected as an antidote for poisoning or an emergency treatment for respiratory failure, although there are other methods of treatment that are more commonly used and much more effective. While there are other means of obtaining caffeine to use in these pharmaceuticals, decaffeination of coffee is the most common.

A negative side exists, as most people know. In large amounts caffeine "produces many undesirable side effects—from nervousness and insomnia to rapid and irregular heartbeats, elevated blood sugar and cholesterol levels, excess stomach acid and heartburn," Varro Tyler, Ph.D., explains in *The Honest Herbal*. He advises "moderation in the use of all caffeine-containing products."

But there's more. There is an as-yet unverified report of evidence linking coffee and cancer of the pancreas. The villain in this case is coffee, but not caffeine.

Benchmark: The pros and cons of coffee safety dovetailed with its enormous worldwide use lend it utility as an interesting herbal benchmark. In compiling a ranking of herb toxicity (see the table A Sampling of Dangerous Herbs on pages 148 through 157) for his *Handbook of Medicinal Herbs,* James Duke, Ph.D., a botanist with the U.S. Department of Agriculture, chose coffee as the benchmark. "I feel that two cups of coffee per day is safe enough not to be dreadfully harmful," he wrote. "On a safety scale of zero to three, I rate coffee 'two,' not real safe, not real poisonous."

CULTIVATION

While no one maintains a coffee plantation in this area of the world, ornamental coffee plants can be grown in warm, humid areas of this country. They sprout readily from seeds and thrive wherever the temperature doesn't dip below 60°F. The atmosphere must be humid, and the plants need as much light as they can stand (without getting scorched).

Coffee plants like fertile soil with a high organic content. While adequate soil moisture is important, proper drainage is equally important to forestall root rot. If conditions become too dry, the plant will get scrawny, and the leaves will yellow and fall off. Plants should be treated with a diluted liquid fertilizer regularly, especially if they are confined to containers. The most common pest problems come from scale insects, spider mites, and mealybugs; they may be dealt with appropriately.

Coffee plants have been known to grow indoors as houseplants. But in areas where cold winters force people to use lots of heat in the house, coffee plants won't fare well because of the dry air.

COLTSFOOT

Tussilago Farfara   **Compositae**

Who ever heard of a plant whose leaves develop only *after* its flower has drooped and gone to seed? There is one. Even the great Roman herbalist Pliny was duped by it: He asserted that it bore no leaves. But it *does* bear leaves, and they *do* develop only after the plant has gone to seed.

The plant is coltsfoot.

And while some of the best herbalists of the past didn't fully understand its life cycle, they did embrace it for what they regarded as its very effective medicinal virtues—virtues that earned it its Latin name and several nicknames as well. Contemporary research, however, suggests that coltsfoot isn't really a safe healer.

HISTORY

For more than 2,000 years, coltsfoot has been regarded as one of the best herbal remedies for coughs. The ancient Greeks called it *bechion,* the Romans *tussilago;* both words mean "cough plant" (so you can see its early reputation). It was also called the coughwort.

Coltsfoot has been used in many herbal remedies over the years. A strong tea made by boiling the leaves was given to coughing or wheezing patients; the tea was strained and sweetened with honey or licorice. People suffering from inflammations, swellings, burns, erysipelas (also known as St. Anthony's fire), and wheals (swellings or welts on the skin, usually itchy) were treated with poultices of crushed coltsfoot leaves and roots. Water distilled with the leaves was also used to treat certain delicate ailments: "The burning heat of piles or privy parts are eased also by applying cloths dipped in coltsfoot water," noted the seventeenth-century British herbalist Nicholas Culpeper. The water vapors were also inhaled.

Native American Indians and American settlers also put this herb to work fighting coughs and congestion. They made soothing teas with the leaves and then strained it, and in severe cases of congestion even soaked blankets in the hot liquid to wrap around the patient.

Before matches were readily available, people would scrape the thick, felty substance from the underside of coltsfoot leaves, wrap it in rags, soak it in a solution of saltpeter, dry it in the sun, and use it as tinder. The fuzz produced on the seeded flower was used by Scotland highlanders as pillow stuffing.

USES

It was as a healing herb that coltsfoot made its mark, but its contemporary use is in question.

Medicinal: The principal active ingredient in coltsfoot is a

SUSPECTED CARCINOGEN

DESCRIPTION

Coltsfoot is a perennial herb. Because of its quickly growing root network, it spreads rapidly and is extremely difficult to get rid of.

Growth begins early in spring, when the creeping root underneath sends up a woolly, scaly shoot. Each shoot produces a single flower. Leaves appear only after the flower fades.

Flowers: Composite, yellow, 1⅜ in. across; composed of tiny disk florets in center surrounded by numerous ray florets; opens in sunny weather, closes under overcast skies and at night.

Leaves: Arise from base of stem; broad, flat, hoof-shaped, mildly toothed, 4–8 in. wide; edged with creamy white color; covered with a woolly, whitish fuzz.

Fruit: Mass of fluffy-topped seeds.

Height: To 6 in. in flower.

FLOWERING

Early spring.

RANGE

Native to northern Europe, Asia, and North Africa; naturalized from Nova Scotia and Quebec to New Jersey and West Virginia.

HABITAT

Stream banks, in fields, and on ridges or embankments.

COLTSFOOT—continued

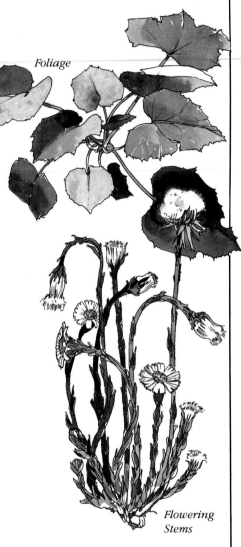

Foliage

*Flowering
Stems*

GROWING CONDITIONS

- Plant hardiness zones 4–6.
- Moist, average soil.
- Full sun.

throat-soothing mucilage. Its reputation is deserved. What is questionable are the methods employed by herbalists to get the mucilage out of the plant and onto the trouble spot. As noted, teas have been used, and a number of proprietary tea mixtures used to treat similar conditions are available in Europe, as are liquid extracts of the herb.

A seemingly reasonable approach—inhaling the vapors of coltsfoot leaves steeping in a pan of hot water—has been debunked by Varro Tyler, Ph.D., author of *The Honest Herbal.* "The useful mucilage is not volatile and would not reach the affected tissues," he says.

As wrongheaded as it may seem, a favorite *remedy* for asthma and bronchial congestion is to dry and smoke coltsfoot roots. It has been recommended—though not here—since the days of Dioscorides and Pliny. Certain herbal tobaccos—blends of lavender, rosemary, thyme, chamomile, and other flowers—are still marketed as expectorants and throat soothers, particularly in Britain. Dr. Tyler clears the smoke away: Smoking coltsfoot for throat conditions is not rational therapy at all, for the "mucilage would be destroyed by burning, and the effect of the smoke on already irritated mucous membranes would be increased irritation."

Toxicity: The deepest shadow over coltsfoot is cast by a study conducted by Japanese scientists in 1976 on the toxicity of coltsfoot flowers, which are widely used in Japan as an herbal remedy. The researchers found that rats fed diets containing high concentrations of coltsfoot developed cancerous tumors of the liver; they concluded that "the young, preblooming flowers of coltsfoot are carcinogenic, showing a high incidence of hemangioendothelial sarcoma [cancer] of the liver (66 percent)." Dr. Tyler indicates that the rest of the plant could be similarly harmful and concludes that neither the leaves nor the flowers can be considered safe for medicinal use.

Culinary: Coltsfoot has had some limited culinary uses. Historically, it was used in herb salads; the young leaves were also cooked and served as a side dish of greens or fried in batter and served with a tangy mustard sauce. A beer called cleats and a wine called clayt were also made from the herb. It has virtually no modern uses.

CULTIVATION

Coltsfoot is too easy to grow. Because of its tendency to overrun an area, it is not a favorite in perennial gardens. It can, however, work well along creek or stream banks and in natural habitat gardens. It thrives in almost any soil and prefers full sunlight. Propagation, should you find it necessary, is easy through division, root cuttings, or seeds.

Thyme

Zatar

Oregano

Calendula

Basil

Rosemary

Summer
Savory

Clary

Chamomile

Nasturtium

Sage

Tarragon

Chives

Dill

Purple
Ruffles
Basil

Tricolor
Sage

Squash
Blossom

Basil

Fennel

Creeping Savory

Sweet Cicely

COMFREY

Symphytum officinale   **Boraginaceae**

Throughout history comfrey has been acclaimed a great healer. In the last 100 years, it has been seen—in addition—by a few visionaries as a crop to feed the world's hungry.

Then, fairly recent scientific studies indicated that comfrey might be carcinogenic, and this herb fell from grace. Now it stands caught in the crossfire of opposing opinions.

HISTORY

Comfrey's reputation as a healing herb has lasted for a *long* time—since around 400 B.C. The Greeks used it to stop heavy bleeding and to treat bronchial problems. Dioscorides, a Greek physician of the first century, prescribed the plant to heal wounds and mend broken bones. In fact the word comfrey is derived from the Latin *conferta,* meaning "grow together." Even the generic name of this plant offers the same allusion. *Symphytum* is Greek and means coming together. The Roman Pliny, a naturalist and contemporary of Dioscorides, on experimenting with the roots, remarked that they were so sticky that when lumps of meat were cooked with them the pieces would all become glued together in one lump. It isn't so surprising then that people were convinced that comfrey could close wounds and knit broken bones. They made poultices for external wounds and drank tea for internal ailments: stomach disorders, diarrhea, bleeding, and more.

Men and women found more to do with this herb than heal their wounds and illnesses. The leaves were cooked in soups and stews or tossed into salads. Farmers cultivated comfrey as fodder for livestock.

Moved by the suffering caused by the Irish potato famine in the 1840s and driven by a vision of the world being saved from hunger by comfrey, Henry Doubleday, an Englishman, established a charitable association to research the cultivation and use of comfrey. The association bearing his name is still in existence today and publishes pamphlets and books on comfrey's history, use, and cultivation.

The setback came in 1978. A study found that rats fed a diet containing dried comfrey leaves and roots developed liver tumors after six months. Initially, the news prompted even the Henry Doubleday Association to caution against all but the external use of the herb. More recently, however, the association has sponsored additional research along the lines of the 1978 study and seems set on refuting its findings.

USES

Debate about the safety of comfrey for internal use is far from over. Nevertheless, comfrey is an externally useful medicinal herb,

SUSPECTED CARCINOGEN

DESCRIPTION

Comfrey is a hardy, upright, leafy perennial that dies down in the winter and comes back strong every spring. Inchthick rhizomes are black outside and white within. They contain a fleshy, juicy mucilaginous substance that gives comfrey yet another of its nicknames—slippery root. (See photo on page 274.)

Flowers: Borne on short, one-sided, curved racemes; tubular corolla with five lobes; blue, yellow, or whitish; ½ in. long; five-lobed calyx; five stamens.

Leaves: Entire, lanceolate to ovate-lanceolate, join stem at bases, lower leaves up to 10 in. long, deep green, hairy.

Fruit: Four nutlets.

Height: 3–5 ft.

FLOWERING

May through frost.

RANGE

Native to Europe and Asia; naturalized on every other continent.

HABITAT

Rich soils along stream banks and in moist meadows.

COMFREY—continued

and it has other beneficial uses as well.

Medicinal: In terms of "knitting" bones together, poultices of comfrey have been replaced by plaster and gauze, but for bruises and external wounds and sores, this herb is an effective remedy. The healing compound in comfrey is allantoin. Scientists have found allantoin in the milk of nursing mothers and in the fetal allantois, a tubelike sac that eventually becomes part of the placenta. Allantoin in some way affects multiplication of cells and tissue growth; wounds and burns do heal faster when allantoin is applied. Currently, pharmacologists add allantoin to ointments and creams used to treat various skin problems.

In addition to comfrey's tissue regenerative abilities, it seems to be effective in destroying harmful bacteria. Applying comfrey extract to infections on both farm animals and humans has quickened the healing process.

Individual claims abound for its use in treating athlete's foot, bedsores, burns, insect bites, various skin problems such as eczema and psoriasis, bruises, and sprains. Used externally, comfrey truly is a healing herb. Fresh leaves can be mashed with a blender and applied to the skin, or a solution from the dried leaves can be made by steeping them in hot water. If using the dried rhizome, grind it and dissolve it in hot water to form a mucilage. Whatever you do, do not boil comfrey. The high temperature can break down the allantoin.

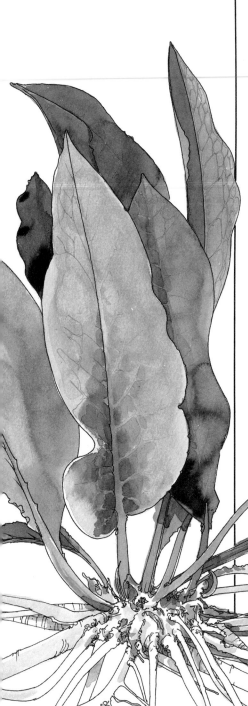

Internal use is still not recommended.

Culinary: Billed as "the world's fastest protein builder" and as a rare plant source of vitamin B_{12}, comfrey once enjoyed a place in the daily diet of many a vegetarian. It was used as a salad green and a potherb. If its status as a suspected carcinogen wasn't sufficient cause to end this practice, knowing that comfrey is in fact a poor source of vitamin B_{12} should be.

An Australian study, conducted in 1983, confirmed that comfrey is indeed one of those very rare plants that contains vitamin B_{12}. But it also demonstrated that you'd have to eat more than 4 pounds of comfrey a day to get the minimum daily requirement of B_{12}. Unless you are a hayburner, eating 4 pounds a day of *anything* is not smart.

Ornamental: You can be sure comfrey won't harm you in the garden. Since it is an easy, fast-growing plant to raise, comfrey is well-suited to background and foundation plantings. Its main drawback is that most varieties are clumsy and rough. It tends to overrun other plants. Plant comfrey in a semiwild area where it can display its handsome leaves and stunning flowers.

Cosmetic: Comfrey can benefit healthy skin. The mucilage soothes and softens, while the allantoin promotes the growth of new cells. To keep skin youthful and beautiful, add comfrey to lotions and creams or soak in a nice, warm comfrey bath. (See the entries Bathing with Herbs and Lotions from Herbs for information on creating herbal baths and lotions.)

Dye: The leaves of comfrey produce a brown dye in wool mordanted with iron. (See the entry Dyes from Herbs for information on how to make dyes.)

CULTIVATION

Do grow this plant for its fine benefits. You can propagate comfrey by seed, by dividing roots in the fall, or by taking cuttings at any time. Set plants 3 feet apart in the ground. Choose the location carefully as comfrey is a tough plant to get rid of once it has established itself. Comfrey grows fairly easily and requires little maintenance once you get it started.

Harvesting and storage: The value of comfrey for medicinal or cosmetic use lies in its allantoin content. Allantoin concentrates in the fastest-growing part of the plant. In the winter months, from January through March, the fastest-growing part is the rhizome. By spring, it is the new young leaves. Harvest accordingly. The rhizome or leaves can be dried and stored in a tightly sealed container.

THE SAFETY OF COMFREY

Two research studies are the basis for the controversy over comfrey's safety. One demonstrated that rats fed a diet that was 8 percent comfrey leaves developed liver cancers within six months. The other showed that certain alkaloids in comfrey cause chronic liver problems in rats.

The Henry Doubleday Research Association, long a champion of comfrey, was cautionary when the studies were first reported, but now is critical of them. A pamphlet it published, *The Safety of Comfrey*, concludes that "...although there are alkaloids of the liver damaging type in comfrey, there are such small quantities in the leaves that reasonable consumption of mature leaves, or of comfrey tea, even over a number of years, is unlikely to cause any problems."

One pharmacognosist, Varro Tyler, Ph.D., of Purdue University, has advised against eating comfrey or drinking comfrey tea. But another commented that he could see no problem in drinking comfrey tea, unless one were to drink 15 to 20 cups daily.

GROWING CONDITIONS

- Plant hardiness zone 3.
- Soil pH 7.1.
- Moist, rich soil.
- Full sun to partial shade.

COMPANION PLANTING

The notion that plants—particularly strong-smelling ones—have some effect on others in the garden may be as old as gardening itself. Through the ages, gardeners and herbalists have claimed that depending on where they are grown and with what other plants, herbs can do everything from keeping pesky caterpillars at a distance, to improving another plant's flavor, to causing a neighbor to shrivel up and die.

Until very recently, you'd be hard-pressed to find a researcher who could keep a straight face on the subject of such plant interactions. Today, researchers not only consider these ideas but routinely conduct experiments that address gardeners' age-old questions: Why does a plant fail in one location and thrive in another where soil, water, and light seem the same? Could a neighboring plant actually influence its growth or attract or repel certain insects?

These issues are of special interest to us here because many of the plants in question are herbs. If the claims are true, then care must go into planting arrangements. Herbs must be kept away from the plants they might damage. Beneficial ones should be freed from the formal garden, to grow among the fruits, vegetables, and flowers they encourage. Such planting schemes, where two or more plants are interplanted for their mutual benefit, are called companion planting.

So far, experimental work on companion plants is inconclusive. Most researchers agree that an interplanted garden—one with many different kinds of plants chosen for sheer variety—can be healthier than a single-cropped one. Since different species flower and fruit at different times, there tends to be less competition for nutrients and moisture. Furthermore, the welter of odors, colors, and textures a heavily interplanted garden has seems to confuse pests, so it's more difficult for them to find their favorite dinner. Whether a specific companion herb can directly affect a specific neighboring plant is another question.

A number of controlled experiments show that some common garden herbs and vegetables do indeed influence the health and growth of their neighbors. How many plants exert this power and to what extent remains to be discovered. There's plenty to do before the last word is heard. What is clear is that there are five ways plants can affect one another: by improving the health and flavor of their neighbor, by interfering with the growth of their neighbor, by repelling pests, by trapping pests, or by attracting beneficial insects such as pest predators, parasites, and pollinators. Common garden herbs fall into each of these categories.

HERBS FOR TASTIER VEGETABLES

Gardeners have always claimed that certain vegetables or fruits seem to taste better if grown near a particular companion plant. Often the claims seem based on culinary association: An herb that enhances a vegetable's taste in cooking is said to have the same effect when planted near that vegetable in the garden. Thus, basil improves tomatoes, and dill helps cabbages.

It's possible something is at work here: There may be at least a bit of truth to these associations. Herbs that shade the soil might keep neighboring crops from becoming parched and woody. For this reason, chervil makes sense as a companion to radish. A plant that makes few nutrient or water demands on the soil undoubtedly would be a better companion than a heavy feeder. It is sensible, therefore, to recommend planting mustard near beans.

A chemical reaction may even be taking place between the plants. Early gardeners looked fondly on the dandelion as a companion in the orchard and vegetable patch. We now know that dandelions not only attract pollinating insects but they give off ethylene, a gas that encourages fruitset and ripening. Could it be that a tree surrounded by dandelions will produce more apples, faster, than one surrounded by clover?

ENEMY HERBS

Gardeners are only human, and they hold grudges. Indeed, you might say, they've held a few horticultural grudges for hundreds of years! Many plants, from tiny herbs to full-grown trees, have been blacklisted as dangerous companions in the garden. Herbals and garden writings are filled with indictments of dozens of plants. Grass "destroys" trees; sage doesn't fare well with onion; there's a "naturall enmitie" between cabbage and grape.

Crazy as it seems, there may be truth to many of these claims. Scientists are uncovering evidence that some plants practice chemical warfare against certain of their neighbors. They do this by exuding chemicals or phytotoxins that inhibit the growth or development of these plants. For example, the black walnut tree exudes a chemical called juglone that prevents many plants from growing in its shadow, among them most vegetables, azaleas, rhododendrons, blackberries, lilacs, peonies, and apple trees. The phenomenon is called *allelopathy,* and a great deal of research is being devoted to it.

Among the details research has confirmed is that the chemicals

---

A GLOSSARY

Allelopathy: The process by which one plant releases chemicals or phytotoxins that inhibit the growth or development of another growing nearby.

Alternate hosts: Plants or animals that insects feed on when their preferred food isn't available. Most insects are fairly limited in their diet, but almost none relies totally on one source of food. Ideally, you should eliminate alternate hosts of pests and maintain alternate hosts for beneficial insects.

Autoallelopathy: The process by which a plant produces chemicals (phytotoxins) that inhibit the growth of members of the same species. Thus, the roots of an apple tree might release substances that would harm other apple trees growing nearby.

Beneficial insects: Insects that work for the gardener's benefit by attacking pests, pollinating flowers, or feeding on weeds. Surprisingly, most insects are beneficial, though not always in any dramatic way.

Companion plant: A plant chosen for intercropping with a given crop because of its ability to enhance or complement the other's growth.

Interplanting: Also called intercropping. The practice of growing two or more crops at the same time in the same field or garden bed. Crops may be interplanted within rows or in alternate rows, blocks, circles, or even mixed plantings that have no geometric pattern.

(continued on page 109)

HERBS FOR HELPING OTHER PLANTS

Listed below are some of the plant combinations that gardeners have long recommended. None has been scientifically proven, but some do seem to make good common sense as interplants. Test them yourself.

Herb	Plant(s) It Enhances	Herb	Plant(s) It Enhances
Anise	Coriander	Lovage	Bean
Basil	Pepper and tomato	Marigold	Potato, rose, and tomato
Beebalm	Tomato	Mint	Cabbage and tomato
Borage	Bean, strawberry, and tomato	Mustards	Bean, grape, and fruit trees
Chamomile	Cucumber, onion, and most herbs	Onion	Beet, cabbage, lettuce, and strawberry
Chervil	Radish	Oregano	Bean
Chives	Carrot, grape, rose, and tomato	Rosemary	Bean
		Rue	Fig
Coriander	Anise	Sage	Cabbage, carrot, strawberry, tomato, and marjoram
Dandelion	Fruit trees		
Dead nettle	Potato	Savories	Bean and onion
Dill	Cabbage, onion, and lettuce	Tansy	Blackberry, raspberry, and rose
Garlic	Rose	Tarragon	Most vegetables
Horseradish	Potato	Thyme	Eggplant, potato, and tomato
Hyssop	Cabbage and grape		
Larkspur	Bean and cabbage	Yarrow	Most aromatic herbs

ENEMY HERBS

These are the herbs that gardeners over the past 1,000 years have named as "harmful" to certain neighboring plants. Don't let this scare you. Any plant deserves to remain innocent until proven guilty. So far, there's almost no scientific "proof" to back up most of these claims. The only plant that should perhaps concern the gardener is wormwood, which does contain fairly substantial amounts of toxins.

Herb	Plant(s) It Harms	Herb	Plant(s) It Harms
Anise	Carrot	Larkspur	Beet
Chives	Bean and pea	Mustard	Turnip
Chrysanthemum	Lettuce	Onion	Bean, pea, and sage
Coriander	Fennel	Rue	Basil, cabbage, and sage
Dill	Carrot and tomato	Sage	Onion
Fennel	Bean and pepper	Tansy	Collard
Garlic	Bean and pea	Wormwood	Most vegetables

COMPANION PLANTING—continued

are fairly specific and only harm certain species. Often they are present in such small amounts that their effect on other plants is hardly noticeable. Furthermore, these toxins have to travel through the soil or air, reach the target plant, and be absorbed, all without losing their poisonous powers. More often than not, the material evaporates or leaches away, or some chemical change renders it innocuous before it ever reaches its target.

Still, there is some convincing evidence of allelopathy in several controlled field studies. Among the herbs that have been implicated are French marigold (*Tagetes patula*) against beans, tansy on collards, some chrysanthemums on lettuce, and wormwood on peas and beans. Clearly, all the facts aren't in yet. But if you find that a plant is failing in your garden and all the usual explanations don't seem to work, consider what's growing next door! It could be that some neighboring herb or flower or tree is the culprit.

HERBS THAT REPEL PESTS

We know that many, perhaps even most, insects rely on taste and smell to find dinner. To find the right plant, for example, the flea beetle and imported cabbage moth need to "smell cabbage." Spray the plant with some thyme or sage extract, and these pests seem confused. They lay fewer eggs there and don't light on the cabbages to feed. Would interplanting cabbage with thyme or sage have the same effect? Hundreds of gardeners claim it does. They plant basil near beans and have fewer bean beetles; garlic near roses and have fewer aphids; parsley by asparagus for fewer beetles; and wormwood here and there to repel slugs.

There's remarkably little scientific documentation on the matter, however, considering the number of claims made. In many studies of specific aromatic herbs, the companions have had absolutely no effect on pests. In some cases they reduce pest numbers but not enough to really reduce the damage. In a few, they actually seemed to attract the very pests they were meant to discourage!

Still, some herbs have performed well. Those that show promise and may eventually be scientifically "certified" repellent plants include nasturtiums against whiteflies; southernwood against cabbage butterflies; tobacco against flea beetles; catnip, coriander, nasturtiums, and tansy against Colorado potato beetles; catnip and nasturtiums against green peach aphids; catnip and tansy against squash bugs; and French marigolds (*T. patula*) against some nematodes, Mexican bean beetles, and possibly against Colorado potato beetles.

Lots of work remains to be done in this area. But to most herb enthusiasts, such scientific confirmation isn't important. They swear by the benefits of repellent plantings.

A GLOSSARY—*continued*

Parasitic insects: Insects that, as larvae, live in and feed on other insects. Parasites lay their eggs on another insect; when the larvae emerge, they consume their host. Tachinid flies, chalcid, braconid and ichneumonid wasps are parasites that help control many common garden pests.

Pheromones: Chemical substances released by insects and interpreted as signals by other individuals of the same species. Insect pheromones may serve as sex attractants, alarms, or territorial markers. Some plant chemicals mimic these pheromones, bringing about a certain behavior in certain insects.

Phytotoxin: Plant-produced chemicals that are harmful to other living things. Phytotoxins are responsible for allelopathic reactions. They give some plants protection from hungry insects or other animals.

Predatory insects: Insects that during some stage of their growth attack, kill, and eat other insects. Predators range in size from tiny mites to large ground beetles and hover flies. Some, such as lady beetles and lacewings, can be purchased and released in the garden. Unless the appropriate plant and insect hosts are available, predators will soon move on.

HERBS THAT REPEL PESTS

Certain plants are believed to repel insects. Use the list below to help you map out your next planting arrangement.

Pest	Repellent Plant(s)
Ant	Peppermint, spearmint, tansy, and wormwood
Aphid	Most aromatic herbs, including catnip, chives, coriander, eucalyptus, fennel, garlic, larkspur, marigold, mustard, nasturtium, peppermint, and spearmint
Asparagus beetle	Basil, parsley, and tomato
Cabbage butterfly	Southernwood
Cabbage looper	Dill, eucalyptus, garlic, hyssop, peppermint, nasturtium, onion, pennyroyal, sage, southernwood, spearmint, thyme, and wormwood
Cabbage maggot	Garlic, marigold, radish, sage, and wormwood
Carrot fly	Leek, lettuce, onion, rosemary, sage, tobacco, and wormwood
Codling moth	Garlic and wormwood
Colorado potato beetle	Catnip, coriander, eucalyptus, nasturtium, onion, and tansy
Corn earworm	Cosmos, geranium, and marigold
Cucumber beetle	Catnip, marigold, nasturtium, radish, and rue
Cutworm	Spiny amaranth
Flea beetle	Catnip, peppermint, rue, spearmint, southernwood, tansy, tobacco, and wormwood
Imported cabbageworm	Dill, garlic, geranium, hyssop, peppermint, nasturtium, onion, pennyroyal, sage, southernwood, tansy, and thyme
Japanese beetle	Catnip, chives, garlic, and tansy
Leafhopper	Geranium and petunia
Mexican bean beetle	Marigold, rosemary, and savories
Mouse	Wormwood
Mole	Castor bean and narcissus
Peach borer	Garlic
Rabbit	Garlic, marigold, and onion
Slug and snail	Fennel, garlic, and rosemary
Spider mite	Coriander
Squash bug	Catnip, nasturtium, peppermint, petunia, radish, spearmint, and tansy
Squash vine borer	Radish
Tomato hornworm	Dill, borage, and opal basil
Whitefly	Nasturtium, peppermint, thyme, and wormwood

COMPANION PLANTING—continued

HERBS FOR TRAPPING PESTS

While some companion plants protect their neighbors by repelling pests, others sacrifice themselves, luring pests away from other plants. In some cases, the trapping plant destroys the pests as well: As they feed, they get sick or lose their ability to lay eggs.

Eighteenth-century growers recommended radishes as a "trap" for cabbage maggot. Many gardeners claim that mullein traps stinkbugs in apple orchards, and borage lures Japanese beetles away from other plants. They plant goldenrod to trap cucumber beetles and nasturtiums for aphids. Unfortunately, none of these claims has been proven by researchers. It's up to the gardener to do his own tests and make up his own mind about the merits of herbal traps.

HERBS THAT ATTRACT BENEFICIAL INSECTS

Not all of the insects in the garden are bad guys. Indeed, most are working for the gardener in the battle to maintain plant health. Beneficial insects fall into three basic groups: the predators that hunt and kill other insects; the parasites that lay their eggs on other insects so that their young may dine on the host's lifeblood; and the pollinators that transfer pollen from male to female flowers. In the ideal garden, there are enough beneficial insects to keep pests under control and to insure that as many flowers as possible set seed.

Like the pests, these helpful species have their own favorite places to lay eggs and feed. Plants that supply the good guys with the shelter, nectar, and pollen they need at some point in their lives are called nursery plants. If the beneficial insects find nursery plants in your garden, they will stick around.

Dozens of herbs are ideal nursery plants. Creeping predators, such as spiders and ground beetles, seek out dark, cool, moist spots. Dense, low-growing plants like thyme, rosemary, and most of the mints should attract these insects. Shelter is also important for the flying insects, but they require nectar and pollen, too. Lacewings, lady beetles, parasitic flies, and predatory and parasitic wasps need this plant food to supplement their diet of mealybugs, aphids, and the like.

Lacewings, whose larvae consume caterpillars, beetle grubs, aphids, and some pests' eggs, seem to favor shady, sheltered spots for egg laying. Plant ferns, evergreens, and all sorts of nectar-rich flowers to keep them in the garden.

Parasitic wasps, such as the chalcid, ichneumonid, and trichogramma, are invaluable for their control of caterpillars, aphids,

GOOD BUGS TO HAVE IN THE GARDEN

How can you distinguish the helpful insects from the harmful ones? It's not always easy to determine if insects are eating the plant or some minuscule pest on the plant. Here's help!

Beetles: Ground beetles and lady beetles stand out as the most effective predators in this group, although blister beetles, fireflies, soldier beetles, tiger beetles, and rove beetles are also good bug eaters. Ground beetles are associated with nightshade and amaranth. Lady beetles like to lay their eggs on tansy and yarrow.

Flies: Hover flies or syrphids are the brightly colored flies we see flitting about the garden. Their larvae parasitize aphids and other small, soft-bodied pests. They need the pollen provided by flat, open flowers such as daisies or marigolds. Tachinid flies are important parasites of European corn borers, Mexican bean beetles, gypsy moths, and other caterpillar pests. Most flowering plants in the carrot family attract them.

Lacewings: These are lovely light green creatures that as larvae and adults prey upon small, soft-bodied pests such as aphids and mealybugs. Tree of heaven (*Ailanthus* spp.) and various evergreens are favorite shelters for lacewings.

(continued on page 113)

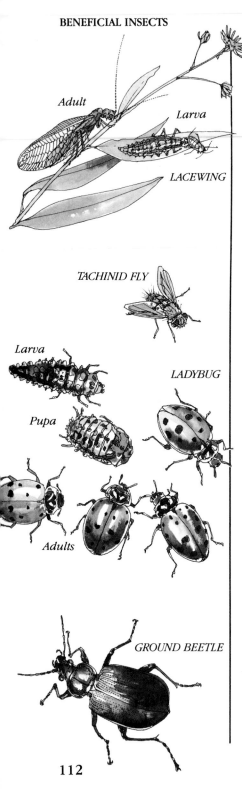

Adult

Larva

LACEWING

TACHINID FLY

Larva

LADYBUG

Pupa

Adults

GROUND BEETLE

COMPANION PLANTING—continued

and other soft-bodied pests. But they must have nectar. Since most are very small and could drown in the nectar of larger flowers, these wasps need small, open flowers such as Queen Anne's lace, dill, and anise. All flowering members of the carrot family host most parasitic wasps. Milkweed and catnip also help sustain some species.

Plant composite flowers—daisy, goldenrod, chamomile—and mint family members—spearmint, peppermint, catnip—to attract predatory wasps, hover flies, and robber flies. As adults, paper wasps, yellow jackets, mud daubers, and hornets eat nectar and pollen, but they catch caterpillars, grubs, and other insects to feed their young. The predatory and parasitic flies prey on all sorts of insects, from tiny leafhoppers and grubs to grasshoppers and butterflies. Interplant closely to provide them with a sheltered area for egg laying.

Many of these same predators and parasites serve double duty as first-class pollinators. Without them (and bees and butterflies) we'd have no garden fruits or seeds. Plants in the carrot, mustard, mint, and daisy families attract them. Interestingly, the showiest blossoms, which we favor, aren't necessarily the insects' favorites. Inconspicuous flowers, like savory, chamomile, and thyme, will attract more beneficial insects than the most stunning roses and the prettiest chrysanthemums.

Surround your vegetable and flower gardens with a mixture of nursery plants, particularly herbs. Combine perennials and annuals, tall-growing and low-growing species. Select varieties for blooming time so different flowers are blooming all the time. Marigold, allysum, marguerite, chamomile, tansy, and feverfew bloom over a long period and make good edging plants. Thyme, the savories, lavender, hyssop, basil, rosemary, and oregano also have prolonged blooming and are fairly easy to control as border plants. Most of the carrot family members are mid- to late-summer bloomers, but two-year-old parsley and carrot will provide some earlier flowers, as will fennel and dill that is started early. Include members of the mustard, mint, borage, and mullein families as well.

BOTANICAL SPRAYS AND DUSTS

Because of their strong odors and seeming freedom from insect attack, aromatic herbs have long been used as insecticides and repellents. A plant that pests didn't attack would be made into a dust or spray, which would be applied to valued but pest-susceptible plants. Persian farmers knew the pest-killing powers of pyrethrum, found in several species of chrysanthemum (*C. coccineum, C. cinnerarifolium*). American Indians were among the first to concoct nicotine insecticides from tobacco leaves. Other widely used botanical insecticides include sabadilla dust, ryania and ryania powder, and quassia wood chips.

All of these plant-derived substances are poisons. Thus, they have harmful effects on the environment. For example, they aren't always too selective in the insects they destroy—predators may die along with pests. Nicotine spray, dust, or even smoke kills just about any insect in its path and may at the same time transmit disease to the infested plant. Pyrethrum is only slightly more discriminating. It poisons just about all caterpillars, aphids, thrips, and many beetles—regardless of whether they are eaters of plants or pests.

Far safer than these poisons are the repellents that keep insects from becoming serious pests.

Most plants contain both insect-repelling and insect-attracting chemicals. They send off signals to bring in some insects and keep others at bay. A compound on the hairs of tomato leaves repels Colorado potato beetles. Yet, at the same time, this or some other compound is attracting tomato hornworm. The same mustard oils that attract all sorts of cabbage pests can sicken or even kill flies, mosquitoes, spider mites, and Mexican bean beetles.

Because of the relative safety of these substances, research in this area is flourishing. The goal is to identify any effective chemical in any traditional repellent plant, including tansy, the mints, marigold, rue, onion, and garlic. If the chemicals are there, a spray, dust, or mulch made from the herbs might be effective. Success depends on whether there is enough of the repellent present and whether it will remain viable long enough to be effective. Even if the "repellents" only mask the crop's attractive odor, they could reduce pest problems.

Several experiments offer encouraging results. Sprays of both sage and thyme deterred imported cabbageworms. A garlic spray seems to repel black pea aphids. Corn seeds treated with an emulsion of butterfly milkweed sends away hungry corn wireworms. Peppermint waste left over after oils have been distilled is effective against Colorado potato beetles.

The possibilities for home-brewed herbal repellents are endless. When pest problems arise, look for herbs that aren't bothered by the insect, and try concocting a tea or emulsion from them. The general rule of thumb seems to be: the stronger the smell, the more likely success. You may wish to combine several herbs, hoping that at least one will contain something your pest won't like. Stay away from toxic substances such as foxglove, larkspur, tobacco, rhubarb, and the like.

GOOD BUGS—*continued*

Wasps and bees: By far the most beneficial of all garden creatures, they are pollinators as well as parasites. Braconid wasps are small (half an inch or less) wasps that attack corn borers, sawflies, and all sorts of larval pests. The tiny white cocoons you find on the back of a tomato hornworm were put there by a braconid wasp. Flowering carrot family plants, such as Queen Anne's lace and yarrow, attract these insects.

The even smaller chalcid wasps (less than a quarter inch long) parasitize lots of caterpillar pests. The trichogramma egg parasite you can buy for biological control is a type of chalcid wasp. Like most other wasps, it can be encouraged to stay around the garden if you provide a border or strip of yarrow, wild carrot, and other flowering plants. Wasps also seem to benefit from nearby evergreens.

Ichneumonid wasps are varied in their appearance and size, but most species are important parasites of larval pests. Fennel, wild mustard, and some evergreens feed and shelter ichneumonids during part of their life cycle.

To encourage bees, our best garden pollinators, plant fennel and all sorts of flowering carrot family plants.

COOKING WITH HERBS

If the secret to your favorite recipe for tomato sauce is a predominance of basil and your neighbor swears only by oregano, which recipe is correct? Both, of course, because the seasoning and flavoring of food with herbs and spices is mostly a matter of personal taste. We choose harmonious flavors by tasting and smelling as we cook. The choice between basil and oregano can depend on the sweetness of the tomatoes; whether they're fresh, frozen, or canned; if the sauce will be served hot or cold; what food will be served with the sauce; and what sort of mood you're in.

So if seasoning is in the taste buds of the beholder, why bother at all with a culinary section? Because of basics. By acquainting yourself with or refreshing your knowledge of how to use herbs, classic combinations, storage methods, and individual flavor personalities, you'll become a more skillful and creative cook.

GENERAL TECHNIQUES AND PRESERVATION

The following tips and suggestions shouldn't be regarded as the last word on using herbs in cooking. Be sure to check the entries on individual herbs for additional ideas and tips.

Using fresh herbs: Some say it started in California at restaurants like Spago and Chez Panisse. New Yorkers claim it began in the Village and spread from there, and others say James Beard had been doing it for years.

Regardless of where it started, any red-blooded lover of food has realized that there's a new culinary aroma in the air, and that aroma is herbal. In restaurants, markets, and in the home, fresh herbs are becoming commonplace. They're being sprinkled, pureed, and sautéed with everything from appetizers to desserts.

In fact, in many recipes, fresh herbs are taking center stage. For instance, press fresh marjoram into the flesh of fish before a quick grilling and the beautiful pattern, aroma, and taste that the marjoram offers will outperform any sauce.

Or think of pesto, the popular herb paste. We used to make it for pasta and only when we could gather enough fresh basil. Now we create pestos with oregano, dill, or coriander leaf and the medium with which we use them (chicken, fish, pasta, or vegetables) gets second billing.

Because fresh herbs are inspiring, they will continue to sprout up in a variety of recipes and cooking styles. And because cooking is an ongoing, creative process, fresh herbs will continue to be enjoyed by a growing and eager audience.

To serve four people with a sauce, soup, stew, or sauté, use about 2 teaspoons of minced fresh herbs. To reach the fullest aroma, rub the leaves between your hands, then mince them using a sharp knife or by snipping them with kitchen shears. Mince large amounts of herbs in a food processor.

Whole fresh leaves should be rubbed between your hands before adding to marinades, soups, stews, and punches. The amount of leaves to add will vary depending on their size, but use the 2-teaspoons-for-4-servings rule and try to visualize how many whole leaves will make that amount.

For the best flavor in long-cooking foods like soups and stews, add fresh herbs during the last 20 minutes or so of cooking.

Conversely, fresh herbs may not have a chance to release their flavors in uncooked foods like salad dressings and marinades or during microwaving. Be sure to taste these foods before serving since it may be necessary to add more herbs.

Tips for keeping fresh herbs fresh: Bouquets of fresh herbs can be set into jars filled with an inch or two of water, covered loosely with plastic wrap, and refrigerated. They'll last this way for about two weeks.

Smaller sprigs of herbs should be wrapped in paper towels, sealed in plastic bags, and placed in the crisper drawer of the refrigerator, where they'll last for about two weeks. Be sure the leaves are completely dry, or brown spots may develop.

Using dried herbs: Although this is the most common condition for culinary herbs, the common *collection* is changing. Where once our staples were bay leaves, dried oregano, and cinnamon, our culinary exploration is encouraging us to reach out.

We now own saffron for our fiestas and filé for our gumbos. Dried seeds like coriander and cardamom and dried roots like ginger and horseradish are now the norm for the well-stocked, creative cupboard.

Herbs preserve most flavorfully when they're picked (1) before they flower, and (2) early in the morning just after the dew has dried. Always use plants that are healthy and free from dark spots and other imperfections.

Generally use about 1 teaspoon of dried herbs to serve four people, or about half the amount you would use of fresh. Smell the herbs before using them to make sure they're aromatic. Then rub them between your hands or grind them coarsely in a spice-grinder, coffee grinder, or with a mortar and pestle. Use them immediately. Dried herbs can also be steeped in warm stock or other liquid, to

MAXIMIZING THE FLAVOR

- To develop the flavor for dried herbs, soak them for several minutes in a liquid that can be used in the recipe—stock, oil, lemon juice, or vinegar.

- When using herbs in salad dressings, allow the flavor of the combination to develop by soaking for 15 minutes to an hour.

- Work the flavors of herbs into meat, poultry, and fish by rubbing them in with your hands before cooking.

- For steamed or boiled vegetables, add the herbs to melted butter and allow to stand for 10 minutes before seasoning the vegetables with it.

- To intensify the flavors of whole spices, toast them briefly in a dry, heavy skillet before using.

- Dried and fresh herbs may be used interchangeably in most recipes. Use three to five times more fresh herbs than dried, depending on the strength of the herb.

COOKING WITH HERBS—continued

GRATING, GRINDING, AND CRUSHING

An electric spice grinder is very handy for grinding whole spices. Small spice graters for whole nutmeg or allspice are useful and also come in handy for grating lemon and orange peel. For crushing herbs and spices and blending them into other ingredients, a mortar and pestle are very efficient.

If you use a blender to grind spices and herbs, try this method: A pint canning jar with a standard-size mouth will fit perfectly into many blender bases. Just put the spices in the jar, place the blade, rubber, and screw bottom of the blender container onto the jar as you would a lid. Turn the jar upside down, place in the blender base, and proceed with grinding the spices.

cover, before adding them to recipes. This will enhance their flavors. Remember to taste, and, if necessary, adjust the flavor before serving.

Tips for drying herbs: Herbs may, of course, be dried in commercial dryers. But if you don't have one, there are lots of alternatives. For starters, use your oven on its lowest setting. Spread the herbs on cookie sheets, set the sheets in the oven, and leave the oven door ajar to help encourage circulation. Stir and check the herbs occasionally. They're dry when the leaves crumble when pinched and rubbed.

Bouquets of herbs can be hung to dry. Choose an airy, dry place like an attic, and hang the herbs upside down. Tie a paper bag over the bouquet to keep it from the light and to catch falling herbs. The bouquet may take up to two weeks to dry, but check its progress daily.

Microwaving is another alternative. Start with a clear, sunny day, because in humid weather the herbs may reabsorb moisture when removed from the microwave. Brush soil from the leaves and stems with a stiff paintbrush. Then place about a cup of herbs in a single layer between paper towels, and microwave on high for about three minutes. (Delicate herbs like thyme should be turned every 30 seconds.) If the herbs aren't completely dry after three minutes, reset the timer for 20 seconds, and start the microwave again. Don't let the herbs get too hot, or they'll taste scorched. They're ready when they feel brittle and rattle when you shake the paper towels, or when the leaves pull easily from the stem.

Herbs like parsley, coriander leaf, and rosemary dry well in the refrigerator. Simply place an unwashed bouquet in a paper (not plastic) bag. Close the bag and leave it in the refrigerator for about a month. The bouquet will be surprisingly green, but dry and aromatic.

To store herbs, remove the leaves from the stems. Make sure they're completely dry, or mold could occur. Then scoop the herbs into tightly covered glass jars away from the light and heat, and they'll be flavorful for about a year. Don't make the easy mistake of storing them above or next to your stove, for the heat will dissipate their flavors.

Roots and thick stems can be dried in a commercial dryer, your oven, or a microwave. For faster drying, chop them into pieces first. Store them in tightly covered glass jars away from the light and heat, and always try to grind them as you need them, using a coffee grinder, spice grinder, or mortar and pestle.

To dry seeds, gather ripe flower heads and lay them out in an airy, dry, dark place. When the seeds are dry, you'll be able to shake them right out of the flower heads.

Pods like chilies and peppers are dried whole in a commercial dryer, in the oven, or by stringing them together and hanging them in a dry, airy place. Store them in jars or by hanging. Grind as needed in a coffee grinder, spice grinder, or mortar and pestle for use in chili powder or paprika.

Garlic cloves and onion pieces can also be dried using a commercial dryer or your oven. Store the dried pieces in a tightly covered glass jar. Grind as needed for garlic powder or onion powder.

Using frozen herbs: Clever chefs are learning that the herbal pantry is not limited to fresh or dried herbs. The freezer provides a hospitable environment for many herbs and spices because its low temperature helps them keep their flavors longer.

What's more, if you need to grind your dried spices ahead of time, freezing will preserve their flavors longer than keeping them at room temperature.

Many frozen herbs can be used as you would fresh—about 2 teaspoons to serve four people. Take the herbs from the freezer and toss them (without defrosting) into soups, stews, and sauces. If you're using frozen herbs in salads or other uncooked foods, drain them first. (Frozen minced herbs will need more draining than sprigs.) Note that flavors can change during freezing, so be sure to taste and, if necessary, adjust before serving.

Tips for freezing herbs: Tough stemmed herbs like basil, tarragon, and sage should have their leaves removed for freezing. Brush off the soil with a stiff paintbrush rather than washing because too much water may dilute flavors. Once the leaves have been brushed and removed, lay them out flat on a cookie sheet and freeze them for several hours. Then place them gently into freezer containers or bags, and they'll be easy to remove individually as needed.

The big question when freezing herbs is whether or not to blanch. Although the color of the herbs will usually stay greener if they're blanched, flavor and aroma will often be sacrificed.

Basil is an exception: It should be blanched, or it will turn black. Most other herbs will freeze well unblanched for up to six months if it is done just after harvesting. After that time, blanched or unblanched, they'll begin to deteriorate.

To blanch, simply place the leaves in a strainer and pour boiling water over them for one second. Then lay them on paper towels and let them cool in the air before freezing. Don't be tempted into cooling the leaves by plunging them into ice water, because it could dilute their flavor.

Delicate herbs like thyme and dill freeze well in sprigs. Simply arrange them in freezer containers or bags and seal. Use whole frozen sprigs or snip them as needed.

COMBINATIONS FOR FREEZING AND DRYING

If you use basil and thyme together in cooking, why not preserve them together, too? Here are some ideas for other tasty combinations:

- basil, thyme, and Italian parsley
- marjoram, lovage, and thyme
- coriander leaf and chilies
- chives and dillweed
- dill, mint, and parsley
- oregano, thyme, and Italian parsley
- tarragon and lovage
- sage, thyme, and chives
- lemon verbena and tarragon
- mint, lemon balm, and dill
- dill, lovage, and chives
- oregano, basil, and thyme
- chives and marjoram
- oregano, epizote, and parsley
- mint and zatar

COOKING WITH HERBS—continued

COMBINATIONS FOR FLAVORED VINEGARS

- rosemary, raisins, orange peel, garlic, and white wine vinegar

- sage, parsley, shallots, and red wine vinegar

- borage, dill, shallots, and white wine vinegar

- chilies, garlic, oregano, and cider vinegar

- mint, honey, cardamom seed, and white vinegar

- coriander leaf, garlic, and rice vinegar

- rose petals, violet petals, and rice vinegar

- dill, nasturtiums, garlic, and cider vinegar

- savory, chive blossoms, and cider vinegar

- fennel leaf, garlic, parsley, and white wine vinegar

Herbs can also be minced by hand or with a food processor and frozen in ice cube trays. When the cubes are frozen, transfer them to plastic bags and use as needed.

Another way to freeze minced herbs is by making herb pastes. Add fresh leaves or sprigs to a food processor and begin to mince. While the motor is running, add oil, a bit at a time, until the mixture has formed a paste. Freeze the paste in ice cube trays or in tablespoon amounts wrapped in plastic.

Making herbed vinegars: Herb-flavored vinegars add magic to any recipe that asks for vinegar. They offer aroma to foods just as rhythm adds excitement to music, without overpowering the harmony of the recipe.

Choose white vinegar, white wine vinegar, red wine vinegar, apple cider vinegar, or rice vinegar, depending on the herbs you're adding. Heat the vinegar but don't boil it; then pour it into a glass jar to which you have added fresh herb sprigs or leaves. Use about three 2-inch sprigs for each cup of vinegar. Garlic, shallots, or chilies can be used, too, by adding one for each cup of vinegar.

Let the vinegar cool, then cover it, and store in a cool, dark place for up to a year. Use the vinegar in salad dressings and marinades and to deglaze pans.

Making flavored oils: Flavored oils can be a dieter's dream. The secret is that you can use less because the oil is more flavorful. For example, on a salad to serve four people, you might make a dressing using 2 tablespoons of oil. But if you use a flavored oil, you can cut the amount in half, and the dressing will be so flavorful, nondieters will be jealous.

Gently heat olive oil, peanut oil, or other vegetable oil until it's warm and fragrant. This will take three to five minutes, depending on how much oil you're heating. Then pour the oil into a glass jar to which you have added fresh herb sprigs, herb leaves, garlic, or chilies. Use about three 2-inch sprigs, one clove of garlic, or one chili for each cup of oil. Let the oil cool, cover, and store it in a cool, dark place for about six months. Use the oil to sauté and in marinades and salad dressings.

Making herb butters: Like flavored oils, herb butters allow calorie counters to use less because there's more flavor. They also jazz up a breakfast table or an appetizer tray with wonderful colors and tastes. Try serving herb butters in tiny ramekins (crocks), shaping them in butter molds, or cutting them with a butter curler.

Combine about 1 tablespoon of minced fresh herbs with ½ cup softened sweet butter. Wrap the mixture in plastic and store it in the refrigerator for about a month or in the freezer for about three months. Use the butter on warm biscuits or toast, steamed vegetables, poached chicken, or fish. Use it to sauté.

CLASSIC HERB AND SPICE COMBINATIONS

Our tastes are expanding and as they do, the flavors of many countries are finding their way into our kitchens. When we use a pinch of Indian curry powder to spike a sauce or a dash of Spanish saffron to spice a soup, we are enriching ourselves with the classics of other cultures.

Bouquets garnis are the little bundles of aromatic herbs and spices used to flavor soups, stews, and sauces. The idea behind a bouquet garni is to keep the herbs contained so that flavor, but not flecks, will permeate the food. The little bundles can be made up of several fresh herb sprigs tied together with string; fresh or dried herbs tied in a cheesecloth bag; fresh or dried herbs placed in a tea ball; or fresh or dried herbs tucked between two pieces of celery and tied with string. When using a bouquet garni that is tied together with string, make the string long enough that you can tie the loose end to the pot handle. Then when you need to remove the bouquet, it will be easy to find.

Classically, bouquets garnis contain parsley, thyme, and bay with occasional additions of whole peppercorns, whole allspice, whole cloves, celery leaf, tarragon, or marjoram. Be encouraged to expand on the bouquet concept by creating your own removable bundles. For instance, combine cinnamon stick, orange peel, lemon peel, and nutmeg to flavor warm apple cider. Or use lemon peel, whole peppercorns, and garlic together to spice up simmering vegetables.

Bouquets garnis can be made ahead in cheesecloth bags and frozen. Add them to simmering food directly from the freezer.

Fines herbes are a combination of chervil, parsley, thyme, and tarragon, freshly minced and added to omelets, sautés, cheese sauces, and other recipes at the very last minute of cooking. The allure of fines herbes is in the freshness of the herbs and the satisfying flavor they create when combined.

Quatre epices simply means "four spices" and is used in French haute cuisine to flavor roast meats, poultry, hardy vegetables, or desserts. The four spices are a ground combination of any of the following: cloves, mace, nutmeg, ginger, cinnamon, black pepper, or white pepper. Without the peppers, quatre epices become good old American pumpkin pie spice.

Curry powder does not grow on trees. Instead, it is an aromatic combination of many ground spices that can include coriander seed,

(continued on page 122)

COMBINATIONS FOR FLAVORED OILS

- oregano, thyme, garlic, and olive oil
- chervil, tarragon, shallots, and peanut oil
- fresh ginger, cardamom seed, coriander leaf, and safflower oil
- saffron, garlic, and olive oil
- dill, garlic, and sunflower oil
- basil, chili, garlic, and olive oil
- lemon verbena, lemon thyme, and walnut oil
- lovage, garlic, celery leaf, and olive oil

COMBINATIONS FOR HERB BUTTERS

For breakfast butters:
- mint and dill
- beebalm and lovage
- lemon verbena and a dash of grated orange peel
- costmary and tansy

For savory butters:
- basil and minced, roasted sweet pepper, oregano, thyme, and pureed shrimp
- marjoram and garlic
- garlic, sesame seeds, and chives

119

WHAT HERBS GO BEST WITH . . .

The question usually comes up just after "What's for dinner?" While it is true that most herbs go with most foods, there are some pairings that are especially successful. Listed below are common foods and some of the herbs that best flatter them. While the table isn't the final word, it can be a starting point for your own culinary experiments.

Asparagus

Chives	Savory
Lemon balm	Tarragon
Sage	Thyme

Beans, dried

Cumin	Parsley
Garlic	Sage
Mint	Savory
Onions	Thyme
Oregano	

Beans, green

Basil	Mint
Caraway	Sage
Clove	Savory
Dill	Thyme
Marjoram	

Beef

Basil	Onion
Bay leaf	Oregano
Caraway	Parsley
Cumin	Rosemary
Fenugreek	Sage
Garlic	Savory
Ginger	Tarragon
Marjoram	Thyme

Broccoli

Basil	Marjoram
Dill	Oregano
Garlic	Tarragon
Lemon balm	Thyme

Cabbage

Basil	Dill
Caraway	Fennel
Cayenne	Marjoram
pepper	Sage
Cumin	Savory

Carrots

Anise	Ginger
Basil	Marjoram
Chervil	Mint
Chives	Parsley
Cinnamon	Sage
Clove	Savory
Cumin	Tarragon
Dill	Thyme

Cauliflower

Basil	Marjoram
Caraway	Parsley
Chives	Rosemary
Cumin	Savory
Dill	Tarragon
Garlic	

Chicken

Anise	Lovage
Basil	Marjoram
Bay leaf	Onion
Borage	Oregano
Chives	Parsley
Cinnamon	Rosemary
Cumin	Saffron
Dill	Sage
Fenugreek	Savory
Garlic	Tarragon
Ginger	Thyme

Corn

Chervil	Saffron
Chives	Sage
Lemon balm	Thyme

Eggplant

Basil	Onion
Cinnamon	Oregano
Dill	Parsley
Garlic	Sage
Marjoram	Savory
Mint	Thyme

Eggs

Anise	Marjoram
Basil	Oregano
Caraway	Parsley
Cayenne pepper	Rosemary
	Saffron
Chervil	Sage
Chives	Savory
Coriander	Tarragon
Dill	Thyme
Fennel	

Fish

Anise	Marjoram
Basil	Oregano
Borage	Parsley
Caraway	Rosemary
Chervil	Saffron
Chives	Sage
Dill	Savory
Fennel	Tarragon
Garlic	Thyme
Ginger	

Fruit

Anise	Lemon balm
Cinnamon	Mint
Clove	Rosemary
Ginger	

Lamb

Basil	Marjoram
Bay leaf	Mint
Cinnamon	Onion
Coriander	Parsley
Cumin	Rosemary
Dill	Saffron
Garlic	Sage
Ginger	Tarragon
Lemon balm	Thyme

Mushrooms

Coriander	Rosemary
Marjoram	Tarragon
Oregano	Thyme

Parsnips

Basil	Parsley
Dill	Savory
Marjoram	Thyme

Peas

Caraway	Savory
Chervil	Tarragon
Chives	Thyme
Rosemary	

Pork

Anise	Oregano
Caraway	Rosemary
Cardamom	Saffron
Dill	Sage
Garlic	Tarragon
Ginger	

Potatoes

Basil	Marjoram
Caraway	Oregano
Chives	Parsley
Coriander	Rosemary
Dill	Sage
Fennel	Tarragon
Lovage	Thyme

Rice

Basil	Saffron
Fennel	Tarragon
Lovage	Thyme

Spinach

Anise	Cinnamon
Basil	Dill
Caraway	Rosemary
Chervil	Thyme
Chives	

Squash

Basil	Marjoram
Caraway	Dill
Cardamom	Oregano
Cinnamon	Rosemary
Clove	Sage
Ginger	Savory

Stuffing

Garlic	Rosemary
Marjoram	Sage
Onion	Thyme
Parsley	

Tomatoes

Basil	Oregano
Bay leaf	Parsley
Chives	Rosemary
Coriander	Sage
Dill	Savory
Garlic	Tarragon
Lovage	Thyme
Marjoram	

Turkey

Basil	Saffron
Garlic	Sage
Marjoram	Savory
Onion	Tarragon
Oregano	Thyme
Rosemary	

Veal

Basil	Onion
Bay leaf	Parsley
Chervil	Rosemary
Chives	Sage
Ginger	Savory
Marjoram	Thyme
Mint	

COOKING WITH HERBS—continued

Because many herbs and spices are quite powerful, it is wise to add them with some restraint. If, however, you do find you have underestimated the power of a seasoning, this may be remedied in a number of ways:

- Strain as much of the herbs and spices as possible out of the dish.

- Add a peeled, whole, raw potato just before serving.

- If possible, add more of the bland ingredients, or make a second, unseasoned batch of the recipe and combine it with the overseasoned one.

- Serve the dish chilled to blunt the taste of the overseasoning.

cumin seed, nutmeg, mace, cardamom seed, turmeric, white mustard seed, black mustard seed, fenugreek seed, chilies, ginger, white peppercorns, black peppercorns, garlic, allspice, cinnamon, cayenne, and fennel seed. Curry powder is famous in East Indian cooking where, depending on the spice combination, it is called *garam masala*. It is also imported to Southeast Asian cuisines, especially Thai. Note that Thai curries (except for Thai Muslim curry) omit the sweeter spices like cinnamon, ginger, nutmeg, and mace and include lots of fresh basil. Thai curry powders are commonly combined with a liquid and used as pastes.

To enliven its exceptional aroma, curry powder should always be heated before eating.

Chili powder is a combination of ground spices and herbs that always contains dried chilies plus a selection of garlic powder, oregano, allspice, cloves, cumin seed, coriander seed, cayenne, black pepper, turmeric, mustard seed, and paprika. As with all dried spice and herb combinations, chili powder is best when ground as needed and heated before eating. If you must make chili powder ahead, store it in a tightly covered glass jar and keep the jar in a cool, dark place.

Chinese five spice powder is a dried, ground combination of Szechuan peppercorns, cinnamon, cloves, fennel, and star anise. It's used as a seasoning for pork and chicken and as a condiment. Five spice powder is most flavorful ground as needed and heated before serving. If you're using five spice powder as a condiment, toast it first in a dry sauté pan. If you must store five spice powder, keep it untoasted in a tightly covered glass jar in a cool, dark place.

Pickling spice often includes dillweed and/or dill seed plus a choice of dried chilies, mustard seed, bay, allspice, white peppercorns, black peppercorns, cinnamon, cloves, coriander seed, turmeric, cardamom, ginger, celery seed, garlic, mace, and nutmeg. Sound confusing? Simply choose your spices according to what you're pickling. For instance, for cucumber pickles, use dillweed, dill seed, mustard seed, celery seed, garlic, and black peppercorns. Now imagine that you're pickling carrots. Think about what flavors enhance them. You could choose cinnamon, nutmeg, bay, and peppercorns.

SALT-FREE BLENDS

Are you one of the millions who monitor salt intake for health reasons? Don't despair! You aren't doomed to a tasteless diet.

The four basic tastes we perceive are sweet, salty, sour, and bitter. Imagine what can happen if one of those tastes, in this case salt, is removed. If you're thinking "bland," you're right. But you can achieve high flavor levels without salt. By raising the flavor levels of sweet, sour, and bitter, you can create wonderful blooms of flavor that will stimulate your taste buds. Here are some salt-free flavor combinations for marinades, sauces, and for sprinkling.

For beef:
- lemon juice, minced fresh rosemary, and freshly ground black pepper
- minced fresh thyme, ground cloves, grated orange peel, and freshly ground black pepper
- garlic, herbed vinegar, and freshly ground black pepper
- mashed green peppercorns, minced onions, and minced fresh marjoram

For poultry:
- minced fresh ginger, freshly grated orange peel, and minced fresh sage
- minced fresh marjoram, minced fresh thyme, and apple cider vinegar
- minced fresh tarragon, minced shallots, and lemon juice
- minced fresh basil, white wine vinegar, and garlic

For fish:
- minced fresh dill, lemon juice, and mustard seed
- minced fresh lovage, celery seed, lemon juice, and freshly ground black pepper
- fennel seed, mustard seed, bay, and grated lemon peel

For green vegetables:
- minced fresh savory, minced fresh chives, and minced onions
- minced fresh dill, bay, and rice vinegar
- minced fresh basil, freshly grated nutmeg, and minced fresh marjoram

For yellow and orange vegetables:
- cinnamon, nutmeg, orange juice, and minced fresh thyme
- minced fresh ginger, cinnamon, apple cider vinegar, and minced fresh lovage or celery leaf
- minced fresh beebalm and minced fresh thyme

PEPPER PARTICULARS

- World pepper consumption is about 124,000 tons a year, according to the American Spice Trade Association.

- Twenty percent of that pepper comes from India; 60 percent from Indonesia; 17 percent from Brazil; and 3 percent comes from Malaysia.

- India and the Soviet Union have a trade agreement in which they swap Indian pepper for Soviet construction equipment.

- In 1984, the consumption of pepper (red, white, and black) in the United States was 155,300,000 pounds.

HERB AND SPICE SALES UP

Herb and spice sales have increased 33 percent since 1976. The sale of basil alone has increased by 407 percent; fennel by 159 percent; and cinnamon by 124 percent.

These increases may be connected to reduced salt intake by health-conscious consumers, reports Frost and Sullivan, a New York business research company. Frost and Sullivan adds that heavy users of herbs and spices tend to have more education and higher incomes than the average person.

COOKING WITH HERBS—continued

EDIBLE FLOWERS

The following list of beautiful and edible flowers is from *Rodale's Organic Gardening* magazine:

beebalm
borage
calendula
chive blossoms
daylily
English daisy
forget-me-not, *Myosotis
    scorpioides* or *M. sylvatica*
fuchsia
geranium
hollyhock
impatiens
lavender
lilac
mint flower
nasturtium
pansy
portulaca
redbud
rose
snapdragon
squash blossoms (especially
    nice for stuffing or frying)
violet
zucchini blossoms (especially
    nice for stuffing or frying)

For cheese and eggs:
- minced fresh dill, minced fresh chives, minced fresh parsley, and paprika
- freshly grated nutmeg, dry mustard, and freshly ground black pepper
- minced fresh oregano, garlic, and minced fresh thyme

For beans, rice, and other grains:
- chilies, cumin seed, minced fresh oregano, and garlic
- saffron, garlic, and minced fresh parsley
- minced fresh mint, minced fresh parsley, grated lemon peel, and caraway seed

SWEETNESS ENHANCERS

Many herbs and spices sweeten the foods around them without adding calories. Use them alone—a pinch of cinnamon to sweeten tomato sauce—or in combination with traditional sweeteners—cardamom adds extra sweetness to cakes and cookies, for example. Experiment with these natural sweeteners:

- angelica stem in salads
- beebalm in beverages
- costmary and mint in sparkling waters
- lemon balm and lemon verbena in frozen desserts
- violet and rose in condiments
- vanilla (just a drop) in savory sauces
- rosemary in fruit salads, fruit compotes, and fruit tarts

EDIBLE FLOWERS

Many flowers can add color and an outdoorsy, perfumelike flavor to your cooking. They are frequently used as floating garnishes for beverages and soups and to add color to trays and individual plates. But their flair reaches far beyond. For example, edible flowers can be minced and added to cheese spreads, herb butters, or to pancake, crepe, or waffle batter. Use them whole in salads, stuffed, or fried in a light cornmeal or flour batter.

The key word here is edible, which is a nice way of saying nontoxic.

CORIANDER

Coriandrum sativum   **Umbelliferae**

To find out that coriander was named after the bedbug because it emits the same unpleasant odor that bedbugs produce is enough to make one lose his appetite when considering a Moroccan dish flavored with coriander seed. Coriander is supposed to *increase* the appetite. Also ironic is the fact that coriander is a fragrant ingredient in various perfumes and cosmetics. This herb offers more than a few surprises.

HISTORY

The history of this herb contains many more interesting facts, and they have accumulated over a great period of time, for coriander has been cultivated for more than 3,000 years. Seeds of coriander have been found among the funeral offerings in ancient Egyptian tombs. From Egypt, in all probability, the herb came into use by the ancient Hebrews, who made it one of the bitter herbs involved in the ritual of Passover.

Greek and Roman physicians, including Hippocrates, made medicines from it, but it was also prized as a spice and as an ingredient in a Roman vinegar used to preserve meat. The Chinese used coriander as far back as the Han dynasty 207 B.C.–A.D. 220. At that time, it was thought that coriander had the power to make a person immortal. The Chinese developed several compounds from coriander with this in mind.

Others developed coriander concoctions with lust in their mind, for they believed that it aroused passion. This rumor may have begun in an Arabian fantasy, *The Thousand and One Nights,* in which coriander was referred to as an aphrodisiac.

USES

This herb has had some potent properties assigned to it over the years. It does have a bold flavor and fragrance, but as a medicine it's pretty slight stuff.

Medicinal: People drink infusions of coriander seeds or chew on the seeds themselves to soothe upset stomachs or aid digestion. Poultices made from crushed seeds are recommended for relieving the pain of rheumatism. The fruits contain a volatile oil responsible for the actions coriander produces, but unfortunately those actions aren't very effective. The *U.S. Dispensatory* describes coriander as "a rather feeble aromatic and carminative."

DESCRIPTION

The coriander plant is a bright green annual with slender, erect, finely grooved stems. It has a hairless, shiny appearance.

Flowers: Tiny, white to pinkish, mauve, or reddish, 5–10 rays, in flat, short-stalked umbels; outer flowers larger than the inner ones.

Leaves: Compound, pinnate, lower leaves roundish and lobed, upper ones finely divided into very narrow segments.

Fruit: Seeds, brownish yellow, spherical, ribbed, less than ¼ in. long, musty odor, in symmetrical clusters.

Height: 2–3 ft.

FLOWERING

Spring or mid- to late summer, depending on sowing time.

RANGE

Native to eastern Mediterranean region and southern Europe; cultivated in Morocco, Mexico, Argentina, Canada, India, and the United States. In the United States, it is found mostly in South Carolina.

CORIANDER—continued

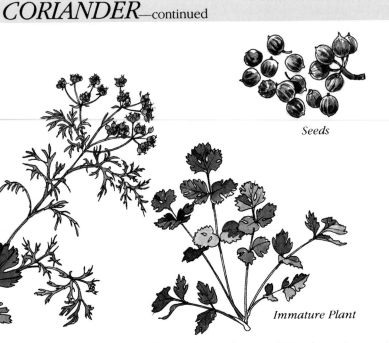

Seeds

Immature Plant

Coriander does have valid use in modern medicine but primarily as a flavoring agent to mask the taste of other compounds in medicines and to calm the irritating effects on the stomach that certain medicines produce.

Culinary: As a flavoring, coriander is more often appreciated in foods than in medicines. You can use the leaves, fruits, or roots.

Coriander leaves have a bold taste that combines a strong sage flavor with sharp citrus notes. Mince the fresh leaves and add them to foods or use them whole as a lacy garnish. The roots taste like the leaves but with an added nutty flavor. They are also used fresh and are minced before using. Coriander seeds diverge a bit. They have no sagelike flavor at all, just the simple taste of citrus. Add them whole or ground to foods.

Given coriander's bold sage flavor and tangy citrus taste, it is not surprising that this spice sets a spark in the cuisines of Southeast Asia, China, Mexico, East India, South America, Spain, Central Africa, and Central America. The root is popular in Thai cooking, where it is minced and added to salads and relishes.

The flavor of coriander combines nicely with those of beets, onions, sausage, clams, oysters, and potatoes. Whole or ground seeds add character to marinades, salad dressings, cheese, eggs, chili sauce, guacamole, and pickling brines. Try the leaf, root, seed, or all three with marinated mushrooms, tomato salads, stews, pilafs, lentil stew, pasta salads, and curries.

Available commercially: Whole or ground seed, but whole is preferable. Leaves and roots are occasionally available in specialty stores and some supermarkets.

Storage note: Store dried leaves and seeds separately.

Commercial use: Coriander is used by the food and beverage industries as a flavoring for foods, sugared confections called comfits, liqueurs, and gin.

Aromatic: Yes, a mature coriander plant does reek of bedbugs, but this passes. Once the fruits fully ripen, their fragrance changes to one that is pleasantly like citrus, *and* they become *more* fragrant with age. Mix them in potpourris to give them a lemony scent.

Commercially, the essential oil is extracted and used to scent perfumes and cosmetics.

Companion planting: Coriander reportedly enhances the growth of anise.

Other: Coriander could be justified as a garden plant if only for the job it does in attracting useful insects like the bees and other pollinators. Coriander honey is justly famous for its flavor. Some people make an ersatz coriander honey by mixing a small quantity of oil of coriander into clover honey.

CULTIVATION

Since coriander roots are long and difficult to transplant, you will do best to sow the seeds directly into beds as soon as the danger of frost has passed (April or May in most parts of the United States). In very mild climates, seed, which is slow to germinate, may be sown in the fall. Put seed in drills ½ inch deep and 5 to 9 inches apart. When seedlings appear, thin, if necessary, to allow at least 4 inches between plants. Caraway, a biennial, is often interplanted with coriander because of its complementary habit of growth.

Weeding or mulching of coriander is important early in the season. Don't overfertilize coriander. Too much nitrogen in the soil produces a less flavorful plant.

Harvesting and storage: Harvest your coriander promptly when the leaves and flowers have become brown, but before the seed has had a chance to scatter. The odor of the seed will be changing at that time, so this task should not be unpleasant. Cut the whole plant and hang it to dry, gathering the seed as it falls or threshing it out for further drying. Seed that has not been dried has a bitter taste.

When harvesting fresh leaves, cut only the small, immature leaves for the best flavor. Dried leaves store poorly, but the seeds will store well if kept in stoppered jars.

CHEF TIPS

- Create a marinade for 1 pound of fish or shellfish by combining ½ teaspoon of ground coriander seed, 2 ground allspice berries, the juice of 1 lemon, and a splash of fruity olive oil. Marinate for 30 minutes, then broil or grill.

- To make a relish for spicy poultry or lamb, combine 1 cup of coriander leaves, ½ cup of mint leaves, 2 cloves of garlic, the juice of 1 lemon, a minced hot chili, and a handful of blanched peanuts in a food processor. Add a bit of olive oil during processing until smooth.

- Add ½ teaspoon of ground coriander seed to the batter (for one loaf) of gingerbread or banana or carrot bread.

GROWING CONDITIONS

- Soil pH 6.6.
- Moderately rich, light, well-drained soil.
- Full sun to partial shade.

COSTMARY

Chrysanthemum Balsamita   Compositae

DESCRIPTION

Costmary is a leafy perennial with a balsamlike fragrance. (See photo on page 513.)

Flowers: Minute disk and rays, ½ in. across; heads gathered in loose clusters at top of stem; yellow.

Leaves: Gray-green, silvery, hairy, oblong, serrated margins, two small lobes at base of some leaves; upper leaves 1½–5 in. long, lower leaves to 12 in.

Fruit: Tiny seeds.

Height: To 3 ft.

FLOWERING

Late summer.

RANGE

Native to southern Europe and western Asia; now rarely found wild, but cultivated in Europe and North America.

CHEF TIPS

- Mince and add to tuna, egg, or shrimp salads.
- Add young leaves to a glass of lemonade.
- Make tea from dried leaves.

GROWING CONDITIONS

- Plant hardiness zone 4.
- Soil pH 6.2.
- Fertile loam.
- Full sun to partial shade.

Costmary seems to be nearly a forgotten herb, so rarely grown now when compared to its flourish in English gardens in the sixteenth century. Yes, nearly forgotten, until you pull down grandmother's Bible and find a brittle leaf pressed between the pages. The edges look like they've been nibbled. The leaf still releases a faint scent of balsam. Then you remember. You remember grandmother's stories about the history of this herb, and you remember how she used the plant herself in cooking and in sachets.

HISTORY

Its name comes from the Latin *costum,* meaning oriental plant. Costmary was originally found growing in the Orient. It was introduced into England in the sixteenth century, where it became popular and could be seen growing in gardens everywhere.

Like clary, costmary was a beer drinker's herb. Its leaves spiced their pints of ale. Fresh leaves were also added to salads and to hearty soups and stews.

The seventeenth-century British herbalist Culpeper reported that costmary "maketh an excellent salve to cleanse and heal old ulcers, being boiled with olive oil, and Adder's Tongue with it. After straining, a little wax is added to thicken it." Herbalists recommended costmary to treat ague, to strengthen the liver, for disorders of the stomach, and as a diuretic. It was officially listed in the *British Pharmacopoeia* until 1788 as a gentle laxative, and it was used often in the treatment of dysentery, two seemingly contrary uses.

The one custom that most endears a person to costmary is its use as a bookmark. Since colonial days, costmary leaves have marked the pages of Bibles and prayer books, hence its nickname, Bible leaf. It did not serve as just an innocent bookmark, however. Sleepy churchgoers benefited from the scent and flavor. When the sermon became long and boring and their eyelids drooped and heads began to nod, they would pull the leaves from their prayer books and sniff them or nibble on the edges, and they would be revived—at least for a little while. You could probably determine which parish had the most boring clergy by the amount of costmary grown in the area's gardens.

USES

You could still use costmary as a bookmark. Perhaps students who slumber over their texts would benefit by this leafy marker. A couple of whiffs every now and then might perk their spirits, and with sprigs of rosemary around their heads to help their memory, they'd surely do well in their studies.

Medicinal: Costmary's properties are very much like those of tansy, and it is tansy that is used medicinally more often. However, should you want to try costmary for any of its historic recommendations or in place of tansy, make an infusion from the leaves.

Culinary: Costmary's tender leaves have a mintlike flavor. Use them to flavor refreshing beverages, iced soups, and fruit salads. The young leaves are tasty in green salads and make pretty garnishes.

Substitute: Tansy or mint.

Aromatic: The pleasant balsamlike fragrance of costmary is perhaps currently its greatest virtue. The dried leaves make a good addition to potpourris and sachets. Use it to create a fragrant bath, either alone or mixed with other herbs.

Ornamental: You don't find costmary in too many gardens these days—at least not in formal ones—but it is still cultivated in herb gardens here and there in Europe and North America. Lovely button-like flowers bloom in the spring if costmary is grown in a sunny spot. It does well in the shade also but will not produce flowers. A tall plant, you can use it most effectively in the back of the garden. It serves as a nice green background for shorter flowering plants.

Cosmetic: Its astringent and antiseptic qualities recommend costmary as a cosmetic herb. Try an infusion of costmary leaves as a skin lotion after cleansing with soap and water.

Craft: Costmary can be used to make herb baskets (see the entry Crafts from Herbs).

CULTIVATION

Propagation by division is really the only option, since costmary produces little or no seed. Divide plants in the spring and space them 2 feet apart. Costmary spreads rather easily once you've started them and will probably require dividing and transplanting every few years.

Costmary grows easily in most soils from sandy to clayey, but prefers a fertile loam. It does not require a lot of fertilization. It will do best in a dry area in the sun.

Do not bother to mulch costmary, as it spreads above the ground.

Harvesting and storage: Harvest small quantities of leaves at a time from one plant, as few leaves are produced up the stem—most grow from the base of the plant. Collect them before they yellow. The leaves take only a short time to dry at a temperature of about 100°F. Once dried, they will store for a long time without problem.

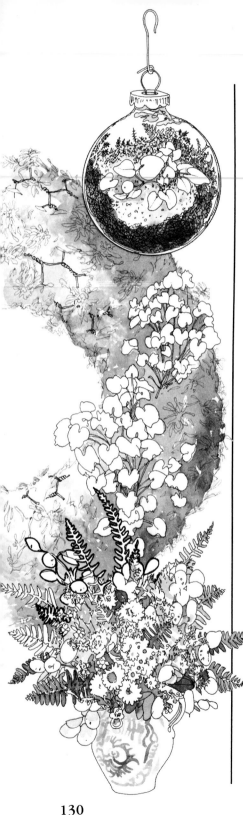

CRAFTS FROM HERBS

Herbs invite but don't intimidate. Nearby, inexpensive, abundant. Rich in textures, colors, and fragrances. There's a special satisfaction from turning such homey materials into an elegant piece of craftwork.

The pleasure is not all in the result; the process itself soothes and refreshes. There are no acid baths, no deafening machinery with finger-eating blades. Herbs are quiet and fragrant, and the herb crafter's hands smell of rosemary and thyme.

But the greatest charm of herb crafts may perhaps be described as their quirkiness. A finished project shows immediately what's growing by your garage or roadside or what a neighbor happened to plant too much of. Each piece becomes absolutely personal, local, and distinctive, a refuge of the individual spirit in a formularized, mass-produced world.

LIVING HERB WREATHS

Wreaths make year-round pleasure for Peggy Armstrong, an herb crafter from Ohio. Peggy starts her living wreaths in the spring when she has lots of young plants and is ready to start her other herb plantings; the wreaths become circular herb gardens she happens to hang on the wall. During the summer they thrive hanging against the cedar boards on the outside of her house. When they come inside for a visit, lying on a tray of stones, a hurricane lamp in the center, they make a fragrant centerpiece for a table. One of her favorite wreaths is a treat for the palate as well as the eye, a perfect gift for a good cook:

1. Soak several handfuls of sphagnum (not milled) in water until wet throughout, about 15 minutes. Cut a strip of ½-inch-mesh chicken wire 12 inches wide and 30 inches long. Bend the long sides of the wire, so they curl up to form a trough. Squeeze enough water out of the sphagnum, so it won't drench the table while you work; then pack it tightly into the trough. (A good dense mass of sphagnum will give the plants a firm base and will hold water well.)

2. Bend the trough sides together until they overlap slightly to form a sausage. Fasten the sides together by bending the loose prongs (sticking out where the mesh was cut) to form little hooks that can catch in the mesh hole on the opposite side of the seam. Do the same with the ends of the sausage to form a wreath.

3. Make seven little wells in the sphagnum, evenly spaced about the wreath, by poking through the wire. Plant a young herb in each, anchoring wayward runners with hairpins, if necessary. Peggy uses plants from 3-inch pots whose creeping stems are about 6 inches long. She encourages wreath makers to choose plants boldly

in hopes of discovering striking effects. She has certainly not been timid or tradition bound; some of her wreaths include a bright cascade of petunias.

4. Hang the wreath in strong but indirect sunlight. Peggy puts hers on the west side of her house. When the moss starts to dry out, she soaks the whole wreath for 15 minutes in a tub of water with a dash of plant fertilizer. If herb tendrils start growing in odd directions, prune them back or wire them into shape. In about six weeks, you should have a fully covered wreath.

LIVING CHRISTMAS BALLS

These little globes have some of the same magic as ships in a bottle. Fortunately they're easier to make. They can hang near windows (but out of direct sun) or on Christmas trees, and they make unusual holiday gifts.

1. Find glass Christmas balls 2½ inches in diameter with chimneys at least ½ inch in diameter. Pull off the metal tops and save them. Soak the balls overnight in a half-and-half solution of bleach and water. Then, wearing rubber gloves, swirl each ball in the solution, letting the bleach slosh around inside. Rinse them with plain

PLANTS FOR LIVING WREATHS

For culinary wreaths:
chives (plant at the bottom center if the wreath is to be hung)
creeping sage
marjoram
oregano
thymes, especially creeping wooly thyme

For fragrant wreaths:
lavender
prostrate rosemary
santolina
scented geranium

To add color:
marigold
petunia

Hook sides of trough together.

Plant seedlings into wreath.

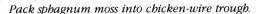

Pack sphagnum moss into chicken-wire trough.

CRAFTS FROM HERBS—continued

THE LANGUAGE OF HERBS AND FLOWERS

To help you create tussie-mussies with meaning, here is a list of suitable plants and the meanings traditionally ascribed to them:

aloe—healing, shelter from harm
angelica—inspiration
basil—love, good wishes, hate
bay—achievement and fame
beebalm—virtue
borage—bravery
calendula—sadness, hopelessness
chamomile—wisdom, fortitude
chervil—sincerity
chives—usefulness
costmary—sweetness
dill—good cheer, survival in the face of odds
elder—misfortune, zealousness, sympathy
fennel—grief, power, and endurance
geranium, scented—happiness

(continued)

water. The color should wash off easily. If any trace remains of the color or the cloudy inside coating, rub it off with a paper towel. To reach the inside, use a long-handled cotton swab or a bit of paper towel stuck on the end of a pencil.

2. Mix crumbled charcoal (available wherever aquarium supplies are sold) into a soilless potting mixture (half sphagnum and half perlite, for example). You'll need about 1 teaspoon of charcoal and ¼ cup of potting mixture per ball. Rest the ball in a cup to keep it from rolling around while you work on it. Form paper into a funnel, insert it into the ball's chimney, and pour in the charcoal-soil mix. It should fill a quarter to a third of the ball.

3. Push bits of trailing moss through the opening, and position them with a pencil or needle-nosed tweezers to form a loose carpet over the soil.

4. Take a 1¾-inch-long cutting of partridgeberry, preferably including some berries (the red will make the final ball more festive), and remove the bottom pair of leaves. Using tweezers, poke the cutting through the chimney and into the soil. Make sure at least one node is below ground. Put the point of a long-necked squeeze bottle into the ball and mist the soil.

5. Put the cap and hook back on the ball and if the mood strikes, tie a ribbon around the ball's chimney. Hang it in indirect light and mist the soil when the moss begins to look faded. The ball will make a perfect rooting chamber for the partidgeberry and the moss.

TUSSIE-MUSSIES: BOUQUETS WITH MEANING

"Making things that are pretty is one thing, but making them meaningful is another," says Lane Furneaux, a master of both arts. From her herb garden in Dallas, she's reviving enthusiasm for tussie-mussies, pretty bouquets of herbs and flowers. What is special about a tussie-mussie is that each plant in it has a meaning.

These little nosegays have been familiar British accessories for centuries, but the Victorians raised them to the level of language, particularly the coy exchanges of flirtation. A young dandy might reassure a distant lady with a tussie-mussie of forget-me-nots (for true love) and rosemary (for remembrance) and perhaps southernwood (for constancy). If she didn't find the bouquet convincing, she might send back yellow roses (for infidelity) and larkspur (for fickleness). He'd best rush for the white violets (innocence) or a lot of rue (repentance). After laying waste to several flower borders, they might get the matter sorted out, or perhaps she would finish the liaison with one scorching handful of fumitory (for hatred).

geranium, unscented—folly
goldenrod—encouragement
iris—pure heart, courage,
    faith
lady's mantle—protection
lavender—devotion
lemon balm—sympathy,
    regeneration
marjoram—joy
mint—refreshment
mugwort—pleasant journeys
parsley—merriment
rose—love, success
rue—grief
sage—long life, wisdom
salad burnet—cheerful
    disposition
santolina—full of virtue
savory—interest
southernwood—constancy
sweet woodruff—humble
    spirit
tansy—hostility
tarragon—lasting involvement
thyme—daring
violet—modesty, devotion
yarrow—health

Today's revival of tussie-mussies seems to have sidestepped the lovers' quarrel (an herb patch is unlikely to replace the telephone) and concentrated on creating pretty and meaningful—and fragrant—bouquets for brides, new mothers, departing friends, new neighbors, or anyone in need of a kind word. The little bouquets have even entered politics. As legislation to form the National Herb Garden wobbled through Congress, various legislators received pleas for support in the form of tussie-mussies. The legislation did pass, which might give pause to anyone inclined to dismiss the power of a handful of flowers. To create your own flower power, here is Lane Furneaux's advice.

Selecting the plants: "Tussie-mussies are something you make with what you have," Lane emphasizes. Using only the plants from the backyard or a nearby field makes the bouquets absolutely distinctive and expressive of the maker. She describes seeing a tussie-mussie in *National Geographic* whose maker was not identified. She wrote to ask about the maker, commenting that the style didn't look American to her, and if she had to guess, she would say that it had been made in England, at Claverton in Bath. Several weeks later, she received an astonished phone call from the staff; she had guessed exactly right. She urges newcomers to relax: "Every garden has what it needs for a tussie-mussie."

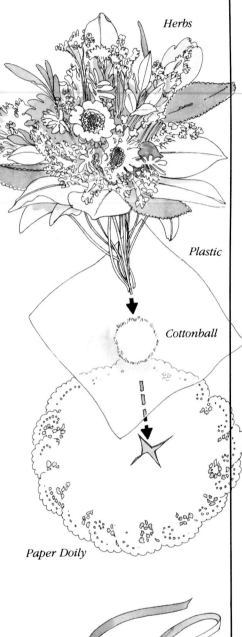

Herbs

Plastic

Cottonball

Paper Doily

Ribbon

CRAFTS FROM HERBS—continued

The plant that represents the main message is Lane's starting point. This is the flower that will go into the center. She strolls through her garden searching for plants that express her theme, preferably something colorful. Perhaps opal basil flowers for good wishes, a rose for love, or a pair of roses for an anniversary bouquet. She selects other plants with complementary meanings, and finally she just picks anything that is in particularly good condition or would make a good combination for the flowers. These last plants she looks up on returning indoors, and often she discovers that their sentiments would be perfect for the occasion. She has made tussie-mussies with as few as 2 kinds of plants and as many as 36. (The 36 went into a tussie-mussie for Nancy Reagan to whom Lane had a lot to say.)

Arranging the plants: According to Lane arranging the plants is like writing a letter. It's an activity so intuitive and personal that rules become irrelevant. Here is her approach:

Starting with the plant symbol for the main sentiment, the one that will go at the center, she surrounds it with a little frame of foliage, perhaps some kind of mint for fragrance. Next a ring of something wispy is added for contrast. With a strongly symmetrical center, Lane arranges little bunches of the remaining plants asymmetrically around the outer part. (Some tussie-mussie makers use only one sprig for each sentiment, but bunching the sprigs makes a more dramatic display.) In this outer section, Lane looks for ways to accent the center color. The bouquet is finished with an outer rim of leaves, perhaps from different kinds of scented geraniums. Lane will alternate a triangular leaf with a round one, for example. Or perhaps make two rings of contrasting leaf shapes.

Assembling the bouquet: Put the sprigs in water, and then wash them, in Lane's words, "just as if they were something to eat." Groom them, cutting off spent blossoms or chewed leaves, until each sprig is perfect. Lane strips the lower leaves, although this is a matter of personal style. At Claverton, for example, tussie-mussie makers retain the leaves, crushing them together when the stems are wrapped. It makes for a bulkier base but more fragrance.

For a bouquet that will be carried, spread out a square of plastic wrap and put a little puff of moist cotton in the center. Then fold up the square so that it engulfs the stems of the bouquet, twisting it around the stems like the flaps of a folded umbrella. Cover it with a spiral of florist's tape.

Tussie-mussies are often set in a paper doily. Cut an X in the middle of the doily, fold down the points, and put the stems through the hole in the doily. Lane secures them with a ¼-inch florist's pin through each point of the X-cut. If the bouquet is eventually going into water, the doily can get pretty soggy. Lane creates a little wax protector for the doily by dipping the points of the X-cut in paraffin before inserting the bouquet stems.

Decorate the assembly with ribbon. Lane uses three colors to spiral up the stem and tie over the pins. She lets long ends trail down.

A tussie-mussie should stay fresh for several hours when wrapped this way. To keep it longer, snip off the base of the plastic container, or better yet, unwrap the stems. Set them in a glass of water. If you have included a large number of plants that dry well, set the tussie-mussie in a glass *without* water and wait. When the bouquet dries, remove any sprigs that didn't dry gracefully and rewrap the stems.

A final note. Include a message with the tussie-mussie explaining what you intend the plants to symbolize. Even a fellow speaker of the floral language might appreciate clarification on plants that have several meanings. And never give anyone unlabeled basil, which can mean either love or hate.

WOVEN HERB BASKETS

The easiest way to make these unusual craft baskets is to start with plenty of fresh herbs, weave them while they're at their most pliable, and then let them dry. These highly textured baskets with a heathery blending of colors make a dramatic container for any number of displays—pinecones, glass balls, rag dolls, or dried flowers.

The following design comes from the irrepressibly creative herb crafter Peggy Armstrong:

1. Start with a moss basket (the wire frame baskets that florists stuff with sphagnum moss and plant with hanging plants). Garden centers carry several sizes, particularly in the spring. Collect herbs with long stems and, ideally, feathery foliage but with few pronounced branches. Leave flowering stalks on, but break off any part of the stem that's too woody to bend.

2. To weave the first row, select one or two leafy stems. Anchor one end of the bunch by poking it very far down into a crack between two ribs at the base of the basket frame. Weave the herb stem(s) over and under the wire ribs. Press the stem(s) down against the base as firmly as possible. The stem(s) will probably go all the way around the base with a bit left over. Then just use the same stem(s) to start the next row. Weave under the ribs you went over the first time and vice versa.

3. When the first stem(s) have been completely woven in, select

GOOD HERBS FOR BASKETS

costmary
flax
goldenrod
mints (for fragrance)
mugwort
Queen Anne's lace
salvia (for color)
Silver King artemisia
southernwood
sweet Annie
tansy

135

CRAFTS FROM HERBS—continued

another one or two stems. To anchor, lay the stem(s) over the previous row so they overlap about an inch, going under and/or over the same ribs as the previous row. Then continue weaving around the basket. When you reach the beginning again, start the third row, passing the herbs under the ribs you have just gone over and vice versa. That's the basic pattern; you'll just keep repeating it until you reach the top. *The most important part of the process is packing down the layers firmly.* Otherwise large holes will appear in the basket as the stems dry and shrink. As you weave higher on the frame, one bunch of stems will not reach all the way around. Don't worry. Just select another bunch, let it overlap, and go on weaving.

4. After you have woven about an inch of the basket, increase the size of the herb bundle by one stem. Thus you might be weaving with three stems instead of two. About every inch up, increase the size by another stem. (The thicker bunches will give a sturdier, more dramatic basket, but it's impossible to use them near the base. There the ribs are so close together that thick bunches can't bend sharply enough to get around them.) In selecting these thick bunches, don't waste the prettiest stems by burying them in the middle. Put them where they will show on the basket's outside or inside. By composing the stem bunches carefully, you can streak colors from the top to the bottom of the basket, or give the basket's inside a different character from the outside.

5. When you've woven three-quarters of the way up the frame, add a handle. Peggy makes a semicircle of grape vines or plaited herb stems and wires each end against a rib with florist's wire. Continue weaving herb bunches through the ribs, going over or under the handle-and-rib as if it were just another rib.

Weave herbs into a wire-frame basket.

Add a handle by wiring each end to a rib of the basket.

Finished Basket

6. When you come to the top, fasten southernwood around the top edge with florist's wire to hide the metal rim.

7. Prop the basket upside down, perhaps on jars so it can dry.

DRYING HERBS AND FLOWERS FOR DECORATION

In drying flowers we play a trick on Mother Nature—and discover the laugh is on us. At first a dried arrangement seems like such a magnificent way to break the rules: When everything turns dry and brown for the winter, we can have tufts of silvery, fuzzy leaves, tiny blue petals, clumps of tawny flowers, hundreds of echoes of summer. But consider the "unnatural" trick: The principal way of drying herbs and flowers is just a matter of warm air, a light breeze, and a couple of days. It's Mother Nature's trick after all.

Air-drying—for the right flowers: Colonial Williamsburg, a sort of carnival of preservation technology, preserves its herbs and flowers in the simplest way possible. Staff members tie them in bunches, hang them in a dark attic with a dehumidifier, and wait. There are other ways to dry plants, says Libbey Oliver, who supervises Williamsburg's flower arranging, but air-drying produces a look appropriate to the colonial atmosphere. (Silica drying—described later—she considers more Victorian.) Air-drying is certainly the simplest drying technique, but like any other simple task, it can be refined into an art.

Here, step-by-step, is how to do it:

1. Choose plants that work. The most common mistake that beginners make, says Libbey, is to try to air-dry the wrong things. The technique just doesn't work on some plants, particularly those with large petals that shed (like tulips or full-blown roses) or those with delicate structures that shrivel (like Queen Anne's lace).

2. Pick flowers at the right stage. Some do best when picked half open; they open more as they dry. Others do best when left to dry as much as possible on the vine (see the accompanying list, Flowers for Air-drying).

3. For flowers, strip the leaves: the less plant material on each stem, the faster the piece will dry. Of course, no stripping is necessary in drying foliage.

4. Tie 8 or 10 stems in a bundle and hang them upside down. Libbey uses a rubber band to make a slipknot around the bundle and then hooks the open loop around a clothespin on a clothesline in her drying attic.

The drying area should be dark and well-ventilated. Air movement is the key. Heat won't be much help if the moisture has no place to go. Williamsburg's drying attic has dark paper over the

FLOWERS FOR AIR-DRYING

Flowers to pick before fully open:
delphinium (spike should be half open, half in bud)
goldenrod
peony (dry the buds)
pokeberry
safflower (pick when some flowers are still in bud; let top leaves remain)
strawflower

Flowers to pick when fairly open:
celosia (before seeds appear)
chive flowers
marigold (will dry into dark gold pompoms)
salvia

Flowers to leave on stalk until very dry:
globe amaranth
pearly everlasting
tansy
yarrow (yellow is best)

Foliage to pick in prime condition:
artemisia

Pods to let dry on plant:
love-in-a-mist
rue seed heads (pick either green or dried)

Cut

Wire

CRAFTS FROM HERBS—continued

windows and vents at each end. During the summer flowers dry in an average of 10 days.

5. As soon as the flowers are dry, pack them in boxes. Libbey adds a few mothballs. The important rule here is to arrange the flowers so you'll never have to dig through a heap to find the ones you want. Therefore, put only one kind in a box and label each box clearly.

Drying powders—for finicky flowers: If hanging flowers in the attic just produces a drift of petals on the floor, try one of the powder methods. The slowest method is to bury the flower in fine sand in an open box. The sand holds the bloom open and the petals in shape while the air dries the flower. Borax, clean sand mixed with borax, plain Kitty Litter, and numerous other powders will do this. Flowers dry in this mixture in two to five weeks.

One powder—silica gel—actually draws water out of the plant. Finding it may be a challenge. Try drugstores, hobby shops, and florists. Silica gel costs perhaps $6 per pound, but after each batch of flowers, the powder, which looks like a laundry detergent, can be dehydrated in a warm oven and then reused. Flowers dry in this mixture in two to seven days. Afterward they may be particularly sensitive to humidity and may reabsorb moisture and droop if placed in a humid part of the house. The ideal way to display them in such a case is under a Victorian bell jar.

Whatever the drying powder, the method of packing is the same:

1. Pick flowers for powder drying when they're not quite fully open. Cut off the stem right under the blossom. Poke a piece of florist's wire into the center of the flower, and pull it through until it forms a wire "stem." Bend one end of the wire into a little nubbin so it won't pull through the stem and out the bottom. (The flowers will be too fragile to wire once they're dried, but the wire is essential if you want to stand the flowers in a vase.)

2. Cover the bottom of a wide, low container with a thin layer of drying powder, and nestle the flowers into the powder, with the wires curling around them. Don't let the blossoms touch. Gently pour in the remaining powder, completely burying the flowers. If the powder is silica gel, seal the container tightly. For other powders, leave the container open.

3. Try to catch the flowers when they're dry enough to hold their color, but not so dry that they fall apart. Flowers with thin petals may dry in two days, while fleshier flowers like snapdragons may take a week. Don't leave flowers in silica gel "an extra day," because they can overdry. Excavate them from the powder very gently because they'll be extremely brittle. If a petal breaks off, reattach it with a spot of white glue.

**PLANTS FOR DRYING
WITH DRYING POWDERS**

carnation
dahlia
delphinium
forget-me-not
hollyhock
larkspur
marigold
rose
zinnia

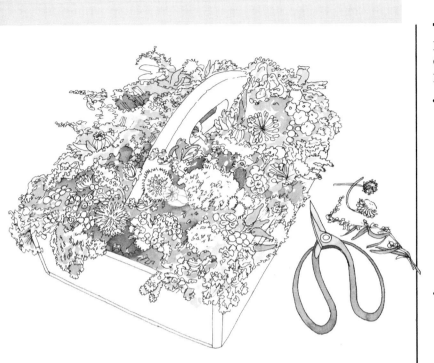

DRIED HERB WREATHS

Pastels. Little pinpricks of color. Airiness, softness.

Dried herbs have opened up thousands of possibilities for wreaths. The herbs may not be evergreen, but they're practically ever ready. Instead of discarding the wreath in January, add a Valentine's Day bow and use it as a centerpiece. Hang a hatchet in it for George's birthday . . . . We are just beginning to glimpse the decorative possibilities of wreaths.

We are also just beginning to glimpse the range of techniques. Here are two approaches from skilled herb workers; you can invent at least a dozen more.

Eileen Weinsteiger's dried herb wreaths: Eileen Weinsteiger takes care of the display herb and vegetable gardens at the Rodale Research Center. Create your own wreath following Eileen's instructions:

1. Select a wreath base of straw or Spanish moss. These are available at garden centers or can be made by bending heavy-gauge wire into a circle and lashing a filling material to it with florist's wire.

2. Pick a "background" plant—something that you have tons of and that will go well with all the flowers you intend to use in the wreath. The pale fluff of Silver King artemisia, for example, makes an excellent background. Insert it in the straw, stem by stem, until the whole wreath is covered.

HINTS ON COLONIAL-STYLE DRIED ARRANGEMENTS

- Pick a dry day to work with dried flowers: They may absorb moisture on rainy days and become a little too flabby to handle. Even on a good day, you will find the arrangement "wilting" as you put it together. Don't panic; just turn up the heat in the workroom, or set the herbs in silica gel for several hours or overnight until they recover.

- To achieve arrangements of rich texture, use some dried flowers that are spiked in shape (like celosias); some that are round and fairly big (like marigolds); and some small, dainty flowers (like pearly everlastings).

- Choose two or three shades of the same color. For example use a red and a pink, or three flowers of various shades of yellow. That range will make the colors seem richer.

- For the Williamsburg look, choose mostly flowers with strong colors. It's a matter of personal taste, of course, but Libbey Oliver thinks that too many plants with neutral tones (like the German statice) can make an arrangement look washed-out.

(continued on page 140)

CRAFTS FROM HERBS—continued

- Fill the containers with sand to hold the flowers and give them some stability. For little finger vases, use plugs of florist's foam.

- Start working with the low core of the arrangement; dried flowers are fragile, so you don't want to reach among the tall stems any more than necessary. Libbey starts with low flowers, putting them in compactly. Dried flowers don't have quite the substance of fresh flowers, so she makes a fairly dense mass at the base to get a dramatic effect, perhaps with a lot of goldenrod or artemisia.

- After constructing a dense core for the arrangement, insert airier plant material higher up, perhaps long stems with a small part of celosia on it.

3. Now add the accents, perhaps little bouquets of colorful dried flowers, spaced around the wreath connected by stretches of more neutral flowers. Or perhaps a whole circle of harmonious dried flowers with a few contrasting colors stuck here and there. You might wire in several florist's tubes so you can add fresh flowers, replacing them when they fade.

Peggy Armstrong's dried herb wreaths—any shape: Your imagination and flower supply are your only limitations in making this wreath:

1. Cut a long strip of heavy-gauge wire for the spine of the wreath or garland, and bend a hook into each end.

2. Assemble a bunch of dried flowers, perhaps 3 inches across, representing a balanced arrangement of the foliage and color accents you want in the wreath. Using fine florist's wire, bind the stems to the big wire.

Just keep adding bunches until you've covered the wire. The most important part is keeping the bunches close to each other. Otherwise there will be gaps when the wire is bent. (Peggy prefers to keep the composition simple. She advises people to use no more than three basic colors.)

3. When you have filled the wire or run out of flowers, bend the garland into whatever shape you want. You can have a wreath, a heart, a circle with Mickey Mouse ears, or whatever. Peggy has even wound herb garlands around the poles of umbrellas at a poolside party.

DANDELION

Taraxacum officinale   Compositae

Most people view the dandelion as a common lawn pest. But in other places and other times, it has been valued as a source of food and medicine.

HISTORY

The derivation of the name *Taraxacum officinale* is clouded by two points of view. Some botanists claim that *taraxacum* comes from the Persian *tark hashgun,* or wild endive. The more common theory is that the name is taken from the Greek *taraxos,* meaning disorder, and *akos,* meaning remedy.

The plant first appears in the tenth-century medical journals of Arabian physicians. By the sixteenth century, British apothecaries, who knew the drug as Herba Taraxacon or Herba Urinaria (for its diuretic effect), considered dandelion as a valuable drug. By the nineteenth century, dandelion had also become a potherb in Europe and America.

The plant picked up a number of common names that reveal something of its personality: Swine's snout, yellow gowan, Irish daisy, puffball, and peasant's cloak have all survived the passage of time. The name blowball conjures an early memory of a childhood game played on a lazy afternoon. You would give the mature seedhead your best blow of air and then count the seeds remaining to see how many children you were destined to have. Priest's crown, a medieval name, refers to the green and eager bud that first resembles a golden-haired seminarian and then matures into a distinguished pastor whose hair turns white and finally falls out. Our word dandelion comes from the French *dent de lion,* or lion's tooth, for the deeply jagged shape of the leaves.

USES

Medicinal: As an herbal medicine, dandelion root has held a distinguished place among European herbalists for centuries. The dried root is listed in the *U.S. Pharmacopoeia,* but little scientific evidence exists to place dandelion in the category of a medicinal herb.

The juice of the dandelion root is still used by European herbalists to treat diabetes and liver diseases. They regard dandelion as one of the best herbs for building up the blood and for curing anemia. It is said to act as a diuretic. It also is prescribed as a mild laxative, as an aid in digestion, and as an appetite stimulant.

Culinary: Dandelion wine has a taste suggestive of sherry and a reputation as an excellent tonic for the blood. Make it as you would

DESCRIPTION

This herbaceous perennial develops from a long, milky taproot about as thick as your little finger. The taproot is white on the inside and dark brown on the outside.

Flowers: Golden yellow flower head 1½–2 in. in diameter on smooth, hollow stem protruding from the center of leaves; closes in evening, opens in daylight.

Leaves: 2–12 in. long, very jagged along margin, fleshy, smooth, mostly hairless, dark green; spring directly from root; grow in rosette close to ground.

Fruit: Fluffy, downlike puffball; round seed head contains a cluster of as many as 200 achenes; narrow seeds with parachutelike tufts, carried by the wind.

Height: 6 in.–1 ft.

FLOWERING

Late spring.

RANGE

Native to Europe and Asia; naturalized throughout the temperate regions of the world.

CHEF TIP

Create a filling for savory pastries by combining minced dandelion leaf, ricotta cheese, feta cheese, and a pinch of mint. Fill pastries and bake in a moderate oven until browned.

any folk wine. To improve the flavor, add ginger, sliced lemon, and orange rind. Use 1 gallon of boiling water and 3½ pounds of sugar to each gallon of flowers. Add a wine yeast for best results.

In many parts of the world, dandelion roots are roasted as a coffee substitute or as an addition to hot chocolate. Dandelion coffee is prepared from autumn roots that have been thoroughly cleaned, dried by artificial heat, roasted until they are the color of coffee, and then ground for use. You can mix roasted dandelion root with coffee, much as chicory root is.

Young, tender dandelion leaves, called greens, taste a lot like chicory. They are used in salads, and older leaves are steamed or sautéed like spinach. The bright yellow flowers can be minced and added to butters and spreads for color. The flowers are also used as garnishes and to lend color to herb vinegars.

Available commercially: Dried root.

Cosmetic: Dandelion is reported to be a tonic herb externally as well as internally. Use the leaves in herbal baths and facial steams.

Dye: The flowers of dandelion can be used to make yellow dyes for wool. If the whole plant is used, you will obtain magenta. (See the entry Dyes from Herbs.)

Companion planting: While most people go around ripping dandelions out of the lawn, some gardeners recommend that you leave them to grow near fruit trees.

CULTIVATION

Dandelion greens are more nutritious than spinach. Cultivated varieties produce greens with a milder flavor than the weed. Seeds can be collected from the wild plant for sowing in shallow drills, 12 inches apart, the following spring. For the best results, prepare narrow, raised beds of loose, nitrogen-rich soil that has been lightened with sawdust or fine wood chips. This will make it easier to pull the roots out of the earth.

Harvesting and storage: The harvest time for dandelions will depend on the part of the plant you intend to use and the purpose you have in mind. Fresh flowers are used to make dandelion wine.

Leaves taken in the spring will need to be blanched to reduce the bitterness. Wash and allow them to drain. If you do not intend to use the greens immediately, store them in the refrigerator as you would ordinary salad greens. Very young, tender leaves are less bitter than larger ones and can be used fresh in salads. Or, if you wait until fall to take the leaves, the bitterness will have dissipated naturally, and you can eat them without having to blanch them first.

GROWING CONDITIONS

- Any temperate hardiness zone.
- Any soil.
- Full sun to partial shade.

DANGERS OF HERBS

Lobelia

Sassafras

Pokeweed

Herbs are wonderful plants, nature's miracle plants some call them. By definition, they are useful to man, for food or physic, color or fragrance, or simply for their beauty. But the herbal realm is not without its dark side.

Each year, countless numbers of people experience the dark side of herbs, generally in the form of some malady caused by an herb. It may be a rash or a bout of nausea. In the extreme, the herb causes a brush—or worse, a face-to-face meeting—with death. The unpleasant fact of the matter is that some herbs are downright dangerous. A corollary unpleasant fact is that some people don't give any herb—dangerous or benign—the appropriate respect.

Among the dangers that surround herbs and their uses are these:

Misidentification: An herb lover collects plants from the woods, a wayside weed patch, a farmer's pasture. He or she gets the plants home, brews tea or prepares a wild salad. That first mouthful may bring an unpleasant surprise.

Herb writer Jeanne Rose reported in her book *Herbs and Things* that "a group of friends in a commune in Connecticut gathered green hellebore by mistake instead of wild onions. They made a soup and each ate a bowlful. They all became violently ill and were all hospitalized."

Writing in the *New York Times,* health writer Jane Brody recounted the story of an elderly couple in Chehalis, Washington, who heard about and decided to try comfrey tea as an arthritis remedy. "The wife picked what she thought was comfrey and prepared tea, which the couple drank with lunch," Brody reported. "Within an hour they were overcome with nausea, vomiting, and dizziness. The husband discovered that what his wife had picked was not comfrey but a similar-looking plant called foxglove, the source of the toxic heart drug digitalis. By the time the ambulance arrived, his wife was dead and his own heart rhythm was so unstable that hospital treatment could not save him."

Plant identification, in the words of one pharmacognosist, is "neither an exact science nor an easy one." Plants of the same species can display variations that will give pause to an experienced plant taxonomist; an amateur armed with a paperback book or two may be totally confused. Don't be hasty or overconfident. Be sure you *know* what that plant is before you ingest it.

Mislabeling: Perhaps you buy dried and packaged herbs in a health food store. There is no guarantee, unfortunately, that the package's label is accurate.

"Most of the plants are collected in Eastern Europe, Asia, and

DANGERS OF HERBS—continued

PLANTS ARE DRUGS

A lot of people think of herbs in terms of seasonings, of dye plants and craft plants, and of pleasant, fragrant gardens. The FDA, after all, classifies herbs as foods or food additives, rather than drugs. But pharmacognosists consider plants to be drugs and often refer to them as such.

"Herbal teas are drugs, not foods," states Ara Der Marderosian, Ph.D., professor of pharmacognosy at the Philadelphia College of Pharmacy and Science. "They are crude complexes containing many impurities and active components with a variety of possibly undesirable effects. Some are actually too dangerous to be used at all."

South America, in places where people are not very well educated, where there are very poor quality controls," explained Varro Tyler, Ph.D., a noted pharmacognosist. "For example, the only 'active' part of chamomile is the flower head, not the leaves or stem. But when workers in Argentina go out into the field to pick chamomile, they use machines that cut the whole plant. So the chamomile you buy might contain leaves and stems, in addition to flower heads."

Occasionally, incidents suggest more deceptive forces may be at work. Brody reported in her *Times* article that a man who suffered adverse reactions to a regimen of gotu kola (*Centella asiatica*) discovered that the gotu kola he was buying at a health food store consisted of ground kola nuts (*Cola acuminata*). His symptoms resulted from the high percentage of caffeine found in kola (but not in gotu kola).

Incidents such as these spur calls for more stringent labeling requirements. The American Society of Pharmacognosy, for example, has recommended that the Food and Drug Administration (FDA) require labels on packages of herbs to include the scientific name of the plant, as well as the country of origin and a specific lot number that could be traced to a voucher specimen maintained for reference purposes. As Tyler says, "That would solve the identity problem; questions concerning safety, efficacy, and potency would still remain, of course."

Misinformation: You buy an herbal—it may be old, but this is just as likely to happen with a brand new one—and you follow its advice or directions. It is a principal danger of herbs that many herbals contain nothing but misinformation.

Tyler criticized such books in his book, which he titled (pointedly) *The Honest Herbal.* "One of them tells us that lily of the valley (*Convallaria majalis* L.) '... not being poisonous, does not leave any harmful results if it is taken over a long period.' Yet all modern authorities characterize the plant as poisonous," Tyler pointed out, "and convallatoxin, the principal glycoside contained in it, is regarded as the most toxic cardiac glycoside in existence."

Brody cited the example of three young women who suffered severe diarrhea after drinking senna tea as a substitute for coffee. They didn't know that senna (*Cassia* spp.) was a common folk laxative.

The point here is how important it is to have trustworthy, up-to-date, and complete information. We've come a long way since the days of herbalists Gerard and Culpeper. These Elizabethans may be entertaining to read, but they are no match for modern pharmacognosists when it comes to the facts of herbal safety.

THE VAGARIES OF SELF-MEDICATION

But people do use these plant/drugs. And they use them *as* drugs, figuring they can circumvent a trip to the doctor or avoid having to use an "unnatural product."

"He who self-medicates has a fool for a doctor."

That is the judgment of James Duke, long an herbal researcher for the U.S. Department of Agriculture. Herbs, unfortunately, tend to bring out the doctor in us. We figure we'll cure what ails us with a cup of herb tea or a home-concocted herbal prescription. The dangers of self-medication are several:

1. You may not really know what is wrong with you.

2. Your regimen of self-medication may be inappropriate for your ailment, even if you have properly diagnosed it.

3. Your self-medication program may delay more radical, but nevertheless necessary and appropriate, treatment.

4. Your self-medication may conflict with drugs prescribed by a doctor—allergy medication, for example, or blood pressure medication.

5. Your self-medication may cure your minor ailment, but aggravate another health problem, like high blood pressure.

These dangers prevail whether you are using herbs or more contemporary over-the-counter drugs. But using herbs as the remedy can intensify the hazards of self-medication. Misidentification, mislabeling, or misinformation enter in. The variable potency of herbs does too.

R. F. Chandler, Ph.D., professor of pharmacy at Dalhousie University in Halifax, Nova Scotia, is a member of Canada's Expert Advisory Committee on Herbs and Botanical Preparations. He summed up the concerns about self-medication: "First, most of us aren't trained to diagnose symptoms of illness. If you start following your own hunches, herbal treatments may or may not have any benefit. But our major fear is that by diagnosing and treating yourself, you may delay detection of serious illness well beyond the point where conventional drugs can help you."

DANGEROUS HERBS

The fillip to the dark side of herbs is that some herbs are, quite simply, *dangerous*. Quite a number are overtly poisonous. Poke kills. Aconite kills. Some others may not kill you but *will* make you deathly ill or take you on a trip you won't soon forget. A final category of danger encompasses those herbs that through prolonged use may

THE POTENCY OF HERBS

How potent are herbs?

It varies. It varies not just from species to species but from plant to plant.

"Whether plant drugs are purchased or self-collected," says pharmacognosist Varro Tyler, Ph.D., "it is important to remember that their active constituents may vary considerably, depending on: the conditions under which the plant was grown, the degree of maturity at the time of collection, the manner of drying, the conditions of storage, and other similar factors."

What this means is that the self-medicator may innocently underdose or overdose, simply because different specimens of the same herb may be widely divergent in potency.

"These variables are overcome, in the case of crude drugs used in conventional medicine, by conducting chemical or physiological assays or tests and then standardizing the product by adding drug material of greater or lesser potency," Tyler explains. "The more potent the medicine, the more important it is that some sort of control be utilized to assure proper dosage. Unfortunately, herbs are seldom subjected to such procedures."

DANGERS OF HERBS—continued

OVERDOING IT

A common danger of herbal self-medication is "overdoing it."

"What happens is that some people think they can make a good thing better," says California herbalist Nan Koehler. It's the thinking that prompts people to take three aspirins instead of two. If a cup of tea is good, they figure two must be better. Or if a tea is good, some stronger extract of the herb must be better. They'll experiment with decoctions or tinctures instead of infusions.

Sometimes, she continues, they'll substitute an essential oil for the whole herb. "I must caution that while herbs contain essential oils, any concentrated form of these oils can be extremely irritating. When I first became interested in herbs, I decided to try out some essential oils. I put just a few drops of essential oil of cinnamon in my bathtub, and my skin got violently red. I didn't realize that these oils can burn you. But they do. Essential oil of peppermint or pennyroyal will do the same thing. And, of course, you can die from taking these oils internally."

Don't make a minor ailment a major one by overdoing the herbal medication.

give you cancer or damage your organs.

The table that follows lists 36 herbs that are, in one way or another, dangerous.

The listing is derived from *Prevention* magazine's list of dangerous herbs, from the FDA's unsafe herb list, and from a toxicity ranking in James Duke's *CRC Handbook of Medicinal Herbs*.

"We take a very cautious attitude toward the use of potent medicinal herbs," says Mark Bricklin, executive editor of *Prevention*. The magazine's dangerous herbs list, he points out, "is not complete, but covers most of the common herbs as well as some uncommon ones." The toxicity of the included herbs varies greatly, he says, and it includes some herbs because they may present a danger to people with diabetes, heart trouble, or other diseases.

The FDA list has three categories: unsafe herbs, herbs of undefined safety for food use, and safe herbs. The latter category is often called the GRAS list, for Generally Recognized As Safe. The phrase "for food use" is the key since the FDA regards herbs not as drugs but as foods or food additives.

"It must be realized," the FDA report points out, "that no matter what recognized use there may be for any herb, such as GRAS or regulated flavor or spice, exaggerated usage or abuse outside of the context of customary usage may introduce safety problems, which in no way reflect on the safety of the herb when used in moderation. Too much of any herb is toxic."

Duke's ranking grew out of hundreds of phone calls about the safety of individual herbs. For many years Duke was chief of the U.S. Department of Agriculture's Medicinal Plant Resources Laboratory. Even after the laboratory was closed down in 1981, he continued to get calls. "Some inquiries came from those who might be called 'champions of herbs,' " he wrote, "others from 'enemies of herbs,' but perhaps most came from confused citizens barraged with overzealous statements, pro and con. Within one year alone, I was asked about more than 100 herbs by the FDA, trying to protect consumers from certain herbs, and/or the late HTA [Herb Trade Association], trying to educate consumers about the utilities of the herbs. Often one faction would be promoting an herb or concept the other faction was denouncing."

Duke came up with the idea of comparing individual herbs to coffee, a widely consumed decoction. "On a safety scale of zero to three," explained Duke, "I rate coffee 'two,' not real safe, not real poisonous. A score of zero means I think [the herb being rated] is much more toxic than coffee; perhaps deadly in small doses. For a score of one, I would discourage all but the most cautious experimentation. A score of two means I am as leery of this herb as I am of coffee. Two cups a day would seem to me to be as safe (or as dangerous) as two cups of coffee. A score of three indicates that it seems to me to be safer than coffee, that I would not be afraid to drink three cups a day. Much more than three cups of anything seems immoderate."

The individual ratings, according to Duke, were based on what he knew of the herbs "as 1983 draws to a close." In assigning his ratings, he had to weigh likely uses, the safety of plant parts, and other variables. He added that his ratings could change in the face of new information.

"For the reader's enlightenment," Duke supplemented his own ratings with ratings based on published writings by two other "herb experts": Tyler, whom Duke characterized as "rather conservative," and Rose, whom Duke characterized as "rather liberal."

In *The Honest Herbal,* Tyler included a table listing all the herbs he discussed, rating their applications with a plus (+) for safe and effective, a minus (–) for unsafe or ineffective, or a plus or minus (±) where the safety or effectiveness data are inconclusive. The table included a safety column and an effectiveness column. Thus, an application could get a plus for safety, but a minus for effectiveness. Duke converted this rating into his own: A zero in Duke's listing (and in the table that follows) means that Tyler gave the herb minuses in both the safety and effectiveness columns of his table. A one means Tyler listed a minus in the safety column. A two indicates Tyler gave a plus for safety, "tempered with a minus somewhere else." Finally, a three means Tyler gave only positive ratings.

Duke derived Rose's rating from her book *Herbs and Things.* In it Rose used a rating system consisting of special symbols (typesetters call the symbols dingbats; Duke called them asterisks). Rose explained: "Those substances marked [with three dingbats] are either poisonous and/or hallucinogenic. Those substances marked [with two dingbats] are potentially dangerous. They can cause irritation, allergic reaction, gastric distress, or other discomfort. Those substances marked [with one dingbat] are poisonous or dangerous in large doses or if used over a long period of time." By extension, those herbs not marked at all can be assumed to be safe.

Duke converted Rose's rating inversely. Rose's three became Duke's zero; her two became his one, and so on.

We have supplemented the various ratings with comments drawn from the published writings of the raters.

147

A SAMPLING OF DANGEROUS HERBS

Herb	Prevention	Safety Ranking[1]				Comments[2]
		FDA	Duke	Rose	Tyler	
Aconite (*Aconitum Napellus*)	unsafe	x	0	0	x	DUKE: *Very toxic.* Aconite is poisonous and should not be used without medical advice. Overdose should be avoided as there is no sure antidote. One mg. of aconitine is said to have killed a horse, 2 mg. may kill a human. The poison aconitine can be absorbed through the skin. ROSE: It is very unreliable and causes strange hallucinations. It should be handled and used with great caution.
Aloe (*Aloe barbadensis*)	unsafe	GRAS	3	2	3	PREVENTION: Fresh juice of the aloe plant helps heal minor wounds and burns, as scientists have verified. But taken internally, it's a violent purge. FDA: Aloe has cathartic action but is today infrequently administered for medicinal use.
American hellebore (*Veratrum viride*) or	unsafe	x	0	0	x	DUKE: Internally violently narcotic; applied locally, the fresh root [of black hellebore] is 'violently irritant.' . . . There are many cases of human poisoning from confusion with other herbs, through consuming the seeds, and through medicinal overdoses. Symptoms include dry or scratchy throat and mouth, salivation, nausea, stomachache, vomiting, colic, diarrhea, irregular slow pulse, weak heartbeat, dyspnea, vertigo, ringing ears, mydiasis, disturbed vision, excitement in fatal doses, coronary arrest, and collapse.
Black hellebore (*Helleborus niger*)	unsafe	x	0	0	x	ROSE: Green hellebore is a cardiac depressant, in contrast to black hellebore, which is a cardiac stimulant. The fresh leaves cause intense itching on contact with the skin, and if gathered and cooked . . . it can be a poisonous sedative, resembling aconite in action.
Angelica (*Angelica Archangelica*)	unsafe	GRAS	2	1	1	PREVENTION: Its sweet name contrasts with its devilish nature: It contains carcinogens. Women have been poisoned in futile attempts to induce abortion with it.

| Herb | Safety Ranking[1] | | | | | Comments[2] |
	Prevention	FDA	Duke	Rose	Tyler	
						TYLER: . . . may induce photosensitivity (to the sun), resulting in a kind of dermatitis. Studies have shown that these compounds are photo-carcinogenic (cancer-causing) in laboratory animals and are acutely toxic and mutagenic even in the absence of light.
Arnica (*Arnica montana*)	unsafe	unsafe	1	0	3	FDA: Aqueous and alcoholic extracts of the plant contain, besides choline, 2 unidentified substances which affect the heart and vascular systems. Arnica is an active irritant which can produce violent toxic gastroenteritis, nervous disturbances, change in pulse rate, intense muscular weakness, collapse, and death. TYLER: Scientific studies of the effects of alcoholic extracts of arnica on the heart and circulatory system of small animals have verified the folly of using the drug internally for self-medication. Not only did it exhibit a toxic action on the heart, but in addition, it caused very large increases in blood pressure. External application of the drug is quite a different matter.
Autumn crocus (*Colchicum autumnale*)	unsafe	x	0	x	x	*PREVENTION*: Herbalists prescribed it to *lower* sexual excitement. And well it might with its nausea, colic, intestinal pain, and kidney damage. DUKE: Overdoses of colchicine [an alkaloid in the plant] may cause intestinal pain, diarrhea, vomiting, and may even cause death. . . . As little as 7 mg. colchicine has proved lethal, but the usual lethal dose is closer to 65 mg.
Bayberry (*Myrica cerifera*)	unsafe	x	2	3	2	*PREVENTION*: Is the bark useful as medicine? Not by any scientific measure, and rats get cancer when injected with it. The berries make nice candles, though. DUKE: Bayberry wax is said to be irritant and sensitizing.
Bloodroot (*Sanguinaria canadensis*)	unsafe	unsafe	1	x	x	*PREVENTION*: Used by American Indians as a skin dye and to treat breast cancer; it shouldn't be used by reputable healers. FDA: Contains the poisonous alkaloid sanguinarine, and other alkaloids. DUKE: In toxic doses, bloodroot causes burning in the stomach, intense thirst, paralysis, vomiting, faintness, vertigo, collapse, and intense prostration with dimness of eyesight.

(continued)

149

A SAMPLING OF DANGEROUS HERBS—continued

Herb	Safety Ranking[1]					Comments[2]
	Prevention	FDA	Duke	Rose	Tyler	
Blue cohosh (*Caulophyllum thalictroides*)	unsafe	x	1	x	1	PREVENTION: It cannot safely be used to stimulate menstruation or hasten childbirth, as some books suggest. It has a toxic effect on the heart muscle and may hurt the intestines. DUKE: Children are said to have been poisoned by eating the blue seeds. Powder of dried blue cohosh must be handled carefully as it is strongly irritating, especially to the mucous membranes. Should be avoided by pregnant women. TYLER: Discretion dictates that blue cohosh not be used for medical self-treatment.
Broom (*Cystisus scoparius*)	unsafe	unsafe	1	0	1	PREVENTION: Although claimed by some to be a mood alterer when smoked, broom slows the heartbeat without making it stronger. It's a dangerous drug. DUKE: Toxicity symptoms suggest nicotine poisoning: circulatory collapse with tachycardia, paralysis of the ileus, nausea, diarrhea, vertigo, and headache. ROSE: It is . . . used as a cardiac stimulant and narcotic but can be poisonous in large doses, paralyzing the respiratory and motor centers and causing convulsions and death. TYLER: There are . . . safer and more effective drugs for . . . actions attributed to [broom].
Coltsfoot (*Tussilago Farfara*)	unsafe	undefined safety	2	3	1	PREVENTION: If you want an herb for a cough, try slippery elm bark or marsh mallow root, not this herb that contains potent toxins that cause liver cancer. FDA: The only therapeutic value the leaves possess is a demulcent effect due to their mucilage. TYLER: Neither the flowers nor the leaves can safely be used for medicinal purposes.
Comfrey (*Symphytum officinale*)	unsafe	undefined safety	2	3	1	FDA: The rhizome contains allantoin. It contains the alkaloids, *consolidine* and *symphytocynoglossine*, which are depressants to the central nervous system. Comfrey contains large quantities of mucilage and some tannin. TYLER: Both root and leaf of this plant have been shown to be carcinogenic in rats when fed in concentrations of as little as 0.5% and 8% of their diet,

150

Herb	Safety Ranking[1]					Comments[2]
	Prevention	FDA	Duke	Rose	Tyler	
Deadly nightshade (*Atropa Belladonna*)	unsafe	unsafe	0	0	x	*PREVENTION:* A component of witches' brew, its nickname means beautiful lady. But its nicknames of deadly nightshade and dwale (for "trance") are more apt. It's poisonous. FDA: Poisonous plant which contains the toxic solanaceous alkaloids, hyoscyamine, atropine, and hyoscine. DUKE: Sap of the plant can cause dermatitis. People handling the berries can develop vesiculo-pustular eruptions on the face with disorders of visual accommodation. ROSE: Its properties are sedative, narcotic, anodynic, and, like all medicines that act through the central nervous system, small doses stimulate and large ones paralyze. . . . Belladonna poisoning manifests itself within 15 minutes of ingestion by dryness of mouth, burning throat, dilated pupils, intense thirst, double vision, giddiness, burning in the stomach, nausea, hallucinations, rambling talk, and a feeble rapid pulse.
Eyebright (*Euphrasia officinalis*)	unsafe	x	2	1	0	*PREVENTION:* Though the poet Milton had an angel clear Adam's sight with it, this flower that looks like bloodshot eyes may hurt yours, particularly if it's unsterilized. DUKE: German experimentation suggested that 10 to 60 drops of the tincture could induce confusion of the mind and cephalalgia; violent pressure in the eyes with lacrimation, itch, redness, and swellings of the margins of the lids, dim vision, photophobia, weakness, sneezing, coryza, nausea, toothache, constipation, hoarseness, cough, expectoration, dyspnea, yawning, insomnia, polyuria [excessive urination], and diaphoresis. TYLER: . . . none of these constituents is known to possess any useful therapeutic properties for the treatment of eye disease. . . .
Foxglove (*Digitalis purpurea*)	unsafe	x	0	0	1	DUKE: Many fatalities have resulted from foxglove ingestion. . . . Symptoms of digitalis poisoning include nausea, diarrhea, stomachache, severe headache, irregular heartbeat and pulse, tremors, convulsions, and death. ROSE: Digitalis is cumulative, and relatively small doses, taken often, induce the symptoms of poisoning.

(continued)

A SAMPLING OF DANGEROUS HERBS—continued

Herb	Safety Ranking[1]					Comments[2]
	Prevention	FDA	Duke	Rose	Tyler	
Goldenseal (*Hydrastis canadensis*)	unsafe	undefined safety	1	3	2	*PREVENTION:* It makes you feel better when you stop taking it. This extremely bitter herb makes some people nauseated. It has no effect below "near-toxic" doses. DUKE: An overdose (even externally) can cause severe ulceration of any surface it may touch. Such notes should discourage those who recommend goldenseal as a douche. ROSE: This marvelous natural drug is a nontoxic, nonirritating antiseptic that both heals and soothes the surfaces of the body and it may be used as frequently as one wants. TYLER: . . . unless extremely large, near-toxic doses are administered, the effects are too uncertain to be therapeutically useful . . . interesting but valueless drug.
Hemlock (*Conium maculatum*)	x	unsafe	0	0	x	DUKE: Following lethal doses, animals rapidly begin to show symptoms; among them: paralysis of the tongue, mydriasis, head pressure, giddiness, nausea, vomiting, diarrhea, and collapse into central paralysis, first the feet and legs, then the buttocks, arms, then paralysis of swallowing and speech . . . death ensues through central respiratory paralysis. ROSE: In ancient times it was used to poison criminals. Socrates, condemned to die, drank this poisonous juice of his own hand. . . .
Jimsonweed (*Datura Stramonium*)	unsafe	unsafe	0	0	x	*PREVENTION:* People have died trying to get high on this plant. Hallucinations may be paid for with an irregular heartbeat, elevated blood pressure, and convulsions. FDA: A poisonous plant. It has been misused for producing hallucinogenic effects. DUKE: Usual consequences of poison are dimness of vision, dilation of the pupils, giddiness, delirium, sometimes amounting to mania. Those who indulge in jimsonweed seed may be taking off on a one-way trip. ROSE: A person who uses this drug becomes unconscious and must be watched and kept from hurting himself. He may think he's flying. The first symptom is a dry throat, then gaiety, laughter, black objects appear green. The experience is usually

Herb	Prevention	FDA	Duke	Rose	Tyler	Comments[2]
Juniper (*Juniperus communis*)	unsafe	GRAS	1	3	2	*PREVENTION*: It's not toxic in the tiny doses used to flavor gin (though you may think so next morning). But small, repeated doses may cause convulsions and kidney damage. DUKE: Internally, symptoms from overdose are pain in or near the kidney, strong diuresis, albuminuria, hematuria, purplish urine, accelerated heartbeat and blood pressure, and, rarely, convulsive apparitions, metrorrhagia, and, more rarely, abortion. TYLER: Since much safer and more effective diuretic and carminative drugs exist, the use of juniper in folk medicine should also be abandoned.
Licorice (*Glycyrrhiza glabra*)	unsafe	GRAS	1	3	2	*PREVENTION*: Don't worry about a licorice shoestring or two, but anyone with heart or blood pressure disorders should avoid this entirely. DUKE: While licorice extract may alleviate peptic ulcers, swelling of the face and limbs may be a side effect. TYLER: Although licorice does have a flavor pleasing to many and may also have some utility in treating coughs, it must be remembered that it is also a potent drug. Large doses over extended periods of time are quite toxic.
Life root (*Senecio aureus*) (*S. vulgaris*)	unsafe	x	1	x	1	*PREVENTION*: Its name reflects its old use, easing the pain of childbirth. Research reveals that it has little effect on the uterus, and worse yet, can damage the liver. TYLER: . . . it is not useful to discuss in detail the therapeutic potential of life root or the desirability of self-medicating with it for conditions in which it may be effective. Because of the presence of senecionine, the drug is simply not safe to use.
Lobelia (*Lobelia inflata*)	unsafe	unsafe	1	0	1	*PREVENTION*: It's deadly. Sometimes sold as an aid to weight loss, it may work since "most individuals do not eat much when nauseated," says one book. It may be fatal. DUKE: Remember the warning: *Death has resulted from improper use of this drug as a home remedy*. ROSE: This is a very useful and valuable remedy, but must be used with great care since it has caused death when misused.

(continued)

153

A SAMPLING OF DANGEROUS HERBS—continued

Herb	Safety Ranking[1]					Comments[2]
	Prevention	FDA	Duke	Rose	Tyler	
Lobelia—continued						TYLER: In normal doses, it produces dilation of the bronchioles and increased respiration, but overdoses result in respiratory depression, as well as a host of other undesirable side effects including sweating, rapid heartbeat, low blood pressure, and even coma followed by death.
Mayapple (Podophyllum peltatum)	unsafe	unsafe	1	0	x	PREVENTION: Whether it's American mayapple or the European Satan's apple, mandrake is toxic. The European type destroys the heart, and the American harms the intestines. FDA: European mandrake is a poisonous narcotic similar in its properties to belladonna.
or						
European mandrake (Mandragora officinarum)	unsafe	unsafe	0	x	x	DUKE: In large doses it [mayapple] causes nausea and inflammation of the stomach and intestines which have proved Fatal. Amerindians once used the young shoots for suicide. ROSE: [Mayapple] is a powerful irritant to the intestine, acting as an emetic and purgative. If misused it can be dangerous. The rootstock is poisonous. . . .
Mistletoe American (Phoradendron serotinum)	unsafe	unsafe	1	0	1	PREVENTION: Kiss under it, but don't kiss it. The [ingestion of] berries and leaves may cause an agonizing disruption of the heartbeat and eventual death. DUKE: Fatalities have been reported following ingestion of the berries. Children frequently suffer epileptiform convulsions following ingestion of the berries.
or						
European (Viscum album)	unsafe	unsafe	1	0	1	TYLER: All of the recent scientific studies emphasize the similar toxic nature of plant material, especially the berries but also the leaves, from both American and European mistletoe. So the use of either product as a home remedy or as a beverage should definitely be avoided.
Pennyroyal American (Hedeoma pulegioides)	unsafe	GRAS	2	x	2	DUKE: Both [American and European pennyroyal] oils consist of 85 to 92% pulegone and are, therefore, quite toxic, causing severe liver damage, even in relatively small amounts.
or						
European (Mentha Pulegium)	unsafe	GRAS	2	3	1	TYLER: While pennyroyal oil may indeed induce abortion, it does so only in lethal or near-lethal doses. Such amounts would ordinarily not be obtained from

Herb	Prevention	FDA	Duke	Rose	Tyler	Comments[2]
Pokeweed (*Phytolacca americana*) (*P. decandra*)	unsafe	undefined safety	0	x	0	*PREVENTION*: The word on this plant is "don't," and it should be written in neon. It has no known good effects. And children who've eaten the inky berries have died. FDA: Narcotic effects have been observed. Has been employed internally in chronic rheumatism but is not therapeutically useful and is no longer prescribed. Overdoses have sometimes been fatal. DUKE: I think Tyler's hyperbole [see below] might help spare another pokeweed incident. TYLER: Pokeroot is not therapeutically useful for anything. It may act as an emetic and cathartic, but it does so because it is extremely toxic....
Rue (*Ruta graveolens*)	unsafe	GRAS	2	0	2	*PREVENTION*: You'll rue the day you smell rue! So it may be effective as claimed as an insect repellent. It's also likely to cause a rash on you; may upset stomach. DUKE: An acro-narcotic poison in excessive doses internally; externally irritant and rubefacient. Oil, very dangerous, has been said to cause abortion. Handling of the foliage, flowers, and/or fruit can produce burning, erythema, itching, and vesication. ROSE: The oil is a dangerous abortifacient and large doses may produce nerve derangement. It is poisonous but rarely causes death. TYLER: While there is little question about the antispasmodic action of rue, there is appreciable doubt about the utility and safety of the drug, especially in the fresh state. Medicinal use of the plant, fresh or dried, is not recommended for anybody, and under no circumstances should it be taken by pregnant women.
St. John's-wort (*Hypericum perforatum*)	x	unsafe	1	1	3	DUKE: In sheep, may cause shedding of wool, swelling of the face, generalized skin irritation, loss of appetite, and sometimes loss of eyesight. ... Illustrations of animals poisoned by photosensitization are quite dramatic. TYLER: Much of the activity reported for the plant is due . . . to the presence of hypericin, a reddish dianthrone pigment. Very small doses of hypericin produce a tonic and tranquilizing action in human beings, apparently by increasing capillary blood flow. Reducing capillary fragility is another recorded action of the compound.

(continued)

A SAMPLING OF DANGEROUS HERBS—*continued*

Herb	Safety Ranking[1]					Comments[2]
	Prevention	FDA	Duke	Rose	Tyler	
Sassafras (*Sassafras albidum*)	unsafe	x	2	3	1	*PREVENTION*: As little as a teaspoon of the volatile oil causes degeneration of the heart, liver and kidneys. Do you really want that cup of tea? DUKE: Safrole [a chemical constituent of sassafras], sassafras, and sassafras oil are prohibited from use in foods. TYLER: . . . Safrole was recognized as a carcinogenic agent in rats and mice. Both sassafras oil and safrole were prohibited by the FDA from use as flavors or food additives. An overriding consideration . . . is that the plant material has no real medical or therapeutic utility.
Sweet flag (*Acorus Calamus*)	unsafe		1	0	1	*PREVENTION*: This irislike flower has fallen into disrepute since animal studies showed it to cause heart and liver damage as well as cancer. FDA: Oil of calamus, Jammu variety is a carcinogen. DUKE: Oil of Calamus has been shown to be carcinogenic, probably due to its asarone or safrole content. . . . [It] has been shown to possess considerable toxicity in long-term feeding studies in rats. TYLER: While the small-animal studies did involve feeding the drug for extended periods of time and therefore may not be directly applicable to occasional human consumption, the fact is that calamus has no therapeutic ability which is not provided more effectively and more safely by other drugs. This is also true of its use as a flavoring agent, which can no longer be condoned.
Tansy (*Tanacetum vulgare*)	unsafe	x	2	2	2	DUKE: The oil is quite toxic and should be used only with extreme caution. Ten drops of the oil could be lethal. . . . Tansy is said to be prohibited for botanical dealers, and cannot be sold as a dried herb by mail. . . . Symptoms of internal tansy poisoning include rapid and feeble pulse, severe gastritis, violent spasms, and convulsions. ROSE: It is dangerous if used in large quantities and overdoses have caused fatal incidents. It is safer if used only externally. TYLER: In this enlightened era, there is absolutely no

Safety Ranking[1]

Herb	Prevention	FDA	Duke	Rose	Tyler	Comments[2]
Wahoo (*Euonymus atropurpurea*)	x	unsafe	1	x	x	FDA: The poisonous principle has not been completely identified. Laxative. DUKE: This species is probably toxic.... Ingestion of the fruits may cause vomiting, diarrhea, weakness, chills, and convulsions following in about 12 hours by unconsciousness. No deaths are reported in the U.S.
Wormwood (*Artemisia Absinthium*)	unsafe	unsafe	1	0	1	*PREVENTION:* Once an ingredient in absinthe, it's a central nervous system depressant. FDA: Contains a volatile oil which is an active narcotic poison. DUKE: Habitual use or large doses cause convulsions, insomnia, nausea, nightmare, restlessness, tremors, and vertigo. TYLER: Wormwood acquired its sinister reputation as a subtle poison when it became the principal flavoring ingredient in a 136-proof alcoholic beverage called absinthe.... Practically every civilized country in the world banned the preparation or consumption of absinthe.
Yohimbe (*Corynanthe johimbi*) (*Pausinystalia johimbe*)	x	unsafe	1	0	1	FDA: Used as an aphrodisiac. ROSE: ...it causes a tingling sensation in the genitals. TYLER: The drug dilates the blood vessels of the skin and mucous membranes and thereby lowers blood pressure.... The drug also should not be taken by persons suffering from hypotension, diabetes, or from heart, liver, or kidney disease. Psychic reactions resembling anxiety have been shown to be produced....

NOTE: Rankings by Duke, Rose, and Tyler reprinted with permission from *CRC Handbook of Medicinal Herbs.* Copyright 1985 by CRC Press, Inc., Boca Raton, Fla.

1. 0 = Very dangerous. 1 = More dangerous than coffee. 2 = As dangerous as coffee. 3 = Safe. x = Rating not available. GRAS = Generally recognized as safe.
The rationale behind these ratings is detailed in the text of the entry Dangers of Herbs under the heading Dangerous Herbs.

2. These comments are taken directly from *Using Medicines Wisely* (a volume in the Prevention Total Health System series), the FDA's unsafe herb list, James Duke's *CRC Handbook of Medicinal Herbs*, Jeanne Rose's *Herbs and Things*, and Varro Tyler's *The Honest Herbal*, respectively.

DEADLY NIGHTSHADE

VERY TOXIC

Atropa Belladonna   Solanaceae

Every family has a black sheep, and in most, the black sheep isn't really black but gray. In the plant world, however, the Solanaceae family—that nice one that gave us those delicious tomatoes, eggplants, potatoes, and peppers—has a whole flock of black sheep. There's henbane, jimsonweed, and European mandrake. The blackest of these blackguards is deadly nightshade.

DESCRIPTION

Deadly nightshade is a shrublike perennial herb with several cylindrical, purplish stems, bearing leaves and flowers.

Flowers: Bell-shaped, five-lobed, dull purple, drooping, to 1¼ in. long, bloom individually from axils of leaves, five-pointed green calyx cups base of corolla, remains after petals fall.

Leaves: Alternate, ovate, pointed, entire, dusky green on upper surface, paler green underneath, conspicuous veins, purplish midrib, 3–9 in. long, 2–4 in. wide, upper leaves accompanied by smaller leaf.

Fruit: Roundish berry, turns from green to deep purple to black, ½ in. in diameter, yields purple juice

Height: Usually 2–3 ft. but can reach 6 ft.

FLOWERING

Midsummer.

RANGE

Native to Europe, Asia, and North Africa; cultivated in central Europe, England, the United States, and northern India; naturalized in the eastern United States.

HABITAT

Meadows, forests, and waste places.

HISTORY

Much of the dark history of deadly nightshade is revealed by its name. According to mythology, Atropos, one of the three Greek goddesses of fate, used the poisonous berries of this herb to cut the thread of life. So the generic name of deadly nightshade became *Atropa. Belladonna* is derived from the Italian words for beautiful lady. The most common and perhaps most plausible explanation for why nightshade was given this species name is that Italian women placed drops of the plant's juices in their eyes to dilate their pupils and make them more beautiful. Another legend, though, tells that men once believed that deadly nightshade changed from an herb into a beautiful lady, delightful to gaze on but dangerous.

During the Middle Ages, men and women believed that deadly nightshade was the favorite plant of the devil. This is not surprising when one considers the stories told of this plant. Belladonna was said to be an ingredient in the refreshments of wild orgies at which women would strip off their clothes, dance, and throw themselves into the arms of eager men. Sorcerers and witches added the juices of this plant to their brews and ointments. Witches rubbed a lotion containing belladonna and aconite into their skin, believing that it helped them to fly. Given the physiological effects of both of these herbs, in a way, it probably did make them fly. Deadly nightshade's toxicity did not go unnoticed either. Men used this herb frequently to kill.

USES

In spite of this plant's wretched past, it does have some redeeming qualities as a medicinal herb. Those qualities, however, are unlikely to manifest themselves in a home remedy. Deadly nightshade is truly deadly.

Medicinal: As poisonous as this plant can be, extracts of it are added to over-the-counter as well as prescription drugs. The leaves of belladonna have been official in the *U.S. Pharmacopoeia* since 1820. Modern medicine uses certain isolated compounds: atropine, hyoscyamine, and scopolamine and tinctures made from the leaves.

Scopolamine has had some interesting uses in its time. It was once combined with morphine and given to women during childbirth, but when infant mortality noticeably increased, this practice was ceased. The law made use of this drug for a brief time, administering it as a truth serum to suspected criminals.

Ironically, though deadly nightshade is itself toxic, one of its compounds, atropine, is an effective antidote for certain poisons. In 1967 in Tijuana, Mexico, bread became contaminated with parathion, a deadly insecticide, and doctors administered atropine to save the lives of those who had eaten it. During World War II, atropine was the only antidote against a deadly nerve gas developed by the Germans. Fortunately, it never had to be used.

Today, atropine is an important drug of ophthalmologists. Perhaps we owe thanks to those *bella donnas* who signaled one of the uses of this drug with their beautiful eyes. Atropine also helps to control mucous secretions in the throat and respiratory passages, and it serves as an antidote to such depressant poisons as muscarine, opium, and chloral hydrate. As an antispasmodic, it is prescribed for conditions such as gastritis, pancreatitis, and chronic urethritis.

Extracts of deadly nightshade are used to treat Parkinson's disease, psychiatric disorders, convulsions, epilepsy, and whooping cough. They are added to drugs taken for asthma, colds, and hayfever. Certain laxatives and liniments contain belladonna preparations. So, you see, this herb really does benefit man if handled properly. If handled improperly, which can easily occur when experimenting with this herb at home, it can kill.

Toxicity: Men and women have been poisoned merely by eating rabbits and birds that have fed on the berries of deadly nightshade. Children tempted by the dark, delicious-looking berries have died after eating only three. Symptoms include dilated pupils, flushed skin, dryness of the mouth and throat, nausea, vomiting, weakness, delirium, rapid heartbeat, and sometimes paralysis and coma. A person who has merely handled the plant may also show some signs of poisoning as the plant's chemicals are absorbed through the skin.

CULTIVATION

Don't even consider growing this deadly plant in your garden. As Elizabethan herbalist John Gerard warned:

> . . . Follow my counsell, deale not with the same in·
> any case, and banish it from your gardens and the
> use of it also, being a plant so furious and deadly:
> for it bringeth such as have eaten thereof into a
> dead sleepe wherein many have died . . . .

POISONED?

Julia Morton in *Major Medicinal Plants* reports an interesting method for determining deadly nightshade poisoning in an individual. Take a few drops of the person's urine and place them in a cat's eye. After a half hour, if the cat's eye dilates fully under light, it can be assumed the person ate some nightshade.

DILL

DESCRIPTION

Dill looks like a smaller version of fennel, its relative. Its taproot is singular and spindly like a carrot. One long, hollow stalk comes from the root, whereas fennel's taproot is branched and has many stalks. (See photos on pages 101 and 375.)

Flowers: Flat, terminal, compound umbels, 6 in. across; numerous yellow flowers with tiny petals rolled inward from either side.

Leaves: Feathery, bipinnate, blue-green; leaflets threadlike, pointed.

Fruit: Ribbed, flattened, and elliptical, ⅛ in. long, three longitudinal ridges on the back; produced in great quantities; germinating capacity lasts for three years.

Height: 3 ft.

FLOWERING

July through September.

RANGE

Native to the Mediterranean and southern Russia. Naturalized in North America.

CHEF TIPS

- When mincing, preserve the delicate flavor of dillweed by snipping it with scissors rather than ripping it with a knife.
- Create a chilled dill sauce for fish by combining 1 cup of plain yogurt, 3 tablespoons of minced fresh dillweed, and 1½ teaspoons Dijon mustard.

Anethum graveolens   **Umbelliferae**

Dill is simple to grow and beautiful to look at, and therefore deserves a place in either an herb or vegetable garden. In the gardens of ancient Athens and Rome, dill held a permanent spot. Fragrant dill garlands crowned war heroes on their return home. Aromatic wreaths of the yellow flowers hung in Roman banquet halls.

Although at one time dill had medicinal uses, they have been forgotten over the years. Today, dill seed is used as a pickling spice, while dillweed, the light, feathery leaves, is used to flavor fish sauce and salad dressing.

The name dill comes from *dilla,* Norse for "to lull," and indeed dill was once used to induce sleep. It was taken to relieve flatulence and as a milk stimulant for nursing mothers. Dill was believed to work as a charm against witches; mystics could combat an "evil eye" spell by carrying a bag of dried dill over the heart.

USES

Medicinal: European and American herbalists use both the leaves and the seeds to dispel flatulence, increase mother's milk, and treat congestion in the breast resulting from nursing. Dill is also said to be stimulating to the appetite and settling to the stomach and has been used to relieve babies with colic. To prepare an infusion, steep 2 teaspoons of seeds in 1 cup of water for 10 to 15 minutes. Take ½ cup at a time, 1 or 2 cups per day. You can also make dill water by adding 8 drops of oil to 1 pint of water, with doses ranging anywhere from 1 to 8 teaspoonfuls.

The essential oils of dill differ in flavor and odor depending on whether they have been taken from the mature seed or the dillweed. The quality of dill oil can vary greatly depending on the relative percentages of seed oil and oil from the weed. Another variable is the maturity of the seeds.

Culinary: Dill has a dominant personality and a well-rounded tang. The feathery leaves are used fresh in salads and as garnishes. The seeds of the plant have a stronger flavor and are used whole or ground in longer-cooking recipes.

Dill is delicious with fish (especially salmon), lamb, pork, poultry, cheese, cream, eggs, cabbage, onions, cauliflower, parsnips, squash, eggplant, spinach, potatoes, broccoli, turnips, cucumbers, carrots, green beans, tomatoes, avocados, eggs, and apples. It is particularly popular in the salads, soups, sauces, spreads, and fish recipes of Russia and Scandinavia.

Available commercially: Fresh and dried leaf, but fresh is preferable. Whole or ground seed, but whole is preferable.

Storage note: Dillweed is easiest to handle when frozen on its stem. As needed, simply snip some off with scissors and return the rest to the freezer.

Craft: If you can spare some dill from the kitchen, both the foliage and flower heads dry nicely and add a light, airy touch to herb and flower arrangements.

Companion planting: Dill is supposed to enhance the growth of cabbage, onions, and lettuce.

CULTIVATION

Dill can be situated along the garden perimeter to attract bees or used as a backdrop for shorter plants. Wherever you place dill, be sure to pick a permanent spot; the plant is self-seeding, and chances are good that new plants will shoot up every year if you let the flowers go to seed. Consider a protected location; wind can destroy the tall stalks. Or you can tie plants to a stake to keep them upright.

Seeds are best sown right in the ground; transplanting is not always successful. Plant early in the spring after the danger of frost is gone, in rows 2 to 3 feet apart. Within the rows, place seeds in shallow drills from 10 to 12 inches apart, or thin the young seedlings to this spacing when they are approximately 2 inches tall. If you grow dill chiefly for the foliage, you can sow the seeds just 8 to 10 inches apart; do so every three weeks for a constant supply of dillweed.

If you're growing dill for the seeds, keep in mind that seeds may not be produced until the beginning of the plant's second year. If dill is planted early enough, however, seeds should appear at the end of that summer. Weeding is the only care required.

Harvesting and storage: Once the plants are well established, you can begin clipping the leaves close to the stem. Do so either early in the morning or in the evening. Dillweed will last only a couple of days in the refrigerator before it droops and loses its flavor. For year-round use, dry it by spreading the leaves over a nonmetallic screen in a warm, dark place for a couple of days. Then place the dried leaves in an airtight container. An easier alternative is to freeze the freshly picked leaves.

Harvest the seeds when the flower matures, anywhere from two to three weeks after blossoming. The seeds will be a light brown color. Those seeds on the lower side of the flower umbel will be ripe, while the others will ripen as they dry. Handle the sheaves gingerly to keep the seeds from falling off the flower head and into your garden. Cut the stems with enough length, so that they can be tied in a bunch and hung in a dark place. Spread paper beneath them to catch the dried seeds as they fall. If the seeds do not fall, you'll have to pull them off by hand.

GROWING CONDITIONS

- Soil pH 6.0.
- Moderately rich, well-drained, moist soil.
- Full sun.

DOCK

Rumex spp.   Polygonaceae

The *Rumex* genus is a divided family. The sorrels are the cultivated members; the docks are the wild. The sorrels are used primarily in cooking, adding a lemony taste to salads, for example, while the docks are used as medicinal plants.

DESCRIPTION

The *Rumex* species includes weedy perennials. They generally grow from long, carrot-shaped taproots, often a ruddy brown outside, but yellow or orange within.

Flowers: Many small, greenish yellow or reddish in spreading panicles; six stamens.

Leaves: 1 ft. long or more, lance-shaped, wavy edged, light green; lower leaves larger than higher ones.

Fruit: A three-angled achene.

Height: 1–4 ft.

FLOWERING

June through August.

RANGE

Native to Europe; naturalized in North America.

HABITAT

Rich, heavy soil in disturbed ground; moist clearings, ditches, streams, roadsides, and meadows.

GROWING CONDITIONS

- Soil pH: acid.
- Any soil.
- Full sun.

HISTORY

Once classified under the genus *Lapathum,* a derivative of the Greek word meaning "to cleanse," dock was used as a purgative. The leaves were applied to burns, blisters, and nettle stings. (The cure for nettle stings was thought to be more effective when accompanied by the words "Nettle in, dock; dock in, nettle out; dock rub nettle out.")

Herbalists recommend dock root as an astringent tonic and for diseases of the blood and liver. It was used to "purify the blood" (often a euphemism for the treatment of venereal disease) and to treat scrofula and skin problems. The American Indians applied crushed yellow dock roots to cuts and boils. The roots have been used throughout history as a laxative and also as a remedy for anemia because they reputedly draw iron out of the soil.

European peasants used dock and sorrel leaves to avoid scurvy; both are high in vitamin C. The leaves were served as potherbs.

USES

Yellow dock is most often used medicinally. Its main value is as a laxative. To make an infusion of dock, place 1 teaspoonful of the dried root in a cup, add boiling water, and steep for 30 minutes. Take 1 or 2 cups a day. In Appalachia it is still used externally to combat ringworm and hives.

You should not eat fresh dock leaves. Although they are rich in vitamin C, they also contain oxalic acid, which can aggravate gout. However, they are relatively safe when boiled in water that has been changed twice, since this cooks away much of the acid.

CULTIVATION

Dock grows as a weed and is hard to control. Even French sorrel is difficult to eradicate once established, but it's worth growing in a contained area. Plant it in a sunny location in well-drained, loamy soil. In spring, sow seed either directly in the garden or in flats. When seedlings are 1 to 2 inches tall, thin to 6 inches apart.

Dig up dock roots in late summer, autumn, or early spring. Split them with a knife, then dry them. Sorrel leaves can be harvested any time during the growing season. Use them fresh.

DYES FROM HERBS

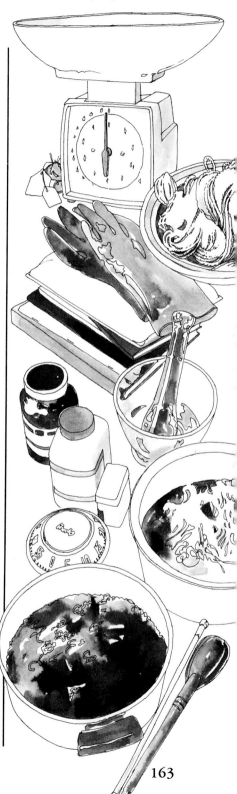

It isn't surprising that herbs—the source of foods, flavors, fragrances, medicines—provide colors as well. Stirred with skeins of wool, the leaves, flowers, and roots of many herbs impart reds, blues, greens, yellows, browns, and grays.

Dyeing your own yarns can be a creative and enriching experience. Imagine wandering through the herb garden gathering plants, simmering them in large enamel pots to release their hues, gently moving skeins of wool through the colored waters, and the result— yarns of such pleasing colors.

MATERIALS

Before you get started, you will need the following materials:

1. *Fibers.* You can dye wool, cotton, linen, or silk, but wool is the easiest (and the directions that follow assume you are dyeing wool). Finished fabrics can also be dyed, but it is difficult to achieve even coloring throughout the cloth.

2. *Cotton thread.* The skeins should be tied loosely so they may be boiled, yet still be recovered as skeins.

3. *Soap.* Mild soap or dish detergent for washing the skeins free of all grease, dirt, or chemicals that might repel dyes.

4. *Water.* Lots of water, preferably soft. The minerals in hard water can affect the clarity of the dye. Rainwater is ideal if you can collect it. If you use tap water and it is hard, add a water softener.

5. *Pots.* Stainless steel or enamel is best. They will not affect the color of the dyes. To dye a pound of fiber at a time, you will need a pot that can hold 4½ gallons of water in addition to the yarn.

It's best to set aside pots specifically for dyeing rather than using your cooking pans. Although most of the materials you use are perfectly safe, some of the mordanting chemicals are poisonous.

6. *Stirring rods.* Rods to stir and lift the yarn. Glass is best, but you can use plastic or wooden dowels. Wooden rods do absorb dye, so you will need a separate one for each dye that you create.

7. *Sieve.* A sieve, cheesecloth, or a colander for straining the dye bath and removing plant material.

8. *Mordants.* Alum, chrome, tin, and iron. Cream of tartar is a supplement to these chemicals.

9. *Measuring spoons and cups.* Stainless steel, plastic, or glass is best.

10. *Thermometer.* It should read temperatures at least up to 212°F.

11. *Scale.* A letter scale will do.

DYES FROM HERBS—continued

BLACKS

alder
black walnut
yarrow

BLUES

elder
elecampane
indigo
Oregon grape
woad

BROWNS

burdock
cascara sagrada
comfrey
fennel
geranium
hops
juniper
madder
onion
pokeweed
poplar

GOLDS

agrimony
amaranth
dock
goldenrod
lavender cotton
mullein
onion
plantain
poplar
ragwort
safflower
salsify
yarrow

GRAYS

elder
poplar
raspberry
sunflower
yarrow

12. *Rinsing containers.* A sink, buckets, or large containers for washing and rinsing the fibers.

13. *Rubber gloves.* You don't have to use them, but they will protect your hands.

14. *Recording materials.* Notebook, tags, and a file box.

PREPARING THE YARN

Before dyeing your wool, you will need to wash and mordant them. The following process is for skeins of yarn:

Tying: During both the washing and dyeing processes, the yarn gets swirled and agitated. To keep the strands together and prevent them from tangling, tie some cotton thread around the skein in a figure-eight fashion. Tie it tightly enough to keep the yarn together, but loosely enough that the dye can flow around the individual strands of yarn. In addition, if you knot the two ends of the skein together and then tie them loosely around the skein, you will easily find them later on when you work with your yarn.

Washing: And now, even though it looks clean and new, wash the skeins to remove any traces of dirt, oil, or chemicals that would repel the dye. Use a mild soap. The water should be warm (about 95°F) but not hot. Squeeze the soapy water through the skein for several minutes. Rinse in water of the same temperature. After rinsing, squeeze the water from the skein, then roll the yarn in a towel to remove more moisture. Hang the yarn to dry in a shady location, or if you are ready to mordant the yarn, you can use it immediately.

Mordanting wool: To set the colors and prevent them from fading or bleeding, you must mordant the yarn by simmering it in a diluted chemical bath. The most commonly used mordants are alum, chrome, tin, and iron. Cream of tartar is used with some of the mordants to brighten colors. The mordant affects the shade of color you will get, so choose one according to what result you want (see the table A Sampling of Herbs for Dyeing).

If your yarn is dry, soak it in cool water for several minutes before placing it in the mordant solution.

When mordanting is complete, you may either dye your yarn right away or dry it in a shady spot and store it, except with chrome-mordanted skeins. Chrome reacts easily with light, and yarns treated with it should be dyed immediately.

Alum (potassium aluminum sulfate): Alum is the most stable and most commonly used mordant.

For 1 pound of wool, use 4 ounces of alum (3 for fine wool), 1 ounce of cream of tartar, and 4 gallons of soft water.

Boil a little of the water and dissolve the alum and cream of tartar in it. Start heating the remaining water, mixing in the mordant. When the water becomes lukewarm, add the wool. Slowly heat the water to boiling. Then lower the heat and simmer the water and wool for one hour. Let the mordant bath cool, then remove the wool, or let it soak in the solution overnight.

After it has soaked and cooled, pull the skein out of the bath, squeeze it gently, roll it in a towel to remove more water, and hang it in a shady spot to dry.

If you will be storing the mordanted wool, tag it with the date and the mordant used.

Chrome (potassium dichromate): Chrome warms the hue of colors, enhancing yellows and reds and muting greens.

The process here is much the same as with alum, but chrome is very light-sensitive, so the solution and the yarn must be kept out of the light. Because of this sensitivity, wool mordanted with chrome should be dyed immediately. Storage carries the possibility that light might affect the yarn and result in uneven dyeing.

For 1 pound of wool, use ½ ounce of chrome, ¾ ounce of cream of tartar, and 4 gallons of water.

Boil a little of the water and dissolve the chemicals in it. Stir it into the remaining water. Cover the pot with a lid and heat the solution. When it is lukewarm, add the wool. Bring the solution just to a boil, then turn down the heat and simmer everything for ¾ to 1½ hours, depending on the coarseness and thickness of the wool. Every now and then move the wool in the solution with a stirring rod.

At the end of the simmering period, let the solution cool, remove the skeins, and gently squeeze the water out of them. Rinse in cool water, then squeeze it and roll it in a towel to remove moisture. Keep the yarn wrapped in the towel until you are ready to add it to the dye bath.

Tin (stannous chloride): Tin brightens most colors, but it is harsh on fibers and can make them brittle. After mordanting, it is best to rinse the yarn in soapy water.

Follow the same procedure as for chrome mordanting, using ½ ounce of tin and ½ ounce of cream of tartar or oxalic acid crystals. Dissolve the cream of tartar or oxalic acid crystals in a little boiling water, add that to the remaining water, then add the tin to the solution.

When simmering is complete, rinse the yarn in warm, soapy water, then in warm, clear water, then in slightly cooler, clear water, and once more in a slightly soapy solution.

Tin can be added directly to the dye bath to add brilliance to the color of the wool. Appropriately, this is called blooming. If you want

GREENS

agrimony
angelica
barberry
bayberry
betony
coltsfoot
comfrey
dock
fennel
foxglove
goldenrod
horsetail
marjoram
mullein
rosemary
sage
salsify
sunflower
tansy
uva-ursi
weld
yarrow

ORANGES

bloodroot
chicory
golden marguerite
madder
sunflower
weld

PINKS

bloodroot
pokeweed
sorrel
woad

PURPLES

blackberry
geranium
grape
lady's bedstraw

165

DYES FROM HERBS—continued

REDS

dandelion
dock
hops
lady's bedstraw
madder
pokeweed
potentilla
St.-John's-wort
sweet woodruff

RUSTS

pokeweed
safflower

TANS

barberry
onion
Oregon grape
raspberry
sunflower
sweet woodruff
uva-ursi

YELLOWS

agrimony
barberry
broom
chamomile
dandelion
dock
fennel
fenugreek
golden marguerite
goldenrod
grindelia
horseradish
lady's bedstraw
onion
safflower
saffron
sage
St.-John's-wort
salsify
sunflower
tansy
yarrow

to try this, add 2 teaspoons of tin dissolved in water to the bath 20 minutes before dying is complete.

Iron (ferrous sulfate): Iron grays the color of yarn and so is called a saddener. Rather than making a mordant solution, you add the iron to the dye bath at the end of the dyeing process.

Use ½ ounce or less of iron and 1 ounce of cream of tartar. Dissolve both together in boiling water. When you've finished dyeing your wool, pull it out of the bath while you stir in the iron/cream of tartar solution. Put the wool back in the bath and simmer for 20 to 40 minutes, depending on the color you want.

Iron also is hard on wool, so rinse the skeins two or three times. Squeeze out the water and dry the yarn in the shade.

Other options: A few herbs, such as tea, sumac, and black walnut, contain their own mordant (usually a tannin). With these dyes you will not need to go through the mordanting procedure unless you want to vary the shade of the dye somewhat.

Besides the mordants, you can either acidify or alkalize the dye pot, often affecting the color greatly, say from red to blue. Use vinegar to acidify and clear ammonia to alkalize.

A shortcut in mordanting: To save work, time, pots, and water, simply add the mordant directly to the dye bath. This can be done with all mordants and all dye baths. The limitation is that you will only get one color out of the bath. When using premordanted wool, you can put skeins with different mordants into one dye bath and get different shades of color.

THE DYE BATH

Once you have finished preparing the yarns to be dyed, you can begin working with the herbs. Many herbs can be used fresh or dried, but you will usually obtain brighter colors with fresh herbs, and you will probably enjoy working with them more.

Harvesting herbs: Plant material should be harvested when it is at its peak in order to obtain the brightest colors. Gather flowers when they are coming into full bloom and berries when they are ripe. Roots are best harvested in the fall, leaves in the spring. Bark should be harvested in the spring also, but if you let the spring pass without harvesting, bark taken in the fall will also produce nice dyes.

Remember, all herbs are not created equal. The amount of color they contain varies depending on environmental conditions and the season in which the plants are harvested. A person using plants grown along the coast of Massachusetts will obtain very different

(continued on page 171)

Bloodroot

Madder

Woad

Calendula

White
Yarrow

Agrimony

Scotch
Broom

Yellow
Yarrow

Indigo

Indigo

Uva-Ursi

Golden Marguerite

*Variegated
Elderberry*

DYES FROM HERBS—continued

colors from someone in the mountains of Virginia who makes dyes from the same species.

Quantities: With some experience you will know exactly how much plant material to use, but as a general guideline, collect 1 peck of plant material to dye 1 pound of yarn. With nut hulls, wood, bark, or berries, use 1 pound; and with roots, ½ pound. It is always safer to have a little more than a little less.

For each pound of wool, cotton, or linen, use 4 to 4½ gallons of soft water to prepare the dye bath.

Preparing the bath: Now it is time to chop leaves, stems, or roots; separate the petals from the flowers; or break up the nut hulls, wood, or bark to ready them for the dye bath. Preparation varies somewhat from herb to herb. Several good books are available with specific dye recipes (see the Bibliography), but the following guidelines will get you started:

Tough leaves, roots, nut hulls, and bark: These should be soaked overnight in 2 gallons of water. On the next day, strain the liquid and save it. Put the plant matter in another 2 gallons of water. Bring to a boil, then simmer for one hour. (Bark may take a little longer.) Strain out the plant matter and combine the two quantities of water.

Flowers, fruits, and tender leaves: Because these plant parts are delicate and easily damaged, they don't need any soaking at all. Place them in 4 to 4½ gallons of water; bring to a boil; and then simmer for 30 minutes to 1 hour, until the material has given up its color. Strain out the herbs.

THE DYEING PROCESS

After all the preparation, you are finally ready to dye your yarns, and this is where it gets exciting. The stark fibers soon will bloom with nature's colors.

Dyeing: If your yarn is dry, soak it for about an hour in lukewarm water before dyeing. Then place it in the dye bath, which should also be lukewarm, and slowly raise the temperature to a simmer. Move the yarn around in the bath with a glass or wooden rod and simmer for about one hour. Dyes made from flowers may take only about a half hour, while dyes from bark and roots may take up to two hours. Pull the yarn from the bath every now and then to check on the color. Dyeing is complete when you are happy with the color. Remember, the color of the yarn will get lighter as it dries, so leave it in the dye bath until its color is a little darker than what you want.

If the bath gets low during the dyeing process, lift out the wool and add water of the same temperature until the original level is reached. Replace the skein and continue dyeing.

WOOL-HANDLING TIPS

Handle wool carefully. Stirring and drastic temperature changes can cause shrinkage and matting of the fibers.

1. *Never agitate wool.* Never stir the dye pot—poke. Lift and turn wool gently. Always have plenty of water around the yarn so the yarn swims and dives freely, without help.

2. *Never shock wool by fast temperature changes.* When transferring wool from one pot of water to another in mordanting or dyeing, the temperatures of the water should be close. During the rinsing process, cool wool gradually by rinsing it in successively cooler baths of water. Also, when raising the temperature of the mordant or dye bath, do it slowly.

3. *Do not hang saturated wool.* When lifting wool from the mordant, dye, or rinse, do not hold it over the water.

4. *Do not wring or twist wool.* Squeeze it gently to remove the water.

DYES FROM HERBS—continued

DYEING TIPS

- You do not have to cover the dye pot with a lid except when using chrome. However, covering your pots does prevent steam from escaping and helps to contain any odor.

- Dye the entire amount of yarn needed for a project in one dye bath. You won't be able to produce the exact same shade again.

- If you don't work in 1-pound quantities, ¼-pound skeins are easy to work with. For the mordant and dye recipes given in this entry, use one-quarter the amount of ingredients.

- Adding white wine vinegar to the water at the rinse stage (about ¼ cup per gallon) helps to soften wool.

When you have finished with one skein, don't throw that dye bath away! You won't have used up all of the color in it, so go ahead and throw in another skein.

Rinsing: The dyed skein must be rinsed a few times in waters of successively cooler temperatures. The first rinse bath should be the same temperature as the dye bath. Continue to rinse the skein until the rinse water remains clear. Remove the yarn, squeeze out the water, and roll it in a towel to absorb more of the remaining moisture. Hang the skein in a shady spot to dry.

Simultaneous dyeing: You will be more successful with some herbs if you create the dye bath and dye the yarn at the same time—hence the name of this procedure, "simultaneous dyeing." Rather than brew a dye bath, strain out the plant material, then add the yarn, wrap the plant material in a thin cotton bag, and simmer it with the yarn. This procedure is used with delicate plant parts like flowers.

KEEPING RECORDS

Before you start to knit, weave, or embroider with your beautifully colored yarns, you ought to record what you've done. Dyeing does involve experimentation, given the great number of variables possible: different stands of herbs, different mordants, different methods. Testing and recording allows you to keep track of what you've done so that you can repeat it or try to vary it in some way. Of course, because so many variables do exist in this process, you won't ever get exactly the same shade twice, but you can gain some control over what you do if you keep records.

Testing: How well the color of the yarn holds up under bright light is certainly an important quality of your dye. One way to test this is to hang a set of yarn samples in a south-facing window and keep a second set covered in a notebook. After a month, compare the two sets. Or you might want to wrap the yarn around a file card and keep half of it covered and expose the other half to direct sun. Again, after a month uncover all the yarn and check the results.

Recording: You actually shouldn't save this step until the very last. Take notes throughout all of the stages of preparation and dyeing, beginning with the gathering of herbs. In your dye notebook, record the herbs used and when and where they were gathered. Make note of the amounts of plant material used, the type and amount of mordant, the quantity of water, and so forth. Record the time spent soaking and simmering the plant material to create the dye bath and the time spent simmering the yarn in the dye. Note the results of your light test, and finally write in any remarks you might have: pleasures, displeasures, surprises. Beside each entry, you might want to attach a snippet of dyed yarn.

A SAMPLING OF HERBS FOR DYEING

Herb	Color	Plant Part	Fresh or Dried	Mordant	Color Fastness
Agrimony (*Agrimonia Eupatoria*)	Brassy yellow	Leaves, stems	F	Alum	Very good
	Gold	Leaves, stems	F	Chrome	Very good
Barberry (*Berberis vulgaris*)	Yellow	Inner bark	F or D	None	Good
	Yellow	Roots, bark	F or D	Tin	Good
	Dark green	All	F or D	Iron	Very good
	Tan	All	F or D	Alum	Very good
Betony (*Stachys officinalis*)	Chartreuse	All	F	Alum	Good
Bloodroot (*Sanguinaria canadensis*)	Orange	Roots	F	None	Good
	Rust	Roots	F	Alum	Good
	Reddish pink	Roots	F	Tin	Good
Broom (*Cytisus scoparius*)	Green-yellow	Tops	F	Alum	Good
	Bright yellow	Flowers	F	Alum	Good
	Deep yellow	Flowers	F	Chrome	Good
Chamomile, Roman (*Chamaemelum nobile*)	Yellow	Flowers	F	Chrome	Good
	Bright yellow	Flowers	F	Alum	
Comfrey (*Symphytum officinale*)	Brown	Leaves	F	Iron	
Dandelion (*Taraxacum officinale*)	Soft yellow	Flowers	F	Alum	Good
	Yellow	Flowers	F	Tin	Good
	Magenta	All	F	None	
Dock (*Rumex* spp.)	Deep yellow	Roots	F	Alum	Good
	Red	Young leaves	F	Chrome	
	Gold	Late leaves	F	Chrome	
	Yellow	Leaves	F	Alum	
	Dark green	Leaves	F	Iron	
Elderberry (*Sambucus* spp.)	Violet	Berries	F	Alum	Good
	Blue-gray	Berries	F	Tin	Good
	Blue	Berries	F	Chrome	Good
	Soft yellow	Leaves	F	Alum	
	Deep yellow	Leaves	F	Chrome	
	Gray	Bark	F	Iron	
Fennel (*Foeniculum vulgare*)	Mustard yellow	Flowers, leaves	F	Alum	Fair
	Golden brown	Flowers, leaves	F	Chrome	Good
	Brown	Tops	F	Iron	
Feverfew (*Chrysanthemum Parthenium*)	Greenish yellow	Leaves, stems	F	Chrome	

(continued)

Herb	Color	Plant Part	Fresh or Dried	Mordant	Color Fastness
Foxglove (*Digitalis purpurea*)	Chartreuse	Flowers	F	Alum	Good
Golden marguerite (*Anthemis tinctoria*)	Yellow-buff	Flowers	F or D	Alum	Good
	Golden orange	Flowers	F or D	Chrome	Excellent
	Yellow	Flowers	F or D	Tin	Excellent
Goldenrod (*Solidago* spp.)	Yellow-green	All	F	Iron	Fair
	Yellow	Flowers	F	Alum	Good
	Gold	Flowers	F	Chrome	Good
	Bright yellow	Flowers	F	Tin	Good
Lady's bedstraw (*Galium verum*)	Red	Roots	F or D	Alum	Good
	Purplish red	Roots	F or D	Chrome	Good
	Plum	Roots	F or D	Iron	Good
	Dull yellow	Tops	F	Alum	
Lavender cotton (*Santolina Chamaecyparissus*)	Gold	Leaves, flowers	F	Chrome	Good
	Yellow	Leaves, flowers	F	Alum	Good
Madder (*Rubia tinctorum*)	Orange	Roots	F	Tin	Excellent
	Lacquer red	Roots	F	Alum	Excellent
	Garnet red	Roots	F	Chrome	Excellent
	Brown	Roots		Iron	
Marigold (*Tagetes* spp.) (*Calendula* spp.)	Gold	Flowers	F or D	Chrome	Good
	Yellow-tan	Flowers	F or D	Alum	Good
Marjoram (*Origanum Majorana*)	Green	Whole tops	F	Alum	
	Olive green	Whole tops	F	Chrome	
Nettle (*Urtica dioica*)	Greenish yellow	All	F	Alum	
	Tan	All	F	Chrome	
Onion (*Allium Cepa*)	Tan-brown	Red skins	F or D	Tin	Good
	Gold	Red skins	F or D	Chrome	Good
	Reddish orange	Red skins	F or D	Alum	Good
	Dark tan	Red skins	F or D	Chrome	Good
	Burnt orange	Yellow skins	F or D	Alum	Good
	Brass	Yellow skins	F or D	Chrome	Good
	Yellow	Yellow skins	F or D	Alum	Good
	Bright orange	Yellow skins	F or D	Tin	Good
	Brown	Yellow skins	F or D	Iron	Good

Herb	Color	Plant Part	Fresh or Dried	Mordant	Color Fastness
Oregon grape root (*Mahonia Aquifolium*)	Purplish blue	Fruit	F	Alum	
	Buff-brown	Roots	F	Alum	
	Tan	Roots	F	Chrome	
	Khaki yellow	All	F	Alum	
Plantain (*Plantago major*)	Dull gold	All	F	Alum	Good
	Camel	All	F	Chrome	Good
Pokeweed (*Phytolacca americana*)	Red	Fruit	F	Alum	Fair
	Brown	Fruit	d	Alum	Fair
	Red	Fruit	F	Tin	Fair
	Rust	Fruit	F or D	Chrome	Good
	Pink	Fruit	F	Alum	Good
Potentilla (*Potentilla verna*)	Brown-red	Roots	F	Chrome	
	Purple-red	Roots	F	Iron	
Rosemary (*Rosmarinus officinalis*)	Yellow-green	Leaves, flowers	F	Alum	Good
Safflower (*Carthamus tinctorius*)	Yellow	Flowers	F or D	Alum	Good
	Brass	Flowers	F or D	Iron	Good
	Rust	Flowers	F or D	Tin	Good
Sage (*Salvia officinalis*)	Yellow-buff	Tops	F	Alum	
	Deep yellow	Tops	F	Chrome	
	Green-gray	Tops	F	Iron	
St.-John's-wort (*Hypericum perforatum*)	Medium yellow	Tops	F	Alum	
	Bright yellow	Tops	F	Chrome	
	Orange-red	Flowers	F	Tin	
	Brown-red	Stems	F	Alum	
Sweet woodruff (*Galium odoratum*)	Tan	Stems, leaves	F	Alum	Good
	Red	Roots	F	Alum	
Tansy (*Tanacetum vulgare*)	Yellowish green	Young leaves	F	Alum	Fair
	Greenish yellow	Flowers	F	Alum	Fair
	Dark green	Tops	F	Iron	
Uva Ursi (*Arctostaphylos Uva-ursi*)	Camel	Leaves	F	None	Good
	Green	All	F	Alum and iron	
Woad (*Isatis tinctoria*)	Blue	Young leaves	F	None	Good
	Pink	Young leaves	F	Alum	
Yarrow (*Achillea Millefolium*)	Yellow	Flowers	F	Alum	Good
	Olive green	All	F	Iron	

ECHINACEA

Echinacea angustifolia   **Compositae**

With its delicate, pastel petals, this pretty, little, daisylike flower is not the type of plant you would think to grow for its medicinal applications. Yet during the 1920s, echinacea was one of this country's most popular "plant drugs."

DESCRIPTION

Also known as the purple coneflower, the Sampson root, and, in some circles, the Kansas niggerhead, the echinacea is a lovely perennial that resembles a black-eyed Susan. Its stout, sturdy stems are covered with tiny, bristly hairs, and its roots are long and black. (See photo on page 274.)

Flowers: Composite flower head, solitary, 3–4 in. across; cone-shaped center composed of numerous tiny, purple, tubular florets; surrounded by 12–20 spreading purple ray florets.

Leaves: Pale to dark green; lower leaves ovate, pointed, coarsely toothed, 3–8 in. long; upper leaves shorter and narrower.

Height: 1–2 ft.

FLOWERING

Mid- to late summer.

RANGE

Native to the prairies from Texas to southern Canada.

HABITAT

Prairies and open woods, at roadsides, and in fields.

HISTORY

According to Melvin Gilmore, an American anthropologist who studied native American medicine in the early part of this century, the echinacea was used as a remedy by the Indians more than any other plant in the plains states. All the Indians used the plant to treat snakebite and the bites of poisonous insects. Native Americans also used the juice of the plant to bathe burns and added the juice to the water sprinkled on coals during traditional "sweats," taken for purification purposes. According to *Growing and Using the Healing Herbs* by Gaea and Shandor Weiss, some Indians used echinacea juice to make their hands, feet, and mouths insensitive to heat in order to hold, walk on, or "swallow" hot coals and fire during ceremonies.

Throughout the development of this country, herbalists have extolled the virtues of echinacea. And at one time it was actually prepared and packaged as a drug. In 1885, Dr. H. C. F. Meyer, who had learned of the plant's therapeutic value from the Indians, attracted the attention of Lloyd Brothers of Cincinnati, a pharmaceuticals manufacturer. Shortly thereafter, the firm introduced several echinacea-based anti-infective agents. By 1920, echinacea was the firm's most popular drug plant. With the advent of new and more effective anti-infectives in the 1930s, however, echinacea fell from popularity among drug companies.

USES

To this day, herbalists continue to grow and use echinacea for its healing qualities.

Medicinal: The American Indians are credited with discovering which part of the plant yielded its medicinal properties: the roots. They contain a substance called caffeic acid glycoside, which reacts with other substances in the body's cells and facilitates the wound-healing process. In folk medicine, this unidentified substance was used as a "blood purifier" to cure a wide variety of ailments: rheumatism, streptococcus infections, bee stings, poisonous snakebites, dyspepsia, tumors, syphilis, gangrene, eczema, hemorrhoids, and a host of pains and wounds.

While it is not found in any modern commercial drugs, many American herbalists still regard echinacea as one of the very best blood purifiers, as well as an effective antibiotic. According to naturopathic doctor Michael Tierra, echinacea neutralizes acid conditions in the blood characteristic of lymphatic stagnation. Dr. Paul Lee, founder of the Platonic Academy of Herbal Studies, describes echinacea as "our leading herb on the list of immuno-stimulants."

Ornamental: If you're not interested in walking on hot coals or otherwise healing yourself with its roots, you can simply enjoy the beauty of echinaceas in your yard or garden. They have a very slight fragrance and propagate into beautiful, meadowlike beds, if you let them. Because they are easy to care for, can stand hot weather and humidity, and provide a profusion of blooms, echinaceas are suitable for most North American outdoor gardens. They work well in perennial and cut-flower gardens; the natural wild species are lovely additions to native-plant gardens and informal areas.

CULTIVATION

Echinaceas are hardy plants and will grow in any ordinary gardening soil, but they prosper in soil treated with compost and rock phosphate in the spring.

Echinaceas are easy to start from seed, provided you wait until the air temperature is about 70°F before you sow. In the garden, echinaceas should be spaced about 1½ to 2 feet apart. Weeds should be kept in check through mulching and shallow surface cultivation; dying flower heads should be snipped off. Normally the plants do not need staking, since they tolerate hot, humid temperatures so well. While the soil needs to be moderately moist, you should not have to water unless there is an extended dry spell. (If you live in the Southwest, you will need to water periodically.)

If you experience cold, dry winters, you might want to cover the plants with a bed of hay or evergreens to prevent any instance of root damage, but this is not absolutely essential. In most cases, prospering plants are hardy and will survive winters unattended. Every four or five years, it's a good idea to dig up echinaceas, divide them, and replant them in newly fertilized soil.

Pests and diseases: Leaf spot or Japanese beetles could infest your plants. (See the entry Growing Herbs for information on controlling pests and diseases.)

Harvesting and storage: If you intend to use the roots for herbal healing purposes, it is best to wait until after the plant has endured several hard frosts and begins to die back. The root should then be cleaned and dried. The crown of the plant can be replanted after the root has been harvested, but the new plant will not be as medicinally potent.

Echinacea purpurea

GROWING CONDITIONS

- Plant hardiness zones 3–9.
- Fertile, well-drained soil.
- Full sun to light shade.

177

ELDERBERRY

Sambucus spp.   **Caprifoliaceae**

One of the human race's earliest plant companions (found in Stone Age sites), the elderberry has developed reputations for great powers of good—one physician was said to tip his hat in respect every time he passed the plant—as well as great powers of evil—in some parts of the world, no prudent carpenter would make a cradle of elderberry wood for fear of bringing harm to the baby.

DESCRIPTION

The name elderberry (or elder) encompasses perhaps 13 species of deciduous shrubs native to North America and several venerable European shrubs that followed settlers here. (See photos on pages 170 and 376.)

Flowers: White or whitish, wheel-shaped, to ¼ in. in diameter; in large terminal clusters.

Leaves: Odd pinnate, opposite; leaflets toothed.

Fruit: ¼ in. juicy, berrylike drupes of amber, red, black, purple, or blue.

Height: To 12 ft.; more treelike species to 50 ft.

FLOWERING

Summer.

RANGE

Native to North America, Europe, western Asia, and North Africa.

HISTORY

The elderberry has been involved in human history for centuries, and one story suggests that it takes its name from a unique medicinal dimension. The generic name *Sambucus* may come from the Greek *sambuke,* a musical instrument, supposedly made from elderberry wood. For centuries the plant has had the reputation of healing the body, but in the elderberry's golden age, it made music to heal the spirit.

During its long association with humanity, the elderberry's traditions have become an incredible jumble of conflicting currents. It provided the wood for Christ's cross; it was the home of the goddess Freya. If seen in a dream, it meant illness was on the way; it was such a healthful plant that seventeenth-century herbalist John Evelyn called it a remedy "against all infirmities whatever." It would ward off witches if gathered on the last day of April and put up on the windows and doors of houses; it was very attractive to witches and thus should be avoided after dark.

Elderberries worked their way into every aspect of living from dyeing hair black (perhaps one of the original Grecian formulas) to showing berries just at the right time to signal the beginning of wheat sowing. Shakespeare had something to say about it. One of his characters called it "the stinking elder." The Shakers used it as a medicinal herb. The wood of old stems, hard and fine grained, was prized by the makers of mathematical instruments. The list could go on for pages; elderberries stand in our gardens as old friends.

USES

Medicinal: Elderberry shrubs are not the place for the amateur herbal enthusiast to experiment. They contain cyanogenic glucosides, substances that release cyanide, and an unidentified cathartic, found primarily in the leaves and roots of some species.

The danger comes mainly from the roots, stems, and leaves, says

Dr. Kenneth Lampe, author of the *AMA Handbook of Poisonous Injurious Plants*. (Children got sick from playing with elderbei whistles or blowguns.) *Ripe, cooked* berries are harmless, as any fan of elderberry jelly and pie knows. Lampe says the flowers are "probably nontoxic" and that "limited amounts" of raw fruit are "generally considered to have no adverse effect."

Turning to the flowers then, the blooms of the sweet elder and the European elder were listed in the *U.S. Pharmacopoeia* from 1831 to 1905. Dr. John Gathercoal, who studied natural medicines at the University of Illinois in the 1940s, explained that a strained, sterilized tea was used as a mild stimulant, carminative, and diaphoretic. For specific recipes the herbalist John Lust has suggested making elder-flower tea from sweet elders with 1 teaspoon for a cup of water; from European elders with 2 tablespoons of flowers per cup (which he has recommended drinking up to three times a day). Evidence that the tea has medicinal benefits is a bit thin, but there seem to be no indications that moderate consumption is harmful.

Culinary: Elderberry's tart, deep purple berries are used in jams, jellies, chutneys, preserves, and wine. The dried blossoms are used in tea blends.

Available commercially: Dried blossoms.

Substitute: Black currants or serviceberries (Juneberries) for the berries.

Ornamental: "Elders are seen to best advantage in extensive

CHEF TIP

Add 1 cup of elderberries to pear or apple pie filling.

ELDERBERRY—continued

CHANGING TIMES

"It is needless to write any description of this, since every boy that plays with a pop-gun will not mistake another tree for the Elder," wrote Culpeper, the maverick British herbalist of the seventeenth century. He was referring to the centuries-old tradition of cutting young branches from the elderberry and poking out the cottony center to leave a rough tube, perfect for whistles and blowguns. Children now and then got sick from holding the elderberry branches in their mouths, but this didn't stop them. Only modern merchandising seems to be doing that; now that children are armed with simulated steel guns that light up or beep and whir, the elderberry is falling into disuse and needs an explicit description.

landscapes where they can be massed and viewed from some distance," advises the New York Botanical Garden's *Encyclopedia of Plants* (sounding not at all startled by the idea of growing them). "They are generally too vigorous and coarse for small properties; they do not lend themselves to the ornamentation of intimate gardens."

Cosmetic: Elder-flower water was one of those traditional half-homespun elegances that belonged on a lady's dressing table along with potpourris and lace-edged handkerchiefs and tortoiseshell combs. Its virtues were vague, but wide-ranging, dealing with all the offenses to femininity, including sunburn and freckles. For a touch of yesteryear, toss a handful of dried elderberry flowers into bathwater. An old-style herbalist would assure the bather that the flowers would soften the skin and serve as an excellent remedy for irritable nerves.

Dye: Yellow and violet dyes can be made from the leaves and berries. (See the entry Dyes from Herbs for specific information.)

False pretense: Although hardly a use to recommend, for several hundred years, various sorts of scoundrels added elderberry juice to cheap port to make it look and taste more expensive. In Portugal, the practice reached scandalous proportions and was outlawed so zealously that it was illegal even to grow elderberries. The adulterators were somewhat vindicated around the turn of the century when a sailor remarked to a doctor that a drunken binge on (so-called) fine port was a great remedy for rheumatism. Instead of dismissing this as just another farfetched excuse, doctors investigated the claim and began prescribing elderberry juice in port. It may not have been necessary to drink as much as a sailor to achieve the benefits. Modern medicine does not substantiate the claims.

CULTIVATION

One northwestern herb grower sounded incredulous when asked whether he had ever grown elderberries. Then he remembered his manners and pulled himself together, gently replying that elderberries were not uncommon in the wild and just collecting the berries or leaves is an option.

Yes, collecting certainly is an option for many people and a very pleasant one. However, gardeners have done far stranger things than grow elderberries, and a number of landscapes include a lush informal clump of the shrubs. In Europe, elderberries are beloved ornamentals, says Holly Shimizu, curator of the National Herb Garden in Washington, D.C. She reminisces about working in a botanical garden in Belgium where the elderberry collection was quite extensive. Named horticultural varieties are available for several species.

One of the easiest ways to propagate an elderberry shrub is from suckers, says Shimizu. The plants sucker freely, to put it mildly. They will also grow from seed or cuttings, both hardwood and leafy.

Shimizu has her sweet elderberry in rich, moist soil where it does well, growing prolifically. However, it doesn't require such luxurious treatment. The plants seem to be more vigorous in wetter rather than drier soil, but they forgive a lot of shortcomings in their location and their care.

Their vigor can be a problem. Shimizu's plant relentlessly sends up shoots that must be pulled out, and she characterizes it as an "extremely high maintenance plant." It would be good for a wild garden, she says. "It's not suited for an area of the garden with a lot of little treasures nearby." If it sprawls, chop it back. It will take severe pruning.

Harvesting and storage: There are modern harvesting techniques, which are simple, and old techniques, which are not. Cutting branches or, perish the thought, chopping down the whole plant, presented serious dangers according to many folk traditions. In Denmark, the *Hylde-Mkoer* (elder-tree mother), a spirit, lived in elderberry plants and would haunt anybody who cut one down. The British, however, discovered that the spirit was willing to bargain. Take off your hat and kneel, one source advises, and try to sound respectful: "Give me some of thy wood and I will give thee some of mine when it grows in the forest." In this system, silence meant consent. (It is presumed that consent was not uncommon.)

For anyone modern enough to approach an elder without permission or with a hat on, British herbalist Maude Grieve describes brash harvesting techniques. (She also describes the polite ones in a delightful section of *A Modern Herbal.*)

For flowers: Pick the flowers when they're in full bloom. They can be used fresh, "pickled" by the addition of about 10 percent common salt, or dried. She recommends drying them by stirring them in a heated copper pan or by placing in a cool oven with the door open.

For bark: Strip the bark from young trees in autumn and dry at moderate heat. She also has cured bark in the sun, taking it indoors at night. (Be reminded that the bark contains toxins.)

For leaves: She collects them only in June and July on clear mornings after the dew has dried. The leaves can be used fresh or dried. (Be reminded that the leaves contain toxins.)

ELDERBERRY SPECIES

Sambucus caerulea: Tall, sometimes 30 ft. high, occasionally 50 ft.; five to seven leaflets. Yellowish flowers in airy, mounded bunches. Blue-black berries that look paler because of a natural waxy coating. Native from British Columbia to California, but adaptable. Reported hardy in southern New England.

S. canadensis: 4–10 ft. high; usually seven leaflets. White flowers in flat-topped bunches. Deep purple or black berries. In the wild, sweet elder often grows in moist soil. From Nova Scotia to Florida, west to Manitoba, Kansas, and Texas.

S. Ebulus: Grows to about 3 ft. and dies back in winter; five to nine leaflets. Cream-colored flowers with a pinkish tinge and purple anthers. Black berries. Native to Europe, western Asia, and North Africa, but has been found growing from Quebec to New Jersey.

S. nigra: Reaches 30 ft. under ideal conditions; leaves usually have five leaflets.

GROWING CONDITIONS

- Moist, fertile soil.
- Full sun to partial shade.

ELECAMPANE

Inula Helenium   **Compositae**

Known primarily for its bitterness and pungency, elecampane was widely used by the ancient Romans as a cure for postbanquet indigestion. "Let no day pass without eating some of the roots of elecampane . . . to help digestion, to expel melancholy, and to cause mirth," the Roman scholar Pliny wrote many centuries ago. If it promotes mirth, as Pliny suggested, perhaps people of today should consider sampling this herb.

DESCRIPTION

A tall, striking perennial plant, the elecampane is commonly known as the wild sunflower. It is sturdy and almost unbranching, the stout, round stem coarse and woolly. (See photo on page 378.)

Flowers: Resemble sunflowers; terminal composite flower heads, 3–4 in. across; numerous, slender, yellow ray florets surround center of disk florets.

Leaves: Toothed, bristly on upper surface, velvety on under surface; basal leaves elliptical to oblong, to 2 ft. long, stalked; stem leaves pointed, oblong-ovate, heart-shaped at bases, stalkless.

Fruit: Achenes; brown, quadrangular, with a ring of pale reddish hairs—the pappus.

Height: 4–6 ft.

FLOWERING

Summer months.

RANGE

Native to central and northern Europe and northwest Asia; naturalized in some parts of North America, from Nova Scotia to North Carolina and westward to Missouri.

HABITAT

Damp soils near ruins, along roadsides and woodland edges. Provided with a moist, shady spot, this plant will grow well in any garden soil.

HISTORY

There are many fables about the origin of this herb's name. Its classical Latin name *inula* is a derivation of the Greek word *helenion*. Interestingly, the Latin variation, *helenium,* is now applied to the same species. Some say *helenium* originated with Helen of Troy, who is said to have had a handful of the plant when Paris stole her away. Another legend describes the plant springing from the goddess Helena's tears. A third postulates that it was named after the island Helena, where the best plants grew.

In Rome, ancient poets and writers specializing in agriculture and natural history were well-acquainted with elecampane. The acclaimed ancient physician Galen brought this mysterious medicine of Rome into brief focus when he wrote that elecampane root is "good for the passions of the hucklebone." Perhaps this is what prompted Pliny to praise it for causing mirth.

A plant that supposedly blossomed in the domain of the Roman gods, survived the Norman Conquest, and was used extensively during the Middle Ages, elecampane has earned many nicknames—from elfdock, elfwort, and the wild sunflower to horseheal and scabwort. Scabwort came from the herb's alleged effectiveness in healing scabs on sheep. Horseheal developed in much the same way: Early veterinarians believed it cured many ailments suffered by horses.

USES

Planting elecampane in a garden, to grow proudly alongside the geraniums and the daisies, is perfectly natural. But it's likely that most people don't realize that it's also perfectly natural for this herb to be sitting next to the Vicks and the throat lozenges in the medicine cabinet.

Medicinal: Herbalists throughout the world have used elecampane's thickened root for treating diseases of the chest. Rarely used alone, the dried, crushed root is said to be an effective ingredient in

many compound medicines.

American Indian herbalists found the plant to be particularly useful in treating bronchial and other lung ailments. One Indian remedy for such problems was made by combining a half-pound each of elecampane root, spikenard root, and comfrey root. The roots were mashed well, combined with a gallon of water and boiled down to a quart. The liquid was poured off into a half-gallon container, and 8 ounces of alcohol and a pint and a half of honey were added. The Indians recommended a teaspoonful of the brew every two hours.

In China, where the native species of the plant is known as *hsuan-fu-hua,* elecampane is used in the form of syrup, lozenges, and candy as a soothing treatment for bronchitis and asthma.

Besides relieving lung problems, elecampane is also thought to aid in soothing stomach cramps and other digestive ailments. Mixing the powdered root with sugar or steeping it in tea is believed to help regulate menstrual cycles. The root also works as a diuretic and at one time was used as a treatment for water retention, then known as dropsy.

Elecampane can still be used as a remedy for coughs and other minor respiratory ailments. To make a tea for this purpose, simmer an ounce of the root in a pint of water, and let cool.

Culinary: The rootstock has been traditionally used as a flavoring for sweets; it has also been candied and eaten as a sweet itself.

Ornamental: While it has traditionally been a favorite in herb gardens, elecampane can also make a striking addition to many types of outdoor gardens and natural habitats.

Craft: Elecampane can be striking in dried arrangements, too. Cut the flower heads when the plant reaches its brown stage.

CULTIVATION

Elecampane is easily propagated from offshoots or 2-inch root cuttings, taken from a mature plant during the fall. Cover the cuttings with moist, sandy soil, and keep them in a room with an air temperature that remains between 50° and 60°F. The roots will develop into plants by early spring; make sure you set them out after all danger of frost has passed.

The plant prefers a clay loam that is moist and well drained, and a slightly shaded locale. If you intend to harvest the plant's roots for medicinal purposes, do so in the fall of the plant's second growing year, after two hard frosts.

GROWING CONDITIONS

- Plant hardiness zone 3.
- Moist, moderately fertile soil.
- Full to light shade.

EPHEDRA

DESCRIPTION

Ephedras are among the oldest, most primitive plants. Related to horsetail (*Equisetum*), ginkgo (*Ginkgo*), and the conifers, they are gymnosperms or naked-seeded plants. Most species are shrubby plants that resemble stunted pine trees or plumed horsetails. Some grow upright, while others trail along the ground. They may be gray, reddish, or bright green, depending on the species. Their tough, jointed stalks and branches have no bark.

Flowers: Minute green blossoms.

Leaves: Scales or tufts attached to the nodes of the branches.

Fruit: Male fruits greenish cones; female fruits typically red berries.

Height: 5–36 in., depending upon the species.

FLOWERING

Early summer.

RANGE

The arid regions of the world. North American species are found in the southwestern United States and Mexico, with some species as far north as the Dakotas.

GROWING CONDITIONS

- Soil pH: alkaline.
- Dry soil.
- Full sun.

Ephedra spp.   Ephedraceae

The several members of this medically important genus go by the American names Mormon tea, squaw tea, cowboy tea, popotillo, and desert herb, and by the Chinese name *ma-huang.*

HISTORY

The Chinese species, *Ephedra major, E. sinica,* and *E. trifurca,* have been known in the Orient for over 5,000 years. Long valued as a decongestant, *ma-huang* has been the subject of much study. In the early part of this century, Chinese researchers isolated the substance ephedrine from the plant, and today China remains the principal supplier of this important asthma drug.

The American species contain only trace amounts of ephedrine, but these desert plants have nevertheless played a part in folk medicine. *E. nevadensis* was equally popular with the Indians and the settlers, who both attested to its health-giving properties.

USES

The most common use of the American species is in making a pleasant piney tea. In fact, the herb may have been called Mormon tea since it brews up into a tasty beverage that served as a substitute for the coffee and black tea scorned by the Mormons. A conflicting legend claims that the name refers to a Jack Mormon who, frequenting the bars and brothels of the West, concocted the tea as a cure for syphilis and gonorrhea. In fact, the tea was served in brothels in the 1800s.

Medicinal: The Chinese species contain much more ephedrine than the American species. It is present throughout the entire plant but is traditionally taken in the form of a tea made from the dry branches.

Attempts to extract the same drug from the American species have been disappointing, but weak as it is, Mormon tea is still considered a good decongestant, tonic, diuretic, and fever and cold medication. To make a medicinal tea, steep ½ ounce of the dried branches in 1 pint of boiling water for 5 to 20 minutes.

CULTIVATION

These plants aren't usually cultivated except in special botanical collections. The plants grow very slowly and are not easy to raise. Propagation is by division, seed, or layering.

You can collect ephedra at any time, in any season. Pick large branches and put them in a paper or burlap bag. Hang the bag near a heater or lay it in the sun until the stems are bone-dry.

EUCALYPTUS

Eucalyptus spp.   **Myrtaceae**

If you are a native of the Pacific Southwest, you've undoubtedly admired these graceful trees with their shimmering, silvery leaves and creamy bark more than once. But while they are lovely to look at, the many varieties of eucalyptus offer an abundance of practical uses as well—not the least of which is providing meals for the Australian koala bear.

HISTORY

Eucalyptus varieties—there are more than 500 species of *Eucalyptus*—constitute more than three-quarters of the vegetation on the Australian continent, and so their history in that country is rich and varied. The aborigines and early settlers of Australia ground and ate the roots of the more diminutive species and later discovered that "lerp" or "manna," a sugary secretion of parasites that infect some of the trees, made an excellent base for foods and beverages.

One of the most critical values of the trees was as a source of drinking water. The aborigines discovered that eucalypts (a name used to encompass all members of the genus) store water in their roots. A thirsty soul could dig up a length of root, blow vigorously into one end, and catch the liquid that bubbled out the other end. Ironically, many early settlers died of thirst when water was all around them, stored in eucalyptus roots.

Eucalypts made their world debut during the nineteenth century. As a source of hardwood timber, eucalypts also became important to the economies of many countries. In a few countries the blue gum tree (*E. globulus*) was pivotal in an unusual attack on malaria. Planted in mosquito-infested marshes, the trees soon dried the marshes through their heavy feeding, effectively killing the mosquitoes. The blue gum thus earned the name Australian fevertree.

USES

Medicinal: The Australian aborigines were probably the first to discover that eucalyptus oil, called eucalyptol, was very effective in certain medicinal applications. The oil, derived from the mature leaves, roots, and bark, is a colorless or pale yellow liquid with a camphoraceous odor and a spicy, cooling taste. It's an active germicide, possessing antiseptic and astringent qualities. A favorite cure among herbalists for abscesses and other skin ailments is a eucalyptus-leaf poultice. You can use the oil as an antibacterial, but don't apply it full strength; always dilute it with water, vegetable oil, or rubbing alcohol (no more than 2 teaspoons of the oil in a pint).

The most widely known medicinal use of eucalyptus oil is for respiratory ailments. Herbals recommend inhaling steam laced with

DESCRIPTION

There are more than 500 species of *Eucalyptus,* ranging from bushy, 5-ft. shrubs to towering, 480-ft. giants. The majority of eucalypts are evergreens, and all produce an oil with a strong, haunting fragrance. The most common and certainly the most recognizable among the eucalyptus species is the blue gum (*E. globulus*).

The bark of the blue gum is smooth and blue-gray in color; it peels off in thin strips as the tree matures to reveal a creamy trunk. The peeling occurs on the upper portions of the tree, leaving the base covered.

Flowers: Occur near leaf axils; in umbel-like groups of three or four; groups solitary or clustered; no sepals or petals; flower bud in two parts, upper part (opercullum) falls away during growth to reveal numerous stamens and style supported by the bud receptacle; depending on species, stamens may be white, cream, pink, yellow, orange, or red.

Leaves: Young leaves opposite, broad, stalkless, silvery bluish gray; mature leaves alternate, stalked, swordlike, thick, dark, lustrous green; 4–12 in. long.

Fruit: Capsules containing several seeds.

Height: To 480 ft.

RANGE

Native to Australia and Tasmania; cultivated in southern Europe, South Africa, Tahiti, India, Latin America, and in the United States in California and other southwestern states.

EUCALYPTUS—continued

the oil to relieve the symptoms of bronchitis, asthma, croup, and the like. Eucalyptus oil remains an effective expectorant and is used in many commercial lozenges, rubs, and liquids to clear mucus from the nose and lungs and to relieve upper respiratory distress.

You can make a simple eucalyptus infusion at home by steeping a handful of fresh or dried leaves for 20 minutes in a quart of boiling water. Breathe in the vapors of the steaming tea. The infusion can be drunk or used in a vaporizer.

Toxicity: Large doses can cause nausea, vomiting, diarrhea, and muscle spasms.

Aromatic: The refreshing fragrance of dried eucalyptus leaves adds interest to potpourris. The oil is used in both home-prepared and commercial air fresheners, deodorants, and insecticides; 1 teaspoon of oil in ½ pint of warm water, rubbed into the skin, makes a powerful insect repellent for both humans and animals.

Ornamental: Several species of eucalypts make excellent yard and garden trees, where climatic conditions are favorable. Varieties such as the silver dollar are attractive and produce fragrant blossoms that attract bees, a plus if you grow fruit trees as well. The blue gum makes a good shade tree, but its large limbs tend to break easily in high wind.

Cosmetic: An infusion of the leaves provides an antiseptic skin lotion. Eucalyptus can also be used in an herbal bath. (See the entries Lotions from Herbs and Bathing with Herbs for more information.)

Craft: It's usually the leafy branches of eucalypts that you think of adding to dried herb and flower arrangements, but consider also the branches of dried seedpods. Those *E. globulus* have a unique appearance and add an interesting and unusual touch to wreaths and arrangements.

CULTIVATION

If you want a eucalyptus in your yard, it's best to transplant a hardy young tree. Eucalypts transplant easily, and while they prefer a light loam, they will adapt to a wide variety of acid or alkaline soils. Eucalypts are heavy feeders, so it's wise not to place them too close to other plants that might suffer from nutrient depletion. They grow rapidly—even more quickly in areas where they have access to plenty of moisture. It's better to err on the side of underwatering, though, particularly in the case of indoor and greenhouse specimens; too much moisture makes the leaves blister. Pests are normally not a problem since the natural aromatic oils of eucalypts tend to repel insects. In the greenhouse, as outdoors, eucalypts prefer full sunlight and nighttime temperatures above 50°F.

GROWING CONDITIONS

- Plant hardiness zones 8–10.
- Soil pH: tolerates a wide range of pH.
- Light, loamy soil.
- Full sun.

EYEBRIGHT

Euphrasia officinalis   Scrophulariaceae

Herbalists suspect that the ancients knew of eyebright's healing powers because the name Euphrasia is of Greek origin, derived from *Euphrosyne* (gladness), the name of one of the three graces, who was characterized for her mirth and joy. It is believed that the plant acquired this name because of its reputation for curing eye ailments: It brought much gladness by preserving the eyesight of the sufferer.

HISTORY

In addition to its widespread use as an eye medication, eyebright has been used as a tea and a memory tonic, and in Queen Elizabeth's time, as an ale. In *Paradise Lost,* the poet Milton relates that the Archangel Michael used eyebright to cure Adam of the eye infliction suffered by his eating of the forbidden fruit.

USES

Medicinal: Although most herbals tout the use of eyebright as an eye medication, modern scientific studies have yet to establish the effectiveness of the herb. What's more, there may be a danger in applying a homemade, unsterilized preparation to the eye.

The dried herb was once smoked to relieve chronic bronchial colds.

CULTIVATION

As a semiparasite, eyebright takes part of its nourishment from the roots of other plants, particularly grass. Because the leaves of totally parasitic plants are devoid of any green color, eyebright is deceptive. Its bright green leaves give it the appearance of a normal, self-sufficient plant. But below the ground, tiny root suckers spread out, lie on the rootlets of the grasses, and absorb nourishment. There is no permanent damage to the grass, however. Because both plants are annual, they renew themselves each year.

Eyebright is difficult to transplant and prefers its natural habitat—grassy, dry earth. It has the unusual distinction of taking on a different appearance in various environments. In the mountains or near the sea, the plant will grow only an inch or so high, with the stem scarcely branched. But in a rich, chalky soil, eyebright grows to 8 or 9 inches and looks like a small shrub.

All parts of the plant except the root have been used. To gather eyebright fresh, cut the plant just above the root when it is in full flower and the foliage is in good condition. For drying, do the same; then hang it upside down in a cool, dark place where there is plenty of air circulation.

DESCRIPTION

Euphrasia officinalis is an elegant annual.

Flowers: Shoot out in terminal spikes with leafy bracts interspersed; white or purple, variegated with yellow spots or stripes; corolla two lipped, the upper lip arching over the stamens; the lower, tubelike portion tipped with four teeth and enclosed in a green calyx.

Leaves: Leafy stems bear stiff, ovate leaves, opposite at the base of the plant and alternate toward the top; leaves deeply cut around the margin, pointy at the tips; to ½ in. long and ¼ in. broad.

Fruit: Many ribbed seeds from small, flattened capsules.

Height: 2–8 in.

FLOWERING

July through September.

RANGE

Found predominantly in the meadows, dry pastures, and heaths of England; some grassy areas of Europe and Western Asia; only rarely domesticated in North America.

GROWING CONDITIONS

- Soil pH: alkaline.
- Poor soil; must be grown in conjunction with grass because it is a semiparasite.
- Full sun.

FENNEL

Foeniculum vulgare   **Umbelliferae**

DESCRIPTION

Fennel is a semihardy perennial, often cultivated as an annual, grown for its leaves, seeds, and stems. The branching erect stem is round, smooth, striated, and a glaucous blue-green in color. The tapering root resembles a carrot. (See photo on page 102.)

Flowers: Small, yellow, in compound umbel.

Leaves: Alternately branch out from joints of the stem; on broad petioles; deep green; pinnately divided into feathery segments.

Fruit: Ovate, ribbed.

Height: 4 ft.

FLOWERING

July through October.

RANGE

Native to the Mediterranean region; widely naturalized.

Fennel's filigreed leaves and stunning flower umbels dance with the wind. It stands tall to make a good border. Or, when intermittently placed among shorter specimens, it can create an unusual garden skyline.

When shopping for fennel plants or seeds at your local garden center or supermarket, you're likely to find at least two types. The perennial *Foeniculum vulgare,* which is synonymous with *F. officinale,* is commonly known as wild fennel. *F. vulgare dulce,* known as sweet fennel, Florence fennel, or finocchio, is an annual but has quite the same growing habits. But sweet fennel's celerylike stem swells to a greater size, and it is preferred for culinary purposes.

Fennel's taste is close to that of anise or licorice. Its flavor mingles particularly well with vegetable dips, cream sauces, and grilled fish. When eaten raw, as you would celery, or in a salad, the anise flavor is pronounced. Its character is subdued by cooking.

HISTORY

An early Greek name for fennel was *marathron,* from *maraino,* which meant "to grow thin." The seventeenth-century British herbalist Culpeper wrote that all parts of the fennel plant "are much used in drink or broth to make people lean that are too fat." In medieval times people kept a stash of fennel seeds handy to nibble on through long church services and on fast days; the seeds were considered to be an appetite suppressant. Others employed fennel to prevent witchcraft. Bunches of fennel were hung over the doors of country cottages on Midsummer's Eve for this purpose.

The Romans named the plant *foeniculum,* which is derived from the Latin word *foenum,* which means "hay." This name eventually evolved into the one we know it by. The Romans ate the young shoots, and fennel was mentioned frequently by the Anglo-Saxons in their cooking and medicinal recipes prior to the Norman Conquest. The emperor Charlemagne is responsible for introducing the plant into central Europe. Fennel was one among many herbs cultivated on his imperial farms. In the 1600s it was eaten along with fish and meat to aid digestion.

USES

Medicinal: Fennel has been used as a carminative, a weak diuretic, and a mild stimulant. Fennel tea is said to soothe the stomach. All parts of the plant are considered to be safe for human consumption and work well as a spice or a vegetable. The volatile oil of the seed, however, can be irritating or even dangerous to those with allergies or skin sensitivities.

Oil of fennel includes 50 to 60 percent anethol, which is also the chief constituent of anise oil, and 18 to 22 percent fenchone, a pungent, colorless liquid.

The Greek physicians Hippocrates and Dioscorides both recommended fennel to increase the flow of milk in nursing mothers. Serpents were believed to eat the plant to restore their sight after shedding their skins, and it came to be regarded as a remedy for visual ailments.

To the medieval mind, fennel was one of nine sacred herbs with the power to cure the nine causes of medieval diseases. Culpeper believed that fennel helped break kidney stones, quieted hiccups, prevented nausea and gout, cleared the liver and lungs, and served as an antidote to poisonous mushrooms.

Fennel tea was used to cure colic in babies; with the seeds the famous "gripe water" was concocted, which relieved infants of flatulence. The tea was gargled as a breath freshener, taken to expel worms, and applied as an eyewash. A poultice was used to relieve swelling in the breasts of nursing mothers.

Culinary: Fennel tastes like a softer and nuttier version of anise. The leaves, tender stems, and seeds are used from the sweet fennel variety; the stalks and bulbs are used from Florence fennel.

Use fresh leaves in salads and as lacy garnishes; the tender stems are eaten like celery. The seeds, whole or ground as needed, are popular in desserts, breads, cakes, cookies, and beverages. Florence fennel stalks and bulbs can be minced for use in salads and soups.

Fennel fares well with fish, sausages, duck, barley, rice, cabbage, sauerkraut, beets, pickles, potatoes, lentils, breads, eggs, and cheese. The leaves and seeds lend aroma and flavor to herb butters, cheese spreads, salad dressings, and Chinese marinades.

Available commercially: Sweet fennel—whole and ground seed (whole is preferable), fresh leaves, and stalks. Florence fennel—fresh.

Substitute: Anise, in slightly less proportion, for seeds and leaves.

Storage note: Sweet fennel leaves lose flavor when dried.

Aromatic: Fennel oil is sweetly aromatic in both odor and taste. It is used commercially in condiments and creams, perfumes, liqueurs, and soaps.

Cosmetic: According to modern herbalist Jeanne Rose, fennel is cleansing and medicating. An infusion of the ground seeds can be used to make a steam facial.

Dye: The flowers and leaves of fennel can be used to make yellow and brown dyes for wool. (See the entry Dyes from Herbs for more information.)

CHEF TIPS

- Heat will destroy the delicate flavor of fennel leaves, so add to cooked recipes at the very last moment.

- Add ground seed to hot or chilled tomato soup.

- Mince a bulb of Florence fennel and add to a salad of avocado and grapefruit.

GROWING CONDITIONS

- Plant hardiness zone 6.
- Soil pH 6.5.
- Average, well-drained soil.
- Full sun.

CULTIVATION

Heavy clay will hinder the seed's growth. Plant directly in a humus-rich soil that drains well. Sow them lightly in drills 6 inches apart. The beds should be kept moist for two weeks, until the first leaves appear. After that, take care not to overwater. For a continuous crop, make succession plantings through mid-August, which will yield a fall harvest. If you're eager for fennel's arrival, plant seeds in autumn to insure early germination in spring.

Fennel can have a damaging effect on its neighbors in the garden, including bush beans, caraway, tomatoes, and kohlrabi. Conversely, it can be harmed if planted close to certain herbs; coriander will prevent seeds from forming, and wormwood can reduce seed germination and stunt the plant's growth.

Harvesting and storage: Each part of the fennel plant is edible. You can begin snipping the leaves once the plant is well established. Clippings can be frozen for later use; as with other herbs, the leaves hold up well when chopped and stored loosely in containers. It takes approximately 80 days for the stems to fully mature, but they are edible as soon as they begin to fatten. Just cut them off at the crown. For the plumpest stems, pinch off the emerging seed head and give them several more days. Some say that the stems are at their best when the plant is just about to bloom.

Harvesting the seeds requires precise timing. You have to watch the plant closely to notice when the seeds turn from yellowish green to brown. They will fall even in a gentle breeze. With scissors, simply snip the entire seed head and let it drop into a paper bag. Store in a warm, dark place for further drying. Once the seeds are thoroughly dried, they can be transferred to jars for year-round keeping.

FENUGREEK

Trigonella Foenum-graecum   **Leguminosae**

Fenugreek is well-known in the Mediterranean and Middle East not only as a human food and medicinal plant but also as a fodder crop. In fact, the Latin name *foenum-graecum* means "Greek hay," and it is sometimes used to disguise the smell of moldy fodder.

Fenugreek was used as a fodder crop even before its medicinal powers were exploited in ancient Egypt. Benedictine monks brought the plant to Western Europe during the ninth century.

USES

In addition to its use as an animal feed, fenugreek has many medicinal and culinary purposes involving the seeds and occasionally the leaves.

Medicinal: Fenugreek has been used to cure just about everything under the sun. Here and there around the world, the plant is recommended as an expectorant, laxative, febrifuge, and stomachic. The herb is employed as a folk cure for diabetes, anemia, and rickets. Applied externally, fenugreek poultices have been said to soothe boils, wounds, and ulcers. The herb was a primary ingredient of the popular Lydia Pinkham's health tonic.

Research suggests that at least some of these old-time remedies have merit. The seeds contain up to 30 percent mucilage, which does indeed make them a good poultice. The mucilage may be responsible for fenugreek tea's value as a laxative and as an aid in curing ulcers and other stomach problems. To make fenugreek tea, steep 1 ounce of seeds in 1 pint of boiling water. The tea might also soothe a sore throat or, according to some herbalists, reduce a fever. If you like, add a little honey or peppermint extract to improve the odor and taste.

Culinary: Fenugreek's nutty flavor combines the taste of celery and maple. The seeds are used whole or ground as needed in East Indian, Pakistani, and African cuisines, and are used in chutney and halvah. Fenugreek enhances meats, poultry, marinated vegetables, and curry blends.

Available commercially: Whole seed.

Dye: The seeds produce a yellow dye in wool mordanted with alum.

CULTIVATION

Broadcast seed thickly in a rich soil that has been deeply plowed. Seed can be sown when the soil temperature reaches 55°F. In cold, wet soil, root rot may occur.

Harvest the pods when ripe, but before they begin to shatter. Remove the seeds and dry them in the sun.

DESCRIPTION

An annual herb, fenugreek has tender stems and leaves that vaguely resemble clover.

Flowers: White, pealike, ½ in. long; hairy calyxes; occur singly or in pairs at the leaf axils.

Leaves: Compound; three leaflets oblong, toothed, ¾–2 in. long.

Fruit: Curved seed pod, 2–3 in. long; 10–20 smooth brown seeds.

Height: 1–2 ft.

FLOWERING

Midsummer.

RANGE

Native to western Asia and the Mediterranean; naturalized in North America.

CHEF TIPS

- Add whole fenugreek seed to pickling brine.
- Sprout seeds and add to salads.
- Use fenugreek with care because too much can cause food to be bitter.

GROWING CONDITIONS

- Plant hardiness zone 6.
- Rich soil.
- Full sun.

FEVERFEW

Chrysanthemum Parthenium   Compositae

Here's an herb that makes a medical claim with its name. Feverfew comes from the Latin *febrifugia,* or "driver out of fevers." The Romans believed in its powers, but by medieval times it had fallen out of favor. Only lately has this helpful member of the chrysanthemum family been rediscovered, this time not as a fever cure but as an anti-inflammatory and migraine headache cure of remarkable power.

DESCRIPTION

A member of the daisy family, feverfew grows as a vigorous hardy biennial, or a perennial, on a branched and tufted root. The finely furrowed stems are also many branched.

The plant is sometimes confused with chamomile, which has a dome-shaped central floret receptacle and very feathery leaves. Chamomile is procumbent in habit, while feverfew stands up straight. (See photo on page 33.)

Flowers: Grow at ends of stems; small, white, numerous, and daisylike; yellow centers composed of many tubular disk florets; 10–20 white rays surround disk; bloom in tight, flat-topped clusters.

Leaves: Strongly and bitterly scented, hairless, alternate, stemmed, 4 in. long, yellowish green to yellow. Lower leaves: bipinnate leaflets in egg-shaped segments with deeply incised lobes; upper leaves: pinnate divisions into two or three pairs of toothed segments.

Fruit: Inconspicuous, oblong shape, truncated base, smooth-furrowed sides, and crowned, toothed membrane.

Height: 2–3 ft.

FLOWERING

Midsummer through fall.

RANGE

Native to central and southern Europe; naturalized in most parts of the temperate zone, including North America.

HISTORY

The ancient Greek physician Dioscorides valued the herb for its effect on the uterus. It was often used in childbirth to help in the delivery of the afterbirth if contractions were not regular. Its use against fevers has been well documented.

In more recent times, in the southwestern United States and in Finland, it has been taken as a tonic, while a Cuban variety is used as an antiperiodic. In its long history this herb has been used as an ingredient in making confectionaries and wines; as an aromatic to ward off disease; and as an insect repellent.

The seventeenth-century herbalist John Parkinson claimed it aided in recovery from opium overdose, and Cotton Mather recommended it for toothache. It has also been used against ailments as diverse as "female hysteria," infant colic, melancholia, shortwindedness, vertigo, arthritis, kidney stones, constipation, and insect bites.

USES

Feverfew has only recently become available in health food stores in the United States, although the British have long used it for self-medication. As a headache remedy it is not new, having been recommended by the British herbalist Gerard in 1633, but recent scientific findings now support claims of its effectiveness.

Medicinal: In 1978 scientists suggested in the *Lancet,* a British medical journal, that since feverfew has long been used against both migraines and arthritis, it might share properties with aspirin. Two years later, the *Lancet* confirmed this educated guess with results from a subsequent study. In 1985 the *British Medical Journal* reported yet another study with findings that demonstrated that feverfew helps alleviate the pain of migraines. Researchers speculate that substances in the plant appear to make smooth muscle cells less responsive to body chemicals that trigger migraine muscle spasms.

These findings don't suggest that migraine sufferers can toss away their conventional drugs, but they do show that feverfew does help some sufferers. "If you take feverfew by eating the leaves, it should be in very small doses—from 50 to 60 milligrams, which is

three or four of the little feverfew leaves each day," says Varro Tyler, Ph.D., dean of the School of Pharmacy, Nursing, and Health Sciences at Purdue University. "Commercial preparations—capsules, for example—are hard to find, but some botanical wholesalers list them." To hide the bitter taste characteristic of the herb, some migraine sufferers mix the leaves into foods.

Ornamental: Low-growing varieties of feverfew can be used as annuals in rock gardens, window boxes, and porch boxes for summer and fall blooming. The flower looks very much like a cluster of small daisies.

Craft: Dry the stems of feverfew to add to herb and flower arrangements.

Dye: The fresh leaves and stems produce a greenish yellow dye in wool mordanted with chrome.

Other: One active ingredient in feverfew is thought to be pyrethrin. If it is, the effectiveness of feverfew as an insecticide and insect repellent would be explained.

CULTIVATION

It stands to reason that a plant that can grow from a chink in a wall will require only the most casual methods of cultivation. Ordinary, well-drained soil and full sunshine will meet its needs, and a little shade can be tolerated. Propagation can be by cutting, division, or seed. Root division is done in early spring.

Divide feverfew by sectioning each old plant into three parts and transplanting these. To use cuttings, dig part of the heel of the old plant along with the new shoots that form at its base in the spring. Cuttings may be taken from October through May. Shorten the foliage by 3 inches and plant the cutting in light soil in a shady spot. Cover with sand and drench with water.

To start feverfew from seed, sow it indoors in flats or pots in February or March, or two weeks before all danger of frost will have passed. Keep the seedlings at a daytime temperature of 65° to 70°F and 50°F at night. Transplant the seedlings in June, spacing them 9 to 12 inches apart. In mild areas, seed may be sown directly outside in the early spring or fall.

The double-flowered variety is most popular in ornamental gardens. Take care, however, not to place it among other flowering plants that require pollination: Bees hate the smell of it and will stay away from the whole garden it occupies. A compact plant, feverfew is useful for window boxes and small flower beds.

The leaves are available from either wild or garden plants throughout the growing season. The leaves may also be frozen; they lose some pungency if dried.

GROWING CONDITIONS

- Plant hardiness zone 5.
- Soil pH 6.3.
- Average, well-drained soil.
- Full sun to partial shade.

FLAX

Linum usitatissimum   **Linaceae**

This multipurpose herb, also known as linseed, offers something for the weaver, the painter, the physician, and the cook. Fibers from the stalk are spun into linen; oil from the seeds is used in paint and linoleum; both the seeds and the oil are used medicinally; and the seeds are baked in bread.

It stands to reason that such a versatile plant would figure in legend. In Teuton mythology flax was said to be under the protection of the goddess Hulda, who taught mortals the art of growing, spinning, and weaving flax. In the Middle Ages, flax flowers were believed to be a protection against sorcery. A more recent Bohemian belief held that if children danced among flax at the age of seven, they would become beautiful.

DESCRIPTION

Flax bears a solitary, erect stem that branches off at the top.

Flowers: Terminal, light blue, five petals; ½ in. across; striated and minutely scalloped at the extremities; wither quickly after opening in the morning.

Leaves: Alternate, stalkless, pale green; shaped like a spearhead; ¾–1 in. long.

Fruit: A globular pod; distinct cells contain 10 brown seeds, about ¼ in. long.

Height: 20 in.

FLOWERING

June through August.

RANGE

Widely cultivated in the northwestern United States, Canada, and Europe.

HABITAT

Roadsides, railroad lines, and waste places.

HISTORY

Flax began serving civilization before the time of recorded history. The strong fibers were used by the Swiss Lake Dwellers, the earliest Europeans for whom remains exist. The Egyptians held flax in high esteem, wrapping their mummies in linen and decorating their tombs with carvings of the flax plant itself.

The Bible tells us that the flax plant's fibers were the primary source of clothing for biblical characters. In the New Testament Christ wore linen as He lay in his tomb.

In the *Odyssey* Homer mentions sails made of linen. Pliny, the Roman naturalist, said, "What department is there to be found of active life in which flax is not employed?"

Bartholomew, the medieval herbalist, described how linen was made. The flax was soaked in water, dried in the sun, then bound in "praty bundels" and afterward "knockyd, beten and brayd and carflyd, rodded and gnodded; ribbyd and heklyd, and at the last sponne." He writes of using it for clothing, sails, fishnets, threads, ropes, strings, measuring lines, bed sheets, bags, and purses.

For at least two centuries, flax was one of the main sources of fabric for American clothing, much of it in the form of homemade linen and linsey-woolsey. Making linen from flax is not really that much more difficult than making cotton or wool yarn.

USES

Flax's many uses are important enough that, though in decline, it is a major farm crop in Russia, Canada, and the northern plains states of the United States. In this country it is all grown for linseed oil, with the fibers from the straw being utilized for fine papers. Its decline can largely be blamed on the rise of water- and rubber-based paints.

GROWING CONDITIONS
- Light, well-drained soil.
- Full sun to partial shade.

Its commercial value, however, can't overshadow its importance as an herb.

Medicinal: A discussion of flax's curative virtues must be prefaced with a word of caution. Immature seedpods are especially poisonous, but all parts of the plant contain cyanogenetic nitrates and glucosides, particularly linamarin. Overdose symptoms include increased respiratory rate, excitement, gasping, staggering, weakness, paralysis, and convulsion.

Flax's main constituents include 30 to 40 percent fixed oil, mucilage, wax, tannin, gum, and protein. Linseed oil has been recommended as an ingredient of cough medicines; as a tea, it has been used as a remedy for colds, coughs, and irritations of the urinary tract. The tea can be made from 1 ounce of ground or whole seeds to 1 pint of boiling water. The active principle seems to be the mucilage. Add a bit of honey and lemon for taste. The tea is said to be mildly laxative.

Linseed meal, made from crushed seeds, has been useful as a poultice. The boiled seeds are wrapped in a clean cloth and placed on sprains or burns. Herb folklorist Cyrus Hyde of Well-Sweep Herb Farm in New Jersey recalls a flax-seed poultice from his childhood. The ground seeds were mixed with a little water and a chunk of butter to make a balm for soothing festering sores.

Culinary: Flax seed has long been an ingredient of hearty bread.

Ornamental: Flax is most typically grown in herb gardens as an ornamental border plant. Though the individual flowers are small and bloom for a short period of time, the blossoms are profuse in number and, in aggregate, appear over many weeks. The plant used in this way is a perennial form, which grows in a low clump. The plant grown for seed and for linen is an annual.

Craft: Flax can be woven into dried herb baskets. (See the entry Crafts from Herbs for instructions on making herb baskets.)

Linen: The linsey-woolsey of America's colonial days was hardly fine fabric, but it was durable. Historically, some climates and soils have proved more suitable for producing fine linen than others, Belgium being perhaps the most famous. The process described by Bartholomew is much the same as that used by makers of homespun linen today.

The flax plants, which have been pulled and allowed to dry (with the seed heads cut or combed out), are soaked in water for several weeks to rot the woody stems around the fibers, a process called retting. When the stems are sufficiently rotted, the plants are dried. Then a device called a flaxbrake is used to break the stems in several places. Next, a wooden swingling knife is used to scrape or "scutch" the broken stems, removing the woody shards of stem from

Seed Capsule

Seedlings

Immature Plant

the fibers. These are passed through the teeth of a hetchel (or hacksel), straightening them and pulling out all the remaining stem pieces. The resulting material resembles a fine, fluffy horsetail. The fibers are then spun into yarn.

Other: The seeds were once used much as we now use car wax—a spoonful of them was mixed in the family horse's feed to put a shine on his coat, according to Hyde. The protein-rich seeds are sometimes used in livestock feed and are added to bird feed.

The seeds are notoriously slippery. Herb lore has it that people literally have drowned in vats of the seeds: They dropped in and had no way of extricating themselves.

A curious use is related by Hyde: "Until not many years ago, the seeds were converted into something of a homemade mousse. They were soaked in water to make a thick mucilage, which was then applied to the hair before styling. Once the stuff dried, it was combed out, leaving the hair with the desired topography."

CULTIVATION

Flax is easy to grow, whether you start the seeds in the ground or under glass. If you will be planting seeds directly in the ground, remove weeds and avoid heavy, clay soils. After the plants are established, weed carefully by hand; the roots are shallow and easily disturbed. Sow the seeds either in early spring or late fall and thin the seedlings to about 4 inches apart.

For greenhouse growing plant the seeds in September. They will sprout best when set in a container of porous soil in which the plants will stay. Thin the seedlings to leave six or seven in each pot. They will grow in full sun or partial shade and prefer a temperature from 55° to 60°F by day and 50°F by night. Take care when watering. Allow the soil to dry somewhat between waterings—especially in the early stages of growth, when the days are short and light levels relatively low.

Don't apply fertilizer until the plant is full grown and ready to flower. You can use an occasional dose of a diluted liquid fertilizer.

Pests and diseases: Grasshoppers and cutworms may bother your plants. (See the entry Growing Herbs for information on controlling pests.)

Harvesting and storage: Seeds can be harvested at the same time as the fiber—just before the flower blooms. Either leave the seeds to ripen on the cut sheaths, or allow them to mature fully on the plant a while after the flowers drop. The flax fibers are softer and stronger if harvested when the blossoms have just fallen and the stalk begins to turn yellow. Care must be taken to keep the seeds dry, as they are damaged by dampness.

196

FOXGLOVE

Digitalis purpurea   Scrophulariaceae

One day in 1775, Dr. William Withering, enroute from Birmingham to Stafford, stopped to change horses. During the stop he was asked to examine a woman suffering from dropsy. He did so and found her case to be quite severe. Expecting her to die shortly, he was surprised to hear weeks later that she had recovered completely. He visited her again and found out that she had been drinking an herbal tea to cure her dropsy. He studied the tea closely and eventually deduced that foxglove, an ingredient in the tea, yielded an active principle called digitalis that effected the woman's recovery.

In 1785 he published *An Account of the Foxglove,* which thrust foxglove into the forefront of medicinal treatments for the heart. Since then this herb, the source of digitalis, has become a very important medicinal plant.

HISTORY

The medicinal use of foxglove began much earlier than Dr. Withering's account of it. It was cultivated for herbal medicines as far back as 1000 A.D. The English used it as a cough medicine, a treatment for epilepsy, and a cure for swollen glands. Some suspect that Vincent van Gogh took digitalis for epilepsy, and that the yellow vision this drug creates may have influenced his art. After Withering's discovery, foxglove was widely used as a cardiac sedative and diuretic, but occasional overdoses and fatalities discouraged the use of the drug.

USES

Potent indeed. Digitalis is far too powerful to be used without medical supervision. Grow foxglove, by all means, but purely for ornamental purposes.

Medicinal: Digitalis contains several glycosides, digitoxin being the one primarily responsible for foxglove's actions on the heart. Both the powdered leaves of the herb and extracted digitoxin are employed medicinally. Digitoxin is 1,000 times more powerful than the powdered leaves. Digitalis increases the force of heart contractions, making it beneficial in congestive heart failure for which it is most often used. The increased contraction of the heart helps to empty the ventricles, giving the heart more time to rest between contractions and to fill up again with blood from the veins. This in turn helps to reduce blood pressure in the veins, a benefit in the treatment of hypertensive heart disease. In addition, digitalis elevates low arterial blood pressure caused by impaired heart function. The

UNSAFE

DESCRIPTION

This stunning biennial is unmistakable when in bloom. It's not always as easy to spot in the first year of growth, when it is just a rosette of green leaves. In that first year after seeding, look for large (up to 10 in. long), fuzzy leaves growing in a low mound. (See photos on pages 273, 376, and 513.)

Flowers: Borne on one side of spike, tubular, bell-shaped, hanging, 1½–3 in. long, faintly five-lobed, lavender on outside surface, white with crimson spots on inner surface, hairs on inner surface at mouth of corolla, four stamens, five-pointed calyx.

Leaves: Alternate, 6–12 in. long, 3–4 in. wide, ovate to lanceolate, toothed, wrinkled, hairy, deep green, conspicuously veined; lower leaves have long stalks.

Fruit: Dry, oval-shaped, hairy capsule, ⅝ in. long; contains many red-brown seeds.

Height: 4–8 ft.

FLOWERING

June and July.

RANGE

Native to the British Isles, western Europe, and Morocco; naturalized in North and Central America. Widely cultivated.

HABITAT

Along roadsides and edges of woods.

improved circulation alleviates water retention and reduces edema.

Drugs derived from Grecian foxglove, *Digitalis lanata,* have been used widely since the late 1940s. Digoxin, not digitalis powder, is the main product from the leaves of this plant. It is 300 times stronger than the digitalis powder made from *D. purpurea,* and it is also quicker acting and more stable.

Toxicity: Foxglove has killed many people who have ingested it. The signs of poisoning include blurred vision; strong, slow pulse; vomiting; dizziness; diarrhea; tremors; and possibly convulsions.

Ornamental: For all of its medical benefits, scientists and doctors certainly prize this herb, but gardeners love it, too, for the beauty of its blossoms. Foxglove fits nicely into almost any garden setting, from the small cottage planting to the larger landscape. Blooming in the early summer, it is among the first tall plants to provide color. The plants naturalize easily along forest edges and beside hedges. A few of the smaller varieties work nicely in rock gardens, while some of the larger cultivars, reaching up to 6 feet tall, are spectacular against a background wall or foliage planting.

Dye: The flowers yield a chartreuse color to wool mordanted with alum.

CULTIVATION

Foxgloves can be grown from seed. Since the seeds are so tiny, mix them with sand before broadcasting in the cold frame or nursery bed. Cover them very lightly with soil and keep continuously moist.

You must sow seeds in the late spring or early summer in order to have plants strong enough to survive the winter. However, if they are started too early, they may bloom that first fall rather than waiting until the following summer. Germination occurs within two weeks after sowing. When seedlings are 2 to 3 inches tall, transplant them to the garden. Allow about 1 foot between plants, in rows 1 to 2 feet apart. It is also possible to obtain plants by division in the early fall or spring.

Foxglove tolerates a wide variety of soils and growing conditions. The only thing they absolutely have to have is good drainage to prevent root rot. The plants can tolerate freezing temperatures; however, in the far North, they need some protection from winter cold and snow.

Pests and diseases: Foxglove may be bothered by Japanese beetles or mealy bugs, and it is susceptible to mosaic virus, curly top, wilt, anthracnose, and leaf spot. (See the entry Growing Herbs for information on controlling pests and diseases.)

GROWING CONDITIONS

- Plant hardiness zones 4–8.
- Soil pH: acid.
- Fertile, moist, humusy soil.
- Full sun to partial shade.

GARDENING WITH HERBS

There are two ways to landscape with herbs: Work them into the overall design as decorative elements, or feature the herbs in special period or theme gardens. If you don't have the room or desire for an herb garden, herbs can still make a valuable contribution to your landscape.

A low hedge of lavender or rosemary can set off a fence or wall or line a path, perfuming the air when anyone walks through. If you're tired of mowing grass, a colorful lawn of creeping thymes, chamomile, and/or pennyroyal requires almost no maintenance. (Remember, though, that an herb lawn won't hold up under heavy traffic—if you want to walk on the lawn, it's best to set down stepping stones.) On a smaller scale, creeping thymes, with their pleasantly pungent fragrance and pink, white, rose, or lilac flowers, can be planted between the bricks or stones of a path, spreading to form a colorful ground cover.

Ground covers for shady sites need not be limited to ivy or pachysandra, either. Plant sweet woodruff, with its starry white flowers, mint-scented pennyroyal, or heavenly sweet violets under your shade trees. If part of your yard is heavily shaded, angelica, lemon balm, sweet cicely, evening primrose, valerian, chervil, goldenseal, lungwort, and the hellebores will add color and texture. Reclaim a swampy site with lovage, marsh mallow, mint, elecampane, queen of the meadow, and beebalm.

Herbs can also be worked into a flower border or vegetable garden. Bright-flowered beebalm; gold, white, or cherry yarrow; garlic chives with its clusters of star-shaped, rose-scented flowers and handsome straplike foliage; variegated sage; daisy-flowered feverfew; blue-green rue; blue-spired aconite; and foxglove with its majestic spikes of flowers in shades of red, pink, yellow, and white are particularly suited to the mixed border. So much variety to choose from makes it easy to design a striking border.

In the vegetable garden, annual and biennial herbs like nasturtiums, basil, parsley, anise, dill, borage, chervil, coriander, calendula, and summer savory add diversity and possibly protection from insects. But to avoid grief at tilling time, confine the perennial culinary herbs, such as sage, thyme, and their like, to a site of their own at one end of the garden, just like those other perennial crops, asparagus, strawberries, rhubarb, and artichokes.

LANDSCAPING

If you use herbs on a larger scale or feature them in a design or

GARDENING WITH HERBS—continued

A BIBLE GARDEN

The Bible is full of references to herbs. Myrrh and frankincense were two of the gifts brought to the Christ child by the magi. Mandrake is mentioned in Genesis 30:14 as a plant that would insure conception. Dandelions, endive, chicory, and sorrel are the bitter herbs traditionally eaten during Passover.

At the Cathedral of St. John the Divine in New York City, these herbs, along with others like coriander, mustard, saffron, and aloes, grow among quince trees, pomegranates, lilies, and various other fruits, flowers, and trees of the Bible.

The Bible garden occupies a quarter of an acre. Stone benches provide places where visitors can sit, enjoy the colors, textures, and fragrances of the garden, and be soothed by them. To visit this garden, just walk in. It is open from sunrise until sunset. The Cathedral of St. John the Divine is located at Amsterdam Avenue and West 112th Street.

garden, good commonsense landscaping rules apply, as they do in any type of garden design. Before you start to design, remember that all gardens involve work. The more formal the design and the larger the scale, the more weeding, clipping, mulching, and watering you'll need to do. Scale down those visions of grandeur until they reach manageable proportions.

When you begin the actual design, bear in mind that it's a lot easier—to say nothing of cheaper—to make mistakes or changes on paper than in the garden. Measure the garden site, then transfer the outline to graph paper, making the layout to scale. Mark down trees, buildings, and other obstructions, and note the direction north. Make sure to leave enough space for comfortable paths, and keep beds narrow enough to work in—4 to 5 feet is about maximum—but wide enough to look effective. Once you have the basic design down, choose the herbs that will bring it to life. The choice can be based on color, height, climatic conditions, or type of plant—for example, those suitable for a colonial or dye garden.

It's wise to keep basic rules in mind when choosing plants. First, always plant groups of a given herb together. Individual plants will get lost, creating a blurred, jumbled effect, while masses of plants will stand out and create a unified design. Second, plant in descending order of height. If your design features a border backed by a wall or fence, plant the tallest herbs in back, the lowest herbs in front. If you're planning an island bed, put the tall plants in the center, the low plants around the edge. Third, keep perspective in mind. If you're planting a knot garden, make sure the garden "floor" contrasts with the knotted "cord," or the pattern will be lost. If your design is meant to be viewed from a distance, use plants that will show up—large ones with bright flowers or silver foliage.

Finally, a word about maintenance. Herb gardens, like any others, look best when the plants are full and lush. This is vital when an herbal hedge or solid block of plants is integral to the design. It's good gardening practice to grow extra plants in a nursery area or corner of the vegetable garden, so you'll always have spares to fill in gaps.

PERIOD GARDENS

Period gardens are complex because they are limited to the designs, materials, techniques, and plants of a given historical era. Before embarking on a historical design, read everything you can on the period of your choice, as well as on garden design in that period. An Elizabethan knot garden design is included here as a starting place. But there are other possibilities.

A medieval garden is a delightful refuge. It should be walled, if possible, and include a fountain. Surround the fountain with an herbal lawn studded with flowers—irises, clove pinks, lilies, daisies, primroses, sweet violets, and columbines.

If you have a tree in the garden, you can build a circular seat around it. But the most traditional seating arrangement is a turf seat under an arbor. The turf seat—a medieval inspiration—is an earth-filled rectangular box surfaced with a creeping herb such as one of the prostrate thymes or creeping chamomile. Its walls can be brick, stone, wood, or plaited wicker (wattling).

The vigorous formality of a colonial garden may seem far removed from the enclosed tranquillity of a medieval bower, but the symmetry of a successful colonial garden is soothing. To make a colonial herb garden, lay out raised, board-sided beds along a central walk. The two sides of the garden should be identical. The walk should lead to something—a sundial, bench, or view. If possible, fence the garden, or hedge it with santolina, lavender, rosemary, or southernwood.

Colonists often planted herbs randomly with vegetables and flowers. An all-herb garden should be planted informally within the rigid framework of the design. Colonial herbs include burnet, comfrey, dill, basil, clary sage, lemon balm, parsley, nasturtiums, rue, madder, woad, mint, fennel, saffron, coriander, chamomile, angelica, caraway, borage, chervil, tarragon, licorice, lovage, tansy, sweet cicely, catmint, and calendula.

One thing to bear in mind when attempting a historical re-creation is to limit yourself to materials available in the period you're reproducing. For example, wood, wattling, stone, gravel, brick, and clay were the usual building materials used in the colonial days. Local materials were usually used in garden construction, down to sheep-shank edgings for beds. This sort of attention to detail, combined with a sound design and diligent maintenance, will guarantee you a successful herb garden.

THEME GARDENS

A theme garden is one in which the plants are unified by a common feature, such as flower color or function. Five such garden designs are included here to inspire you—a medicinal garden, dye garden, fragrance garden, everlasting garden of ornamental plants for drying, and kitchen garden. Other possibilities include a white garden, with silver-foliaged and white-flowering herbs; a seasonal garden, with herbs that bloom in your favorite season; an herb tea garden; and a "meaningful garden," with message herbs so popular

THE NATIONAL HERB GARDEN

Herbs have been so important to mankind and civilization that it is only appropriate that a national garden should exist in their honor. The National Herb Garden, located in the U.S. National Arboretum at 3501 New York Avenue, N.E., Washington, D.C., is it.

A visit begins with a walk around the knot garden, whose interlocking chains have been formed from various dwarf evergreens.

Next, stroll through the historic rose garden, designed using rose species that originated before the year 1867. These include some of the most beautiful and most fragrant roses known.

After walking through the rose garden, you reach the specialty herb gardens. There are ten of these arranged in an oval. Each garden has a particular theme, based on historical significance or use. The Dioscorides garden features herbs known and used by the famous Greek physician. Herbs used to make natural dyes are highlighted in the dye garden. The Early American garden displays herbs that were important to the colonists. Continue walking along the garden path to view the American Indian garden, the medicinal garden, the culinary garden, the industrial garden, the fragrance garden, the oriental garden, and the beverage garden.

in Victorian bouquets (such as rosemary for remembrance or borage for courage).

Theme gardens can also have literary significance. There are Shakespearean gardens all over this country, featuring plants mentioned by the bard. Biblical gardens, featuring wormwood, rue, hyssop, aloe, anise, mint, dill, coriander, mustard, saffron, cumin, and roses—all herbs mentioned in the Bible—are popular. Some include plants associated with the Virgin, such as rosemary, costmary, lady's mantle, and lady's bedstraw.

THE KNOT GARDEN

(AUTHENTIC SIXTEENTH-CENTURY DESIGN)

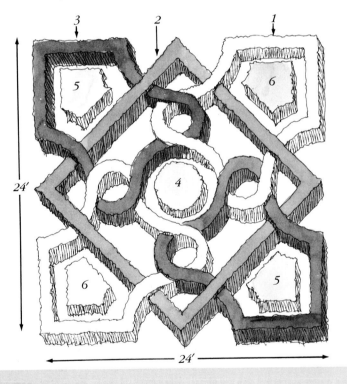

PLANTS FOR A KNOT GARDEN

Because a knot garden is basically an indulgence, you can play with it in whatever way you wish. You could emphasize the formal geometry of this pattern by using a single plant throughout. You could use all one plant for the central accents and keep three kinds in the borders. Or you could reduce the borders to two kinds—one for the square and a second for the "loops" of the knot. You can play with the background, too. A single mulching material—cocoa bean hulls—is used here to accent the greens, blues, and grays of the herbs. You could use different stone chips to make a mosaic—white marble chips in some sections, black in others, and gray-blue crushed granite in others. Or you could use brilliantly colored fish-tank gravels to create patterns that would have thrilled the Elizabethans.

Another option is to simplify and reduce the size of the knot garden. A striking knot can be made in a 9- or 10-foot square. The thing to bear in mind is that knot gardens were originally intended to be viewed from above—as when one looked from one's terrace or castle window. The narrower and lower the herb borders, the closer you'll have to get to the knot for it to be effective—and the more maintenance it will require to keep those herbs in bounds.

The plants:

1. GREEN SANTOLINA (*Santolina virens*): A perennial, to 2 feet tall, with rich green, aromatic leaves and yellow flowers in early summer. Plan on one plant per foot of border. Keep plants clipped back to about a foot—a hard clipping in early spring, followed by a light trim every two weeks from late May through July should keep them looking neat.

2. MUNSTEAD LAVENDER (*Lavandula angustifolia* spp. *angustifolia* 'Munstead'): A compact perennial, only 1 foot tall, with aromatic gray foliage and bright lavender flower spikes in summer. Plan on one plant per foot of border. Trim only if needed to keep plants in bounds during the growing season, but prune back hard in early spring for bushy growth. Will probably need winter protection, such as a covering of evergreen boughs.

3. GERMANDER (*Teucrium Chamaedrys*): A perennial, to 2 feet tall and wide, with dark green foliage and pink flowers in midsummer. Plan on one plant per foot of border. Clip it as you would green santolina.

4. LAVENDER COTTON (*Santolina Chamaecyparissus*): A perennial, to 32 inches tall and wide, with finely cut, aromatic silver-gray foliage and yellow cottonball blooms in summer. Plant as a specimen. Prune back hard in spring to keep it from becoming woody, then shear lightly for a mounded effect.

5. HYSSOP (*Hyssopus officinalis*): A perennial, to 3 feet tall, with aromatic green foliage and white, blue, or pink flowers in summer. Plant on 2-foot centers. Shear to desired shape.

6. BLUE BEAUTY RUE (*Ruta Graveolens* 'Blue Beauty'): A perennial, to 2 feet tall, with blue-green, ferny, aromatic foliage and yellow flowers in summer. Plant on 2-foot centers. Shear to desired shape.

Other plants that make handsome knot borders include dwarf and edging box, American germander, 'Hidcote' lavender, mother-of-thyme, lemon and golden lemon thyme, gray Roman and fringed wormwood, sage, winter savory, sweet marjoram, rosemary, and southernwood. Creeping thymes can be used in place of sand, stone, or mulch to fill in the design between the borders. The entire knot garden can be framed in brick or stone (preferably set no wider or higher than the borders).

Knot gardens are not low-maintenance propositions. Besides requiring constant pruning, winter protection, and standard good cultural practices, they need a supply of backup plants. Nothing looks quite as dreadful as a ratty knot garden border, with brown or empty patches where herbs didn't make it through the winter. Keep a nursery of "squares" of all the plants you use in the knot in an out-of-sight border so you'll always have replacements ready.

THE MEDICINAL GARDEN

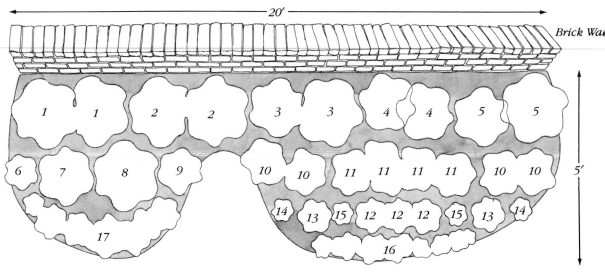

PLANTS FOR THE MEDICINAL GARDEN

These days, plants for the medicinal garden are chiefly for show. While you may make a cup of comfrey or chamomile tea, or try your hand at horehound drops, or gather a bouquet of aconite, foxglove, and feverfew, many medicinal plants are poisonous and are best admired for their historical significance and left in the garden. The half-kidney shape of this garden subtly reinforces its medical theme.

The plants:

1. VALERIAN (*Valeriana officinalis*): A perennial, 3½ to 5 feet tall, with pinnate leaves and clusters of fragrant white, pink, or lavender flowers from June through September. Plant on 2-foot centers. Oil from the roots has been used as a sedative and painkiller.

2. GENTIAN (*Gentiana lutea*): A perennial, to 6 feet tall, with deep-veined leaves and showy yellow flower clusters in late summer. Plant on 2-foot centers. The root has been used as a digestive aid, vermicide, and antiseptic wound treatment.

3. MULLEIN (*Verbascum thapsus*): A biennial, 3 to 6 feet tall in flower, with a basal rosette of large, woolly leaves and a large spike of lemon yellow flowers from June through September. Plant on 2-foot centers. The flowers have been used to treat coughs, congestion, and tuberculosis and were smoked to soothe pulmonary diseases.

4. ELECAMPANE (*Inula Helenium*): A perennial, to 6 feet tall and 3 feet wide, with large basal leaves, smaller upper leaves, and yellow daisylike flowers in summer. Plant on 2-foot centers. The rhizome has been used to treat respiratory diseases.

5. AMERICAN HELLEBORE (*Veratrum viride*): A perennial, to 7 feet tall, with broad, ribbed leaves and a spike of yellow-green flowers in midsummer. Plant on 2-foot centers. The rhizome has been used as a sedative, emetic, and to treat hypertension. All plants are poisonous.

6. COMFREY (*Symphytum officinale*): A perennial, 3 to 5 feet tall, with large, hairy basal leaves

and white, rose, purple, or yellowish bell-shaped flowers from May through frost. Plant on 1½-foot centers. The root has been used to reduce inflammation and to heal broken bones.

7. LOBELIA (*Lobelia inflata*): An annual, to 3 feet tall, with toothed leaves and blue or white flowers in July and August. Plant on 1½-foot centers. The entire plant has been used to treat asthma, as a nerve stimulant, and as a tobacco substitute.

8. FEVERFEW (*Chrysanthemum Parthenium*): A perennial, to 3 feet tall and wide, with aromatic, fingered foliage and creamy white, buttonlike flowers midsummer through fall. Plant on 1½-foot centers. The flowers have been used as a sedative and tonic.

9. BETONY (*Stachys officinalis*): A perennial, 2½ feet tall in flower, with a basal rosette of round-lobed leaves and spikes of white, pink, or reddish purple flowers from mid- to late summer. Plant on 1½-foot centers. The leaves have been used as a poultice, emetic, tonic, nervine, and sedative.

10. ACONITE (*Aconitum Napellus*): A perennial, to 3 feet tall, with deep green, finely divided leaves and dark blue hooded flowers in large spikes in July and August. Plant on 1½-foot centers. The rhizomes have been used as a sedative, painkiller, and to treat rheumatism. All parts are poisonous.

11. FOXGLOVE (*Digitalis purpurea*): A biennial, 3 to 4 feet tall, with large, wrinkled leaves and huge spikes of white, cream-yellow, pink, rose, lavender, or purple bell-shaped flowers, often with speckled throats, which bloom in June and July. Plant on 1½-foot centers. The leaves have been used as a heart stimulant and to treat dropsy. All parts are poisonous.

12. ARNICA (*Arnica montana*): A perennial, to 2 feet tall in flower, with a basal rosette of long leaves and yellow daisylike flowers in midsummer. Plant on 1-foot centers. The flowers have been used as a compress for bruises, wounds, and inflammation. All parts are poisonous.

13. ECHINACEA (*Echinacea angustifolia*): A perennial, to 2 feet tall, with long, narrow leaves and lavender daisylike petals curving back from tall orange cones; plants flower in mid- to late summer. Plant on 1-foot centers. The roots are still used by some herbalists as an anti-infective.

14. MANDRAKE (*Mandragora officinarum*): A perennial, to 1 foot tall, with a basal rosette of wrinkled leaves and greenish yellow bell-shaped flowers borne singly in late spring. Plant on 1-foot centers. The root has been used as a painkiller and sedative. All parts are poisonous.

15. WHITE-WOOLY HOREHOUND (*Marrubium incanum*): A perennial, 2 to 3 feet tall and 15 inches wide, with hairy leaves and whorls of white flowers in summer. Plant on 1-foot centers. The leaves and flowers have been used for coughs and colds.

16. ROMAN CHAMOMILE (*Chamaemelum nobile*): A perennial, 1 foot tall in flower; with 2- to 4-inch-tall mats of feathery, fruit-scented foliage and white daisylike flowers from June through August. Plant on 6-inch centers. The flowers have been used as a sedative and hair rinse.

17. AUTUMN CROCUS (*Colchicum autumnale*): A perennial bulb, to 1 foot tall and 3 to 4 inches wide; straplike leaves wither in summer and are followed in September by rose-purple flowers. Plant on 6-inch centers. The seeds and corms have been used to treat gout and rheumatism. All parts are poisonous.

PLANTS FOR THE DYE GARDEN

Even though dye plants formed an integral part of most dooryard gardens before the invention of chemical dyes, they were never "domesticated" like their more civilized culinary and fragrant cousins. As a result, they retain a rustic, meadow-plant feel and should be given a simple setting. Ours features half-barrel and rectangular, board-sided raised beds, with the framing staked in place. A split-rail fence or dry-stone wall makes the perfect backdrop to the dye garden. Some dye plants are familiar annual flowers—marigolds, zinnias, and calliopsis—and these have been incorporated in the design for added color until the herbs fill in. In subsequent years, they can be removed or space left for them, as desired.

The plants:

1. QUEEN OF THE MEADOW (*Filipendula ulmaria*): A perennial, to 4 feet tall, with large, bright green, lobed leaves, and fragrant, white, feathery plumes in June and July. Plant on 2-foot centers. The roots yield a black dye; the leaves and stems, harvested when the plants are just coming into bloom, yield a greenish yellow with alum used as a mordant.

2. WELD (*Reseda luteola*): A biennial, 5 feet tall in flower, with a basal rosette of long, slender, lance-shaped leaves and long, slender, yellow flower spikes in summer. Plant on 2-foot centers. The whole plant in full flower yields a lemon yellow dye with alum used as a mordant; a golden yellow with chrome; and an orange with alum and tin.

3. GOLDEN MARGUERITE (*Anthemis tinctoria*): A perennial, one of the most ornamental herbs, 2 feet tall and white, with aromatic, feathery green leaves and masses of 2-inch, yellow daisylike blooms from June through August. Plant on 15-inch centers. The flowers yield a yellow dye with alum used as a mordant; a gold dye with chrome.

4. MARIGOLD (*Tagetes* spp.): An annual, with deep green, aromatic, feathery foliage and single to double flowers in yellow, gold, orange, burgundy, and rust; also bicolors and white. Choose bushy plants in the 2-foot range, and plant on 15-inch centers. They'll bloom summer through frost. The fresh or dried flowers yield yellow, gold, orange, brown, gray, or green without a mordant; yellow with alum used as a mordant.

5. LADY'S BEDSTRAW (*Galium verum*): A perennial, to 3 feet tall, but often creeping, with whorls of narrow, pale green leaves and small yellow flowers in panicles in July and August. Plant on 15-inch centers. The roots yield light red with alum used as a mordant; purplish red with chrome. The flowering tops yield yellow with alum or chrome used as a mordant.

6. MADDER (*Rubia tinctorum*): A perennial, to 4 feet tall, but often prostrate, with whorls of leaves and greenish yellow, inconspicuous flowers in early summer. Plant on 15-inch centers. The 3-year-old roots, dried, yield a rose-red or lacquer red with alum used as a mordant; garnet red, orange, or rust with chrome; bright red or Turkey red (on cotton) with tin. The fine reds of old quilts and oriental rugs were created with madder dyes.

7. SAFFRON (*Crocus sativus*): A perennial bulb, saffron is indicated by dotted lines, as it sends up 1½-foot-long, thin, straplike leaves in spring, which die in midsummer. In September saffron bears 2-inch, lilac cup-shaped flowers with bright orange stigmata. Plant on 4- to 6-inch centers. The stigmata yield yellow with alum used as a mordant; gold with chrome. Because the tiny stigmata must be hand-harvested in great quantity to yield dye, saffron dyes have always been the property of the elite and the stuff of legend.

8. SOAPWORT (*Saponaria officinalis*): A perennial, domesticated varieties 1 to 2 feet tall, with 2- to 3-inch, lance-shaped leaves and large pink blooms in panicles from July through September. Plant on 15-inch centers. Soapwort is not a dye plant but is included in the dye garden for authenticity's sake, as the roots were used to make a soapy lather in which the yarn was washed before dyeing.

9. SAFFLOWER (*Carthamus tinctorius*): An annual, to 3 feet tall, bushy plants with toothed, bright green lance-shaped leaves and striking

206

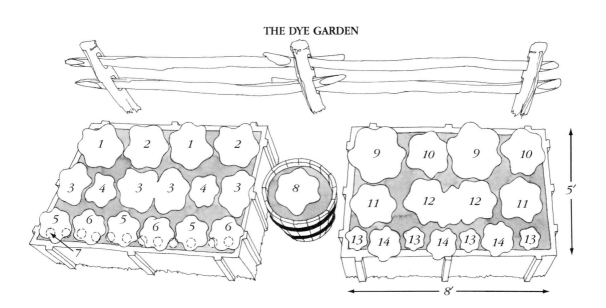
THE DYE GARDEN

scarlet-orange-yellow thistle-shaped flowers in summer. Plant on 2-foot centers. The fresh or dried flowers yield yellow with alum used as a mordant; red in an alkaline solution. It is often called poor man's saffron.

10. GOLDENROD (*Solidago* 'Goldenmosa'): A perennial, to 3 feet tall, with erect stems, slender, spear-shaped leaves, and handsome golden yellow plumes in August and September. Plant on 2-foot centers. The flowers and leaves yield yellow, gold, tan, yellow-green, avocado, olive green, bronze, brown, and khaki; yellow with alum used as a mordant; old gold with chrome. This much-maligned plant is not the source of hayfever (the real villain is ragweed). It is one of the most attractive dye plants. While 'Goldenmosa' is suggested, try any of the tall, domesticated varieties.

11. WOAD (*Isatis tinctoria*): A biennial, 3 feet tall in flower, with a basal rosette of 1-foot-long blue-green leaves and large panicles of cloudlike yellow blooms in May and June, fol-

lowed by clusters of black berries that can be used in dried arrangements. Plant on 2-foot centers. The young leaves, picked fresh and fermented, yield blue; mature leaves treated in the same manner yield blue-black; weak solutions yield green. The only temperate-climate source of blue dye (tropical indigo also yields blue), woad is indisputably the most stunning dye plant in flower. It's also one of the most historic, having been used by the Picts of England as a styptic for battle wounds, causing them to appear in what was taken by the disconcerted Roman invaders as blue war paint.

12. ST.-JOHN'S-WORT (*Hypericum perforatum*): A perennial, to 2 feet tall, with yellow flowers in July and August. Plant on 2-foot centers. The flowering tops yield yellow and gold; the whole plant yields yellow-green with alum used as a mordant; gold with chrome; bronze with blue vitriol; yellow-green with iron and tin.

13. ZINNIA (*Zinnia elegans*): An annual, 6 to 36 inches tall, with opposite, spear-shaped leaves

and double blooms to 7 inches across, with quilled, pointed petals, in white, pink, orange, red, green, purple, yellow, and multiples, from summer through frost. Plant one of the 1½-foot cultivars on 1-foot centers; remember to choose a color or colors compatible with the reds, yellows, and golds of the rest of the bed. The flowers yield yellow with alum used as a mordant; bronze with chrome; bright gold with tin; gray-green with iron; khaki with blue vitriol.

14. CALLIOPSIS (*Coreopsis tinctoria*): An annual, 8 to 48 inches tall, with spindly, needlelike leaves and yellow, purple-red, or bicolor daisylike blooms summer through frost. Plant on 1-foot centers. The fresh flowers yield bright yellow with alum used as a mordant; bright orange-yellow with tin; rusty orange with chrome. If picked after frost, the flowers yield dull gold with alum; brown with chrome and iron; dull rust with chrome and tin.

PLANTS FOR THE FRAGRANCE GARDEN

The bloom season in the fragrance garden extends from the first sweet violets in April until the nasturtiums are killed by late fall frosts. Summer is a blaze of color—blue, white, lavender, apricot, and gold. But fragrant flowers are only half the story. The delightfully scented foliage of rosemary, scented geranium, lemon balm, lavender, catmint, the thymes, and nasturtiums can be enjoyed all season. The design brings the plants to nose level for a heady feeling when you're sitting on the bench; the violets form a soft carpet underfoot.

The plants:
1. SWEET VIOLET (*Viola odorata*): A perennial, 6 inches tall in spreading clumps; blooms in April and May with the classic violet fragrance. Violets prefer partial shade so they are planted under the bench and in the shelter of the brick wall. Plant all violet 'Royal Robe', or mix them with 'Red Giant', 'White Czar', and 'Rosina'.
2. SNOW WHITE BEEBALM (*Monarda didyma* 'Snow White'): A perennial, 3 feet tall; blooms in July and August. Give these plants a 2-foot circle; they will spread. Both the tubular flower clusters and the leaves are fragrantly lemony.
3. HIDCOTE LAVENDER (*Lavandula angustifolia* subsp. *angustifolia* 'Hidcote'): A perennial, 1½ feet tall and up to 1½ feet wide; blooms in June and July with deep violet-blue flower

spikes. Both the flowers and the silver-gray foliage are highly fragrant, with the intensely pungent lavender scent. Place 1 foot apart to form a solid "hedge."
4. MOTHER-OF-THYME (*Thymus serpyllum*): A perennial, creeping ground cover 3 inches tall; bears tiny lavender flowers in June and July. The small, shiny evergreen leaves are fragrant, with the pungent, salty smell of thyme. Plant 1 foot apart; plants will trail over the brick edging for a cascade effect.
5. LEMON THYME (*Thymus* ×*citriodorus*): A perennial, clumping herb 4 inches tall; bears small rosy blooms in June and July. The light green leaves have a wonderful lemon fragrance. Give them 1-foot circles.
6. SCENTED GERANIUM (*Pelargonium* spp.): A perennial in Zones 9 and 10, where it may reach 3 feet tall. In colder areas cuttings or pot plants must be set out after all danger of frost has passed; plants will probably reach 1½-foot height and width in one growing season. Pink through lavender flowers are borne in summer. The soft, fuzzy green or bicolored foliage is highly fragrant. There are hundreds of scented geraniums; plant all of one kind or mix them. Favorites include lemon-scented geranium (*P. crispum*), with tiny crinkled leaves; *P. crispum* 'Variegatum', with creamy white leaf margins;

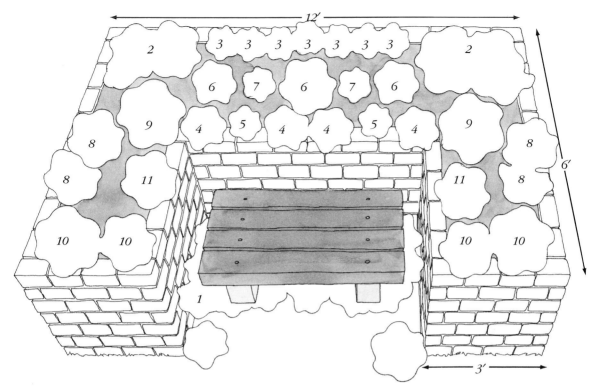

rose-scented geranium (*P. graveolens*), with large, fingered leaves; and peppermint-scented geranium (*P. tomentosum*), with downy, maple-like leaves. Give plants 1½-foot circles.

7. LEMON BALM (*Melissa officinalis*): A perennial; may reach 2-foot height and width in flower; blooms July through September. Flower heads should be cut back to keep plants from wantonly self-sowing. Scalloped green foliage is strongly lemon scented. Plant in 1½-foot circles.

8. BLUE WONDER CATMINT (*Nepeta mussini* 'Blue Wonder'): A bushy perennial, 12 to 15 inches tall, which covers itself with 6-inch blue flower spikes in spring and early summer. Fuzzy foliage smells minty. Shear plants back after flowering for rebloom in fall. Give plants 1-foot circles.

9. GARLIC CHIVES (*Allium tuberosum*): A perennial, to 2 feet tall; spreads in clumps. Straplike blue-green foliage contrasts nicely with the more leafy herbs. Plants cover themselves with rose-scented clusters of starry white flowers in late summer. Cut the bloom stalks before the seeds ripen, or you'll have a forest on your hands in subsequent seasons. Plant garlic chives on 1½-foot centers.

10. NASTURTIUMS (*Tropaeolum majus*): An annual; 1 foot tall by 2 feet wide; will cascade over the brick edging. Sea green leaves are succulent and shaped like inverted umbrellas. Both leaves and flowers, which are borne summer through frost in saturated shades of red, apricot, orange, and gold, are strongly scented, with a unique, nose-pinching, pepper-perfumy smell. Sow after all danger of frost has passed. Plant on 1½-foot centers.

11. WHITE-FLOWERED ROSEMARY (*Rosmarinus officinalis* 'Albiflorus'): A perennial in Zones 8 through 10; otherwise, sink pots in the bed or plant out and pot again in fall. Can reach hedge proportions, but won't north of Zone 8, where it is unlikely to reach 2-foot height. There are several good white-flowered varieties, blooming in early summer. The main attraction, however, is the graceful branches of deep green needles with their delightfully pungent, piny scent.

209

THE EVERLASTING GARDEN

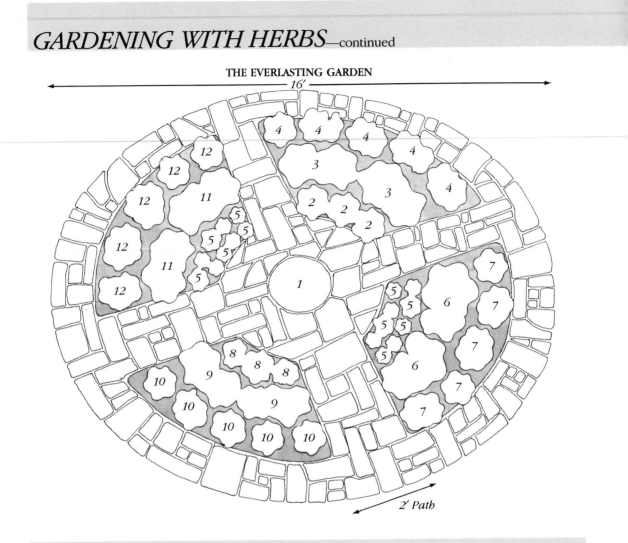

16'

2' Path

PLANTS FOR THE EVERLASTING GARDEN

This garden is everlasting in two senses: first, it is composed of perennials; and second, all of the plants may be dried for everlasting arrangements. To dry the flowers or foliage for bouquets or wreaths, cut the stems on a dry day after the dew has evaporated. Because flowers will continue to mature as they dry, cut them before they are fully open. Unless the foliage is ornamental when dried, strip off the leaves; otherwise, you face increased drying times and the danger of mildew. Tie the stems in loose bunches (but make the ties tight—stems will shrink as they dry). Hang the bunches upside down in a dark, warm, well-ventilated room (such as an attic or pantry) for a couple of weeks. Flowers with woody stems can be placed upright in a glass. (See the entry Crafts from Herbs for more information.)

Many other plants can be chosen to add color and texture to an everlasting garden. Most of these are considered ornamental flowers rather than herbs. They include the green flowers and foliage of ambrosia; the white, pink, mauve, rose, and purple flowers of statice; the reds, yellows, oranges, and purple-blacks of strawflowers; the silvery foliage of 'Silver King' artemisia; the white flowers of pearly everlasting; the aromatic, gray-green foliage of eucalyptus; and the handsome mauve and green pods of love-in-a-mist. Other herbs that are handsome dried include camphor-scented artemisia, beebalm, dill, elecampane, sage, and hops.

The plants:

1. LAMBROOK SILVER WORMWOOD (*Artemisia Absinthium* 'Lambrook Silver'): A perennial, to 3 feet tall, with finely dissected, metallic silvery foliage, which emerges green in spring, and stalks of tiny, yellow, fluffy flowers in midsummer. The foliage is used in arrangements.

2. HIDCOTE LAVENDER (*Lavandula angustifolia* subsp. *angustifolia* 'Hidcote'): A perennial, 1½ feet tall and up to 1½ feet wide; blooms in June and July with deep violet-blue flower spikes. Plant on 1-foot centers. Both the flowers and the silver-gray foliage are highly fragrant and can be dried for arrangements.

3. GOLDENROD (*Solidago* 'Golden Baby' or *S.* 'Goldenmosa'): A perennial, 'Golden Baby' grows 2 feet tall, while 'Goldenmosa' can reach 3 feet; both have erect stems, slender, spear-shaped leaves, and handsome golden yellow plumes borne profusely in August and September. Plant on 2-foot centers. The flowers are used in arrangements; pick them early or they'll turn to loose fluff.

4. YARROW (*Achillea Millefolium*): A perennial, 2 feet tall, with aromatic, feathery foliage and flat clusters of creamy white flowers from June through September. Plant on 1½-foot centers. The flowers are used in arrangements.

5. SWEET MARJORAM (*Origanum Majorana*): A perennial, 1 foot tall and 4 to 6 inches wide, with small, rounded leaves and showy, deep purple flower heads. Often acts like an annual in temperate areas. Plant on 6-inch centers. The flowers are used in arrangements.

6. TANSY (*Tanacetum vulgare*): A perennial, 3 feet tall, with feathery foliage and yellow buttonlike flowers from July through September. Plant on 2-foot centers. The pungent foliage is used in arrangements.

7. CORONATION GOLD YARROW (*Achillea filipendulina* 'Coronation Gold'): A perennial, to 2 feet tall with fernlike foliage and flat clusters of golden yellow flowers in summer. Plant on 1½-foot centers. The aromatic flowers are used in arrangements.

8. MUNSTEAD LAVENDER (*Lavandula angustifolia* subsp. *angustifolia* 'Munstead'): A perennial, 1 foot tall, with aromatic, gray foliage and bright lavender flower spikes in summer. Plant on 1-foot centers. Both flowers and foliage can be used in arrangements.

9. FEVERFEW (*Chrysanthemum Parthenium*): A perennial, to 3 feet tall and wide, with aromatic, fingered foliage and ivory buttonlike flowers midsummer through fall. Plant on 1½-foot centers. The flowers are used in arrangements.

10. CERISE QUEEN YARROW (*Achillea Millefolium* 'Cerise Queen'): A perennial, to 2 feet tall, with aromatic, feathery foliage and flat clusters of bright cherry red flowers from June through September. Plant on 1½-foot centers. The flowers are used in arrangements.

11. BLUE BEAUTY RUE (*Ruta graveolens* 'Blue Beauty'): A perennial, 2 feet tall, with aromatic, blue-green, ferny foliage and yellow flowers in summer. Plant on 2-foot centers. The aromatic seed heads, which can be picked in the green or brown stage, are used in arrangements.

12. MOONSHINE YARROW (*Achillea filipendulina* 'Moonshine'): A perennial, to 2 feet tall and 1½ feet wide, with fernlike foliage and flat clusters of cream-yellow flowers in summer. Plant on 1½-foot centers. The flowers are used in arrangements.

THE KITCHEN GARDEN

PLANTS FOR THE KITCHEN GARDEN

This kitchen garden is designed to be ornamental, but it is composed—with the exception of borage—of the most common culinary herbs. The borders of the central path are undulations of purple, green, and pink (if you let the 'Dark Opal' basil flower). Plants in the outer borders are on 1½-foot centers so each can be shown to best advantage. A mulch of bark chips or cocoa hulls will accent form and foliage color, as well as keep dirt off the bricks. Mints are invasive. Control them by sinking metal edging strips, preferably a foot deep, around their planting area, or by planting them in sunken bottomless

buckets. In either case, leave an inch or so of rim or edging above the ground to control prowling stems. The focal point of the garden is the borage, with its fuzzy foliage and lovely star-shaped blue, pink, or lavender flowers.

The plants:

1. DARK OPAL BASIL (*Ocimum Basilicum* 'Dark Opal'): An annual, to 15 inches tall, with dark purple leaves and pink flowers in July and August. For heaviest production of the spicy, fragrant leaves, clip off the flower heads; leave them for the most ornamental effect. Plant on 1-

foot centers.

2. PURPLE SAGE (*Salvia officinalis* 'Purpurascens'): A perennial, 12 to 30 inches tall, powder green older leaves, new leaves powder purple, with purple flowers in June. The foliage has a hearty, sausagelike smell; let it grow in subsequent years to fill the borders, or keep it cut back to leave space for the 'Dark Opal' basil. Plant on 1-foot centers.

3. CURLY PARSLEY (*Petroselinum crispum*): A biennial, treated as an annual. Bushy 1-foot-tall plants with dark green, moss-curled leaves. Remove after the foliage dies back at the end of the first season—the following year, the plants' energies will be directed toward producing 3-foot stalks of yellow-green umbels in summer, rather than the flavorful, vitamin-rich leaves. Plant on 1½-foot centers.

4. CHIVES (*Allium Schoenoprasum*): A perennial, forming spreading clumps 1 to 1½ feet tall of tubular, deep green leaves, with striking balls of pink to pale lilac flowers in June. Plants do tend to spread, but are easily controlled by division. Plant on 1½-foot centers.

5. COMMON THYME (*Thymus vulgaris*): A perennial, shrubby plant, to 14 inches tall, with small, deep green leaves and tiny mauve flowers in June and July. The name may be common, but the fragrance and fine, salty, pungent flavor are unbeatable. Plant on 1½-foot centers.

6. SPICY GLOBE BASIL (*Ocimum Basilicum* 'Spicy Globe'): An annual, rounded mound of tightly packed, pungent, light green foliage to 1 foot tall. Bears light green flower heads in July and August. The most visually appealing basil; you want to pet it. A similar variety is Burpee's

'Green Globe'. Plant on 1½-foot centers.

7. BERGAMOT MINT (*Mentha ✕piperita* var. *citrata*): A perennial, 2 to 3 feet tall, with long, deep green, purple-tinged leaves, purple flowers in midsummer, and a strong citrus scent. Confine the roots. Harvest or shear back to the desired height. Shear before flowering—mint is invasive enough without encouraging seeding. Plant on 2-foot centers.

8. APPLE MINT (*Mentha suaveolens*): A perennial, to 4 feet tall, with rounded, gray-green, hairy leaves, lavender flowers in midsummer, and a rich fruity scent. Confine the roots. Harvest or shear back to the desired height. Shear before flowering. Plant on 2-foot centers.

9. SPEARMINT (*Mentha spicata*): A perennial, to 2½ feet tall, with spear-shaped, bright green leaves, pink, white, or lilac flowers, and the inimitable spearmint scent. Confine the roots. Shear before flowering. Plant on 2-foot centers.

10. PEPPERMINT (*Mentha ✕piperita*): A perennial, to 3 feet tall, with long, dark green, purple-tinged leaves and purple stems, lilac-pink flowers in midsummer, and the strong, incomparable peppermint fragrance. Confine the roots. Harvest or shear back to the desired height. Shear before flowering. Plant on 2-foot centers.

11. BORAGE (*Borago officinalis*): An annual, 2½ to 3 feet tall, with strong, hairy, large green leaves and star-shaped, drooping, predominantly blue flowers (though they may also be pink and lavender) in midsummer. Flowers and leaves are edible; both are used in salads and fruit salads, while the flowers are refreshing in drinks. The flavor is reminiscent of cucumber. Plant on 1½-foot centers.

PUBLIC HERB GARDENS

The best way to learn about herb garden design is to visit herb gardens that are open to the public. Listed on the next page are a few notable gardens. *The Travelers' Guide to Herb Gardens,* available from the Herb Society of America, 2 Independence Court, Concord, MA 01742 ($3.75 ppd.) lists 480 public herb gardens in the United States and Canada..

California
The Herb Garden
Los Angeles State and County
Arboretum
301 North Baldwin Avenue
Arcadia

Fragrance Garden
Strybing Arboretum
Golden Gate Park
San Francisco

Colorado
Denver Botanic Garden
1005 York Street
Denver

Connecticut
Capriland's Herb Farm
534 Silver Street
Coventry

Henry Whitfield House
Old Whitfield Street
Guilford

Florida
Medicinal Plant Garden
College of Pharmacy
University of Florida
Gainesville

Georgia
Callaway Gardens
Highway 27
Pine Mountain

Illinois
Botanic Garden
Chicago Horticultural Society
Glencoe

Maine
Merry Gardens
Mechanic Street
Camden

United Society of Shakers
Route 26
Poland Spring

Massachusetts
The Herb Garden
Hancock Shaker Village
Pittsfield

Old Sturbridge Village
1 Old Sturbridge Village Road
Sturbridge

Michigan
Fox Hill Farm
440 West Michigan Avenue
Parma

Minnesota
Landscape Arboretum
University of Minnesota
3675 Arboretum Drive
Chanhassen

Missouri
Shaw's Garden
Missouri Botanical Gardens
4344 Shaw Boulevard
St. Louis

New Jersey
Duke Gardens Foundation
Route 206 South
Somerville

Well-Sweep Herb Farm
317 Mt. Bethel Road
Port Murray

William Trent House
539 South Warren Street
Trenton

New York
Biblical Garden
Cathedral Church of St. John
the Divine
New York City

Garden of Fragrance
Rochester Museum and Science
Center
657 East Avenue
Rochester

Medieval Herb Garden
The Cloisters
Fort Tryon Park
New York City

Robison York State Herb Garden
Forest Home School
Cornell University
Ithaca

Ohio
Western Reserve Herb Garden
Garden Center
11030 East Boulevard
Cleveland

Oklahoma
Anne Hathaway Municipal
Herb Garden
Woodward Park
Tulsa

Pennsylvania
Fragrant Garden
John J. Tyler Arboretum
515 Painter Road
Lima

Drug Plant and Herb Garden
Morris Arboretum
9414 Meadowbrook Avenue
Chestnut Hill

Old Economy Village
14th and Church
Ambridge

Rhode Island
Garden of Dye and Textile Plants
Old Slater Museum
Pawtucket

Virginia
Colonial Williamsburg
Williamsburg

Monticello
Route 53
Charlottesville

Mt. Vernon Kitchen Garden
Washington's Home
Mt. Vernon

Washington
Pioneer Herb Garden
Washington State Capitol Museum
211 West 21st Street
Olympia

Washington, D.C.
The National Herb Garden
U.S. National Arboretum
3501 New York Avenue, NE

Wisconsin
Boerner Botanical Garden
Whitnall Park
5879 South 92nd Street
Hales Corner

GARLIC

Allium sativum   Liliaceae

Garlic is a medicinal and culinary herb that inspires extraordinary affection in people. In medieval times, it was eaten as a vegetable, rather than in discreet amounts as a condiment. Whole bulbs are pickled and put up in jars in Southeast Asia. In the United States, garlic lovers even have a national club, the Order of the Stinking Rose.

HISTORY

Garlic was once thought to possess magical powers against evil and was widely used in charms and spells. The poet Homer's Odysseus used it to keep the sorceress Circe from turning him into a pig. The Egyptians swore on a clove of garlic when they took a solemn oath.

Many of the legends surrounding it have to do with strength, speed, and endurance. Egyptian slaves ate garlic as they built the pyramids. The Israelites nibbled it before their escape from Egypt and later longed for the herb during their wilderness wanderings. The Romans took it to strengthen them in battle since it was the herb of Mars, the Roman god of war. European legend says that if a man chews on a garlic bulb during a foot race, no one will be able to get ahead of him (and it's doubtful anyone would want to draw close).

Medicinally, garlic has been prescribed since prebiblical times. In the Far East, ancient herbalists used it to treat high blood pressure and respiratory problems. It is mentioned in the Calendar of the Hsai, which dates back to 2000 B.C. An Egyptian medical listing of 1550 B.C. recommends garlic as a remedy for 22 problems, including headaches, bites, worms, tumors, and heart ailments. The Roman scholar Pliny said it would cure over 60 ailments. Within the past 500 years, doctors have brought along a few cloves on house calls as a charm and disinfectant. However, because of what one British herbalist calls its "intolerable Rankness," the English never really grew very fond of it. The seventeenth-century British herbalist Culpeper was reserved in describing its powers. It killed worms in children, he said, protected against various plagues, eased earaches, counteracted some poisons such as hemlock and henbane, and took away skin blemishes. But he warned: "Its heat is vehement; and in choleric men it will add fuel to the fire. In men oppressed by melancholy, it will attenuate the humour. Therefore, let it be taken inwardly with great moderation; outwardly you may make more bold with it."

The culinary home of garlic is southern Europe, of course, and it also figures in folk medicines. It is the main ingredient of Four Thieves Vinegar, a legendary remedy that has been sold in France

DESCRIPTION

Garlic is an onion with a compound bulb made up of 4 to 15 cloves or bulblets. These are enclosed in a papery sheath that is tan-colored in early varieties and pinkish in later ones. (See photo on page 273.)

Flowers: Very small, white to pinkish, six segments, six stamens, sterile; in terminal globe-shaped umbel.

Leaves: Arise from the base; four to six; linear, long, to ½ in. wide.

Fruit: Seeds; rarely produced.

Height: To 2 ft.

FLOWERING

Spring and summer.

RANGE

Origin uncertain; may be indigenous to southern Siberia. Naturalized widely.

GARLIC—continued

OLD-TIME GARLIC REMEDIES

Here are a few old-time remedies for various aches and pains.

Garlic cough syrup: Recipes for this syrup abound. The British herbalist Maude Grieve recommends pouring a quart of boiling water on a pound of fresh, sliced garlic. Let this steep for 12 hours, then add sugar until the consistency is syrup. To improve the taste, add honey and vinegar boiled with caraway and fennel seeds. For children, she suggests a milder syrup of 1½ ounces of sugar dissolved in 1 ounce of fresh garlic juice.

Garlic tea: Gargle garlic tea for a sore throat, and swallow it if you have the flu. Chop several cloves of garlic and let steep in ½ cup of water for six to eight hours.

Tincture: To lower blood pressure, herbalists recommend a few drops of tincture of garlic. Soak ½ pound of peeled cloves in 1 quart of brandy. Shake a few times each day. After two weeks, strain. The liquid (or tincture) will keep for about one year. Take up to 25 drops a day as needed.

Smelling salts: To relieve hysteria, sniff crushed garlic.

Garlic oil: To soothe an earache, place a few drops of warm garlic oil in the affected ear. Make the oil by slicing a garlic clove, adding a small amount of olive oil, and heating briefly. Strain before use.

since the early eighteenth century. According to the story, four condemned criminals were recruited to bury those who had died during a plague in Marseilles, and they themselves never fell ill because they drank a mixture of crushed garlic and wine vinegar.

In this country wild garlic was well-known to the Indians, and domestic varieties were brought over by the settlers. The pioneers were said to have put garlic in their horses' nostrils to counteract the effects of high altitude.

USES

Garlic is a useful plant to have around: Hundreds of dishes call for it; several claims made for its medicinal benefits have recently been substantiated; and then there are scores of odd uses for the stuff. If you haven't seen a vampire lately, you can thank the garlic in your kitchen. Or, if you need to get rid of a lovesick boyfriend, garlic can also help. A legend of the American West says that the girl must go to an intersection in a road and place there a piece of garlic with two crossed pins. She entices the boy to walk over the charm, and he will lose interest in her.

Medicinal: Recent findings show that this plant has powerful ingredients that earn it a place in the modern medicine bag.

Infection: Herbalists have long claimed that garlic was a good germ killer. In India, garlic is used to wash wounds and ulcers. During World War I, army doctors daubed garlic juice on sterilized sphagnum moss and applied it to infected wounds.

Now we have research findings to explain these cures. The very component that gives garlic its strong odor is the one that destroys or inhibits various bacteria, fungi, and yeast. Called allicin, its antibacterial action is equivalent to that of 1 percent penicillin. Allicin forms in the garlic when the cloves are crushed and a parent substance, alliin, meets up with an enzyme, allinase. The result is that potent smell and some equally potent antibacterial powers. Unfortunately, allicin is quite unstable, and cooking the garlic may reduce its effectiveness.

Experiments have shown that garlic is effective against some influenza viruses, fungi, and yeasts, such as the one that causes athlete's foot. It is more effective than penicillin against typhus. It works against staph and strep bacteria, against the organism responsible for cholera, and against the bacillus species that causes typhus, dysentery, and enteritis.

Experienced herbalists recommend care in using garlic rubs and poultices. If placed directly against the skin, these may cause irritation or even blistering. Apply the crushed garlic cloves, extracted juice, or the oil to a piece of gauze that has been placed over the infection.

Worms and parasites: Garlic is a traditional cure for worms and other parasites in pets and people. Perhaps you have heard of giving your dog a clove of garlic every day for just this reason. An old-time remedy for pinworms was an enema of raw garlic juice.

Such treatments may not be as farfetched as they sound. Several of the sulfur compounds in garlic are at least mildly noxious to parasites. However, it's not known if they are present in sufficient concentrations to do much good.

Respiratory ailments: In the traditional medicine of both China and Europe, garlic is recommended for various respiratory ailments. Tuberculosis used to be treated with an inhalant of garlic oil or juice. A widely used treatment for whooping cough was a rubdown of garlic and lard on the chest and back. Some herbalists even recommended putting a clove in the patient's shoes; it was believed that the healthful aspects of garlic could be easily absorbed through the soles of the feet. It is possible that the irritating quality of garlic's volatile oils may indeed help open the lungs and bronchial tubes because these oils are readily absorbed into the bloodstream. A more direct remedy is to take a teaspoon of garlic syrup to relieve congestion.

High blood pressure: The Chinese have long used garlic to treat high blood pressure and other cardiac or circulatory ailments. Now Western physicians are beginning to experiment with it. Re-

217

GARLIC—continued

GARLIC BREATH

Whether you have just taken a few drops of garlic tincture or eaten a plate of creamed garlic, your breath will smell pretty rank. Young, fresh garlic leaves less of an aftertaste than older cloves, and elephant garlic seems to be milder yet. Still, garlic breath is the unavoidable occupational hazard of garlic eating.

Getting rid of this smell is the subject of many folk cures. Here are a few: Chew on a sprig of parsley immediately after eating garlic; nibble cardamom or fenugreek seeds; eat a strawberry; or take a long bath in very warm water (the garlic oils will evaporate).

search in the 1970s showed that oils extracted from garlic inhibit blood clotting. Studies in India gave garlic and onions credit for reducing both the cholesterol levels in the blood and the clogging of arteries. Just how garlic works on cholesterol isn't yet understood. Scientists have isolated a substance from onions, which decreases blood pressure when injected intravenously. We still don't know whether this agent has the same effect when swallowed, or whether it is also present in garlic.

Stomach cancer: Investigators in China are looking at the role garlic may play in preventing gastric cancer. They compared the counties with the lowest and highest rates of stomach cancer deaths and found that the residents of the healthiest county regularly ate up to 20 grams a day of garlic. They proved to have "significantly lower" levels of nitrite in their stomachs as well.

Other medical uses of garlic have yet to be supported by research. We don't yet know whether garlic truly is useful against colic, colds, kidney and bladder troubles, toothaches, or snakebites.

But for those who wish to try home remedies, garlic is one of the safest herbs. Given in moderation (and not to small children), garlic is very unlikely to cause a dangerous reaction. While it may not help the problem, it seems unlikely that it will harm the patient. Use as much as your friends can tolerate.

Culinary: Garlic's taste is vibrant and oniony. The bulb of the plant, which is broken into cloves, is important in most of the world's cuisines and adds dimension to all foods except desserts. Add minced garlic to herb butters, cheese spreads, breads, beans, broccoli, cauliflower, crackers, salads, stuffings, sauces, marinades, salad dressings, stews, soups, meats, fish, poultry, game, herb vinegars, and flavored oils and pickles. Preparing eggplant, tomato sauce, Caesar salad, and pesto is unthinkable without garlic.

Available commercially: Fresh whole; dried in flakes, or powder. Whole is preferable.

Storage note: Store fresh garlic in an airy place, not in the refrigerator.

Craft: As with other members of the genus *Allium,* the flower heads of garlic dry nicely and make an attractive addition to herb and flower arrangements.

Companion planting: The pest-controlling powers of garlic are well-known. Companion planters claim that garlic helps keep pests, particularly aphids, off roses. It is also recommended as an interplant with cabbages, eggplants, tomatoes, and fruit trees. Although scientists haven't been able to prove its benefits, they do know that garlic contains some fungicides and feeding deterrents. In one study one application of garlic spray kept black pea aphids at bay for up to 30 days. Researchers in the Northwest have found that a garlic spray also keeps hungry deer away from tender saplings.

Other: Japanese scientists discovered that grated garlic breaks dormancy in some bulbs, tubers, and woody plants. When gladiolus corms were treated with garlic paste, they sprouted in 41 days, compared to an average of 51 days for untreated bulbs. Sulfur and other chemicals have been used in this way, but they can be damaging if not given in very small amounts. Garlic seems to have no phytotoxicity and is effective on far more plants.

CULTIVATION

You can start garlic from seeds or cloves, the latter choice being much faster and easier, but more expensive.

Plant garlic cloves in early spring for a garlic harvest the following fall. Since it is quite cold-hardy, you can plant garlic as soon as the ground can be worked, up to six weeks before the last frost. This early start gives plants a chance to develop their leaves while days are still short and temperatures cool. During the warmer weather, when the days are longer, bulbs develop. In all but the coldest regions, you can even plant bulbs in autumn, so they get an early start the following spring.

The soil should be rich, somewhat dry, and deeply cultivated. Plant cloves 2 inches deep and about 6 inches apart; for the large elephant garlic, plant bulbs 1 foot apart. Full sun produces the largest bulbs, but garlic will tolerate some shade.

When flower stalks appear in early summer, cut them back so that the plants can devote their energy to developing bulbs. Allow a few plants to blossom, just so you can enjoy their beauty.

Harvesting and storage: Eventually, the tops will begin to bend and turn brown. If by midsummer they have not done so, don't wait; knock them down yourself. Withhold water and a few days later lift the plants. Place them on a screen in the shade for several days, then shake the dirt free.

Storage requirements are the same as for onions. A cool, dark, dry spot is best. Take care not to bruise the bulbs since this will invite molds and insects; you might even separate the bulbs so they don't bump against one another. One easy, attractive way to store garlic is to braid the leaves into a rope or a wreath by tying the cloves to a straw or wire frame. Or, twist off the dried leaves and drop the bulbs into a nylon stocking, tying a knot between each one. Hang this up and whenever you need a new bulb, snip one off just below a knot.

GENTIAN

Gentiana lutea   Gentianaceae

Humankind has valued *Gentiana lutea,* the yellow gentian, more for its bitter-tasting root than for its beautiful flowers—perhaps out of a puritanical belief that the sweet in life comes only after bitterness. For our less straitlaced times, the soul-restoring sight of the gentian blossom may be a better medicine than the root. Still, it is used in commercial bitters and to flavor Moxie, an old-time soft drink.

DESCRIPTION

A perennial herb, gentian emerges from a root that is 1–2 ft. long and 1–2 in. thick. When fresh, it is yellow inside and brownish outside; when dried, it is much darker. The taste is extremely bitter. Often the root is ringed, forked, and wrinkled.

Flowers: Large, bright yellow, to 2 in. across, usually cleft into five sections; in whorls of 3 to 10 from axils of the uppermost leaf pairs.

Leaves: Occur at each joint of the stem; opposite; smooth, waxy, stiff oval to oblong, light to bright green, to 1 ft. long, 6 in. wide; five prominent veins mark underside; upper leaves small, no leafstalks; lower leaves large, short leafstalks.

Fruit: A two-valved capsule of oblong shape; abundant.

Height: To 6 ft.

FLOWERING

July and August.

RANGE

Native to the mountains of Europe; cultivated in the northwestern United States and Canada.

HABITAT

High bogs and wet pastures at 3,000–8,000 ft.

GROWING CONDITIONS

• Plant hardiness zone 7.

• Soil pH: neutral to acid.

• Moist, well-drained, humusy soil.

• Full sun to partial shade.

HISTORY

The botanical genus got its name from Gentius, a second-century B.C. king of Illyria, who supposedly introduced its use in healing. But gentian was an ingredient in medicines described on an Egyptian papyrus dating from 1200 B.C. Both the Greeks and the Arabs used gentian preparations in cures for stomach and liver ailments, as a tonic, for prevention of pestilence, for protection against fainting, and to kill intestinal worms. It has also been used against hysteria and ague and for washing wounds and raising white blood cell counts.

USES

It is tempting to speculate that if a substance tastes bad enough, anything you eat subsequently will taste terrific. Maybe this is the basis of the popularity through the ages of bitter appetizers and aperitifs. Gentian has long been the most popular ingredient of these preparations; it is distinguished by a lovely orangish pink hue and for having no aftertaste.

Medicinal: The bitter taste of gentian root is so strong that it endures drying, grinding to powder, and dilution.

Among the numerous chemical substances present in yellow gentian root are some that have been found to increase the gastric secretions of dogs. While some medical authorities believe that all they do in healthy humans is irritate the mucous membrane of the digestive tract, others speculate that in people suffering from a sluggish appetite due to anorexia, old age, illness, or chronic indigestion, these substances do indeed stimulate the appetite. Commercial bitters employ gentian for this reason, but it may be the alcohol base itself that stimulates the appetite. Experiments with small animals show that gentian substances may increase the secretion of bile.

Pregnant women and anyone with high blood pressure are advised against taking gentian root. When taken in too large a dose, it can cause nausea and vomiting. The usual dose is 10 to 30 grams, given 30 to 60 minutes before meals to increase appetite and start stomach secretions. To make your own bitters, infuse a small section of root (2 ounces or less) in at least 1 pint of boiling water. Add brandy or dilute further with water. Take 1 tablespoonful or less. Add honey and cardamom seed for flavoring, if you wish.

Ornamental: Gentians of all kinds, including *G. lutea,* are valued for their looks in rock gardens, woodland plantings, and informal wild gardens. They are flowers of spectacular beauty, and only their finicky culture (and our lack of experience with them) keeps them from wider use. In Europe, gentians rank with primroses in popularity among alpine rock gardeners.

Several North American relatives are often grown for ornamental effect. The pine barren gentian, *G. autumnalis* or *G. Porphyrio,* is bright blue and comparatively easy to cultivate from New Jersey to South Carolina. The closed gentian, a bottle gentian, *G. Andrewsii,* grows from Manitoba south to North Carolina; some have white flowers, although blue ones are more common. *G. clausa* and *G. Saponaria* are much like the closed gentian. Western gardeners grow *G. calycosa,* which has a pale to dark blue flower on a foot-high stem. *G. sceptrum* has blue flowers dotted with green and can grow up to 4 feet high. *G. Catesbaei,* which grows in swamps from Virginia to Florida, has blue, club-shaped flowers.

CULTIVATION

Gentians can be raised from seeds, but the process is hardly foolproof. Without frost, the seeds will not germinate, and even with frost, germination can take up to a year. In Europe, they often are raised in cold frames before being transplanted to the garden.

Some experts say that you would do better to start gentians from crown divisions or carefully transplanted roots. Most species need rich, acid, loamy soil. In order to transplant the endless root, dig very deeply to loosen the soil.

The main consideration when growing gentians is location. Once planted in a place that satisfies them, they require little care if given abundant moisture, shelter from cold, dry winds, and strong, direct sunshine. They benefit from an annual top dressing of fresh acid soil or peat moss. In very cold climates with inadequate snow cover, they need light mulching with hay or evergreen boughs to protect them.

Harvesting and storage: The roots are harvested in late summer or autumn and must be cured by thorough drying before use.

If dried slowly and then powdered, the root will retain its desired bitterness and color. Good-quality roots are dark reddish brown, tough, and flexible, with a strong, disagreeable odor. The taste should be sweet at first, and then deeply bitter.

GERMANDER

Teucrium Chamaedrys   Labiatae

The cunning miniature hedges that edge Elizabethan-style knot gardens are made of clipped germander. The glossy, dark green germander leaves look like those of a stately boxwood hedge, but one specifically designed for the landscaping of the Little People. Unlike boxwood, however, germander has had many other uses, from curing gout to treating fever.

DESCRIPTION

There are as many as 100 varieties of this perennial. *Teucrium Chamaedrys* is slender with four-sided, mintlike, hairy stems that trail the ground, then rise.

Flowers: On small stalks in groups of two or three or in whorls of six or more at upper leaf axils; ¾ in. long; two-lipped corolla, purple to purple-red, dotted with white; hairy, angular calyx shaped like a top, with five rounded, tapering, purplish, hairlike teeth.

Leaves: Opposite, oval or wedge-shaped, veined, bright green above and paler on the underside, with serrated edges tending toward small lobes; on short leafstalks; leaves at very top of plant are actually bracts and have smooth, uninterrupted margins.

Fruit: Four small nut forms, each containing a single seed.

Height: 2 ft.

FLOWERING

July through September.

RANGE

Naturalized in North America and Europe. Cultivated throughout the temperate zone.

GROWING CONDITIONS

- Plant hardiness zones 5–9.
- Soil pH 6.3.
- Average, well-drained soil.
- Full sun to partial shade.

USES

Medicinal: The active principle of germander was usually obtained by steeping the leaves in boiled water. The herb was used to heal wounds. It was also used as a digestive tonic, antiseptic, diuretic, stimulant, fever cure, astringent, and as a cure for asthma, quinsy, sore throat, bronchitis, dropsy, melancholy, palsy, jaundice, and more. Infusions were said to bring on delayed menstruation and to cure worms, as well as to soothe coughs. The most time-honored use, however, was as a cure for gout and rheumatism. Belief in its pain-curing properties persists into modern times.

Despite the folk cures, no substantial research has been done on the chemical properties of the herb. While there is no known toxicity or counterindication, neither is there any established medicinal value for germander.

Other: In earlier times the sprightly, garliclike aroma of germander leaves made it useful as a room freshener and as a part of wreaths. It was used as a substitute for hops in beer. Its uses as a low hedge and an ornamental plant continue to this day. According to herb folklorist Cyrus Hyde, germander is known as "poor man's box" because it can be trained into a hedge like the more expensive box.

CULTIVATION

Germander can be started from seed, but it takes as long as 30 days to germinate. A better early-season propagation approach is to use cuttings. Set the cuttings in sandy soil under glass. Layering techniques can also be employed. In the fall divide the plants.

After the plants are established, set them about 1 foot apart in a well-drained, slightly acid soil. An ideal medium contains peat, sand, and organic matter. If germanders are grown in pots, select a sunny location.

Shrubby germanders, especially those used to edge herb beds, need pruning to encourage branching and to shape them. This is done in the spring. In northern states, give winter protection if snow cover is light. Either mulch or burlap screening will do.

GINGER

Zingiber officinale   Zingiberaceae

Forty-four hundred years ago, Greek bakers were using ginger imported from the Orient to make gingerbread. The Spanish were cultivating ginger as early as the sixteenth century, and the conquistadors introduced it to the New World via Jamaica. It became so popular among Europeans that in 1884 Great Britain imported over 5 million pounds of the root.

USES

Today, Chinese cooks rarely stir-fry vegetables without first browning a piece of the fresh, pungent root. Ginger is spicy to the tongue, and yet it's also soothing to the digestive system.

Medicinal: Ginger is used to soothe indigestion and take the wind out of flatulence. Researchers have found that ginger is effective against motion sickness. It is a safe and effective herb.

Ginger is a mild stimulant, promoting circulation. On a cold winter day, a cup of ginger tea is warming and invigorating. Pour 1 pint of boiling water over 1 ounce of the rhizome and steep for 5 to 20 minutes. Drink it hot or warm, 1 or 2 cups a day.

Culinary: Ginger's flavor seems to be half spice and half citrus. The root of the plant is used fresh or dried in the recipes of China, Japan, Southeast Asia, East India, the Caribbean, and North Africa. Add it to beverages, fruit salads, meats, poultry, fish, preserves, pickles, sweet potatoes, winter squash, carrots, beets, pumpkin, rhubarb, and peaches. Combine it with onions and garlic. Ground ginger enhances sweet puddings, quick breads, muffins, cakes, and cookies.

Available commercially: Fresh, dried ground, or dried pieces.

Storage note: Keep fresh ginger refrigerated, wrapped first in a paper towel, and then in tightly wrapped plastic; it will last for several months.

CULTIVATION

Ginger is grown commercially throughout the tropics. Elsewhere, it's easy to grow in a container. Plant a rhizome purchased either from a nursery or a grocery store in a large pot filled with equal parts of loam, sand, peat moss, and compost. Give it plenty of warmth, moisture, and humidity. During warm months, move the potted ginger to a semishaded location outdoors.

To harvest, pull the plant from its pot 8 to 12 months after planting, cut off the leafstalks, and remove the fibrous roots. Cut off as much ginger root as you can use and replant the rest.

DESCRIPTION

An herbaceous tropical perennial, ginger grows from an aromatic, tuberous rhizome that is knotty and branched and whitish or buff-colored, depending on the strain.

Flowers: In dense, cone-like spikes 3 in. long at the end of a 6–12-in. stalk; corolla composed of two ¾-in., yellow-green segments and one purple lip, spotted and striped with yellow; occur between 1-in. long, overlapping, green bracts.

Leaves: Grasslike, 6–12 in. long, to ¾ in. wide, alternate, pointed, lanceolate.

Fruit: Fruiting is unknown.

Height: 2–4 ft.

FLOWERING

Rarely flowers in cultivation.

RANGE

Origin is uncertain, probably native to India and southern China; introduced to southern Florida.

CHEF TIP

Toss 1 slice of peeled fresh ginger into a marinade for each pound of meat or poultry.

GROWING CONDITIONS

- Plant hardiness zone 9.
- Fertile, moist, well-drained soil.
- Partial shade.

GINSENG

Panax quinquefolius   **Araliaceae**

DESCRIPTION

Ginseng's thin, single stem rises from the ground and then separates into a whorl of compound leaves. The plant's stem grows from a bud that forms at the top of the root. After several years of activity, the budding part of the root would grow out of the ground if the rest of the root didn't shrink a comparable amount. This simultaneous growing and shrinking produces wrinkles around the neck of the root that can be used to estimate the plant's age.

Flowers: After three or four years: 4 to 40 green flowers at the center of the "umbrella"; mostly in single, terminal umbels, $1/12$ in. across; five petals, five stamens, two styles.

Leaves: Young plants: one or two leaves; after three or four years: three to six leaves; each leaf divided into five toothed or lobed leaflets radiating from a central point.

Fruit: Bright red berries, each with two or three white seeds inside.

Height: 6–16 in.

FLOWERING

Depending on location, June through August.

RANGE

Manitoba and Quebec; west through Alabama to Oklahoma; south to Florida.

HABITAT

Hardwood forests; prefers north or northwestern slopes.

To be perfectly frank, the ginseng root looks like any of a number of wrinkled old roots a gardener might grub out of a weed patch, and the slow-growing plant won't stop sightseers in their tracks. Its glossy green leaves have something of the ground cover about them, but they are obviously inferior to, say, pachysandra because they're too tall and sparse. (That's daytime of course. At night, the legends tell us, the plants glow, mysteriously rise from the ground, and flit around the forest, a more interesting spectacle.) However, the plants ordinariness may be part of its charm. One of the most appealing parts of any story is when the ugly duckling turns into a swan. And this ground-cover reject has certainly turned into a swan of an herbal remedy, recommended for at least 2,000 years, touted as a prolonger of life and cure for literally all human ills, not to mention being the cornerstone of a multimillion-dollar ginseng trade.

HISTORY

Considering the origins of ginseng, an evolutionary botanist might chat excitedly about the curious pattern of plants whose close relatives are found only on the absolute opposite sides of the globe, one in temperate America, the other in the temperate Far East. Are they offspring of a common ancestor or offspring who were separated when continents split apart? If we think in a geologic time, we see continents floating around on the oceans as casually as leaves drift in mud puddles. All a bit disconcerting. It's a relief to consider Chinese folk stories about ginseng's origins.

Ginseng began as a divine gift to a deserving but miserable young wife, according to one story. After several years of marriage, she had no children and was frantic with disappointment. Custom made it particularly bitter; after three childless years, her husband would be permitted to take a concubine. She dreamed about an old man in the mountains who could give her an herbal remedy. She searched him out, took the remedy, and bore a child. When she journeyed back to see him, she thanked him so prettily that he (who, of course, was a deity in disguise) filled the woods with this miraculous plant (which of course was ginseng).

People in northern China probably began using ginseng in prehistoric times. When medicinal traditions were written down in the *Shen-nung pen-ts'ao-ching* sometime in the first century A.D., ginseng was among the remedies. The entry is terse, only 44 words, but notes that ginseng is used for "enlightening the mind, and increasing the wisdom. Continuous use leads one to longevity. . . ."

Chinese herbalists noticed that some roots resembled a human figure and considered these signs of a medicine that could enhance the whole of human health. This idea that a plant's appearance contained clues to its medicinal benefits is called the Doctrine of Signatures and has popped up in numerous dissimilar cultures. Medieval European herbalists discussed the same system, which they took as a sign of divine skill and generosity in constructing the universe. Ideas may float around like continents.

The root that promised wisdom and long life, not to mention its reputation as an aphrodisiac . . . who could resist? Ginseng madness struck China. Both the Chinese and the Tartars wanted the plants enough to kill for them; wars broke out over good ginseng territory. One Tartar lord is said to have surrounded an entire province with a wooden fence in an attempt to protect growing grounds. Storage areas had to have armed guards; smuggling the root was punishable by death.

The power of ginseng, both medicinal and economic, impressed the Europeans who were beginning to learn about the Far East, but at first, it was no more than one among many colorful, exotic tales. In 1642, the adventurer Samedo Alvaro brought back the story, but soon afterward the picture changed abruptly. In 1704, an explorer named Sarrasin brought to Paris what he claimed was ginseng root found in the New World. It was like the first hint of a gold strike. Meanwhile, a Jesuit in China, Father Jartoux, was corresponding with another Jesuit, Father Lafiteu, who lived among the Iroquois near Montreal. Jartoux sent a sample root; Lafiteu eventually discovered a patch of the American plant, and in 1718 shipped a boatload to Canton where it brought the outrageous price of $5 per pound.

This was one of the great eras in botany; Linnaeus was inventing his classification of plants, naming everything he could, sometimes naming a beautiful flower after a friend, sometimes naming funny-looking plants after enemies to make complex horticultural insults. When he got to ginseng in 1753, he called the genus *Panax,* from the Greek *pan,* meaning all, and *akos* or ills, hence a plant that cured all ills.

Some Americans and Europeans became convinced of the plant's curative powers. The illustrious Virginia planter, William Byrd II, noted that it "frisks the spirits . . . and comforts the bowels exceedingly." He added a reassuring note (which might have halved its price had other ginseng eaters agreed with him): "All this it performs without any of those naughty Effects that might make men too troublesome and impertinent to their wives."

It was certainly curing financial problems for some Americans. Ginseng prices were circulated on handbills; it was a commodity

SUPPLY AND DEMAND

The Chinese, probably on account of its scarcity, have a very extraordinary opinion of the virtues of this root, so that it sells for many times its weight in silver. Americans, on the contrary, disregard it, because it is found plentifully in their woods.

Robert Thornton
British doctor
1814

GINSENG—continued

**CLEAR THINKING
CIRCA 1908**

It has been asked why the Chinese do not grow their own Ginseng. . . . Ginseng requires practically a virgin soil, and as China proper has been the home of teeming millions for thousands of years, one readily sees that necessary conditions for the plant hardly exist in that old and crowded country.

A. R. Harding
*Ginseng and
Other Medicinal Plants*
1908

traded on the frontier along with furs. Thomas Jefferson lists it in his inventory of native plant resources. Ginseng and Virginia snakeroot made up most of Virginia's medicinal exports. In 1773, a sloop out of Boston took 55 tons of ginseng to China and sold it for $330,000. Philadelphia records show that Daniel Boone sold ginseng to a company in the city. The Shakers came to use it. It was the financial mainstay of Moravian communities in Ohio.

The high point for exporting ginseng collected from the wild was in 1824, when over 750,000 pounds left the United States. But the plant was no longer plentiful, thanks to the clearing of woods and the rapacious collecting. In 1905, Wisconsin passed a law that roots could not be dug until after August 1, so the plants would have a chance to set seed. The tricky art of ginseng farming was beginning. The father of the industry was a man named George Stanton, who transplanted wild roots onto his property in New York. His farm eventually grew to 150 acres. Grower associations were formed, with newsletters informing members of new horizons, like the development of ginseng ice cream.

Insurance policies were also available for ginseng growers. They needed it. Ginseng is not an easy crop to grow. Unscrupulous

seed and plant merchants promoted it as a get-rich-quick scheme; one can still find articles about farmers who toss in some plants, pull a weed or two in the summer, and then stand back while the profits roll in.

Nonsense.

To begin with, growing ginseng requires a big capital investment. Even in the late 1970s, stratified seed cost $85 a pound—that's about $10,000 in seed alone to plant an acre. The plants need shade, so growers construct lath sheds or drape the fields with black nylon mesh or polypropylene tarps. Shading, maintenance, and harvesting costs could add another $10,000 in cost per acre. And, obviously, the roots aren't ready to dig for several years, so the farmer has plenty of time to watch the fields eat his money before he sees any return. At least 10 fungus diseases attack the roots, and harvesting and curing require delicate handling. The roots' value comes in part from their shape; breaking an "arm" off a root lowers the value.

Improbable as it sounds after considering the hazards, there *are* commercial ginseng growers, mostly in Marathon County, Wisconsin. Eighty percent of the ginseng exported from this country comes from there, and the techniques have evolved into a high art. It may be too subjective to explain easily, and there isn't much incentive in the current market for a grower to try to explain trade secrets. As one extension agent in Wisconsin put it, "God and the growers know what they're doing, but neither one is talking."

USES

Medicinal: It's hard to evaluate the medicinal qualities of a plant that has been said to help every human ailment. You might think that science is close to an overview; just consider the flood of research papers and books published on ginseng: bibliographies list hundreds of items. Biologically active compounds have been identified in the plant, but whether and how these might be useful remains unclear.

According to the Food and Drug Administration (FDA), it's very much a muddle. The agency categorizes ginseng for tea as "Generally Recognized as Safe," but that's as far as it goes. As long as it's just for flavoring and fun, the FDA permits ginseng sales. But dealers who claim the plant has any medicinal virtues are disciplined.

The evidence may not have brought the two sides together on this debate, but here is a sampling of the medicinal claims made for ginseng and some of the evidence that supports or denies them.

Perhaps the broadest health effect claimed for ginseng is that it is an "adaptogen," a substance that protects against stress, physical and mental. Put another way, adaptogens help body functions return

PULLIN' 'SANG

The most valuable ginseng is that which grows in the wild. Throughout the southern highlands, hardy individuals—men and women, young and old—earn extra money by collecting roots from the wild. "Pullin' 'sang" is what they call the work.

It isn't as easy as stumbling over a fallen log. The hunters must know the plant and its habitat. They must be fit. "To harvest one pound," explained Georgia ginseng trader Hoyt Bonds, "a man must walk not less than 20 miles over a two-day period, and in the process, kill 3 rattlesnakes and 10 copperheads." Another 'sang hunter, Allen Brown, reported being charged by a bear on an outing. "I almost got run over," he said.

And if the natural obstacles aren't enough, the hunters and traders must also parry governmental regulations. They are required to plant, on the spot, the seeds of each plant they dig up, since the plant is an endangered species.

For their trouble, the 'sang hunters can earn as much as $115 per pound of root collected, which Brown says translates into about $150 for a full weekend's work. The root is sold to regional traders, who in turn sell it to exporters. More than 90 percent—with an export value of roughly $30 million—is funneled into Hong Kong.

BUT THERE'S NO GINSENG IN IT!

It should come as no surprise—ginseng being the All-Time Great Snake Oil, and snake oil being what it is—that many of the ginseng compounds and preparations sold in the United States don't have any ginseng in them. None at all. (Well, maybe there was a ginseng root in the room when the stuff was packaged.)

Two studies have come to this conclusion.

The first, published in the *Journal of Pharmaceutical Sciences* in 1978, was conducted by two scientists from the Philadelphia College of Pharmacy and Science. It reported that a full quarter of the ginseng products tested contained nary a trace of the botanical.

A year later, *Whole Foods,* a magazine published for the natural food industry, came to the same conclusion, reporting that "60 percent of the ginseng products analyzed in a recent sampling were judged 'worthless.' . . . Twenty-five percent of the sampled products apparently contain no ginseng at all!"

The industry response to the studies seems to have been largely rhetorical. No mechanism exists to assure the consumer that what is advertised on the packaging is what is inside it. And this is true not only of ginseng but of most herbal products as well.

to normal more quickly than they would otherwise. Hence ginseng is supposed to increase physical endurance. Koreans give it to race-horses. Mice given a ginseng booster have survived endurance tests up to 70 percent longer than unboosted mice.

But here we get to a wrinkle in the research. A lot of the information comes from Russian researchers, who usually use the so-called Siberian ginseng, *Eleutherococus senticosus*. It's a prickly shrub, a member of the same family as other ginsengs, but not of the same genus, related about as closely to them as monkeys are to people. Siberian ginseng supposedly shares biochemical properties with regular ginseng. If we accept that it shares enough, we may accept the research as relevant. And the reports do suggest some kind of endurance enhancements. The Russian Ministry of Health reports that telegraph operators measurably improved their performamce after taking Siberian ginseng, making fewer mistakes. The Olympic training diet includes it, and reportedly cosmonauts carried it into space.

An adaptogen also might soften the blows of aging. The claim itself has certainly aged well; almost 2,000 years ago the great Chinese medical directory said that ginseng increased longevity. Hints of such effects are coming out of modern laboratories. Researchers found that a culture of human amnion cells grew denser on a medium containing a ginseng extract because the cells lived longer. Actually, reports show ginseng extracts increasing and decreasing cell division, perhaps depending on the dosage. Other studies exist along these lines; they are certainly intriguing but alas by no means conclusive. It's not easy to translate the effects of an extract on cells in culture into the effect of a cup of tea consumed by a whole organism.

Another area of research concerns ginseng's reputed ability to protect cells from radiation damage. Rats treated with ginseng and then exposed to prolonged radiation lived twice as long as expected. In particular their blood withstood the radiation better. These effects have been observed for both Siberian and Korean ginseng (the latter a true ginseng).

Ginseng has been explored as an aid in preventing heart disease. The *American Journal of Chinese Medicine* reported that in both rats and humans, ginseng seemed to moderate the effects of a high-cholesterol diet. However, ginseng extracts given to shock patients raised blood pressure. Again, research does not seem to have unraveled the plant's mysteries.

The list of adaptogenic effects could go on for pages. Varro Tyler, Ph.D., dean of the School of Pharmacy, Nursing, and Health

Sciences at Purdue University, sums up the evidence as showing "favorable modification by ginseng of the stress effects of temperature changes, diet, restraint, exercise, and the like . . . ."

As for treating specific diseases, Dr. Tyler notes that "useful pharmacologic effects in such conditions as anemia, atherosclerosis, depression, diabetes, edema, hypertension, and ulcers have also been documented." Researchers certainly have many conditions to investigate. James Duke, a botanist with the U.S. Department of Agriculture, reports folk traditions for more than 70 conditions that have been treated by ginseng.

Some tests have looked at the root's ancient reputation as an aphrodisiac. Preparations of the plant have promoted the formation of sperm in rabbits, ovary growth and ovulation in frogs, and egg-laying in hens. Korean scientists have studied mating behavior in ginseng-boosted rats, reporting that the plant "facilitated" mating behavior.

Out of all this, we may be no nearer to obtaining useful suggestions for using the plant. Not all the tests were carefully designed, and some of the studies were old-fashioned, sloppy, and misleading. For those that did document effects, there is little agreement on the form and the dosage. The evidence about ginseng may not be overwhelming, but it is satisfying to see folk wisdom and modern science coming closer together.

CULTIVATION

Unless you have the naturally perfect garden spot, ginseng needs to be pampered. It's usually grown from seed and the complications begin immediately. Just planting the seed won't work; it needs a cold period of at least four months. Some growers dip the seeds in hydrochloric acid to help break through their tough outer coating. The seedlings can be grown in a greenhouse or seedbed and transplanted to their final location when they are two years old.

The seedlings should be planted in shady, moist locations with good drainage. A wooded hillside is ideal, although growers build lath structures to mimic the dappled forest shade for field-grown ginseng. The plants need a soil pH of about 5.0 to 6.5. In the winter they need to be mulched, mimicking the leaves that would fall on the forest floor in their native habitat. A substantial number of rots can attack the root. Again, good drainage is critical.

In five to seven years, the roots should reach marketable size. There's no need to harvest them then; one Russian scientist reported seeing a ginseng root that had 400 yearly growth rings.

In short, ginseng is a difficult crop to grow.

A TESTIMONIAL

I never found it worth a damn for anything but to get money out of.

Jake Plott
Georgia ginseng trader

GROWING CONDITIONS
- Plant hardiness zone 4.
- Soil pH 5.0–6.5.
- Humus-rich, well-drained loam.
- Partial shade.

GOLDENROD

Solidago spp.   **Compositae**

One gardener's lifelong enemy is another's lifesaving herb and another's treasured border plant. That perverse rule of horticulture, or perhaps just of human nature, is beautifully illustrated by the goldenrods.

DESCRIPTION

The common name goldenrod embraces a genus of plants with more than 130 species. They are erect perennials with somewhat woody stems that seldom branch.

Flowers: Disk flowers surrounded by ray flowers in ¼-in.-wide flower heads; profuse; in compound clusters; form showy spikes, racemes or panicles; yellow.

Leaves: Simple alternate, toothed or smooth edges.

Fruit: Angled or nearly cylindrical achenes.

Height: 3–7 ft.

FLOWERING

August and September.

RANGE

Native chiefly to North America; a few species are native to Europe, Asia, the Azores, and South America.

HABITAT

Open fields and roadsides.

GROWING CONDITIONS

- Plant hardiness zone 4.
- Average to poor, well-drained soil.
- Full sun.

HISTORY

Goldenrod has long been associated with wound healing, often by peoples who were not obviously associated with each other like the American Indians and the Chinese. (The Latin *solida,* "whole" and *ago,* "to make" combine to form the genus name, *Solidago.*)

The plant appears in British folklore as a healing herb for both the body and the pocketbook. The golden plants were supposed to point toward equally golden hidden treasure. They were also supposed to mark hidden springs.

The sweet goldenrod was one of the early herbal equivalents of sugar coating on a pill; the pleasant smell and aniselike taste of the tea could disguise disgusting flavors and odors of other ingredients.

USES

Medicinal: Three species in particular, *S. nemoralis* or gray goldenrod, *S. odora* or sweet goldenrod, and *S. virgaurea* or European goldenrod, have been used as astringents, diuretics, and diaphoretics.

Gray goldenrod has been taken as a carminative. Sweet goldenrod, also considered a carminative by some, has been used as a stimulant. A tea of the leaves has been administered for flatulence and vomiting, and a local application has been used to soothe a headache. The flowers reportedly have laxative properties, and a tea made from them has been used in treating urinary obstructions.

Uses for European goldenrod make the longest list. It has been used to treat periodontal disease, arthritis, chronic eczema, and kidney inflammation. It has also been taken to reduce heavy menstrual flow. Some herbalists use the crushed fresh leaves in healing wounds, sores, and insect bites. In Chinese medicine the species we call European is prepared as a headache remedy and for treating flu, sore throat, malaria, and measles.

Twentieth-century herbalist John Lust recommends steeping an ounce of flowering tops of European goldenrod in a pint of water or teaspoon of sweet goldenrod leaves in a cup of water.

In general, modern science offers no evidence that goldenrod is an effective medicine for anything. However, there seems to be no record of serious illness connected with the plant. One obvious caution: If you're allergic to the pollen, don't experiment with goldenrod as a medicine.

Ornamental: While most Americans look on goldenrods as roadside weeds, Europeans cherish them. The British plant them in colorful perennial borders and have named varieties. These horticultural varieties of goldenrod are moving toward bigger flower heads and shorter plants. The so-called dwarf goldenrod varieties only grow a foot high and are recommended for the front of borders, an incredible concept for an American.

Craft: The flower heads of goldenrod dry to a nice golden color, certainly not as bright as the plant's fresh color, but still one that is highly recommended for dried herb and flower arrangements.

Dye: The flowering heads of goldenrod will create varying shades of yellow, depending on what mordant is used and on the generally willful flukiness of natural dyes. Cyrus Hyde of New Jersey's Well-Sweep Herb Farm suggests adding onion skins and sage to the dye pot if the goldenrod yields too brassy a yellow for your taste.

Might-have-beens: Goldenrod gum, or goldenrod gumdrops for that matter, have not taken the country by storm, but they once were part of a farm merchandising dream. In 1948 an agricultural experiment station in Texas published detailed instructions for sweet goldenrod farming as well as suggestions on how to pace the harvest so it wouldn't overrun the processing operation. The acres upon hypothetical acres of goldenrod were going to be processed for the plant's oil, which was to be sold as an ingredient for chewing gums, candies, and deodorants.

CULTIVATION

Goldenrod does best in poor soil, according to Holly Shimizu, curator of the National Herb Garden in Washington, D.C. In rich soil, they tend to grow tall and flop over (an annoyed weed-control specialist may grumble that that's not so bad). Shimizu says she has had no pest problems.

Although some people start a goldenrod collection by marking particularly lush weeds and then returning in the fall to dig them, Shimizu recommends buying them from nurseries that carry native plants. Plants are available, as are seeds of horticulturally selected varieties. Digging wild plants, even common ones, is a habit she doesn't encourage.

Harvesting and storage: Collect the plant when it's flowering and dry it carefully. Spread it out to dry soon after harvesting because it turns black and musty if left in a heap.

231

GOLDENSEAL

Hydrastis canadensis   **Ranunculaceae**

Goldenseal costs an arm and a leg in the health food store—enough that a few people can make a living growing it or digging it in the wild. The lore of its culture and its secret woodland locations are passed on with selective care in the backwaters of the United States, where it may be referred to as poor man's ginseng.

You'll do best if you act with moderation—in how much you dig of it (it's becoming endangered); in how much you consume (it may be toxic); and in the claims you believe when listening to tales of its powers.

HISTORY

Goldenseal is associated with the American Indian. Under the name "yellow puccoon," it kept early Cherokee Indians from being regarded as red men. They stained their faces and their clothes with the juice from the root.

The Cherokees also mixed powdered goldenseal root with bear grease and employed the mixture as an insect repellent. The Indians were always sure to save enough of the plant to cure almost every affliction known to man—red, yellow, or white. Unfortunately, the miracle root couldn't save them from European invasion, and once that had taken place, both the Indians and goldenseal were doomed to near extinction.

Early on, the pioneers followed the Indians' example in using goldenseal to treat watering eyes, wounds, and rashes. They also chewed it to relieve mouth sores. Quickly, it became an herb of almost mystic powers. American herbalist Jethro Kloss called it "one of the most wonderful remedies in the entire herb kingdom," adding, "When it is considered all that can be accomplished by its use, and what it actually will do, it does seem like a real cure-all."

More recently, it has been used to prevent morning sickness, for liver and stomach complaints, to check internal hemorrhage, to increase appetite and the secretion of bile, as a laxative, as a mouthwash, and for urinary and uterine problems. It was said to prevent pitting of the skin in smallpox and to cure ringworm. It was also used as an astringent, a diuretic, a canker-sore cure, a poison ivy cure, a cure for dyspepsia, and a disinfectant.

Early in the 1900s, there was concern that the country might run out of the plant. As much as 300,000 pounds of the root were harvested each year. The U.S. Department of Agriculture, citing its medicinal value, published bulletins outlining how to cultivate it.

Goldenseal remains scarce. As scarcity has grown, the cost of

DESCRIPTION

Goldenseal is a small perennial plant with an erect, cylindrical, hairy stem. The stem emerges from a rhizome that is seldom more than 2 in. long and ¼–¾ in. thick. Fleshy in texture and marked with seal-shaped scars from flower stems of earlier years, the twisted, knotted rhizome is covered with yellow-brown bark and is bright yellow inside. (See photo on page 377.)

Flowers: Solitary, terminal, on flower stalk, ½ in. across; no corolla; greenish white calyx composed of three small, frail sepals that look like petals; numerous stamens; sepals fall off when flower opens.

Leaves: Solitary basal leaf, one or two heart-shaped leaves near top of the stem; deeply divided into five lobes (sometimes seven); lobes pointed and irregularly but finely toothed; to 12 in. across; covered with soft down.

Fruit: Oblong orange-red berries, with the withered flower style remaining at their top; clustered; two shiny black seeds inside.

Height: 6–12 in.

FLOWERING

May.

RANGE

Native to North America.

HABITAT

Moist, rich woodlands, damp meadows, and open and forested highlands.

goldenseal has doubled many times in accordance with the classic law of supply and demand. And that is despite the fact that the plant is no longer officially recognized as a medicinal herb. Recently, the mistaken idea that it could mask heroin use in tests drove the price up yet again.

USES

Before you get carried away with the claims made for goldenseal, remember that you are dealing with a potentially dangerous substance whose effectiveness has been exaggerated. The mechanism for many of its purported cures still awaits study.

Medicinal: The most active ingredient, and the one that accounts for any chemical effectiveness, is hydrastine. It does exert a minor influence on circulation and on muscle tone and contractions in the uterus and in other smooth muscle areas. However, as a promoter of uterine contractions and for use to reduce uterine bleeding, it is less effective than ergot, a fungus with pharmacological properties. Hydrastine has a mild antiseptic effect.

As for goldenseal's effect on the nervous system, the evidence is that in small doses a second ingredient, canadine, is a mild sedative and muscle relaxant, but that it is not very useful.

A goldenseal eyewash has been shown scientifically to be mildly antibiotic, especially against *Staphylococcus aureus;* the eyewash is also astringent and can reduce inflammation.

Goldenseal extracts seem to lower blood sugar levels, which may make them useful for treating stress and anxiety.

Toxicity: The medical jury is still out on the controversial herb that inspires so much passion among its advocates and so much cynicism among its critics. Note well, however, that in large doses goldenseal's major component, hydrastine, is *toxic and dangerous.* To be absolutely safe, you should not take goldenseal internally. Eating fresh plant material may ulcerate and inflame the mucous membrane of the mouth. Hydrastine remains in the system for a long time and accumulates. Large quantities of it will overstimulate the nervous system and may produce convulsions, respiratory failure, miscarriage, or the overproduction of white blood cells. Other possible toxic reactions include nausea, vomiting, diarrhea, and a burning skin sensation. In extreme cases, paralysis as a result of depression of the spinal cord and the peripheral nervous system may be fatal.

Ornamental: The goldenseal plant has limited ornamental use. It can be included in wildflower collections for woodland settings or collections of native plants. Don't let your neighbors know that

233

GROWING CONDITIONS

- Rich, humusy, moist soil.
- Partial to full shade.

you're growing it or you may end up with empty woodland beds and wealthy neighbors.

Dye: Perhaps the Cherokees were right to value goldenseal's yellow juice over its medicinal powers. Used with mordants, the root will produce permanent dyes ranging from pale yellow to orange. Mixed with indigo, it will give an attractive green color to wool, silk, and cotton. It can also be used in watercolors and oil paints.

CULTIVATION

Goldenseal is a sensitive plant and very difficult to cultivate, so it is usually gathered from the wild. If you have already had success with other wild plants, try starting it from seed in the fall, using propagation beds shaded with laths to get it going. Later, move it to a permanent woodland location.

It requires about five years from seed to harvestable maturity, and three or four years if you start it from root bulbs or pieces of sprouted rhizome. Budded pieces of rhizome are easiest to grow. Set them in woodland soil, spaded and enriched with leaf mold, compost, peat moss, sand, bonemeal, and cottonseed meal to a depth of 10 inches. The soil should feel light and moist.

In winter, mulch the seedlings with leaves, hay, or chopped legume vines, and in the summer mulch with aged sawdust. Thirty-two plants are said to produce 2 pounds of root in three years.

When starting goldenseal from sprouted rhizomes, wait until the mother plant dies back after frost. Uproot the rhizome carefully, removing the dirt. Sever the shoot, and replant the underdeveloped roots that have developed from the rhizome, setting them ½ inch deep and 8 inches apart. At the same time, the rhizomes themselves may be harvested and sun-dried for medicinal use, assuming that they are at least in their fourth year of growth.

Several specialty seed houses and plant growers sell goldenseal rhizomes or seed. The larger rhizomes may be transplanted at any time of year, but moving them is risky.

Harvesting and storage: For dried leaves and stems of goldenseal to be used in infusions, harvest in the late summer after they have dried on the plant. After a late autumn harvest, the rhizome is washed and then dried slowly. When dry, it is a dark yellow-brown.

The root will remain in storage for a number of years and can be refreshed by soaking in water. For longer storage or easier use, the root is sometimes ground, or powdered. When buying the root, check for the distinctively sweetish, licorice odor and for a bitter taste. Goldenseal powder is often adulterated with bloodroot and many other members of the buttercup family.

Silver-gray artemisias (top) offer a pleasing contrast to other herbs in the garden.

Lavender's form and color (left) make it a stunning herb in any garden design.

Sweet woodruff (right) nestles among trilliums in a woodland setting.

Germander (bottom front), crimson pigmy barberry (center front), dwarf hyssop (starting bottom left), and Jean Davis lavender (starting bottom right) form the knot garden at Well-Sweep Herb Farm in Port Murray, New Jersey.

Creeping thyme and yellow-flowered sedum spill over rocks in this garden.

237

Lamb's ears, thyme, and lavender surround the sundial in the National Herb Garden in Washington, D.C. Fall-blooming clematis covers the arched trellis.

Parsley, sage, and basil add striking color and texture to any garden.

Tea roses, planted near the Dutch lavender (foreground), beautify this fenced area.

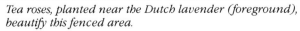

GRINDELIA

Grindelia spp.   Compositae

Among the 60 species of grindelia, many have common names such as gumplant, gumweed, tarweed, or resin weed. That's because they share a sticky substance that forms on the flower heads. In some parts of the world, children use this substance as chewing gum. The plant has medicinal uses as well, most notable of which is its ability to soothe or cure poison ivy and poison oak eruptions.

Although the herb didn't come into use in Western medicine until the latter part of the nineteenth century, American Indians treated liver problems with a tea made of its root. An infusion has been used to treat stomachache, gonorrhea, pneumonia, dyspepsia, dyspnea from heart disease, smallpox, and urinary ailments.

USES

Medicinal: The *National Formulary* lists *G. camporum, G. humilis,* and *G. squarrosa* as the sources of the drug called grindelia. A balsamic resin makes up 20 percent of these plants, and, according to the *U.S. Dispensatory,* the resinous components make the drug effective, if only feebly so. According to the dispensatory, the drug "has been used in the treatment of acute bronchitis, especially when there is a tendency to asthma. Its action is probably simply that of a stimulating expectorant, but some believe it exerts also an antispasmodic effect."

In animal studies of grindelia, very large doses produced drowsiness, decreased the heart rate, and increased blood pressure. Moreover, large doses can cause some urinary irritation since the active principles are excreted from the kidneys.

By far the safest way to use grindelia is as an external ointment or in a solution applied to rashes from poisonous plants and minor burns. *G. squarrosa* is particularly useful for this purpose. Boil 1 ounce of plant material—leaves, stems, flowers—in 1 pint of water for 10 minutes. Cool, strain, and soak a cloth in the cooled liquid. Apply the cloth to the affected area of skin.

CULTIVATION

Since the plant is too scrubby to be much of an ornamental, it is seldom cultivated except for medicinal purposes or occasionally to enliven wild plantings in alkaline soil. If there are no wild plants in your area, try starting it from seed in poor soil. The herb can also be started with cuttings or divisions.

DESCRIPTION

Grindelias are coarse and shrublike plants. The roots are usually perennial, but the plants sometimes have a biennial, or even an annual, tendency.

A distinctive mark of the whole genus may be found on the limb of the calyx, or flower covering, where two to eight bristlelike, narrow spikes, called awns, stand rigid until they fall as the flower matures.

Flowers: Numerous, sticky, yellow; disk flowers surrounded by ray flowers; occur in heads, either solitary or in cymes or panicles, depending on variety; usually a bell-shaped whorl of bracts around the flower.

Leaves: Slightly toothed, spade-shaped, green or blue-green leaves, alternate, clasping the stems.

Fruit: A small achene.

Height: To 3 ft.

RANGE

Dry prairies from Saskatchewan south to Mexico. Some form of grindelia may be found in almost all the states east of the Rockies, but most species occur west of the Mississippi.

GROWING CONDITIONS

- Plant hardiness zone 7.
- Light, moderately rich soil.
- Full sun.

GROWING HERBS

Although herbs may have an air of mystery about them, growing herbs doesn't. It's as straightforward as growing flowers and much less demanding than growing vegetables. The majority of herbs are relatively pest- and disease-free and require little more than a well-drained, sunny site, plenty of room, and moderately fertile soil to thrive. Annuals need more pampering and a richer soil to complete their bloom-and-boom life cycle in a single summer; perennials must be protected over winter and periodically divided. But whether your herb project is modest—putting parsley and basil in the vegetable beds or adding foxglove, beebalm, and lavender to the perennial border—or ambitious—setting up a medicinal or Elizabethan herb garden—it will require a very reasonable commitment of time and effort. Ultimately, herb gardening is just gardening.

SITE AND SOIL

If you don't have the sunny, well-drained site most herbs prefer, there's no need to abandon herb growing. Grow herbs in raised beds or containers for better drainage, or plant angelica, beebalm, boneset, sweet flag (calamus), elecampane, lovage, meadowsweet, and the mints, which will grow in damp soil. If your site is shaded, choose sweet cicely, pennyroyal, violets, sweet woodruff, lemon balm, chervil, valerian, ginseng, evening primrose, lungwort, the hellebores, or goldenseal. If, on the other hand, your conditions are *too* "good"—dry soil and glaring sunlight—you'd probably do best with Mediterranean herbs such as the thymes, sages, santolinas, artemisias, lavender, rosemary, winter savory, and hyssop.

The best soil for herbs is a humusy loam—average garden soil with compost, well-rotted strawy manure, shredded leaves, or other organic matter turned in to improve drainage and texture. Organic matter will hold water in quick-drying sandy soils and speed drainage in waterlogged clays. It will release nutrients slowly, so herbs will be fed without being glutted with fast-action fertilizers. Add leaves and manure the fall before planting so they can break down over the winter; fine compost can be tilled or forked in before spring planting or used as a topdressing on the prepared beds or rows.

The ideal pH range for most herbs is pH 6.5 to 7.0 (slightly acidic to neutral). If your soil is more acidic or you're growing lavender, thyme, rosemary, or rue, which prefer a higher pH, you can increase the soil alkalinity with dolomitic limestone, wood ashes, bonemeal, or eegshells. Add dolomite and eggshells the fall before planting; bonemeal or wood ashes a few weeks before spring sowing. Adding plenty of organic matter is the best way to lower the pH of a soil that's too alkaline.

Once the soil has warmed and seedlings are up (or transplants are in), an organic mulch will help retard evaporation and reduce the need for irrigation. Two or three inches of straw or salt hay is ideal. Avoid sawdust (unless it's extremely well rotted) and bark chips, which are fine on paths but will rob soil nitrogen if used as mulch. Grass clippings will add a boost of nitrogen as they break down, but they can form an impenetrable mat unless they're mixed with a looser material like straw. Don't put clippings against plant stems or they'll burn them.

PLANTING

Most herbs can be started from seed, sown directly in the garden, or started indoors in flats or pots. Borage and the umbelliferous herbs—anise, caraway, chervil, coriander, cumin, dill, fennel, and parsley—resent transplanting and should be sown where they will grow, if at all feasible. If necessary, parsley (at least) can be transplanted successfully by breaking up flats into seedling "clumps" and setting the clumps into the ground. The trick is to plant them out before the plants are more than a couple of inches tall and to resist the urge to separate, or even touch, the roots.

To sow seed indoors, prepare flats or pots by lining the bottom of each with paper toweling (one sheet thick), then adding a layer of fish-tank gravel or perlite for drainage. Next, add a moistened growing medium (1 part potting soil or fine compost, 2 parts sand or vermiculite, and 1 part peat moss in a common mix), leveling and firming it in the container. Plant seeds in rows about 2 inches apart in the flat, or in clusters of three in individual pots. Perennial herb seed is often extremely fine, so you may want to mix it with sand before sowing to reduce thinning chores later. Be sure to label each container with the type of herb and the date of sowing.

Most seeds need darkness to germinate, so cover the rows with a thin coat (the rule of thumb is two to three times the seed diameter) of fine soil or sand. Seeds that need light in order to germinate include angelica, the chamomiles, chervil, dill, feverfew, lemon balm, mugwort, the savories, and yarrow. Just press them lightly against the medium; don't cover them. Mist the flats or pots gently to avoid disturbing the seeds, then cover them with glass, plastic, or damp newspapers, and put them in an area that remains at 65° to 70°F day and night.

The time to start seedlings indoors is usually six to eight weeks before setting out. Some perennial herbs take four to eight weeks to germinate, however, and this must be added to the starting time. Perennial seeds can need other specialized treatment, such as chill

GROWING HERBS IN THE SHADE

How many times have you heard someone complain, "Oh, my yard is so shady, I can't grow anything"?

Rarely is a location so shaded that nothing will grow in it. Think of all the woods you've seen, thick with undergrowth; you can find herbs that will flourish in a shady spot. Some herbs, like sweet woodruff, actually prefer shade. Others, such as thyme, will grow in partial shade, even though they prefer full sun. Their growth habit in the shade will simply be taller and more open.

Try growing some of the following herbs. (Those in italic prefer shade, while the rest will grow in full sun to partial shade.)

aconite
agrimony
angelica
beebalm
betony
black hellebore
bloodroot
blue cohosh
cardamom
castor bean
catnip
chamomile
chervil
comfrey
coriander
costmary
(continued on page 243)

GROWING HERBS—continued

ing and stratification as well, which explains why so many are vegetatively propogated and sold as transplants.

Once the first seedlings are up, remove the covers from the flats and pots and move them to a sunny window or under fluorescent light racks. Seedlings need 12 to 15 hours of light daily for the best growth. If you aren't providing overhead light, don't forget to turn the containers! Thin crowded rows by snipping "extra" plants off at the soil surface with scissors—don't disturb the roots by pulling up plants. In individual pots cut off all but the strongest seedling. Keep the soil moist until the seedlings are about 2 inches tall; then allow the soil surface to dry between waterings.

Before setting out your transplants (usually after all danger of frost is past), harden them off gradually by putting them outside in a sheltered location. Begin by leaving them out only an hour or two a day, and increase the time until, after 10 days, the plants can be left outside all day. If the seedlings are flats, cut a block around each plant with a sharp knife before you begin to harden the plants off (think of cutting a tray of brownies).

If you direct-seed in the garden, you obviously won't have to worry about how much light your seedlings are getting or about

SOWING SEEDS

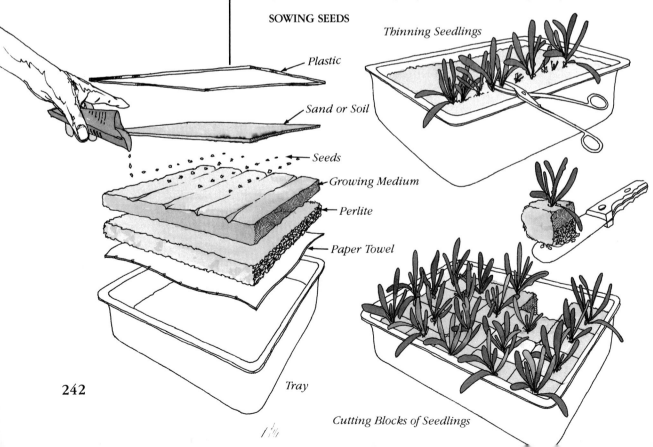

Thinning Seedlings

Plastic

Sand or Soil

Seeds

Growing Medium

Perlite

Paper Towel

Tray

Cutting Blocks of Seedlings

hardening off and transplanting. You will, however, still have to worry about watering and thinning, and you'll also have to cope with weeds. The trick to successful direct-seeding is a well-prepared seed-bed. Clods should be broken up and the soil raked smooth and fine so that the seeds are in close contact with soil and moisture and the seedling roots can grow down without impediment.

For more specifics on planting and culture, see "Rodale's Guide to Growing Herbs," which begins on page 246, and individual herb entries. Before planting any perennial herb, make sure it is hardy enough to survive the winters in your area. Consult the Plant Hardiness Zone section of the guide and the USDA Hardiness Zone Map (see page 245), which is divided into zones based on average annual minimum temperatures across the country. If your area is too cold for a favored perennial, you can bring it indoors over the winter, grow it as a container plant, or try (repeat: *try*) to carry it over under a heavy mulch and/or by growing it in a protected site that warms early in the spring and cools late in the fall.

VEGETATIVE PROPAGATION

With perennial herbs, as with most perennials, vegetative propagation is a means of rejuvenation as well as of multiplying plants.

Division: When a perennial herb becomes invasive or the center of the plant dies out, leaving a fringe of foliage circling a virtual "bald spot," it's time to divide the roots. Early spring, just before or as the first new growth begins, is the best time to divide herbs such as tarragon, yarrow, sweet woodruff, artemisia, horehound, tansy, beebalm, evening primrose, oregano, and lungwort. Other candidates for division are chives, horseradish, lovage, monkshood, the mints, chamomile, bergamot, meadowsweet, valerian, costmary, the hellebores, licorice, and soapwort (bounding bet). If you don't get around to it in the spring, herbs can also be divided in the fall.

A sharp shovel is best for dividing herbs like yarrow that form broad, dense mats of foliage. Cut shovel-width divisions of vigorous growth from around the edges of the plant and lift them out of the ground. If your goal is to get a lot of new plants, you can then subdivide these clumps; but they'll be more vigorous if they're larger. Once you've divided the perimeter of the plant, dig up and compost the woody center of the clump. Replant and water-in the divisions as soon as possible.

The bulbous roots of chives and garlic chives can be pulled apart or separated with a trowel. Fleshy-rooted herbs such as horseradish, ginger, and lovage may have to be forked out of the ground, then

dill
fennel
feverfew
flax
foxglove
gentian
germander
ginger
ginseng
goldenseal
hyssop
lemon balm
licorice
lobelia
lovage
mayapple
mint (all varieties)
parsley
pennyroyal
pipsissewa
plantain
rosemary
St.-John's-wort
salad burnet
sweet cicely
sweet flag
sweet woodruff
tansy
tarragon
thyme
tropical periwinkle
valerian
violet
wintergreen
wormwood

In gardening, as with many endeavors, there are no guarantees. If you want to grow a particular herb, experiment with it in your garden and see how it grows. You just might be pleasantly surprised.

243

Cutting

sliced apart with a sharp knife before replanting.

Layering: Propagating noninvasive herbs such as rosemary, marjoram, the chamomiles, horehound, hyssop, sage, santolina, clove pink, winter savory, and the thymes is even easier and more foolproof. In summer, select a branch near the base of the parent plant that's flexible enough to bend to the ground. Strip the lower branches and foliage from the part of the stem that will touch the soil. Press the stem firmly into the soil and pin it in place with a piece of wire bent in a U. If you like, you can layer several branches from the same plant. Keep the soil evenly moist until the new plant is established at the end of the growing season. Once roots have formed, cut the connecting stem from the parent plant and transplant the layer to its new location. The big advantage of layering is that the new plants remain attached to their parents during rooting, so losing them to neglect or shock isn't a possibility.

Cuttings: Riskier, but much faster, are stem cuttings. The list of herbs that can be propagated from cuttings is long, including scented geraniums, lavender, rosemary, lemon verbena, curry plant, hyssop, clove pink, rue, santolina, artemisia, sage, pineapple sage, myrtle, and the shrubby thymes. From cutting to rooting should take only two to three weeks. Spring and late summer are the best times to take cuttings—spring for planting out the same season, late summer for overwintering indoors or for rooting plants as Christmas presents.

The method is straightforward: Choose healthy growth that is
(continued on page 268)

Layering

Division

WHAT'S YOUR ZONE?

The U.S. Department of Agriculture's plant hardiness zones are determined by the average annual frost-free days and minimum winter temperatures, and they're accurate in a general way. They are not *specifically* accurate, however. If you live on a high hill and face north, you may actually be in the next colder zone, while someone a few miles away in a sheltered, south-facing part of a valley floor could be in the next warmest zone.

Besides such local variations, there are na-tional variations. Zone 6, for example, is as diverse as Maine and Nevada. Eastern Zone 6 is subject to lots of rain, and plants that like it moist will do well there. But the same plants may not do well at all in Nevada, where the land is thousands of feet above sea level and dry as dust.

Use the zones as a general measure of plant hardiness, rather than as a climate guide. You know your local climate, rainfall patterns, and environmental conditions better than any map.

HARDINESS ZONE MAP

Zone 1	below -50°F
Zone 2	-50° to -40°
Zone 3	-40° to -30°
Zone 4	-30° to -20°
Zone 5	-20° to -10°
Zone 6	-10° to -0°
Zone 7	0° to 10°
Zone 8	10° to 20°
Zone 9	20° to 30°
Zone 10	30° to 40°

Average Minimum Temperatures for Each Zone

245

Herb	Plant Type[1]	Plant Size	Bloom Time	Plant Hardiness Zone
Aconite (*Aconitum Napellus*)	P	3 ft. tall	July–August	2–7
Agrimony (*Agrimonia Eupatoria*)	P	To 5 ft. tall	July–August	3
Aloe (*Aloe barbadensis*)	TP	1–2 ft. tall; to 3 ft. in flower		
American hellebore (*Veratrum viride*)	P	2–8 ft. tall	Midsummer	1–10
Angelica (*Angelica Archangelica*)	B	5 ft. tall in flower; foliage forms basal rosette	June–July	3
Anise (*Pimpinella Anisum*)	A	2 ft. tall	Summer	
Arnica (*Arnica montana*)	P	To 2 ft. tall in flower; foliage forms basal rosette	Midsummer	
Autumn crocus (*Colchicum autumnale*)	P	To 1 ft. tall; 3–4 in. wide	September	5
Basil (*Ocimum Basilicum*)	TA	2 ft. tall; 8 in. wide	July–August	
Bay (*Laurus nobilis*)	TP	To 40 ft. tall; to 5 ft. in pot culture	Spring	8
Beebalm (*Monarda didyma*)	P	3 ft. tall; 16 in. wide	July–August	4–9
Betony (*Stachys officinalis*)	P	2½ ft. tall in flower; foliage forms basal rosette	Mid–late summer	4
Black hellebore (*Helleborus niger*)	P	1 ft. tall; to 15 in. wide	January–March	4–8

Soil pH	Soil Requirements	Light Requirements	Propagation Method	Pests and Diseases
5–6	Rich, deep, moist	Partial shade to full sun	Division in fall or seed	Crown rot, powdery mildew, mosaic virus, verticillium wilt, and cyclamen mites
Very tolerant	Average, dry	Light shade	Seed or division	Powdery mildew
Neutral	Average, well-drained	Full sun to light shade	Offsets	
1–10	Moist	Light shade	Division or seed	
6.3	Rich, moist, well-drained	Partial shade	Sow fresh seed or transplant in spring when soil temperature reaches 55°F.	Spider mites, aphids, earwigs, leaf miners, and crown rot
6.0	Poor, light, dry, well-drained	Full sun	Seed sown in spring after danger of frost is past; does not transplant well	
4	Sandy, dry, humusy	Full sun	Division or seed sown in early spring (seed may be slow to germinate)	
	Humusy, moist	Full sun to partial shade	Division of corms in summer every 3 years	Leaf smut
6.0	Rich, moist, well-drained	Full sun	Sow fresh seed or transplant in spring after danger of frost is past	Japanese beetles and slugs
6.2	Moderately rich, well-drained	Full sun to partial shade	Cuttings	Scale
6.5	Rich, moist, humusy	Full sun to partial shade	Division in spring every 3–4 years	Powdery mildew and rust
	Average, moist, well-drained	Full sun to partial shade	Seed or division	
6.5–7.0	Rich, moist, well-drained	Partial shade to full sun	Seed or division in spring	Black spot and crown rot

(continued)

247

Herb	Plant Type[1]	Plant Size	Bloom Time	Plant Hardiness Zone
Bloodroot (*Sanguinaria canadensis*)	P	6 in. tall	March–April	3
Blue cohosh (*Caulophyllum thalictroides*)	P	To 3 ft. tall	April	
Boneset (*Eupatorium perfoliatum*)	P	3–5 ft. tall	August	5–9
Borage (*Borago officinalis*)	A	2 ft. tall; 16 in. wide	Midsummer (depends on seeding time)	
Burdock (*Arctium Lappa*)	B	1½–6 ft. tall	July–October	1–10
Calendula (*Calendula officinalis*)	HA	1½ ft. tall and wide	Spring–fall	
Caraway (*Carum Carvi*)	B	2 ft. tall in flower; foliage forms basal rosette	Spring	3–4
Cardamom (*Elettaria Cardamomum*)	TP	To 6 ft. tall		
Castor bean (*Ricinus communis*)	TA or TP	8–10 ft. tall; 4–6 ft. wide	Summer	8–10
Catnip (*Nepeta Cataria*)	P	1–3 ft. tall; 16 in. wide	June–August	3–4
Cayenne pepper (*Capsicum annuum*)	TA	9–12 in. tall and wide	Summer	
Chamomile, German (*Matricaria recutita*)	HA	30 in. tall	Summer	
Chamomile, Roman (*Chamaemelum nobile*)	P	1 ft. tall in flower; foliage in mats 2–4 in. tall	June–August	3–4
Chervil (*Anthriscus Cerefolium*)	HA	2 ft. tall in flower; foliage forms basal rosette	Summer (depends on seeding time)	

Soil pH	Soil Requirements	Light Requirements	Propagation Method	Pests and Diseases
Acid	Rich, moist, humusy, acid	Full sun to partial shade (woodland plant)	Division or seed	
Neutral	Rich, moist, humusy	Shade	Division or seed	
Very tolerant	Rich, moist	Full sun	Division	
6.6	Fairly rich, moist, light	Full sun	Seed sown in spring after danger of frost is past	
	Deep, loose, well-drained	Full sun	Seed sown in spring or fall	
6.6	Average, well-drained	Full sun	Seed sown 4–6 weeks before last frost date	Mildew, slugs, and snails
6.4	Light, dry	Full sun to light shade	Seed sown in spring or fall	Aphids
	Moist	Shade	Division or seed	
	Rich, moist, well-drained	Full sun to partial shade	Seed sown in spring after danger of frost is past	Generally pest- and disease-free
6.6	Average, sandy, well-drained	Full sun to partial shade	Seed sown in spring or summer or division in spring	
6.8	Rich, moist, humusy	Full sun	Seed sown indoors 8–10 weeks before last frost date	Generally pest- and disease-free; if treated as a perennial in greenhouse, virus can be a problem
6.7	Sandy, well-drained	Full sun to partial shade	Seed sown in early spring; will reseed readily	
7.0	Light, dry	Full sun to partial shade	Division, seed, or cuttings	
6.5	Moist, humusy	Partial shade	Seed sown in spring or late summer	Aphids

(continued)

249

Herb	Plant Type[1]	Plant Size	Bloom Time	Plant Hardiness Zone
Chicory (*Cichorium Intybus*)	P	3–4 ft. tall in flower; 22 in. wide	June–September	3
Chives (*Allium Schoenoprasum*)	P	1½ ft. tall	June	3
Clary (*Salvia Sclarea*)	B	3–4 ft. tall in flower; foliage forms basal rosette	June–July	
Coltsfoot (*Tussilago Farfara*)	P	To 6 in. tall in flower	Early spring	
Comfrey (*Symphytum officinale*)	P	3–5 ft. tall	May–frost	3
Coriander (*Coriandrum sativum*)	HA	2–3 ft. tall; 6–12 in. wide	Spring–fall (depends on seeding time)	
Costmary (*Chrysanthemum Balsamita*)	P	3 ft. tall	Late summer	4
Dandelion (*Taraxacum officinale*)	P	1 ft. tall; foliage forms basal rosette	April–May	3
Dill (*Anethum graveolens*)	HA	3 ft. tall; 2 ft. wide	Midsummer (depends on seeding time)	
Dock, curled (*Rumex crispus*)	P	1–4 ft. tall	June–August	3
Echinacea (*Echinacea angustifolia*)	P	To 2 ft. tall	Mid–late summer	3–8
Elecampane (*Inula Helenium*)	P	4–6 ft. tall; 2 ft. wide	Summer	3
Ephedra (*Ephedra distachya*)	P	2–4 ft. tall	Early summer	6

250

Soil pH	Soil Requirements	Light Requirements	Propagation Method	Pests and Diseases
6.4	Average to poor, well-drained	Full sun	Seed sown in early spring or division	
6.0	Moderately rich, well-drained	Full sun	Division in spring every 3 years	
Limey	Average to sandy, dry, well-drained	Full sun	Seed sown in spring	Root rot
	Average, moist	Full sun	Division, seed, or root cuttings	
7.1	Rich, moist, alkaline	Full sun to partial shade	Seed sown in fall or early spring or division	
6.6	Moderately rich, light, well-drained	Full sun to partial shade	Seed sown in spring when soil temperature reaches 55°F; does not transplant well except in cool, moist weather	Wilt and mildew
6.2	Rich, humusy	Full sun to partial shade	Division	
	Any soil	Full sun to partial shade	Seed sown in spring or fall	
6.0	Moderately rich, moist, well-drained	Full sun	Seed sown in spring or fall	
Acid	Any soil	Full sun	Seed	
	Fertile, well-drained	Full sun to light shade	Division, or seed sown in spring or fall	Leaf spot and Japanese beetles
	Moderately rich, moist	Full sun to light shade	Division, or seed sown in spring	
Alkaline	Dry	Full sun	Division, seed, suckers, or layering	

(continued)

Herb	Plant Type[1]	Plant Size	Bloom Time	Plant Hardiness Zone
Eyebright (*Euphrasia officinalis*)	A	To 8 in. tall	Summer	
Fennel (*Foeniculum vulgare*)	P or A	4 ft. tall; 1–2 ft. wide	July– September	6
Fenugreek (*Trigonella Foenum-graecum*)	A	6–24 in. tall	Midsummer	
Feverfew (*Chrysanthemum Parthenium*)	P	2–3 ft. tall and 1–2 ft. wide	Midsummer-fall	5
Flax (*Linum usitatissimum*)	A	20 in. tall	Summer	
Foxglove (*Digitalis purpurea*)	B	3–4 ft. tall and 1 ft. wide	June–July	4–8
Gentian (*Gentiana lutea*)	P	To 6 ft. tall	Late summer	6
Germander (*Teucrium Chamaedrys*)	P	2 ft. tall and wide	July–September	5–9
Ginger (*Zingiber officinale*)	TP	2–4 ft. tall	Depends on conditions	9
Ginseng (*Panax quinquefolius*)	P	1½ ft. tall	June–July	4
Goldenrod (*Solidago* spp.)	P	3–7 ft. tall	August–September	4
Goldenseal (*Hydrastis canadensis*)	P	To 1 ft. tall	May	6
Horehound (*Marrubium vulgare*)	P	2–3 ft. tall; 15 in. wide	Summer	4

Soil pH	Soil Requirements	Light Requirements	Propagation Method	Pests and Diseases
Alkaline	Poor soil; must be grown in conjunction with grass because it is a semi-parasite	Full sun	Seed	
6.5	Average, well-drained	Full sun	Seed sown in spring; will reseed readily; resents root disturbance	
	Rich	Full sun	Seed sown in spring when soil temperature reaches 55°F.	Root rot in cold, wet soil
6.3	Average, well-drained	Full sun to partial shade	Seed sown as soon as soil can be worked in spring	Generally pest- and disease-free
	Light, well-drained	Full sun to partial shade	Seed sown in spring	Grasshoppers and cutworms
Acid	Rich, moist, humusy	Full sun to partial shade	Seed sown as soon as soil can be worked in spring, or start indoors	Mosaic virus, curly top, wilt, anthracnose, leaf spot, Japanese beetles, and mealybugs
Limey	Moist, well-drained, humusy	Full sun to partial shade	Cuttings, division, or seed sown as soon as ripe	
6.3	Average, well-drained	Full sun to partial shade	Cuttings, layering, or division in spring	Usually none serious; may get mildew, leaf spot, rust, and mites
	Rich, moist, well-drained	Partial shade	Division of rhizomes in spring	
5.0–6.5	Humusy, well-drained	Partial shade	Seed sown as soon as berries ripen	Soil diseases
	Average to poor, well-drained	Full sun	Division in spring every 3 years	
	Rich, moist, humusy	Partial to full shade	Seed, or division in fall	
6.9	Deep, sandy, well-drained	Full sun	Seed sown in early spring or division	*(continued)*

Herb	Plant Type[1]	Plant Size	Bloom Time	Plant Hardiness Zone
Horseradish (*Armoracia rusticana*)	P	3 ft. tall	Midsummer	
Horsetail (*Equisetum hyemale*)	P	6–20 in. tall	April	2
Hyssop (*Hyssopus officinalis*)	P	2–3 ft. tall	June–August	4–5
Indigo (*Indigofera tinctoria*)	P	3–5 ft. tall	Late summer	10
Lady's bedstraw (*Galium verum*)	P	3 ft. tall, but often creeping	July–August	2–4
Lavender (*Lavandula angustifolia*)	P	30 in. tall; 2 ft. wide	June–July	5–8
Lavender cotton (*Santolina Chamaecyparissus*)	P	2 ft. tall; 1 ft. wide	June–July	6–8
Lemon balm (*Melissa officinalis*)	P	2 ft. tall and wide	July–September	4–5
Lemon verbena (*Aloysia triphylla*)	TP	5 ft. tall	Late summer–fall	9–10
Licorice (*Glycyrrhiza glabra*)	P	3–5 ft. tall	Midsummer	9
Lobelia (*Lobelia inflata*)	A	1–2 ft. tall	July–August	
Lovage (*Levisticum officinale*)	P	5 ft. tall; 3 ft. wide	June–July	3
Madder (*Rubia tinctorium*)	P	4 ft. tall, but often prostrate	Early summer	7
Marjoram, sweet (*Origanum Majorana*)	TP	1 ft. tall; 4–6 in. wide	August–September	9–10
Marsh mallow (*Althaea officinalis*)	P	4–5 ft. tall	Late summer	6

254

Soil pH	Soil Requirements	Light Requirements	Propagation Method	Pests and Diseases
6.8	Rich, moist, heavy	Full sun	Root cuttings planted in spring, seed, or division	
Acid–neutral	Moist, humusy	Full sun to partial shade	Division	
6.7	Light, well-drained	Full sun to partial shade	Division, stem cuttings, or seed sown in spring or fall	
	Well-drained, humusy	Full sun	Seed, suckers, or cuttings	
	Deep, light, rich, well-drained	Full sun to light shade	Division in spring or seed	
7.1	Light, well-drained	Full sun	Cuttings in spring or summer or division	Usually none serious, but may have root rot, leaf spot, and root-knot nematodes
Alkaline–neutral	Poor, light, well-drained	Full sun	Cuttings, layering, division, or seed	Susceptible to root fungal problems in warm climates, especially if not in a well-drained soil
7.0	Average, well-drained	Full sun to partial shade	Cuttings in spring or summer, layering, division, or seed	Powdery mildew
6.5	Rich, moist	Full sun	Cuttings in summer	Spider mites and whiteflies
Neutral	Rich, moist	Full sun to partial shade	Division in fall or seed	
	Humusy	Full sun to partial shade	Seed sown in spring after last frost date or cuttings	
6.5	Rich, moist, well-drained	Full sun to partial shade	Seed sown in fall or division in spring	Leaf miners and aphids
Neutral	Deep, well-drained	Full sun	Division or seed	
6.9	Light, dry, well-drained	Full sun	Seed, division, or cuttings	Damping-off
Neutral	Moist to wet, light	Full sun	Seed or division	

(continued)

Herb	Plant Type[1]	Plant Size	Bloom Time	Plant Hardiness Zone
Mayapple (*Podophyllum peltatum*)	P	1–1½ ft. tall	April–May	3
Mint (*Mentha* spp.)	P	To 2 ft. tall	July–August	5
Mugwort (*Artemisia vulgaris*)	P	To 6 ft. tall; 16–20 in. wide	Summer	3
Mullein (*Verbascum thapsus*)	B	3–6 ft. tall in flower; foliage forms basal rosette	June–September	4
Myrtle (*Myrtus communis*)	P	5–10 ft. tall; 4–7 in. wide	Spring–fall	9
Nasturtium (*Tropaeolum majus*)	A	1 ft. tall and 2 ft. wide; or climbing to 6 ft.	Summer–frost	
Oregano (*Origanum vulgare*)	P	1–2 ft. tall	July–September	5
Orris (*Iris ×germanica* var. *florentina*)	P	30 in. tall	May–June	5
Parsley (*Petroselinum crispum*)	B	1½ ft. tall; 8 in. wide	Early summer	9
Pennyroyal American (*Hedeoma pulegioides*)	A	4–16 in. tall; prostrate	August–September	
European (*Mentha Pulegium*)	P	1 ft. tall in flower; otherwise prostrate	Late summer	5
Pipsissewa (*Chimaphila umbellata*)	P	To 10 in. tall	May–August	5
Plantain (*Plantago major*)	HP	6–18 in. tall in flower; foliage forms basal rosette	June–September	3

Soil pH	Soil Requirements	Light Requirements	Propagation Method	Pests and Diseases
	Rich, moist, humusy	Partial shade	Division or seed	
6.5	Rich, moist, well-drained	Full sun to partial shade	Division, cuttings, or layering	Verticillium wilt, mint rust, mint anthracnose, spider mites, loopers, and mint flea beetles
	Averge to poor, well-drained	Full sun	Division in spring or fall or seed	
	Poor, well-drained	Full sun	Seed sown in early spring or fall	Usually none serious; rot if soil is wet
7.0	Moderately rich, well-drained	Full sun to partial shade	Cuttings, seed, or layering	Mites, scale, and mushroom root rot
	Average, moist, well-drained	Full sun	Seed sown in early spring as soon as soil warms; resents root disturbance	Aphids, leaf spot, and wilt
6.8	Average, well-drained	Full sun	Cuttings in summer, or division in spring	Root rot, fungal diseases, spider mites, aphids, and leaf miners
7.0	Rich, well-drained	Full sun	Division in summer after flowering	Iris borers and bacterial soft rot
6.0	Moderately rich, moist, well-drained	Full sun to partial shade	Sow seed or transplant when soil temperature reaches 50°F.	Crown rot, carrot weevils, parsley worms, and nematodes
Acid	Average, dry	Full sun	Seed sown in early spring; will reseed readily	
Neutral	Rich, moist, humusy	Full sun to partial shade	Seed	
Acid	Rich, humusy	Partial shade	Division or cuttings	
	Average, well-drained	Full sun to partial shade	Seed sown in spring	

(continued)

257

Herb	Plant Type[1]	Plant Size	Bloom Time	Plant Hardiness Zone
Pokeweed (*Phytolacca americana*)	HP	4–9 ft. tall	July–September	3
Potentilla (*Potentilla verna*)	P	3 in. tall, trailing	May–June	4–8
Rosemary (*Rosmarinus officinalis*)	TP	5 ft. tall; 3–6 ft. wide	Early summer	8
Rue (*Ruta graveolens*)	P	3 ft. tall	June–August	4–9
Safflower (*Carthamus tinctorius*)	A	12–30 in. tall	Summer	
Saffron (*Crocus sativus*)	P	1½ ft. tall	September	6
Sage (*Salvia officinalis*)	P	12–30 in. tall; to 2 ft. wide	June	4–8
St.-John's-wort (*Hypericum perforatum*)	P	2 ft. tall	July–August	5
Salad burnet (*Poterium Sanguisorba*)	P	3 ft. tall in flower; foliage forms 1-ft. basal rosette	May–June	3
Savory, summer (*Satureja hortensis*)	A	1½ ft. tall	Midsummer–frost	
Savory, winter (*Satureja montana*)	P	1½ ft. tall; 6–16 in. wide	July–mid-September	6
Scented geranium (*Pelargonium* spp.)	TP	3 ft. tall		10
Soapwort (*Saponaria officinalis*)	P	1–2 ft. tall	July–September	3–8
Sorrel (*Rumex acestosa*) (*R. scutatus*)	P	1½ ft. tall; flower stalks 3–4 ft. tall	*R. acestosa:* Late summer *R. scutatus:* Early spring	5

258

Soil pH	Soil Requirements	Light Requirements	Propagation Method	Pests and Diseases
	Moist, humusy	Full sun to partial shade	Seed	
Acid or alkaline	Average, well-drained	Full sun to partial shade	Division in spring	
6.8	Light, well-drained	Full sun to partial shade	Cuttings, layering, or division	Botrytis, root rot, spider mites, scale, mealybugs, and whiteflies
7.0	Clay loam, well-drained	Full sun	Cuttings, division, or seed	Root fungal problems in warmer zones; can prevent by providing good drainage
	Average to poor, dry	Full sun	Seed sown in spring when soil has warmed	
	Light, well-drained	Full sun to light shade	Division of corms in summer every 3 years	
6.4	Moderately rich, well-drained	Full sun	Cuttings, layering, division, or seed	Wilt, root rot, slugs, spider mites, and spittlebugs
Acid or alkaline	Average to poor	Full sun to partial shade	Seed, cuttings, or division in fall	
6.8	Average, well-drained	Full sun to partial shade	Division in spring or seed; reseeds readily	Root rot
6.8	Average	Full sun	Seed sown indoors 1 month before last frost date	
6.7	Light, dry, well-drained	Full sun	Cuttings, layering, division, or seed	Root rot
6–7	Rich, dry, well-drained, humusy	Full sun	Cuttings in spring or summer	Bacterial wilt, botrytis blight, and whiteflies
	Average to poor, well-drained	Full sun to light shade	Division or seed	Usually none serious
6.0	Rich, moist	Full sun to partial shade	Division in early spring, or seed sown in early spring	Leaf miners and slugs

(continued)

259

RODALE'S GUIDE TO GROWING HERBS—*continued*

Herb	Plant Type[1]	Plant Size	Bloom Time	Plant Hardiness Zone
Southernwood (*Artemisia Abrotanum*)	P	5 ft. tall; 2–3 ft. wide	August	4–8
Sweet cicely (*Myrrhis odorata*)	P	3 ft. tall	May–June	3
Sweet flag (*Acorus Calamus*)	P	To 3 ft.	Midsummer	3–10
Sweet woodruff (*Galium odoratum*)	P	8 in. tall	April–May	3
Tansy (*Tanacetum vulgare*)	P	3–4 ft. tall	July–September	4
Tarragon (*Artemisia Dracunculus*)	P	2 ft. tall; 16 in. wide	Should not flower	4
Thyme (*Thymus vulgaris*)	P	1 ft. tall	June–July	5–9
Tropical periwinkle (*Catharanthus roseus*)	A	To 2 ft. tall and wide	May–October	
Valerian (*Valeriana officinalis*)	P	3½–5 ft. tall when in bloom; otherwise 1 ft. tall; 12–16 in. wide	June	4
Violet (*Viola odorata*)	P	6 in. tall	April–May	5–8
Wintergreen (*Gaultheria procumbens*)	P	4 in. tall, creeping	July	4
Woad (*Isatis tinctoria*)	B	3–5 ft. tall in flower; foliage forms basal rosette	May	
Wormwood (*Artemisia Absinthium*)	P	1–3 ft. tall	July–August	4
Yarrow (*Achillea Millefolium*)	P	3 ft. tall in flower; otherwise 6–10 in. tall	June–September	2

1. A = annual; HA = hardy annual; TA = tender annual; B = biennial; P = perennial; HP = hardy perennial; TP = tender perennial

Soil pH	Soil Requirements	Light Requirements	Propagation Method	Pests and Diseases
6.7	Average, well-drained	Full sun	Division in spring or fall or cuttings	Aphids
	Moist, well-drained, humusy	Partial shade	Seed or division in fall (must use fresh seed)	Mites
	Rich, marshy	Sun or shade	Division in spring or fall	
5.0	Moist, well-drained, humusy	Shade	Division in spring or cuttings	None serious; fungal problems in late summer
6.3	Average	Full sun to partial shade	Seed sown in spring or fall or division	
6.9	Rich, sandy, well-drained loam	Full to partial shade	Division in spring or cuttings; must be divided every 2–3 years	Root rot and mildew
6.3	Light, dry, well-drained	Full sun to partial shade	Layering, cuttings, or division	Root rot, fungal diseases, and spider mites
	Average, well-drained	Full sun to partial shade	Seed or cuttings	Usually none
Wide range	Rich, moist, humusy	Full sun to partial shade	Division in spring or fall or seed	
Acid–neutral	Rich, moist, humusy	Partial shade	Offsets, seed, or division in spring	Downy mildew, anthracnose, leaf spot, crown rot, cutworms, and slugs
Acid	Moist, humusy, peaty or sandy	Partial shade	Layering, suckers, division, cuttings, or seed	
	Rich, well-drained	Full sun	Seed sown in spring or late summer	
6.6	Clay loam, well-drained	Full sun to partial shade	Cuttings, seed, or division	
6.1	Moderately rich, well-drained	Full sun	Division in spring or fall every other year	Few problems; occasional powdery mildew, rust, and stem rot

HERB PESTS

Pest	Description	Herb(s) Affected	Control
Aphid (*Aphis, Macrosiphum, Myzus* spp.) (*many other species*)	Soft-bodied, pear-shaped insect less than 1/10 in. long; may have clear wings or be wingless; green to bluish black DAMAGE: insect pierces plant tissue and extracts sap; transmits viral diseases; leaves turn yellow	Angelica, caraway, chervil, lovage, nasturtium, oregano, southernwood, and sunflower	Foil mulch; insecticidal soap spray; diatomaceous earth or rotenone dusts; ladybugs; lacewings; syrphid flies
Carrot weevil (*Listronotus oregonensis*)	Brownish insect, 1/5 in. long with hard shell; pale, legless, brown-headed larva DAMAGE: larva tunnels into herb's top and root, destroying most of plant's tissue	Parsley	Crop rotation; clean cultivation
Cutworm (Noctuidae)	Grayish to black worm, sometimes with markings, 1–2 in. long; curls up when disturbed; nocturnal; adult is mottled, night-flying moth DAMAGE: chews stems at or below ground level	Flax and violet	Protect seedlings with cardboard collars; circle plants with diatomaceous earth for serious infestations
Cyclamen mite (*Steneotarsonemus pallidus*)	Microscopic, orange-pink, shiny mite with 8 legs DAMAGE: foliage shows purplish areas; leaves are distorted; flowers are streaked and blotchy; buds don't open	Aconite	Destroy infested plants immediately; mite predators *Typhlodromus bellinus* and *T. reticulatus*
Earwig (*Forticula auricularia*)	Reddish brown insect with short, leathery forewings and pincers on tip of abdomen; 3/4 in. long DAMAGE: nymph feeds on plant shoots and eats holes in foliage and flowers	Angelica	Handpicking; tachinid flies (*Bigonicheta spinigennis*)
Iris borer (*Papaipema nebris*)	Gray or violet caterpillar 1–1½ in. long; adult is gray moth with 1-in. wingspan DAMAGE: caterpillar eats insides of leaves, burrowing down from top; blades and rhizomes brown and rot	Orris	Run hands up leaf blades to crush borers; Bt (*Bacillus thuringiensis*); remove borer-infested rhizomes

Pest	Description	Herb(s) Affected	Control
Japanese beetle (*Popillia japonica*)	Shiny metallic green beetle with copper brown wings, about ½ in. long; larva is inch-long white grub DAMAGE: adult eats leaves, resulting in lacy skeletons of veining, as well as flowers; grub feeds on roots and underground stems	Basil, echinacea, and foxglove	Milky spore disease (*Bacillus popilliae*); fall tiphia (*Tiphia popilliavora*)
Leaf miner (*Liriomyza* spp.)	Small, black fly, usually with yellow stripes; tiny yellowish larva DAMAGE: maggot feeds between upper and lower leaf surfaces, causing white tunnels or blotches on leaves	Angelica, lovage, oregano, and sorrel	Remove and destroy affected leaves before maggots mature; cover plants with screening to prevent infestations
Mealybug (*Pseudococcus* spp.)	Yellowish wingless female covered with dense white cotony powder; ⅒ in. long; male is tiny fly DAMAGE: feeds by sucking sap; secretes honeydew, which attracts ants and promotes sooty mold	Foxglove and rosemary	Insecticidal soap spray; swabbing with alcohol; knocking off with a strong stream of water; mealybug destroyer *Cryptolaemus montrouzieri*; green lacewing larvae
Mint flea beetle (*Longitarsus menthaphagus*)	Small, dark, oval beetle that jumps vigorously when disturbed; tiny white larva DAMAGE: adult eats tiny rounded holes in leaves, so foliage looks riddled; larva feed on plant roots	Mints	Lime, diatomaceous earth, or rotenone dusts; keep weeds out of garden and vicinity; cover seedbeds with gauze or Reemay
Parsley worm (*Papilio polyxenes asterius*)	Green caterpillar 2 in. long; has yellow-dotted black band across each segment; larva of the black swallowtail butterfly DAMAGE: feeds on parsley leaves	Parsley	Handpicking; Bt (*Bacillus thuringiensis*)
Root-knot nematode (*Meloidogyne* spp.)	Microscopic worm with pearly egg masses DAMAGE: stimulates injured plant tissue to form galls, which block the flow of water and nutrients to the plant, leading to stunting, wilt, and yellowing; roots appear scabby	Lavender and parsley	Add organic matter to encourage parasitic fungi; plant rotation; monocropping with marigolds

(continued)

HERB PESTS—continued

Pest	Description	Herb(s) Affected	Control
Scale (Coccideae)	Legless, wingless female 1½–⅛ in. long, covered with a waxy or cottony substance; male may have pair of wings DAMAGE: feeds by sucking sap, causing stunting and chlorosis; honeydew secretions attract ants and promote sooty mold	Bay, myrtle, and rosemary	Vedalia ladybug; insecticidal soap spray
Slug (*Limax maximus*) (*Deroceras reticulatum*) (*many other species*)	Grayish or grayish brown, legless, slimy mollusk, ½–4 in. long, antennae, nocturnal DAMAGE: feeds on foliage, scraping holes in leaves and causing extensive damage	Basil, calendula, sage, sorrel, and violet	Handpicking; stale beer traps; boards placed in damp areas as traps and checked each morning
Snail	Gray, pinkish, black, brown, or mottled mollusk, with soft, slimy body and coiled shell, ½–3 in. long, antennae; chiefly nocturnal DAMAGE: same as for slug	Calendula	Handpicking; stale beer traps; diatomaceous earth dusts; copper bands around tops of boards that frame raised beds
Spider mite (*Tetranychus urticae*) (*many other species*)	Microscopic, 8-legged, often web-spinning arachnid; some 2-spotted; green, yellow, brown, or red DAMAGE: feeds by sucking plant juices; leaves show pinprick spots and puckering; weakens plants	Angelica, germander, lemon verbena, mints, oregano, rosemary, sage, and thyme	Cold water spray on leaves; insecticidal soap spray; slurry of flour, buttermilk, and water; lacewings, ladybugs, predatory mites *Phytoseiulus persimilis* and *Amblyseium californicus*
Spittlebug (*Philaenus leucophthalmus*)	Brownish or green, triangular insect, ½–⅓ in. long; nymph is green; surrounded by masses of frothy bubbles DAMAGE: sucks plant juices; may cause wilting and death	Sage	Remove bubble masses; keep weeds cleared from garden and surrounding area
Whitefly (*Trialeurodes vaporariorum*)	Small, mothlike, dusty, white-winged adult; legless, yellowish nymph DAMAGE: nymph and adult suck juices from leaves, buds, and stems, weakening plants	Lemon verbena, rosemary, and scented geranium	Insecticidal soap spray; yellow sticky traps; parasitic wasp *Encarsia formosa*; pyrethrum

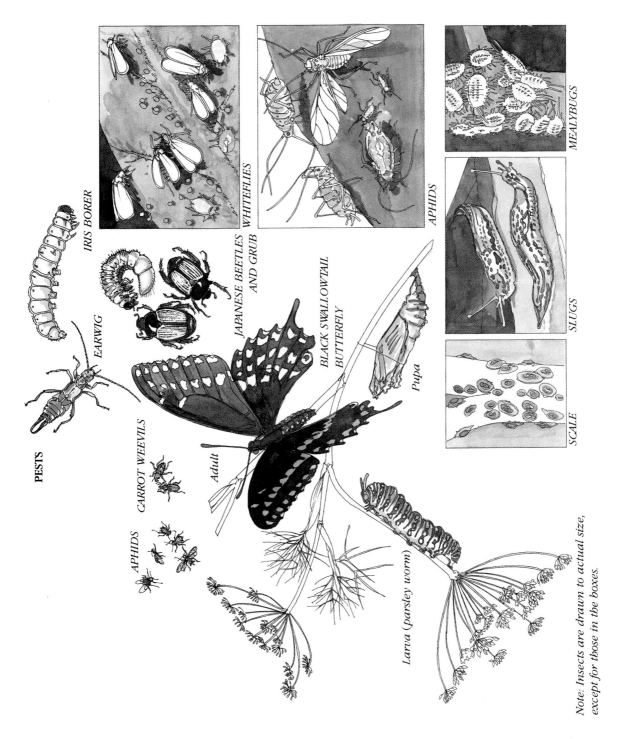

PESTS

IRIS BORER

EARWIG

APHIDS

CARROT WEEVILS

Adult

BLACK SWALLOWTAIL
BUTTERFLY

Pupa

Larva (parsley worm)

JAPANESE BEETLES
AND GRUB

WHITEFLIES

APHIDS

MEALYBUGS

SLUGS

SCALE

Note: Insects are drawn to actual size,
except for those in the boxes.

265

HERB DISEASES

Disease	Description	Herb(s) Affected	Control
Anthracnose (*Collectotrichum* spp.)	Small, water-soaked spots on aboveground parts, which turn a light color and may drop out; elongated tan cankers on stems; fungus	Foxglove, mints, and violet	Rotate plants every 2 years; don't cultivate when plants are wet; remove diseased plants promptly
Bacterial soft rot (*Erwinig* spp.)	Soft decay of fleshy tissues, causing them to become watery or slimy; shoots wilt and blacken at base	Orris	Remove diseased plants promptly; avoid injuring plants; keep soil as acidic as plants will tolerate
Bacterial wilt (*Pseudomonas solanacearum*)	Plants wilt and die; no yellowing occurs; stem sap produces strings; vascular system browns	Coriander, foxglove, nasturtium, sage, and scented geranium	Remove diseased plants promptly; avoid injuring plants; keep soil as acidic as plants will tolerate
Black spot (*Diplocarpon rosae*)	Black circles up to ½ in. in diameter on both sides of leaves, with indistinct, fuzzy edges; tissue around spots turns yellow; leaves drop; fungus	Black hellebore	Space plants far enough apart to provide good ventilation; don't cultivate when plants are wet; mulch; remove diseased leaves; water plants in the morning
Botrytis blight (*Botrytis* spp.)	Small yellow, orange, or brown splotches on leaves, flowers, roots, or bulbs, spreading and becoming coated with fuzzy gray mold; hard black blisters on plant stems; fungus	Rosemary and scented geranium	Remove dead flowers and yellowed foliage
Crown rot (*Pellicularia rolfsii*)	Fibrous fans of white fungus near bases of plants; red or light brown crust on soil surface around plants; plants yellow, wilt, and die	Aconite, angelica, black hellebore, parsley, and violet	Rotate plants every 3 years; dig up and burn diseased plants
Curly top (*Ruga verrucosans*)	Leaves pucker and curl down, cupping or looking like small balls; young plants are stunted and die; virus	Foxglove	Protect plants from beet leafhoppers, which carry the disease, by close spacings and covering plants with gauze or Reemay
Damping-off (*Rhizoctonia solani*) (*Pythium debaryanum*)	Kills seedling roots; affected plants are water-soaked and look shriveled	Sweet marjoram	Pasteurize soil; provide warm, well-drained seedbeds
Downy mildew (*Phytophtbora* spp.)	Yellow spots on upper surface of leaves; downy or violet-gray mold on undersides; leaves wither and die; fungus	Calendula, coriander, germander, queen of the meadow, tarragon, and violet	Do not crowd plants; cultivate only when plants are dry; remove diseased plants promptly; rotate plants every 3 years

Disease	Description	Herb(s) Affected	Control
Leaf smut (*Entyloma ellisii*)	Black, sooty spots or stripes on leaves; leaves twist and curl; plant eventually dies; fungus	Autumn crocus	Remove diseased plants promptly; do not plant corms in infested soil
Leaf spot (*many species*)	Tiny, greenish yellow spots on upper side of leaf, which form a white spot surrounded by a red band; may drop out to give a shot-hole appearance; fungus	Echinacea, foxglove, germander, lavender, nasturtium, sunflower, and violet	Remove diseased plants promptly; disinfect garden tools; don't cultivate when plants are wet; allow wide spacings; water soil, not foliage
Mosaic virus (*Marmor* spp.)	Yellow and green mottled, curled leaves; stunting; leaves grow upright in rosettes; misshapen flowers	Aconite and foxglove	Control aphids and keep garden and surrounding area weed-free; remove diseased plants promptly
Powdery mildew (*Erysiphe cichoracearum*)	White, powdery mold on upper surfaces of leaves and petioles; foliage wilts and browns, then drops; fungus	Aconite, agrimony, beebalm, calendula, coriander, germander, lemon balm, queen of the meadow, sunflower, tarragon, and yarrow	Remove diseased plants promptly; thorough fall cleanup
Root rot (*Rhizoctonia solani*)	Rotted, yellowish brown to black roots and underground stems; outer layers of root slough off, leaving a central core; fungus	Clary, fenugreek, lavender, mullein, myrtle, oregano, rosemary, sage, salad burnet, tarragon, thyme, and winter savory	Rotate plants every 3 years; provide good drainage; remove diseased plants promptly; thorough fall cleanup
Rusts (*Puccinia* spp.)	Reddish, orange, or black waxy pustules on stems and foliage; leaves may drop prematurely; plants look unsightly; fungus	Beebalm, germander, mints, sunflower, and yarrow	Remove diseased plants promptly; dust plants with sulfur; thorough fall cleanup
Stem rot (*Phytophthora cactorum*)	Dead areas develop at bases of plants; plants wilt, fall, and die; fungus	Sunflower and yarrow	Remove diseased plants promptly; rotate plants every 3 years
Verticillium wilt (*Verticillium albo-atrum*)	Yellowed splotches on leaves gradually brown; entire plant affected at once, midday wilting; leaves drop, beginning at the bottom of the plant; chlorosis; stunting; fungus	Aconite, coriander, foxglove, mints, nasturtium, and sage	Rotate plants every 3 years; avoid high-nitrogen fertilizers; remove diseased plants promptly

GROWING HERBS—continued

mature but not yet woody (i.e., that still bends easily but isn't too succulent) and is not in bloom. Cut stems 3 to 4 inches from the tips using a sharp propagating or razor knife. Strip the leaves and small branches from the bottom third to half of each stem, and immediately insert it into a moist rooting medium (the only exception is scented geranium, which roots best if allowed to callus over for about eight hours in a cool place—overnight is ideal). Use a loose, sterile medium such as 1 part dampened peat to 3 parts perlite. Stick the cuttings into the medium so that their leaves almost touch, but don't allow them to overlap.

Once all of the cuttings have been set in the medium, water gently to firm the soil around the stems, and cover the flat or pot with a clear plastic bag. Keep the bag up off the cuttings with Popsicle sticks or pencils inserted in the medium around the perimeter of the container. Place the flat or pots in bright light—but not direct sunlight—and mist the plants daily to maintain high humidity. Promptly remove any dead cuttings. New top growth is a sign of rooting. When it begins, remove the plastic and water the cuttings normally for a few days before transplanting.

PESTS AND DISEASES

Herbs are not immune to pests and diseases, but they seem less susceptible—perhaps because of their high concentrations of aromatic oils or their undomesticated nature—than most garden plants. Like vegetables and flowers, herb seedlings must be protected from cutworms and damping-off; aphids, whiteflies, and spider mites prey on many; slugs and snails tend to their usual voracious tendencies; and rots, mildews, and wilts take their toll, usually of plants spaced too closely together in poorly drained soil. Good gardening practices, including prompt cleanup and rotation, will take care of many problems; specific pests, ailments, and controls are listed in the pests and diseases tables (see pages 262–67).

HARVESTING AND STORAGE

How you harvest herbs depends on what you're harvesting and what you plan to do with them. If you need a few snippets of parsley, chives, and basil for a salad, or some thyme and oregano for the spaghetti sauce, the most sensible time to collect them is when you're ready to fix the salad or sauce. If your aim is to preserve a quantity of a given herb for future use, however, a few general rules apply.

Drying Herbs on Screens

The best time to gather herbs is in the morning of a dry, sunny day after the dew has dried from the plants. If you are harvesting leaves, the peak time for flavor and fragrance is just before the plants flower in the spring. Harvests can continue as need and plant growth permit, until early fall. Trim off any flower heads from basil and mint for continued top-quality leaf production. Annuals can be harvested until a fall frost kills them, but perennials should be allowed to grow unimpeded for 40 to 60 days before the first frost so they can harden off before winter. If, as in the case of lavender, you are harvesting flowers, cut flower stalks before the blooms are fully open since they will continue to open as they dry. Similarly, for seed harvests of coriander, anise, fennel, dill, and the like, cut the stalks before the seeds begin to shatter from the heads.

For a harvest of leaves, always cut stems; don't just strip off individual leaves and desert the naked stems in the garden. You can cut as much as three-quarters of the current season's growth in a given harvest. Naturally, harvest only disease-free growth. If your harvest is small, you can rack-dry it in a well-ventilated room out of direct sunlight. Use a screen, bamboo tray, or cheesecloth-covered cookie sheet (paper towels do fine as a covering, too). Lay the stems down in a single layer so the leaves don't overlap. Turn or stir the herbs once or twice a day until dry and crumbly.

Drying herbs: If you're contemplating a larger harvest, there are several effective techniques for drying your herbs. To air-dry herbs, tie bunches tightly with string or rubber bands (stems will shrink as they dry), and hang them in a warm, dark, well-ventilated area as dust-free as possible. If dust is a problem, poke a hole in the bottom of a brown paper bag and insert the herb cluster lantern-style. To dry seeds, wrap unpunched paper bags around the stems and secure them; the seeds will fall into the bag as they dry. All drying takes about two weeks.

If you haven't the room or time for air-drying, the oven is an option. With a gas oven, simply leave on the pilot light—the oven temperature will be 85° to 90°F—and spread a single layer of herbs on cookie sheets or brown paper on the oven racks. Turn the herbs once or twice daily; they'll dry in one to three days. If your oven is electric, turn it on its lowest setting and proceed as for gas; the herbs will dry in a matter of hours. Oven drying works particularly well for succulent herbs like basil.

Storage: Whatever method you choose for herb drying, storage techniques are the same. When the leaves are crisp and fully dry, strip them from the stems. Put them in glass bottles (dark bottles are

Hanging Herbs to Dry

GROWING HERBS—continued

INVASIVE HERBS

A word of warning is in order about invasive herbs.

Division can keep rampant perennials like comfrey and the artemisias under control. But some herbs—tansy and mint, for example—grow out of control and will overrun the garden if left unconfined.

Unconfined is the key word. The easiest way to confine them is by setting up barriers when you plant. Sinking metal lawn edgers into the soil around plants that spread from underground runners will keep them in bounds. So will planting them in large plastic pots with the bottoms cut off and the tops just at the surface of the soil. The barriers must go down at least a foot, however, or the roots will just duck under them and go their merry way.

The worst offenders are 'Silver King' and 'Silver Queen' artemisia, horseradish, tansy, the mints, comfrey, hops, and costmary.

recommended, if available) or canning jars; plastic bottles can be air- and moisture-permeable. Store out of direct sunlight, which bleaches and deteriorates the herbs. The same storage techniques work for the flowers and seeds.

If you would prefer fresh herbs to dried, the leaves can be harvested and frozen as you would freeze any leafy green. A clever alternative is to puree the herb in a blender with water to liquefy, pour the puree into ice cube trays, and freeze. When frozen, pop the herb cubes into labeled freezer bags. The flavor and aroma of herbs can also be preserved in vinegars, jellies, and other condiments; edible flowers can be candied. For details, see the entry Cooking with Herbs.

WINTERIZING

After a year's enjoyment of herbs in the garden and a bountiful harvest for year-round use, it's time to turn your thoughts toward putting the garden to bed for the winter. Harvest the last of the annuals before frost strikes in the fall, and pull up unusable parts to enrich the compost heap.

Once frosts arrive and the ground has frozen, mulch heavily to protect perennials from winter heaving (when alternate freezing and thawing of the soil pushes plants right out of the ground). Straw is the ideal winter mulch since leaves may drift over the crowns of small plants and suffocate them. Draw the mulch up to, but not over, the plants. Gray-leaved plants that hold their leaves over winter—lavender, santolina, thyme, the artemisias—need additional protection in cold climates. Laying evergreen boughs over the plants will help ensure their survival with minimal dieback.

Late fall, before the onset of frosts, is also the time to think about bringing tender perennials indoors for the winter. Those that are in pots should be moved to a shaded location, such as an open porch, about two weeks before you bring them in so they can adjust to the transition. Examine each plant closely for insect infestations. If you see pests such as whiteflies or aphids, spray with insecticidal soap.

A week before you bring in potted plants, pot up any tender perennials that are in the ground. Be extremely careful to disturb the roots as little as possible. Move them into the shade and proceed as for potted plants. Once plants are indoors, they need at least four hours of direct sunlight a day. If you don't have a sunny plant window, a fluorescent light setup may be the solution. For more information, consult the entry Herbs as Houseplants.

Valerian

Sage

*Ginseng
Root*

Black Horehound

Garlic

Thyme

German Chamomile

Foxglove

Golden Barberry

Green Barberry

Soapwort

Echinacea

Comfrey

Tropical Periwinkle

274

HAWTHORN

Crataegus laevigata   **Rosaceae**

Heart patients look to hawthorn. It could become the source of an important cardiac medicine.

The ancient Greeks and Romans regarded the hawthorn as a symbol of hope and happiness. As such, it was often used for bouquets and corsages in wedding ceremonies. The Romans believed hawthorn kept evil spirits away, so they placed leaves of it in their babies' cradles. Contrarily, during the Middle Ages, people thought hawthorn an evil herb. Branches brought into a home meant that someone in that house would die.

USES

The pendulum of opinion is swinging back. Today, hawthorn is viewed as a potentially important drug source.

Medicinal: Scientists have discovered that hawthorn dilates blood vessels, allowing blood to flow more freely and thus lowering blood pressure. In addition, it acts directly on the heart muscle to help a damaged heart work more efficiently. Hawthorn works slowly and appears to be toxic only in large doses, making it a relatively safe, mild tonic.

When it comes to treating an organ as vital as the heart, of course, self-medication is foolish, no matter how safe the herbal remedy. It is hoped that continuing scientific research will confirm hawthorn's benefits. In Germany several medications containing hawthorn extracts are already on the market.

Ornamental: With their attractive foliage, flowers, and berries, hawthorns offer beauty to any landscape. Of moderate size and tolerant of a range of environmental conditions, they adapt well to almost any landscape, too. Plant them individually or in hedges.

CULTIVATION

Hawthorns can be grown in a range of environments from closed urban sites to open, exposed, windy locations near the sea. They tolerate a wide variety of soils, but they do best in a limestone soil that is rich, loamy, and moist.

Hawthorns are best propagated from seed, except for certain horticultural varieties that must be grafted or budded. Smaller hawthorns transplant better than older, larger ones.

Pests and diseases: Check your plants for aphids, borers, leaf miners, spider mites, scale, cedar-apple rust, fireblight, fungus leaf blight, powdery mildew, and twig blight.(See the entry Growing Herbs for information on controlling pests and diseases.)

DESCRIPTION

The genus *Crataegus* consists of deciduous trees and shrubs with thorny branches. In North America alone, between 800 and 900 species have been described. Because hawthorn flowers in the spring, it has been called May or Mayblossom. The ship Mayflower was named after the hawthorn.

Flowers: In clusters, five sepals, five petals, many stamens, usually white or cream but sometimes pink or red.

Leaves: Alternate, lobed or toothed; vary in size and shape.

Fruit: Pomes, spherical to egg-shaped, red, contain one to five nutlets.

Height: To 15 ft.

FLOWERING

May.

RANGE

North America throughout the United States; Europe; North Africa; and western Asia.

HABITAT

Hedges and open deciduous woods.

GROWING CONDITIONS

- Plant hardiness zone 3.
- Soil pH: alkaline.
- Rich, loamy, moist soil.
- Full sun to partial shade.

HEALING WITH HERBS

Healing with herbs is a very controversial subject. There are many people who regard herbal healing as antiquated hocus-pocus.

If you ask your family physician about herbs, for example, he or she may very well lecture you on the folly of trying to remedy even minor ailments with herb teas or poultices, citing the uncertainties of diagnosis and the shortcomings of the "medicaments." Ask a pharmacist and you may get a lecture on the impurities of the material and the vagaries of dosages.

On the other hand, you may have read about or heard about or even know someone who claims to have had successful healing experiences with herbs. They can't explain how or why they worked. They just worked.

These two approaches to healing exist in today's society, as they have throughout much of history. One can be called rational, the other empirical.

Rationalism is a search for knowledge based on established laws and principles, rather than on what is directly perceived. Empiricism is a search for knowledge based on practical experience, rather than principles. All of the sciences, including medicine, can be approached from either perspective. The dominant approach in medicine now is rationalism, though many modern-day holistic practitioners, including almost all current folk healers, opt for the empirical perspective.

Inherent in modern folk medicine is the philosophy of "vitalism." *Vitalism is the belief that life is unique, and that it possesses qualities that cannot be defined in simple terms of anatomy and physical makeup.* Vitalism is inherent in the modern holistic viewpoint and has been an important part of the empirical perception of medicine.

Thus, in the empirical approach to healing, crude medicines are made using plants gathered from the garden, meadows, and woodlands. Teas and poultices made from leaves, bark, roots, and flowers are administered to cure all manner of ailments. This is folk medicine, practiced by naturopaths, herbalists, and a great many ordinary folk.

In the rational approach, the active principles of plants are extracted or chemically duplicated. This is the orthodox, scientific medicine administered by M.D.s and pharmacists.

Surprisingly, a recent survey revealed that close to 50 percent of all prescriptions—issued by rational physicians—contain drugs that are either directly derived from natural sources or synthesized from natural models as the sole ingredient or as one of the several ingredients. To a pharmacognosist, there is no meaningful difference between a drug that has been synthesized and the natural substance on which its design was based. And the decision—made by drug companies—as to whether a given medicinal substance ought to be used in its natural state or synthesized is almost entirely an economic one. One herbal "drug," for instance, might be so easy to grow and harvest that it would not be worth the investment to synthesize it. Another natural "drug" might be very difficult to obtain in the wild but very easy to synthesize in the laboratory. Still another herbal "drug" might be expensive to collect in the wild, but its bioactive molecules may either be unidentified or simply too complicated to synthesize, so the wild sources must be used.

Traditional herbalists are strongly opposed to the use of bioactive molecules rather than the use of preparations made from whole herbs. They argue that even if the active ingredients are chemically identical, the other constituents naturally found in the plant are there for a purpose, either to help the active ingredients or to help protect against possible overdoses or side effects.

Asked what he thought of popular or traditional herbalism, one pharmacognosist explained that while it certainly had some validity, doctors cannot use herbs unless they are absolutely certain of their purity and potency and of the availability of the active principles to the body. It is impossible, therefore, for them to use preparations made from whole herbal materials because their properties simply cannot be measured in an herb when it is still in its "crude" form, he said. To do otherwise with a potent herbal substance such as atropine or digitalis, for example, would be to risk a possibly fatal overdose— or a possibly fatal *underdose.*

As for commonly used herbs such as garlic, peppermint, sage, and so forth, pharmacognosists generally will acknowledge that they *do* have certain medicinal properties, but they point out that these herbs are relatively weak and not sufficiently dependable to use in a medical setting.

HOMEMADE HERBAL MEDICINES

Natural food stores and vitamin suppliers sell all sorts of ready-made herbal medicines. Still, it's far cheaper and more satisfying to make your own remedies with homegrown herbs picked right from your garden. You can combine the herbs to fit your own needs and tastes and make just the amounts you need. Furthermore, you can guarantee the purity of the herbs since you would know they hadn't been treated with any toxic chemicals.

Just remember that many of the herbs in your garden have toxic properties, and some are absolutely poisonous. Take care to identify

PHARMACOGNOSY

Herbal medicine does not begin and end with folk traditions. Although its roots have been traced back thousands of years and for most of its history herbalism has been closely linked with religion, astrology, and superstition, there is also a purely scientific approach to the world of herbs, known as pharmacognosy.

A pharmacognosist has expert knowledge of the chemical constituents of plants, how to go about identifying new chemicals and even molecules that occur in plants, and how various cultures use plants to their benefit, with particular interest in their medical applications. A pharmacognosist may, for instance, travel through a rural area such as Appalachia or a remote jungle area, learning how the residents use plants for healing and observing their actual use. He would collect these herbs and, being a rationalist, take them back to his laboratory and subject them to various sophisticated analyses.

Most typically, a pharmacognosist is interested in isolating and describing the active ingredients, or bioactive molecules, of plants. And his or her investigations might lead to attempts to synthesize these bioactive molecules, or to experiment with changing them slightly to achieve certain desired effects, such as increased activity, less toxicity, or greater stability.

HEALING WITH HERBS—continued

BOTANICALS IN MODERN MEDICINE

At the turn of the century, just about any medicine you took was made from plants.

Botanical materials made up some 80 percent of all pharmaceuticals in those days. Most prescriptions were made directly from "crude botanicals," but chemical and drug companies were already becoming more sophisticated; they had begun identifying the active principles in plants. Wherever possible, these principles were being duplicated in the chemistry laboratory, then marketed as "purer" medicines.

Over the years, some plant drugs have gone out of favor or been abandoned altogether. They may be costly to process and store; medicinal plants are particularly subject to the quirks of an international economy, and to the growing and gathering conditions in producing countries. Moreover, depending on the weather and soil, the concentration of a plant's active ingredients can vary greatly. So, wherever possible, pharmaceutical manufacturers have replaced these crude medicines with ones made in the laboratory.

Laboratory-made drugs haven't entirely replaced their natural predecessors. For many diseases, Mother Nature still holds the best cures. Today, at least 25 percent of the medicines in our pharmacopoeia still come from higher plants.

plants accurately and if you aren't sure of one, then DON'T use it. Read the entries on individual herbs and the entry Dangers of Herbs (with its accompanying table A Sampling of Dangerous Herbs). Use *all* plants judiciously; use *some* plants not at all. Remember, too, that medicines that are healthful when taken in small quantities can be very harmful in larger doses. Finally, don't try to treat yourself for serious ailments without first consulting a doctor or other qualified health professional. Certain herbal medications may not work well in conjunction with other drugs you may be taking.

Picking and storing medicinal herbs: Herbalists have their own preferences for just when and how to collect each herb. A common suggestion is to gather herbs on a sunny morning, just after the dew has evaporated, but before the sun begins to bake them. Wet plants can mold or mildew. Fresh herbs are best for flavoring foods, but dried ones serve quite well for most medicines. In fact, careful drying concentrates some of the active principles. This is a happy fact, since we so often get sick in winter when many of our herbs aren't available.

To dry medicinal herbs, hang them upside down in an airy barn or other shady place. Direct sun bleaches them and bakes out the volatile oils. The ideal temperature range is 90° to 100°F. If the temperature isn't right or if there isn't steady air circulation, the herbs may mildew, fade, or spoil.

Roots and heavy, succulent stems contain too much moisture for this sort of hang drying. Clean these parts and chop them into 1-inch pieces. Dry them in a food dehydrator or indoors on a propped screen, near but not directly on a heat source.

Leaves and stems are sufficiently dry when they crackle between your fingers. Flowers should be light yet still holding their shape. Roots are ready for storage when they snap or chip easily. All parts should smell and look pretty much like they did when first picked: the color only slightly muted and the smell as strong or stronger.

It is best to bottle the dried herbs without any further processing. Grinding or powdering them seems more efficient, but it tends to release the herbs' oils and to make them weaker medicines in the long run. For example, the whole cloves stored on your kitchen shelf have a lot more punch than the bottle of ground cloves beside them.

Store dried herbs in opaque glass, wood, hard plastic, or other nonmetallic containers that are approved for food storage. Keep them in a cool, dry, dark place.

When it comes time to use the herbs, rub leaves between your hands. For a finer powder or to process roots and stems, use a mortar and pestle.

Teas: The most common way to turn healthful herbs into medicines is by brewing up a tea. Medicinal teas barely resemble mild-flavored packaged herb beverages. They are much more potent drinks, and many aren't the least bit pleasant tasting. They are made by steeping about 1 ounce of dried tops (leaves, flowers, and stems) per pint of boiled, hot water. Commercially prepared herb tea bags, in contrast, contain only about one-seventh that amount of herbs per pint of water. Usually the dried herb is preferred since it has more concentrated oils.

As a general practice, when you wish to substitute dried herbs for fresh herbs in a recipe, you should decrease the quantity of each herb by half. Similarly, if you want to substitute fresh herbs for dried herbs, double the quantities called for unless the recipe directs otherwise. Fresh herbs contain much more water than dried herbs, and so they are proportionally less potent.

When it is brewed for 15 minutes to several hours, the tea is called an *infusion*. Infusions are usually made in fairly large quantities, then kept in a bottle for use over a day's time. One pint—if you drink ½ cup three times daily—should be enough for one day.

Some herbalists distinguish between infusions and *tisanes,* which are teas prepared one cup at a time for immediate use. Tisanes are steeped briefly—for no longer than it takes to make a cup of tea—so they require more of the herb in order to make a strong enough concentrate.

Here are some guidelines for brewing infusions and tisanes:

Use a glass or ceramic container. Aluminum, iron, tin, or other metals will leach into the tea, so don't use pots made from these metals. Although copper and stainless steel may be okay, herbalists recommend you stay with a clean glass, ceramic, pottery, or (unchipped) enameled pot.

Use pure water. Don't pollute your tea with chlorine or other chemicals in the water you use. Fresh spring water or distilled water is best for making medicinal teas.

Use boiled, not boiling, water. Boil your water first, then remove it from the heat and add the herb.

Use the proper proportions. A typical medicinal tea requires 1 ounce of dried herb (about 2 handfuls) to 2 cups of water, or 2 ounces of fresh herb to 2 cups of water. Let the infusion steep for 15 minutes to several hours, depending on the herb's potency and how strong a tea you want to make. The herb will soak up about ½ cup of the water, leaving you with roughly 1½ cups of beverage.

Cover the pot tightly. If you smell the aroma of the brewing tea, the herb's essential oils are escaping into the air, rather than being retained in the liquid.

MAJOR BOTANICAL MEDICINES

The plants listed below are widely used by the pharmaceutical industry. Although some have traditional healing uses, they require processing to extract the drug for which they are known. To try and concoct a homemade form of a prescribed drug is not a good idea. *Poisonous plants are delineated with an asterisk.*

Aloe (*Aloe barbadensis*): The juice from the leaves, dried and powdered, is both a strong cathartic and an antiseptic that stimulates new tissue to form. The juice is used in skin lotions and soaps.

***American hellebore** (*Veratrum viride*): The roots yield drugs sometimes given in small doses to slow the heart rate or to treat pregnant women suffering from acute hypertension.

***Autumn crocus** (*Colchicum autumnale*): The corm contains colchicine and other alkaloids used to reduce the inflammation from arthritis and gout.

Balsam of Peru (*Myroxylon balsamum* var. *pereirae*): Resin from this tree, a thick flammable liquid that smells like vanilla, but tastes bitter, has bactericidal and mildly antiseptic properties. It is used in fungicidal, antiseptic, and anti-itch creams, and in some dental cements.

(continued)

HEALING WITH HERBS—continued

MEDICINES—*continued*

*Belladonna (*Atropa bella-donna*): In small enough doses, belladonna is a relaxant, sedative, and antidiuretic. The drug is used for Parkinson's disease, epilepsy, stomach ulcers, and kidney stones. Ophthalmologists use belladonna drops to dilate the pupils.

Benzoin tree (*Styrax benzoin*): The whitish resin from this tree is the principal ingredient in benzoin tincture (friar's balsam). The cosmetics industry uses it to fix the scents in perfumes, lotions, and soaps.

*Calabar bean (*Physostigma venenosum*): The active principles paralyze the central nervous system. A derivative is occasionally used to counteract antidepressants and sedatives, or to treat arthritis and bursitis. Another is applied to the eye to relieve intraocular pressure caused by glaucoma.

Camphor tree (*Cinnamomum camphora*): Camphor, a yellow oil, permeates the tree. Abroad, camphor is used as an antiseptic and anthelmintic. Here, it is mainly used in lotions to relieve pain and itching.

Castor bean (*Ricinus communis*): Once a widely used cathartic, castor oil is now primarily a base for eye ointments and drops, contraceptive foams, and skin creams. An active principle has shown some promise against tumor cells and leukemia in experimental animals.

(continued)

Strain the finished infusion before capping and storing.

Decoctions: A decoction, simmering herbs in water, is the most effective method for drawing the healing elements from coarse plant parts such as bark, roots, stems, and heavy leaves. To make a decoction, use the same proportion of herb and water as you would to make an infusion—1 ounce of dried herb to 1 pint of water. The heavier herb parts require a higher heat than that used for infusions. Add the dried herbs to water that has been brought to a boil in a medium-size pot. Keep the water just below boiling for about 30 minutes and let the herbs simmer gently. Some treatments may require heating for up to one hour, but 30 minutes is the general rule.

Syrups: Honey-based herbal syrups are a simple and effective way to preserve the healing qualities of some herbs. Syrups can soothe sore throats and provide some relief from coughs and colds. Some serve as laxatives or general tonics.

To make an herbal syrup, combine 2 ounces of dried herb with 1 quart of water in a large pot. Boil that down until it is reduced to 1 pint, then add 1 to 2 tablespoons of honey. If you use fresh fruit, leaves, or roots in making syrups, you should double the amount of herbs. Using these general guidelines, you can make herbal syrups with just about any herb. Store all herbal syrups in the refrigerator for up to one month.

Compresses, poultices, and plasters: Some herbs do their best work outside the body, acting through the skin. Traditionally, these are the very "hot" herbs—mustard, cayenne, garlic, ginger, and the like—or the "cool" ones—borage, comfrey, aloe, slippery elm. Applied to the skin, they are used to treat congestion, tension, aching muscles, swelling, sprains, and all sorts of other ailments of the mind and body. Herbalists are careful to distinguish among several kinds of external remedies. All should be applied in a warm room in order to keep the recipient of such treatments comfortable.

Compresses are made by soaking a towel in a hot herb tea and laying it on the affected area. To avoid burning the patient, make sure the liquid is not hotter than 180°F, and wring out the towel thoroughly. Cover the compress with a dry towel. Leave the hot compress in place for several minutes, until it no longer feels quite warm, then replace it with another. Keep the area under compresses for up to 30 minutes, depending on the condition and the herb being used. Generally, you can stop the compress application when the treated skin becomes uniformly flushed, or if a tingling sensation or feelings of relief develop. Interrupt the regimen if the area becomes red or if the patient feels discomfort.

The herbs used for compresses can be those with stimulating and warming properties, or those with soothing and cooling qualities. A stimulating herb such as cayenne or ginger is used in a compress to increase circulation and energize areas of the body that are congested or debilitated. A soothing compress can help dissipate excess heat or nervous energy or calm swelling from sprains or bruises.

A *poultice* is made from dried, powdered, or macerated herbs mixed with hot water or herb tea. Sometimes oatmeal or flour is mixed with the herbal matter to make a paste (use 2 ounces of herbs with 20 ounces of oatmeal). The resulting herbal mass is put directly on the skin. A warm cloth, towel, or bandage is then applied to hold the herbs in place. Poultices are effective for drawing out infection and foreign bodies and relieving muscle spasms and pain. Don't use mustard, cayenne, or other very hot, irritating herbs in this fashion, as they can actually burn the skin. Burdock, comfrey, crab apple, flax seed, and slippery elm are safe traditional poultice herbs.

A *plaster* consists of herbs or an herb paste set within the folds of cloth, usually cheesecloth or muslin, which is applied to the injured area. You can make an herbal bandage or miniplaster to use for small injuries, when an antiseptic and healing effect is desired. Stronger herbs, such as cayenne and mustard, are best applied as plasters, rather than poultices, so they don't touch the skin.

Oils and ointments: In most aromatic herbs, the essential oil contains active ingredients. Manufacturers use steam distillation to extract the oil, which is then used in pharmaceuticals, cosmetics, foods, and so on. Concentrating the potency of many pounds of plants in just a few drops, these extracted oils are particularly strong, and sometimes people don't realize just how potent they are and misuse them (see the entry Dangers of Herbs).

You can easily make a less concentrated, and therefore safer, oil at home. Macerate 2 ounces of the dried herb (4 ounces of fresh), and mix with 1 pint of olive, safflower, or other pure vegetable oil. After several days in a warm place, strain and bottle the oil.

Another method involves gently heating the herbs. Combine the herbs and oil in a pot large enough to hold them. Heat the mixture gently, uncovered, for 1 hour, allowing the oil to get no hotter than 200°F. Strain and bottle when cooled.

Thicker herbal creams and ointments can be made by adding 1 to 1½ ounces of melted beeswax to any herb oil. Some recipes call for rendered lard (tallow) instead of oil. Simmer 1 ounce of crushed dried herbs in ¾ of a pound of fat. When the herbs have broken down well, strain the fat and allow it to set. To make a still firmer ointment, melted beeswax may be added while it is still warm. Calendula or comfrey ointment is widely recommended as a first aid cream.

Tinctures: Until about 50 years ago, there were hundreds of

MEDICINES—*continued*

Cinchona (*Cinchona* spp.): The bark and roots are the source of quinine and quinidine. Synthetic drugs have replaced quinine as an antimalarial, but it is used in some over-the-counter cold remedies, hair tonics, and suntan lotions. Quinidine is used like digitalis to regulate the heartbeat.

Ephedra (*Ephedra* spp.): The active principle of this shrub is ephedrine, a heart stimulant and bronchiole dilator prescribed for emphysema, asthma, and similar conditions. It is a nasal spray ingredient and, as an oral medicine, is used to treat some epilepsies.

*Foxglove (*Digitalis purpurea*): Digitalis made from the dried, powdered leaves is an important drug for treating congestive heart failure. The much more potent pure digitoxin is also prescribed. It is easy to overdose on either drug.

Great scarlet poppy (*Papaver orientale* var. *bracteatum*): Flowers and leaves contain various alkaloids, including thebaine, a source of codeine.

*Grecian foxglove (*Digitalis lanata*): Drug companies use this species to extract the lanatoside C and the fast-acting digoxin.

Ipecac (*Cephaelis ipecacunha*): Emetine, an active principle found in the roots, is used as an expectorant and, more commonly, an emetic. Syrup of ipecac is a standard means of inducing vomiting to treat poisoning.

(continued)

MEDICINES—*continued*

Japanese mint (*Mentha arvensis*): Volatile oil from the leaves is nearly 90 percent menthol; this mint is the source of most of the menthol in medicines and cosmetics.

Licorice (*Glycyrrhiza glabra*): A licorice derivative is used to shrink peptic ulcers. Another is an effective expectorant. Serious side effects make establishing dosages tricky.

*Mayapple (*Podophyllum peltatum*): Roots, and to a lesser extent the green fruit and leaves, of this common wildflower yield a very strong purgative, usually used in combination with milder laxatives. Derivatives are useful against cancerous tumors and have inspired semisynthetic cancer drugs.

Mexican yams (*Dioscorea composita*): Oral contraceptives, cortizone creams, estrogen, progesterone, and other drugs are made from the active principles.

*Opium poppy (*Papaver somniferum*): Unripe pods, leaves, and other parts are the source of morphine, codeine, thebaine, narcotine, papaverine, noscapine, and other alkaloids. Although they are addicting, morphine and codeine are still used in cases of severe, chronic pain. Codeine is an ingredient in some cough medicines, as is the relaxant noscapine. Papaverine is prescribed for relief of intestinal spasms or asthma attacks.

Pareira (*Chondrodendron tomentosum*): An active principle, tubocurarine, is a muscle
(continued)

tinctures listed in the *U.S. Pharmacopoeia* (the official listing of pharmaceutical raw materials and recipes in regular use, which is issued annually by the U.S. government). Although tinctures are no longer readily available to the general public, they remain very useful to the herbalist. Tinctures are an excellent medium for preserving and concentrating the healing qualities of herbs.

Tinctures are effective in very small amounts because they are so concentrated. Several drops to 1 tablespoon is the general dosage. Be cautious in the use of tinctures; they are potent.

Do not confuse the concentrates called "fluid extracts" of herbs, available commercially today, with tinctures. These fluid extracts are even more potent than tinctures—often 10 times as strong.

To make a tincture, combine 4 ounces of the powdered or finely cut herb with 1 pint of spirits, such as brandy, vodka, or gin, in a large jar or jug with a secure-fitting lid. (Never use rubbing or isopropyl alcohol, or methyl or wood alcohol, both of which are poisonous!) Shake the mixture several times daily over a two-week period. By the end of this time, the herb will have released its properties to the alcohol. Let the herb settle, then strain off the liquid into another clean bottle for storage.

Herbal baths for gentle healing: The herbal bath, a very old form of medical treatment, is a safe and effective way to use herbs for healing. Besides being healing, herbal baths are enjoyable. Baths can relax the ill person, as the healing qualities of the herbs permeate the body through the skin. If you doubt the efficacy of herbal baths, try pressing a slice of garlic against the sole of someone's foot. After a short while, smell his breath—you should smell the garlic. (For more information on herbal baths, see the entry Bathing with Herbs.)

Lotions and washes: Some of the most sensual and delightful ways to use herbs are in refreshing lotions to use after shaving, with a massage, and for cleansing. Lavender is one of the most preferred scents in such preparations. Herbs that are demulcent, astringent, aromatic, styptic, or antiseptic are good choices for after-shave lotions or washes. (For more information on herbal lotions, see the entry Lotions from Herbs.)

SOME MEDICINAL HERBS

Here is a rundown of medicinal herbs that pose fewer health risks than most, when used occasionally. Nothing is entirely safe, however, and preparations made from these herbs should be used with care. More detailed information about each one is presented in their individual entries.

Aloe (*Aloe barbadensis*)

Uses: Cleanser, antiseptic, moisturizer, and anti-inflammatory; for burns, blisters, and scrapes.

Part used: Juice squeezed from the leaves.

Preparation: Fresh juice applied externally.

Remarks: Safe and effective for external use; not recommended for internal use.

Arnica (*Arnica* spp.)

Uses: Anti-inflammatory analgesic; for sore muscles and sprains.

Part used: Flower heads.

Preparation: Dilute the tincture (no more than 2 tablespoons in 1 cup of water) to use with a compress. Oil or ointment as a liniment.

Remarks: Safe and effective for external use; not recommended for internal use.

Barberry (*Berberis* spp.)

Uses: Antibacterial, astringent, laxative, and antipyretic; for lowering fevers, strengthening the bowels, and stimulating the liver.

Part used: Rhizome or roots.

Preparation: Infusion is prepared from ½ ounce to 1 pint of water. Take 1 to 4 cups daily, before meals. Because barberry tea is so bitter, it should be taken in small doses, a mouthful at a time, for example. A decoction is taken as needed, 1 tablespoon at a time.

Remarks: One herbalist calls barberry "one of the most beneficial medicine plants of the West." A pharmacognosist, on the other hand, says there is "no reason to recommend barberry for its therapeutic properties."

Betony (*Stachys officinalis*)

Uses: Astringent; for sore throats, coughs, and diarrhea.

Parts used: Leaves and tops.

Preparation: Infusion taken a mouthful at a time throughout the day; no more than 2 cups a day total.

Remarks: Effective but due to the high tannin content, *may* prove carcinogenic in long-term use.

Boneset (*Eupatorium perfoliatum*)

Uses: Aperient, cathartic, diaphoretic, emetic, febrifuge, and tonic; to break up colds and flu and to induce sweating.

Parts used: Leaves and tops.

Preparation: Infusion taken 3 ounces at a time, three times

MEDICINES—*continued*

relaxant used in surgery and to ease the spasms of cerebral palsy. Synthetic products have partly replaced the natural one.

Senna (*Cassia* spp.): Active principles in the leaves and unripe pods are powerful cathartics. Many over-the-counter laxatives contain some form of senna.

Serpentwood (*Rauwolfia serpentina*): The root and to a lesser extent the stem and leaves of this shrub contain reserpine, a drug used to treat hypertension, as well as schizophrenia and other psychoses.

Strophanthus (*Strophanthus gratus*): Seeds of this vine contain ouabain, a fast-acting cardiac stimulant.

Thyme (*Thymus* spp.): The oil of some species is effective against salmonella, staph, streptococcus, and other germs. It is used in some mouthwashes and disinfectants.

Tragacanth (*Astragalus gummifer*): The gummy substance oozing from the roots and woody parts of this shrub is an ingredient in toothpastes and spermicidal jellies and creams. It is used as a binding agent in pills and to help in the absorption of steroid glycosides in some vitamins.

Tropical periwinkle (*Catharanthus roseus*): Two alkaloids have proved to be important. Vinblastine sulfate is used to treat Hodgkin's disease and choriocarcinoma, a type of skin or lymph cancer. Vincristine works against breast cancer, childhood leukemias, and Wilms' tumor, a cancer affecting children's kidneys.

HEALING WITH HERBS—continued

THE FUTURE OF HERBAL RESEARCH

Plant-derived products account for more than $5 billion in medicine sales. Nevertheless, experts estimate that just 4 percent of the world's plants have been analyzed for pharmacological activity. That leaves 96 percent, or over 1 million species to investigate.

HOW PURE ARE THE HERBS YOU BUY?

Are the herbal products on the shelf what their labels say they are? Have they been sprayed with pesticides?

Unfortunately, you have no way of knowing. Vague, even incorrect labeling is more common than it should be. Herbs imported from other parts of the world often have contaminants added. Government labeling requirements are lax, and terms such as natural or even organic have no real meaning. The government does have regulations for safe limits on the residues of some pesticides, and proper cleansing does remove most toxic materials.

But the best way to get what you want may be to grow it yourself.

daily. To encourage sweating, drink 4 or 5 cups of the hot infusion while in bed.

Remarks: Pharmacognosists question boneset's effectiveness against colds and flu.

Burdock (*Arctium Lappa*)
Uses: Tonic and diuretic; for sluggishness, psoriasis, and acne.
Parts used: Roots, seeds, and leaves.
Preparation: One cup of an infusion of the leaves is taken three or four times daily as a tonic. Similarly, a decoction—1 ounce of roots and/or seeds to 1½ pints of water, boiled down to 1 pint— is taken 3 ounces at a time, also three or four times daily. For rashes, pimples, eczema, and other skin ailments, use a decoction of equal parts of burdock root and yellow dock as a wash, and, at the same time, as a tea.
Remarks: Pharmacognosists question burdock's effectiveness, but not its safety.

Calendula (*Calendula officinalis*)
Uses: Antibacterial; for cuts, scrapes, and burns.
Part used: Flowers.
Preparation: Compress or ointment on stings, ulcers, or wounds. Wash wounds with an infusion. A strong tea can be used as a sitz bath for hemorrhoids.
Remarks: Pharmacognosists question calendula's effectiveness, but not its safety.

Catnip (*Nepeta Cataria*)
Uses: Sedative, diaphoretic, and carminative; for insomnia, colds, colic, upset stomachs, nervous headaches, and fevers.
Part used: Tops.
Preparation: Infusion—be sure not to boil the herb, warn most herbalists—taken in doses up to a cup, as needed. In excessive doses it can produce nausea. A recommended combination is catnip with chamomile and peppermint, sweetened with honey; excellent for relieving symptoms of colds, headaches, and indigestion.
Remarks: Despite what this herb does to your cat, catnip does appear to be a safe and effective natural tranquilizer.

Cayenne pepper (*Capsicum annuum* Longum Group)
Uses: Carminative, stimulant, and tonic; for stomach upsets, toothaches, rheumatism, inflammation, sores, wounds, symptoms of a cold, and muscle aches.
Part used: Fruit.

Preparation: Infusion—1 teaspoon to 1 cup of water—can be taken in ½-ounce doses. For a sore throat, the infusion can be used as a gargle. As a tonic, to benefit the heart and circulation, ¼ teaspoon of the dried, powdered fruit can be taken in water or juice three times daily, four days a week. For toothache, place cotton soaked in the oil on the cavity; use sparingly as the oil is potent.

Externally, a compress is effective for rheumatism, inflammation, sores, or wounds. A liniment for sprains and congestion can be made by gently boiling 1 tablespoon of cayenne pepper in 1 pint of cider vinegar; bottle the unstrained liquid while it's hot. To make a muscle rub, mix a little crushed cayenne pepper with rubbing alcohol.

Remarks: Prolonged application of liniments and rubs to the skin can cause irritation, even burns or blisters. Excessive consumption can cause stomach upset.

Chamomile (*Matricaria recutita* or *Chamaemelum nobile*)

Uses: Anodyne, antispasmodic, calmative, carminative, diaphoretic, and tonic; for colds, headaches, and nervousness.

Part used: Flowers.

Preparation: Take an infusion 1 cup at a time, two or three times daily, for cramps, dizziness, gas, indigestion, and nervous stomach. Taken before mealtime, it stimulates the appetite; taken at bedtime, it calms nervousness and helps to defeat insomnia. Small amounts are good for colicky babies. Mixed with peppermint in an infusion, it is a soothing and relaxing tea whenever minor illness appears.

Remarks: "It has no known toxicity," reports a pharmacognosist. "The only problem is an occasional allergy."

Comfrey (*Symphytum officinale*)

Uses: Vulnerary, antiseptic, demulcent, and tonic; for healing wounds and burns, and for reducing the swelling of boils, bruises, and sprains.

Parts used: Leaves and roots.

Preparation: A strong decoction is used with a compress for bad bruises, swellings, sprains, and boils. Make a poultice by mixing fresh, chopped leaves with boiling water; then, after cooling them, sandwich the leaves between layers of cheesecloth. Apply the poultice to sore breasts, wounds, ulcers, and burns. Blend a small portion of a strong decoction with honey and either vitamin E or wheat germ oil to make an ointment for minor burns and wounds.

HERBAL MEDICINES AND THE LAW

New botanical medicines are harder to come by in the United States than they are in the Soviet Union, India, China, and most European countries.

That's because drug testing and patent laws here tend to discourage the development of new botanical medicines. Exhaustive studies proving a drug's safety and effectiveness are required before it can be sold. The costs and paperwork for such investigations are staggering.

Plant-derived drugs have additional burdens. Plant gathering expeditions are pricey but manageable as long as the company can patent any new drug yielded by such expeditions. But patenting is tricky since a whole plant can't be patented. Even obtaining protection for an isolated active principle is difficult. Placed on the market without patent protection, a new medicine can be duplicated by any firm. Thus, the chance of the discoverer recouping research costs is slim indeed. Although the government sponsors some research in botanical drugs, patenting disputes keep most of these discoveries from ever reaching the market.

Although European countries are currently more hospitable to herbal medicines, that is changing. By 1989, West Germany will follow the U.S. lead and begin requiring any botanicals on the market to be proven not only safe but also effective. Thus herb preparations will only be marketable *(continued)*

HEALING WITH HERBS—continued

HERBAL MEDICINES AND THE LAW—*continued*

as "foods," and it will be impossible to label them with directions for use or supply the usual warnings that come with any drug.

Canada is leading the way in another direction. The Canadian Ministry of National Health plans to introduce a new class of drugs, designated Folklore Medicines (FM). FM drugs would be labeled as such, complete with the botanical name and formal certification, plant part used, and type of preparation. Standards would be enforced, so that the active constituents in the drugs would remain stable. A voluntary code of ethics and advertising would enlist the help of retailers in avoiding the sort of advertising that preys on people desperate for help. Such regulations would offer a middle ground on which herbal medicines could stand. They would practically guarantee that the herbs on the shelf had been screened for *safety*, even if their efficacy remained unproven.

Remarks: Although most herbalists highly recommend comfrey for both internal and external uses, pharmacognosists believe regular, long-term internal use may lead to cancer.

Dandelion (*Taraxacum officinale*)

Uses: Diuretic, laxative, carminative, tonic, and antiseptic; for digestive disorders, arthritis, circulatory problems, and healing wounds.

Parts used: Leaves and roots.

Preparation: Fresh leaves are eaten raw in salads. The infusion can be taken hot or cold, a cup at a time, three or four times daily. Similarly, a decoction of the root can be taken hot or cold in 6-ounce doses, three or four times daily.

Remarks: "Dandelion is both a nutritive herb and one of nature's best medicines," contends one herbalist. However, pharmacognosists, while accepting its safety, question its effectiveness.

Echinacea (*Echinacea angustifolia*)

Uses: Tonic, antiseptic, alterative, and febrifuge; for headaches, rheumatism, bladder infections, dizziness, fevers, wounds and sores, and hemorrhoids.

Parts used: Rhizome and roots.

Preparation: One tablespoon of a decoction is taken three to six times daily for bladder infections, headaches, dizziness, and fevers. It can be used with a compress on wounds and painful swellings.

Remarks: Judged to be safe and effective by pharmacognosists.

Eucalyptus (*Eucalyptus* spp.)

Uses: Decongestant, astringent, antiseptic, and stimulant; for cold symptoms and respiratory congestion.

Parts used: Leaves and oil.

Preparation: An infusion of the leaves can be added to bathwater as a stimulating astringent. The classic eucalyptus remedy for congestion is to inhale the vapors of the infusion. The oil can be added to rubbing alcohol to use as an astringent lotion, to the bath, or to water to make an infusion.

Remarks: Eucalyptus oil is particularly potent. Keep it away from the eyes. Never put it directly on the skin unless it has been well diluted with oil, alcohol, or water. Eucalyptus teas should be very diluted.

Fennel (*Foeniculum vulgare*)

Uses: Carminative, aromatic, calmative, and decongestant; for flatulence, coughs, colds, sore throats, and bad breath.

Parts used: Seeds and roots.

Preparation: Seeds taken fresh or dried; seeds or leaves as tea. An infusion of the seeds is taken 1 cup at a time, three times a day to soothe the stomach and intestines and to relieve flatulence. The infusion can be gargled to remedy a sore throat or hoarseness. A syrup, made by combining up to 3 drops of the oil with 1 tablespoon of honey, is a natural cough remedy.

Remarks: Judged by pharmacognosists to be safe and effective as a stomachic and carminative.

Fenugreek (*Trigonella Foenum-graecum*)

Uses: Demulcent, emollient, expectorant, stomachic, restorative, and flavoring; for asthma, fever, boils, cold symptoms, heartburn, and to strengthen the body following an illness.

Part used: Seeds.

Preparation: A decoction is taken a cup at a time, three times a day, for asthma, bronchitis, coughs, fever, and heartburn. It can be gargled to remedy a sore throat. A syrup is used for hoarseness. A poultice of seeds is used for boils and other sores.

Remarks: Pharmacognosists question fenugreek's effectiveness.

Feverfew (*Chrysanthemum Parthenium*)

Uses: Carminative, stimulant, and tonic; for migraine headaches.

Part used: Leaves.

Preparation: Eat three or four of the little leaves each day to forestall migraines. The leaves are bitter; the taste can be masked by mixing the leaves into foods. An infusion can be drunk 1 to 2 cups a day in tablespoon doses.

Remarks: Judged by pharmacognosists to be safe and effective against migraines.

Garlic (*Allium sativum*)

Uses: Alterative, antibiotic, and antiseptic; for infections, respiratory problems, sore throats, atherosclerosis and high blood pressure, and gastrointestinal ailments.

Part used: Bulb.

Preparation: Express small amounts of juice from a clove into hot water to make infusion, into honey to make syrup. Mash the clove and apply to insect stings. Commercially prepared garlic perles can be taken as a nutritional supplement. Herbalists recommend eating raw garlic cloves; cooking destroys their medicinal potency.

Remarks: Garlic reduces the tendency of blood platelets to clot, lessening the risk of heart attack or stroke. The active components of garlic are odoriferous; deodorized varieties have some of the activity removed.

A GLOSSARY

Abortifacient: A substance that causes abortion.

Adaptogen: An herb that maintains health by increasing the body's ability to adapt to environmental and internal stress. Adaptogens generally work by strengthening the immune system, nervous system, and/or glandular system.

Alterative: A substance that gradually alters or changes a condition. Often, it is a medicine that cures an illness by gradually restoring health.

Analgesic: A substance that relieves pain by acting as a nervine, antispasmodic, rubefacient, antiseptic, antibiotic, or counterirritant.

Anodyne: A medicine that relieves pain.

Anthelmintic: A substance that expels or destroys intestinal worms. Such medicines are also called *vermifuges.*

Antibiotic: A substance produced by a microorganism that is capable of killing or inhibiting the growth of bacteria or other microorganisms.

Antidote: A substance that counteracts the action of another, particularly a poison.

Antiperiodic: A substance that prevents the periodic recurrence of a disease, such as malaria.

Antipyretic: A substance that tends to reduce or prevent a fever. Such medicines are also referred to as *febrifuges* and *refrigerants.*

(continued)

A GLOSSARY—*continued*

Antiseptic: A substance that destroys bacteria; usually applied to the skin to prevent infection.

Antispasmodic: A medicine that relieves or prevents involuntary muscle spasms or cramps, such as those occurring in epilepsy, painful menstruation, intestinal cramping, or even "charley horses."

Aperient: A mild and gentle-acting laxative medicine.

Aromatic: A substance with a strong, volatile, and fragrant aroma. Medicinally, aromatics are used to relieve flatulence, open nasal passages, or eliminate phlegm, and are often added to medicines to improve their palatability. Just the fragrance and flavor alone can provide a psychological lift.

Astringent: A substance that causes dehydration, tightening, or the shrinking of tissues and is used to stop bleeding, close skin pores, and tighten muscles.

Balsamic: A substance that heals or soothes.

Bitter tonic: A substance with an acrid, astringent, or disagreeable taste that stimulates the flow of saliva and gastric juice. Such tonics are taken to increase the appetite and to aid the digestive process.

Calmative: A substance that allays excitement; usually less strong than a sedative.

Carminative: A substance that checks the formation of gas and helps dispel whatever gas has already formed.

(continued)

Gentian (*Gentiana lutea*)

Uses: Cholagogue, stomachic, and tonic; to stimulate appetite, aid digestion, and improve circulation.

Parts used: Rhizome and roots.

Preparation: As a bitter tonic, take a decoction; dosages range from ¼ to 1 teaspoon three times daily to ½ to 1 cup daily. Because of the bitterness, it is often combined with aromatic herbs.

Remarks: Pharmacognosists find gentian safe and effective.

Ginger (*Zingiber officinale*)

Uses: Aromatic, carminative, diaphoretic, stimulant, decongestant, and antispasmodic; for flu, bronchitis, sinus congestion, intestinal ailments, morning sickness, and motion sickness.

Part used: Root.

Preparation: A tea made by simmering 3 or 4 thin slices of the root in a pint of water for 15 to 20 minutes is a bracing and stimulating wintertime drink. For indigestion, gas, nausea, or morning sickness, as well as colds, coughs, and sinus congestion, take an infusion, sipping about 1 ounce at a time throughout the day. The powdered rootstock, taken in capsule form— empty capsules are available in some health food stores or drugstores—is as effective an antidote to motion sickness as Dramamine.

A tea, made of 5 ounces of rootstock in 2 quarts of water, is good to use as a stimulating footbath and with pain-relieving compresses. Compresses on the forehead relieve sinus congestion; on the chest they relieve chest congestion.

Hawthorn (*Crataegus laevigata*)

Uses: Antispasmodic, cardiac, and vasodilator; to dilate blood vessels and to lower blood pressure.

Parts used: Fruit (haw), leaves, and flowers.

Preparation: A tea—taken 1 cup at a time, two or three times a day, is good for nervous conditions and insomnia. Extended use will lower blood pressure.

Remarks: Judged to be safe and effective by pharmacognosists.

Hops (*Humulus Lupulus*)

Uses: Nervine, stomachic, and sedative; as a sleep aid.

Part used: fruit (strobiles).

Preparation: Drinking 1 cup of an infusion three times daily can calm the nerves and settle a nervous stomach. Use a pillow stuffed with hops to relax yourself at bedtime and bring on sleep.

Remarks: Hops are best used fresh; they lose their potency rapidly in storage. Pharmacognosists judge hops both safe and effective.

Horehound (*Marrubium vulgare*)

Uses: Diaphoretic, expectorant, decongestant, diuretic, stimulant, and antiseptic; for coughs and colds and for fevers.

Parts used: Leaves and tops.

Preparation: For fevers, drink a hot infusion frequently, taking a cup at a time. The infusion and the syrup are good for all symptoms of a cold—coughs, lung congestion, sore throats. Take ½ to 1 teaspoon of the syrup, three times a day.

Remarks: Use of the syrup for children is recommended. Judged to be safe and effective by pharmacognosists.

Horseradish (*Armoracia rusticana*)

Uses: Diaphoretic, diuretic, expectorant, and stomachic; for colds, coughs, neuralgia, stiffness, hoarseness, and to stimulate circulation and appetite.

Part used: Fresh root.

Preparation: Combine 1 ounce of chopped fresh horseradish root and ½ ounce of bruised mustard seed in 1 pint of boiling water, steeping the herbs for four hours; take 3 tablespoons three times a day.

To make a syrup, grate 2 cups of fresh horseradish and soak in enough honey to slightly cover the horseradish for four to eight hours. Strain, then add a little water to the strained-out horseradish, and simmer for 10 minutes. Strain and add this liquid to the honey mixture. Take 1 teaspoon three times a day. This is a standard remedy for hoarseness.

Externally, chopped or grated fresh horseradish can be mixed with a little water and applied as a heat-producing and pain-relieving compress for neuralgia and stiffness.

Hyssop (*Hyssopus officinalis*)

Uses: Stimulant, diaphoretic, expectorant, and vulnerary; for coughs, rheumatism, fevers, and sore throats.

Parts used: Leaves and tops.

Preparation: A warm infusion of the leaves and tops, taken by the mouthful, up to 2 cups a day, is recommended for colds, fevers, coughs, and sore throats. Some herbalists recommend combining hyssop with horehound in an infusion for the same ailments.

Remarks: Hyssop is judged by pharmacognosists to be safe and effective as an expectorant.

A GLOSSARY—*continued*

Catarrh: An inflammation of any mucous membrane, but especially one affecting the respiratory tract.

Cathartic: A laxative or purgative that causes the evacuation of the bowels. A laxative is a gentle cathartic, while a purgative is much more forceful and is used only in stubborn conditions.

Cholagogue: A substance that promotes the discharge of bile from the system.

Corroborant: Another term for a tonic or other substance that is invigorating.

Counterirritant: An irritant that distracts attention from another, usually an agent applied to the skin to produce a superficial inflammation that reduces or counteracts a deeper inflammation.

Demulcent: Oily or mucilaginous substances that soothe and moisten, providing a protective coating and allaying irritation.

Deobstruent: A substance that clears obstruction from the natural ducts of the body.

Detergent: In medicine, as in the laundry. a substance used for cleansing.

Diaphoretic: A substance taken internally to promote sweating, usually through expansion of capillaries near the skin. Also called *sudorifics,* they have been used along with sweat baths to promote general and specific health.

(continued)

HEALING WITH HERBS—continued

Diuretic: A substance that promotes the flow of urine.

Emetic: A substance that induces vomiting.

Emmenagogue: A medicine taken internally to promote menstruation.

Emollient: A substance that, applied externally, softens and soothes the skin.

Expectorant: A substance that, taken internally, helps the body expel phlegm through coughing, sneezing, or spitting.

Febrifuge: A substance that helps dissipate a fever. Sometimes called *antipyretic.*

Flatulence: Gas in the stomach or bowels.

Hemostatic: Any substance used to stem internal bleeding.

Hepatic: Any substance that affects the liver, whether helpfully or harmfully.

Holistic: In reference to health, the way of prevention and treatment that takes into account factors such as diet, attitude, emotions, relationships, activities, and constitution. Holistic therapies aim at treating the whole person. They include herbology, nutrition, fasting, massage, psychotherapy, exercise, creative arts, dreaming, meditation, bathing, acupuncture, and counseling.

(continued)

Licorice (*Glycyrrhiza glabra*)

Uses: Expectorant, demulcent, and laxative; for congestion, all kinds of intestinal and stomach ulcers, and constipation.

Parts used: Rhizome and roots.

Preparation: Often the root is chewed; a piece up to 3 inches long can be taken, as needed. The decoction can be taken in 1 tablespoon doses, as needed. As a sweet herb, licorice root is added to bitter tonics to make them more palatable. As a sweetener, demulcent, and expectorant, it is added to cough syrups.

Remarks: Licorice is a mild laxative, especially effective for elderly people and children, reports one herbalist. Too much licorice can cause edema. People with high blood pressure and people on steroid drugs should avoid licorice altogether.

Marsh mallow (*Althaea officinalis*)

Uses: Demulcent, diuretic, emollient, alterative, and vulnerary; for coughs, hoarseness, sore throats, and skin conditions.

Parts used: Roots, flowers, and leaves.

Preparation: An infusion of the leaves and flowers can be taken frequently, 1 cup at a time. More commonly recommended is a decoction of the root taken 1 cup at a time, three times a day. Use the decoction or syrup for coughs, hoarseness, and sore throats; use the infusion or decoction for all sorts of lung ailments. A poultice of the root or the infusion or decoction with a compress is used for skin inflammations.

Remarks: Marsh mallow is high in mucilage and derives its healing value from that.

Myrrh (*Commiphora* spp.)

Uses: Astringent, antiseptic, emmenagogue, carminative, expectorant, and stimulant; for spongy gums, pyorrhea, and all throat diseases.

Part used: Resin.

Preparation: Take an infusion in ½-cup doses, three or four times a day. Use a tincture in water as a gargle for bad breath, sore gums, mouth ulcers, and thrush.

Remarks: Judged by pharmacognosists to be safe and effective.

Onion (*Allium Cepa*)

Uses: Anthelmintic, calmative, expectorant, diuretic, and antiseptic; for indigestion, nervous disorders, kidney problems, high blood pressure, asthma, and headaches.

Part used: Bulb.

Preparation: To make a cold extract, soak a chopped onion in 1 cup of water for 24 hours. Drink ½ cup daily. A decoction, made by chopping an onion and simmering it gently in a cup of water, can be taken in 1 tablespoon doses, three or four times a day. The juice can be taken in 1 teaspoon doses, three or four times a day, or added to honey to make a syrup good for hoarseness and coughs.

Onions are eaten raw for their nutritive and medicinal values. Slices of raw onion can be applied to an insect sting. A poultice of chopped onions can be applied to bruises or sprains. For chest congestion, consume clear soup made with lots of onions, or the strained liquid poured off a mixture of honey and onions heated but not boiled on the stove for several hours.

Remarks: Like garlic, the onion reduces the tendency of blood platelets to clot, which may lessen the risk of a heart attack or stroke should a clot block an already narrowed artery.

Parsley (*Petroselinum crispum*)

Uses: Diuretic, carminative, expectorant, nervine, and tonic; to remedy water retention, kidney problems, bad breath, and digestive problems.

Parts used: Leaves, stems, and seeds.

Preparation: For kidney problems and water retention, an infusion of the leaves or a decoction of the seeds can be taken, 1 cup at a time, two or three times daily. Fresh parsley juice can be drunk, 2 ounces at a time, twice daily. Eaten raw, parsley is good for bad breath.

Remarks: Pharmacognosists say the leaves have no medicinal value, and that the seeds are only mildly effective.

Passionflower (*Passiflora incarnata*)

Uses: Sedative and calmative; for insomnia, restlessness, and nervous headaches.

Parts used: Flowers and fruiting top.

Preparation: Use an infusion—1 cup taken during the day—for back, eye, and general nervous tension, headaches, spasms and muscular twitching, and insomnia.

Remarks: Though not recognized as safe or effective in the United States, passionflower is used in sedatives sold in Europe.

Peppermint (*Mentha ✕piperita*)

Uses: Aromatic, carminative, stomachic, diaphoretic, and stimulant; for chills, upset stomach syndrome, and headaches.

Part used: Leaves.

Preparation: An infusion should be taken in 1 cup doses, three

HEALING WITH HERBS—continued

Rubefacient: A substance that increases blood circulation to the area where it is applied, usually on the skin but sometimes internally.

Scrofula: An infection and enlargement of the lymph glands. Thanks largely to modern sanitation, scrofula is no longer common.

Sedative: An agent that reduces nervous tension; usually stronger than a calmative.

Sialagogue: A substance that causes an increase in the flow of saliva.

Simple: An herb used by itself as a complete form of prevention or treatment, called *simpling*. Simples are usually very mild, locally grown, or indigenous plants.

Soporific: A substance that tends to induce sleep.

Specific: A medicine that has a special effect on a particular disease.

Stimulant: A substance that increases or quickens the various functional actions of the body, such as hastening digestion, raising body temperature, and so on. It does this quickly, unlike a *tonic,* which stimulates general health over a period of time. And unlike a narcotic, it does not necessarily produce a feeling of general well-being, which a narcotic does by depressing nerve centers.

(continued)

times a day. To open up the sinuses, drop 5 to 10 drops of peppermint oil into 2 quarts of hot water, then breathe the vapors in through the mouth and nostrils.
Remarks: One of the oldest household remedies, peppermint is judged by pharmacognosists to be safe and effective as a stomachic and carminative.

Rose (*Rosa* spp.)
Uses: Stomachic, aperient, astringent, and antiscorbutic; for cold and flu symptoms.
Part used: Fruit (hips).
Preparation: Use the infusion—taken frequently, a cup at a time—for colds and flu. The syrup is good for sore throats.
Remarks: The vitamin C content of the rosehip makes it a good natural remedy for colds and flu. Considered by pharmacognosists to be safe and effective.

Rosemary (*Rosmarinus officinalis*)
Uses: Tonic, diaphoretic, antiseptic, astringent, stomachic, and carminative; for headaches, insomnia, nervous disorders, and digestive ailments.
Parts used: Leaves and flowers.
Preparation: An infusion, taken 2 ounces at a time, three times a day, is good for gas, colic, indigestion, and fevers.
Remarks: The volatile oil of rosemary is irritating to the stomach in excessive amounts. One herbalist recommends drinking no more than 3 cups a day.

Sage (*Salvia officinalis*)
Uses: Antispasmodic, astringent, tonic, and vulnerary; for cold symptoms and digestive upsets.
Part used: Leaves.
Preparation: Use an infusion, taking 1 tablespoon at a time, hot or cold, as needed, up to 2 cups a day, for all cold symptoms, as well as dizziness, nausea, headaches, gas, and weak digestion. Use the tea as a gargle for sore throat and laryngitis. As a tonic add ½ ounce of fresh sage leaves to the juice of one lemon or lime; sweeten the honey and infuse in a quart of boiling water removed from the heat; strain and serve either hot or ice cold.

Thyme (*Thymus vulgaris*)
Uses: Antiseptic, anti-inflammatory, carminative, and antispasmodic; for infections and inflammation, mastitis, fever, digestive ailments, headaches, and nervousness.
Part used: Tops.
Preparation: An infusion, taken frequently, a mouthful at a time,

up to 2 cups a day, is good for all throat and bronchial problems, as well as stomach and intestinal problems.

Uva-ursi (*Arctostaphylos Uva-ursi*)

Uses: Diuretic, urinary antiseptic, and astringent; for nephritis, cystitis, urethritis, and kidney and bladder stones.
Part used: Leaves.
Preparation: An infusion is taken in ½-cup doses as needed, up to 3 cups a day. Some herbalists recommend adding marsh mallow root or some other mucilaginous diuretic.
Remarks: Though considered safe and effective as a diuretic, uva-ursi should not be used during pregnancy.

Valerian (*Valerian officinalis*)

Uses: Antispasmodic, nervine, and calmative; for calming the nerves.
Parts used: Rhizome and roots.
Preparation: An infusion can be made using about ¼ teaspoon of the root in 1 cup of water. Some herbalists recommend taking ½-cup doses three times a day.
Remarks: Valerian is a natural tranquilizer that won't interact with alcohol. Large doses, however, can bring on depression. Though not approved in the United States, valerian compounds are widely sold as tranquilizers in Europe.

Witch hazel (*Hamamelis virginiana*)

Uses: Astringent, hemostatic, and tonic; for bruises, muscle aches, burns, sores, and oozing skin conditions.
Parts used: Leaves and bark.
Preparation: An infusion of the leaves or a decoction of the bark can be used on a compress for bruises, muscle aches, burns, sores, and oozing skin conditions. The tincture, diluted in water, is a good gargle or mouthwash for minor infections.
Remarks: Witch hazel is considered safe and effective by pharmacognosists.

Yarrow (*Achillea Millefolium*)

Uses: Astringent, anesthetic, carminative, diaphoretic, hemostatic, and tonic; for wounds, toothaches, diarrhea, gas, and intestinal ailments.
Parts used: Tops and leaves.
Preparation: The infusion is taken 1 cup at a time, three or four times a day. The decoction is a good wash for wounds and sores, even chapped hands.
Remarks: Yarrow is considered safe and effective as a carminative and diaphoretic by pharmacognosists.

A GLOSSARY—*continued*

Stomachic: A medicine that gives strength and tone to the stomach or stimulates the appetite by promoting digestive secretions.

Styptic: A substance that stops or checks external bleeding. It is usually an *astringent,* which shrinks the tissues, thus closing exposed blood vessels.

Sudorific: A substance that promotes sweating. Much like *diaphoretic.*

Thoratic: A medicine used to remedy respiratory ailments.

Tonic: A substance that invigorates or strengthens the system. Often tonics act as *stimulants* and *alteratives.* Bitter tonics stimulate the flow of gastric juices, increasing the appetite and promoting the intake of food, which strengthens and invigorates. Whether an herb is regarded as a tonic, a nutritive builder, or a stimulant often has to do more with the dose or quantity used than with its actual properties.

Vermifuge: A medicine that destroys intestinal worms and helps expel them. Also called *anthelmintic.*

Vesicant: A substance that causes blisters or sores. Poison ivy is a vesicant.

Vulnerary: A substance used in treating wounds, usually an antibiotic, antiseptic, styptic, and/or plant that promotes healing through cell regeneration.

HERB

Plantain

"A *tree* can't be an herb, can it? I mean, this book's got poplars and willows in it! They can't be *herbs,* can they? And cloves and cinnamon? Aren't they spices? Dandelion? *Plantain?* Those are *weeds,* for crying out loud. My neighbor's lawn is undergoing chemotherapy to get rid of them. Now you are saying these are *herbs.*"

What makes a plant an herb *is* an oft-asked question, and one that an encyclopedia of herbs should answer.

The definition for herb that we use in this book is one that's usually a dictionary's second one: "A plant or plant part valued for its medicinal, savory, or aromatic qualities." The Herb Society of America, as good an arbiter of such things as any, has always held that an herb is "any plant that may be used for pleasure, fragrance, or physic," or some variation on that theme. As defined here, the term herb includes a broad spectrum of plants—trees, shrubs, and forbs.

Historically, most plants categorized as herbs make it on the basis of some medicinal concoction derived from the root, leaf, bark, flower, or fruit. Paging through an old herbal (which properly is a book dealing with the medicinal aspects of plants), you will find the names of hundreds of plants. Could such a definition take in too many plants?

Henry Beston, in his short but delightful book *Herbs and the Earth,* suggested just that. He said:

> In its essential spirit, in its proper garden meaning, *an herb is a garden plant which has been cherished for itself and for a use* and has not come down to us as a purely decorative thing. To say that use makes an herb, however, is only one side of the story. Vegetables, quasi-vegetables, herbal what-nots, and medicinal weeds are not "herbs" and never will be "herbs," for all the dictionaries. It is not use which has kept the great herbs alive, but beauty and use together. Clumsy food plants, curlicue salad messes and roots belong in the kitchen garden, in the *jardin potager,* and not with the herbs. They spoil the look of an herb garden, taking from it its inheritance of distinction; they confuse it; they destroy its unique atmosphere.

Beston's remarks advance imposing standards, although beauty, in the eye of the beholder, can encompass even "vegetables, quasi-vegetables, herbal what-nots, and medicinal weeds."

A contrary stance was taken by the late Euell Gibbons in his book on wild herbs, *Stalking the Healthful Herbs.* While agreeing that the great distinction of herbs stems from their beauty, he presented a more egalitarian view of beauty:

> Everyone appreciates the conspicuous and flamboyant beauty of the larger wildflowers, but how many have thrilled to the sheer beauty of the thrice-pinnate foliage of the common yarrow that grows by every roadside? How many have ever seen the intricate beauty of the many wildflowers that are so tiny they must be studied under a magnifying glass? Once the eye is trained to see these things, one finds that nature has surrounded us with breath-taking beauty that largely goes unobserved and unappreciated.

Gibbons made his mark by finding beauty and utility in what-nots and weeds, cherishing them for themselves. Even what-nots and weeds find utility and place in an herbal landscape.

WHAT ARE SPICES?

There are no clear-cut divisions between herbs and spices.

Contemporary writing on the subject of spices tends to focus on them as seasonings. *Rodale's Organic Gardening,* for example, offered its readers the following rules of thumb for telling spices and herbs apart:

- Leaves, both fresh and dried, are normally called herbs, while seeds, roots, fruits, flowers, or bark are spices.
- Herbs more frequently grow in temperate regions, while spices come from the tropics.
- Herbs are green and often have more subtle tastes; spices tend to be shades of brown, black, or red, with a dramatic, pungent flavor.

"A good example of some of these differences is the coriander plant *(Coriandrum sativum),*" continued the magazine. "Its fresh or dried green leaves are referred to as Chinese parsley or the *herb* cilantro. The brown seed from the same plant is known as the *spice* coriander."

Historically, spices have not been used exclusively as seasonings. They were valued for aromatic and healing qualities as well. If you accept the broad definition of herb ("A plant or plant part valued for its medicinal, savory, or aromatic qualities"), then you see that spices are herbs.

And so they are treated in this book.

WE SAY "ERB";
THEY SAY "HERB"

How do you pronounce it? That's easily the most-asked question about herbs. Is the H aspirated or not?

The answer is that it depends upon where you live.

If you are in England, do as the British do. Aspirate that H.

If you are an American, however, don't posture. Swallow that H. "Erb" is what we say.

HERBAL BOTANY

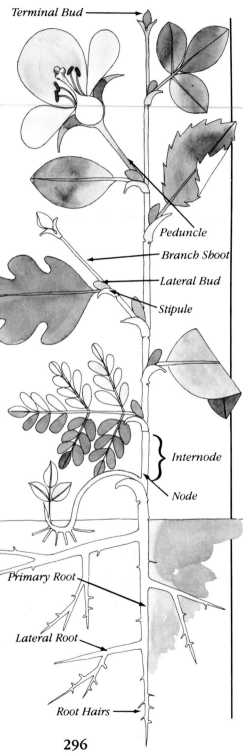

Terminal Bud

Peduncle

Branch Shoot

Lateral Bud

Stipule

Internode

Node

Primary Root

Lateral Root

Root Hairs

Botany is serious science. A branch of biology, it deals with the properties and life phenomena exhibited by plants. A botanist studies the inner structure, growth functions, and reproduction processes of plants, their diseases, their evolution and breeding, and so forth.

Plant structure and nomenclature—both elements of botany—are appropriate and important topics for a popular encyclopedia about herbs. Plant identities are based on plant structure. The structure helps the botanist classify and then name individual plants. If you are going to travel comfortably and knowledgeably in the herbal realm, you should know some botany.

PLANT STRUCTURE

Varied as they appear, all the plants discussed in this book share certain structural features. They have roots, leaves, stems, flowers, and seeds. A few are woody shrubs and trees; most are herbaceous, but they are all higher plants: They flower and produce seeds.

Flower structure: A plant's flowers, no matter how small and seemingly insignificant they may be, are typically the key to its identity. Flowers, unlike leaves for example, are fairly uniform features. They usually remain the same regardless of changing light, water, or other environmental conditions. If a species has five-petaled flowers in one garden, it will have the same sort of five-petaled flowers in another garden thousands of miles away.

A bit of knowledge about flower structure, then, is crucial for identifying unknown plants. It's also necessary if you plan on doing any plant breeding or seed saving.

Petals are the showiest, most colorful parts of most flowers. The color and markings on the petals attract pollinating insects and birds. All the petals together make up the *corolla*.

Sepals are the leaflike structures that enclose the flower before it opens. Sepals may be separate "leaves," or several lobes fused together. Usually they are green, but in some plants such as the dogwood, they almost resemble petals. All the sepals together make up the *calyx.*

Stamens are the male flower parts. They lie just inside the petals. Each stamen consists of a *filament* supporting the *anther* where pollen is found.

Pistils are the female flower parts. They lie in the center of the flower. Each pistil consists of an *ovary,* containing tiny *ovules* and one or more *styles,* or stalks, each supporting a *stigma.*

Pollen from the anther is received by the stigma and travels down the style to fertilize the ovules. The ovules eventually develop into seeds, and the ovary becomes the fruit.

The flowers of most cultivated plants contain the male and female parts they need for pollination. But single-sex flowers are also fairly common. These are either male or female (staminate or pistillate). Corn, asparagus, and cucumber produce single-sex flowers.

In some species, individual plants are single sexed because they produce only male or female flowers, but not both. Many fruit trees fall into this category. Pollination, hence fruiting and seed production, can only occur if a plant of the opposite "sex" is planted nearby. If you want red berries on your holly tree, you must be sure to plant a female tree and have a male one nearby. In the herb garden, however, flower sex isn't an issue: The failure to bloom can't be blamed on having a male. It simply indicates poor care or poor growing conditions!

Flower clusters: There are dozens of ways in which flowers may occur on a plant. The cluster they form is called an *inflorescence*. Some of the more typical inflorescences are shown in the illustration below.

Fruits and seeds: Botanically speaking, a fruit is simply the fully fertilized and ripened ovary of a flower. It may be quite large and tasty, like an apple or a plum, or small like a single grain of buckwheat. Among garden herbs, many are inedible, woody structures you hardly notice. The pods of a milkweed plant, the "wings" of a maple seed, and the capsules on an iris are all fruits. What you might

A GLOSSARY

Annual: A plant whose complete cycle of development from germination of the seed through flowering and death occurs in a single growing season. See also Biennial and Perennial.

Axis: The central stalk or branch of a plant from which lateral parts arise radially. Plural *axes*.

Basal: At the base, as in a basal leaf, which arises at the base of a stem.

Biennial: A plant that requires two seasons to complete the growth cycle, usually generating vegetative growth the first year, then flowering, fruiting, and dying in the second. See also Annual and Perennial.

Bract: A modified leaf, often scalelike, that forms either on the flower stalk or as part of the flower head. Bracts are many times mistakenly referred to as flowers.

(continued)

FLOWER STRUCTURE

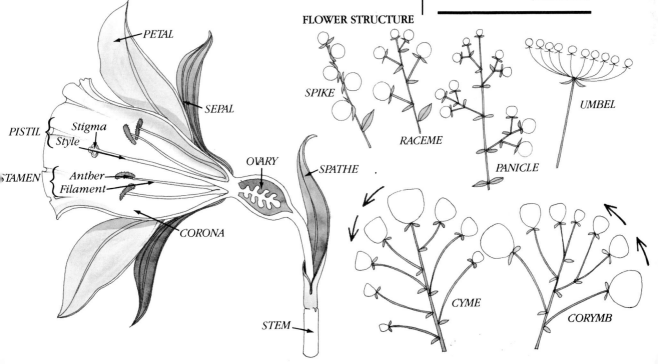

HERBAL BOTANY—continued

A GLOSSARY—*continued*

Catkin: A downy or scaly spike of flowers produced by certain plants. The pussy on the willow is a familiar example.

Cleft: A leaf divided to or nearly to the midrib.

Composite: A flower actually made up of many separate flowers, complete of themselves, which are united in a single head. This is the characteristic flower of the Compositae or daisy family.

Corona: A crownlike appendage at the center of the corolla.

Corymb: A short, broad, flat-topped flower cluster with individual pedicels emerging at different points along the axis, in which the outermost flowers open first. See also Umbel.

Crucifer: Flower of four petals arranged in a crosslike formation. This is the characteristic of the Cruciferae or the mustard family.

Cultivar: An unvarying plant variety maintained by vegetative propagation or by inbred seed.

Cutting: A piece of plant without roots; set in a rooting medium, a cutting develops roots and can then be potted as a new plant.

Cyme: A short, broad flower cluster in which the central flowers open first and which always bears a flower on the tip of the axis.

(continued on page 300)

think are the seeds of dill or parsley are actually the dried fruit, with the seed within.

Among herb plants, a few fruits are useful in dried arrangements. The money plant or honesty (*Lunaria annua*) is grown for the ornamental quality of its disklike fruit, called a *silique*. When dry, it separates into two parts, with a thin, silvery membrane between. Seeds are found on both sides of the membrane. If you look closely at other members of the mustard family, you'll find that they, too, produce silique fruits, but they are usually quite small.

The fruits of the carrot family also split open when mature. They divide into two parts, but without a central membrane. Each half of the fruit contains one seed. Often, the seed is so tightly attached to the carpel, that the seed and fruit are indistinguishable. Such is the case of the parsley "seeds" we plant. They are actually the one-seeded halves of the fruit. This type of fruit is called a *schizocarp*.

The fruits of the daisy family are also easily mistaken for seeds. Called an *achene,* this type of fruit is like a nut that doesn't readily open, even when mature. If you carefully crack it open, however, you'll find a single seed within. Such is the case of the sunflower fruits: Break open a "seed" and you'll find the true seed, attached by a stalk, within. Agrimony and strawberry "seeds" are also achenes; the juicy red "fruit" we eat isn't a true fruit at all but really a fleshy part of the receptacle.

Lily, iris, poppy, bachelor's button, onion, chives, and many other garden herbs produce capsules containing three or more seeds. Some of these capsules, such as poppy, open from the top, and others open lengthwise.

The fruits on most of the other herbs are hardly noticeable. Mint family members produce tiny nutlets, hardly distinctive and not necessary to identify the plants in that family. Mullein and other members of its family (Scrophulariaceae) have small, two-parted capsules shaped like a heart or teardrop.

Leaves: You might think you know what a leaf is, until you begin to really look at the leaves on plants in and around your garden. A single pine needle is a leaf. The tendrils of peas, the fleshy pads on a cactus, and an entire head of cabbage are all leaves, too.

What are leaves, then? They are the main light-trapping, energy-making organs of plants, with a distinctive anatomy designed for photosynthesis. Their shape, size, and special features vary greatly from plant to plant.

Leaf features aren't nearly as important in identifying garden flowers and herbs, as they are in naming trees and shrubs. Still, it's helpful to be familiar with some of the most common leaf types, so

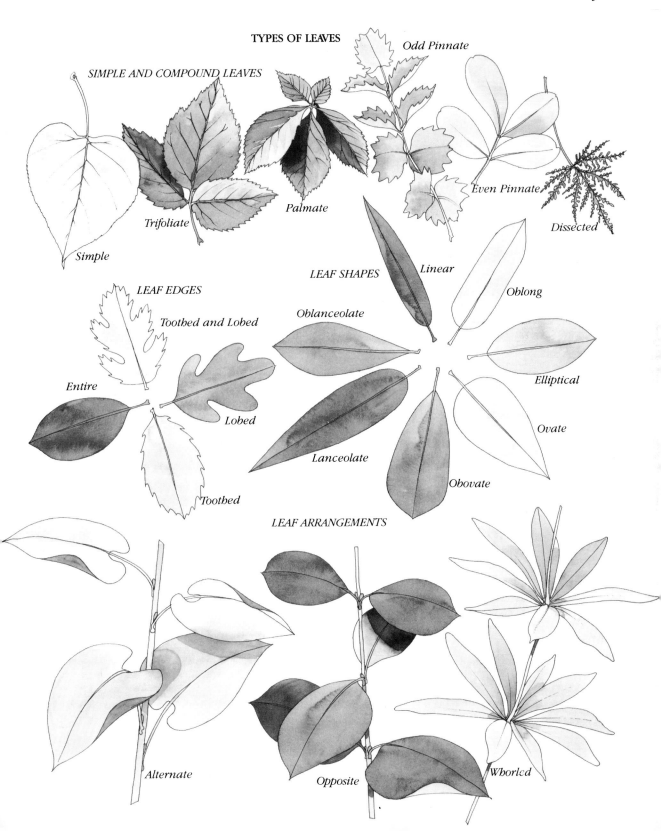

TYPES OF LEAVES

SIMPLE AND COMPOUND LEAVES

Odd Pinnate

Even Pinnate

Dissected

Trifoliate

Palmate

Simple

LEAF SHAPES

Linear

Oblong

Oblanceolate

Elliptical

LEAF EDGES

Toothed and Lobed

Ovate

Entire

Lobed

Lanceolate

Obovate

Toothed

LEAF ARRANGEMENTS

Alternate

Opposite

Whorled

HERBAL BOTANY—continued

A GLOSSARY—*continued*

Deciduous: Not persistent; falling off at maturity or at certain seasons, as the leaves of a nonevergreen tree or the petals of many flowers.

Decumbent: Reclining on the ground, but with tip ascending.

Disk flower: The small, tubular flowers in the central part of a floral head, as in most members of the daisy family. See also Ray flower.

Dissected: Divided deeply into many slender segments.

Division: Propagation of a plant by separating it into two or more pieces, each of which has at least one bud and some roots.

Entire: With a continuous margin, without toothing or divisions.

Floret: A tiny flower that makes up a dense head or cluster.

Fruit: The mature, fully developed ovary of a flower and anything that matures with it, usually one or more seeds.

Genus: A group of closely related species. Plural *genera.*

Herb: (1) A plant that lacks a permanent, woody stem, and that usually dies back to ground level during cold weather. May be annual or perennial. (2) A plant valued for its medicinal, savory, or aromatic qualities.

Herbaceous: (1) Not woody, dying to the ground each year; of plants or stems. (2) Leaflike in color and texture; of plant parts.

(continued)

you can make your way through a plant guide or a good catalog description.

There are two kinds of leaves, *simple* and *compound.* A simple leaf is all of one piece. A compound leaf consists of a number of separate parts *(leaflets)* that may, in themselves, look just like leaves. It's often hard to decide whether a single blade is a simple leaf or a leaflet on a compound leaf. Each of the roundish leaves on a rose, for instance, aren't leaves, but leaflets. Five leaflets attached to a single stalk form the compound rose leaf. Other garden plants with compound leaves include most carrot family members such as parsnip, angelica, and caraway, as well as strawberry and ginseng. The best test to determine whether you are holding a compound leaf or a branch of individual leaves is a check of their placement on the stem or branch. Leaflets of a compound leaf will be arranged in one plane; leaves are usually attached in several different planes.

When all of the leaflets connect to their stem at one point, the leaf is *palmately compound.* If they attach along the stem, then the leaf is *pinnately compound.*

The leaves of most cultivated garden plants consist of two parts: the *blade,* or thin sheet we usually call the leaf, and the *petiole,* or stalk. The petiole attaches to the plant's stem. At the base of the petiole, there may be two small, leaflike outgrowths called *stipules.* The upper angle between the petiole and the stem is called the *axil.* Sometimes a bud called the axillary bud forms there.

If there is no petiole and the blade is simply attached directly to the plant's stem, then the leaf is *sessile.* This is the case with zinnia and mullein.

The arrangement of leaves along the stem may be *alternate* or *opposite,* or the leaves may form in clusters or *whorls.*

The leaves of grasses, orchids, irises, lilies, even onions, don't have petioles either. They have a *sheath* that wraps around the plant's stem where the leaf joins. These plants are distinguishable in many other ways as well, including the pattern of their leaf veins.

Veins: The pattern that veins make in the leaf or leaflet blade is an important tool for plant identification. The leaves of the grasses, lilies, and other plants described above have *parallel* veins.

Most garden herb leaves have *netted* venation, either pinnate (branching off a central midrib), or palmate (forming a fan out from a central point on the stalk.

Stems: The stem gives its plant support and connects it with nutrient-absorbing roots. It's also a storage place where food and water can be saved. All along the stem are nodes, or swollen parts where leaves, buds, and branches form. Some herbs, including rosemary and sage, can be propagated from stem cuttings with nodes. Cut a 4-inch piece of stem, strip off the lower leaves, and plant the cutting upright in moist soil. Roots should soon follow.

Among cultivated plants, stems take on many different forms both above and below ground.

A *crown* is a mass of compressed short stems that grow just below the soil surface. Strawberry and asparagus are propagated by their crowns.

A *runner* is a stem that grows horizontally along the ground. At various points along the runner, shoots and roots grow. Strawberry and thyme send out runners.

A *bulb* isn't a root but rather a type of stem, compressed and covered with scalelike leaves. The parallel-veined plants, such as irises, lilies, and some grasses, are propagated by bulbs. In some, such as crocus, the bulb is more flattened and squat. This is called a *corm*.

A *bulblet* forms aboveground in the leaf axils or, as in bunching onions, in the flower. Left to its own devices, it will fall to the ground and possibly start a new plant. It can also be harvested and stored in a cool spot for later planting.

A *rhizome* is a runner that grows underground. It might be quite thick and short, as in the iris, or longer, as with bluegrass, the mints, tarragon, and the thistles. Where the rhizome is enlarged at its ends (as in a potato), *tubers* form. Plants that produce rhizomes tend to

A GLOSSARY—*continued*

Hybrid: The offspring of two parent plants that belong to different species.

Lanceolate: Shaped like a lance; several times longer than wide; pointed at the tip and broadest at the base.

Leaf margin: The edge of a leaf.

Lobe: A segment of a cleft leaf or petal.

Midrib: The main rib or vein of a leaf or leaflet; the continuation of the petiole.

Node: The place or joint on a stem that normally bears a leaf or leaves.

Ovate: Irregularly oval; more or less rounded at both ends and broadest below the middle.

Palmate: With the lobes or division arising from a common point.

(continued on page 303)

TYPES OF STEMS

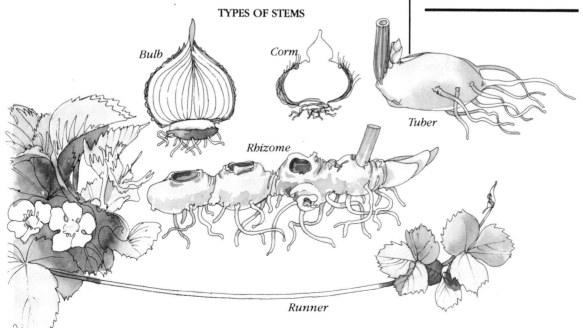

Bulb

Corm

Tuber

Rhizome

Runner

301

HERBAL BOTANY—continued

TYPES OF ROOTS

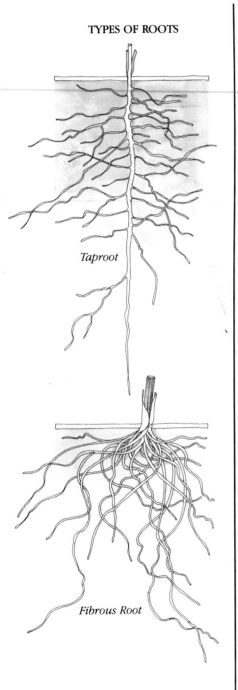

Taproot

Fibrous Root

spread rapidly. For better control in the garden, you may wish to plant them in bottomless cans.

Roots: Since they are usually underground, these most important structures are typically overlooked by gardeners. Roots are the anchors that keep the plant upright, the plant's means of absorbing water and nutrients from the soil, and a major storage organ. Roughly one-third of the entire mass of the plant is roots. The plant's health and well-being depend on their health.

Most herbs have *fibrous root systems* that are fairly shallow. This makes it easy to transplant and makes many well-suited to pot culture. The shallower the roots are, however, the more subject they are to drought and to variations in water and fertilizers.

Members of the carrot family have *taproots*, long, fleshy storage roots. These plants are better able to withstand fluctuating conditions. Of course, they can't be propagated by division and don't even transplant very easily. Fortunately, most members of this family are prolific self-sowers.

PLANT NAMES

Suppose you are speaking to someone about herbs. You are talking about valerian. But the other party is talking about garden heliotrope. Without the common ground botanical names provide, you may never know you both are speaking of one and the same plant, *Valeriana officinalis.*

What the botanists have done is really quite remarkable, for they have achieved an international accord, establishing a uniform system for classifying and naming plants. Botanists everywhere speak the same language. There are disagreements and points of controversy, but in the main, the system works well.

The generic (for genus) and specific (for species) names are the heart of the binomial system of identifying plants. The system was first proposed by Carl von Linné, a Swedish biologist and botanist who is better known by the Latinized form of his name, Carolus Linnaeus. In a sense, the binomial system is like the bureaucratic system for handling people's names—last name first, first name last. Or more correctly, the genus name first and the species name (or epithet) second.

The generic name of a plant loosely corresponds to the family or surname of a person. Within botanical families, which might be said to loosely correspond with humanity's clans, there are groupings of similar plants, all given a generic name to identify them as to group membership. In the family Compositae there is the genus *Artemisia*. Just as we tell the Smiths apart by giving them different first names, the botanist tells the *Artemisias* apart by giving them additional names called species epithets, only these names come second. So we have *Artemisia vulgaris* (mugwort), *Artemisia Dracunculus* (tarragon), *Artemisia Abrotanum* (southernwood), *Artemisia Absinthium* (wormwood), and others.

The generic name is often derived from the Greek language, but other languages are represented as well. Sometimes the name is representative of the original plant name, of the person who discovered the genus, the place in which it was discovered, some hero of Greek mythology or ancient legend, or whatever else flitted through the mind of the person giving the name. Thus we have the *Artemisias* named for Artemis, the daughter of Zeus; and the *Achilleas*, named after Achilles, the fellow with the bad heel. The genus name *Rosmarinus* is constructed of the Latin *ros*, for "dew," and *marinus*, which means "of the sea," to denote the seaside habitat of the plant.

The species epithets are supposed to describe the plant, but this ideal is sometimes missed. Occasionally, the epithet commemorates the name of the discoverer or the area to which the plant is native. Especially among the herbs, we see many plants with a species epithet *officinalis* or *officinale*, which means that the plant had some commercial value, generally to the apothecary. *Vulgaris* or *vulgare* describes the species as being the common or ordinary variety of the genus.

When a variation occurs within a species, the variation is described in a word, and that word is tacked onto the binomial name with a "var." in roman type. Thus a variety of the common yarrow which has red, rather than white, blossoms is named *Achillea Millefolium* var. *rubrum*.

Two vagaries of the system that can be puzzling are (1) the variations in some of the common specific names, like *vulgare* and *vulgaris*, or *officinalis* and *officinale*, and (2) the occasional capitalization of a species name.

In the first situation, the difference in species name is simply a rule of Latin. The two elements of the binomial must agree in gender, and the species element is the one that must agree with the genus element. It might be worth mentioning in passing that Latin was originally selected as the standard language for the botanical classification system because at the time Linnaeus advanced the binomial system, Latin was the language that was almost universally

A GLOSSARY—*continued*

Panicle: An open flower cluster that blooms from top to bottom and does not end in a flower; a branched raceme.

Pedicel: The stalk of one flower in a flower cluster.

Perennial: A plant that continues the cycle of new growth, flowering, and fruiting for at least three years. See also Annual and Biennial.

Persistent: Not deciduous; remaining attached to the plant (even after withering).

Procumbent: Trailing or lying partly on the ground, but not rooting.

Raceme: A simple elongated stem bearing stalked flowers, with the lowest flowers blooming first.

Ray: A primary branch of an umbel or umbel-like flower cluster; in composites, the corolla of a ray flower.

Ray flower: Floret of Compositae, in which the corolla is an expanded blade above a short tube. See also Disk flower.

Regular flower: A flower with petals and sepals arranged evenly around the center, like the spokes of a wheel, always radially symmetrical.

Rosette: A crowded cluster of leaves, usually basal, circular, and at ground level.

Scale: A small, modified leaf, usually covering a bud or at the base of a pedicel. In true bulbs, the scales are leaf bases, swollen with stored food.

(continued)

A GLOSSARY—*continued*

Scape: A leafless flower stalk arising from ground level; it may bear bracts or scales but no leaves and be single or many flowered.

Seed: A fertilized, ripened ovule, most always covered with a protective coating and contained in a fruit.

Solitary: Borne singly or alone, not in clusters.

Species: A population of plants or animals whose members are potentially able to breed with each other, and which is reproductively isolated from other populations. Plural *species.*

Spike: A simple, elongated stem bearing sessile flowers or heads, the lowest opening first.

Stolon: A horizontal shoot that runs along the ground and takes root, giving rise to new plants at the node.

Terminal: At the tip of the main stem of a plant.

Toothed: Having the margin shallowly divided into small, toothlike segments.

Tube flower: Floret with tubular corollas, usually five lobed or five toothed at the tip, in the center of the heads of most Compositae.

Umbel: A cluster of flowers formed by stalks of nearly equal length sprouting from a common point, with individual flowers forming a flat or nearly flat surface. See also Corymb.

Variety: A subdivision of species; incorrectly, but popularly, a form produced in cultivation.

understood by the better-educated classes. Even today, Latin is the basic language of scientific nomenclature.

The second puzzler is simply an example of a traditional exception to the rule. The rule is that the species epithet never be capitalized—except when the species name is a former genus name. The dual capitalization came about years ago, when some botanist reviewed a plant's classification and determined that it was in the wrong genus and moved it. He may have kept the old generic name as the species epithet to go with the new generic name, in which case he capitalized both elements of the binomial. Too, species epithets derived from a specific location or a person's name used to be capitalized.

The contemporary and widely recommended practice is to list all species epithets in lower case; this eliminates confusion and misspellings. It is acceptable practice still, however, to follow the traditional practice (and former international rule) of capitalizing certain species epithets. *Hortus Third,* a 1,300 page "dictionary of plants cultivated in the United States and Canada," prepared by the staff of the Liberty Hyde Bailey Hortorium at Cornell University, still lists them this way, and herbs are sufficiently traditional to warrant a continuation of the practice in this book.

The family names are usually based on the name of a prominent genus in the family. The root of the genus name is supplemented with the suffix *aceae.* Thus the genus *Viola* lends *viol,* and the family name is Violaceae. There are eight family names that predate this convention and they are so well-known that botanists accept either the traditional name or the new name. Among the eight are four that are well-known to herb lovers: Compositae, which botanists call Asteraceae, Cruciferae (Brassicaceae), Labiatae (Lamiaceae), and Umbelliferae (Apiaceae). As with species names, this book sticks to the traditional family names.

One bit of shorthand that is seen quite often is the abbreviation of the genus name to the first letter, as in *A. Millefolium.* The abbreviation is only used when it is clear what the genus is and when a complete binomial is being used. One wouldn't talk about the *A.'s;* one would talk about *Artemisias.* But in listing several species in a genus, one would spell out the genus only in the first name.

The botanical system of classifying and naming plants is at base quite simple, which is the major reason it works so well. Perhaps the trouble people have with it stems from the fact that it is based on a language foreign to them. *Cochlearia Armoracia* can twist your tongue if you've never seen the words before, but the more you say it and use it, the easier it becomes.

HERBS AS HOUSEPLANTS

Herbs work hard as houseplants. They're not content to be merely decorative, like a fern or an ivy. In addition to good looks, herbs give you flavor, fragrance, or both. Running your hand over a piny rosemary or pungent, clove-scented thyme as you pass by can bring a room to life. And nibbling a leaf of fresh mint, basil, or chives can bring *you* to life.

Visually, there's an herb for every taste. Some are downright cute—a little mound of 'Spicy Globe' basil or a mat of fluffy lemon thyme covered with pink flowers. Others are more stately, like a potted bay shrub with its dark, glistening leaves and dignified carriage. Some, like spearmint, with its ramrod stems and crisp, toothed foliage, and chives, with its clump of tubular stems, are positively architectural. And then there are those like rosemary, with fuzzy, white, arching branches covered with dark evergreen, needlelike leaves, and parsley, with its mossy curls of foliage, which are simply beautiful.

But why grow herbs indoors? There are plenty of convincing reasons if "because I like them" isn't good enough. If you're an apartment dweller, your home is probably your garden. If you want to grow herbs well, there's no place like home. For those of us who live outside the Deep South, winter puts an end to outdoor herb growing but not to our craving for fresh herbs. The plants may go dormant until spring, but our taste buds don't! And some perennials simply wouldn't make it over the winter in most of the country. Bay, for example, is expensive, slow-growing, and very temperature-sensitive. Rosemary, lemon verbena, tricolor sage, marjoram, and scented geraniums are other finicky—but wonderful—herbs. Unless you have more money than sense, you'd be well advised to pot them up and bring them in over the winter or to grow these in pots year-round.

If you have some extra space and a fluorescent light setup, winter is also an ideal time to root cuttings for spring transplanting. You can increase your stock of lemon verbena, rosemary, lavender, thyme, and scented geraniums. By spring, you'll have the makings of a whole herb garden—or a border or edging. No need to wonder if the mail-order plants will arrive all right or if the local nursery has that cultivar you particularly like.

To simplify things, we can divide "houseplant" herbs into two categories: herbs grown indoors all year, which are basically decorative and fragrant plants; and herbs grown indoors in winter, which are usually food plants.

THE BEST HERBS FOR INDOORS

Basil (*Ocimum Basilicum*): annual, to 2 ft. tall. Needs full sun; 6.0 optimum pH. Give basil well-drained soil, and water whenever the soil surface begins to dry. Harvest by snipping the growing tips frequently to keep plants bushy and prevent flowering. Prefers daytime temperatures in the 70s and nighttime temperatures in the 60s. Don't let the temperature drop below 50°F. Plants will remain productive for three to six months if prevented from flowering. Try handsome compact cultivars such as 'Spicy Globe' and 'Green Globe'.

Bay (*Laurus nobilis*): perennial tree or shrub, to 40 ft. tall (though not indoors). Needs full or part sun; 6.2 optimum pH. A slow grower, bay will take years to reach 2 ft. in a pot. Allow the soil to dry between waterings. Pot up one size in the spring. Prefers daytime temperatures in the 60s and nighttime temperatures in the 50s, but can take temperatures in the low 40s. Allow plants plenty of room for good air circulation. Harvest by cutting off individual older leaves as needed or to dry.

(continued)

HERBS AS HOUSEPLANTS—continued

Chives (*Allium Schoenoprasum*): perennial, to 1½ ft.
tall. Needs full sun; 6.0 optimum pH. Prefers daytime temperatures in the 70s amd nighttime temperatures in the 60s,
but can take temperatures in
the low 40s. Water when the
soil begins to dry, and give
plants room for good air circulation. Repot whenever plant
looks crowded (you can divide
clumps and pot up individually
as well). Plants will live several
years in pots. Harvest by cutting
off individual leaf blades to
within 1 inch of the soil surface.
Because chives makes such
slow growth from seed, it's best
to buy a pot that's already established. Or divide and pot up a
clump outdoors in the fall;
leave the pot outside until the
foliage has been killed back by
frost, then bring the pot inside
where it will make vigorous
new growth.

Dill (*Anethum graveolens*): annual, to 3 ft. tall. Needs full sun;
6.0 optimum pH. Prefers daytime temperatures in the 60s
and nighttime temperatures in
the 50s, but can take temperatures in the mid-40s. Give
plants room for good air circulation, and water whenever
the soil surface begins to dry.
Sow directly and thin to three
seedlings per 6–in. pot or five
per 8–in. pot; plants may need
staking. Productive for two to
four months indoors; harvest by
cutting individual lower leaves
once plant reaches 1 ft. tall. Dill
is a difficult plant indoors. The
best cultivars for pot culture are
'Aroma' and 'Bouquet'.

(continued on page 311)

HERBS ALL YEAR

If you're going to have a plant in your house all the time, it's got
to look good. And it helps if it's not too demanding. If you're going to
grow herbs indoors and you want them to look good, you've got to
stop thinking of them as herbs—for a minute, anyway. Think of them
as houseplants. How will they look together? Do some make a particularly effective grouping? How will they look in flower? What are
you going to put them in? And where are you going to put them?

The first rule of thumb is: If you're growing a plant for its
ornamental appeal, it must look nice. One way to do this is to put
them in an attractive container—a window box, ornamental tub, or
planter box. Trailing varieties often look well in hanging baskets.
Another technique is to plant them individually in similar containers.
Groups of plain clay pots or dark Japanese-style planters are visually
effective and focus attention on the plants—their colors, shapes, and
textures—rather than on the container. Carefully chosen baskets can
add another dimension of texture without distracting from the herbs.
But if you've always wanted to plant herbs in that huge brass pot with
nymphs and mermaids all over it, do it. Just put it in another place, so
the spotlight is on the planter, not on the clash between the planter
and the clay pots all around it.

Another way to play with herbs is to group them according to
some unifying characteristic: herbs with white or blue flowers, gray-
leaved herbs, fragrant herbs. It's better to mix herbs of different
growth habits, rather than having a forest of tall herbs in one corner,
trailing herbs on the sideboard and end tables, and a cluster of
miniatures across the room on a table by themselves. Mixing lets you
see more of the plants.

You can also train myrtle and some cultivars of scented geranium into standards: dwarf "trees" with a single "trunk." Myrtle and
other herbs also lend themselves to topiary and espalier; however,
before you start turning out thyme turtles, you'd do well to read up
on the techniques and make sure you're willing to devote the time
and care needed to maintain these high-tech plants. It would be
good, too, if you prepared a spot to showcase the results.

There's one more thing to bear in mind: Potted plants don't have
to stay indoors forever. You can move your bay, lemon verbena, and
rosemary onto the patio for a summer breather, or sink them and
your scented geraniums—pots and all—into the flower bed. They're
a snap to unearth again in the fall, without root loss or transplant
shock. Just make sure they haven't gained a few bugs before you
bring them back inside!

(continued on page 311)

The Bonnefort Cloister herb garden at the Cloisters in New York City contains only species of herbs that were known and used during the Middle Ages, including queen of the meadow (photo upper right) and betony (photo upper right, opposite page). During the Middle Ages herbs were valued highly as sources of food, fragrance, medicine, dye, and flavoring.

HERBS AS HOUSEPLANTS—continued

HERBS IN WINTER

If you're growing herbs specifically for winter, chances are some of those herbs will be culinary herbs. You may be bringing in a clump of chives or a rosemary, or a spring-planted pot of parsley or ginger. Or you may be rooting cuttings of perennials like mint, sage, and oregano in midsummer for the winter windowsill. Or you may be sowing seeds of dill, basil, and marjoram in late August for the plant table. But a goal every gardening cook probably has in mind is: fresh herbs for winter salads, stir fries, and sauces, right at your fingertips.

When growing herbs for the winter kitchen garden, there's one cardinal rule: Make sure you grow enough. One perky little parsley or bright green basil may cheer you up on a snowy morning, but it is unlikely to go far toward perking up winter salads or spaghetti. Here's where a plant table comes in handy. Most herbs need strong sunlight to grow and produce well, and space at south-facing windows is usually at a premium. Setting up fluorescent lights over a

← *The Cuxa Cloister garden at the Cloisters in New York City.*

BEST HERBS —*continued*

Garlic chives (*Allium tuberosum*): perennial, to 2 ft. tall. Needs full sun; 6.0 optimum pH. Culture as for chives. A beautiful plant, with straplike, dark green foliage and clusters of pure white star-shaped flowers that smell like roses.

Ginger (*Zingiber officinale*): perennial, to 3 ft. tall. Needs shade. Ginger enjoys high temperatures, high humidity, and moist soil. Plant a fragment of rhizome—underground stem —with "eyes" on it in a roomy, shallow pot. When the rhizomes fill the pot, harvest by lifting them.

(continued)

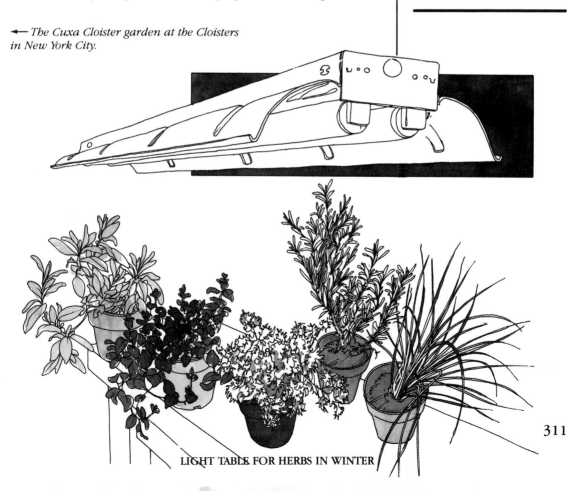

LIGHT TABLE FOR HERBS IN WINTER

311

BEST HERBS —*continued*

Marjoram

(Origanum Majorana): perennial, to 1 ft. tall. Needs full sun; 6.9 optimum pH. Prefers daytime temperatures in the 70s and nighttime temperatures in the 60s, but can take temperatures in the high 40s. Marjoram needs good drainage and can be kept on the dry side. Allow plenty of room for air circulation. Cut plants back often to maintain bushy habit, as they are rapid growers. Potted plants remain productive for one to two years; after they become woody, root new 4–in. tip cuttings. Heavenly fragrance is pervasive—use sparingly in cooking.

Mints

(*Mentha* spp.): perennial, to 2 ft. tall. Needs full or part sun; 6.5 optimum pH. Mints prefer daytime temperatures in the 60s and nighttime temperatures in the 50s, but can take temperatures in the low 40s. Give them good air circulation and high humidity, and water when the soil surface begins to dry. When crowded, repot into a container wider than it is deep, or divide into sections and pot each section. Mints remain productive for six months or more in pot culture. Harvest by trimming or cutting individual stems. Peppermint (*M. ×piperita*), spearmint (*M. spicata*), and pineapple mint (*M. suaveolens* 'Variegata') make good pot plants.

(continued)

shelf or table adds more growing space, so you can grow a more realistic number of high-use plants: parsley, basil, dill, chives, oregano, and the mints. If you enjoy cooking and don't have an attached greenhouse, a winter plant table is practically indispensable. And it lets you save the pretty plants—marjoram, thyme, rosemary, and lemon balm—for the windows!

CULTURE

Growing herbs indoors means dealing with seven major aspects of plant culture: light, temperature, air circulation, soil, fertilization, water, and pests. There are also the techniques for bringing plants in and propagation. Because herbs are less tolerant than most houseplants—they insist on conditions being "just so"—it helps to review their needs before heading out to the nursery or garden. Nobody wants a winter's worth of pale, spindly, spider-mite-infested herb plants.

Light: Most herbs thrive on light—at least five hours of direct sunlight a day. (Exceptions are the mints, bay, parsley, rosemary, thyme, myrtle, and santolina, which can take partial shade; and ginger and lemon balm, which actually *like shade*.) Natural sunlight can be supplemented or replaced with fluorescent light. A two-tube, cool white fixture hung 6 to 8 inches above the herbs and left on for 14 to 16 hours a day will keep your plants bushy and productive. You can maximize natural exposure by putting shelves in your south-facing windows, but don't crowd plants in or you'll have circulation problems.

Don't forget to turn the plants on windowsills regularly. Turning keeps the plants shapely and makes sure all sides get enough light.

Temperature: Most herbs like temperatures on the cool side—daytime temperatures of 65°F and night temperatures of 60° or even 55°F. Bay, dill, and the mints are the most insistent on daytime temperatures in the 60s and night drops to the 50s, and parsley does best between 60° and 65°F day and night. The other common household herbs do fine with daytime temperatures in the 70s and night lows in the 60s. If your house is cool, most herbs can survive temperatures in the mid- to low 40s (though scented geraniums and basil can't take it below 50°F). Obviously, foliage pressed against a frozen windowpane will freeze and die. Move the plants away from the glass in freezing weather, or slip a sheet of paper between the plant and the pane.

Air circulation: Herbs are extremely sensitive to dry, stagnant air—the kind, unfortunately, in many tightly sealed, centrally heated houses. Stale air promotes fungal diseases and insect infestations. On the other hand, a blast of crisp winter air may be bracing to us, but it (or a constant draft) is anathema to herbs. Try to keep the air moving around the plants by cracking a window in an adjoining room or by opening doors for better cross-ventilation. Another preventive measure is to give the plants plenty of space so air can circulate around them. Don't crowd the pots, and don't let the foliage from neighboring plants touch! Finally, if the air is very dry, you can set the pots on pebble-lined trays filled with an inch or less of water. But make sure the pots are over—not *in*—the water.

Soil: Herbs in pots need a reasonably rich soil mix with good drainage. Some successful mixes are:

> 2 parts compost, 1 part vermiculite, and 1 part perlite
> 1 part sand and 1 part peat moss
> 1 part compost, 1 part sand, and 1 part perlite
> 7 parts loam, 3 parts peat moss, and 2 parts coarse sand
> 1 part potting soil, 1 part sand, and 1 part peat moss.

Experiment until you find a mix you're happy with. One word of warning: If you habitually have problems with plant diseases, you might be best off not using soil in your mixes. Or add sterilized soil if there's a source at hand.

On the subject of soil, be sure your plants have enough of it. No herb should be grown in a pot less than 4 inches in diameter; 6 inches is even better. For plants that spread by underground stems, like the mints and ginger, wide, shallow pots are ideal. And for herbs with long taproots, like bay and parsley, a deep pot or bucket is a necessity.

Fertilization: Fertilizing potted herbs involves a balancing act. You want to fertilize them enough to keep them productive but not so much that they get leggy and begin to lose their flavor. Once-a-month applications of seaweed or fish emulsion (which can smell pretty foul in a closed house, remember!) at half-strength should give them enough nutrients to keep growing.

Water: Herbs like regular waterings, but they're finicky. Waterlogged soil and pots standing in water tend to bring on root rot and other fungal diseases. Hence the need for a well-drained potting mix (leave the clay in the yard). Water most herbs thoroughly when the soil surface starts drying out. Let bay, marjoram, oregano, sage, and thyme dry out between waterings. But *never* let rosemary completely dry out—just one "dry spell" can kill it. The mints, lemon

BEST HERBS —*continued*

Oregano *(Origanum vulgare)*: perennial, to 1½ ft. tall. Needs full sun; 6.8 optimum pH. Prefers daytime temperatures in the 70s and nighttime temperatures in the 60s, but can take temperatures in the high 40s. Give plants good drainage and keep them on the dry side. Cut back often to contain spreading habit and improve air circulation. To insure getting culinary oregano, buy plants or take 4-in. tip cuttings. Plants will remain productive in pots for one to two years. When they become woody, replace them.

Parsley *(Petroselinum crispum)*: biennial, to 1½ ft. tall. Needs full or part sun; 6.0 optimum pH. Grows best between 60° and 65°F, but can take temperatures in the low 40s. Can be grown from seed; germination takes 9 to 21 days. Cover seed with ¼ in. of soil. Sow in late spring in a big container—a 3-gallon bucket is ideal. Set the pot outdoors and keep it watered until fall. Bring it indoors before the first fall frost, giving it cool temperatures and plenty of sun. Plant several to have plenty through spring. Harvest parsley by cutting the outer leaves, leaving the central rosette to produce new growth. The fine flavor of flat-leaf (Italian) parsley is stronger than that of curly parsley, but both make handsome pot plants. Parsley remains productive for six to nine months in pot culture.

(continued)

BEST HERBS —*continued*

Rosemary (*Rosmarinus officinalis*): perennial, to 6 ft. tall. Needs full or part sun; 6.8 optimum pH. Prefers daytime temperatures in the 70s and nighttime temperatures in the 60s, but can take temperatures in the low 40s. Don't let plants dry out completely or they'll die. Prune or pinch back frequently to maintain bushy habit. Propagate by 4–in. tip cuttings. Rosemary needs good drainage. If the needlelike evergreen leaves turn brown, the plant is being overwatered. Woody growth and yellowed leaves are signs that the plant is potbound.

Sage (*Salvia officinalis*): perennial, to 2½ ft. tall. Needs full sun; 6.4 optimum pH. Common culinary sage has spear-shaped, pungent, pebbly, gray-green foliage and blue flowers. Purple sage, with purple foliage; tricolor sage, with purple, white and green variegated foliage; and pineapple sage (*S. elegans*), with pineapple-scented foliage and red flower spikes, are also handsome pot plants. Sage must have good drainage but can withstand infrequent waterings. Prefers daytime temperatures in the 70s and nighttime temperatures in the 60s, but can take temperatures in the low 40s. Allow plenty of room for air circulation. Sage remains productive for one to two years in pots. Grow from tip cuttings. Prune regularly to maintain bushy shape. Be sure to have enough on hand for stuffing the Thanksgiving and Christmas turkeys!

(continued)

balm, ginger, and scented geraniums enjoy more moist conditions than their brethren. Always use room-temperature water so you don't shock the plants.

Pests: Herbs aren't attacked by pests often, but close, dry, indoor conditions can bring on infestations of spider mites, whiteflies, and aphids in succulent species, and scale on woody plants like bay, rosemary, and lemon verbena. Soap sprays can control spider mite, whitefly, and aphid attacks. To make such a spray, dissolve 1 to 2 tablespoons of a mild flaked soap like Ivory or Oxagon in 1 gallon of warm (not hot) water. Spray diligently once a week until the pests are brought under control. Be sure to coat the undersides of the foliage. Needless to say, wash the soapy residue off the leaves before adding them to food! Yellow sticky traps work well for whiteflies. Scale can be controlled by scraping off the insects or by daubing them weekly with alcohol-dipped cotton swabs. Isolate any infested plants, and if you can't control the infestation, get rid of them. This may seem drastic, but it's preferable to having an entire houseful of insect-ridden plants.

Bringing plants in: Perennial plants that won't survive the winter outside in most of the United States and Canada—rosemary, bay, lemon verbena, oregano, marjoram, camphor, and scented geraniums—must be brought indoors over the winter if they're to see another summer. Other perennials, such as chives, garlic chives, thyme, the mints, winter savory, and lavender, make the transition to indoor conditions fairly easily. When preparing to move plants inside for the winter, remember to acclimatize them first.

Dig the plants, causing as little root damage as possible, and pot them carefully. Then water the herbs and set them in a shady place outdoors for three days to a week so they can gradually adjust to the dual shocks of pot culture and decreased sunlight. Check the plants vigilantly for pests, and isolate them for a couple of weeks before mixing them in with your other houseplants, just in case an infestation has slipped by you. This shading-and-checking routine is necessary even when moving in plants that have spent the summer outdoors in their pots, like bay, rosemary, parsley, and lemon verbena.

The best time to pot most outdoor herbs is after the fall harvest and before the first frost. They should be safely indoors by the time frost strikes. Chives and garlic chives, however, benefit from induced dormancy before "coming in from the cold." Divide the clumps, pot them, and let them remain outside until frost kills the foliage. Then bring them in for a new burst of lush, stocky growth.

Propagation: Start annual seeds (such as basil and dill) as well as parsley and perennials that will come true from seed (marjoram and thyme, for example) in the same mix you plan to pot them in. Sow the seed in late August or early September, water the flats, cover them with plastic wrap, and put them where temperatures will drop no lower than 60°F. (The top of the refrigerator is warm and out of the way.) When the seeds sprout, remove the plastic and move the flats into full sun. Keep the soil moist but not soggy. When seedlings have their second set of true leaves, transplant them to 4-inch pots, and when the first pots are outgrown, move the plants to 6-inch pots.

For cultivars that will not come true from seed or herbs like lemon balm that are difficult to germinate, start with plants or take cuttings. Rosemary, the mints, thyme, lavender, lemon verbena, scented geraniums, culinary oregano, and sage can be propagated by taking 4-inch tip cuttings, stripping off the lower leaves and sticking the stems in moist perlite. Take the cuttings two to three weeks before the first fall frost (or earlier; they take two to three months to root). If your home has especially low humidity, you can cover the flats with glass or plastic to promote higher moisture levels. Again, be sure to keep the perlite moist but not soggy.

STANDARDS

BEST HERBS —*continued*

Savory, winter (*Satureja montana*): perennial, to 1½ ft. tall. Needs full sun; 6.7 optimum pH. Winter savory prefers daytime temperatures in the 70s and nighttime temperatures in the 60s, but can take temperatures in the low 40s, Water when the soil surface begins to dry, and give plants plenty of room for air circulation. Prune regularly to keep plants productive. Winter savory will remain productive in pots for one to two years.

GROW A STANDARD

Suitable herbs for growing standards (dwarf trees with a single trunk) include myrtle, rose, bay, scented geranium, rosemary, and lemon verbena. The mature plant's stem must be able to support the foliage head, so only selected species will do.

• Stake the plant.

• Clip off all side branches (though not leaves) that appear below the desired height.

• As the top branches develop leaves, pinch out their tops to force more branching, thus forming a good crown.

• Shape the head with clippers.

315

HISTORY OF HERBS

The history of herbs is a history of economic botany—plants used by man for food or physic or for aromatic, cosmetic, or dyeing use. Plants are central to this history, to be sure, but it is peopled with warriors and gardeners, wives and mothers, witches and shamans, doctors and quacks, dreamers and schemers.

The cord of the tale has many strands—cultural, social, economic.

Herbs, of course, are celebrated for many uses, but the oldest uses seem to be the medicinal ones. Perhaps this is because much of the lore of herbs is derived from herbals—the plant medicine books—and it is to these ancient volumes that we tend to turn in determining whether or not a plant may properly be called an herb. There are, of course, other herbal uses explained, but even the culinary and aromatic qualities seem tied to the curative, salutary, or hygienic properties of the plants.

HERBS IN CHINA, INDIA, AND EGYPT

The oldest known systems of medicine in the world today are those of China, India, and ancient Egypt.

Chinese medicine: The system of Chinese polypharmacy, which has survived into modern times, is widely acclaimed as one of the most complete and effective herbal traditions extant today.

The oldest of the Chinese pharmacopoeias, *Pen-ts'ao* (*Herbal*), is reputed to be the work of the Emperor Shen-nung, a great cultural hero who is said to have lived from 3737 to 2697 B.C. Shen-nung is said to have compounded and self-tested hundreds of herbal preparations, aided by a transparent abdomen that enabled him to observe the workings of his internal organs. The freakish condition was undoubtedly a gift of legend, rather than of nature. Recorded in the *Pen-ts'ao* are 365 medical preparations; all but 51 are herbal.

The emperor who succeeded Shen-nung was also interested in medicine and prepared his own medical text. The book *Huang-ti Nei-ching* (*The Yellow Emperor's Classic of Internal Medicine*) is less of an herbal and more of a comprehensive review of the state of medical arts in China. It is presented as a dialogue between the Yellow Emperor, Huang-ti, and his chief minister, Ch'i Po. Huang-ti is said to have ruled from 2697 to 2595 B.C.

The authenticity of both these works is in question. The ancient Chinese had a propensity for attributing their writing to older sources in the hope of bolstering their value, and such is probably the case here. Studies have placed the two in the first millennium before Christ, making them not as old as the Ebers Papyrus. Despite the discrepancies of the dates, the *Pen-ts'ao* and the *Huang-ti Nei-ching* are valuable and legitimate old herbals.

From the third century B.C. to the seventh century A.D., Chinese medicine was highly influenced by the philosophy and example of Taoist sages who believed in preventing disease through moderation. The Chinese used acupuncture, herbs, massage, diet, and gentle exercises to correct imbalances within the body.

Indian medicine: The Indian medical system is known as Ayurveda, the "science of life." According to mythology, the science of Ayurveda came from the realm of the gods. Eventually, it was taught to a small group of human disciples. These physicians then taught the science of life to other human physicians. Eventually, it spread throughout India and much of the ancient world.

Ayurveda was incorporated into most texts of the Vedas, the ancient scriptures upon which Hindu culture and religion is based. The Vedas are thought to have existed since 10,000 B.C. Although no written records remain from that far back, it is certain that Ayurveda was already highly developed by 1000 B.C. It continued to evolve until about A.D. 1100. By the twelfth century A.D., due to invasions, Ayurveda lost its state patronage and diminished slightly. But still it evolved, particularly along the lines of mineral and botanical medicine, until well into the sixteenth century.

In the *Rigveda,* one of the ancient Hindu scriptures, over 1,000 medicinal plants are listed, and a special group of sages who knew the secrets of plants is described. These ancient doctors are said to have made artificial limbs, cured wounds, used the soma plant as an anesthetic (soma is now thought to be a mushroom, *Amanita muscaria*), performed cauterization, and opened obstructed bladders with surgical instruments. The *Charaka Samhita,* one of the most famous Indian medical texts dating back to preliterate times, was preserved for many generations by oral tradition. Written down at last in the first century A.D., the text mentions 500 herbal drugs.

The Indian system like the Chinese system, works to maintain health and prevent disease through a balance of diet, exercise, thought, and environment. Treatments include not only herbs and other natural substances, diet, and exercise but also mental and physical practices intended to help the sick person develop positive emotions and qualities. These practices, called yogas, have their parallel in Chinese medicine. All of these disciplines are devoted to regulating the body's vital energies and to refining the mind.

Many references to Indian herbs and treatments are found in the famous herbal written by the Greek Dioscorides during the first century A.D. This herbal, which attests to the influence of Indian

MATERIA MEDICA OF LI-SHIH-CHEN

The first major Chinese medical work to be translated into Western languages was the *Materia Medica of Li-Shih-Chen.* It was first published in 1596.

A compendium of remedies, it lists 12,000 prescriptions and formulas and analyzes 1,074 plant substances, 443 animal substances, and 354 mineral substances. The book is still studied by traditional Chinese physicians.

THE EBERS PAPYRUS

A trove of ancient herbal information was discovered in a remarkable Egyptian medical document dated to 1550 B.C.

This comprehensive roll, discovered by the German Egyptologist Georg Ebers in 1874, is about 65 feet long and contains extensive information about surgery and internal medicine. More important to the herb historian are listings of some 800 medicinal drugs, including anise, caraway, cassia, coriander, fennel, cardamom, onions, garlic, thyme, mustard, sesame, fenugreek, saffron, and poppy seed.

The Egyptians used these aromatic plant materials in medicine, cosmetic ointments, perfumes, aromatic oils, cooking, fumigation, and notably in embalming.

HISTORY OF HERBS—continued

THE HANGING GARDENS OF BABYLON

The Hanging Gardens, in what is now Iraq, have been called one of the seven wonders of the world. Legend has it that the gardens were built by King Nebuchadnezzar II for his favorite wife, who was homesick for trees and mountains on the featureless Mesopotamian plains. Legend lies, however, in calling the gardens "hanging"—unless, of course, the occasional trailing vine constitutes hanging.

The Hanging Gardens were really terraced roof gardens, built over a massive, arching stone foundation and huge storage rooms. The roofs were waterproofed with layers of bitumen, reeds, bricks, and lead, and soil was then added to a depth suitable for trees. Deep wells supplied water to the gardens by means of a hydraulic machine.

Did Nebuchadnezzar grow herbs on his roof gardens? Babylonian records show that the citizens of the day had thyme, coriander, saffron, anise, poppy, mandrake, rosemary, and hemp, as well as such ornamentals as roses, lupines, and anemones. Surviving accounts describe the effect—the manufactured mountain towered above the Babylonian plain—rather than the plants, but surely any pleasure garden would have had at least a few of the aromatics.

medicine on the West, is only one example of a continuous flow of medical information from India to the Mediterranean area from Roman times onward.

Egyptian medicine: At roughly the same time that the Chinese and Indians were developing their herb-based healing traditions, the Egyptians were doing the same.

In ancient Egypt, medicine united magic, prayers, spells, and sacrifices with empirical treatments and some surgery. A host of medical documents recorded on papyrus have survived and have given modern scholars a fairly complete picture of Egyptian medical practices. While most of the papyruses have been dated to between 2000 and 1000 B.C., they refer to older traditions that had previously been transmitted orally.

Perhaps more than its medicine, however, ancient Egypt is known for developing embalming to a high art. To appease the gods of death, the bodies of important people were preserved by cleansing the interior of the abdomen and rinsing it with fragrant spices, including cumin, anise, marjoram, cassia, and cinnamon. Embalming yielded a mighty impact in another realm through its need for exotic herbs and spices. It stimulated world trade.

GARDENS AND LEGENDS

Fortunately, more has come down to us than lists of ancient remedies, interesting as these are to horticulturists and historians. The arts and letters have preserved some tantalizing garden fragments, like the frieze of the Assyrian king Ashurbanipal (c. 670 B.C.) and his queen in their pleasure garden. And archaeologists have been quite successful in corroborating some ancient legends—such as the existence of the Hanging Gardens of Babylon.

The slightly later Persian pleasure gardens gave us the word paradise and altered the way gardens would look in the East and West for over a thousand years. The Greek historian Xenophon described the paradise gardens of kings Darius the Great (521 to 486 B.C.) and Cyrus (d. 401 B.C.), stressing the straightness of rows and angles and the regular spacing in the plantings. The paradise gardens had trees and sweet-scented herbs and flowers, usually with geometric water courses and pools laid out symmetrically.

When Alexander the Great (356 to 323 B.C.) conquered Persia, the concept of a well-ordered pleasure garden spread to Greece and throughout the Hellenistic world, eventually reaching Rome and, from there, finding its way to the medieval castle and cloister.

Of course, Greece had gardens long before Alexander's adventures. They are featured even in the epic poem the *Odyssey.* The

TRADE ROUTES

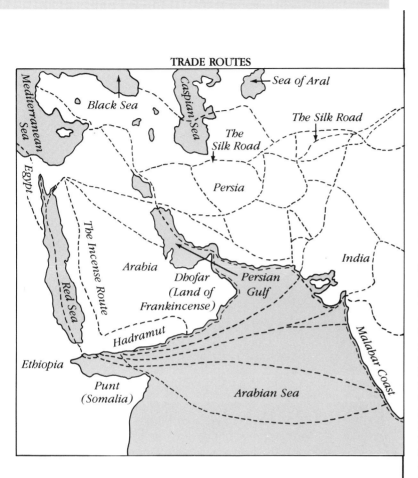

Mediterranean Sea

Black Sea

Caspian Sea

Sea of Aral

The Silk Road

The Silk Road

Egypt

Persia

The Incense Route

Arabia

Red Sea

Dhofar (Land of Frankincense)

Persian Gulf

India

Malabar Coast

Hadramut

Ethiopia

Punt (Somalia)

Arabian Sea

most famous is the garden of Theophrastus, the father of botany and student of Plato and Aristotle. Theophrastus (c. 371 to 287 B.C.) wrote a "History of Plants" that mentions some 450 plants, systematically categorizing them as trees, shrubs, or herbs and noting that some plants were specific to certain areas. Though Theophrastus contributed much to the study of plants, especially to plant classification, it was the Romans who developed the true art of European gardening.

The Romans perfected the idea of the enclosed courtyard garden. They incorporated the geometrical symmetry and water features of the Persians and the potted plants of the Egyptians and added homegrown innovations, such as elaborate topiary (usually of boxwood). Even city houses had garden rooms, open to the sky and painted with landscape murals to extend the feeling of the shrubs and flower beds. But it was in their villas that the Roman's genius for garden design was best expressed.

SPICE TRADING ROUTES

The Arab lands lay between the spice-producing Eastern countries and the spice-consuming Western countries. In the millenia before Christ, the Arabs took full advantage of their proximity and established a virtual monopoly on trade between East and West. All of the overland routes passed through their turf. Sea voyages were dangerous and time-consuming.

In about A.D. 40, the secret of the wind systems over the Indian Ocean was unlocked by a Greek merchant named Hippalus. He observed that twice a year the prevailing winds—called monsoons—changed direction. From April through October, the prevailing southwesterly favored the trip from Egypt to India. Then from October through April, the northeast monsoon was favorable for a return voyage. Hippalus showed that by taking advantage of these winds, a round trip between Egypt and the pepper-producing Malabar Coast of India could be completed in less than a year. Until Hippalus's discovery, such a voyage was taking at least two years.

The discovery of the monsoons allowed the Romans to sail directly from a land they controlled, Egypt, to the source of the spices and other goods they wanted. It sharply reduced the importance of the overland spice routes.

319

HISTORY OF HERBS—continued

GALEN'S THERIAC

Some of the most effective herbal medicines, called "simples," feature but a single herb. The concept of the simple seems wonderful, but the application of simpling turns out to be tough for people to embrace warmly.

Throughout history, physicians (and pharmacists) have favored the complex, potent, make-'em-well-right-now bolt of medicine. A cup of herb tea, efficacious as it may be, is not usually the drug of choice. And *the patients themselves* favor what the doctor touts. The simple is usually the choice of those who—through economic hardship or isolation—have no other choice.

The all-time bolt of medicine had to be Galen's Theriac, truly a witches' brew. Beyond its opium base, it contained more than 70 ingredients, including dozens of herbs, minerals, chunks of animal flesh, honey, and wine. The pharmacist was required to compound subrecipes first, then mix them together. At a minimum, the mélange was expected to mature for 40 days; longer was better.

Theriac, which was also called Galene, survived along with Galen's principles and theories for centuries. Elizabethan herbalist John Evelyn reported on a ceremonial compounding of Theriac he witnessed in Venice in 1645.

Villa gardens were usually geometrically precise, with colonnades and statuary (the Romans were enthusiastic collectors of Greek statues), topiary and plane trees, and canals and fountains. They also had raised beds; irises, narcissus, rose poppies, verbenas, hyacinths, and violets were grown in what we naively consider a modern innovation, as were coriander, dill, parsley, fennel, rosemary, and many other herbs.

As the Roman Empire expanded, it carried its concept of the villa and its enclosed garden farther and farther across Europe. Archaeologists have uncovered "classic" villa gardens in Herculaneum and Pompeii, at Fishbourne in England, and at Conimbriga in Portugal. And where they brought their gardens, the Romans also brought their herbs, flowers, vegetables, and trees—and their knowledge of herbal medicine.

GRECO-ROMAN MEDICINE

The roots of Roman medicine, from which bloomed most European medicine for the next 1,000 years, were in Greek medicine.

To herbalists, the two great figures in Roman medicine were Galen (A.D. 130 to 200) and Dioscorides (first century A.D.), both Greeks. Galen, physician to Marcus Aurelius, wrote a "recipe book" of 130 antidotes and medicines. Dioscorides, also a physician, traveled with the Roman legions. He wrote the first true herbal, an attempt to describe the medicinal plants of the Mediterranean area and their functions. His book *De Materia Medica* describes, very sketchily, about 500 plants. Because the descriptions are short and vague, it's quite a trick to match them to the appropriate Mediterranean plants. Galen's work is no more instructive. And these men, along with Theophrastus, were the final authorities on European herbalism! Until well into the sixteenth century, when a new world of plants brought back by explorers forced a reevaluation of botany and medicine, Dioscorides was reverently cited by herbalists all over Europe.

The earliest surviving copy of *De Materia Medica* is a Byzantine manuscript prepared in about A.D. 512. Called the Codex Vindobonensis, it features nearly 400 full-page, strikingly natural paintings of plants. The art of the codex is so realistic, especially compared to the crude and stylized pictures in the herbals of the next 1,000 years, that it has been attributed to the greatest botanical illustrator of ancient times, Krateuas, the legendary physician to the tyrant king and poisoner par excellence, Mithridates VI Eupator. The codex formed the high point of herbal illustration until the appearance in 1542 of Leonhard Fuchs's *De Historia Stirpium,* with its exquisite and readily recognizable woodcuts.

HERBS IN THE MIDDLE AGES

Between Dioscorides and Fuchs lay all the Middle Ages, the age of chivalry and monasticism and enclosed gardens, of unicorn tapestries and ladies in their bowers with lutists softly playing in the flowers at their feet, the age of plagues and lepers, famines and crusades. What was the fate of herbals and herb gardening in such romantic and brutal times?

The great repositories of learning in medieval Europe were the monasteries, where literacy was nurtured and manuscripts were dutifully copied. For the most part, herbal literature was on hold. But while most monks contented themselves with copying Dioscorides, faithfully or otherwise, a few were writing down their own thoughts on gardening.

One such original thinker was Walahfrid Strabo (c. A.D. 807 to 840), a dirt gardener in the finest tradition and the abbot of Reichenau in Switzerland. In his poem *Hortulus* ("The Little Garden"), Strabo wrote a celebration of gardening that devoted enthusiastic—but not unrealistic—sections to the cycle of work in the garden ("On the Cultivation of Gardens," "The Difficulty of the Undertaking," and "The Gardener's Perseverance and the Fruits of His Labor"). Strabo

THE PLAN OF ST. GALL

The Plan of St. Gall, drawn in 820, is the idealized layout of a Benedictine monastery.

Shown are four gardens: the cloister garth, where the monks walked and meditated; the cemetery/orchard, where they were buried; the medicinal herb garden; and the vegetable garden.

The medicinal garden was walled and adjoined the infirmary/physician's house. Less than 1,000 square feet altogether, it was a tidy garden of raised beds. Each bed was devoted to a single plant: lily, rose, climbing bean, savory, costmary, fenugreek, rosemary, mint, sage, rue, iris, pennyroyal, watercress, cumin, lovage, and fennel.

Herbs had the featured role in the kitchen garden as well. The plan shows it as a walled, rectangular plot adjoining the gardener's house. Plainer than the infirmary garden, it had raised beds with plank sides and paths between. Herbs reserved for culinary use were coriander, dill, two kinds of poppy, parsley, chervil, and savory. Again, each plant had its own bed.

The plan may seem to have leaned heavily toward herbs, but herbs were a medieval staple. For dyeing clothes and illuminating manuscripts; for chasing moths from cloth and fleas and lice from people; for preventing and curing disease; for adorning a church; or for disguising spoiled food, everyone used herbs. And grew them.

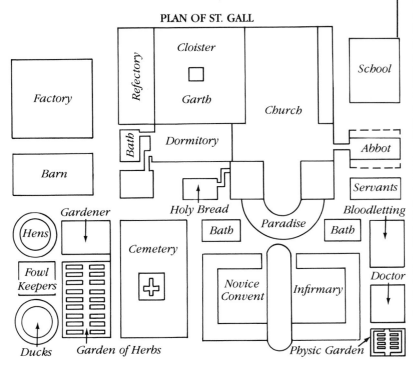
PLAN OF ST. GALL

HISTORY OF HERBS—continued

ST. ANTHONY'S FIRE

St. Anthony is the saint who protects against fire, epilepsy, and infection. A religious hermit, he lived in Egypt, where he died in A.D. 356. During the Crusades, his remains were moved from Egypt to Dauphiné, France, the site of the first recognized epidemic, in 1039, of what was to become known as St. Anthony's Fire.

In the most common form of the "fire," the victim suffered intense, firelike pain in the limbs, which eventually would turn gangrenous. Delirium and hallucinations were common. So was death.

St. Anthony was saddled with the Fire when the Order of St. Anthony was established in Dauphiné, along with a hospital to care for Fire victims.

It wasn't until 1676 that the cause of St. Anthony's Fire—a fungus that infects certain cereal grains, principally rye—was isolated. The fungus, *Claviceps purpurea,* or ergot, had been recognized as a poison as far back as 600 B.C., but it wasn't until the millers conscientiously monitored the grains they ground for ergot that the Fire was brought under control (although occasional outbreaks have occurred, even into the twentieth century).

Ergot today is the source of important drugs used in obstetrics, internal medicine, and psychiatry. The nature of the hallucinations victims of St. Anthony's Fire experienced can be imagined; lysergic acid diethylamide (LSD) is a synthetic derivative of ergot.

also devoted sections to his favorite plants, which included sage, rue, melon, wormwood, fennel, lily, poppy, and mint. He gave the growth habits and uses of his plants, and he, like the Romans, grew them in raised beds.

And what of the lady's pleasure garden and the lutist in the flowers? Paradise gardens were alive and well in the Middle Ages. Even Albertus Magnus, the great Dominican theologian, turned his attention to the requirements of a pleasure garden in *On Vegetables and Plants* (c. 1260). Albertus described the garden as centering on a lawn, around which were sweet-smelling herbs (he recommended rue, sage, and basil). But this was only the "floral carpet." There were also fruit and shade trees and "furniture," such as a fountain and bench of flowering turf.

The pleasure garden was almost invariably enclosed, and it was usually small—less than 1,000 square feet. As in their Persian forerunners, water features heightened the enjoyment of the medieval gardens. And fresh fruit provided consolation when the great flush of spring bloom was over. Aromatic herbs such as rosemary and lavender remained popular. Occasionally, peacocks or other ornamental fowl were allowed free reign. And the turf seats—built up against the walls or under trees and sided with brick, boards, and even wattle-and-daub—seem to be an innovation.

GRECO-ARABIC MEDICINE

The history of herbs and medicine in these Dark Ages (from 641, the fall of Alexandria, to 1096, the First Crusade) was dominated in western and northern Europe by the monastery on the one hand and the herb lady on the other. The monasteries perpetuated the healing doctrines and herbal knowledge of Galen and Dioscorides, while the folk healers stirred a pot of ancient herbal lore, pragmatic healing know-how, and pagan sorcery. The latter are preserved in history as quacks or, worse, witches who brewed everything from harmless folk remedies to venomous abortives, from love potions to disgusting elixirs and outright poisons.

Of course, the Church itself adopted versions of the primitive superstitions, such as tying bundles of herbs to doors to keep out the witches or wearing amulets of dried dung to ward off disease.

In the Mediterranean region at this time, the Arabs dominated. When they overran North Africa in the seventh century, the Arabs seized countless Greek and Roman medical texts, which were collected in Baghdad and closely studied by Arab physicians. Under the influence of this Greco-Roman medical trove, Arabian medical practice flourished, stirring changes and spurring advances.

Although the Arabs were initially quite empirical in their approach, drawing on Hippocratic principles, in the end, the Galenic concept of medicine, based on mechanical laws of anatomy, logic, and physiology, prevailed. Galen believed doctors should be guided by theory rather than observation, and the Arabs, guided by the example and writings of ibn-Sina, who was known in the West as Avicenna, accepted that concept. Ibn-Sina was a flamboyant and extraordinarily successful physician. His Canon of Medicine was an attempt to order all medical knowledge according to Aristotelian and Galenic principles. Until well into the seventeenth century, Avicenna's canon was the highest medical authority. It was this canon that the medical iconoclast Paracelsus tossed into the fire in 1527, signifying his rejection of Galenic medicine.

A school of medicine established in the eighth century in Salerno, Italy, became the prime vehicle for the learnings of Arab physicians. The Arabian Muslims believed that God in his wisdom had provided medicines aplenty in nature (a belief that finds its counterpart in the Old Testament). Arab physicians enthusiastically researched plant medicines and developed a vast amount of information on healing plants from Europe, Persia, India, and the Far East. The Arab businessmen also took an active interest in herbs: They were the first occidental pharmacists and had opened their shops in Baghdad by the early ninth century. Another Arab contribution was the use of astrology in medicine. In Arabic culture, astrology was regarded as a science that could help in the selection of medicines and the treatment of diseases.

After the Crusades, Arabian pharmaceutical expertise took root in Europe. Highly sweetened and exotically spiced preparations made with plants from faraway lands became popular healing agents. However, the study of native plants still found no favor. Herbalists who had inherited the common sense of the old folk medicine tradition were legally and socially separated from the so-called proper practice of medicine. Folk remedies and the old local traditions of herbal wisdom became more and more of a threat to the medical academies.

The Crusades, of course, are generally credited with pulling western and northern Europe out of the Dark Ages. They certainly introduced the material goods of the Middle East and through it, the Orient, to Europeans. Paramount among these luxuries of the East were spices. These spices produced fortunes and helped to spur world exploration.

Consider the nature of life in the Middle Ages. Frederick Rosengarten, Jr., described it as follows in *The Book of Spices.*

Depicts ancient Greek and Arabian medical authorities. A woodcut from Ortus Sanitatis, *published in Mainz, Germany, in 1491*
Courtesy of Hunt Institute for Botanical Documentation, Carnegie-Mellon University, Pittsburgh, Pa.

WHAT IS AN HERBAL?

An herbal is a book that both describes plants and tells how to use them, usually medicinally, although cosmetic and even culinary uses are sometimes given. Herbals were written for the layperson and served the function of a combination medical encyclopedia and corner drugstore. In an age when both books and doctors tended to be rare and expensive, the herbal held a valued place in every literate household, ranking second in importance only to the Bible. The housewife who concocted remedies from her herbal was the only doctor her family was ever likely to see.

323

HISTORY OF HERBS—continued

PARACELSUS

In the early 1500s, a Swiss physician named Philippus Aureolus Theophrastus Bombastus von Hohenheim burst on the medical scene. He learned about medicinal plants and minerals from his father, a physician and chemist. Using the name Philippus Aureolus Paracelsus, he traveled throughout Europe, researching folk remedies. An advocate of writing in the common tongue, he departed from the tradition of writing herbals and pharmacopoeias in Latin. Such departures from tradition were his stock in trade.

He lauded folk healers, comparing them favorably to his more celebrated colleagues. He rejected Galen's theory that all disease stems from either excess or deficiency of the body humors. He catalyzed the movement toward mineral medicines, a movement that would be taken up much later by chemists of the nineteenth and twentieth centuries. He also predicted the discovery of pharmacologically "active principles" in plants.

Paracelsus believed that all medicinal substances, plant or otherwise, contained an essential principle that was pure and entirely beneficial. It was the role of the physician-alchemist, he proclaimed, to discover these subtle secrets of nature and make them available to humanity.

Remembered primarily as the greatest alchemist, Paracelsus changed the course of Western medicine.

Food was neither wholesome nor palatable. Cattle, slaughtered in October, were salted and kept until the following spring. Spices were believed to have a beneficial preservative action in meat. Potatoes were unknown and very few other vegetables could be obtained, either in or out of season. There were few lemons to flavor beverages, no sugar to sweeten them. Neither tea nor coffee nor chocolate was available. Spices, however, such as pepper, cinnamon, ginger, and cardamom, when mixed with the coarsest, dullest, even the most repulsive fare, could make it more palatable. Spices were used to camouflage bad flavors and odors, and it was also believed that their consumption would prevent illness. Spiced wines were popular; in fact, the more spices in the wine, the more delectable it was thought to be.

Initially, the great trading centers of Europe were in Italy, thanks to the Italian associations with the Arabs prior to the Crusades. The Polo brothers, Nicolo and Maffeo, left one of those centers, Venice, for the Far East in about 1260, taking Nicolo's young son Marco with them. A quarter-century later, Marco Polo's tales of life and luxury in the Far East provided more fuel for the drive to find new routes to the Orient. The virtual closing of land routes caused by the spread of the Ottoman Empire drove spice prices higher and higher. It was another goad for world exploration. Black pepper, cinnamon, cardamom, sandalwood, nutmegs, cloves, mace, and other exotic spices: These were the commodities in demand.

Eventually, in the late 1400s, Portuguese ships, commanded by Bartholomeu Dias and Vasco da Gama, circumnavigated Africa, opening a direct sea route to India and beyond and developing a new distribution of exotic spices. Spanish ships, commanded by Christopher Columbus, crossed the Atlantic and discovered a whole new world. And from this New World came new plants, from the love apple (better known today as the tomato), to Jesuit's bark (the bark of the cinchona tree, which has yielded the malarial-fighting drug quinine), to tobacco.

THE AGE OF HERBALS

Over the next century, centered on the reign of Queen Elizabeth I (1558 to 1603), stretched the Great Age of Herbals.

The era of herbals opened in 1530 in Germany, where Otto Brunfels and Leonhard Fuchs, two of the fathers of German botany, published herbals with illustrations that have never been equaled in all the herbals that have followed. Brunfels's work is notable in that his artist displayed the plants realistically—wilted leaves and all. Leonhard Fuchs's *De Historia Stirpium* (1542; a German edition was published in 1543), on the other hand, focused on perfect specimens. Fuchs's herbal had more than 500 woodcuts with large, clear, readily recognizable plants and no text crowded around the illustration—truly a first in herbal publishing. Unfortunately, his text is largely a compilation of previous writings, including, of course, those of Theophrastus and Dioscorides. A physician and professor of medicine, Fuchs seems to have felt compelled to write his herbal because of the general ignorance of herbs even among his fellow physicians. He also made an effort to be thorough; in addition to the indigenous European plants, he describes and pictures at least a hundred "new discoveries," including corn, snap beans, and marigolds.

One of the most popular of the European herbalists was the Belgian Rembert Dodoens, whose *Cruydeboeck* appeared in Dutch in 1554, was revised and published in Latin as *Stirpium Historiae Pemptades Sex* in 1583, and continued to surface in many other languages, including English, where both a full-length and an abridged version (Ram's *Little Dodoens*) found their way onto many a bookshelf. Dodoens, a physician and professor like Fuchs, supplied his artists with fresh plants and supervised their work.

Beautiful as the European herbals are, however, it is the English herbals that make for florid and spicy reading, and sometimes the lives of their authors were at least as colorful as their writing. John Gerard is the best known and, with the exception of Culpeper, the most controversial of the English herbalists. The controversy stems chiefly from the disreputability of some of Gerard's "eyewitness accounts" and the circumstances surrounding the publication of his *Herball or Generall Historie of Plantes* (1597).

Generally, Gerard was a reliable witness, listing wildflower locations around London and their flowering times, disproving old wives' tales, and scrupulously listing the names of those to whom he is indebted for exotic plants and new cultivars. But when he erred, it was in the grand tradition. He claimed, for example, to have *seen* barnacles hatching out geese (a popular belief at the time).

Gerard, like so many of the herbalists, was connected to medicine as well as gardening; he belonged to the Barber-Surgeons' Company. Accordingly, he prescribed such undoubtedly effective cures as peony seeds in a heady drought of wine or mead to ward off "The Night Mare," and rosemary to "comfort the brain."

Gerard died in 1612, and in 1633 Thomas Johnson, a botanist and author in his own right, brought out a revised edition of Gerard's

GERARD'S CRIBBED HERBAL

One of the most famous of all herbals is the one known as *Gerard's Herbal.* First published in 1597, it is much quoted, even today, and is still in print in facsimile editions.

But the book wasn't entirely John Gerard's own work. He apparently got hold of an unfinished translation of Rembert Dodoens's herbal from Latin to English, the translator having died before he had finished the work. Gerard altered the arrangement of the herbs, then added his own comments, and published the work, with the remark: "Dr. Priest, one of our London College, hath (as I heard) translated the last edition of Dodoens, which meant to publish the same, but being prevented by death his translation likewise perished."

Gerard, of course, did not merely crib Dr. Priest's work. *The Herball* bears Gerard's own unmistakable stamp; it is full of his friends, the rare exotics thriving in his garden (he grew over 1,000 species), and English flora and botanico-medical lore in general. It is also full of his remedies.

HISTORY OF HERBS—continued

herbal. He corrected much of Gerard's misinformation, enlarged *The Herball* to cover 2,850 plants, and illustrated it with woodcuts from the most prestigious botanical publisher of the day.

The most ambitious of the English herbalists was John Parkinson, whose massive *Theatrum Botanicum* (*The Theater of Plants, or An Universall and Complete Herball*) covers roughly 3,800 plants in almost 1,800 pages. It was published in 1640 when Parkinson, who billed himself as "Apothecary of London and the King's Herbarist," was 73. The title page bears personifications of Europe, Asia, Africa, and America, to indicate that the plants described had been drawn from the four corners of the earth. In the true herbal tradition, Parkinson incorporated the works of two Continental herbalists (one of which, Caspar Bauhin's *Pinax*, provided a system of nomenclature for the plants) and took most of his illustrations from Gerard.

The *Theatrum Botanicum* is distinctive as well as comprehensive, however. Parkinson groups his plants into 17 "Classes or Tribes," including "Venomous Sleepy and Hurtfull plants and their counter poysons," "Hot and sharpe biting Plants," "The Unordered

From E. Rosslin's Kreuterbuch, *published in Frankfurt, Germany, in 1536, is this scene of herbs being gathered, processed, and administered to a patient. In the center of the illustration, the physicians consult.*
Courtesy of Hunt Institute for Botanical Documentation, Carnegie-Mellon University, Pittsburgh, Pa.

Tribe," and "Strange and outlandish plants." He provides his readers with an antidote for love potions and a Rabelaisian recipe "to entertain...[an] unbidden unwelcome guest to a man's table, to make sport with him and drive him from his too much boldnesse."

The follies perpetrated in the herbals of Gerard and Parkinson—and there are some—are trifling compared to the whoppers perpetrated in the herbal of Nicholas Culpeper, surely the most outrageous—and perhaps the most popular—of all the herbalists. Culpeper was a nonconformist, a Puritan apothecary when virtually the entire medical establishment of the day was loyalist. His goal was to take medical knowledge out of the hands of the College of Physicians—those "proud, insulting, domineering Doctors, whose wits were born about five hundred years before themselves"—and put it within the reach of the apothecaries, who actually did most of the prescribing, and the families who could not afford to consult any doctor. To this end, he translated the *London Pharmacopoeia* from Latin to English and published it in 1649 as the *Physicall Directory,* earning the ire of the medical establishment and the devotion of the reading public.

Unfortunately for those who trusted his advice, Culpeper was more than a bit of a crank. He subscribed wholeheartedly to the Doctrine of Signatures, which held that the key to a plant's use lay in its appearance. At the time, it was universally believed that the sole purpose of plants was to serve man—the only trick was determining what they were good for. The Doctrine of Signatures suggested that God had left little clues in the shape or coloring of a plant to indicate its medicinal value. If a plant had lung-shaped leaves that were spotted, why, it must be meant to cure diseased lungs!

Culpeper was also fascinated by astrological botany, which allied plants to the planets according to color and shape and then connected the astrological influence of the planet with its plants. The combination of astrology and signatures created quite a witches' brew, and Culpeper distilled it lavishly in his herbal *The English Physician* (also called *The Complete Herbal*), published in 1651. Despite—or perhaps because of—its dubious and sensational contents, Culpeper's herbal was enormously successful.

Culpeper's work can also be regarded as the swan song of herbals and herbalists, for the scientific era was beginning. Even as Culpeper was promoting superstition, scientists were beginning to examine and disprove it. One of the foremost of these was Sir Thomas Browne, "Dr. of Physick," whose *Vulgar Errors* (1646) and *Pseudodoxia Epedimica: or, Enquiries Into Very Many Received Tenets and Commonly Presumed Truths* (1658) attacked many of the "truths"enshrined in the herbals.

Courtesy of Hunt Institute for Botanical Documentation, Carnegie-Mellon University, Pittsburgh, Pa.

PARKINSON'S VEGETABLE LAMB

The title page of John Parkinson's *Theatrum Botanicum* was embellished with a small representation of a plant that existed only in the mind. The fantastic plant apparently had grown to legendary proportions in Europe in Parkinson's time, and he was extremely fond of it.

He gave a fulsome description of the "vegetable lamb" in his book. The plant bore a lamblike fruit atop its stem that "feeding on the grasse round about it until it hath consumed it and then dyeth or else will perish if the grasse round about it bee cut away of purpose."

The vegetable lamb apparently is based on misreadings of the ancients' descriptions of cotton.

HISTORY OF HERBS—continued

HALLUCINOGENS

Hallucinogens are drug plants that affect the mind more than the body, distorting the senses and producing the sensation of entering another world. Examples of them are found all over the world—from marijuana, native to the Middle East, Asia, and Africa, to deadly nightshade found in Europe, to the various hallucinogenic mushrooms found in the Americas.

In primitive cultures, such as those discovered by the Europeans exploring the New World, hallucinogens are the favored medicines. This is because sickness and death are viewed as being a consequence of interference from the spirit world, rather than being induced physically or organically. The hallucinogens seemingly permit the shaman or medicine man, and sometimes even the patient, to communicate with the spirit world.

Moreover, hallucinogens, as vehicles to the spirit world, play significant roles in religious life, in rites of passage, in societal relationships. Thus, the Algonquin Indians gave wysoccan, a medicine that induced derangement and memory loss, to young men so they would enter manhood with no recollection of childhood. Tribes of the Southwest and Mexico use various *Datura* species in divination, prophecy, and healing rituals. The Mixtecs of Mexico ingest puffballs so that their questions can be answered by the voices of heaven.

Given impetus by such works as those of Browne and by the influx of new plants brought about by the age of exploration, the apothecaries also turned their attention to a more empirical treatment of plants. In 1673, the Worshipful Society of Apothecaries established the Chelsea Physic Garden on roughly 4 acres along the Thames. They hoped to advance medical botany and grow as many of the exotic imports as possible to determine their medicinal value. Accordingly, they grouped the plants systematically in beds, walled the garden and, in 1722, hired Philip Miller, the most prominent horticulturist in England, as gardener. Miller's *The Gardener's Dictionary* may arguably be regarded as the most successful of all gardening books, and it was enthusiastically received in edition after edition both in England and in the Colonies.

THE NEW WORLD

About the time these Englishmen were collecting their herbal lore into book form, other Englishmen were moving to the New World, joining Spaniards and Frenchmen who were already there in exploring and exploiting the land and its resources. They were taking, along with everything else, their healing and savory plants. As had been true throughout history, the first settlers in the new land counted on the herbs primarily for their salutary qualities. Their healing properties combated illness; their scents disguised the poor sanitation; their flavors masked bland or spoiling food.

Along with their cherished herb plants, the colonists brought their gardening styles with them from Europe. The Elizabethans did not have separate gardens for herbs, flowers, and vegetables. Instead, everything was thrown together in a "kitchen garden." The colonists followed this practice, putting the garden just outside the door (for convenience and safety) and fencing or hedging it in (to keep out livestock and other unwanted guests). The garden was set up geometrically in raised beds edged by boards. Plants were grown cheek-by-jowl, with no attempt at ordered rows or monocropping. Today, we could call the colonists' gardening "methods" intensive gardening and interplanting, using herbs and flowers as companion plants to confuse or repel pests.

To the colonists, however, the herbs were at least as important as the vegetables, and they grew an impressive variety. Lavender, rosemary, thyme, savory, sage, germander, hyssop, southernwood, lavender cotton, dill, chamomile, caraway, fennel, lemon balm, mint, basil, parsley, borage, chervil, tarragon, rue, comfrey, and licorice were all in colonial gardens. Dye plants such as alkanet, calendula, saffron, tansy, woad, and madder colored colonial costumes, and potherbs, including sorrel, purslane, skirret, burnet, and cress contributed to "sallets" (almost invariably cooked) and pottages.

But the New World was just that, a new land with a population and a plant world of its own. The new arrivals discovered that the native peoples had a vast herbal knowledge of their own. They discovered that some of their plants didn't thrive in the new land, while others did quite well. The upshot was the development of a new body of herbal lore, a body recorded largely by the naturalized Americans.

Undoubtedly the first written record of the native American herb lore was made by Juan Badianus, a native Mexican Indian doctor. Badianus had been educated by priests and in 1552 wrote a manuscript, in Latin, recording native medical practices.

The exchange of herbal knowledge between the new and the old worlds was begun in the seventeenth century by two Englishmen, William Wood and John Josselyn. In 1634, Wood published in London a book titled *New England Prospect,* reporting his observations on the New World. The book included a chapter, "Of the Hearbes, fruits, woods, waters . . . ." Josselyn's book was published in London in 1672, and its almost interminable title admirably captured the gist of the text: *New England's Rarities Discovered: In Birds, Beasts, Fishes, Serpents, and Plants of that Country. Together with The Physical and Chyrurgical Remedies wherewith the Natives constantly use to Cure their Distempers, Wounds and Sores. Also A perfect Description of an Indian Squa in all her Bravery; with a Poem not improperly conferr'd upon her. Lastly A Chronological Table of the most remarkable Passages in that Country amongst the English.*

Other writings and research on the uses of plants followed, of course. In the late seventeenth century, the first arboretum was established in America by a Bavarian named Johann Kelpius, who was residing in Germantown, outside of Philadelphia. Kelpius was interested in testing the medicinal plants he had heard about from the Indians.

Philadelphia was also the home of two respected, college-educated physicians, mutual colleagues, who examined the Indian materia medica and came to opposite conclusions. The better known of the two, Dr. Benjamin Rush, actively disparaged the rich heritage of folk healing among the Indians. After studying Indian healing techniques, Rush concluded, "We have no discoveries in the materia medica to hope for from the Indians in North America. It would be a reproach to our schools of physics if modern physicians were not more successful than Indians, even in the treatment of their own diseases." In contrast, Dr. Benjamin Smith Barton studied the Indians' healing materials and techniques and soon after published *Col-*

Comfrey

HISTORY OF HERBS—continued

PATENT MEDICINES

In 1813, Samuel A. Thomson obtained a patent on "Thomson's Improved System of Botanic Practice of Medicine." His objective was to allow him to "sell" his system of medicine, while at the same time to legally prevent buyers from altering it in any way.

Thus began the era of the patent medicine, a notable though not necessarily illustrious period. An entrepreneur, looking for a fast buck, would create a "medicine" unlike any other and obtain a patent on it. Proof that the medicine worked was not necessary to get the patent, only proof that it was unique. But the patent did confer a measure of legitimacy on the compound, and that's all the entrepreneur was looking for.

The practice of adding alcohol and sometimes opium, cocaine, or marijuana to these medicines became prevalent. The unscrupulous practice of marketing them with vague and glorious claims became widespread. Most patent medicines were useless, often intoxicating placebos, sold with grand promises.

lections for an Essay towards a Materia Medica of the United States. His work spawned a flurry of compilation activity, and soon a variety of guides to Indian medicines was available.

Colonial interest in herbs continued unabated through the Revolution and extended to the presidency. Thomas Jefferson grew 26 kinds of herbs in his 1,000-foot kitchen garden at Monticello. Like his colonial predecessors, Jefferson interplanted herbs and vegetables. He grew garlic, parsley, sage, mint, lemon balm, thyme, tansy, chamomile, rosemary, lavender, burnet, hyssop, marjoram, sorrel, shallots, horseradish, rue, southernwood, mustard, cresses, and wormwood, among others. After years of searching, he finally procured plants of true French tarragon while he was president. Jefferson's favorite, however, was the nasturtium. As we do today, he used the flowers and leaves in salads and pickled the buds as "capers." In 1824, his nasturtium bed stretched 10 by 19 yards—surely a glorious sight in high summer. (We must remember, however, that in Jefferson's day there were no "bush" nasturtiums; the sprawling vines were grown in hills like squash, and it would not have taken as many as it might at first appear to cover 190 square yards.)

THE DECLINE OF HERBAL MEDICINE

Although these colonial days marked what would perhaps be the heyday of herbal healing, they marked a concurrent unfolding of scientific advances that would end their prominence in established medicine.

"Orthodox" medicine in this country was nothing if not aggressive, with a fairly typical course of action consisting of massive doses of poisons, violent cathartics, and purgatives, coupled with epic (up to 140 ounce) bleedings. The doctor wanted to make something happen, but what happened all too frequently was that the patient died. No wonder this brand of medicine was called "heroic."

And no wonder that alternative therapies flourished. One of the most significant in this country was founded by Samuel A. Thomson (1769 to 1843), a New Hampshire native. Thomson's early experiences with orthodox medicine made him a foe of bleeding and of mineral-based medicines. His therapy was based, he said, on helping the body to heal itself. He used steam and hot baths to induce sweating and herbal regimens to purge the body and promote healing. Although he was entirely self-taught, Thomson nevertheless called himself "doctor."

What made Thomson significant was that he established a whole school of folk healing. Faced with destitution and the avowed opposition of medical orthodoxy, Thomson hit upon a scheme to simulta-

neously provide himself with a livelihood, protect his healing therapy from unwelcome additions or changes, and spread the word to
those who needed it. In 1813, he patented "Thomson's Improved
System of Botanic Practice of Medicine." He then sold, for $20,
"family rights" to and some instruction in the system and, for another
$2, a copy of the *New Guide to Health or Botanic Family Physician.*
Purchasers became members of one of many Friendly Botanic Societies that he organized. To them were available herbal medicines
that Thomson prepared and distributed through agents.

As the century progressed, as Thomson and other herb-oriented
healers battled the medical establishment, the chemists worked in
their laboratories, isolating more and more essential principles. Encouraged by their successes, they began efforts to create synthetic
duplicates of these alkaloids, thus bypassing the plant.

HERBAL REGENERATION

Scientific and technological developments in the twentieth century have led to the increasing use of synthetics in pharmaceuticals.
But there remains a large proportion of medicinal substances that can
be derived reasonably only from plants. According to one expert, "At
least 25 percent of the prescriptions dispensed by the modern-day
physician contain active ingredients from plants." Furthermore, said
Norman R. Farnsworth, Ph.D., a pharmacy scientist at the Illinois
Medical Center in Chicago, "Essentially all of the plants yielding
useful drugs, or which are found in prescriptions as extracts, are rich
in medicinal folklore." Were it not for folk medicine, there would
not be as many excellent drugs available to modern science.

The old herbals have been rediscovered and reprinted, and each
year brings its harvest of new herbals and herb books. Herb nurseries
and newsletters; herb wreaths, potions, and potpourris; herb gardens
of every size, shape, and specialty—not to mention herb teas and,
yes, even some time-honored herbal remedies—all have found a
place in the pattern of modern life.

Perhaps the true romance of herbs, the secret of their continuing
fascination for us, is that they link us so concretely to past glories:
renaissance Europe and Elizabethan England; Byzantium, Greece,
and Rome; Egypt and China; and even our own vigorous colonial and
federal heritage. To the Unicorn Tapestry and illuminated manuscripts. To Dias, da Gama, and Columbus. To Thomas Jefferson
relishing his nasturtiums. And even if brushing past a rosemary plant
doesn't conjure a vision of a Roman villa garden, we must find, like
Gerard, that its fine, pungent fragrance "comforteth the heart and
maketh it merry." Perhaps after all, that's the *real* secret of herbs.

Elecampane

HOP

Humulus lupulus   **Cannabaceae**

Maybe it isn't just the alcohol in beer that makes you drowsy. The hop, an ingredient of beer, has a long and deserved reputation as a sedative. Simply resting one's head on a pillow stuffed with this herb will put any insomniac to sleep. Or so they say.

Sedative or not, its status as an ingredient of beer has made the hop an herb that's anything but sleepy. Few herbs can claim to be grown and used on the scale of the hop. It is of considerable agricultural significance around the world.

HISTORY

Once used as a kitchen herb and mentioned by the Roman scholar Pliny for its edible shoots, the hop came to be used widely for brewing in France and Germany in the ninth and tenth centuries. The value of hops to brewers was as a preservative; beer brewed with hops could be kept longer before it was sold.

Hops were introduced into North America by the Massachusetts Company in 1629, and by 1648 production had spread to Virginia. It wasn't until 1800 that hops became an important field crop, however. Throughout the nineteenth century, hop growing moved progressively westward. An epidemic of downy mildew put most New York State growers out of business in the 1920s, and the eastern dominance in the market ended. In the United States today, most hops are grown in Washington, Oregon, California, and Idaho.

While brewers added hops to their beer recipes, herbalists mixed hops into herbal remedies—and not just a few. Over the centuries, hops have been used as an anodyne, a fever cure, an expectorant, a means to get rid of intestinal worms, a diuretic, a sedative, a tonic, an agent for the removal of obstructions of the spleen, a stimulant for estrogen production, and in the treatment of rheumatism, jaundice, insomnia, hysteria, nervous heart conditions, excess uric acid, flatulence, itches, intestinal cramps, ringworm, and diarrhea, among other conditions. Hop poultices have been used to cure numerous skin infections and conditions, including boils and discoloration.

Hops aren't used for these ailments today, but the herb does have a few valid medicinal properties.

USES

Not all hops germinate equally. Female flowers are the ones of economic importance. The female flower, a conelike growth called a strobile, is the part used in brewing and in most medicinal applica-

DESCRIPTION

The hop's angled, fibrous vine, like the native wild grape, is remarkable for the speed and persistence of its growth. The stem grows from the root each year and soon begins twining from left to right. No fruit forms until the third year, but the root is strong and perennial. (See photo on page 32.)

Flowers: Male and female flowers on separate plants. Female flowers: inconspicuous, paired blooms on short spikes, mature into strobiles, which are conelike structures composed of overlapping, papery, greenish white, roundish bracts or scales that contain the fruit; slight garlic odor. Male flowers: inconspicuous, white; five sepals, five stamens; form loose bunches or panicles 3–5 in. long.

Leaves: Resemble grape leaves; opposite, heart-shaped, coarse, hairy, with finely serrated edges; leaves high on vine sometimes grow singly and alternate.

Fruit: Achenes; appear sprinkled with a yellow, grainy substance that is actually glandular hairs.

Height: 20–25 ft.; have been known to reach 40 ft. in one season.

FLOWERING

Mid- to late summer.

RANGE

Originally native to Europe, Western Asia, and North America.

HABITAT

In vacant fields and along rivers.

tions. There are male flowers, but they grow on separate plants, and since they have no commercial value, they are quite ruthlessly eliminated from the commercial hop nurseries.

By far, the most common use for hops has been as a flavoring and preservative for beer. Much has been claimed for it medicinally, but then people have always claimed that whatever they liked to drink was good for them.

Medicinal: Do you have trouble sleeping at night? Make a hop-stuffed pillow to lay your head on. Be sure to moisten the pillow with water or alcohol to keep it from rattling, or it will do more to keep you awake than put you to sleep. Abraham Lincoln and King George III are both reported to have used such pillows, but the odor is strong and, to some, unpleasant enough to drive away any thoughts of pleasant dreams.

Hops deserve their reputation as a sedative. Early reports that workers in hop fields tired easily tend to confirm the sedative action, although no scientific studies have been conducted on humans. Experiments with frogs, birds, and mice show that hops do depress the central nervous system.

Hops also have been found to have antiseptic properties and, when applied externally as a hot poultice, are said to reduce inflammations.

The primary chemical constituents responsible for the medicinal properties of hops and for the bitter taste are humulone and lupulone. These compounds are contained in the yellow glandular substance found on the hairs of the fruit.

Ornamental: You can use hops to decorate screens, arbors, and pergolas. A Japanese variety, *Humulus japonicus* var. *variegatus,* not a beer hop, and a yellow-leafed variety, *H. lupulus* var. *aureus,* have especial ornamental potential.

Craft: Cut and dry the flower heads to add to wreaths and dried arrangements.

Other: In Scandinavia, a coarse cloth is made from the vines

333

HOP—continued

after they have soaked for a whole winter to soften the fiber enough for it to be separated. The flexible vine can be used to weave baskets.

JUDGING THE QUALITY OF HOPS

To evaluate the quality of hops, growers—and buyers—generally look for a light yellowish green color, a full, pleasant aroma, and a degree of stickiness in the cones. If the color is too green or the aroma haylike, the hop was harvested too soon. If the color is somewhat rusty or the smell harsh, it was probably harvested too late. The stickiness is simply a measure of the essential oils and resin in the hop; the more the better.

CULTIVATION

In commercial agriculture, hops are grown in bizarre, pole-studded fields called hopyards. A network of wires is strung from pole to pole, about 18 feet overhead, and more wire dangles from the network to the ground. The hop vines are trained to these trellises in early spring when they have just begun trailing. The plants grow with remarkable vigor, sometimes as much as 6 to 12 inches in a single day. At maturity, the vines often extend 25 feet in length. The vines are harvested intact, then hauled to a stationary picker that separates the conelike strobile from the vine and foliage. The cones are dried very carefully in a kiln.

Hops are generally started from cuttings or suckers taken in early summer from the healthiest old plants. Commercial growers select a section of the rhizome that is at least ⅜ inch thick. The cuttings are started in a nursery area. After a year there, the plants are moved, usually in October or November, and replanted in groups 6 feet apart. The groups, or "stools," consist of three to five plants.

Hop plants require deep, humusy, well-drained soil; you should dig deeply before planting. Air circulation should be very good to prevent mildew.

Seeds can be used for propagation, but these will not always reproduce true to variety.

Train the plants to long poles, wire, or strings. Major growth does not begin until the second year, and the plant bears well only in the third and following years.

Spider mites and aphids are the most common pests of hops. If this becomes a problem in your area, wash the vines thoroughly.

Downy mildew, which caused so much trouble for New York hop growers 65 years ago, is still one of the most common diseases of hops. Others include sooty mold, root rot, and some viruses.

Harvesting and storage: Gather strobiles when they are amber brown and partly dry.

If you do plan to store them, dry them immediately after harvesting in an oven at a temperature of 125° to 150°F. The best way to preserve the flavor of medicinal hops is by making a tincture.

Hops lose their flavor and medicinal effectiveness very quickly. They are quite unstable in the presence of light and air. One study demonstrated that nine months of storage cost 85 percent of the hop's original chemical vitality. Obviously, hops should be used as promptly as possible.

GROWING CONDITIONS

- Plant hardiness zone 3 (hardy to -35°F).
- Soil pH 6.0 to 7.0.
- Deep, well-drained, humusy soil.
- Full sun.

HOREHOUND

Marrubium vulgare   **Labiatae**

You thought you had recovered from your head cold enough to risk an evening at the symphony, but toward the end of the final movement of the Mahler, the tickle in your throat became impossible to control, and your paroxysms of coughing were causing your fellow concertgoers to focus their frowns on you. At intermission the gentleman on your right reached into his pocket and produced a decorated metal box, extending it open in his hand. You unwrapped the little round cough drop and, as he instructed, held it far back on your tongue.

A vaguely bitter, aromatic warmth seemed to suffuse your entire head, soothing the rawness of your throat and reaching into nasal passages with its spicy, and somehow woodsy, fragrance. "What is it?" you whispered.

"Horehound," your companion replied. "My grandmother's people used to make their own. I couldn't manage without the things when cold season's here."

HISTORY

Horehound takes its name from Horus, the Egyptian god of sky and light. In ancient Greece the herb was credited with curing the bite of mad dogs, and among the Hebrews, it was one of the ritual bitter herbs of Passover. Folk legend through the ages held that horehound could break magic spells.

Horehound was also said to relieve chronic hepatitis, tumors, tuberculosis, typhoid, paratyphoid, snakebite, worms, itches, jaundice, and bronchitis. You could take your choice and either put it in your eyes or sniff it to improve your eyesight. People also believed it removed obstructions from the liver and the spleen and, with the addition of oil of roses, that it would cure earaches. Horehound was thought to be both a diuretic and a diaphoretic. It has been used to battle cankerworms when they attack trees.

In more recent times, expectations for horehound have been reduced somewhat, which is probably just as well since it lets us focus on one of the few claims that appears to be reliable—horehound's ability to soothe a hoarse throat and to promote expectoration. Horehound syrups and cough drops were used as early as the 1600s in England and later found favor with the Shakers in this country.

USES

Few people have put horehound to the test for removing magic spells in the last few years, but it remains an ingredient of over-the-

DESCRIPTION

Horehound's branching stems give it a bushy look, accentuated by the extreme wooliness of the stems and leaves. The squareness of the stems reveals the plant to be a member of the mint family. (See photo on page 273.)

Flowers: White, in dense whorls; tubular corolla has two lips; tubular calyx divided at margin into 10 hooklike segments; four stamens.

Leaves: Opposite in pairs; lower ones stalked, upper ones stalkless; 2-in. long, soft, hairy, round to oval, serrated edges; upper surface veined, lower surface woolly.

Fruit: Barbed seeds catch on clothing and animal fur; in clusters of four, lie inside small nutlets at the base of the spiny calyx.

Height: 2–3 ft.

FLOWERING

Summer.

RANGE

Native to southern Europe, central and western Asia, and North Africa; naturalized in North America.

HABITAT

Dry, sandy places, wastelands, sheep pastures, vacant lots, and abandoned fields.

CHEF TIP

Add horehound and fennel seed to iced tea and lemonade.

HOREHOUND
COUGH SYRUP

Make an old-time cough remedy by mixing horehound tea with honey.

Make an infusion by steeping 1 ounce of fresh or dried horehound leaves in a pint of boiling water. Allow it to steep only 10 minutes. Strain off the leaves, then measure the quantity of liquid remaining. Add twice as much honey as liquid, mix well, and bottle.

To soothe a cough, take 1 teaspoon at a time, about four times a day.

counter and some prescription drugs, especially cough syrups. It is best known as an old-fashioned candy flavoring. Some other herb products often combined with it are oil of roses, slippery elm, marsh mallow, ground ivy, coltsfoot, licorice root, hyssop, and rue. Either honey or sugar can be added to horehound tea or extract to make candy, cough drops, and cough syrup.

Medicinal: The primary constituents thought to be responsible for the medicinal actions of horehound include a volatile oil, tannin, and a bitter principle called marrubiin. (Marrubiin does not exist in the living plant but is formed during the extraction process.) Scientists have found that marrubic acid, formed from marrubiin, stimulates the flow of bile in rats. This may account for horehound's use as a purgative and a bitter to produce gastric action. In large doses horehound also serves as a laxative, but in very large doses it can cause irregular heartbeat, so use it with some caution.

Its value as a cough soother and expectorant is better substantiated. Marrubiin and vitamin C may play a part in the action, as might the high concentration of mucilage, which eases sore throats. Horehound has also been found to promote the secretion of mucus.

Make a decoction from 1 teaspoon of horehound leaves in a cup of boiling water; take only 1 tablespoon at a time and no more than 1 cup a day.

This plant should not be confused with black or stinking horehound (*Ballota nigra*). True to its name, this is a strong-smelling weed, and it may be toxic in large quantities.

Culinary: Horehound's furry leaves have a menthol-like taste, and an infusion of them is the base for both confections and throat lozenges. At one time horehound was a popular culinary herb in England, where it is still occasionally used to flavor ales and, more often, teas.

Candied horehound can be made by adding sugar to an infusion of the leaves and boiling until the mixture reaches a thick consistency. Pour into a shallow pan and cut into squares when cool.

Available commercially: Dried leaf, lozenges, and candy.

Other: *Marrubium vulgare* has been used as a substitute for hops in beer, especially in England. Horehound ale is sold in Europe.

When grown as an ornamental, horehound usually finds its place in the herb garden. It attracts bees, however, and would be a useful addition to any garden where bees are needed.

CULTIVATION

Horehound grows easily, so easily in fact that it may take over your garden if left unrestricted—especially if allowed to flower without being picked so that it self-sows. It prospers in a dry soil and can survive on as little as 12 inches of water a year. Clearly, mulching is not required.

You can start this plant from seed sown ⅛ inch deep in early spring or from division. For an earlier harvest, start seed inside and set out seedlings 10 to 20 inches apart. You should have good-sized plants by the following year.

Recent experiments show that germination is best with daily fluctuations in temperature between 50° to 77°F and 95° to 104°F. However, researchers found that cool-moist stratification at 35°F (moistening the seeds and incubating them at 35°F for four to eight weeks) also did the trick.

Harvesting and storage: Horehound does not produce flowers until the second year, but the plant can be cut for drying or use during the first year. Take only about a third of the plant's top growth in that first year. Marilyn Hampstead of Fox Hill Farm in Parma, Michigan, recommends cutting the second-year plants just when the flower buds form.

You can hang bunches of horehound to dry, but the plant loses its flavor quickly; so to retain that flavor, remove the leaves and chop them. As soon as they have dried, place them in tightly sealed jars.

GROWING CONDITIONS

- Plant hardiness zone 4.
- Soil pH 6.9.
- Deep, well-drained, sandy soil.
- Full sun.

HORSERADISH

Armoracia rusticana   **Cruciferae**

For centuries, this perennial herb was thought of as a medicine, not a condiment. The French called it *moutardes des allemands,* mustard of the Germans, and indeed, the Germans and the Danes were the only Europeans of the Middle Ages to use the root at the dinner table.

Simply put, horseradish assaults the tongue and nose so powerfully that its use and culinary reputation spread only very cautiously. Once horseradish caught on, it became a staple in many households, particularly in America. By 1861 "a stick of horseradish" had found its way into Isabella Beton's *Book of Household Management* as one condiment not to be forgotten for a picnic. Used as a condiment, it is most often allied with roast beef.

HISTORY

The origin of horseradish is obscure. It is believed to be native to eastern Europe and western Asia, from the Caspian Sea through Russia and Poland to Finland. In the 1500s it was known throughout England as "Red Cole," or *Raphanus rusticanus,* and it grew wild in several sections of the country. Although it was used as a medicine only, Elizabethan herbalist John Gerard noted that "the Horse Radish stamped with a little vinegar put thereto, is commonly used among the Germans for sauce to eate fish with and such like meates as we do mustarde."

Not until the 1600s did horseradish become an acceptable condiment in England—and even then, only for "country people and strong labouring men," according to John Parkinson, an herbalist of the time, who added that "it is too strong for tender and gentle stomaches."

USES

Medicinal: The fresh root of horseradish has been used by herbalists as an internal and external medicine for centuries.

The chief active constituent of horseradish root is allylisothiocyanate, or mustard oil. The root also contains an antibiotic substance and vitamin C; the vitamin remains in the root, without weakening, for as long as it is kept in cool storage.

Externally, chopped or grated fresh horseradish has been mixed with a little water and applied as a heat-producing and pain-relieving compress for neuralgia, stiffness, and pain in the back of the neck.

The classic internal use of horseradish is to treat kidney condi-

DESCRIPTION

This herbaceous perennial of the mustard family is often cultivated as an annual to yield the best-quality root. The long, white, tapering root produces a 2–3-ft.-high stem in the second year.

Flowers: Small, white, in terminal racemes from leaf axils; four petals, four sepals, six stamens; petals narrow at bases.

Leaves: Abundant; lower ones long stalked, oblong, lobed or toothed, to 1 ft. long; upper ones smaller, lanceolate, short stalked.

Fruit: Plant generally described as sterile but has produced viable seeds after first year; ovoid to ellipsoid capsules.

Height: 2–3 ft. in second year.

FLOWERING

Midsummer.

RANGE

Native to eastern Europe and western Asia; widely cultivated in North America.

tions in which excessive amounts of water are retained. Horseradish is believed to be one of the more potent herbal diuretics. A traditional preparation consists of 1 ounce of chopped fresh horseradish root, ½ ounce of bruised mustard seed, and 1 pint of boiling water. Let the horseradish and mustard seed soak in the water in a covered vessel for four hours, then strain, and take 3 tablespoons three times a day. Horseradish can also be eaten spread on some bland food like bread or fish, mixed with vinegar, or diluted in almost any way imaginable. One favorite way to take it when you want to flush fluids out of your system is to mix it with white wine.

A syrup made of grated horseradish, honey, and water is one of the standard remedies for hoarseness.

Culinary: Horseradish is best known for the sharp, mustardy taste of the condiment prepared from its root. The condiment is made by grating the fresh root and adding vinegar. Another commercial version adds mayonnaise. Horseradish is an excellent foil for fish, smoked fish, beef, sausages, poached chicken, egg salad, potato salad, salmon salad, and beets. It is especially important in Russian cooking, and in the Middle East it is enjoyed as a sliced and pickled snack. Tender horseradish leaves can be added—in moderation to tossed salads of mild-tasting greens.

Foliage

Seed Capsule

Flower

Flowering Stem

Roots

HORSERADISH—continued

- Help preserve the crisp texture of low-salt cucumber pickles by adding two 2-inch batons of fresh horseradish root to each quart jar.

- Add grated fresh horseradish to mayonnaise for spreading on sandwiches and dressing salads.

Available commercially: Fresh whole root; prepared root in jars, often colored with red beet juice; or dried ground root.

Substitute: Dry mustard for the dried root.

Storage note: Fresh root can become bitter if stored for more than three months.

Companion planting: Gardeners recommend planting horseradish near potatoes to make them more disease resistant. No scientific study supports this claim, but none refutes it either.

Other: For its stimulating and rubefacient properties, horseradish has been used to make an invigorating herbal bath.

CULTIVATION

Horseradish is most often propagated by root cuttings. These should be straight, young roots, about 8 or 9 inches long and ½ inch wide. Each cutting should have a bud or a growing point, although pieces will develop new buds (or crowns) in the ground. The roots grow out, not down, and should be placed 12 to 18 inches apart each way and 12 to 15 inches deep. When planting, carefully remove all side roots from each set, then drop the cutting into the hole, and fill in by trickling a fine soil around them.

You will have the best results with a rich soil that is high in organic matter. Since the root is the portion for which the plant is most commonly grown, you should take care to provide a deeply cultivated soil, free of stones that could cause gouges in your crop.

Prepare the soil as early in the spring as possible. In fact, most herb growers recommend you work the soil in January for a February planting. Till deeply and fertilize generously with well-rotted manure and compost. Water the bed well and frequently and keep the bed weed-free.

Horseradish is an herb that spreads rapidly, quickly taking over the area in which it is planted, and it is very difficult to eradicate. Be sure to give it plenty of room, perhaps in an isolated spot in the garden. Or, you could contain it by placing it in the ground in a bottomless 5-gallon container. When you want to remove it completely, take pains to discard every lingering piece of root, as even the tiniest rootlet will produce another plant.

Harvesting and storage: You can begin harvesting horseradish root in late October or early November and continue taking it as long as the weather permits. Some people use the ground as a storage place; others pack the root in dry sand and keep it in a cool, dark location such as the cellar. The root also will stay fresh for months in the crisper drawer of a refrigerator. Be sure to scrub the root thoroughly before you store it for the winter.

- Plant hardiness zone 5.
- Soil pH 6.8.
- Moist, rich, heavy soil.
- Full sun.

HORSETAIL

Equisetum spp. Equisetaceae

Horsetail is the only herb in this book that you can use to sand wood. This remarkable quality is explained by the plant's high silica content. Horsetails are among the oldest of all plants, having dominated the plant world some 200 million years ago. In those times they were giant fernlike trees. The 20 species surviving today are miniature versions of their ancestors. Most are pesky weeds.

USES

Campers can confirm horsetail's reputation as a pot scrubber, but its supposed medicinal virtues are not easily supported.

Medicinal: Medicinally, it has not been widely used. Horsetail enthusiasts recommend taking a fluid extract from the barren green stems in order to cure diarrhea, bladder ailments, water retention, and even tuberculosis. An external application is said to stop bleeding wounds and speed the healing of ulcers. Horsetail contains saponin and glycosides, which may account for its mild diuretic action, but otherwise, no scientific evidence supports claims for its medicinal use.

Toxicity: The plant is toxic if taken in large doses. Children have been poisoned by using the hollow stems as blowguns. Horsetails growing in highly fertilized areas may be particularly toxic because they tend to pick up nitrates and selenium from the soil.

Craft: The cut stems add an interesting and unique touch to herb and flower arrangements.

Dye: Horsetail yields a yellowish green color in wool mordanted with alum and a deeper green when an iron mordant is used.

Other: Its silica content explains horsetail's usefulness as an abrasive. *Equisetum hyemele* is the highest in silica and therefore the most prized for scouring. Collect the leafless stems, dry them briefly in the sun, and tie them in bundles. You can use the stems as scouring pads for shining metal or to give wood its final sanding.

CULTIVATION

Horsetails are seldom cultivated because once established they are nearly impossible to eradicate. Occasionally, certain species are suggested for erosion control along the sides of ponds. A safe way to enjoy the plant while keeping it under control is to plant it in buckets placed just below the surface of a pond.

Horsetails propagate easily by division. Pick the mature barren stalks in the fall when the silica content is highest.

DESCRIPTION

The species of horsetail most common in North America is *Equisetum arvense,* a ferny little perennial with a rhizome that looks like a string of beads. It appears in two different stages. The first stage is fertile, the second sterile.

Flowers: First stage, spike atop stalk. Second stage, none.

Leaves: First stage, sharp-toothed, ringed leaf sheaths, occur at 1-in. intervals along length of yellowish, bamboo-like stalk; joints snap apart easily. Second stage, whorls of needlelike leaves.

Fruit: Spores.

Height: First stage, 4–8-in. Second stage to 18 in.

E. hyemale, or giant scouring rush, grows up to 5 ft. high and has just one form. It has no leaves, just small scales around the joints of ridged stalk.

FLOWERING

April.

RANGE

Naturalized in all parts of the world except New Zealand and Australia.

HABITAT

Moist woods, roadsides, and waste places.

GROWING CONDITIONS

- Plant hardiness zone 2.
- Soil pH: acid–neutral.
- Humusy, moist soil.
- Full sun to partial shade.

HYSSOP

Hyssopus officinalis   **Labiatae**

Hyssop has a strongly medicinal odor that suggests its rightful place must be in the sickroom, and yet it was once used as a pot-herb—with a flavor that is not likely to appeal to the tamer palates of today.

Etymologists aren't certain whether or not this plant is the hyssop mentioned in the Bible ("Purge me with hyssop and I shall be clean; wash me, and I shall be whiter than snow"); that may have been a marjoram or one of a dozen other herbs. Its name comes from the Greek word *hussopos* and the Hebrew *esob,* meaning "holy herb."

DESCRIPTION

Hyssop is a pretty, compact perennial. As a member of the mint family, it is very aromatic, having a medicinal sort of smell. It has upright, many-branched, square stems. The leaves have a mintlike odor when crushed. (See photos on pages 445–46.)

Flowers: In whorls; form dense spikes at top of main stem; lower whorls interrupted; corolla tubular, two-lipped, to ½ in. long, blue or violet; four stamens; tubular, bell-shaped calyxes.

Leaves: Opposite, linear to lanceolate, hairless, 1–1½ in. long; sessile.

Fruit: Four nutlets.

Height: 2–3 ft.

FLOWERING

June through August.

RANGE

Native to Europe and Asia; naturalized throughout North America.

HISTORY

Because of its strong camphorlike odor, hyssop has a history of use as a cleansing herb. The earliest reference to the plant dates to the seventh century, when it was strewn about the floors of sickrooms and used to improve the smell of kitchens. The volatile oil from hyssop is a key ingredient in some liqueurs, including Benedictine and Chartreuse.

USES

Medicinal: Seventeenth-century British herbalist Nicholas Culpeper called hyssop "a most violent purgative" and warned against taking it unless under the care of "the alchymist." During the seventeenth and eighteenth centuries, tinctures and teas of the flowers and leaves were used to reduce perspiration and to cure jaundice and dropsy. Hyssop tea has also been recommended for bronchitis and sore throats. According to Maude Grieve, writing in *A Modern Herbal,* it will "improve the tone of a feeble stomach."

A poultice of fresh ground leaves is said to promote the healing of wounds and bruises. It will supposedly clear a black eye. One tradition says that hyssop cleanses wounds received from rusty metal because penicillin grows on the plant's leaves. But modern herbalists attribute any germ-killing power it might have to the volatile oils.

Although hyssop may not be as effective as its advocates claim, it certainly is a safe herb in any form. You can make a mildly expectorant tea from the flowers, sweetening it to taste.

Culinary: Hyssop's minty leaves and flowers are used to flavor green salads, chicken soup, liqueurs, fruit soups, fruit salads, lamb stew, and poultry stuffing with sage. The leaves and flowers can be dried for use in teas.

Available commercially: Dried as tea.

Substitute: Costmary or mint.

Aromatic: Oil of hyssop occasionally turns up in perfumes. A

CHEF TIP

For a sauce to serve with cheese omelets or on rice, mince ¼ cup of fresh hyssop and add to 4 cups of tomato sauce.

small amount might be added to a heavily scented potpourri, along with thyme.

Ornamental: Like most of the mints, hyssop is quite easy to grow and is rarely bothered by pests or disease. It is such a pretty plant that it deserves a prominent place in every herb garden. The Elizabethans used it to edge knot gardens as they did germander. Clip it frequently, bringing it down to within 6 inches of the ground, so that growth will be full and lush. Feed plants with fish emulsion to help them green up after these cuttings.

In less formal border plantings, hyssop combines nicely with the more feathery herbs such as dill and anise. It's a lovely interplant for roses, particularly those with white or pink flowers.

Cosmetic: According to modern herbalist Jeanne Rose, an herbal bath made with hyssop is soothing and diaphoretic. She recommends mixing it with thyme, mint, and rosemary for best results. In addition, a steaming herbal facial made from hyssop cleanses the skin. (See the entry Bathing with Herbs for more information.)

Companion planting: Gardeners claim that hyssop repels flea beetles and other pests and lures away cabbage moths, but research doesn't confirm this. Still hyssop is less competitive than some other members of the mint family, and it is a good choice for you to try for interplanting in both the flower bed and the vegetable patch, especially near cabbage and grapes.

Other: Hyssop is a bee plant extraordinaire. Butterflies and hummingbirds are also attracted to its flowers. Beekeepers once rubbed their hives with hyssop, as well as juniper, fennel, and thyme, in order to encourage the bees to stay put. At the very least, it is worth planting near the hive to add flavor to the honey.

CULTIVATION

You can start this plant by seeds, cuttings, or division. Choose a sunny spot where the soil is well drained, or even dry. In early spring, sow seeds ¼ inch deep in rows about 1 foot apart. In early summer, thin the seedlings to stand 1 foot apart within the rows. You can propagate by cuttings or division in the spring or fall.

You'll need to prune the plants occasionally and remove the old flower heads, but hyssop plants require relatively little maintenance. After four or five years, the plants may need to be replaced.

Harvesting and storage: For medicinal use cut the stems just before the flowers begin to open. Hang bunches upside down in a warm, dark place. Dried leaves, green stems, and flowers may be chopped and stored in tightly covered glass containers or tins. Harvest only the green plant matter, because the tough woody parts have much less of the characteristic oil.

GROWING CONDITIONS

- Plant hardiness zones 4–5.
- Soil pH 6.7.
- Light, well-drained soil.
- Full sun to partial shade.

INDIGO

Indigofera tinctoria, I. suffruticosa   Leguminosae

DESCRIPTION

Indigos are mainly tropical and subtropical perennial shrubs with an erect stem. The French and Guatemalan indigos differ in the size and shape of their leaflets and pods. (See photos on pages 169–70.)

Flowers: Pealike; purple, pink, or white; in spikes or racemes that emerge from leaf axils; 10 stamens.

Leaves: Alternate, toothless, pinnate, with a terminal leaflet and side leaflets; fine hairs on surface.

Fruit: Usually small, cylindrical pods; some varieties have angled pods.

Height: 3–5 ft.

FLOWERING

Late summer.

RANGE

Indigofera tinctoria requires 60°–80°F temperatures and abundant moisture. Therefore, it is largely confined to the tropics. It grows in India and other parts of tropical Asia, including Java. *I. suffruticosa* (syn. *I. anil*) comes from the West Indies and has, to some extent, become naturalized in Hawaii and the southern United States.

GROWING CONDITIONS

- Well-drained, loamy soil.
- Full sun.

How are the mighty fallen! In another age, explorations were launched, battles fought, alliances formed, and fortunes made and lost, all for a now virtually forgotten herb, indigo.

And why? Because indigo was the sole source of a much-favored blue dye. For many centuries indigo was considered the most important dyestuff in the world, and it brought great prices in trade with the Orient. Though the development of the aniline dye destroyed its commercial value, indigo is not forgotten.

USES

The commercially important indigos were *Indigofera tinctoria*, known as French indigo, and *I. suffruticosa*, or Guatemalan indigo. The entire genus embraces about 700 species, including ornamentals grown in the United States.

Medicinal: *I. patens,* a related indigo species, is made into a root powder used in South Africa to cure toothaches. Many varieties of indigo have been used as emetics, and the Chinese used *I. tinctoria* to cleanse the liver, detoxify the blood, reduce inflammation, reduce pain, and diminish fever. None of these cures has been scientifically documented.

Toxicity: Some species of indigo, notably *I. endecaphylla,* are poisonous, so self-medication with any variety is not wise.

Dye: The juice of indigo is yellow, not blue. The blue hue develops as the juice ferments.

In making indigo dye, leaves are combined in vats with caustic soda or sodium hydrosulfate. A bitter, yellow agent in the plant called indocan prompts the juice to ferment. A paste is exuded in the process, and this is collected, made into cakes, and ground. The blue color develops as the powder is exposed to air.

It is believed that indocan is converted to blue indigotin by enzyme reaction. It becomes a colorfast dye and can be mixed with other plant dyes to produce a wide range of colors.

CULTIVATION

If you live in the Deep South, or in Hawaii, you may succeed in growing indigo, but the varieties that produce dye have little ornamental value. Pick a sunny location with well-drained soil. Root the shrub from suckers in spring or early fall, or from cuttings in summer. Cuttings should be taken with a segment of branch wood. Propagate in a greenhouse, if possible, or in a cold frame. If seeds must be used to start the plants, soak them in almost boiling water overnight. Blooms appear on the current season's shoots, so prune severely.

JIMSONWEED

Datura Stramonium   **Solanaceae**

At one time a staple of witchcraft, this medicinal herb again received wide attention in the 1960s for its reputation as a hallucinogen. The plant does have mind-altering powers, but it extracts a heavy toll on the person using it.

Jimsonweed is poisonous, and it should not be ingested or smoked. Even brushing against it may irritate the skin. Numbing potions of one *Datura* were given to prepare victims for sacrificial murders. So, although its large trumpetlike flowers are showy, this plant is not suited for areas frequented by children. The seeds are the most poisonous part, but the leaves are also potentially lethal. Fortunately, its fetid aroma does not inspire the curious to take a nibble. Adults have rarely been fatally poisoned by accidentally ingesting jimsonweed.

Other names for the plant reflect either its looks or its part in Indian ritual: thorn apple, mad apple, sacred datura, locoweed, Indian apple, and devil's trumpet.

HISTORY

According to legend, the most common name is a corruption of "Jamestown weed." In 1676, a detachment of British troops was sent to Jamestown, Virginia, to quell an uprising. On the way there, the soldiers ate some shoots of the weed and, reportedly, went both AWOL and berserk for 11 full days, saving the Jamestown colonists from possible punishment.

These British soldiers were not the first military group to be led astray by jimsonweed. Legend has it that soldiers of Mark Anthony fell victim to it some 17 centuries earlier, with roughly the same results.

The priests at Delphi were said to be inspired by jimsonweed smoke when delivering their oracles. The ancient Nubians used the weed for chest complaints. In India, where it is a native, thugs used the weed to incapacitate intended victims. It was brought from India to Europe in the first century by jimson-smoking gypsies. Later, the plant was associated with witchcraft and spell casting, partly, it is said, because it caused sensations of flying when inhaled.

In the American Southwest, jimsonweed was part of Indian rituals, but its use was always controlled by the shaman or medicine man. It was used by South American Indians as an anesthetic for setting bones, as part of puberty rites, and as an aphrodisiac for women. In some cultures where the death of a potentate demanded the sacrifice of slaves and wives, the weed was given to the victims to ease their death.

VERY TOXIC

DESCRIPTION

Jimsonweed is a rank, foul-smelling annual or short-lived perennial. Its rubbery stem holds many yellow-green branches. Its root is white and fibrous.

Flowers: Rise from flower stalks at leaf axils; solitary, up to 6 in. long, trumpet-shaped (like enormous, showy morning glories); light blue or white.

Leaves: Alternate, oval-to-triangular, irregularly toothed edges; dark green above, lighter below; 5–6 in. long; strong, sweet odor when bruised.

Fruit: Four-valved capsule; large, fleshy, spiny, and rounded; about the size of a golf ball; contains many black seeds; capsule opens at the top.

Height: 3–6 ft.

FLOWERING

May through August.

RANGE

Native to Asia; naturalized in North and South America and Europe.

HABITAT

Isolated stands in a protected place such as a dry wash, irrigation ditch, or roadside.

JIMSONWEED—continued

USES

This most pharmacologically valuable of the *Daturas* is widely grown commercially for use in medicines. The active principles are extracted and prescribed in carefully controlled doses for a variety of ailments.

The weed has been used to check secretions, stimulate circulation, stimulate breathing during asthma attacks, cure dyspepsia, and overcome muscle spasms. Strangely enough, it was thought to allay symptoms of insanity, epilepsy, and hysteria.

External applications have been used for hemorrhoids, skin eruptions, wounds, and painful joints and muscles. But even external applications can be toxic.

Never take jimsonweed internally in any form. It is not only hallucinogenic but also poisonous. A very small amount can be fatal to a child. In recent years poisonings have been reported in adolescents with some regularity. One case involved six New Jersey boys who had been drinking alcohol. Soon after eating jimsonweed seed, they became ill with symptoms including hallucinations, dry mouth, thirst, blurred vision, flushed skin, inability to urinate, and slurred speech. Certain symptoms lasted several days, while the blurred vision persisted for more than a week.

Other symptoms of jimsonweed poisoning include increased heart rate and blood pressure, heartbeat abnormalities, increased body temperature, headache, dilated pupils, convulsions, and coma. Skin contact may produce rashes.

Jimsonweed contains atropine, hyoscyamine, and a trace of scopolamine, also called hyoscine; all are toxic. The drugs influence the work of transmitters in the brain, affecting the heart, brain, involuntary muscles, and exocrine glands. The weed paralyzes a pulmonary nerve and so relieves the spasms of bronchial asthma when smoked as a cigarette or inhaled as vapor, but it should not be used without medical supervision.

CULTIVATION

Because of the danger associated with ingesting parts of the plant, do not cultivate it near where children may play. For supervised collections in flower beds, it can easily be grown from seed like an annual, or it can be transplanted from an indoor start after the danger of frost is over. Plant jimsonweed in a sunny location at the back of a border. Rich, deep soil is best. Space widely for this large plant, and pick the flowers to keep the blooming season going; otherwise, seedpods will form.

JUNIPER

Juniperus communis   **Cupressaceae**

Why is a suburban yard like a martini? Because both contain juniper. This highly aromatic plant graces the landscape and yields a medicinal oil that has long been used in cure-alls and gin. Common juniper is one of over 50 species in this genus.

HISTORY

Many know juniper chiefly as the source of gin's flavoring. Indeed, the name gin is derived from the Dutch *jenever,* which means "juniper." The Dutch invented this juniper-flavored drink; eighteenth- century Englishmen took to it enthusiastically; and today gin is one of the most popular alcoholic beverages of the Western world.

Juniper's uses haven't been restricted to the gin industry. All parts of the plant have been employed in folk medicine, cooking, and spell casting. The plant's pungent aroma has long recommended it for driving away evil spirits and disease. Legend has it that juniper planted beside the front door will keep out witches; the only way for a witch to get past the plant was by correctly counting its needles.

American Indians also believed in juniper's cleansing and healing powers and used it to keep away infection, relieve arthritis, and cure various wounds and illnesses.

USES

Medicinal: Rheumatism, arthritis, bruises, ulcers, and wounds are said to be relieved by juniper poultices and rubs. Adding a handful of leaves to warm bathwater is said to soothe aching muscles. For poultices berries can be simmered in olive oil or simply mashed and applied to the sore. American Indians simply tied steaming bundles of the boughs to sore limbs. Juniper tincture has been used externally on painful swellings, bruises, and sores.

The primary medicinal use of juniper over the years has been as a diuretic. The plant does work but through an irritating action, and most herbalists advise pregnant women and people with kidney ailments to avoid juniper's use. Pharmacognosists, on the other hand, suggest that everyone avoid juniper because there are other, more effective herbal diuretics that don't have its irritating qualities.

The main active principle in juniper is its volatile oil, found not only in the berries but in the leaves and wood as well. A constituent of the oil, terpinen-4-ol, works on the kidneys and is responsible for the plant's action as a diuretic and potential kidney irritant. The oil is most abundant in the ripe, freshly picked berries. As the fruit dries, its oil content diminishes dramatically.

UNSAFE

DESCRIPTION

The junipers most often cultivated are dwarf, spreading evergreens, although there are some tall-growing varieties. The size, color, and shape vary drastically both with variety and with growing conditions. For the most part, the junipers are low growing with tangled, spreading branches covered with a thin, reddish brown bark. Juice may seep out of the tree and form a sticky gum on the bark.

Flowers: Male and female flowers on separate plants; male flowers yellow, in whorls; female flowers green.

Leaves: Needle-shaped, ½–3/4 in. long, concave, sharply pointed; distinguished by white band above; occur in whorls of three along branches; almost at right angles from branches.

Fruit: Berries ¼–⅓ in. across; green ripening to bluish or purple in second year; usually covered with white wax; each contains two or three angular seeds.

Height: 2–6 ft., sometimes reaching 25–30 ft.

FLOWERING

April through June.

RANGE

Native to Europe; naturalized in North America.

JUNIPER—continued

Toxicity: Juniper should not be used by pregnant women or those with kidney problems. Repeated use can cause kidney damage, as well as convulsions and personality changes.

Culinary: Juniper has a place in the kitchen other than in the gin bottle. The berries are said to stimulate the appetite, and for this reason they can be added sparingly to sauerkraut, pâtés, salads, and hors d'oeuvres. Since their flavor is quite strong, they must be used with discretion.

Crushed or bruised juniper berries are a key ingredient of many wild game dishes. Three or four berries can be added to the marinade for venison, hare, or goose. To spice up other stews, sauces, and marinades, try substituting four juniper berries for each bay leaf. The berries combine well with parsley, fennel, bay, and garlic. Try tossing a few branches on the outdoor grill; the aromatic oils will give the grilled meat a subtle, smoky flavor.

Ornamental: With so many varieties available, it is easy to find a common juniper suited to almost any landscape. Tall, narrow junipers such as *hibernica* and variegated ones such as *aureo-variegata* make fine accent species. *Depressa* is a very low, flat, broad juniper that does nicely in rocky areas or bordering foundation plantings.

CULTIVATION

If you are growing juniper for its berries, be sure to plant both male and female shrubs, or the female won't fruit.

Junipers like sandy or light, loamy soil in sunny locations. The more open the exposure, the stronger the plant's aroma seems to be. Nurseries usually propagate them from seed sown in a cold frame in the spring or fall. Germination takes two or even three years. Cultivars are best propagated from cuttings taken in late summer. They take root easily if constantly misted or placed in the greenhouse.

Transplant seedlings almost any time of year, preferably in early spring or fall. Water frequently until they are well established. Prune the plants in early spring while they are still dormant. Junipers are tough plants and require little care. In fact, common juniper has become a pesky weed, invading the open fields in much of its habitat.

Harvesting and storage: The leaves and branches may be picked any time. Wear gloves because the leaves are prickly. The berries are not ready for eating or medicine making until fall. The plants will have immature (green) and ripe (blue) berries simultaneously, but harvest only the ripe ones. Spread them on a screen to dry in the sun. When dry, their bluish glow will have turned to a dull black.

Juniperus communis
subsp. *hibernica*

Juniperus communis var. *depressa*

GROWING CONDITIONS

- Hardy in all zones.
- Sandy or light, loamy soil.
- Full sun.

LADY'S BEDSTRAW

Galium verum   **Rubiaceae**

A woman was done in each night by her commute from New York City to her home in New Jersey—but she was too wound up to fall asleep easily. Her mother found a remedy at Cyrus Hyde's Well-Sweep Herb Farm—lady's bedstraw, an herb with a reputation as a soporific. The harried commuter was able to nod off on a pillow stuffed with bedstraw. According to Hyde, the heat of a person's head releases soothing, honeylike vapors from the stuffing.

Mary is said to have prepared the Christ child's bed with this herb. Thereafter, it was known as Our Lady's bedstraw, and the formerly white flowerheads turned their present golden hue. The pleasant-smelling stems and leaves have been a traditional mattress stuffing, but people have found other uses for this herb as well.

USES

If your feet ache and swell after standing or walking all day, try a footbath made by steeping the herb in hot water. If your head is abuzz and you can't sleep, try a bedstraw pillow. Most gardeners, however, grow bedstraw as an ornamental or dye plant.

Ornamental: Lady's bedstraw contributes a light, delicate look to the landscape. It is grown by some gardeners as a groundcover since it spreads rapidly on its own. The plant has become naturalized, and it therefore is appropriate for native plant gardens and rock gardens. Airy sprays of bedstraw help to offset the heavy look of large blooms in bouquets of fresh flowers.

Dye: As you might guess from looking at bedstraw's yellow flowers, it produces a dull yellow color in wool mordanted with alum. The roots, however, are used more often for the beautiful shades of red they yield.

Boil either fresh or dried roots for about two hours to extract the dye. An alum mordant will give red; a chrome mordant produces a purplish red; mix alum and chrome for a light orange-red; and with an iron mordant expect a plum dye. One disadvantage to preparing dye from lady's bedstraw is that you must collect lots of the thin roots—4 to 6 ounces per gallon of water.

CULTIVATION

Propagate lady's bedstraw by seed or root division in the spring. Thereafter, it will spread on its own. It grows well in full sun or part-day shade and is not too particular about soil, although it prefers a light, deep, rich, well-drained earth.

DESCRIPTION

Lady's bedstraw is a perennial herb with an erect, nearly square, somewhat woody stem that is slightly branched.

Flowers: Small, bright yellow; in crowded panicles; honey scented.

Leaves: Narrow, linear, ½–1 in. long, bristle tipped; white and minutely hairy on underside; grow in rings of six around stem.

Fruit: Two-lobed, two-seeded, sometimes bristly.

Height: 3 ft.

FLOWERING

July and August.

RANGE

Southern Canada, the northern and eastern United States, most of western Europe, and the coastal areas of Great Britain.

HABITAT

Roadsides, moist thickets, and stream banks.

GROWING CONDITIONS

- Hardy.
- Deep, light, rich, well-drained soil.
- Full sun to light shade.

349

LAVENDER

Lavandula angustifolia   Labiatae

The smell of lavender has the power to conjure memories of other times and other places. You may have first encountered it as a sachet, a soap, or as the gray-green plant itself. We tend to think of lavender as a somewhat old-fashioned, even fusty herb; but it has a clean, spare fragrance that could be called classic. In fact, its name derives from the Latin verb "to wash," and both the Romans and Greeks scented their soaps and bathwater with the herb.

For some, it is the quintessential English garden herb; others think of the "lavender Alps" of southern France, where otherwise featureless hills are washed with a special color and a palpable scent.

Lavender also has modest abilities as a medicinal herb, and it has been used to relieve headaches and revive those with "nervous languor."

HISTORY

In the Middle Ages, lavender was thought to be an herb of love, but it worked both ways: Although it was considered an aphrodisiac, a sprinkle of lavender water on the head would keep the wearer chaste. Traditionally, the herb's fragrance has been exploited in sachets, to protect linens from moths, and to freshen sickrooms. It has also been used to soothe troubled minds and bodies as a medicine for hysteria, nervous palpitations, hoarseness, palsy, toothaches, sore joints, apoplexy, and colic. Herbalists claim that it has powers as a carminative, antispasmodic, and stimulant. It has been used as an ingredient of smelling salts. Up until World War I, lavender was used as a disinfectant for wounds.

Superstition persisted that the asp made his nest in lavender bushes. This superstition was useful to herb dealers because it drove up the price of the plant.

You probably don't think of this herb as a medicinal aid. But in some parts of Europe, it used to quiet both coughs and rumbling digestive systems.

USES

Today, the largest percentage of the blooms goes into perfumery and perfumed products. For this, *Lavandula angustifolia* (English lavender) is particularly prized, but either *L. latifolia* (spike lavender) or their many crosses is used to extend the quantity of the oil in lower-priced products.

Medicinal: The oil varies in quality, depending on when the plants are harvested. The oil from early flowers is pale and contains more valuable esthers than the darker oil of later flowers.

DESCRIPTION

In general, lavender is a bushy, branching shrub, although there are a few subshrubs in the species. The stems of mature plants often become a dense, woody tangle. (See photos on pages 32, 236, 445, and 512.)

Flowers: Small, lavender purple, five-lobed corolla; five-toothed calyx; four stamens; whorls of 6 to 10 flowers form terminal spikes on 6–8-in.-long stalks.

Leaves: Opposite, lanceolate, smooth edged, somewhat hairy, silvery gray, to 2 in. long.

Fruit: Four shiny, dark gray-brown nutlets.

Height: To 3 ft.

FLOWERING

June and July.

RANGE

Native to the Mediterranean region; naturalized in the southern United States; widely cultivated throughout the world.

CHEF TIP

When making apple jelly or raspberry jam, add a sprig of lavender to each jar.

Although there has been little scientific work devoted to lavender, it appears that the oil may have spasmolytic, antiseptic, and carminative powers. The leaves do repel insects.

Lavender is safe but should be used in moderation. One teaspoon of flowers to a pint of water is safe for infusions to be used as a mild sedative. For eczema and psoriasis, add no more than 2 drops of the yellow-colored oil to a cup of a bland oil. A few drops of this mixture in a hot bath is said to relieve neuralgia pain or sore feet. Warm lavender tea can be applied as a compress for the relief of chest congestion. Bruises and bites are treated with lavender compresses in France and Spain.

Medicinal cordials have been made by combining lavender oil, rosemary oil, cinnamon bark, nutmeg, and sandalwood with wine, letting the ingredients steep for seven days. According to British herbalist Maude Grieve, the dose is a teaspoon after an "indigestible" meal, followed by a second dose a half-hour later, "if needed."

Lavender is an ingredient of aromatic spirits of ammonia, used to prevent or relieve fainting spells, and indispensable to Victorian melodrama.

In China, lavender is used in a cure-all medicinal oil called White Flower Oil.

Culinary: Lavender's perfumy flowers and leaves are used in flavored vinegars, jellies, and sparingly in salads.

Available commercially: Dried flowers or leaves.

Aromatic: English lavender's aroma is more complex and delicate than that of French lavender—according to Grieve. She could not hold back her nationalist pride and says in a footnote in *A Modern Herbal,* "The Editor has often come across fields of French lavender in bloom and the scent has been poor compared with English Lavender grown under the worst conditions." French lavender is said to have the suggestion of balsam and rosemary, and it is the variety known to the ancients. Sachets full of dried lavender are still popular for perfuming drawers and closets containing linen and underclothes. Potpourris frequently include the herb. You can simply place oil of lavender on a wad of cotton and hang it to freshen a room and keep moths away. Pillows can be stuffed with lavender. Lavender soaps abound, and you can complement them with lavender shaving creams, toilet water, cologne, and perfume. These are usually made from the very best lavender, especially the English variety.

Cosmetic: Added to the bath or used to make facials, lavender stimulates and cleanses the skin (see the entry Bathing with Herbs). Lavender vinegar is reported to be good for oily skin.

LAVENDER SPECIES

There are at least 28 species in the genus *Lavandula,* but their taxonomy has been snarled and confusing even to horticulturists. What is commonly known as English lavender (and variously called *L. officinalis, L. vera, L. delphinensis,* and *L. Spica*) is in fact most usually *L. angustifolia.* Botanically, there is no such thing as English lavender.

The next most common lavender for commercial use is usually called spike lavender (*L. latifolia*), also known as Spanish lavender or Portuguese lavender.

These two lavenders have crossed to create a huge number of cultivars. Some of the crosses are "mule hybrids"; that is, they are sterile. Many were cultivated in the eighteenth and nineteenth centuries and then allowed to disappear.

The most common cross of *L. angustifolia* and *L. latifolia* is *L. ✕intermedia,* a hybrid sometimes called Lavandin; next to its more oil-stingy parent, *L. angustifolia,* it is the lavender most used in the perfume industry. Another cross, *L. hybrida* var. *Reverchon,* is produced in France and is much in demand for oil used in soap because it contains 15 to 30 percent esthers.

LAVENDER—continued

LAVENDER WANDS

A favorite use for lavender is as an aromatic wand to freshen closets and drawers. A variety that has 18- to 24-inch-long stems is best for this.

Start with 13 long, freshly picked stems. Tie the blooms together with string or florist's wire. Hold the blossoms with the stems pointing up in the air, then bend them down one by one to form an umbrella. Take a ¼-inch-wide satin ribbon at least 3 yards long. Weave the ribbon, satin-side up, in and out of the stems like a basket. The first two rows are the most difficult to do since the stems tend to flop, cross, and slip around.

After weaving four or five rows, bend the stems together to form a handle under the blossoms. Take a toothpick or crochet hook and smooth and tighten the ribbon, starting at the top and working down. Continue to weave the ribbon in and out of the stems until the entire length of the flowers is covered. When you have about 5 inches of woven material, wind the ribbon around the stems. Secure with a pin.

Store in a warm, well-ventilated place to dry for about two weeks. After the wand is dry, tighten the ribbon again and sew it with a few stitches of matching thread.

Ornamental: For interesting potted plants, consider the special qualities of *L. dentata* (with its fernlike leaf); *L. Stoechas* (purple bracts); *L. angustifolia* 'Alba' (white flowers); *L. angustifolia* 'Nana' (dwarfed and compact); *L. angustifolia* 'Triphylla' (small leaflets at the base of the flowers); *L. angustifolia* subsp. *angustifolia* (small stalks and early blooming habit); and *L. angustifolia* 'Rosea' (pink flowers). When ordering plants, note that the species epithets *angustifolia, officinalis, delphinensis, Spica,* and *vera* are used interchangeably.

Lavender makes a handsome edging for walks or ponds and adds to rock gardens. In warmer latitudes entire roadsides are blanketed with it for beautification and soil stabilization.

Craft: Lavender can be used in wreaths, dried flower arrangements, sprays, and other room decorations.

Other: Lavender oil has found a great range of uses over the centuries, including embalming corpses, curing animals of lice, taming lions and tigers, and repelling mosquitoes. Dried lavender has been a flavoring for snuff. Spike lavender, which is a coarser plant, yields an oil that has been used in lacquers and varnishes, especially those used on porcelain. It dilutes the more delicate colors used in china painting. Oil from *L. latifolia* is also used as an adulterant of higher-quality lavender oil.

CULTIVATION

Because of the difficulty involved in getting many of its strains to breed true and also because of its long germination time, lavender is seldom started from seed. Instead, cuttings, measuring 2 to 3 inches long, are taken in the summer from the side shoots. The cuttings are from the growth of one season and may include some older wood at the base. To take a cutting, grasp a healthy shoot and pull it downward so that a piece of the older wood comes along with it. Place the cuttings 3 to 4 inches apart in moist, sandy soil in a shaded cold frame or in pots with lath protection. When they are one year old, set the plants 4 to 6 feet apart (spacing will depend on the eventual size desired) in dry, light, and stony or gravelly soil that is not subject to frost. During the first year the plants should be clipped to keep them from flowering and to encourage branching into lateral shoots. Vigorous plants can grow as bushy as 5 feet in diameter. To encourage lavender to spread over a wide area, see that it has enough lime and add root cuttings to prepared soil.

Protect the plants from both summer and winter winds because spikes of flowers are easily broken in storms.

Full pickings of lavender are possible in the second through the fifth year. After that, some growers replace the plants, carefully rotating to new soil, but others insist that plants will do well in the same place for 30 years. Fungus diseases and caterpillars sometimes attack lavenders. Routine care is minimal, but winter protection must be given where temperatures are low. Hardiest are English and spike lavender. If you are not using the flowers, cut the spent blossoms to keep your plants flourishing.

Container gardening: Lavender can be trained into an attractive potted plant, taking either a symmetrical or somewhat tortured, bonsai form. Even the less hardy lavenders make trouble-free ornamentals for greenhouses and sunny windows. Set them in coarse, porous soil; water them infrequently; and keep the winter night temperature range between 40° and 50°F, with daytime temperatures only 5 to 10 degrees higher. In summer, set the pots out in the sun.

Harvesting and making oil: An acre of lavender in a good year yields 15 to 20 pounds of oil. Harvesting is done rapidly on a dry, still August day before the high sun can carry off some of the fragrance. Flowers should be in early blossom, short of maximum bloom. The flower spikes are cut by machine or with a hand-held hook to 6 inches below the spike. The spikes are immediately laid out to dry on mats and covered to prevent sun scorch. That evening, the mats are rolled up and taken to a still. To make a better-quality oil, the flowers are first stripped from the stalk.

The flowers are placed in a vat over boiling water, and the oil that is given off is directed through a coil to condense. The best oil is produced from lavender harvested after a hot, dry season with much sun. Temperature is crucial from May to August, when the weather should be both hot and dry. The distilled oil is aged for several months before being sold.

Prune and shape the bushes either after the flowering and harvest are over or in early spring.

Harvesting and storage: Well-dried flowers will remain aromatic for a long time. For dry storage harvest the flowers either when they first open or when they are full. Hang them in bunches or set them on screens in a shaded, airy place with a high temperature. You can tie them in bunches and suspend them from rafters in an attic or shed.

Lavender vinegar, intended for the dressing table and not a cruet, is made by adding rose petals, lavender flowers, and jasmine flowers to distilled vinegar. It stores well in airtight bottles.

Lavender oil and spirits (a 5 percent solution of the oil in alcohol) store well in tight containers.

GROWING CONDITIONS

- Plant hardiness zones 5–8.
- Soil pH 7.1.
- Light, well-drained soil.
- Full sun.

LAVENDER COTTON

Santolina Chamaecyparissus   **Compositae**

Although it is a member of the daisy family, lavender cotton, with its grayish foliage and strong aromatic scent, will remind you of lavender. Like its namesake, it can be used in potpourris and sachets, in dried herb arrangements, and as an ornamental in the garden. It is known also by its genus name, santolina.

In Mediterranean regions where lavender cotton is native, the herb was first used medicinally for its astringent properties and as a vermifuge. But as its use spread north to England, it was as an ornamental. Elizabethan gardeners found they could prune lavender cotton into lovely low hedges, and they created the twists and turns of their knot gardens with it.

DESCRIPTION

Lavender cotton is a grayish green, compact, much-branched perennial evergreen, whose many small leaves give the plant a coral-like appearance. (See photo on page 512.)

Flowers: Bright yellow, tiny, tubular; in round, buttonlike heads, ½–¾ in. in diameter, at top of stalk.

Leaves: Alternate, pinnate, silvery gray-green; 1–1½ in. long, ⅛ in. wide; grow crowded on stem.

Fruit: Brown achenes.

Height: To 2 ft.

FLOWERING

June and July.

RANGE

Native to the southern Mediterranean region; widely cultivated.

USES

The medicinal use of lavender cotton has passed, but its ornamental use has flourished.

Aromatic: Lavender cotton is not everyone's idea of an aromatic herb. But many people *do* enjoy the musky fragrance of lavender cotton and add it to potpourris and sachets.

Ornamental: You can enjoy the fragrance of lavender cotton in your garden, too, in knot gardens or as a border. Its compact form and the close growth of the leaves give it the right density for small hedges. The foliage provides a feathery texture and a silvery gray-green color. If you prefer a less formal look, add it to any flower bed for its texture and bright yellow flowers.

Craft: The foliage and flowers of lavender cotton dry well and can be used in herb wreaths, dried arrangements, or other herb crafts.

Dye: Lavender cotton yields golds and yellows to wool mordanted with chrome and alum.

CULTIVATION

Lavender cotton can be propagated from seed, layering, division, or cuttings taken in the spring. A sunny location with light, dry soil is the best environment for this herb. Lavender cotton may perish in a heavy, wet soil, especially over a cold winter. It prefers limy soil but also will succeed in a slightly acidic garden.

Harvesting and storage: To use the flowers or leafy branches in dried herb crafts, harvest when the flowers are in full bloom, cutting the branches 6 inches from the ground. Do not separate the flowering stem from the branches while drying. For foliage, wait until late summer and then trim the top 8 to 10 inches of the branches.

GROWING CONDITIONS

- Plant hardiness zones 6–8.
- Soil pH: alkaline to neutral.
- Poor, light, well-drained soil.
- Full sun.

354

LEMON BALM

Melissa officinalis   Labiatae

Brush this herb's leaves and your fingers will smell of lemon with a hint of mint, a fragrance that has endeared lemon balm to people for at least 2,000 years. But brush carefully—honeybees swarm over the plant; you may end up with a lemon-scented sting.

HISTORY

This rather floppy, coarse-leaved plant has a history with an elegance you would expect of a more refined-looking ornamental.

Lemon balm, often referred to simply as balm, may be one of the plants mentioned in Homer's *Odyssey* (trying to match ancient and modern botanical names would make a good parlor game for classicists). The Roman scholar Pliny noted that bees preferred lemon balm to other plants. The Greek physician Dioscorides put the plant on bites, both scorpion and dog, and then would drop some more lemon balm into wine for the patient to drink. His pages may have been so full of bite remedies because none of them worked terribly well and herbalists kept experimenting. But in the days before antivenom and rabies shots, a comforting drink was about the best anyone could offer.

The Greeks and Romans seem to have been fond enough of the plant, but its real fans were the Arabs. They held that lemon balm was good for heart disorders, as well as for lifting the spirits.

Lemon balm helped colonize the United States, no doubt lifting spirits dragged down by the strange climate, isolation, and distance from home. It was both medicine and flavoring. Old Williamsburg recipes called for it, and Thomas Jefferson grew it at Monticello.

Lemon balm continued to be used as a medicine well into the nineteenth century. In the American edition of Pereiara's *Materia Medica,* balm tea is noted for inducing sweating in fevers and regulating menstruation. However, the entry shows the signs of an herbal remedy on its way out: "The effects of balm are similar to, though milder than, those of the labiate [mint family] plants already described. The mildness of its operation arises from the small portion of volatile oil which the plant contains."

USES

It may be homely, but it sure is useful. That's lemon balm.

Medicinal: Lemon balm was used like a mild form of Valium in past centuries. As the British herbalist Nicholas Culpeper put it in the mid-seventeenth century, lemon balm " . . . causeth the mind and heart to become merry, . . . and driveth away all troublesome cares and thoughts out of the mind, arising from melancholy and black choler . . . ." We could attribute this to the pleasant lemony fragrance,

DESCRIPTION

This loosely branched, upright perennial attracts attention through its scent rather than its appearance. A member of the mint family, lemon balm has the characteristic square stems. (See photo on page 446.)

Flowers: In clusters at leaf axils; tubular, two-lipped, white or yellowish, ½ in. long; four stamens.

Leaves: Opposite, broad, ovate, toothed; 1–3 in. long; lemon scented.

Fruit: Smooth nutlets.

Height: 2 ft.

FLOWERING

July through September.

RANGE

Lemon balm is native to southern Europe and North Africa and now grows wild and is cultivated throughout much of the world.

which is cheery enough by itself. But a study shows that the herb has a sedative effect on the central nervous systems of lab mice.

The oil of lemon balm also seems to inhibit bacteria and viruses. So, could it have done something to reduce the chance of infection when Dioscorides applied it to mad dog bites and scorpion stings? Or when Culpeper used it to cleanse "foul sores"?

Culinary: Lemon balm's character can be described as lightly lemon with a suggestion of mint. The leaves are best used fresh in cooking, but the leaves and stems can be dried and used for tea. The leaves make a mild, lemony tea. For a beverage with more personality, add it and other mints to a base of black tea.

Toss whole or chopped fresh leaves into green salads, fruit salads, marinated vegetables, chicken salads, poultry stuffing, punch, and marinades for fish.

Lemon balm teams well with corn, broccoli, asparagus, lamb, shellfish, freshly ground black pepper, olives, and beans. It is an ingredient of the liqueurs Benedictine and Chartreuse.

Available commercially: Dried as tea.

Substitute: Fresh lemon thyme or lemon verbena. Note that lemon verbena is stronger than lemon balm, so when substituting, use less verbena.

Aromatic: As heavenly as lemon balm may smell, its oil is rarely used in commercial perfumery because a lemony scent is easier and cheaper to synthesize. If you want to dry the plant for potpourris, you can harvest it at its most potent in late summer. The lower parts are richest in essential oil.

Ornamental: The common variety of lemon balm looks somewhat rank and weedy—a mass of coarse green leaves. It is rarely found outside of herb gardens. For more formal settings, consider using a variety with variegated leaves as a border plant.

Cosmetic: Lemon balm reportedly cleanses the skin. Steamy lemon balm facials are recommended for persons with acne. You might want to add the leaves to a cleansing herb bath mixture, too. (See the entries Lotions from Herbs and Bathing with Herbs for more information.)

Other: Lemon balm has been put to a lot of other uses over the years; some are more practical than others. Here are a few of them.

Wine: An 1829 recipe for lemon balm wine calls for 40 pounds of sugar dissolved in 9 gallons of water and poured, when cool, over 2½ pounds of balm and "a little new yeast." This stood open for 24 hours and was fermented under cover for six weeks before it was bottled. A sugar lump was thrown in each bottle. The receipt noted that balm wine improved with age, being better the second year.

Bees: Beekeepers once rubbed lemon balm inside a hive to

encourage a new swarm to stay. They have long considered lemon balm attractive to bees. The Latin name, *Melissa,* comes from the Greek word for "bees." Two thousand years ago Pliny noted that bees like lemon balm more than any other herb because they use it to get their bearings and find the hive again.

Language of flowers: Lemon balm was a symbolic plant used to transmit messages between lovers; it signified sympathy, perhaps because an extract was used to make soothing medicines.

Furniture polish: Here's a household hint from Shakespeare's *The Merry Wives of Windsor:* For a natural equivalent of lemon-scented furniture polishes, rub lemon balm into wood. The plant's oils work like the oily polishes, and the furniture will take on a lemony smell.

Insect repellent: Although the flowers attract honeybees, the plant is reputed to repel certain insects. You can try rubbing down a kitchen table to keep bugs away from the food, or tossing lemon balm into a fire so bugs won't bother the people gathered around it.

CULTIVATION

Lemon balm grows easily from seed and germinates better if the seeds are not covered. Take care to keep them from drying out. Plants can also be grown by layering, by division in spring, or by cuttings taken in the spring or summer.

Lemon balm needs a well-drained soil. The plant grows best in full sunlight but also survives in shade. Don't despair if the plants are too scrawny to spare many leaves the first year; that's normal. By the second year, they should provide an ample harvest.

Pests and diseases: Lemon balm is susceptible to powdery mildew. (See the entry Growing Herbs for information on controlling diseases.)

Harvesting and storage: Harvesting lemon balm is easy, and it is possible—in fertile, well-watered locations—to obtain as many as three cuttings a season. Lemon balm should be harvested before it flowers for optimum fragrance since a good deal of its aroma will be lost in even the most careful drying. To harvest, cut off the entire plant 2 inches above the ground. Try to avoid bruising the foliage.

Lemon balm should be carefully dried within two days of picking—it has a tendency to turn black unless it is dried quickly. Do not harvest if dry, sunny weather is not predicted for several days. Drying is best done in the shade at temperatures between 90° and 110°F. It's best to use trays or sieves for drying the herb, rather than tying it in bunches on a string. If you plan on using your lemon balm for tea, dry both the leaves and the stems.

CHEF TIPS

- Chop fresh leaves and add them to orange marmalade.

- Stuff fresh, aromatic sprigs into the cavity of a whole fish before grilling or baking. Remove the sprigs before eating.

- Make an extra-strong tea by boiling fresh or dried leaves in water, then strain, and stew fresh or dried fruit in it.

GROWING CONDITIONS

- Plant hardiness zones 4–5.

- Soil pH 7.0.

- Average, well-drained soil.

- Full sun to shade.

LEMON VERBENA

Aloysia triphylla   **Verbenaceae**

Here is an herb that migrated from the New World to the Old. Lemon verbena is an unassuming shrub that charmed the Spanish explorers who happened upon it in Argentina and Chile. There, the shrubs grow to 10 or 15 feet tall, but because they are so sensitive to cold weather, North Americans usually confine them to containers.

The delicate lemony aroma works well by itself as a body scent, and it is an aroma that people seem to find intimate. The leaves were used as an after-bath body rub, and the scent naturally found its way into commercial soaps and bath oils. In *Gone with the Wind,* lemon verbena is mentioned as the favorite fragrance of Scarlet O'Hara's mother. And in Charles Willson Peale's portrait of Mrs. Benjamin Rush, the woman wears a sprig of the herb at her bodice.

USES

Today, lemon verbena is thought of as a houseplant, and it is used most often as a delicately flavored tea.

Medicinal: Lemon verbena has not figured as an important medicinal herb, probably in part due to its late introduction to Europe. It has been used in folk medicine to aid digestion and reportedly produces a tonic effect on the stomach and intestines. It is also said to act as a sedative and to reduce fevers.

Culinary: A delicious lemon-lime tea can be made from the dried leaves of lemon verbena, but you can put this flavor to use in many other ways as well. Use it wherever you want a touch of lemon. The fresh or dried leaves brighten the taste of fish or poultry. They can be added to vegetable marinades, salad dressings, jams, puddings, and beverages.

Available commercially: Dried as tea.

Substitute: Lemon balm at twice the amount of lemon verbena.

Aromatic: Simply brush by this plant and you will release its sweet, lemony fragrance. The leaves can be used in potpourris and sachets. Add a sprig to a tussie-mussie or a bouquet of flowers. The next time you have a fancy dinner party, try the old-time custom of placing sprigs of lemon verbena in finger bowls at each place.

Commercially, the oil is extracted and used to make cologne and toilet water. You can extract the oil at home for use in homemade perfumes, aromatic waters, or scented baths. A simple infusion will also work for baths or waters.

Ornamental: With its tiny blooms, lemon verbena is not a showy plant, but its foliage is attractive, and its cheery fragrance should give it passage to any garden. If you are planning a fragrance garden, lemon verbena should be at the top of your list. Keep in mind that it

DESCRIPTION

Lemon verbena is a deciduous woody shrub with a distinctive lemon fragrance. (See photo on page 446.)

Flowers: Lavender; tiny, tubular, two equal lips; four stamens (two short, two long); four-toothed calyx; in spikes or racemes from leaf axils.

Leaves: Light green, lanceolate, pointed, margins slightly toothed or toothless, fringed with hairs, short stalks, 2–4 in. long, ½–1 in. wide; in whorls of three or four.

Fruit: Two seedlike nutlets enclosed by a calyx.

Height: 10–15 ft. outdoors in warm climates; to 5 ft. in cooler latitudes or indoors.

FLOWERING

Late summer and fall.

RANGE

Native to Chile and Argentina; widely cultivated. Grown commercially in France and North Africa.

CHEF TIPS

- Fresh lemon verbena leaves are tough, so be sure to remove them from marinades, beverages, and salad dressings before serving.

- Add dried, finely crumbled leaves to the batter when baking carrot, banana, or zucchini bread.

- To give plain rice a personality, add minced lemon verbena leaves to cooked rice just before serving.

isn't hardy in cold climates and will have to winter indoors.

Lemon verbena can be trained as a standard—a formal shape like that of a lollipop tree drawn by children.

CULTIVATION

Lemon verbena is best propagated by cuttings taken in the summer. Taking cuttings often causes the plant to wilt, so it is best to keep the donor in the shade and make sure it is well watered. Seeds may also be used, but the plant produces them infrequently.

Container gardening: Unless you live in a very mild climate, you will probably grow lemon verbena in a container. The plant does best in a loamy soil of the sort used with geraniums and chrysanthemums. Lemon verbena needs to be kept moist, but do not let the soil get soggy. Because it feeds heavily, apply regular applications of fish emulsion. Pinch the tips of the plant to keep it bushy. Mist or wash the leaves weekly to keep mites from colonizing.

If you've kept your lemon verbenas outdoors during the summer, cut away the very thin branches before bringing the plants in for the winter. These branches will only become weak and straggly and detract from the appearance and vigor of the plant. Still, these discards will effuse that delightful fragrance, so place them in dresser drawers to scent your clothes.

Remember, lemon verbena is deciduous—don't be concerned when it loses its leaves in the fall. At other times of the year, however, leaf loss is a sign that the plants are under stress, perhaps caused by a lack of water or root shock. If this occurs, hold back on watering for a little while. The lack of leaves reduces transpiration, and the plant will not be able to handle large quantities of water. Keep your lemon verbenas on the dry side until they start perking up again. Then return to your normal watering routine.

Many people bring container-grown lemon verbenas outdoors for the warmer months. If you choose to do this, place the pots on a hard surface, such as tile or bricks, to keep the roots from escaping the pots and entering the ground. Potted plants that have rooted will suffer shock to their roots if broken free from the ground, which will ultimately shorten the lives of the plants.

Pests and diseases: Lemon verbena is often infested by spider mites and whiteflies. (See the entry Growing Herbs for information on controlling pests and diseases.)

Harvesting and storage: Marilyn Hampstead of Fox Hill Farm in Parma, Michigan, recommends cutting the plant back halfway in midsummer and again before the first frost. You can also harvest sprigs of leaves all year long.

GROWING CONDITIONS

- Plant hardiness zones 9–10.
- Soil pH 6.5.
- Rich, moist soil.
- Full sun.

359

LICORICE

Glycyrrhiza glabra　　Leguminosae

"Give me the black ones and you get all the rest."

It seems that there's a licorice lover in every crowd. This popular flavoring has been around for a long time, dating back at least to the ancient Assyrians. It is sad to say that licorice candy, however, is often not licorice at all, but takes its flavor from anise oil. Other countries seem to have retained their affection for the real thing—in Italy, for example, licorice fans can buy sticks of the pure, unsweetened extract. Licorice is also a popular ice cream flavor in southern Europe.

If you want the real thing in the United States, you can buy or grow the root yourself. You may be surprised at how strong tasting real licorice is. But once you acquire a taste for licorice, the anise-flavored substitute won't do.

Although we think of this plant as a candy flavoring, its constituents have a remarkable range of pharmacological properties.

HISTORY

A papyrus dating from the time of Roman Empire describes the therapeutic value of licorice, and the root was also mentioned in the first Chinese herbal. Hippocrates, Theophrastus, and Pliny all referred to licorice. It was recommended for soothing throats and slaking thirsts. But licorice was not introduced to Europe until the fifteenth century. The roots became popular chewing sticks in Italy, Spain, the West Indies, and other places where the plant grows.

In North America Blackfoot Indians used wild licorice (*Glycyrrhiza Missouriensis*) as an infusion to treat earaches; other tribes ate it fresh.

Licorice's medicinal uses have included treatment of dropsy; fever; menstrual cramps; menopausal symptoms; irritated urinary, bowel, or respiratory passages; influenza; and hypoglycemia. In addition it has been used as a diuretic, demulcent, expectorant, emollient, antispasmodic, mild laxative, and cough remedy, and to relieve hoarseness, congestion, bronchitis, and ulcers. Licorice was often added to other medicines not only to make them more palatable but also to keep pills from sticking together. It has also been used in poultices.

USES

Licorice root is used to flavor and color a variety of foods and beverages. But by far the greatest quantity of the licorice we import, perhaps as much as 90 percent, ends up in tobacco products.

Medicinal: Perhaps the most common medicinal use is in cough syrups and cough drops; licorice soothes the chest and helps bring up phlegm. Licorice has also been used to treat ulcers, to relieve

---

DESCRIPTION

Licorice is a hardy perennial. An erect, somewhat branching plant, it issues from a stringy taproot, which is brown on the outside and yellow on the inside. The taproot grows to 4 ft. and sends out stolons, which in turn branch into rootlets, creating a tangled mass like the head of Medusa.

Flowers: Resemble sweet pea or vetch, ½ in. long, purple or lavender, in spikes shorter than leaves.

Leaves: Alternate, pinnate; 9–17 oblong leaflets, 1–2 in. long, yellow-green, lighter on underside, slightly damp and sticky underneath.

Fruit: One-celled pod, ½ in. long, smooth, reddish brown to maroon; containing one to six small kidney-shaped seeds.

Height: 3–7 ft.

FLOWERING

Midsummer.

RANGE

Native to Mediterranean region and central and southwest Asia; extensively cultivated in Russia, Syria, Greece, Spain, Iran, Iraq, Italy, India, and, in the United States, in California and the Salt River Valley of Arizona.

rheumatism and arthritis, and to induce menstruation. In this country it was used in powder form as a laxative.

The chief component of licorice, constituting 5 to 20 percent of the plant, is a saponinlike glycoside called glycyrrhizin. A sweetening agent, it is more than 50 times sweeter than sugar and is added to chocolate to extend the sweetness of sugar. A medically active component is a terpene component, which has a structure resembling a steroid. The root extract produces mild estrogenic effects, and it has proven useful in treating symptoms of menopause and menstrual cramps.

Glycyrrhizin stimulates the secretion of the adrenal cortex hormone, aldosterone. In healthy people this licorice constituent can cause headache, lethargy, water and salt retention, potassium secretion, raised blood pressure, and even cardiac arrest. However, its ability to stimulate the adrenal cortex makes it useful in treating Addison's disease, which is characterized by abnormally low activity in the cortex.

GROWING CONDITIONS

- Soil pH: neutral.
- Rich, moist soil.
- Full sun to partial shade.

LICORICE EYE DROPS

Often the modern medicinal uses we have for herbs have risen from old folk uses of those herbs. Such is true of one of the applications of licorice root. Once recommended to treat inflamed eyes, licorice root is being used today in France and China in eye drops that relieve inflammation. Sodium salts of glycyrrhinic acid are extracted from the root and added to the eye drop formula. The cortisonelike action of the licorice root extract is responsible for its healing effects.

LICORICE—continued

In the 1940s Dutch physicians tested licorice's reputation as an aid for indigestion. They came up with a derivative drug, carbenoxolone, that promised to help peptic ulcer patients by either increasing the life span of epithelial cells in the stomach or inhibiting digestive activity in general. Many cures were achieved in the experiments, but negative side effects—the patients' faces and limbs swelled uncomfortably—outweighed the cures.

Certain agents in licorice have recently been credited with antibacterial and mild antiviral effects; licorice may be useful in treating dermatitis, colds, and infections. It also has been used in a medicinal dandruff shampoo. Other modern-day research found that the herb can reduce arthritic activity.

Licorice has long been used in conjunction with other medicinal herbs, either to mask their less attractive taste or to accentuate their action. These include horehound, mullein, peppermint, chamomile, ginger, ginseng, marsh mallow, comfrey, and powdered linseed.

Toxicity: As noted above, the cortisonelike component of glycrrhizin increases the retention of salt and water in the body. This causes dangerous side effects, including abnormal heart action and kidney failure, triggered by potassium depletion. Licorice should be avoided by cardiac patients and those who suffer from hypertension, kidney complaints, or obesity. Pregnant women, who are especially subject to edema, should also avoid it.

In addition, some people are allergic to licorice, even in modest quantities. Cases of toxicity have been reported from less than a gram of glycyrrhizin in chewing tobacco. Licorice has caused paralysis of the limbs, electrolyte imbalance, high blood pressure, and shortness of breath.

Cosmetic: Licorice root is emollient and soothing. Modern-day herbalist Jeanne Rose recommends making a steam facial with licorice, comfrey, and either chamomile or lavender. The licorice helps to open the pores and allows the other cleansing and healing herbs to penetrate the skin.

Other: As a shampoo ingredient licorice root suppresses the secretion of scalp sebum for a week after shampooing, thereby postponing that oily sheen. It is also used in mouthwash and toothpaste as a sweetening and flavoring agent. Sometimes it is mixed with anise and used in liqueurs and herbal teas. When used in making beer and stout, it adds flavor, color, and a foamy head. Licorice has the power to intensify other flavors, and it is used commercially in pastries, ice cream, puddings, soy sauce, and soy-based meat substitutes.

Not only is licorice used to put a head on beer but it is also used as a foaming agent in fire extinguishers. Licorice products figure as wetting, spreading, and adhesive agents in insecticides and as a medium for culturing food yeast. The pulp is a nitrogen-rich fertilizer and mulch, and it is a component of composition board and insulation.

The main use of licorice root, however, remains the flavoring of tobacco. Some tobacco products are 10 percent licorice, and as much as 90 percent of the licorice brought into the United States is used in them. Cyrus Hyde of Well-Sweep Herb Farm, Port Murray, New Jersey, says that a stick cut from the root is satisfying to gnaw on, especially for those on diets (it has a peculiarly satisfying sweetness) and for those giving up smoking (it can be fiddled with like a cigarette).

CULTIVATION

The licorice plant may be grown from seed under the right conditions, but it is usually started in early spring or late fall from divisions of the crown, from sucker cuttings, or, most easily, from root cuttings. Set the cuttings 1 to 1½ feet apart in prepared, deeply tilled soil. Sandy soil from bottomlands, fortified with compost, is ideal. It should be rich, mellow, moist, and free of stones. Water the cuttings frequently directly after you set them out. Later, all you will have to do is control the weeds. Growth goes slowly for the first two years. Only when the plants are three to four years old, and before they have borne fruit or become woody, is the glycyrrhizin content at its peak and ready for harvest.

Licorice can be cultivated in a greenhouse. Put the roots in foot-deep pots of sandy loam with good drainage. If the fall sun refuses to shine, use artificial light to simulate long day length.

Wild licorice is occasionally cultivated from seed for collections of native plants, but no licorice has any real ornamental value. The leguminous plants are useful in the garden for fixing nitrogen.

Harvesting and storage: Cut the licorice plants in late autumn or in early winter when the tops are dry. Harvest by digging a ditch to one side of the plants, and pull the plants toward it. Remove the nitrogen-rich tops for compost. Remnants of rhizome runners left behind in the soil will give you the sprouts for next year's crop. Licorice roots can be extremely persistent and intrusive.

Shade-dry licorice root for six months. Moisture must be reduced by at least 50 percent, and, if possible, by as much as 95 percent. Moist roots are subject to spoilage and molds. The roots, powder, and extract should be stored in well-closed containers at temperatures under 80°F.

LEGEND BECOMES FACT

Among the herbal lore are those fanciful reports from antiquity about the powers of herbs. Some are far-fetched and darn near unbelievable. But modern science is demonstrating that not all such lore is fiction.

Consider the powers of "Scythian root" (licorice), as reported by the Greek historian Theophrastus in his *Enquiry into Plants*.

> [Scythian root] is also sweet. Some call it simply sweet root. It is useful against asthma and in several troubles of the chest and also administered in honey for wounds. It has the property of quenching thirst, wherefore they say that the Scythians with this and mares'-milk cheese can go 11 to 12 days without drinking.

Can anyone go 11 or 12 days without drinking?

If they eat enough licorice, which has been demonstrated to cause water retention, just maybe they can, thinks William A. R. Thomson, M.D., a British physician and writer. "If excretion of water in the urine was reduced as a result, then thirst would not arise, and there would be much less need to drink," he said. "Thus does legend become fact, and the twentieth-century successor of the alchemist of old produces evidence to support the folklore of the great days of ancient Greece."

LOBELIA

Lobelia inflata   **Lobeliaceae**

Lobelia has been drunk and smoked to relieve various ailments, but its powerful effects on the central nervous system have caused it to fall from favor. This is not an herb for home experimentation. All parts of the plant contain toxins, and poisoning may be fatal.

The plant was named for the Flemish botanist Matthais de L'Obel. The American Indians made use of most native lobelias, using *Lobelia inflata,* often known as Indian tobacco, to relieve asthma, to treat dysentery, and possibly to achieve some sort of mental high. The Indians introduced it to the settlers. The Shakers packaged it for sale overseas. Samuel Thomson, an herbalist-physician of the early nineteenth century, recommended lobelia as a muscle relaxant during childbirth; as a poultice for healing abscesses; and for the treatment of epilepsy, tetanus, diphtheria, dysentery, and whooping cough. Many herbalists of the time believed that the vomiting lobelia induced somehow cleansed the patient.

USES

Medicinal: Lobelia is a powerful poison that doesn't belong on the home medicine shelf. Similar to nicotine, it has been used in over-the-counter preparations to help people stop smoking, even though there is no indication that it is effective. It is also advertised as a tobacco that will help you reduce weight—not surprisingly, since taking lobelia in any form induces vomiting.

Lobeline and related alkaloids in the herb act by first exciting and then depressing the central nervous system. Given in the right amount, it opens the bronchioles; however, if too much is administered, it slows respiration and lowers the blood pressure drastically. Symptoms of poisoning include nausea and uncontrollable vomiting, tremors, paralysis, convulsions, coma, and death. As little as 50 milligrams of dried herb or a single milliliter of lobelia tincture has caused these reactions.

The plant can be safely used externally, and some herbalists recommend it to relieve rheumatism and soothe bruises and bites. Make a rub by steeping the plant in vinegar or rubbing alcohol.

CULTIVATION

Indian tobacco is rarely cultivated because there are many prettier lobelias better suited to the garden and home landscape. If you do want to grow it, you can start it from seed sown in the spring or from cuttings. Choose cardinal flower (*L. Cardinalis*) for marshy spots or the electric blue (*L. Erinus*) for the garden bed or border.

UNSAFE

DESCRIPTION

Lobelia inflata is an annual or biennial relative of the bellflowers (Campanulaceae). Its stems are branched and hairy. When one breaks, it exudes a milky, latex juice.

Flowers: In loose spikes at ends of branches; blue, tubular corolla with two-part upper lip; ¼ in. long.

Leaves: Lanceolate, toothed, alternate, with no leaf stalks; to 3½ in. long, 2 in. wide.

Fruit: Two-celled capsule bearing many tiny brown seeds.

Height: 1–3 ft.

FLOWERING

July and August.

RANGE

Native to North America.

HABITAT

Roadsides; dry, open fields; and light woods.

GROWING CONDITIONS

• Humusy soil.
• Full sun to partial shade.

LOTIONS FROM HERBS

What skin cream or lotion could be more pleasant than one containing the qualities and fragrances of fresh herbs? Herbs can improve the cleansing and refreshing qualities of skin cleansers and lotions. After a long day of grime and sweat, nothing feels better than splashing your face with a cool, fragrant herb water.

SKIN-CLEANSING CREAMS

If you wear makeup, cleanse your skin with a cleansing cream, which will remove the makeup more efficiently and more thoroughly than soap. The cream will leave a light emollient film on the skin to keep moisture in, protecting the skin. Does this mean that if you have oily skin, you can't use creams or lotions? No. Just follow up with soap or an astringent lotion to remove the film.

Herbal creams require a base to which an infusion of herbs is then added. A basic cream base can be made from the following ingredients:

1 ounce of lanolin
½ ounce of beeswax
3 or 4 ounces of a vegetable or fruit oil (almond, avocado, or soybean)
1 ounce of herb water (See instructions on page 367.)

Use a double boiler to melt the lanolin and beeswax together. Add the oil slowly, combining thoroughly. Remove the mixture from the heat and whisk in the herb water, incorporating it thoroughly into the cream. If you prefer something more like a lotion than a cream, do not add the beeswax, use either lanolin or cocoa butter, and increase the herb water to 2 ounces.

You can vary the properties of the cream depending on the herbs you use. For example, to create an astringent cream, add a yarrow water. Fennel and comfrey benefit any skin and can be used in any lotion. Prepare an herb water from any of the herbs listed in this section according to the properties desired.

HERBAL FACIALS

Once you've cleaned the surface of the skin, an herbal facial will open your pores and take the cleansing process to the deeper layers of your skin. The facial will bring out impurities that are clogged in those lower layers and will leave your face feeling and looking clean, healthy, and vibrant.

LOTIONS FROM HERBS—continued

ASTRINGENT HERBS

agrimony
bay
bayberry bark
blackberry leaves
chamomile
comfrey leaf and root
dock
elderberry flowers
frankincense
houseleek
lady's mantle
lemon
loosestrife
mint
myrrh
nasturtium
pansy
primrose
queen of the meadow
raspberry
rose
rosemary
sage
violet
wintergreen
witch hazel
yarrow

STIMULATING HERBS

beebalm
calendula
elderberry flowers
horseradish
lavender
lemon verbena
mint
nettle
plantain
raspberry
rosemary
sage
savory
scented geranium leaves

Preparing a facial: Boil 1 quart of water and pour it over ¼ cup of dried herbs in a bowl. Lean over the bowl, close to the water, and make a tent around your head with a towel to trap the steam. Keep this position for at least 10 minutes. When you have finished, rinse your face with warm water, then cold. Apply an astringent or herbal freshening lotion. Your face will feel thoroughly refreshed.

Herbs that are particularly good for facials include chamomile—soothes and cleanses; comfrey—heals; elderberry flowers—stimulates and tightens; fennel—cleanses (good base for any facial); houseleek—heals; lady's mantle—soothes and cleanses; linden—cleanses; nettle—cleanses and increases circulation; peppermint—stimulates and tightens; rosemary—increases circulation; yarrow—excellent astringent.

Jeanne Rose, author of *The Herbal Body Book,* suggests the following combinations of herbs:

For normal to dry skin—licorice root, fennel, chamomile, clover, and comfrey.

For oily to normal skin—To fennel and comfrey add any of the following: lemon peel, lemongrass, rose, witch hazel, or lavender.

To tighten and stimulate—peppermint, anise seed, lavender, and comfrey.

To stimulate—nettle, rosemary, fennel, peach leaves, and pansy leaves.

SKIN-FRESHENING LOTIONS

The final touch to an herbal cleansing routine? A freshening lotion. An herbal skin freshener removes the last traces of dirt and soap that may be left on your skin. Depending on the herbs you choose, the lotion can also help to relieve specific skin problems. It can increase circulation and add the final spark of color and life to a dull, tired complexion.

Preparing a lotion: A skin-freshening lotion is easy to prepare. Simply make an herb water with the appropriate herb.

Refreshing mint lotion: For a stimulating and refreshing lotion, puree fresh spearmint leaves with cold water in an electric blender. Dab on your face and neck. Dried mint may also be used: Add 1 cup of dried, crushed mint to 1 pint of pure water in a quart glass jar with a tight-fitting lid. Put this glass jar in a convenient place and shake once or twice daily for two weeks. Strain and store in small glass vials with tight-fitting lids.

Other lotions can be made from any of the herbs listed with this entry, choosing according to the benefit you desire. The following are suggestions for some specific skin problems:

For wrinkles: linden flowers, lemon balm, or fennel.

To soften skin: elderberry flowers or salad burnet.

For oily skin: calendula, lady's mantle, lavender, lemon, lemongrass, rose, sage, or yarrow (an excellent astringent).

For dry skin: chamomile, clover, comfrey, elderberry flowers, melilot, mint, orange leaves and blossoms, parsley, primrose, strawberry, or violet.

HERB VINEGARS FOR THE SKIN

Herb vinegars, the same ones you use in cooking, are helpful for both dry and oily complexions and act to refine the skin pores. Vinegar tightens skin pores, reestablishes a natural acid balance, and softens the skin. Start with either apple cider vinegar or white wine vinegar. Add 1 cup of petals or leaves for each pint of vinegar and place on a sunny windowsill in a tightly sealed glass bottle. Let the mixture steep for two to three weeks, shaking it vigorously every day. Strain and rebottle. If you like a more diluted lotion, add water.

For a pungent vinegar, use such herbs as sweet basil, thyme, sage, rosemary, dill, or marjoram. Yes, it sounds like a salad dressing, but try it as a facial rinse. For a more delicate floral fragrance, use lavender, violet, rose, carnation, lemon verbena, honeysuckle, sweet pea, or lilac, or experiment with your own combinations.

For an aromatic citrus vinegar, add ½ cup of grated orange peel, ½ cup of orange leaves, and ½ cup of orange flowers to 1 quart of warm vinegar. Place in a glass jar and shake daily for about three weeks. Strain and use as an astringent or hair rinse.

MOISTURIZERS

After cleansers, herbal facials, and freshening lotions, there's one more step—moisturizers. Once you've cleansed the skin and invigorated it with tonics, the moisturizer protects the work you've done and will help you to maintain healthy skin. It keeps the moisture in and the dirt out.

Preparing a moisturizer: A simple herbal moisturizing lotion can be made by adding 2 tablespoons of an herb water to 1 teaspoon of honey or 1 tablespoon of lanolin or glycerin.

If you prefer to use a cream, melt together 1 tablespoon each of lanolin, honey, almond oil, and white wax in a double boiler. Add 2 tablespoons of a strong herb water. Let the mixture cool slightly, then strain and whisk until a cool thick cream is formed. Because the almond oil will go rancid, these moisturizers are not very stable and should only be kept for a few days.

ANTISEPTIC HERBS

bay
chamomile
echinacea
eucalyptus
marjoram
myrrh
sorrel
thyme

HERB WATER

To make an herb water, gather herbs early in the morning; crush about 1 ounce of herbs in 1 cup of water; pour into a ceramic or enamel pot; add another cup of water and cover; slowly bring to a boil and then simmer for a few minutes. Turn off the heat and let the herbs infuse until cool. Strain and store the water in the refrigerator. When using flowers rather than foliage, bruise them rather than crush them, and heat very gently.

An even easier method of creating an herb water is to purchase the essential oil and add it to water. Because essential oils are so concentrated, only a few drops are needed in a pint of water. Vary the concentration to suit your own preferences.

CLEANSING HERBS

chamomile
fennel
lady's mantle
linden
lovage
nettle
parsley
plantain

DECOCTION

When using the tough plant parts—roots, bark, or seeds—in your herbal cosmetics, you will need to make a decoction by boiling the plant matter in water for 5 to 20 minutes. Use this in place of or in combination with herb waters in any recipe.

HERBS FOR ACNE

agrimony
burdock
clover
fumitory
horsetail
iris
lavender
lemon balm
Solomon's seal
southernwood
tansy
white birch bark

EMOLLIENT HERBS

acacia flowers
chamomile
coltsfoot
comfrey
licorice
linden
loosestrife
marsh mallow root
mint
orange flowers
slippery elm

LOTIONS FROM HERBS—continued

Make the herb waters from any of the emollient herbs listed with this entry.

A traditional rinse: Combine equal parts of glycerin and rose water. Glycerin moisturizes the skin, while rose water acts as a mild astringent.

AFTER-SHAVE LOTIONS

If shaving irritates your face, splash on some herbal after-shave lotion. The coolness of the lotion and the healing and invigorating qualities of the herbal oil will feel wonderful against your skin, and you will feel refreshed and ready to start the day.

Wonderful wake-up lotion: This after-shave lotion is styptic, astringent, and stimulating. Use a large jar and fill it halfway with a mixture of 3 parts fresh sage leaves, 1 part fresh yarrow flowers, and 1 part fresh or dried lavender flowers. For a mentholated scent, you can add either 1 part eucalyptus leaves or 1 part peppermint leaves. Fill the rest of the jar with grain or rubbing alcohol and shake. Let the mixture steep for two weeks, shaking it a couple of times every day. Then strain and add water to dilute to the desired strength. If you have dry skin, add 1 or 2 tablespoons of glycerin or almond oil.

Sage and lavender lotion: For an invigorating after-shave lotion, try this recipe. Again, it is easiest to use a big jar. Pour in 2 cups of witch-hazel extract (available in drugstores) and 2 tablespoons of apple cider vinegar. Add 1 ounce of dried lavender flowers and 1 ounce of dried sage, and shake. Let the mixture steep for one week, shaking it daily. Strain and bottle the lotion.

HAIR CARE

You can concoct marvelous herbal lotions for the hair, too.

The three best-known herbs for the hair are rosemary, sage, and chamomile. If you are a brunette, a rosemary or sage rinse will leave a fine sheen in your hair. Make an herb water of one or the other or a combination of both. After shampooing, pour the rinse over your hair, catching the rinse in a bowl or container so that you can repeat this several times. You can add a rosemary or sage water directly to your shampoo.

Chamomile is the herb of choice for lighter hair. Again, make an herb water to use as a rinse, or add the herb water to your shampoo. Chamomile will lighten your hair and soften it.

All of these herbal lotions are easy to prepare. They will help you look and feel great.

LOVAGE

Levisticum officinale   **Umbelliferae**

Lovage tastes like celery but has medicinal powers and is easier to grow. What's more, it is a large, dramatic specimen for the garden.

Over the centuries, lovage has fallen from fashion. It enjoyed greater popularity in the Middle Ages, when it was grown in kitchen and physic gardens. Even the emperor Charlemagne included the herb in his landscape.

USES

Lovage has most often been used as a medicinal herb, although it certainly has plenty of applications in the kitchen.

Medicinal: Early herbalists recommended lovage as a diuretic and carminative, and occasionally as a cure for rheumatism, jaundice, malaria, sore throat, and kidney stones. It was used to promote and regulate menstruation. To this day, some Europeans still use it as a folk cure for minor stomachaches, kidney problems, and headaches.

The roots of lovage were the key ingredient of most of these medicines. Taken in one form or another, lovage roots were thought to have a diuretic effect that would relieve jaundice, colic, stomach problems, and obesity. In the seventeenth century, the British herbalist Culpeper recommended "half a dram of the powdered root, taken in wine," to "warm a cold stomach, help digestion, and consume all raw and superfluous moisture therein." Simply chewing on a bit of the dried root is supposed to keep one alert.

Externally, preparations of roots or leaves were traditionally used on boils. Added to the bathwater, lovage leaves or roots supposedly relieved skin and eye problems. Fresh juice squeezed from the leaves and stems was said to cure pinkeye. An infusion made from the seeds was used to erase freckles.

Contemporary scientists say that the plant, particularly the root, does work as a diuretic. The essential oil is similar to that of angelica and contains effective diuretics. This may explain lovage's often observed effectiveness against flatulence. To make a medicinal tea, steep a teaspoon of fresh or dried root in a cup of boiling water.

Culinary: Lovage leaves, stems, and seeds all taste like celery. The leaves can be used fresh in salads and fresh or dried in soups, stews, and sauces. The stems can be chopped and added to salads; cooked and pureed; candied; or used like celery stalks. The seeds, whole or ground as needed, are used in pickling brines, cheese spreads, salads, salad dressings, and sauces.

Lovage loves potatoes (especially potato salad), tomatoes, chicken, poultry stuffings, rice, creamed soups, savory pies, and

DESCRIPTION

Lovage is a perennial herb. Its hollow stems are ribbed like those of celery, and they divide into branches near the top.

Flowers: Tiny, yellow; in compound umbels 1½–4 in. across.

Leaves: Glossy, dark green, opposite, compound; decrease in size toward top; leaflets wedge-shaped, may be toothed or ridged; celerylike fragrance when bruised.

Fruit: ¼ in. long, grooved; aromatic; resemble seeds.

Height: 5 ft.

FLOWERING

June and July.

RANGE

Native to southern Europe; naturalized throughout North America.

CHEF TIPS

- Lovage has a particularly well-rounded flavor that adds life to many low-salt or no-salt recipes.

- Blanch and marinate lovage stems and serve as a first course, as you would asparagus or leeks.

- Create a garnish from a lovage stem. Start with a 3-in. piece and cut thin slices in it, leaving 1½ in. of stalk. Keep rolling the stem around as you're slicing to make sure all sides are cut. Toss the stem into ice water until the slices curl so that the stem forms a brush. Use it to serve mustards and dips.

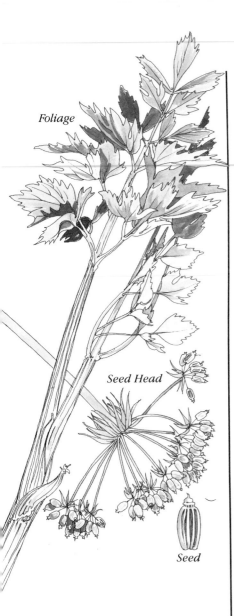

Foliage

Seed Head

Seed

GROWING CONDITIONS

- Plant hardiness zone 3.
- Soil pH 6.5.
- Moist, fertile, well-drained soil.
- Full sun to partial shade.

steamed vegetables.

Available commercially: Dried stems, but hard to find.

Substitute: Celery.

CULTIVATION

This herb is much simpler to grow than celery. Given a fertile, well-cultivated soil in a sunny spot, it will require little care. Lovage dies back to the ground each winter, returning bigger and stronger the following summer. After four years, growth tapers off, and the plants simply hold their own for many years to come.

You can start lovage from seed or by division. Ripe seed is sown in the late summer or early fall. Since you'll probably only want one lovage plant, purchase a seedling from a nursery or ask a friend for a start. Whether you use seedlings or divisions, set them at least 2 feet apart. Wait two years before harvesting the roots or stems.

If you want to encourage bushy growth, clip off the flowers as they appear. Cut the young leaves and stalks frequently. The mature leaves tend to be yellow and bland tasting. Dress plants with a rich compost or rotted manure each spring, and keep them well watered during dry spells.

Pests and diseases: Like celery, lovage is susceptible to leaf miners. Pick off and destroy the infested leaves so this pest won't get out of hand. (See the entry Growing Herbs for information on controlling pests.)

Harvesting and storage: Once lovage is established, the leaves, stems, and roots can be harvested whenever you need them. Gather seeds when the tiny fruits begin to pop open, indicating they are ripe. Lovage stores fairly well in the freezer. For best results, blanch small bundles of leaves by quickly dunking them in boiling water, then plunging them into an ice bath for two minutes. Drain very well, seal in plastic containers, and freeze. The thawed herb will be a bit droopier and softer than when fresh, but it will still prove satisfactory for cooking. If you plan on adding the frozen lovage to soups and stews, chop the blanched herb and freeze it in ice cube trays.

Many herbalists prefer drying this herb. This makes sense especially if you will be using the seeds, as they will dry on the flower heads. To dry the leaves and stems, cut the youngish growth at any time and hang it upside down in a shed or other warm, shady spot. Store the dried leaves and stems in tightly sealed, opaque containers, because light will quickly yellow this herb. To preserve the roots, dig them in the late fall. Wash them, slice them into ½-inch pieces, and dry them on a screen in a warm, shady place.

MADDER

Rubia tinctorum   **Rubiaceae**

Just forget the comedy routine—"What's the madder? I think I'm going to dye."—when you talk about this historically important plant that until the advent of chemical dyes contributed so much to the cloth industry. Although its importance as a commercial dyestuff ended a century ago, madder still means a lot to anyone working with natural dyes as a hobby.

HISTORY

Burial wrappings of Egyptian mummies were colored with madder dye, so we know that the plant was used a very long time ago. Like indigo and other famous natural dyestuffs, however, its time has passed by.

Actually, a study of dyes derived from madder spurred the development of the chemical dye industry, according to British herbalist Maude Grieve in *A Modern Herbal*. One of the constituents of madder root is alizarin, which produces a rose-colored dye. In 1868, two chemical researchers, Graebe and Liebermann, realized that alizarin could be derived from anthracene, a hydrocarbon contained in coal tar. They developed a technique for synthesizing the dye from coal tar on a commercial scale. Such discoveries helped the dye industry to replace dye plants with dye chemicals.

With the renewal of interest in natural dyes, madder may regain a place in the gardens, homes, and small specialty shops of those who work with hand-dyed fabrics.

Greek physicians used madder, both root and stem, in decoctions and infusions for promoting the flow of both urine and menstrual blood. It was also said at various times to cure jaundice, inflammations, and kidney stones; to help in childbirth; to rid the body of worms; to cure dysentery and diarrhea; to help with dropsy; to strengthen bones and cure rickets; and to help wounds and bruises when used externally. It has now become almost obsolete in medicine, but recently it has once more become mildly popular as a facial for the removal of freckles and blemishes.

USES

The constituents of madder make it more useful as a dye than as a medicinal plant.

Medicinal: One very interesting medicinal use relies on the coloring properties of the root. When taken internally, it colors milk, urine, and bones in animals and humans, and bones, beaks, and feet

DESCRIPTION

Madder is a perennial with slender, four-sided, jointed stems. The stems are covered with short prickles to help them climb since they are too weak and succulent to bear the weight of the plant alone. If not climbing, the stems often lie along the ground. (See photo on page 168.)

The reddish brown, succulent root is cylindrical, fleshy, and made up of fibers of various sizes. It ranges up to 3 ft. long with many branches.

Flowers: Less than 1/10 in. in diameter; greenish white to pale yellow, five segments, somewhat bell-shaped; tubular calyxes; in terminal panicles.

Leaves: Prickly along margins and midribs, lanceolate, stalkless or short stalked, 2–4 in. long; in circles of four to six.

Fruit: Resembles burrs; 1/8–1/4 in. in diameter; ripens from red to black.

Height: 4 ft.

FLOWERING

Early summer (first appearance occurs in third year).

RANGE

Native to the Mediterranean area, other parts of southeast Europe, and Asia Minor; naturalized throughout Europe and, less widely, in North America.

MADDER—continued

Pieces of Root

GROWING CONDITIONS

- Plant hardiness zone 7.
- Soil pH: neutral.
- Deep, well-drained soil.
- Full sun.

in birds. Therefore, it has been of use in experiments to determine the characteristics of bone growth.

Madder root has been proven in laboratory experiments to cause contractions of uterine muscles, so its use to bring on menstruation may have some basis in fact. No experiments have tested the other claims made for madder root. The roots, leaves, and seeds of *Rubia tinctorum,* as well as those of *R. sylvestris,* a related species, are used.

Dye: In the nineteenth century, dyeing wool or cotton with madder was done in several steps. The textile was first scoured in a mildly alkaline solution, then steeped in oil emulsions, then washed in sheep dung. Next it was rubbed with oak galls, then treated with alum, and only after that dyed with the partly fermented roots and root powder of madder.

Today less interesting (and less distasteful) mordants are used: tin or chrome for wool, and alum for wool, cotton, and silk, depending on the color desired. The roots are placed in a fabric bag, then soaked overnight in 4½ gallons of water. The wet mordanted wool is added, and the bath temperature is slowly raised to 190°F for alum-mordanted wool or 212°F for tin-mordanted wool, and it is kept there for 40 minutes. Later, the material is washed in soap. Madder yields orange, lacquer red, or garnet red colors. (See the entry Dyes from Herbs for more information.)

Other: According to Maude Grieve, the French once used the prickly madder stalks for scouring pans and polishing metal. The herb is also used as animal fodder.

CULTIVATION

Although it grows wild in some places, madder can also be cultivated. Choose a sunny spot and allow plenty of room.

The plant can be started from seed, but it takes a long time to establish, so root and shoot divisions are usually used. Plant roots or transplant seedlings at least 1 foot apart. Seed is sown in the spring. Germination takes 10 days or so. Two- to three-year-old roots are set out in the late spring or early fall.

After three years grown from seed or two years grown from plants, the roots should be dug sometime after the plant has flowered in the spring, or after the growth dies down in the fall. Harvest is best when roots are three to six years old. Medium-sized roots make the best dye.

Harvesting and storage: In France the roots are dried and the outer layer threshed off and packed separately as an inferior product called *mall.* The stripped roots are heated, unless the weather is unusually warm. Then they are powdered and milled three times.

MARJORAM

Origanum Majorana   **Labiatae**

Herbs don't seem to have quite the significance for us moderns that they did for the ancients. Sweet marjoram, once the plant that sanctified marital bliss, is now most closely associated with turkey stuffing. Still, sweet marjoram is, as the name suggests, a gentle, subtly perfumed, calming herb.

Wild marjoram, winter marjoram, and pot marjoram are closely associated species, but wild marjoram *(Origanum vulgare)* resembles the oreganos. Wild marjoram is used the most in medicine, while sweet (or knot) marjoram is preferred in the kitchen.

HISTORY

The Greeks called the plant "joy of the mountains" and used it to cure rheumatism. Wreaths and garlands of it were used at weddings and funerals. They said it was precious to Aphrodite, the goddess of love, and that this was what made it so gentle—gentle enough to cure sprains as well as to comfort the dead when it grew on their graves. Young Greek couples were crowned with it at their weddings. Legend had it that if you anointed yourself with it before sleeping, you would dream of your future spouse.

USES

A great range of uses has been discovered for marjoram.

Medicinal: As a folk remedy, the herb has been used against asthma, indigestion, rheumatism, toothache, conjunctivitis, and even cancer, but it is doubtful that it has much medicinal value apart from its minor antioxidant and antifungal properties. Marjoram gargles and teas may relieve sinus congestion and hay fever, but try a mild infusion when doing your own doctoring.

Marjoram may irritate the uterus if used during menstruation or pregnancy. Otherwise, it is quite safe.

Culinary: Marjoram is something like a mild oregano, with a hint of balsam. The leaves and flowers are used fresh or dried in recipes; fresh sprigs can be added to salads. The cuisines of France, Italy, and Portugal make the most of marjoram. It is especially good with beef, veal, lamb, roast poultry, fish, patés, green vegetables, carrots, cauliflower, eggplant, eggs, mushrooms, parsnips, potatoes, squash, and tomatoes. Add it to stews, sautés, marinades, dressings, herb butters, flavored vinegars and oils, cheese spreads, soups, and stuffings. It complements the herbs bay, garlic, onion, thyme, and basil. In Germany it is an important seasoning in sausage.

Available commercially: Dried whole or ground leaves (whole are preferable).

DESCRIPTION

Sweet marjoram is a tender perennial usually grown as an annual. It has a dense, shallow root system and an unusually bushy habit. Its square stems branch frequently and are covered with small hairs. (See photo on page 33.)

Flowers: Have knotlike shapes before blossoming; tiny, white or pink; in spherical, clustered flower spikes or corymbs of three to five flowers.

Leaves: Opposite, ovate, entire, fuzzy, pale gray-green, short stalked, ¼–1 in. long; spicy and aromatic.

Fruit: Light brown, very small nutlets.

Height: 1 ft.

FLOWERING

August and September.

RANGE

Native to North Africa and Southwest Asia; naturalized in the Mediterranean region and cultivated in North America.

CHEF TIPS

- Substitute marjoram for oregano when preparing pizza, lasagna, and eggplant Parmesan.

- Add marjoram to a marinade for artichoke hearts, asparagus, and mushrooms.

MARJORAM—continued

Substitute: Oregano, in a lesser amount.

Aromatic: Wild marjoram was once much used as a strewing herb to freshen the air of homes. The French still put sprigs of it into hope chests and linen closets. Soaking in a warm tub of marjoram tea scents the body while relieving aches and pains or chest congestion. Marjoram leaves are also added to potpourris and sachets.

Ornamental: There are variegated varieties of sweet, wild, and pot marjoram. Pot marjoram, *O. Onites,* is most often used for hanging baskets indoors in winter, although its particularly balsamic odor strikes some people as less appealing. When potted and brought inside, it has a lighter green color and cascades over the edges of a hanging container.

The large, purple flower heads of the marjorams make good additions to winter bouquets. The furry, dainty leaves distinguish them in the herb or ornamental garden.

Cosmetic: According to herbalist Jeanne Rose, marjoram has mildly antiseptic properties that benefit the skin. She recommends adding it to herb bath mixtures. (See the entry Bathing with Herbs for more information.)

Craft: Dried sprigs of marjoram can be added to herb wreaths and are especially appropriate for culinary wreaths.

Dye: The tops yield a green dye to wool mordanted with alum and an olive color to wool mordanted with chrome.

CULTIVATION

Because marjoram seeds are small and slow to germinate, they are usually started indoors in midspring for setting out when all danger of frost has passed. Choose a sunny location with rich, well-drained soil, and space the seedlings in clumps of three, every 6 to 8 inches. Five clumps will supply the average family. Because seedlings are small, you should take care that the weeds do not overwhelm them. Weed by hand at first and then hoe frequently. Water sparingly. Pinch the plants back just before they bloom to maintain their shape. Later, when the plants are ready to bloom again, cut them to 1 inch above the ground. In subsequent years, the roots can be divided and brought inside for winter use and for replanting in the spring.

Harvesting and storage: Gardeners in warmer climates may get two harvests a season, but in the North a second cutting may weaken the plants.

Unlike many other herbs, marjoram will retain much of its flavor when dried, but dry it away from sunlight to preserve both color and flavor. Rub the stems on a screen to shred the leaves, and then discard the stems. Store in airtight containers.

GROWING CONDITIONS

- Plant hardiness zones 9–10.
- Soil pH 6.9.
- Light, dry, well-drained soil.
- Full sun.

Chives

Foxglove

Elderberry

Damask Rose Petals

376

Borage

Pink Yarrow

Goldenseal

377

Calendula

Elecampane

Beebalm

378

Nasturtium

MARSH MALLOW

Althaea officinalis   Malvaceae

No, this herb is not an ingredient in that popular campfire confection. But there is a link between the two. Before gelatin and other products were used to give marshmallows their pillowy consistency, this herb's root created the mucilaginous effect.

Marsh mallow is a humble plant, growing wild in waste places, but it has served many cultures as a medicine and even as a staple food in times of famine. The Greek physician Hippocrates described its value in the treatment of wounds. Another Greek physician, Dioscorides, prescribed a vinegar infusion as a cure for toothaches and recommended a preparation of the seeds to soothe insect stings. Horace, a Roman poet, touted the laxative properties of the roots and leaves. Herbalists of the Renaissance period also used marsh mallow for sore throats, stomach problems, gonorrhea, leukorrhea, and as a gargle to treat mouth infections.

USES

Medicinal: Marsh mallow's highest medicinal acclaim is as a demulcent. Internally it has a soothing effect on inflammation and irritation of the alimentary canal and of the urinary and respiratory organs. It was said to ease the passage of kidney stones.

Externally, the dried or powdered roots were applied as a poultice on abrasions or eruptions. The powdered root has been used as a binder in formulating pills.

Culinary: The original marshmallow confection was the French *pâté de guimauve,* made from the plant's root. The uncooked young top and tender leaves of marsh mallow can be added to spring salads. The roots have more substance and can be prepared for the table by boiling and then frying in butter with onions.

CULTIVATION

Given moist soil and full sun, marsh mallow will flourish. It can be easily propagated by seed, cuttings, or root division. Rootstock can be divided in the spring, but dividing in the autumn is preferable. Carefully divide the offsets of the roots after the stalks decay and plant them 2 feet apart.

Harvesting and storage: The leaves are stripped off the branches in July or August when the flowers begin to bloom. They should be gathered on a beautiful morning after the dew has been dried off by the sun. The flowers are taken at their peak, before they begin to wither. Collect the taproots in the autumn from plants at least two years old. To prepare them for storage, remove the lateral rootlets, wash them, peel off the corky bark, and dry them whole or in slices.

DESCRIPTION

This erect perennial has a tapering, woody taproot; woolly stems; and several spreading, leafy branches.

Flowers: Solitary or two or three together; 1–2 in. across; borne from upper leaf axils; five pink or white, obovate, notched petals; velvety calyx, six to nine outer segments, five triangular sepals.

Leaves: Alternate, grayish green; covered on both sides with star-shaped hairs; lower leaves circular, barely three to five lobed, toothed, 1¼–3¼ in. wide; upper leaves ovate to lanceolate, pointed, lobed, toothed.

Fruit: Round, downy, contains many carpels; each holds one seed.

Height: 4–5 ft.

FLOWERING

July through September.

RANGE

Native to Europe; naturalized in eastern North America.

HABITAT

Moist places, particularly salt marshes and damp land close to the sea or its estuaries.

GROWING CONDITIONS

- Very hardy.
- Soil pH: neutral.
- Moist to wet, light soil.
- Full sun.

UNSAFE

Podophyllum peltatum   Podophyllaceae

The annual reappearance of the mayapple's umbrellalike leaves, which form a luxuriant ground cover in moist woods, is a sure sign of spring.

A single, large, white flower is followed by a fruit, which ripens from green to yellow as the summer progresses. This "mayapple" is the only edible part of the otherwise poisonous plant. Although the root has been used medicinally, it is now on the Food and Drug Administration's (FDA) unsafe herb list and should not be ingested.

Confusing *Podophyllum peltatum*'s identity is a long list of common names by which it is known: duck's foot (for the leaf shape), ground lemon, devil's apple, hog apple, Indian apple, racoon berry, and the most common (after mayapple), American mandrake.

You may have heard of magical properties connected with mayapple, its human-shaped root in particular. In the era of psychedelic rock bands, an American group named itself Mandrake Memorial. But these references are to European mandrake, *Mandragora officinarum,* which is no relation to the common woodland plant of eastern North America.

DESCRIPTION

The mayapple is a simple but lovely perennial with a round, smooth stem that bears one or two leaves and a single flower.

Flowers: White, nodding, ¾–2½ in. wide; six to nine smooth, concave, petals; 9–20 stamens.

Leaves: Circular, 5–13 in. wide; light green above, paler underneath; divided into five to nine triangular lobes, each cleft at the top; leafstalks 3–6 in. long.

Fruit: Fleshy, ovoid, 1¼–2 in. long; green when immature; light yellow, spotted, fragrant when ripe; contains 12 or more dark brown seeds.

Height: 12–18 in. tall.

FLOWERING

April and May.

RANGE

Native to North America from Quebec south to Florida and Texas.

HABITAT

Rich, damp, open woodland, pastures, and near streams.

HISTORY

The rhizome of the mayapple was used by North American Indians for inducing vomiting and as a slow-acting but powerful laxative. They also put drops of liquid from the fresh rhizome into the ear to improve poor hearing. Algonquians made a spring tonic from the plant, and some New England Indians used the fruit to remove warts. The early settlers used the powdered rhizome to treat a plethora of common diseases and disorders, including typhoid, cholera, rheumatism, jaundice, dysentery, hepatitis, gonorrhea and syphilis, amenorrhea, and prostate problems.

USES

Medicinal: The active principle, podophyllin, is found throughout the plant, including the seeds and unripe fruit, but it is especially concentrated in the rhizome. The FDA has studied the health effects of this agent and calls it "an unsafe laxative," citing powers that go far beyond the digestive system. The plant-based resin has been found to affect cellular growth and is blamed for deformities in the children of mothers who took laxatives or dieting tablets containing it. Research suggests that this same property may make podophyllin useful as a treatment for skin cancers, but the drug has damaging side effects. It has been used commercially in creams as a wart remover, but again this remedy is unsafe.

Toxicity: Podophyllin is still sometimes used as a laxative, but fatalities have resulted from overdoses. It has been used to abort pregnancies, and American Indians once ingested the young shoots in order to commit suicide. Even handling the fresh or dried rhizome or the podophyllin powder is extremely hazardous, as the poison is absorbed through the skin. The eyes are especially sensitive to mandrake.

The fruit, which ripens in September, is the only edible part of the plant. (However, its seeds are poisonous.) The plumlike, yellow mayapple, with brown spots, has a pleasant aroma and a subacid, strawberrylike flavor.

Ornamental: When grown where it's happy, mayapple will blanket an area, forming a foot-high canopy of attractive, glossy green foliage. Use it in wooded settings with a moist soil high in organic matter, just as it prefers in nature. An Asian species, Himalayan mayapple (*P. emodi* or *hexandrum*), has bright red fruit and bronzed foliage and is twice as medicinally potent.

CULTIVATION

Divide rootstock in the fall or sow seed in the spring. Mayapple requires partial shade and a moist soil high in organic matter.

GROWING CONDITIONS

- Plant hardiness zone 4.
- Humusy, rich, moist soil.
- Partial shade.

Immature Growth Stages

381

MINT

Mentha spp.   **Labiatae**

When summer days burn hot and the heat seems to follow you everywhere, you might be glad the mint is overtaking your garden. Out in the mint patch, the fragrances steam up from the plants. Collect bunches to cool and refresh you. Chew on a peppermint leaf or two and suck in the air for a cool blast. Splash some mint water over your face and on your shoulders. Drop a few sprigs in a glass of iced tea or make a mint julep. Sit back and relax.

DESCRIPTION

One of the most distinctive features of the mints is their square stems. Most species are invasive perennials, which send up new plants from their spreading roots. Since mints interbreed readily, it can be difficult to determine the exact species.

Flowers: Tiny; purple, pink, or white; in whorls, in terminal spikes; four stamens; five-toothed, tubular calyx.

Leaves: Opposite, simple, toothed; very fragrant.

Fruit: Four, smooth, ovoid nutlets.

Height: To 2 ft.

FLOWERING

July and August.

RANGE

Most mints native to Europe and Asia; some indigenous to South Africa, America, and Australia. Naturalized throughout North America from southern Canada to Mexico.

CHEF TIPS

- Mince fresh mint and combine with plain yogurt and sliced cucumbers.

- Add fresh mint to tuna salad, then dress it with lime vinaigrette.

- Prepare an herb vinegar using fresh mint and orange peel. Use the vinegar as a marinade for lamb and in dressings for spring salads.

HISTORY

When Persephone found out that Pluto was in love with the beautiful nymph Minthe, jealousy burned within her, and she changed Minthe into a lowly plant. Pluto couldn't undo Persephone's spell, but he did soften it a little so that the more Minthe was tread upon, the sweeter her smell would be. The name Minthe changed to Mentha and became the genus name of this herb, mint.

Few people considered it a lowly plant. The Pharisees paid their tithes with mint. The Romans crowned themselves with peppermint wreaths. The Roman scholar Pliny thought it the loveliest of herbs: "The very smell of it reanimates the spirit." The Greeks used mint in various herbal treatments and temple rites. They believed it could clear the voice, cure hiccups, and counteract sea serpent stings.

No doubt because of its refreshing scent, mint was always strewn around kitchens and sickrooms. This use of mint played an important role in a tale from Greek mythology: Two strangers walking through Asia Minor were snubbed by villagers, who offered them neither food nor drink. Finally, Philemon and Baucis, an old couple, prepared them a meal. Before setting the table, they rubbed mint leaves across it to clean and freshen it. The strangers turned out to be the gods Zeus and Hermes in disguise. They richly rewarded Philemon and Baucis for their hospitality, changing their humble home into a temple. Mint thus became a symbol of hospitality.

Mint continued to be an important aromatic herb in medieval times. People preferred to strew their homes with water mint *(Mentha aquatica)* because its scent is stronger than that of spearmint or peppermint. *M. Pulegium,* European pennyroyal, was spread about to get rid of fleas. Mint was also added to bathwater for its fragrance (infrequent though baths were in those days!).

Beginning in the eighteenth century, mint became an important medicinal herb. Various species were used as a cure for colic, digestive odors, and a host of other problems. Japanese mint was thought to have antifertility properties. A remedy for mad dog bites called for combining peppermint or spearmint with salt and applying it to the wound.

Peppermint and spearmint came to the New World with the colonists, who also used them medicinally. They drank mint tea for headaches, heartburn, indigestion, gas, and to help them sleep. They also drank mint tea for pure pleasure, especially since it wasn't taxed, but also simply because it tasted good.

USES

Mint can be used in so many different ways that it is hard to find someone who couldn't use it.

Medicinal: Mint is one of those herbs that really works as a home remedy, and it tastes good, too. You won't need a spoonful of sugar to make mint tea go down.

Peppermint, spearmint, and pennyroyal (see the entry Pennyroyal) are used most often, though peppermint is the most effective. Along with Japanese mint (*M. arvensis*), peppermint is the source of the commercially and medicinally important menthol. Spearmint, which does not contain menthol, is used only for flavor.

Probably the most typical complaints mint cures include indigestion, flatulence, and colic. Taking a few drops of mint oil, sipping hot mint tea, or drinking warm milk heated with fresh or dried peppermint leaves is said to calm an upset stomach or relieve muscle spasms such as menstrual cramps. The *U.S. Dispensatory* notes: "[Peppermint] is generally regarded as an excellent carminative and gastric stimulant, and is still widely employed in flatulence, nausea, and gastralgia."

It is the menthol in peppermint that is primarily responsible for this herb's beneficial effects, and the oil of peppermint contains anywhere from 50 to 78 percent menthol. Menthol acts in a couple of different ways. It stimulates the flow of bile to the stomach, which promotes digestion (so don't say no to the afterdinner mints when they're passed around). It also acts as an antispasmodic, calming the action of muscles, particularly those of the digestive system. In this way, it relieves upset stomachs. It can also temporarily reduce hunger, but after a little while the stomach resumes peristaltic action and hunger pangs become even stronger than they were at first. (Those afterdinner mints might find good use as before dinner mints when you want to stimulate the appetite.) Peppermint's antispasmodic effect may help to relieve menstrual cramps as well.

Toxicity: Peppermint is perfectly safe to use medicinally, although it tends to be a little strong for infants and very young children. In the uncertain realm of herbal medicines, it is satisfying to find an herb that does work and can be safely used at home.

Culinary: If you grow several different mints in your garden, you

---

MINT WATER

Twist or bruise 1 cup of peppermint, spearmint, or other mint. Place in a clean half-gallon container. Fill with fresh, cool water. Chill in refrigerator. Strain. Serve on ice.

A MINT JULEP, ANYONE?

When we think of hot, summer southern days, sometimes a scene comes to mind of men sitting on great porches, overlooking even greater, finely manicured lawns, sipping mint juleps from tall glasses. The mint julep was created in the 1800s shortly after the birth of Kentucky straight bourbon. Several recipes were developed for making it, and many stories were told of it, but one thing was certain, a man shouldn't take his mint julep lightly—the mint julep was a sophisticated drink for a refined gentleman.

"A mint julep is not the product of a formula," explained one nineteenth-century southern gentleman. "It is ceremony, and must be performed by a gentleman possessing a true sense of the artistic, a deep reverence for the ingredients, and a proper appreciation of the occasion. It is a rite that must not be entrusted to a novice, a statistician, nor a Yankee."

MINT—continued

MINT REMEDIES

The following are some popular mint-based remedies that you can try.

For flatulence: Take 2 or 3 drops of peppermint oil on a sugar cube, or drink a cup of peppermint tea.

For abdominal pain (including menstrual cramps): Drink warm milk heated with fresh or dried peppermint leaves; take a few drops of mint oil; or sip hot mint tea.

For flu or cold: Drink a tea made from equal quantities of peppermint and elderberry flowers, or peppermint mixed with chamomile.

For insomnia: Drink a cup of spearmint, peppermint, or orange bergamot mint tea.

For fever in children: Drink tea made from equal parts of horehound and spearmint.

For headache: Apply freshly gathered, crushed peppermint leaves to the forehead. Leaves may also be used to soothe tired, sore muscles or arthritic joints.

For toothache: Apply a few drops of peppermint or spearmint oil to the sore tooth and gums.

For bad breath: Chew on fresh mint leaves and stems.

For chapped hands: Wash rough skin with spearmint tea.

For sore mouth or throat: Gargle with spearmint tea.

For beestings or other insect bites: Lay crushed mint leaves on the bite.

will soon begin to appreciate the incredible range of flavors these plants possess. You'll also want to try using mints in ways other than in the traditional jellies, sauces, and teas. From the slightly fruity taste of apple mint, to the perfumy taste of bergamot mint, to the heady flavor of peppermint, there is a mint to please every palate and complement nearly every food.

Peppermint is, of course, the premier mint for flavoring candy, gum, and other sweets. Commercially prepared oil or extract are better for these uses than anything you might concoct at home from the fresh herb. For most other culinary purposes, garden peppermint is a bit strong. When you do use it, harvest only the young leaves; the older leaves and the stems tend to be bitter. The leaves make a fine hot or cold tea, or a garnish for punch or fruit. They are also the best mints for making mint water, a more refreshing drink for a hot day than any soft drink or soda.

Spearmint and curly mint (*M. aquatica* var. *crispa*) are more versatile culinary mints. Milder than peppermint, they enhance all sorts of meat, fish, or vegetable dishes. They mingle well with veal, eggplant, white beans, black beans, lentils, cracked wheat salads, fruit salads, fruit beverages, and creamy vegetable soups. They are old friends of peas, lamb, jellies, sauces, candy, and chocolate. Stuff fresh mint leaves and small garlic cloves beneath the skin of a roasting lamb before you cook it, or use the mint in a marinade. Add spearmint or curly mint to steamed carrots or new potatoes. Welsh cooks even add mint to the boiling water when they prepare cabbage. Dried mint adds a nice touch to split pea soup, diminishing the need for salt.

Apple mint (*M. suaveolens*) and the white-leaved pineapple mint (*M. suaveolens* var. *variegata*) have slightly fruity flavors. They are particularly good choices for garnishing drinks and adding zest to fruit salads or cottage and cream cheeses.

Some connoisseurs believe corsican mint (*M. Requienii*) has the true-blue mint flavor. It is the mint originally used to make crème de menthe. Use it sparingly to make mint water.

When adding mint to foods or when preparing mint tea, use either fresh or dried leaves. A garnish of fresh mint sprigs adds a refreshing touch to both foods and beverages. Mint is popular in Greek, Arabic, North African, Middle Eastern, and Indian food.

Available commercially: Fresh leaves, dried leaves, or extracts (used sparingly in desserts and beverages).

Substitute: Costmary.

Aromatic: "The smelle rejoiceth the heart of man," wrote the sixteenth-century herbalist John Gerard. Mint's sweet perfume

Spearmint

Field Mint

Bergamot Mint

Pineapple Mint

Peppermint

Corsican Mint

385

STARTING FROM SEED

If someone tries to sell you a packet of peppermint seeds, make sure you've still got your wallet and false teeth. There's a flimflam man on the loose.

Peppermint doesn't produce seed. It is a sterile hybrid of *Mentha spicata* and *M. aquatica.* Peppermint *must* be propagated by cuttings, division, or layering. In fact, these are the best ways to propagate all the mints. It's the only way you can be sure you will get the plant you want.

THE BUSINESS OF MINT

Mints are commercially important herbs as sources of flavor and menthol. Japanese mint, peppermint, and spearmint are the species most widely cultivated. Japanese mint, particularly the species *Mentha arvensis* var. *piperescens,* is the primary source of menthol and is cultivated in Japan, Taiwan, the People's Republic of China, Paraguay, Brazil, Argentina, and India. Most of the peppermint oil sold in the United States comes from the English mint *M. ×piperita* var. *vulgaris,* but the finest of all peppermint oils is produced by the white mint, *M. ×piperita* var. *officinalis,* a small plant that grows around Mitchum, England.

seems to expand and improve with age. Thus, the herb, fresh or dried, is an excellent aromatic. In some hot countries, bunches of fresh mint are hung about the house to freshen the air and lend a feeling of coolness. Dried, most mints perform well in sachets and potpourris. Corsican mint and peppermint, because of their high amount of strong, volatile oils, are particularly long lasting.

Bergamot mint is sweeter smelling. Sometimes used to scent perfumes and soaps, another of its common names is eau de cologne mint.

Ornamental: Every gardener wants mints in his or her herb collection. Where there is plenty of room or a desire for a semiwild landscape, they can be allowed to grow unchecked. In large, natural areas where a hardy ground cover is needed, you can just let any of the tougher mints take over: peppermint, horse mint, apple mint, or spearmint. Mow them as they come into flower, and you'll have a lovely thick carpet.

In smaller gardens or where you want to create a more formal impression, plant some of the shorter, small-leaved mints such as Corsican mint. Corsican mint looks lovely in rock gardens and grown between paving stones. With so many species and varieties from which to choose, there is a mint for just about any situation.

Cosmetic: Before you settle down to that iced mint tea, cool your skin with a refreshing mint water. You won't get all hot and bothered making it either—it is so simple to prepare. Just soak a cup of fresh peppermint or spearmint leaves in a quart of cool water, strain, and chill. Use this mint water to wash your face.

"Any of the mints used in the bath will be stimulative and restorative," writes Jeanne Rose in *The Herbal Body Book.* They are cleansing, too, and make effective lotions and facials. Steeped with rosemary in vinegar, mint is reported to help control dandruff. Rose recommends a strong mint infusion for restoring tone and softness to chapped hands.

Companion planting: Old-time gardeners claim that mints repel all sorts of garden pests. Spearmint and peppermint are often listed as good repellent plantings for aphids, flea beetles, and various cabbage pests. While field tests haven't confirmed this, we do know that menthol is an effective repellent, and that some mint species contain fungicides and feeding deterrents as well.

Other: While mints with all of their wonderful uses and their refreshing scent and taste attract lots of people to themselves, they repel certain animal and insect pests. To keep away mice and other rodents, strew rodent-ridden areas with fresh spearmint, peppermint, or European pennyroyal.

MINT SPECIES AND VARIETIES

Name	Leaves	Fragrance/ Flavor	Comments
Mentha aquatica Water mint	Heart-shaped, to 2 in. long	Very strong scent, not as pleasant as other mints	Flowers in ½–1-in.-wide inflorescences, thin stems, tends to lean; grows along streams
M. aquatica var. *crispa* Curly mint	Small, curled, light green	Crisp mint flavor	Grows along stream sides
M. arvensis Field mint	Ovate, stalked, toothed	Pungent, minty fragrance	Flowers in broad clusters, not spikes; common weed in poorly drained soils
M. arvensis var. *piperescens* Japanese mint	Large green leaves	Strong peppermint flavor	Flowers bloom in autumn; major source of menthol
M. longifolia Horse mint	Oblong to elliptical, 2–3½ in. long, white hairs, stalkless	Pungent, minty fragrance	Grows wild in damp ground, not usually cultivated, but parent of many hybrid varieties
M. ✕piperita Peppermint	Longer stalked and less hairy than spearmint	Source of original peppermint flavor	Flower spikes are broader than those of spearmint; purplish stems, rampant grower
M. ✕piperita var. *citrata* Bergamot mint	Large, dark green, with little yellow dots, pointed, wavy edges	Distinct citrusy scent and flavor	
M. Pulegium Pennyroyal	Hairy, ½ in. long, roundish	Mintlike fragrance	Flowers in dense clusters at leaf axils; good ground cover (see the entry Pennyroyal)
M. Requienii Corsican mint	⅜ in. long, bright green	Strong peppermint taste and aroma	Low growth makes for good ground cover; less hardy than other mints; original flavor for crème de menthe
M. spicata Spearmint	Sharply pointed, toothed, lance-shaped	Milder flavor than peppermint	Most common garden mint; sometimes listed as *M. viridis*
M. suaveolens Apple mint	Round, toothed, stalkless, hairy, 1–4 in. long	Slight apple scent, mildly fruity flavor	Sometimes incorrectly given the species name *M. ✕rotundifolia*
M. suaveolens var. *variegata* Pineapple mint	Light green, white-edged, ovate	Mild pineapple flavor	Decorative

MINT—continued

GROWING CONDITIONS

- Plant hardiness zone 5.
- Soil pH 6.5.
- Rich, moist, well-drained soil.
- Full sun to partial shade.

CULTIVATION

Gardeners tend to have more problems getting rid of mint than they do getting it started. With the possible exception of Corsican mint, mints are such rampant growers that they quickly overwhelm other plants. Unless you have a large area you want covered in mint, set up some barriers to their growth. Plant seedlings in bottomless number 10 cans or surround them with metal strips. As long as the barrier is 10 inches deep, it will keep the roots from spreading.

Because of crossbreeding, seeds don't always produce the exact species or variety promised. Propagation therefore is usually by suckers, stolons, cuttings, or division. Peppermint is a sterile hybrid of *M. aquatica* and *M. spicata,* so it must be propagated by cuttings. A wide variety of mints are available as seedlings from mail-order nurseries or herb farms. Plant these in the spring. You can also take cuttings from an existing mint bed in summer. Cuttings root easily in a moist potting soil, or even in water. If you wish to divide established plants, do it in the fall.

Mint thrives in a partly shady spot with plenty of moisture. Allow 1 to 1½ feet between plants. Don't dress the soil with fresh manure, or add too much organic matter, as this will only encourage rust.

Frequent cutting—even mowing of large plots—will keep mints at their prettiest. It encourages stems to branch out and makes for lusher, healthier plants. In the late fall, after your final harvest, cut back plants to the ground. This eliminates overwintering sites for mint pests. If winters are quite severe in your area, you might wish to mulch with straw or pine needles. Most species will begin to get a little woody and weedy after several years. You may wish to dig out old plants after five years, letting the younger ones take over. Most of the mints make fine pot plants and will thrive indoors and out. This keeps them under control and guarantees a fresh supply of leaves whenever you want them. Because of their rapidly growing roots, you'll need to divide and repot every year.

Pests and diseases: Mint is susceptible to verticillium wilt, mint rust, and mint anthracnose. The pests that might bother your mints include: spider mites, loopers, mint flea beetles, mint root borers, grasshoppers, cutworms, root weevils, and aphids. (See the entry Growing Herbs for information on controlling pests and diseases.)

Harvesting and storage: Fresh is best when it comes to mints. Dried or frozen is a good second, if you take time to carefully pick and store the herb.

Since it is such a tough plant, mint can be harvested almost as soon as it comes up in the spring. Young, tender leaves and stems have more flavor than the older ones, which tend to become woody.

MISTLETOE

Viscum album, Phoradendron serotinum   Loranthaceae

The phase of the moon has signaled the beginning of a new year. White-robed figures trudge through a winter oak woods in ancient England, ever peering upward. A cry rings out, and all turn to see a clump of green dangling from a gnarled branch. An older figure—the priest—is called forth, and to him passes a golden sickle. The others meanwhile ring the tree, joyously but ceremoniously singing, "Hey, derry down, down, down, derry." A mantle is spread below, and the priest, bearing his golden sickle, ascends the tree.

What plant could possibly occasion such solemn and mysterious ceremony and such song? The mistletoe, of course. And those white-robed ones who pursued it were none other than ancient Celtic Druids. They claimed that visions had been sent to instruct them to find the pretty parasite, and that if they failed to heed the visions and mistletoe fell to the ground, all manner of misfortune would occur. Once they had gathered it, the Druids used mistletoe in medicine and in fertility rites, and they hung it in their homes to ward off evil.

HISTORY

Many of the legends of mistletoe involve mystery, intrigue, and awe. One legend, for example, explains the French name of the plant, *herbe de la croix,* by saying that when once a tree, mistletoe had been used to make Christ's cross and that afterward it was cursed and denied a place on the earth and so became a parasite. It was an herb of the underworld in Greek and Roman mythology.

The Scandinavians tell that Balder, the god of Peace, was slain with an arrow made of mistletoe. The other gods and goddesses became quite saddened by this and asked that Balder's life be restored. When he did return to life, mistletoe was given to the goddess of love, who decreed that anyone who passed under the plant receive a kiss to show that mistletoe was a symbol of love. How this tradition became associated with the Christmas season goes back to the Druids, who it is said welcomed the new year with branches of mistletoe.

By 1682, mistletoe had moved out of legend and into practical use as a medicinal herb. In France herbalists prescribed mistletoe remedies for epilepsy, nervous disorders, and St. Vitus' dance. Elsewhere it was used for apoplexy and giddiness, to stimulate glandular activity, to serve as a heart tonic, and to aid digestion. Meanwhile in North America, the American Indians were using *Phoradendron serotinum* (known as American mistletoe; *Viscum album* is known as European mistletoe) to stimulate contractions during childbirth. They also used American mistletoe as an abortifacient.

UNSAFE

DESCRIPTION

Both mistletoes are semi-parasitic, freely branched, clumping, tree-born shrubs that live on a wide range of trees.

Flowers: Inconspicuous, unisexual, in short spikes from leaf axils; male and female on separate plants.

Leaves: Evergreen, opposite, oblong to obovate, thick, leathery, ¾–2 in. long. (American), 1–3 in. long (European).

Fruit: Small, white berries with sticky flesh and one seed.

Height: 1–2 ft.

FLOWERING

Midspring to early summer.

RANGE

Phoradendron serotinum can be found from New Jersey and southern Indiana south to Florida and Texas; also Missouri, Ohio, New Mexico, and some in Canada. *Viscum album* grows throughout Europe as far east as China and as far south as the Mediterranean.

HABITAT

American mistletoe has many hosts, although rarely does it grow on oaks. In the western states, it seems to prefer junipers. European mistletoe also has many hosts, but it usually does not choose evergreens.

MISTLETOE—continued

How does mistletoe get up in those trees?

Birds are the true propagators of this plant. Upon spying the delectable white berries, they fly to a plant to eat a few. Some of the berries get carried away to new trees, where they are dropped. The sticky berries adhere to the bark, and after a few days tiny roots emerge. Their flattened tips enable them to work their way through the bark and into the tree, eventually rooting the plant securely to the branch and enabling it to take nutrients from its host.

USES

While European and American mistletoes may have the same purposes hung in doorways at Christmastime, they have very different purposes when taken medicinally.

Medicinal: It is believed that the active ingredient of European mistletoe is a resin, viscin, and that its physiological effect is to temporarily benumb nerve impulses that would otherwise travel from a painful area or organ to the brain. Viscin first raises the blood pressure and then lowers it and speeds up the pulse. In this way, it interferes with the spasms of epilepsy.

American mistletoe, on the other hand, which contains the amines tyramine and beta-phenylethylamine, is believed to stimulate the heart and central nervous system, thus raising blood pressure. These amines also reportedly cause contractions in smooth muscles like those of the uterus; hence the use of mistletoe during childbirth.

According to pharmacognosist Varro Tyler, Ph.D., writing in *The Honest Herbal,* both mistletoes contain toxic proteins very similar in composition. In experiments in which these proteins were isolated and injected into laboratory animals, they produced similar effects: lowered blood pressure, reduced heart rate, and constricted blood vessels in the skin and skeletal muscles. However, no one has studied and followed the effects of these proteins in human beings, so the potential of mistletoe for medicinal use isn't really known.

One area of study that shows some promise is the use of mistletoe in treating tumors. James Duke, Ph.D., author of the *CRC Handbook of Medicinal Herbs,* describes recent research in which cancer cells treated with an extract from *V. album* were unable to reproduce in laboratory cultures. In fact, in Germany and Austria, drugs made from this extract are currently being used to treat certain cancers.

Toxicity: P. serotinum contains toxic amines and proteins called phoratoxins, which can slow the heart rate dangerously, cause hallucinations, cause convulsions, increase blood pressure, cause heart attacks or cardiovascular collapse, and lead to death.

Some people have died after eating the berries of *V. album.* According to the *British Medical Journal,* some people who have taken mistletoe remedies have shown hepatitis-B-like symptoms, although no direct link to active hepatitis has been found. Very large doses of European mistletoe may affect the action of the heart.

In addition to the potential toxicity of mistletoe's regular compounds, the plant may take up poisonous substances from the tree that it lives on. The message from all of this clearly is don't concoct any mistletoe remedies.

Ornamental: Be careful when using this plant as a decoration in the home, too. The berries look inviting to young children who might eat them; it's a good reason for hanging mistletoe high in doorways.

Another good reason to hang mistletoe in doorways is to try to win a kiss from a loved one. The traditional Victorian kissing ring was made from interlocking hoops festooned with colorful ribbon and with the sprig of mistletoe suspended in the middle. Mistletoe is also used in wreaths, sprays, door ornaments, or other trims. The magic of mistletoe continues to keep box loads of it coming to fancy florists and Christmas tree sellers around the first of December.

CULTIVATION

Neither American nor European mistletoe is cultivated, although sometimes in Europe the berries are rubbed onto branches or inserted into splits in the bark to help propagation. Mistletoe is simply gathered from the wild.

THE THIEF

American mistletoe, which derives its nutrients by sending its roots into host trees and stealing precious life juices, appropriately was given the generic name *Phoradendron.* The Greek *phor* means "thief" and *dendron,* "tree." Although European mistletoe lives the same life-style, its botanical name, *Viscum album,* was given to it for its sticky white berries.

European Mistletoe

American Mistletoe

MUGWORT

Artemisia vulgaris   **Compositae**

Mugwort has been surrounded by legends and superstitions for centuries. A crown of mugwort worn on St. John's Eve protected the wearer from evil possession, or so it was believed in the Middle Ages. In China mugwort would ward off evil spirits when hung during the time of the Dragon Festival (the fifth day of the fifth moon).

The herb's most interesting use is in moxibustion, a healing technique that originated in China. A small wad of the weed, called a moxa, is burned on the surface of the skin at a specific acupuncture point to produce a burn scab. The heat of the burning herb is used in conjunction with the familiar acupuncture needles to effect cures. In the 1830s Portuguese sailors brought the moxa to France, where it was temporarily in vogue as a supposed cure for blindness and many other problems.

DESCRIPTION

This soft, green plant has ball-shaped flower heads that are larger than those of most other artemisias, and it has been called one of the more ornamental members of the family. Its purple stems are angular, grooved, and hairy.

Flowers: Greenish yellow to brownish red; in long, terminal, panicled spikes; five stamens.

Leaves: Deeply cut, smooth, 4 in. long; segments oblong, toothed or entire; dark green on top, light gray-green and woolly underneath; basal rosette of pinnate leaves survives winter; sagelike scent.

Fruit: Seeds look like tiny sticks.

Height: To 6 ft.

FLOWERING

Summer.

RANGE

In temperate North and South America. In the United States, it is found south to Georgia and west to Michigan.

HABITAT

Waste places, deserts, and prairies; ditches and roadsides.

USES

Though much less dangerous than its close relative wormwood, mugwort nevertheless is better suited as an ornamental than as a medicine. The use of moxas and acupuncture especially must be left to trained physicians. Mugwort teas and solutions are not safe for internal use.

Aromatic: Europeans once stuffed pillows with mugwort in the belief that this would bring good, and vivid, dreams. Mugwort leaves have a sagelike smell and are used to repel moths.

Ornamental: Variegated and golden-leafed varieties of *Artemisia vulgaris* are attractive additions to the home garden. The leaves of the standard variety go beautifully with lavender and carnations and contrast with dark green mints.

Craft: Mugwort dries well and adds a nice texture to less-formal arrangements needing a slender, somewhat feathery, brown stalk.

Other: Use mugwort in herbal baths to relieve aches in muscles and joints. Modern herbalist Jeanne Rose recommends mixing it with agrimony and chamomile for this purpose.

GROWING CONDITIONS

- Plant hardiness zone 4.
- Average to poor, well-drained soil.
- Full sun.

CULTIVATION

Mugwort can be gathered from the wild but is easily raised from seed. Seeds germinate best at 55°F; because they are small, it is easiest to start them inside or to dig wild plants for transfer to the garden. Plant divisions are made in the spring or the fall.

Harvesting and storage: Gather the plant just as it begins to flower in the summer, cutting it to within 4 inches of the ground. Dry the leaves in the shade and store them in an airtight container.

MUSTARD

Brassica spp.   **Cruciferae**

The mustard family is a big one, and its fold includes scores of common weeds and such vegetables as cabbage, broccoli, and turnip. Relatively few herbalists and gardeners grow mustard for seed; it is a different plant than that cultivated for greens. But gardeners are showing a renewed interest in growing seeds for homemade mustard. Nurseries and seed companies carry black mustard (*Brassica nigra*), white or yellow mustard (*B. hirta*), and brown mustard (*B. juncea*), the common commercial variety. Why grow your own? Because you can have your mustard hot or mild, plain or spiced.

Some catalogs and herb books still use the earlier Latin genus, *Sinapis.*

HISTORY

Black mustard is thought to be the variety mentioned in the Bible. The ancient Greeks valued the herb for its medicinal properties as well as for its spicy flavor. They enjoyed the pungent green leaves as a pot herb and salad. The early Romans pounded the seeds and mixed them with wine to make an early version of our table mustard. The popularity of the condiment spread during the Middle Ages. The English name "mustard" is derived from the Latin *mustum ardens,* or "burning must," which refers to the early French practice of grinding the pungent seeds with grape must (the still-fermenting juice of wine grapes). By the seventeenth century France became the main source of table mustard.

As a medicine, black mustard was preferred over the milder, white-seeded species. Early herbalists recommended taking it internally to relieve digestive problems, and applying it externally to encourage blood flow. The English herbalist John Parkinson suggested the seeds as a treatment for epileptic seizures, and Nicholas Culpeper, another English herbalist, considered it excellent for toothaches and many other ailments.

In this country, the early settlers and Indians used mild and cultivated mustards for food and medicine. They ate the seeds and spring greens. Black mustard seeds were ground to a fine powder, added to animal fat, and applied as a paste to rheumatic joints and sprains. The Mohegan Indians used the black mustard to relieve headaches and toothaches.

USES

The mustards are equally at home in the kitchen and sickroom. They contain no poisonous parts, but the powdered seeds and the oil can be irritating if misused.

DESCRIPTION

Like all Cruciferaes, the mustards are distinguished by their strong smell and by four-petaled flowers that form a rounded Maltese cross. They also have a unique two-part fruit called a silique. Both black and white species are annuals, growing up to 6 ft. and 2 ft. tall, respectively.

Flowers: Small, yellow; four petals form cross; in terminal racemes; four sepals in calyx; two stamens.

Leaves: Alternate, various shapes; lower ones pinnately lobed or coarsely toothed; upper leaves less lobed.

Fruit: Long, slender pod.

Height: Brassica hirta to 4 ft.; *B. nigra* to 6 ft.

FLOWERING

Early summer.

RANGE

The mustards grow anywhere and everywhere. They are quite hardy, and their seeds remain viable for years—even centuries. Black mustard is native to Europe, Asia Minor, India, China, northern Africa, and the Americas. White mustard also grows wild in most parts of the world.

MUSTARD—continued

MAKING MUSTARD

If you have never made mustard, you should try it. It isn't at all difficult. Commercial mustard makers guard their recipes jealously, but you can create your own. Start, if you like, with this recipe, adapted from one in a catalog from Johnny's Selected Seeds of Albion, Maine.

Double-hot mustard: Boil ⅓ cup of cider vinegar, ⅔ cup of cider, 2 tablespoons of honey, 1 tablespoon of chopped roasted hot red peppers, ⅛ teaspoon of turmeric, and ½ to 1 teaspoon of salt. While hot, combine with ¼ cup of yellow mustard seed and ¼ cup of brown mustard seed and immediately grind the mixture in a blender. When smooth, add 1 tablespoon of olive oil. The yield is 1¼ cups.

Tips: The yellow seeds lose some of their heat with time. The finer-flavored brown seeds hold their heat longer. You can adjust the heat of your mustard by altering the proportion of yellow and brown seeds.

Too, you can extend the mustard and simultaneously temper its heat by adding more liquid, cornstarch, or arrowroot. Alternative liquids include dry white wine, vinegar, fruit juice, and leftover pickle juice (provided it isn't too salty).

The most expensive mustard to buy—grainy mustard—is the easiest to make. You need only a blender. A grain or coffee mill is needed to reduce the ingredients to a sufficiently fine texture for a smooth mustard.

Medicinal: The mustard plaster is a time-honored cure for the congested chest. It causes the skin to feel warm and opens the lungs to make breathing easier. The same plaster, made from the powdered seeds of black mustard or the milder species, has also been used to relieve arthritis, rheumatism, toothache, and other causes of soreness or stiffness.

A mustard plaster feels warm because of several active ingredients in the seeds. Most important are the glycoside sinalbin and the enzyme myrosin. When the powdered seeds are mixed with water, these react to form the essential oil—the strong-smelling, hot-tasting (and feeling) stuff we associate with the herb. Left on the skin too long, it will eventually cause blisters. For this reason, the pure powder or oil should never be applied directly to the skin. Instead, put the mustard plaster on a sheet of paper or cloth, and place the sheet on the skin. Remove the poultice as soon as it becomes uncomfortable. Wash the skin thoroughly to be sure no mustard paste remains. Never apply a poultice to very sensitive areas of the body. Some herbalists suggest rubbing castor oil or olive oil on sensitive skin before applying the plaster. You also can tone down the mustard by mixing it with rye flour before adding water, or by using egg white instead of water to prepare the paste.

The ingredients that make mustard effective externally also make it an appetite stimulant and a powerful internal irritant. In very small doses, mustard is said to stimulate the mucous membrane of the stomach and increase the secretions of the pancreas, thereby improving digestion. Larger doses of whole mustard seed will induce vomiting. The seeds' content of oil and fat make them a good laxative. Because of the risk of overdose, remedies made with this herb should be handled with special care. Over a prolonged period, large doses of black mustard could irritate the stomach and intestines.

Culinary: Use whole white (or yellow) mustard seeds in making pickles or chutney. This species is the sort used to prepare the familiar bright yellow hotdog mustard, as well as the English and German types. Brown mustard goes into the French types. Black mustard seed is often used for mustard powder as well as prepared mustard, and the seeds are fried until they pop in making many Indian dishes. Mustard oil is used in Indian cooking to impart a distinctive flavor.

The young leaves of black and white mustards are vitamin rich and tangy. However, most gardeners grow other species for greens, such as brown mustard, *B. juncea*. The young leaves are boiled with onions and salt pork in much of the South; southerners use hot, buttered cornbread to sop up the "pot likker" from the greens.

The leaves of *B. japonica* are an important ingredient in Chinese and Japanese cuisines. There are many different varieties to choose from. Stir-fry or steam them as an accompaniment for bland meats and fish.

Companion planting: Mustards reportedly stimulate the growth of beans, grapes, and fruit trees. No scientific evidence supports or denies this, but research has shown that when planted with collards and brussels sprouts, wild mustard reduces cabbage aphids on both plants and keeps flea beetles away from collards. In addition, mustards release a chemical into the soil that inhibits the emergence of cyst nematodes and prevents root rot.

Other: An infusion of the seeds of *B. nigra* added to a footbath reportedly soothes sore, aching feet.

CULTIVATION

Plants are easily propagated by seed. If you are growing mustard for its leaves, sow at several intervals from spring through early fall. If you want to harvest the ripe seeds, sow in the spring or late summer. A late-summer sowing will give you a head start on the following season; young plants will survive the winter, and by early summer of the following year, they should produce seeds that will ripen by autumn.

Plant the tiny seeds ⅛ inch deep in a sunny spot where soil is rich and well drained. Some gardeners say that white mustard tolerates heavy soil conditions better than black. Thin seedlings to stand 9 inches apart. The plants are heavy feeders, so dress the soil regularly with well-rotted manure or finished compost.

Mustard can easily become a garden pest because it self-sows readily. Don't plant it in your most formal areas, and take care to harvest all the pods before the seeds scatter. Once the seeds drop to the ground, you'll have a tremendous weed problem that could take years to correct.

Pests and diseases: If you find holes in the leaves or stems, your mustards may be infested with mustard beetles. (See the entry Growing Herbs for information on controlling pests.)

Harvesting and storage: Harvest the seeds when the pods have turned from green to brown, but before they begin to split open. Cut and spread the plants on a screen or tray covered with a tightly woven cloth. Within two weeks, you'll find that the seeds ripen—the pods will shatter easily. Abrade the pods between your palms. Winnow the seeds to clean them. Store whole or ground mustard in tightly covered jars.

GROWING CONDITIONS

- Soil pH 4.2–6.0.
- Rich, well-drained soil.
- Full sun.

MYRRH

Commiphora myrrha   **Burseraceae**

Gold, frankincense, and myrrh—these were the gifts of the wise men at the dawn of the Christian era. The aromatic resin of myrrh was valued at least 2,000 years before Christ.

A Syrian legend, later adopted by the Greeks, associates myrrh with the goddess Myrrha, daughter of Thesis, the king of Syria; she was forced by Aphrodite to commit incest with her father and then escaped being murdered by him when the gods transformed her into a myrrh tree. The drops of gum resin that come from cuts on the tree are said to be Myrrha's tears.

According to the Bible, Moses was instructed to anoint priests with an oil that used myrrh as an ingredient. The Egyptians employed myrrh in embalming fluids. It also was used as a cure for cancer, leprosy, and syphilis. Although such is the stuff of legend, myrrh does have some verifiable medicinal properties. It is also still valued as a perfume and incense ingredient.

DESCRIPTION

The myrrh is a little more than a sturdy bush but a little less than a tree. It looks as if its whitish gray trunk were stunted. Its knotted branches support branchlets that come out at right angles and end in sharp spines.

The commercial product of the tree is the resinous sap that oozes from fissures or wounds on the bark. The pale yellow liquid soon hardens to reddish brown crystals that look like tear-shaped pieces of rock candy. This gum has an acrid, aromatic odor and a bitter taste. The surface is powdery and rough, and the pieces are brittle, semitransparent, oily, and marked with white along the surface fractures.

Leaves: Divided into three leaflets, with the one at the tip much larger than the pair below it; leaflets oval, blunt, hairless, roughly toothed.

Fruit: Brown; oval but pointed and furrowed down entire length; calyx of flower remains on fruit as it ripens.

Height: 9 ft.

RANGE

Myrrh remains confined to very hot regions of the Middle East with basaltic soil. The best myrrh, called Turkish myrrh or karam, comes from the Arabian peninsula, Somalia, and Ethiopia, but myrrh is also imported from the East Indies.

USES

Myrrh's aromatic and unguent properties, not its minor medicinal accomplishments, keep it among the world's prized substances.

Medicinal: Aldehydes and phenols in its oil combine with acids in its resin to give myrrh its astringent and antiseptic properties. It is particularly effective when acting on the mucous membranes. It has also been used for sore throats and gums and for mouth ulcers, where its antiseptic and astringent properties may be of real benefit.

Myrrh has been used as a stimulating tonic and to promote peristalsis. It contains constituents that stimulate gastric secretions and relax the smooth muscles, but evidence of its effectiveness as an aid to digestion, a carminative, or an aid in chest or menstrual problems is either in doubt or unknown. There is no experimental evidence to support claims made for it as an expectorant.

Aromatic: When burned, myrrh repels mosquitoes (the Egyptians used it for fumigation). It burns slowly, emitting a mysterious odor that calls to mind an old church or synagogue.

It is an ingredient in soaps and perfumes.

Other: Veterinary medicine has long used myrrh in unguents for wounds, especially for horses.

CULTIVATION

This desert tree is not grown in the United States. Myrrh is available at some drug and health food stores, usually as a tincture and occasionally in gum form.

NASTURTIUM

Tropaeolum majus　　**Tropaeolaceae**

For a garnish or salad ingredient that combines the flavor of watercress with the hues of the rainbow, try nasturtiums. The spectral shout of their blossoms isn't for everyday use, but they can grace special sandwiches, bowls of greens, and punch.

The Spanish conquistadors brought nasturtiums to Spain from Peru in the sixteenth century. The flower traveled to England by the 1590s, and its reputation as a culinary herb gradually spread across the continent.

USES

Culinary: Nasturtiums have a peppery taste. Toss the fresh flowers or the young leaves into salads. The flowers make stunning garnishes. Float them in bowls of punch. The pickled flower buds can stand in for imported capers. Cure them in vinegar.

Ornamental: Nasturtiums are easy to grow. Once they begin to bloom in the summer, they will continue to flower until the first frost in the fall. The leaves are attractive in their own right, with a pleasing shape and texture.

With their low, compact form, nasturtiums can be set attractively in and around rocky areas. The vining varieties will climb trellises and fences, and they can be trained along wires or strings in front of walls. If planted on a bank, they will creep down the slope.

Nasturtiums make wonderful potted plants, indoors or out. Plant them in window boxes or hanging baskets.

Companion planting: Nasturtiums are a well-known companion plant. They are credited with repelling whiteflies, various cabbage pests, and squash bugs. Scientific studies don't give a lot of support to these claims. Nasturtiums did keep green peach aphids away from peppers but were not as effective at reducing Colorado potato beetles on potatoes. They also didn't keep whiteflies away from beans or imported cabbageworms from collards.

CULTIVATION

Grow nasturtiums from seed sown as early in the spring as the soil warms, ½ to ¾ inch deep. A sunny location is best; nasturtiums grown in a shady, moist area will produce an abundance of foliage but few flowers. Once seedlings have established themselves, thin them to 6 to 9 inches apart.

Container gardening: Nasturtiums are easily grown in pots for the windowsill or greenhouse. Sow seeds in a coarse, porous soil that is not overly rich. Place the pots in full sun and water moderately. If you grow nasturtiums in the greenhouse, keep it ventilated.

DESCRIPTION

Nasturtium is a low-growing, bushy or viny annual with saucer-shaped leaves and brilliant blossoms. (See photos on pages 101 and 378.)

Flowers: Funnel shaped, 1–2½ in. across; red, orange, or yellow; five petals, fusing at base to form narrow shafts; eight stamens; five sepals make up calyx.

Leaves: Alternate, round to kidney-shaped, angled or wavy edges, toothless, 2–7 in. wide, dark green.

Fruit: Three fused compartments, each with one seed.

Height: 1 ft. tall, 2 ft. wide, or can reach 6 ft. as vine.

FLOWERING

Through summer until first frost.

RANGE

Nasturtiums are native to South America, where they grow as perennials. They are widely cultivated.

GROWING CONDITIONS

- Average, moist, well-drained soil.
- Full sun.

NEW JERSEY TEA

Ceanothus americanus   **Rhamnaceae**

The American colonists' commando action in Boston Harbor does not seem quite so bold when you consider that the Americans had already learned to brew tea from a number of abundant native plants. New Jersey tea was among them. After being told of the plant by the Indians, dwellers in the thirteen colonies made infusions of both green and dried leaves, producing a beverage much like Chinese green tea.

Since it is somewhat astringent, New Jersey tea was also used as a gargle. For sore throats, a tea was made by boiling New Jersey tea leaves and seeds. The bark of the red roots was used as a sedative, stimulant, and antispasmodic, and for treating respiratory diseases, high blood pressure, and enlarged spleens.

Much later, a commercial preparation of the bark was used to prevent hemorrhaging after surgery. At various times bark preparations have been used for regulating the circulation of lymph, treating enlarged lymph nodes, curing nonfibrous cysts, stopping menstrual hemorrhage and nosebleeds, and treating hemorrhoids and ulcers.

DESCRIPTION

New Jersey tea is a scraggly deciduous shrub. Its leaves are so sparse that the shrub often looks as if it were composed of thorny dead branches.

Flowers: Small, white; on long stalks at end of a very long umbel or raceme; racemes in clusters 1–2 in. across, growing on shoot of current season's growth; racemes look like small, white puffs and if rubbed in water, will make a soaplike foam.

Leaves: Alternate but occasionally opposite, finely toothed, oval to oblong, short stalked; hairy and light green on undersides, dark green and somewhat downy on top.

Fruit: Seedpods resemble acorns with horns; distinctly three lobed; when dry, separate into three nutlets.

Height: 2–3 ft.

FLOWERING

September.

RANGE

Native of North America.

HABITAT

Dry woods, on rocky ledges, and in hardwood forests; adaptable to poor soil.

USES

New Jersey tea today is principally an ornamental plant and only secondarily a medicinal one. As a beverage, it has gone out of favor.

Medicinal: The plant is high in tannin (as is tea from the East) and contains several acids that may explain its use as a blood coagulant. The root bark is definitely astringent, which may be why it works for mouth sores and as a gargle. Experiments conducted in 1922 justify its use to decrease blood pressure and to aid coagulation.

Ornamental: The plant is certainly attractive enough to deserve a place in the back of perennial beds or in foundation plantings of shrubs or shrub borders. Its chief advantage is that it blooms at a time when other flowering bushes are through for the year, so it is a welcome addition to any garden.

CULTIVATION

Nearly all *Ceanothus* species are short-lived, and they must be replaced often when grown as ornamentals. They adapt well in either full sun or partial shade. Prune New Jersey tea in late winter to early spring to control its straggly habit, cutting severely and close to the base to remove all shoots of the season immediately past.

The best way to propagate New Jersey tea is with summer cuttings. The roots are so fibrous and long that they are too hard to dig for transplanting. Cuttings take best in a cold frame or greenhouse.

GROWING CONDITIONS

- Plant hardiness zone 5.
- Light, well-drained soil.
- Full sun to partial shade.

ONION

Allium Cepa   Liliaceae

What plant is most often depicted in Egyptian tomb paintings? What plant did the Greeks and Romans come to have a love-hate relationship with, both praising its healing properties and damning its rank odor? What plant did Alexander the Great feed to his troops to give them strength for battle?

The humble onion.

USES

These bulbs are so widely grown as vegetables that we tend to overlook the fact that they have long been credited with healing powers, and that some varieties make lovely ornamentals.

Medicinal: As a medicine, *Allium Cepa* contains smaller doses of garlic's antibacterial and antifungal components. A paste of onions is said to prevent infection in wounds and burns. Other extracts inhibit blood clotting and seem to reduce cholesterol levels in people who eat high-fat diets. Experiments have shown that rats injected with an onion extract had lower blood pressure. And recent research suggests that onions increase the production of high-density lipoproteins, which in turn are believed to help clear the arteries of fatty deposits.

In addition to these documented benefits, onions boast a host of unproven folkloric applications. To cure baldness, rub a little onion juice on your head and lie out in the sun. To treat burns, lay slices of salted onion on them. To erase freckles, mix onion juice with vinegar and rub on freckles, age spots, or warts.

Culinary: White onions are the most pungent and strong; yellow are milder and sweeter; and red (or purple) are the mildest and sweetest. Sulfur compounds in onions make themselves known long after a meal because they travel through the bloodstream and are expressed through the pores in sweat and through the lungs in exhaled breath. So, it takes time, not just toothpaste and mouthwash, to rid your body of that pungent aroma.

The cured bulb of the plant (called dry onion) is used raw, sautéed, steamed, broiled, boiled, pickled, marinated, stuffed, cooked and pureed, baked, deep-fried in batter, and caramelized. Onions jazz up cheese spreads, savory pies, stuffings, soups, stocks, casseroles, salads, breads, pâtés, meat loaves, steamed vegetable combinations, and stir fries.

Available commercially: Whole dry onions, frozen whole onions, frozen chopped onions, onion powder, charred onion powder, onion flakes, onion salt, and onion juice. Note that most powder, flakes, and salt taste metallic and acrid and are vastly inferior to the fresh bulb.

DESCRIPTION

The onion is a biennial or perennial plant that grows from a bulb. The erect stem carries an umbel of flowers.

Flowers: Small; white, pink, or purple; six segments; six stamens; in globe-shaped umbels.

Leaves: Four to six, narrow, basal, cylindrical, hollow, blue-green.

Fruit: Capsule containing black seeds.

Height: 4 ft.

FLOWERING

June through August.

RANGE

Native to Asia, these hardy bulb plants are grown throughout the world.

CHEF TIPS

- Save time in the kitchen by keeping frozen minced onions on hand. First, mince onions, then blanch them for two minutes, pat dry, and freeze in recipe-size portions. Add them as needed directly to sauces, soups, and stews.

- Create an onion puree to spice up sauces, soups, and stews. Peel and chop onions and add them to a saucepan with a bay leaf and stock to cover. Simmer until tender, let cool, then puree.

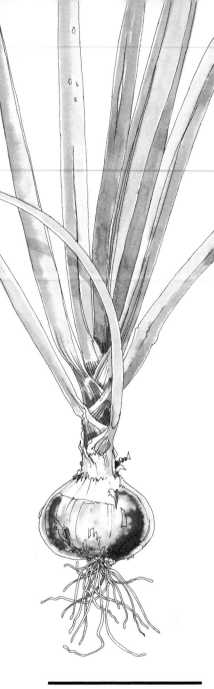

ONION—continued

Ornamental: Many alliums have been bred strictly for their ornamental value. The most familiar species is *A. giganteum* with its huge purple flower. Just let any of your garden alliums blossom, and you'll have ornamentals every bit as nice as this.

Craft: The flowers of leeks, chives, and garlic chives can be dried for use in everlasting arrangements.

Dye: Dyes made from onion skins are famous. Yellows, oranges, and browns can be produced in wool depending on the mordant used and whether yellow or red onion skins are employed. (See the entry Dyes from Herbs for more information.)

Companion planting: Gardeners recommend planting onions with beets, cabbages, lettuce, and strawberries to enhance their growth. They'll also tell you to keep onions away from beans, peas, and sage. Reportedly onions repel cabbage loopers, Colorado potato beetles, carrot flies, and imported cabbageworms.

CULTIVATION

Ordinary onions can be propagated from seed or sets. Seed is cheaper, but sets are faster. Shallots and Welsh onions are best started from sets. For Egyptian onions, plant the bulbs that form in the soil or the largest bulbils taken from the stem tops.

In frost-free climates, onions do well if planted in the fall for an early spring harvest. Elsewhere, they are best planted in the early spring. Sow seeds thickly and evenly, about ½ inch deep. Plant bulbs and bulbils about 1 inch deep, making sure to place the pointed end up and the rooting end down.

Onions need rich, well-drained soil that is loose and moist. As long as sufficient water is provided and weeds are controlled, onions require little care during the growing season.

Pests and diseases: Onions are susceptible to onion smut and downy mildew and attack from onion maggots or onion thrips. (See the entry Growing Herbs for information on controlling pests and diseases.)

Harvesting and storage: Harvest scallions at any time during the growing season. For mature onions wait until the tops begin to yellow and fall to the ground. Knock down the rest of the plants and wait a couple of days before carefully pulling up the plants. If the weather is dry, you can let the pulled onions ripen outside for a day or two before moving them to a dry, unheated shed. Otherwise, bring them in promptly and spread them on a screen. You can keep them there indefinitely; or, once they're thoroughly dry, you can braid them or place them in net bags for the winter. As long as the onions have been thoroughly dried and are not bruised or diseased, they will keep well all winter. Do not store them in the refrigerator.

GROWING CONDITIONS

- Soil pH 6.0.
- Rich, well-drained, moist soil.
- Full sun.

OREGANO

Origanum spp.   **Labiatae**

Oregano. Of what do you think when you hear of that herb?

Perhaps you recall its flavor in your homemade tomato sauce or pizza. If you think of the plant in your garden, do you picture oregano? Or is it marjoram you see? Marjoram looks very much like oregano, and it's in the same genus. The name oregano has caused confusion over the years because you don't come across simply one oregano or even just a few, but rather a whole genus of herbs, all of which have been called oregano because of their culinary use.

HISTORY

The confusion over oregano began early in its history. The Greeks and Romans knew and used oregano, but exactly which species it was is unclear. Perhaps it was *Origanum vulgare,* the common oregano that grows wild in the mountains of Greece. Oregano's name means "joy of the mountain," derived from the Greek *oros,* meaning "mountain," and *ganos,* meaning "joy." Perhaps this is why much later, in the sixteenth century, herbalist John Gerard recommended a decoction of the leaves to "easeth such as are given to overmuch sighing."

Many of oregano's early uses were medicinal rather than culinary ones. The Greeks made poultices from the leaves and placed them on sores and aching muscles. The ancient Roman scholar Pliny recommended oregano poultices for scorpion and spider bites. The great herbal written by the Greek physician Dioscorides in the first century A.D. describes more than one oregano as medicine.

Five hundred years later, herbals continued to recommend the oreganos as cures for various ailments, but the problem of identifying the species of oregano being discussed was yet unresolved. The fact that medieval herbals were all derivative of Dioscorides's writing may have had something to do with this. By the time Londoner John Gerard wrote his herbal in the sixteenth century, he had to devote a paragraph to straightening out the names of the different oreganos and explaining which one his predecessors had meant.

Oregano came to North America with various European colonists and escaped from gardens to grow wild. Today, wildflower guides to the Northeast routinely list the wild oregano.

The oreganos quickly became part of standard medicine in the United States. It was listed in various materia medica as a stimulant and carminative. The tea was used for chronic coughs and asthma. Doctors also used oil of oregano, which was extracted by distilling the herb with water. (Depending upon the season, as much as 200 pounds of oregano is required to produce a single pound of the oil. By the time that much oregano is reduced to such a concentration, it

DESCRIPTION

Oreganos are aromatic, herbaceous perennials with erect, hairy, square stems. See also the entry Marjoram for a description of *Origanum Majorana.* (See photo on page 99.)

Flowers: ¼ in. long, tubular, two-lipped, rose-purple to white; four protruding stamens; in terminal spikelets to 1⅛ in. long.

Leaves: Opposite, toothed or toothless, oval, pointed; up to 2 in. long.

Fruit: Four seedlike nutlets.

Height: 1–2 ft.

FLOWERING

July through September.

RANGE

The Mediterranean region of Europe to central Asia; widely cultivated. *O. vulgare* naturalized in the eastern United States.

CHEF TIPS

- Create an easy appetizer by drizzling a chunk of feta cheese with a bit of olive oil. Then sprinkle on minced fresh oregano and serve with crusty bread and ripe tomatoes.

- Toss thinly sliced red radishes with minced scallions, minced fresh oregano, lemon juice, and olive oil, and serve on a bed of shredded spinach.

OREGANO—continued

WHICH OREGANO?

If you plant the oregano seeds sold by many seed houses, *Origanum vulgare,* you'll end up with a fetching, bushy little plant with all the flavor of lawn grass. Grow this species for its medicinal use or for its pretty pink flowers, which dry well and can be used in floral arrangements.

For flavor in cooking, grow *O. vulgare* subsp. *hirtum* (also referred to as *O. heracleoticum* and *O. hirtum*) or *O. vulgare* 'Viride'. You can also try any of the "oreganos" that really aren't oreganos at all.

One of the most flavorful of these is *Lippia graveolens,* known as Mexican oregano or Puerto Rican oregano. A member of the verbena family, it has cream-colored flowers and ovate leaves. A tender perennial, it can only be grown outdoors in the South and Southwest. Elsewhere in the country, it can be grown in containers indoors in well-drained soil of a neutral pH. Place it in a sunny, south-facing window.

GROWING CONDITIONS

- Plant hardiness zone 5.
- Soil pH 6.8.
- Well-drained, average soil.
- Full sun.

has quite a snap.) A drop or two on cotton was rubbed on an aching tooth. Bald men mixed oregano with olive oil and rubbed it, with hope swelling, into their scalps. The olive oil and oregano mixture was also rubbed onto rheumatic limbs and sprains.

As a cooking herb, oregano did not catch on at first. Looking through eighteenth-century recipes, it's easy to find foods that use "sweet marjoram," but chancing upon oregano in a recipe is more difficult. Some writers maintain that it wasn't until World War II that the flavoring caught on. Servicemen returned from the Mediterranean with a taste for oregano (or at least a taste for Italian cooking), and once pizza embedded itself in the American consciousness, oregano became all-American.

USES

Today, you'd probably find few people who hadn't tasted oregano. After all, how many people do you know who have never eaten pizza or spaghetti with tomato sauce? You'd probably have difficulty, however, finding someone who uses oregano medicinally.

Medicinal: Oregano is still used by some in modern herbal remedies, and many of those remedies are familiar ones from oregano's past. Modern herbalists recommend infusions of the leaves for indigestion, coughs, headaches, and to promote menstruation. Oregano has been described as a tonic and stimulant. The historical toothache remedy that calls for placing drops of oregano oil on the painful tooth is still practiced by some today. An infusion of the flowers reportedly helps to prevent seasickness. Externally, warm poultices of oregano leaves are said to soothe painful swellings.

No clinical evidence supports or refutes any of these claims. If you want to test them yourself, oregano won't cause you any harm.

Culinary: Best known for its appearance in tomato sauce, oregano has a hot, peppery flavor. The leaves of the plant are used in the cuisines of Italy, Greece, Brazil, Mexico, Spain, Cuba, Colombia, and wherever marjoram, its gentler twin, is found.

Oregano enhances cheese and egg combinations, including omelets, frittatas, quiches, and savory flans. It adds dimension to yeast breads, marinated vegetables, roasted bell peppers, mushrooms, roasted and stewed beef, pork, poultry, game, onions, black beans, zucchini, potatoes, eggplant, and shellfish. Its flavor combines well with those of garlic, thyme, parsley, and olive oil.

Available commercially: Dried whole berries or dried ground leaves (whole are preferable).

Substitute: Marjoram, in a greater amount.

Cosmetic: Read labels; you may find oregano or oil of oregano.

Baths: A muslin bag of oregano leaves bobbing in a steaming bath is recommended for relieving aches and stiff joints. The hot water alone might account for the comfort, but the fragrance would certainly lift the spirits.

Craft: The flowers of *O. vulgare* dry nicely and can be used in herb and flower arrangements. Fresh sprigs of oregano make a nice addition to a living culinary wreath.

Companion planting: Gardeners have recommended planting oregano with beans to enhance their growth.

CULTIVATION

To grow oregano for cooking, try to start with a plant or a cutting of a plant, something you can taste before planting. The consensus among serious growers is that *O. vulgare* just is not going to give much flavor unless you happen upon one of the varieties or subspecies. Look for *O. heracleoticum,* says Sal Gilbertie, owner of Gilbertie's Herb Nursery in Westport, Connecticut. This plant varies a great deal when grown from seed, so try to get plants.

Oreganos can be propagated by root divisions in the spring or by cuttings. If you must resort to seed, plant a lot so you can select the plants with prime flavor. The seeds are tiny—130,000 to an ounce. Don't cover them with soil; they germinate better in light. Kept at the optimum germination temperature, 70°F, they should germinate in about four days. Pot them as a clump, suggests Tom De Baggio of Earthworks Herb Garden Nursery in Arlington, Virginia, and keep them a little on the dry side.

Herb grower Betty Ann Laws seeds her oregano directly as long as the temperature will be above 45°F. To keep the seeds from being washed away in a hard rain, she covers them with cheesecloth until the seedlings start to poke through.

Pests and diseases: Oregano is susceptible to root rot and fungal disease, and it can become infested with spider mites, aphids, or leaf miners. (See the entry Growing Herbs for information on controlling pests and diseases.)

Harvesting and storage: To harvest the plant, Betty Ann Laws says sprigs can be snipped when the plant is only 6 inches high. In fact, this makes the plant bushier. In June when the plant is budding so vigorously that it's hard to keep them picked, she cuts the whole plant, leaving only the lowest set of leaves. It sounds rash, but she claims her plants start leafing out again within two weeks. She cuts the plants back drastically again in August.

OREGON GRAPE

Mahonia Aquifolium   **Berberidaceae**

This shrub offers shiny hollylike foliage, clusters of fragrant yellow flowers, and deep purple berries, but herbalists are impressed with the part of the Oregon grape that grows out of sight. Its bitter-tasting root is one of the most versatile of native American herbs.

The name is something of a misnomer. The grapes are not grapes at all, though you can eat them, and they can be cooked down into a jam. The use of Oregon is officially sanctioned, however; it is the state flower of Oregon.

Some seed and plant catalogs still use the former genus name, *Berberis*. While it is in the barberry family, taxonomists have moved it into its own genus, *Mahonia,* perhaps to simplify things. According to *Hortus Third* there are more than 100 species of *Mahonias* and more than 500 of barberries. The genus was named, incidentally, to commemorate Bernard M'Mahon, a distinguished early American horticulturist of Philadelphia, who died in 1816. Other common names include mountain grape, holly-leaved barberry, creeping barberry, and in Spanish-speaking areas, *hierba de sangre*.

DESCRIPTION

The Oregon grape has a striking appearance. This evergreen shrub bears Oregon's state flower.

Flowers: Tiny, bright yellow, six petals, nine sepals, six stamens; in 1¼–3-in.-long racemes; racemes in dense clusters; fragrant.

Leaves: Dense; from 4–6 in. long; five to nine oblong-lanceolate leaflets; leaflets 1–3 in. long, prickly edges like holly, dark green, leathery, lustrous in spring and summer; turn bronze, gold, crimson, and purple in fall.

Fruit: Deep blue and purple berries; ⅓ in long; in drooping clusters; edible when ripe.

Height: 3–6 ft.

FLOWERING

Spring.

RANGE

The Oregon grape is common in coniferous forests throughout the American Northwest, from Colorado and Idaho west to Oregon, and north to Canada; variants can be found in New England and the Atlantic states.

HABITAT

Along roadsides, in pastures and thickets, and under trees in pine mulch.

HISTORY

Long before hardy pioneers traveling the Oregon Trail encountered the plants, the Indians used *M. Aquifolium* for food and medicine. The berries, which have a slightly bitter, but not unappetizing taste, were used to make jelly and wine and to flavor soups. The root of this herb, however, is what earned Oregon grape its great stature among Indian tribes. Medicine men used the crushed, dried yellow rootstock to cure a wide variety of ailments, including ulcers, heartburn, rheumatism, kidney disorders, scrofulous skin conditions, and poor appetites.

The early settlers of the western frontier learned of the rootstock's healing qualities from the Indians, and Oregon grape's popularity as a medicine boomed in the 1800s. One popular Oregon grape remedy concocted by early herbalists called for soaking the roots in beer that had been warmed to just below the boiling point. This tonic was said to relieve hemorrhaging and jaundice.

Oregon grape tonics appeared on the market in the late 1800s, and the herb was listed in official pharmacopoeias until 1950. Europeans, too, learned of the medicinal properties of relatives of this herb (all *Mahonia* species have similar medicinal properties) and considered them excellent blood purifiers.

USES

Medicinal: The active ingredient that makes *M. Aquifolium* such an effective remedy is an alkaloid called berberine (derived from

Berberis). This constituent is found in other powerful healing herbs, such as goldenseal. Berberine stimulates bile secretions, and modern herbalists and homeopaths suggest it promotes good liver function as well as purifying the spleen and the blood. A tincture of Oregon grape is also still used to treat such skin disorders as eczema, acne, herpes, and psoriasis.

The root is most often administered as an infusion, made with ½ ounce of dried root steeped in 1 cup of boiling water. The dosage is 3 tablespoons daily. Herbal manuals warn, however, that persons with overactive livers (a condition brought on by overeating or eating too much rich food) should stay away from Oregon grape.

The purple fruits are said to have a cooling effect when crushed and included in drinks used by herbalists to break fevers. High in vitamin C, the berries were used to prevent and treat scurvy. They can be dried, made into preserves, or converted to a syrup.

Ornamental: Because of their hardiness and attractiveness, Oregon grape makes a wonderful addition to a landscape. The shrubs grow well along fences and driveways and under trees. Many of *M. Aquifolium's* relatives are also popular with gardeners, including *M. repens, M. nervosa,* and *M. Bealei*. The warm-toned wood of the Oregon grape is beautiful, when finished, and is often used for crucifixes and other wooden treasures.

Dye: Yellow and tan dyes can be obtained from the roots and from the stems and leaves combined. The fruit yields a purplish blue color to wool mordanted with alum.

CULTIVATION

Some varieties of *Mahonia* are hosts to wheat rust fungus, and planting them in wheat-growing areas is prohibited. *M. Aquifolium,* however, is immune to the fungus.

M. Aquifolium prefers a shady location and well-drained soils; however, because of its hardiness, it can survive in less-than-perfect conditions. The plant may be propagated through cuttings taken in midsummer; the new plants will be ready to set out the following spring. Oregon grape also grows from seed. Collect the seeds from the berries in the fall and plant them outdoors so they can adapt to cold temperatures. The roots can be dried in a paper bag.

Oregon grape relatives worth considering for the garden are japonica (*M. Bealei*), a dwarf variety (*M. nervosa*), and creeping barberry, with its bluish green leaves (*M. repens*). They work well under trees and in shrubbery borders.

Pests and diseases: Leaf spot, powdery mildew, and rust can do damage to Oregon grape. (See the entry Growing Herbs for information on controlling diseases.)

GROWING CONDITIONS

- Plant hardiness zone 6.
- Well-drained, humusy soil.
- Shade.

ORRIS

Iris ×*germanica* var. *florentina*   **Iridaceae**

Orris is the part of the florentine iris you don't see—the rhizome. Everyone is familiar with the flower, in its extravagant range of colors and forms. (Thousands of varieties and hybrids have been developed from the 300-odd species.) The rootstock is dried to prepare one of the most potent and enduring violet fragrances, and it remains an important fixative and scent.

The ancient Egyptians and Greeks learned that the bland-smelling orris root would take on a remarkable fragrance if dried for at least two years. Medicinally, the root powder and juice were used as a cathartic and diuretic, and to treat convulsions, coughs, upset stomachs, bites, and "saucie face," known to us as acne.

As its name suggests, however, the florentine iris has deeper roots in Florence, Italy. It was here, during the Middle Ages, that the commercial cultivation of orris root first began; the city remains a center for orris root production for perfume making.

DESCRIPTION

One of the longest-cultivated flowering perennials, the iris is available in as many colors as there are in the spectrum. Its name, in fact, comes from the old Greek word for rainbow.

Flowers: Corolla composed of three petal-like sepals called falls, which bend backward, and three true petals called standards, which stand erect and arched; falls purple with brown veins, yellow or white "beards"; standards lilac or blue; three stamens.

Leaves: Slender, sword-shaped, parallel veined, overlap at bases.

Fruit: Many-seeded, oblong capsules.

Height: 30 in.

FLOWERING

May and June.

RANGE

A native of the Mediterranean region, florentine iris has been naturalized in central Europe, parts of the Middle East, South America, and Africa. It grows well throughout North America, except in the humid climate of the Gulf Coast states.

USES

Orris is no longer prescribed by today's physicians or herbalists for treating medical conditions, but medicinal uses were never its strong suit.

Aromatic: Orris powder's heady violet fragrance is effective as a fixative in potpourris. The powder can also be added to aromatic sachets and herb pillows for freshening household linens. Commercially, it is used to produce violet blends. Frangipani, an Italian fragrance, contains orris root among its ingredients. The aromatic power of orris increases with age; in fact, the fresh roots have very little to say to the nose.

Ornamental: Even if you don't explore the uses of dried orris root, the lovely flowers of the florentine iris are attractive enough to earn a spot in any garden.

CULTIVATION

As with most irises, the florentine iris thrives on lots of sunlight and a fertile, well-drained soil. Plant in the early spring; the rhizomes should be divided in the summer after flowering. Make sure that half the divided bulb is left above the surface because it will rot if completely covered by soil. Irises should be divided every few years to insure pretty and abundant blossoms.

Harvesting and storage: If used for aromatic purposes, the rhizomes should be dug up in the autumn and immediately set out to dry. The violet fragrance won't come into its own for two years.

GROWING CONDITIONS

- Plant hardiness zone 5.
- Soil pH 7.0.
- Fertile, well-drained soil.
- Full sun.

PARSLEY

Petroselinum crispum   Umbelliferae

Parsley has the misfortune of being a token herb on plates of steak and fish. But that resilient sprig really is edible, and its high chlorophyll content makes it a natural breath sweetener.

The Romans are said to have used it at orgies to cover up the smell of alcohol on the breath, while also aiding digestion. And there's the unflattering remark that was once made about those who looked as if at death's door: "The man's in need of parsley." (Corpses were sprinkled with parsley to deodorize them.)

Parsley is most often thought of as a garden plant, but it will do well enough on a windowsill, even in a chilly room, to make a contribution of vitamin C to you when you most need it.

HISTORY

In ancient Greece parsley was used in funeral ceremonies long before it was thought of as a garnish. It was also placed in wreaths given to winning athletes because the Greeks believed that the god Hercules had chosen parsley for his garlands. And for athletic horses, the greens were thought to give stamina to win races.

The Greeks also associated parsley with oblivion and death. According to legend, parsley sprang up where the blood of the Greek hero Archemorus was spilled when he was eaten by serpents. The Greeks used the herb to fashion wreaths for graves.

By the Middle Ages, parsley had made its appearance in herbal medicines. It has been given credit for curing a great range of human ills, especially those having to do with the kidneys and liver. It has also been used against plague, asthma, dropsy, and jaundice and as a carminative, an emmenagogue, and an aid to digestion.

USES

Although we tend to think of it only as a decorative green, parsley has been used to attract rabbits and hares and to repel head lice.

Medicinal: Parsley is a course in vitamin therapy all by itself, containing vitamin A, more vitamin C per volume than an orange, several B vitamins, calcium, and iron. Beyond the contribution of its vitamins and minerals, parsley is not significant medicinally, although doctors in the United States continue to prescribe parsley tea for young female patients with bladder problems. The root has laxative properties.

The distinctive odor common to all parts of the parsley plant is the work of volatile oils, one of which, parsley camphor, has been

DESCRIPTION

There are three common varieties of this popular, bright green biennial: flat leaf (Italian), curly leaf, and parsnip rooted (Hamburg). (See photo on page 238.)

Flowers: Tiny, greenish yellow, five petals, five stamens; in umbels.

Leaves: Divided pinnately into featherlike sections; lay flat like celery leaves, or curl into small, frilly leaflets, depending on variety.

Fruit: Small seeds; oval, gray-brown, and ribbed.

Height: 1½ ft.

FLOWERING

Early summer.

RANGE

Parsley grows wild from Sardinia east to Lebanon. It is cultivated throughout the temperate zones.

PARSLEY—continued

extracted for medicinal use.

There is some evidence that this constituent may be toxic in large quantities, causing a decrease in blood pressure and pulse rate, followed by muscle weakness and paralysis and possibly lung congestion and swelling of the liver. Pregnant women should avoid parsley oil and refrain from eating large quantities of parsley. Like many diuretics, parsley can irritate the kidneys.

Culinary: Parsley leaf has a gentle flavor and works especially well at blending the flavors around it. Both the curly leaf and flat leaf (Italian) varieties are used in cooking and as garnishes, but the flavor of the flat leaf is preferable. Parsnip-rooted (or Hamburg) parsley is used like a parsnip.

Parsley works with most foods except sweets. It is an important part of the Middle Eastern tabbouleh. France, specifically Burgundy, features parsley with ham in aspic; with garlic, butter, and escargots; and as *persillade,* a fine mince of garlic and parsley added at the last moment of cooking to sautés, grilled meats, and poultry. The Belgians and Swiss are fond of fondue with deep-fried parsley on the side. The Japanese also deep-fry parsley in tempura batter. The Mexicans and Spaniards use parsley as the prime ingredient in salsa verde, and the English make parsley jelly.

Available commercially: Fresh leaf, dried leaf, and fresh root.

Substitute: Chervil.

Storage note: Frozen parsley is superior to home dried.

Ornamental: As an attractive, bright green, compact plant, parsley has earned a place as a border or edging in both herb and ornamental beds. It can be used as the border of a tussie-mussie.

Cosmetic: Infusions of parsley leaves and stems are said to be soothing and cleansing when added to bathwater. The oil is used in cosmetics, shampoo, perfumes, soaps, creams, and skin lotions.

Companion planting: Placed in the vegetable garden, parsley is supposed to repel asparagus beetles.

CULTIVATION

Seed can be sown in the spring when the soil temperature reaches 50°F. Although hardy, parsley goes to seed in its second year, so it is usually treated like an annual. The superstition that it is bad luck to move parsley plants from garden to garden is based on the fact that parsley is fairly hard to transplant and so should be sown where it is to grow.

Another legend has it that parsley goes to the devil seven times before it grows and can be explained by its extremely slow germination—up to six weeks. You can speed things along by covering seeds with moisture-retaining material, watering frequently, pouring boiling water over the drill before covering it, and treating the seed by soaking, refrigerating, or freezing.

Six plants, set 8 inches apart, will supply the average family and allow enough for freezing or drying. If you let a few plants go to seed late in the season, they may produce seedlings for the next year's crop. You can lift the plants in late September, cut them back, and grow parsley on a window ledge through the winter. Protected window boxes seeded in early autumn will produce a late-autumn crop.

To keep parsley productive, weed it often and thoroughly, frequently cut back the full length of the outside stems, and remove all flower stalks.

Pests and diseases: Parsley is susceptible to crown rot. It may be attacked by carrot weevils, parsley worms, or nematodes. (See the entry Growing Herbs for information on controlling pests and diseases.)

Harvesting and storage: Dry parsley thoroughly in the shade, using an oven or microwave to finish the job. Once dry, it should be crushed by hand and stored in an airtight container. Broad-leaf Italian parsley, *Petroselinum crispum* var. *neapolitanum,* has a slightly stronger taste and so is the better variety for drying. Curly parsley can be frozen.

GROWING CONDITIONS

- Plant hardiness zone 9.
- Soil pH 6.0.
- Moderately rich, moist, well-drained soil.
- Full sun to partial shade.

Curly-leaf Parsley

Flat-leaf Parsley

PASSIONFLOWER

Passiflora incarnata   **Passifloraceae**

DESCRIPTION

Passiflora incarnata is characterized by colorful, showy blooms and coiling tendrils that snake out from the leaf axils.

Flowers: About 2 in. wide; solitary; five each of white or lavender petals and sepals; brilliant pink or purple corona consists of series of rings bearing threadlike processes; five stamens unite to form tube around flower stalk that supports ovary.

Leaves: Alternate; three to five finely toothed lobes; glands readily visible on stalk.

Fruit: A berry; called granadilla or water lemon; round to ovoid, 3 in. long; thin yellow or orange skin; edible yellowish pulp is succulent and sweet; contains many seeds.

Height: 25–30 ft.

FLOWERING

Early to late summer.

RANGE

Native from Florida west to Texas and north to West Virginia, Maryland, Pennsylvania, Ohio, Indiana, Illinois, and Missouri.

HABITAT

Partially shaded dry areas, thickets, fence lines, and the edges of wooded areas.

The association of the passionflower with Christ dates back to Spanish colonial days in South America during the early seventeenth century. Jesuit priests and other explorers from Spain and Italy professed to see symbols of the crucifixion in the plant's blossoms and interpreted this as divine assurance of success in their efforts to convert the natives of the area to Christianity.

The five petals and five sepals of the flower represented the ten faithful apostles (absent are Judas, the traitor, and Peter, who denied he knew Christ); the dramatic corona resembled the crown of thorns that Jesus wore; the five stamens represented Christ's five wounds; the curling tendrils symbolized the cords used to whip him; and the leaves were thought to represent the hands of Christ's persecutors. The missionaries also were encouraged by the fact that the Indians relished the fruit. Many intricately detailed illustrations done at that time made these associations even more realistic. Interestingly, the plant was unknown to the civilized world during biblical times.

Passionflower has long been used as a calmative agent and sedative. The early American Indians applied the crushed leaves as a poultice to treat bruises and other injuries; they also brewed the woody vines and drank the tea to soothe their nerves. Passionflower also has been reputed to be an aphrodisiac, and in fact, the uninitiated might think the name is derived from that reputation. The devout missionaries who discovered the herb, though, would probably not have appreciated this exploitation of their beloved plant!

Passionflower is also known as maypop, an intriguing name of unknown derivation.

USES

Tennessee's state bloom has several interesting properties.

Medicinal: Passionflower extract, derived from the flowers and fruiting tops of the plant, has a slightly narcotic effect when taken internally. Throughout the last few centuries, it was used as a tranquilizer to treat tension, fatigue, insomnia, muscle spasms, and even hyperactivity in children. Smoking passionflower was supposed to impart a marijuana-like high.

Passionflower extract was listed in the *National Formulary* as late as 1936, but since that time it has fallen into disuse. Although it is not recognized as safe or effective in the United States, pharmacognosist Varro Tyler, Ph.D., points out in *The Honest Herbal* that "it continues to be incorporated into quite a few sedative-hypnotic drug mixtures marketed in Europe."

In small doses, passionflower has no known toxicity. For medicinal use, you can add ½ to 1 teaspoon of the dried herb to 1 cup of boiling water. Drink the tea every three or four hours.

Ornamental: The passionflower, like its U.S. cousin *Passiflora lutea,* is a rather weedy specimen and is not of great interest to many gardeners. Still, it may have a place in wild or natural native plant landscapes, where it can show off its unusual blossoms and viny nature.

Other: Used in an herbal bath, passionflower doesn't excite, as its name might suggest, but rather it soothes the body. (See the entry Bathing with Herbs for more information.)

CULTIVATION

Passionflowers grow easily from seed or cuttings. They like deep, fertile, well-drained soil, plenty of water, and a little shade from strong summer sunlight. These plants respond well to soil that is revitalized every spring; this involves replacing the top layer (an inch or two) of soil with new topsoil enriched with fertilizer. For better blossoms, prune worn-out branches and weak or crowded stems and shoots in later winter and early spring. While passionflowers can be potted and grown indoors and in greenhouses, their weedy nature makes them more suitable for outdoor uses.

Pests and diseases: Passionflowers are susceptible to attack from thrips and mealybugs. (See the entry Growing Herbs for information on controlling pests.)

GROWING CONDITIONS

- Plant hardiness zone 7.
- Deep, fertile, well-drained soil.
- Partial shade.

411

PENNYROYAL

Mentha Pulegium, Hedeoma pulegioides **Labiatae**

DESCRIPTION

Although European and American pennyroyal are members of two entirely different genera, they are quite similar in appearance. Both are members of the mint family and have the characteristic square stems. European pennyroyal is a perennial and is more ornamental than the American species. It grows low to the ground and is distinguished from *Hedeoma pulegioides* by its smaller leaves and its four stamens. American pennyroyal is an annual with a more upright growth.

Flowers: Tubular, two-lipped, bluish lilac, ¼ in. long; in whorls at the leaf axils; *M. Pulegium* has four stamens while *H. pulegioides* has two.

Leaves: Opposite, elliptical or obovate, stalked, smooth edged or slightly toothed, with fine hairs; strong, minty odor; leaves of American pennyroyal measure ½–1 in. long while those of European pennyroyal measure about ½ in.

Fruit: Four nutlets.

Height: 4–16 in. (American); 1 ft. in flower (European).

FLOWERING

Late summer.

RANGE

European pennyroyal is native to the Near East and Europe. American pennyroyal is a common wildflower in the eastern United States.

Few things spoil a summer picnic faster than finding yourself in the middle of a cloud of gnats or mosquitoes and whacking your arms and legs every half minute. The defense is strong-smelling insect repellent. But after you've larded your body with it, you tend to lose your appetite. Sure, it keeps the flies away. But you can hardly stand yourself.

Pennyroyal to the rescue! It keeps the insects away, your appetite intact, and your skin pleasantly fragrant.

HISTORY

The use of pennyroyal as an insect repellent isn't a new idea. Pliny remarked on its effectiveness against fleas, and in the eighteenth century, when Swedish botanist Carolus Linnaeus was classifying plants, he derived European pennyroyal's Latin name, *Mentha Pulegium,* from *pulex,* meaning "flea." Across the sea in North America, American pennyroyal, *Hedeoma pulegioides* had similar beginnings. The native American Indians and the white settlers rubbed leaves into their skin to protect themselves from insects.

The history of pennyroyals' medicinal use also developed on both continents. The writings of seventeenth-century herbalist Nicholas Culpeper reflect the opinions of most herbalists on the use of European pennyroyal:

> The herb, boiled and drank, provokes women's courses and expels the dead child and afterbirth. If taken in water and vinegar mingled together, it stays the disposition to vomit. Mingled with honey and salt, it voids phlegm out of the lungs and purges by stool.

In North America several tribes of native American Indians found medicinal uses for the American species of pennyroyal. The Chickasaws soaked the plant in water and placed it on the forehead to relieve itchy and watery eyes. The Mohegans drank pennyroyal tea to soothe the stomach, and the Catawbas used the herb to relieve colds. A nineteenth-century Indian folk healer wrote:

> The hot tea of the plant is a very efficient remedy for all cramps and pains and colic. It is an active sweat producer, or in medical terms, an active diaphoretic. Good for colds and cramping . . . .I prefer the tea from the plant over and above all other forms and modes of preparation.

One cold and flu treatment of that time required that the patient soak his or her feet in a very hot footbath while drinking a cup or two of pennyroyal tea. The patient then was to get into bed under several layers of blankets to encourage sweating until the fever broke.

The white settlers learned of many of these remedies from the Indians and also made use of them. From 1831 to 1916, pennyroyal was an official drug plant to be used as a stimulant, carminative, and emmenagogue. From 1916 to 1931, the oil was officially listed in the *U.S. Pharmacopoeia* as an intestinal irritant and an abortifacient.

USES

Pennyroyal was taken off the list of official drug plants, and it should probably be taken off your list of herbal home remedies, too.

Medicinal: As with the other mints, both European and American pennyroyal teas are drunk to aid digestion and soothe upset stomachs. More often, though, pennyroyal oil has been taken to induce menstruation or to cause abortion. Pennyroyal works as an abortifacient but often at the expense of the mother's life, too. The oils contain 85 to 92 percent pulegone, a toxic chemical, and the amount of oil required to be effective is also the amount that can poison. As little as 2 tablespoonfuls of pennyroyal oil caused the death of an eighteen-year-old girl, and just ½ teaspoonful has been known to produce convulsions and coma.

As for drinking pennyroyal tea to soothe the stomach, the small amount of oil in the tea probably won't hurt you, but it probably won't help you either. If you are looking for a digestive aid, peppermint is the most effective herbal remedy you can use, and it is perfectly safe (see the entry Mint).

Ornamental: Generally, pennyroyal does not find much ornamental use outside the herb garden. Its appearance is a little too weedy for a very formal setting. Of the two, European pennyroyal is a little more decorative. Since pennyroyal grows low to the ground, it works well in rock gardens or along the edges of raised beds.

Other: The best use you can make of pennyroyal is as an insect repellent. Crush the leaves and rub them into your skin to keep away flies, mosquitoes, gnats, ticks, and chiggers. Pennyroyal will leave a pleasant mintlike fragrance on your skin, and it really does work at keeping pests away. As a matter of fact, many commercial repellent sprays and lotions contain pennyroyal oil.

Cyrus Hyde of Well-Sweep Herb Farm in Port Murray, New Jersey, recommends using pennyroyal to keep fleas away from your pets, too: "Try braiding the plant with string to make a flea collar," or scatter some leaves in your pet's bed. For the benefit of your pets and

GROWING CONDITIONS

American pennyroyal:
- Soil pH: acid.

- Average, dry soil.

- Full sun.

European pennyroyal:
- Plant hardiness zone 5.

- Soil pH: neutral.

- Rich, moist, humusy soil.

- Full sun to partial shade.

PENNYROYAL—continued

yourself, if you live in an area where pests can be a problem, it would be worth your while to grow pennyroyal.

CULTIVATION

European pennyroyal propagates easily from cuttings or root division. American pennyroyal can also be started from rooted cuttings, but most gardeners prefer to sow seed in the spring or fall. In extreme northern areas fall-sown seeds may not survive the winter. In all regions many seeds may fail to germinate, so broadcast them quite thickly to assure a good stand. Cover with just ⅛ to ¼ inch of fine soil. Thin established seedlings to stand 4 to 6 inches apart. Plants will spread enthusiastically by sending forth runners that promptly take root just about anywhere, including the tiniest crack in a sidewalk.

Harvesting and storage: Pick sprigs of pennyroyal for fresh use anytime. For peak flavor collect leaves and flower heads when plants are in full bloom, sometime in the early summer. Cut off plants several inches above the ground, and hang to dry in an airy, cool shed. When dry, rub off the leaves and store in airtight containers.

English Pennyroyal   *American Pennyroyal*

PIPSISSEWA

Chimaphila umbellata   **Ericaceae**

This shy woodland wildflower is seldom noticed, but it has been an ingredient in popular soft drinks for decades.

Pipsissewa is an evergreen, a member of the heath family. It grows from coast to coast, primarily in the northern regions. Through history, it also has been known as prince's pine, love-in-winter, butter winter, king's cure, ground holly, noble pine, pine tulip, pyrole, waxflower, rheumatism weed, bitter wintergreen, and fragrant wintergreen. The names suggest the characteristics and versatility of this quiet plant. Its Latin name, *Chimaphila,* comes from the Greek *cheima,* which means "winter," and *philein,* which means "to love"—an appropriate tag for a plant that stays green through the winter.

HISTORY

Pipsissewa was used by the American Indians and the settlers to treat typhus by bringing on perspiration. The plant was used during the Civil War to relieve rheumatism and kidney disorders.

USES

Medicinal: The leaves of pipsissewa are used more widely than the other parts of the plant. The herb is a highly rated natural remedy for kidney problems. According to modern-day herbalist Michael Moore, it is "much less astringent than uva-ursi, with a stronger diuretic action and less irritation of the intestinal lining." He says it can be taken "several times a week for extended periods" to remedy weak kidneys or chronic nephritis.

A typical infusion is 1 teaspoon of chopped leaves, steeped in ½ cup of water, sipped throughout the day. Other health problems that have been said to respond to this herb include scrofula, gonorrhea, and cardiac diseases.

Culinary: Pipsissewa has been an ingredient in commercial root beers and was listed on the label of Hires until recent years. Its flavor is bitter, yet sweet.

CULTIVATION

Taken out of the coniferous forests in which it flourishes, pipsissewa will live as a ground cover on a shady lawn, as a creeping cover on an embankment, or in a rock garden. Provide it with dry, acidic, sandy soil and mulch it with pine needles. Propagate by division or cuttings in a mixture of sand and peat moss. Spring is the time to divide plants, while late summer to fall is the best time to take cuttings for a cool greenhouse or cold frame. Pipsissewa grows slowly.

DESCRIPTION

Pipsissewa is a low-growing evergreen plant that shoots up from a pale yellow underground rhizome. The stems have a wriggly look about them, owing to the scars remaining from previous years' leaves. The woody base lends only slight support, so that the stems tend to trail along the ground.

Flowers: White or pink; five rounded, concave petals; five sepals; 10 stamens; ½ in. across; few together in terminal clusters on long stalks.

Leaves: Rather thick, short-stalked, toothed, glossy; oblong to lanceolate; 1¼–2½ in. long; in whorls of more than two.

Fruit: Globe-shaped capsules, containing many seeds.

Height: To 10 in.

FLOWERING

May through August.

RANGE

Native to the northern latitudes of America, Europe, and Asia.

HABITAT

Woods and coniferous and hardwood forests.

GROWING CONDITIONS

- Soil pH: acid.
- Rich, humusy soil.
- Partial shade.

PLANTAIN

Plantago major   **Plantaginaceae**

Plantain, according to legend, was a maiden who spent so much time by the roadside watching and waiting for her absent lover that she eventually was transformed into this common roadside plant. Considered one of the nine sacred herbs of the ancient Saxons, it symbolized for early Christians the well-trodden path of the multitude who sought Christ. Early American history recalls that the Indians called it white man's foot; the plant, with its rosette of leaves and its stalk of seeds looking like a miniature cattail, seemed to follow the white settlers everywhere they went.

DESCRIPTION

The plantain ranges in appearance from the lawn crawlers that seem to seed overnight, to the miniature versions of cattails scattering their seeds everywhere, to deep green, lilylike plants found along mountain streams. The description that follows is of *Plantago major*.

Flowers: Tiny, yellow-green in slender spikes, 6–18 in. high; phallic appearance of spikes is responsible for plant's reputation as an aphrodisiac in many cultures.

Leaves: To 7 in. long, thick, broadly oval to somewhat heart-shaped; grooved, with five to nine longitudinal veins; form rosette near ground.

Fruit: Small capsule contains 5–26 seeds.

Height: 6–18 in. in flower.

FLOWERING

June through September.

RANGE

P. major is a European native, and the hearty, highly adaptable plant has spread along our roadsides, meadows, marginal areas, and—to the dismay of homeowners—lawns.

USES

Plantain can be your friend and not just a weed. The next time you find it winding its way through your carefully seeded lawn, grab a handful of it and try a few of its positive uses.

Medicinal: If you're stung by a bee while mowing a not-quite-perfect lawn, pick a fleshy plantain leaf, crush it, and apply it to the welt. The Indians found the leaves to be a good treatment for stings and bites.

The *New England Journal of Medicine* printed an account of the successful use of crushed plaintain leaves to stop the itching of poison ivy; the treatment is a folk cure from Maryland's Eastern Shore.

The root can be chewed to ease the pain of a toothache.

Culinary: The tough, fibrous, mature leaves of the plantain are difficult to digest, but the tender young leaves can be eaten in salads or steamed lightly as you would spinach. Watch out, though—the leaves have a mildly laxative effect.

Ornamental: They wouldn't make your list of favorite ornamentals, but there are horticultural varieties of plantain, including rose plantain (*Plantago major* 'Rosularis'), variegated plantain (*P. lanceolata* 'Marginata'), and the tiny Spanish plantain (*P. nivalis*), a candidate for the rock garden.

Cosmetic: An infusion of plantain can be used as a skin lotion. It has stimulating and cleansing properties. Some people are allergic to it, however.

Dye: Using the whole plant, you can color alum-mordanted wool a dull gold or chrome-mordanted wool camel.

GROWING CONDITIONS

- Very hardy.
- Average, well-drained soil.
- Full sun to partial shade.

CULTIVATION

Propagate them by seed in the early spring or fall. You don't need to worry about special growing considerations: All will flourish in any soil and in full sun or partial shade.

POKEWEED

Phytolacca americana   Phytolaccaceae

Pokeweed has been infamous throughout history for its toxic effect on humans. Poisonings were widespread in eastern North America during the nineteenth century, when tinctures made from the root were popular as antirheumatics. And to this day, people are done in when they mistake the inky berries for a wild edible, or the root for that of parsnip, artichoke, or horseradish.

The Indians of Connecticut used the berries to stain splint baskets a dark blue. Indeed, poke provided one of the first natural inks used by settlers of the New World; it proved so enduring that it can still be seen on documents in museums. Pokeweed is used today as a base for fabric dye.

USES

The fruit, seeds, and root are poisonous. In fact, you should wear gloves when yanking it. Many gardeners consider it nothing more than a persistent (if unusually handsome) weed.

Medicinal: Indians of the eastern states used a poultice of powdered pokeroot to treat tumors and skin eruptions, and the colonists followed their example. It was believed that the plant's highly toxic qualities were responsible for its medicinal effect. The Delaware Indians ingested the root as a rheumatism cure. A salve for sores was made by combining roasted poke root, bittersweet, yellow parilla, and elderberry bark to a base of boiled lard and beeswax.

Culinary: While people have eaten the tender young shoots, it is best to keep poke out of the kitchen. Even when the leaves are picked young and boiled, they may be dangerous (see the entry Dangers of Herbs).

Ornamental: American pokeweed *may* serve as a decorative addition to native collections and natural habitats. Pokeweed can serve as a hedge, add color to an area, and in the fall provide a source of food for the many wild birds who enjoy the berries. (Curiously, however, if a bird eats too many of these berries, it will become intoxicated.) But again. keep the toxicity of the leaves and berries in mind as you formulate your landscaping plans.

Dye: The fruits have an attractive color and also offer color to fabrics. Depending on the mordant used, you can dye wool red, rust, brown, or pink.

CULTIVATION

Pokeweed is rarely cultivated as a garden plant. In climates adapted to its growth, it thrives with little care and in a variety of soils. Poke plants prefer strong sunlight but will tolerate limited shade. They are easily raised from seeds.

UNSAFE

DESCRIPTION

Pokeweed is a deciduous, perennial, bushy herb that emits an unpleasant odor.

Flowers: White or purplish, ¼ in. wide, in slender terminal racemes to 8 in. long; 10 stamens.

Leaves: Oblong to ovate-lanceolate, pointed, 4–12 in. long; unpleasant scent.

Fruit: Berries; green when immature, deep purple when ripe; ¼ in. in diameter; toxic.

Height: 4–9 ft.

FLOWERING

June through September.

RANGE

Pokeweed is found from New York and New England to Minnesota, south to Florida, and across to Texas. It has established itself all over Europe and grows from Portugal to the Soviet Union.

HABITAT

The borders of fields, cleared areas, roadsides, and strip-mine areas.

GROWING CONDITIONS

- Very hardy.
- Moist, humusy soil.
- Full sun to partial shade.

POPLAR

Populus spp.   **Salicaceae**

Poplars, cottonwoods, and aspens are closely related trees that often share common names. They reside in the same family as the willows, which they resemble in several ways. The best-known poplar for medicinal use is *Populus balsamifera,* or balm of Gilead, a particularly aromatic shade tree that has winter buds and bark that are useful in treating several ailments. All poplars are more or less effective medicinally. Note that the yellow or tulip poplar is not a member of this family.

DESCRIPTION

All poplars are rapidly growing, soft-wooded, deciduous trees. The size varies greatly from species to species. Most have bark that grows darker as the tree ages.

Flowers: On any one tree, either all male or all female; shaped like catkins.

Leaves: Generally broad and undivided, but range from heart-shaped to delta-shaped; alternate; hairy or smooth, depending on species; various shades of green; winter leaf buds are balsamic, bitter tasting, waxy, and resinous.

Fruit: A small seed capsule; seeds surrounded by tufts of white cottony hair that is easily airborne; North American cottonwoods have more hair than other species.

Height: To 90 ft. or more.

FLOWERING

Spring.

RANGE

Widely distributed throughout the Northern Hemisphere.

HABITAT

Poplars and cottonwoods are generally associated with water; cottonwoods are often found on riverbanks.

Aspens favor higher elevations; occur as weed trees in clear-cut and burned areas.

HISTORY

The best-known medicinal use for poplar buds was in *Pommade de Bourgeons de Peuplien,* a medicine for burns and sores that also included black nightshade, belladonna, henbane, and poppy.

In tincture form, buds have been used for chest and upper respiratory complaints, kidney problems, and gleet and gonorrhea. As an ointment, poplar buds relieved arthritis and rheumatism. Infusions were gargled. Before tea was made of the buds, the buds were soaked in alcohol to remove a bitter resin.

Poplar bark has long been employed as a substitute for quinine in treating fevers. It was also part of brandy-based bitters given for indigestion. American Indians used poplar to treat sore eyes, dropsy, and toothache.

Both the Greeks and Romans used the tree as an ornamental. The Greeks said it came from the Heliades, the grief-stricken sisters of Phaethon, who saw their brother fall from the sky as he drove the sun's chariot. The sisters were turned into poplar trees, and their tears fell into a stream and became amber. The ancients also said Hercules wore a crown of poplar when he went to Hades to bring back the three-headed dog Cerberus. The willows of Babylon mentioned in the Bible were probably poplars.

USES

By far the most commercially important use for the poplar tree is as paper pulp, and hybrids have been bred for this purpose. The lumber, although regarded as inferior, is useful for crates, matches, boxes, and excelsior.

Medicinal: The entire poplar genus contains salicylate precursors, which are related to aspirin and share its properties as an anti-inflammatory, antipyretic, and analgesic. The species vary greatly in their medicinal properties; those with highly resinous buds are usually the most effective. Any ailment helped or relieved by aspirin will probably respond in the same way to the internal use of poplar-bud medications. This includes sore throats, fevers, and headaches, as well as arthritis and rheumatism. There is no evidence that the beneficial ingredients can be absorbed through the skin.

Closed winter leaf buds contain an antioxidant, and a tincture of the buds is put into cosmetics to prevent rancidity. The buds also contribute a balsamic scent. The aroma of poplar buds is heavy and nostril clearing, a little like menthol but without the sensation of coolness.

Toxicity: There has been no report of poisoning from poplar bark, buds, or leaves, but the pollen gives many people allergic rashes and respiratory problems.

Ornamental: Some landscape gardening experts advise against planting poplars because of their relatively short life and the way they litter the ground with their cottony seedpods and fragile twigs. On the other hand, the trees grow fast and cast heavy shade, and most have light-colored, trembly leaves that make a beautiful contrast with ornamental evergreens. Poplars are also planted for their pleasant and fresh scent.

Don't plant ornamental poplars near walls, pavements, or drains, because of damage that can be caused by their strong, invasive roots.

Dye: Gray, gold, and brown dyes for coloring wool can be made from the leaves and twigs. (See the entry Dyes from Herbs for more information.)

CULTIVATION

All poplars prefer a loamy, dampish soil (*P. deltoides* and *P. tremuloides* can do with less water than the others), but they can grow in most soils and do well where other trees will not grow. They are usually started either from nursery stock or hardwood cuttings. Cuttings root without difficulty and can be heeled in directly in the fall or early spring, with only the tips above the ground. Water the cuttings well.

The trees can be grown from seed but may not be true to their breed. Prune only to shape young trees, removing the lower branches until you have established a healthy crown and a well-formed trunk.

Pests and diseases: Poplars are subject to tree cankers, die-back, branch gall, rust, powdery mildew, aphids, caterpillars, scale, borers, and willow beetles. (See the entry Growing Herbs for information on controlling pests and diseases.)

Harvesting and storage: The winter buds used medicinally are sticky, resinous, and highly aromatic. They are dried or, occasionally, used fresh. Tea is made from the bark, which is gathered from pruned or felled trees in the fall, or from pruned twigs in the spring.

GROWING CONDITIONS
- Any ordinary garden soil.
- Full sun.

POTENTILLA

Potentilla spp.   **Rosaceae**

Relatives of roses, the hardy perennials of the genus *Potentilla* include both hated weeds and treasured garden flowers. Of the nearly 500 species, 3 species are listed in the U.S. Department of Agriculture's *Selected Weeds* publication, and 2 others appear on the list of threatened plants, 1 in California and 1 in Oregon. Their medicinal power is suggested by the root of the name, "potent." Members of the genus include silverweed (*P. Anserina*) and tormentil (*P. erecta* syn. *P. Tormentilla*).

DESCRIPTION

Squint at the flowers, and you'll see the potentillas' resemblance to the strawberry. In the middle of the blossom is a bristly tuft of stamens. The leaves are often divided in leaflets, each with saw-toothed edges.

Flowers: ½ in. wide, on long slender stalks; four roundish petals with a short claw, yellow, 16 stamens; calyx cut into four lanceolate, pale green, hairy segments.

Leaves: Palmately compound; five leaflets small, obovate to lanceolate, toothed, hairy, dark green above, paler below; lower leaves alternate, short stalked; upper opposite, attached; stipules at bases of leaves lanceolate or ovate, smooth or toothed.

Fruit: Achenes.

Height: 3 in.

FLOWERING

May and June.

RANGE

Native in the north temperate boreal and arctic regions and somewhat in the Southern Hemisphere.

HABITAT

Damp meadows, hills, and marshes.

HISTORY

In ancient Athens Hippocrates used tormentil to treat malaria victims. (In spite of Greece's postcard-brilliant blue skies and rocky coasts, the country has some swampy land and, before the anti-malaria campaign of this century, chronic fevers were common.) The plant was also commended as a malaria cure in the oldest surviving Western herbal, written by the Greek Dioscorides. If your malarial fever recurred on the third day, Dioscorides would mix a little something involving three tormentil leaves; if the fever recurred on the fourth day, the medicine would have had four leaves. But either way, you also got three spiders in the mixture!

This reputation for driving away fevers may be what led people to believe that tormentil also would drive away witches.

Tormentil was supposedly included in magical flying potions, along with wolfbane, a potentially lethal plant that caused all kinds of weird sensations—including hallucinations of flying.

The great sixteenth-century British herbalist John Gerard advised that powdered tormentil roots be mixed in water taken from a smith's forge where hot steel had been quenched.

The herb also crops up in the history of dentistry. The seventeenth-century British herbalist Nicholas Culpeper recommended packing the root of tormentil into a painful tooth. It was supposed to dry up "the flux of humors" thought to cause toothaches in the days before the discovery of plaque. Mexicans chewed the root of *P. rubra* to clean and strengthen their teeth.

The potentilla's culinary history may be short, but it's hardly sweet. During famines, the roots were boiled for a long time to make them palatable. In the Hebrides silverweed roots were boiled or roasted.

USES

Medicinal: Tormentil acts as a powerful astringent. It was used to treat just about everything from sore throats to gonorrhea. Not much is known about its safety. It is high in tannin, which, in large amounts, damages the kidneys.

Silverweed was also used as an astringent, and a tea was prescribed for many of the same ailments. The tea, made with water or milk and perhaps spiked with other herbs, was taken to relieve cramps.

Ornamental: Gardeners, particularly rock gardeners, plant any of dozens of species, from little furry mats to spidery shrubs. Breeders have crossed species and named selected hybrids. ('Etna' erupts into crimson blooms; the flowers of 'Flamenco' are very red.)

From among many possibilities, North Carolina herb grower Fairman Jayne has chosen *P. tridentata,* which forms a carpet of three-lobed leaves, 3 to 4 inches high. In winter the foliage turns a plum color. In early summer the carpet, green once more, is scattered with little white flowers. Jayne recommends the plant for dry, sunny locations.

He also grows *P. Tabernaemontani,* a low plant with three-part, strawberrylike leaves. This potentilla forms rounded mounds of leaves, so dense that weeds don't push through them. The plant blooms in early spring with bright yellow flowers and sends out a flower or two on warm days in the fall. Jayne says it will grow in sun or partial shade.

The potentillas include a host of little creepers: *P. villosa,* with gray, velvety leaves; *P. rupestris* var. *pygmaea,* a tidier version of a taller European native; *P. alba,* with silver hair under its leaves and white flowers; *P. aurea,* with yellow flowers; and *P. atrosanguinea,* a Himalayan native with dark purple flowers. Many others are available.

Cosmetic: Potentilla's astringent properties recommend it in facial lotions and herbal baths.

Dye: Laplanders used the crushed root to dye leather red. You can use the root to dye wool red-brown, using a chrome mordant, or purple-red, using iron.

Other: It may not be a comforting thought, but the astringent properties that make potentilla medicinally useful also give it the power to tan leather. Orkney islanders mashed up the root for this purpose.

CULTIVATION

Potentillas are best propagated by division. Most are sun-loving and adapt well to a variety of garden soils. "Sometimes I think you can't kill them," says Jayne. "They're the one thing you can depend on." Expect blossoms in the second year.

Potentilla Anserina

GROWING CONDITIONS

- Plant hardiness zones 4–8.
- Soil pH: acid or alkaline.
- Average, well-drained soil.
- Full sun to partial shade.

421

ROSE

DESCRIPTION

If you've pricked your finger on a thorn, you've probably touched a rose. Most roses have thorns along their stems. This plant is usually deciduous but sometimes evergreen. Most species grow as an upright shrub, but some are creeping or climbing.

Flowers: Solitary or in branched clusters or corymbs at the end of short branches; white, yellow, pink, or red; five, rarely four, petals and sepals; semidouble and double varieties have more petals; numerous stamens and pistils.

Leaves: Alternate; usually pinnate; five to nine leaflets including a terminal leaflet; pair of stipules at base of the leafstalk.

Fruit: Berrylike hips contain true fruits, seedlike achenes; hips hard or pulpy, vary in size, turn from green through yellow to shades of red; hips need cold weather to mature.

Height: Depends on the species.

FLOWERING

May through frost.

RANGE

Native to the Middle East; naturalized throughout the world; widely cultivated.

HABITAT

Wild species grow in damp ground throughout North America.

Rosa spp.   **Rosaceae**

When Cleopatra invited Mark Anthony to her palace, she had the floors covered knee-deep in rose petals; such was her belief in the romantic powers of their perfume. Cleopatra won Anthony's affections easily, and in part, at least, she can thank the fragrance of roses and their exquisite beauty. Roses captivate anyone who looks on them or breathes their perfume. Perhaps it is our love affair with roses that has inspired us to define them as the greatest symbol of love and beauty.

HISTORY

It was the Greek colonists who probably first brought the rose from Greece to southern Italy, starting its very long European history. The Romans cultivated *Rosa gallica,* crowning bridal couples with it and using it lavishly in banquet centerpieces. Rose water was prepared as early as the tenth century, and attar, or otto, of roses in the sixteenth. For many centuries the production of attar of roses was an almost exclusively French industry, but it later moved, in part, to Bulgaria.

When William Penn returned to the colonies from England in 1699, he brought with him 18 rosebushes. John Adams was the first to plant roses near the White House, although both George Washington and Thomas Jefferson were very fond of the flower. Long before these people were around, however, American Indians used roses for ornament and for health care. Young braves gathered them for the hair of their brides. They also combined the petals with bear grease to cure mouth sores. Powder made from petals was applied directly to fever sores and blisters. Flowers soaked in rainwater bathed sore eyes, and the inner bark of the root was applied to boils.

When you try to push the long, long history of the rose back beyond the early Indians and the Greeks, you run into legend. For over 3,000 years, it has been known as the queen of the flowers, so it has had enough time to gather lore along with its history, which in record goes back to the Greek historian Herodotus. For example, it is supposed to have developed thorns only after the days of the Garden of Eden were over. The Greeks held that the red rose came from the blood of the goddess Aphrodite whose foot got stuck on a thorn while trying to help Adonis. The Turks, on the other hand, claim the red rose is stained from the blood of Muhammad.

USES

The rose is as much adored today as it was thousands of years ago. Such a beloved flower would flourish in gardens even if it offered no practical uses at all. However, it does offer practical uses in medicines, cosmetics, foods, and fragrances.

Medicinal: Rosehips (the fruit of the plant) are so rich in vitamin C (richer by far than oranges, ounce for ounce) that some people say we should make rosehip tea a part of our daily diet. All health food stores sell rosehips as a staple. One Swiss herbalist recommends rosehip tea for kidney stones as well, but even if they won't help with those, the vitamin content alone justifies their use. They are also rich in vitamins A, B, E, and K, organic acids, and pectin. The acids and pectin make rosehips mildly laxative and diuretic.

The petals are astringent, containing quercitrin, volatile oils, and coloring agents. The coloring agents and the flavor make them useful for adding to medicines, especially syrups. Rose petals have generally been used in tonics and gargles to cure catarrhs, sore throats, mouth sores, and stomach disorders. Several commercial eyewashes contain rose water. The roots, also, have been used for their astringent properties in teas.

Large amounts of petals or hips may give some people diarrhea, although some herbalists recommend roses as a cure for diarrhea. Otherwise, there is no indication that roses are toxic. To benefit from the medicinal properties of roses, prepare an infusion from the hips or the buds. Some species and varieties are more useful medicinally than others (see the accompanying table Rose Species).

Externally, oil of roses is sometimes used to cool inflammations, but given the expense, you might want to save the oil for perfumes and potpourris.

Culinary: Rosehips are tart and cranberrylike. They're famous for their high vitamin C content and are used to make syrups, jellies, jams, conserves, teas, wines, soups (especially in Scandinavian cuisines), purees, pies, tarts, quick breads, and muffins.

Fragrant rose petals are used in salads, as garnishes, candied to decorate pastries, and to make rose water, which is used in East Indian and Arabic cuisines.

Available commercially: Rosehips dried and in tea blends, rose petals, rose water, or candied petals.

Aromatic: One of the best-loved fragrances is that of the rose. Its scent has been captured in perfumes, bath oils, soaps . . . wherever a floral scent can be enjoyed. Rose water and rose oil of the natural variety are very expensive and reserved for special nonallergenic ointments, creams, and fresheners. Varieties of *R. damascena, R. gallica,* and *R. centifolia* are the most fragrant. The finest and most expensive oil used today is obtained from damask roses (*R.*

SUB ROSA

In early times, people were often sworn to silence with a bribe of roses. Thus roses became symbolic of confidences. A rose hung in a room or over a table meant that all information spoken was to be kept secret. Even today, a plaster decoration in the center of a ceiling is called a rose. The expression *sub rosa,* literally "under the rose," means in greatest confidence.

CHEF TIPS

- Substitute fresh rosehips for cranberries in sauce and relish recipes.
- Toss rose petals with fresh fruit and sprinkle with freshly squeezed lime juice.
- Fill dessert crepes with spoonfuls of rose jelly and garnish with candied rose petals.

SHADES OF MEANING

A rose by any name signifies joy, beauty, and love. During the medieval period, people associated the rose with spring and fertility, also pleasure and enjoyment. The specific meanings of roses depend on the color of the flower:

red—passion, desire
pink—simplicity, happy love
white—innocence, purity
yellow—jealousy, perfect achievement

ROSE—continued

A WHITE ROSE

The red rose whispers of
   passion
And the white rose breathes of
   love;
O, the red rose is a falcon,
And the white rose is a dove.
          John Boyle O'Reilly

WHAT'S IN A NAME?

    A rose is a rose is a rose is a
rose, unless it's a multiflora, or a
rugosa, or a hybrid tea, or a
damask, a dog, or a cabbage, or
. . . but we'd better stop there.
    Whole encyclopedias have
been written on the subject of
this one flower. The genus is
one of the most extensive in the
plant kingdom.
    But there isn't much agree-
ment—especially among the
experts—on what's in the genus. Botanists have one system
of classification, based on rose
genealogy, while growers who
develop more and more com-
plexly related hybrids, may
have an alternative system of
their own. Even among themselves, botanists have argued
about the total number of species—that's *species*, now, *not*
varieties or cultivars—claiming
from 30 to over 5,000. The following general classification of
roses groups them according to
their ancestry.
    Species roses include pri-
marily wild roses, which are the
ancestors to all modern roses.
Also included in this group are
some modern hybrids. *Rosa
canina* and *R. rugosa* are two
examples.

(continued on page 426)

damascena), cultivated in Bulgaria.
    A perfumer needs 60,000 roses to procure 1 ounce of pure
essential oil. While this statistic certainly intimidates, at home you
can capture the fragrance of the oil from a far lesser number of roses.
By soaking petals in vegetable oil, you can make a rose-scented oil.
Make rose water by bruising petals in water, heating the mixture
gently for a few minutes, and then leaving it to infuse for a few hours.
(See the entries Scents from Herbs and Lotions from Herbs for
information on making fragrant oils and waters.) Of course, pure
rose oil can be purchased if you don't have the time or the number of
roses to produce your own rose fragrances. (See the entry Scents
from Herbs for a list of companies that sell essential oils.)
    You can also capture the fragrance of roses in potpourris and
sachets. In fact, roses are one of the most common ingredients in
potpourris. Again, the species mentioned above are considered the
most fragrant.
    Ornamental: No one needs to be told about the ornamental
qualities of the rose. The only need is to learn which bush, shrub, or
climber looks best in which spot in the garden or grounds.
    Hybrid perpetuals, hybrid teas, floribundas, ramblers, and large-
flowered climbers will make the most spectacular floral display and
the best cut flowers for indoor arrangements. Wild roses, simple-
flowered roses, and the rose ancestors of the hybrids, when available,
will provide the best background foliage and will lend spots of color
to the garden for short periods of bloom. They may also be mixed
with other shrubs. Trailing kinds, such as *R. Wichuraiana* are useful
in covering banks.
    Cosmetic: If you splash rose water on your skin for fragrance,
you will also benefit from its astringent and cleansing properties,
which help to keep skin healthy.

CULTIVATION

    Roses can be propagated from seeds, cuttings, or buddings, but
the amateur rose grower will do best to stick to nursery-grown stock,
especially if the roses are desired for herbal use only and not for
exhibit or display. If you want to try the other propagation methods,
consult books and articles written specifically on growing roses.
    Generally, roses do best in fairly heavy clay loam that has been
deeply dug and thoroughly enriched with organic matter, but they
will survive in a good, well-drained garden soil. They prefer a pH of
6.5 to 6.8 but will grow in soils ranging from a pH of 6.0 to 7.5.

Hybrid Tea Rose

Wild Rose

Roses are injured by standing in water. Be certain to provide a well-drained location for them. Make sure also that sunshine can reach the bed for at least half a day. Since roses require more attention, more frequent water, and more feeding than other flowers, they are most often given a bed to themselves. They cannot, in any case, bear crowding, for foliage is susceptible to mildew, and the blossoms need sun.

In starting a planting, use dormant stock or potted plants. Dormant roses may be set out in the fall or spring, but spring is the more common time. If you plant them in autumn, mulch them well for the winter. Roses should be planted immediately, so do not purchase stock until your beds have been prepared.

To prepare a bed, dig it to a depth of 1½ to 2 feet. Remove the soil, mix it with organic matter, mix in additives to adjust the pH, if necessary, and fill the bed just slightly lower than the height of the adjacent lawn so that it will hold water when flooded. Let it settle for two weeks before you plant it.

Before planting, cut off any split or broken ends. Also watch for any canes that have very small thorns and seven leaflets and remove these. In the north, canes should be cut back to about 1 foot.

Roses should be planted 1 foot from the edge of a bed and 30 inches, or more, apart, depending on their eventual size. For budded

ROSE—continued

Old garden roses have been cultivated since 1867 and include some of the most fragrant roses. Some types of roses in this group are the albas, Bourbons, centifolias, damasks, gallicas, China roses, hybrid perpetuals, cabbage roses, moss roses, Noisettes, and Portlands.

Climbing roses are those roses cultivated to grow along trellises and arbors.

Shrub roses include cultivars that don't quite fit into the category of old garden roses or the modern roses. Eglantines, hybrid musks, and hybrid rugosas belong to this group.

Floribundas are a group of modern roses that usually have many blooms on their stems.

Grandifloras were developed in the 1950s. These produce large flowers and bloom abundantly.

Hybrid teas, the florists' roses of commerce, have long-stemmed, elegant flowers. They are less floriferous than the floribundas, but bloom from spring through fall.

Miniature roses because of their size can be grown indoors in containers.

GROWING CONDITIONS

- Soil pH 6.5–6.8.
- Well-drained, clayey soil.
- Full sun to partial shade.

roses, holes should be 12 to 18 inches deep and 15 to 18 inches wide. Heap the soil in the middle of the hole, as you would for a fruit tree, and arrange the roots on either side of the hump of soil, making sure that they do not cross. Do not crowd the roots into the hole. Long, scraggly roots should be cut off. Set the collar, the point of the graft, 2 inches beneath the soil surface, and pack the soil around it. This will prevent suckers from the roots from choking the new growth.

For potted roses, the holes need not be much larger than the pots. Plant these as soon as spring weather has settled. Fill the hole with water, insert the plant a little deeper than it stood in the pot, and pack earth firmly around it.

Climbing roses should be provided with some support from the beginning, but they are otherwise planted in the same way. Do not plant them too close to porches, or you may have trouble with slugs.

Prune roses in late winter or early spring to shape the plant, to reduce the number of canes so as to increase the size of the blooms, and to remove old, useless, or dead wood. For bedding or specimen roses that are two years old or older, shorten the length of all canes to 12 to 14 inches, depending on winter damage, if you live in the North. Roses grown in the South can be cut back to 18 to 24 inches. For all of the less highly bred roses, prune minimally to remove woody growth and control excessive, wild growth.

Roses should be cultivated carefully, but frequently, to prevent competition from weeds. They should be top-dressed with rotted manure or compost, or fed manure or compost tea, up to once a week before the blooming season is over and less often after that. Manure and mulch should be applied in the fall. Keep the ground moist, but not wet, watering heavily, but no more than once a week. Mulch in dry weather and in the fall. Remove all mulch in the spring when weather is consistently warm. In regions with no frost, withdraw all water to provoke dormancy during the winter.

Pests and diseases: Roses are susceptible to blackspot, mildew, canker, and rust. Rose pests include aphids, leafhoppers, thrips, Japanese beetles, spider mites, rose bugs, and rose slugs. (See the entry Growing Herbs for information on controlling pests and diseases.)

Harvesting and storage: Petals should be gathered before the flower is completely open. They should be separated from the center, or claw, and dried in the sun, carefully and quickly. Store them in a dry place while they are still crisp. The odor of some kinds, like *R. gallica,* improves with drying.

Rosehips, for medicinal or culinary use, are sometimes dried but are more often made into vinegars or conserves.

ROSE SPECIES

Name	Flowers	Leaves	Comments
Rosa ×alba White rose	Double, white, 2–3 in. across	5 or 7 leaflets, gray-green	An old garden rose; hardy to zone 5; very fragrant
R. canina Dog rose	Single, white or pink, 2 in. across	5 or 7 leaflets, 1 in. long	Species rose; hardy to zone 3; fragrant; high in vitamin C; hips used in preserves and medicines; petals used in tea
R. centifolia Provence rose	Double, pink, nodding, 2½ in. across	5-toothed leaflets, hairy underneath	Old garden rose; hardy to zone 6; very fragrant; used quite often in medicines
R. chinensis China rose	Single, crimson, pink, or white, 2 in. across; many stamens	3–5 toothed leaflets, no down	Species rose; hardy to zone 7; used medicinally as tonic and stimulant
R. damascena Damask rose	Semidouble, clustered, rose-red to pink, 2½–3½ in. across	5 or 7 leaflets, hairy underneath	Old garden rose; hardy to zone 5; very fragrant; cultivated for essential oil; infusion of petals used as laxative and to regulate menstruation
R. Eglanteria Eglantine rose	Single, solitary, bright pink, 2 in. across	5 or 7 leaflets, hairy underneath, apple scented	Species rose; hardy to zone 5; beautiful orange to scarlet hips; dense growth, makes good hedge; used in Iran to cure colic and diarrhea
R. gallica French rose	Single, rich crimson, to 2½ in. across	Toothed leaflets, hairy underneath	Old garden rose; hardy to zone 6; infusion of petals used as astringent, purgative, tonic, douche, and eyewash
R. laevigata Cherokee rose	Single, solitary, white, to 3½ in. across	3 or 5 toothed, glossy leaflets; terminal leaflet larger and longer stemmed	Species rose; hardy to zone 7; fragrant; used in China for diarrhea; hips are astringent
R. multiflora Japanese rose	Often double, clustered, small, white or pink	5–11 leaflets	Species rose; hardy to zone 6; arching, sprawling habit; bright red hips; seeds used in oriental medicine as diuretic and laxative
R. rugosa Japanese rose	Single and double varieties; white, rose, or red, to 3½ in. across	5–9 leaflets	Species rose; hardy to zone 2; fragrant; hips high in vitamin C, B, E, and K; leaves turn red in the fall; can withstand sea spray

ROSEMARY

Rosmarinus officinalis   **Labiatae**

You draw the bathwater, filling the tub high, then gingerly step in, and sink down. Soak. Let the oils rouse the blood under your skin. Breathe in the piny fragrance of the steam rising from the water …ahhhh…. The special ingredient? Rosemary. This is not just an herb for the kitchen spice rack.

DESCRIPTION

Rosemary is a perennial evergreen shrub whose ash-colored scaly bark and green needlelike leaves give it an overall grayish green appearance. (See photos on pages 32 and 100.)

Flowers: Pale blue; ½ in. long; upper lip appears notched or has two lobes, lower lip has three lobes—two small lateral and one larger central lobe; four stamens; flowers grow in clusters of two or three along branch.

Leaves: Resemble needles; ⅓–1½ in. long; opposite; narrow, thick, and leathery; upper surface dark green; white and hairy underneath; prominent vein runs down middle of leaf; margins turn downward; pungent, piny fragrance.

Fruit: Very small, spherical nutlets with smooth surfaces.

Height: 5–6 ft. outdoors; 2– 4½ ft. indoors.

FLOWERING

December through spring. 'Beneden Blue' and 'Tuscan Blue' cultivars start flowering in February. 'Majorca Pink' and prostrate rosemarys bloom almost continuously.

RANGE

Hills along the Mediterranean, Portugal, and northwestern Spain; widely cultivated.

HISTORY

Did you know that if a rosemary bush grows vigorously in a family's garden, it means that the woman heads the household? Surely many healthy rosemarys have been pruned low by humiliated husbands, and many struggling plants have been nurtured by strong-willed wives.

Have you ever thought of twining sprigs of rosemary in your hair to help you remember something? In ancient Greece, students believed this would improve their memory, so they wore rosemary garlands while studying for exams. If you try this, it will at least help others to remember you. Rosemary's history is rich with tales like these.

For centuries people thought that a rosemary plant would grow no higher than 6 feet in 33 years so as not to stand taller than Christ. Another story tells that the flowers were originally white but changed to blue when the Virgin Mary hung her cloak on a bush while fleeing from Herod's soldiers with the Christ child.

Rosemary possessed powers of protection against evil spirits, or so people thought. In the Middle Ages, men and women would place sprigs under their pillows to ward off demons and prevent bad dreams. However, rosemary had many practical applications as well (although, at the time, keeping away evil spirits was probably a very serious matter).

Rosemary was an important medicinal herb. In 1525, Banckes' *Herbal,* the first book devoted exclusively to herbs, was printed in England. It said about rosemary: "Take the flowers thereof and boyle them in fayre water and drinke that water for it is much worthe against all manner of evils in the body." The famous Hungary water made from rosemary oil and alcohol was concocted by a gnarled hermit for Queen Elizabeth of Hungary, who was said to have been cured of paralysis of the joints by rubbing this water into them.

The strong fragrance of rosemary kept homes smelling sweet. During the sixteenth century, wealthy men would pay perfumers to come into their houses and scent the air with a rosemary incense. The perfumer would beat together rosemary leaves and sugar, place the mixture in a perfuming pan, and heat it over hot coals.

But besides the legends, superstitions, and historic uses, rosemary is best known as a symbol of remembrance, friendship, and love. St. Thomas More once said of rosemary, "I lett it runne all over my garden wall, not onlie because my bees love it, but because 'tis the herb sacred to remembrance, and therefore to friendship . . . ." At one time rosemary was used in almost every wedding ceremony. Brides wore wreaths woven with sprigs of rosemary dipped in scented waters, or they carried rosemary in their bouquets. At funerals mourners tossed fresh sprigs into the grave as a sign that the life of the departed would not be forgotten. Tapping a fresh sprig of rosemary against the finger of a loved one was supposed to secure his or her affection. Such a gesture would certainly capture the loved one's attention. Even today, an offering of rosemary signifies love, friendship, and remembrance.

USES

Placing rosemary under your pillow at night might not keep away bad dreams, and tapping someone you admire with a fresh sprig is more likely to frighten that person off than capture his or her love, but rosemary does have many other uses that do produce practical and beneficial results.

Medicinal: Rosemary has long been included in many herbalists' stores of remedies. Herbal physicians have prescribed an infusion of the leaves as a tonic, astringent, diaphoretic, stomachic, emmenagogue, expectorant, and cholagogue. They have recommended it in the treatment of depression, headaches, and muscle spasms. Applied externally, an ointment made from the oil of rosemary is reputed to benefit sufferers of rheumatism, sores, eczema, bruises, and wounds. Do these remedies work? No one knows for certain since none of these claims have been verified clinically. However, a few of rosemary's medicinal properties have been confirmed.

The flowers and leaves contain a volatile oil, which is responsible for the plant's pharmacological actions. This oil is an ingredient in rubefacient liniments and has been used in combination with other drugs as a carminative. It is listed officially in the *U.S. Pharmacopoeia*.

During the fourteenth and fifteenth centuries, rosemary branches were burned in homes to keep away the black death. More recently, during World War II, a mixture of rosemary leaves and

PRESERVING FOODS WITH ROSEMARY

You'd rather not eat foods preserved with BHA, BHT, or TBHQ? Well, the extract of rosemary can be used as an antioxidant; however, the strong odor and bitter taste have prevented this.

Stephen Chang, Ph.D., and Chi-tang Ho, Ph.D., of the Department of Food Science at Rutgers University have patented a process that produces a bland extract of rosemary, which is very effective and was shown to have better stability than BHA and BHT at higher temperatures, making it a useful antioxidant for fried foods.

CHEF TIPS

- When baking, add rosemary to bread dough, using 1 tablespoon for each loaf.

- Create an herb butter by combining 2 teaspoons of rosemary with ½ cup of softened unsalted butter.

- Enhance the sweetness of fruit salads without sugar by adding rosemary.

- For extra aromatics when grilling, add a handful of rosemary to the coals during the last 5 to 10 minutes of cooking.

- Substitute rosemary for mint in a mint jelly recipe. Use it with roast meats and poultry.

ROSEMARY—continued

juniper berries was burned in the hospitals of France to kill germs. These practices may not be as strange as they seem. Research has found that rosemary oil does indeed have some antibacterial effects.

As a medicinal herb, rosemary should be used carefully. According to pharmacognosist Varro Tyler, Ph.D., writing in *The Honest Herbal,* the larger quantities of the pure oil used therapeutically can irritate the stomach, intestines, and kidneys. However, don't let this worry those of you who cook with rosemary. As a seasoning, it is perfectly safe to use.

Culinary: And as a seasoning, rosemary's flavor combines both strong and subtle qualities. It is pungent, somewhat piny, mintlike yet sweeter, with a slight ginger finale.

Its flavor harmonizes with those of poultry, fish, lamb, beef, veal, pork, and game, particularly in their roasted forms. Rosemary enhances tomatoes, spinach, peas, mushrooms, squash, cheese, eggs, lentils, and complements the herbs chives, thyme, chervil, parsley, and bay in recipes. Gentle soups like potato and eggplant benefit from rosemary's robust character, as do marinades, salad dressings, bouquet garnis, and cream sauces.

You can use both the flowers and leaves for garnishing and cooking. Crush or mince the spiky leaves before sprinkling over or rubbing into foods.

Available commercially: Whole or ground.

Substitute: Mint and a bit of ground ginger or sage.

Storage note: Freeze whole sprigs of rosemary. When you need some, slide your thumb and index finger down a sprig, taking off as many leaves as you need. Remember, frozen rosemary is stronger than fresh.

Aromatic: "Take the flowers and put them in thy chest among thy clothes or among thy Bookes and Mothes shall not destroy them," wrote Banckes in his *Herbal.*

Rosemary oil adds a pleasant piny scent to soaps, creams, lotions, perfumes, and toilet waters. (See the entry Lotions from Herbs for more information.) Use rosemary to make sachets for your drawers. (Recipes for sachets can be found in the entry Scents from Herbs.)

Ornamental: Rosemary is a bold yet graceful plant. It looks handsome in any herb garden but also can stand alone in the landscape. The prostrate varieties make lovely ground covers.

Rosemarys are not bothered by reflected heat such as that radiated by sunny walls. Therefore, they can be used as accents on patios and terraces. Set a pot of rosemary at the base of a wall for a striking effect, or plant a prostrate variety so it will creep along a stone wall.

ROSEMARY SPECIES AND VARIETIES

Name	Growth	Flower Color	Comments
Rosmarinus officinalis 'Benenden Blue' Benenden blue rosemary	Upright	Blue	Very narrow leaves, darker than *R. officinalis*
R. officinalis 'Collingwood Ingrami' Wood rosemary or Collingwood Ingrami rosemary	Upright	Dark blue	Shorter, plumper leaves than *R. officinalis;* looser appearance
R. officinalis 'Gray' Gray rosemary	Upright	Pale blue	Grayish foliage, fairly broad leaf
R. officinalis 'Lockwood de Forest' Lockwood rosemary, Santa Barbara rosemary	Prostrate	Blue	
R. officinalis 'Majorca Pink' Majorca pink rosemary	Upright	Pink	Produces long branches that twist around plant, then cascade; blooms almost continuously
R. officinalis 'Miss Jessup' Miss Jessup rosemary	Upright	Pale blue	Golden green foliage
R. officinalis 'Pine Scented' Pine scented rosemary	Upright	Blue	Narrow, light green leaves; strong pine scent
R. officinalis 'Rex' Rex rosemary	Upright	Blue	Very striking appearance; dark leaf color—almost black-green, white beneath; dynamic bloomer
R. officinalis 'Tuscan Blue' Tuscan blue rosemary	Upright	Deeper blue than *R. officinalis*	Larger leaves than *R. officinalis;* faster growth; tall—may reach 10–12 ft. grown outdoors in proper climate
R. officinalis var. *alba* White-flowered rosemary	Upright	White	Along with 'Rex' rosemary is one of the most dynamic bloomers
R. officinalis var. *prostratus* Prostrate rosemary, creeping rosemary, trailing rosemary	Prostrate	Deep blue	Long branches twist, curl, recurve; blooms almost continuously
R. officinalis var. *prostratus* 'Huntington Carpet' Huntington carpet rosemary	Prostrate	Deep blue	Flowers bloom throughout most of year

Cosmetic: "Also if thou be feeble boyle the leaves in clene water and washe thyself and thou shalt wax shiny," wrote Banckes in his *Herbal*.

Baths: Remember, rosemary contains a volatile oil that gets the blood flowing under the skin. A rosemary bath can refresh and stimulate a worn and sluggish body. Make a strong tea from the leaves and add it to the bathwater, or make a steam facial with an infusion of rosemary leaves to perk up your face. (See the entries

ROSEMARY—continued

GARDEN IDEAS

- Create the spokes of an herb wheel with rosemary.
- Plant rosemary in a perennial border.
- Lovely hedgerows can be formed with rosemary bushes.
- Creeping varieties of rosemary look quite attractive planted in hanging baskets with their branches cascading over the edges.

PLANT HARDINESS

Rosemary can be grown outdoors in climates where the winter temperatures do not drop below 10°F. *Rosmarinus officinalis* var. *alba* is the hardiest. Marilyn Hampstead of Michigan's Fox Hill Farm has been able to overwinter this variety, but not consistently.

GROWING CONDITIONS

- Plant hardiness zones 8–10.
- Soil pH 6.5–7.0.
- Well-drained soil.
- Full sun.

Bathing with Herbs and Lotions from Herbs for other bath recipes.)

Hair rinse: If you are a brunette, a rosemary rinse will brighten your hair. One old-fashioned recipe calls for infusing 1 ounce of both rosemary and sage in 1 pint of water for 24 hours, but a simpler rinse can be made by steeping a sprig of rosemary in 1 cup of boiling water for 5 to 10 minutes. Work the rinse into your hair after shampooing.

Dye: Though not usually thought of as a dye plant, rosemary produces various shades of yellow-green with wool. (See the entry Dyes from Herbs for more information.)

Other: Rosemary attracts large numbers of bees, and a very fine honey can be produced from its nectar.

CULTIVATION

To grow rosemary—and surely by now you have fallen in love with this herb and must have one in your garden or home—start your plants from cuttings or by layering. Rosemary can be started from seed, but germination rates are very low, and it takes up to three years to produce a bush sizable enough for harvesting. In addition, plants grown from seed are not as robust as those taken from established plants. The stems are softer, the branches weaker, and the leaf color lacks the sheen and intensity of rosemarys grown from cuttings. If you do choose to grow rosemary from seed, use fresh seeds, preferably ones less than two weeks old. These are the easiest and fastest to germinate. Packaged seeds are difficult to germinate.

Plant rosemary in a sunny location where you want it to stay; rosemary does not transplant well. If your soil is acidic, apply lime, wood ashes, crushed eggshells, or crushed seashells every two to three years. As for fertility, most soils are rich enough for growing rosemary. A very poor soil should be improved with a little fertilization occasionally.

Container gardening: "It is very challenging to grow rosemary in containers," reports Marilyn Hampstead, owner of Fox Hill Farm in Parma, Michigan. "You must accommodate the roots." Because rosemary is an evergreen shrub, the roots easily develop root rot. A well-drained soil is essential. Hampstead recommends a cactus soil that contains a lot of perlite. Using a porous container and being careful not to overwater will also help. However, do not underwater; rosemary can dry out very easily, too. Mist the branches regularly.

Harvesting and storage: Harvesting can be done throughout the year. Hampstead recommends cutting 4-inch pieces from the tips of the branches, being careful not to remove more than 20 percent of the growth at a time.

RUE

Ruta graveolens   **Rutaceae**

The distinctive fragrance of rue is attractive to some herb gardeners and just curious to others. Herb grower Cyrus Hyde is among the former, and he has gone so far as to make a rue sandwich now and then.

Glands distributed over the entire plant contain a volatile oil that accounts for both the unusual smell and the bitter taste of the herb. The oil also has the odd power of photosensitizing the skin of some people, causing small water blisters to break out. Workers at Hyde's New Jersey herb farm have noticed that their skin gets blotchy after working around rue on a hot day.

HISTORY

Rue has a long and colorful history. The genus name, *Ruta,* comes from the Greek "reuo," meaning "to set free," which suggests the herb's reputation in treating disease. Aristotle said it eased the nervous indigestion suffered when eating in the presence of foreigners, and since the Greeks attributed this reaction to witchcraft on the part of the guests, rue was deemed an antimagical herb. They also used it to stimulate the nervous and uterine systems.

The Roman naturalist and writer Pliny tells us that carvers, painters, and engravers ingested rue to improve their eyesight. The plant was also used for many centuries as an antidote to poisons and insect bites. In the first century B.C., King Mithradates of Asia Minor apparently ate rue to immunize himself against being poisoned by enemies, taking the herb in gradually increasing doses. However, this scheme backfired when he attempted suicide by poisoning himself and failed. (In the end, he persuaded a slave to stab him.)

Rue has been used externally to treat insect bites, gout, rheumatism, and sciatica, and internally to treat nervous heart problems, hysteria, worms, gas pains, colic, and to improve the appetite and digestion. Women took rue to correct irregular menstruation, to ease the symptoms of menopause, and to induce abortion.

To treat epilepsy, a bouquet of the herb was hung around the neck of the sufferer. Seventeenth-century herbalist Nicholas Culpeper wrote that "the juice thereof warmed in a pomegranate shell or rind, and dropped into the ears, helps the pains of them. The juice of it and fennel, with a little honey, and the gall of a cock put thereunto, helps the dimness of the eyesight."

During the Middle Ages, rue was considered a reliable defense against witches and their spells. It was also used to ward off the plague. In the sixteenth and seventeenth centuries, rue was scattered

UNSAFE

DESCRIPTION

Rue is an evergreen perennial subshrub. The stems are woody at the base and herbaceous farther up. (See photos on pages 31, 444, and 513.)

Flowers: Yellow to yellow-green, ½ in. wide; petals toothed, concave; in loose clusters at top of plant.

Leaves: Alternate, pinnate, 3–5 in. long; leaflets oblong to spatulate, somewhat fleshy; blue-green, often covered with a white powdery substance; emit strong, pungent odor; lower leaves have much longer stalks than upper leaves.

Fruit: Four or five lobed capsules containing grayish seeds.

Height: 3 ft.

FLOWERING

June through August.

RANGE

Rue's native origin is southern Europe and northern Africa. Although it is no longer found in the wild, it often escapes from European and American gardens to become locally naturalized in poor, dry soil.

HABITAT

Old fields, roadsides, and waste areas.

RUE—continued

VINEGAR OF THE FOUR THIEVES

During the Great Plague of London in 1665, as many as 7,000 people were dying each week. In this plague, as in others that swept Europe, herbs were used in unending combinations and applications to cure the infected, as well as to ward off the disease.

But no one knew with any certainty what was causing the disease, nor how to avoid it other than by avoiding contact with the dead or the dying. A red cross was painted on the doors of homes where a plague death had occurred, providing a warning to the wary and a signal to the unscrupulous.

Among the latter was a small band of thieves, who, fortified—at least in their own minds—by drafts of an herbal vinegar, stole from corpses.

Rue was a primary ingredient. Mixed into a gallon of red wine vinegar were 1½ ounces each of rue, sage, mint, wormwood, and rosemary; 2 ounces of lavender flowers; ½ ounce of camphor; and ¼ ounce each of cinnamon, nutmeg, cloves, garlic, and *Calamus aromaticus.*

on the benches and floors of courtrooms, and judges carried branches of it to guard against "jail fever." The ceremonial bouquets still presented to British judges in this century are a carryover of this tradition.

Long a symbol of sorrow and repentance, rue may have been nicknamed the "herb of grace" in Christian times for the grace given by God following repentance for one's sins. Brushes made of the plant were used to sprinkle holy water before a Roman Catholic high mass.

Rue even played a hand in the design of playing cards—it was used as an early model for the suit of clubs.

USES

In terms of utility, rue can't match its historical richness.

Medicinal: Rue is still used in some folk medicines to relieve gas pains and colic, to improve appetite and digestion, and to promote menstruation. There is some doubt about the safety of rue as a medicine, however.

"Belief in rue as a valuable medicinal agent," wrote pharmacognosist Varro Tyler, Ph.D., in *The Honest Herbal,* "is as ridiculous as the belief that if the gunflints for a flintlock muzzle loader were boiled in a mixture of rue and vervain, the shot would hit its mark no matter how poor the aim of the marksman."

Toxicity: Large doses can cause violent gastrointestinal pains and vomiting, mental confusion, prostration, and convulsive twitching. It should never be taken by pregnant women as it can trigger abortion; animal experiments have shown that several rue extracts may accomplish this through their action on the uterine muscles. Overexposure to sunlight after ingesting rue can result in severe sunburn, and handling the fresh herb or its juice can cause redness, swelling, and even blistering of the skin, not unlike a poison ivy rash.

Ornamental: Rue isn't often grown in ornamental gardens, but its unusual blue-green foliage makes it a standout in herb gardens. And, while not spectacular, their muted yellow blooms are certainly pretty. It also grows well in a container, indoors or outside. Several cultivated varieties are available, including 'Variegata', with white-edged leaves, and 'Jackman's Blue', a compact grower with rich blue foliage.

Craft: The dried seed heads of rue add interest and texture to herb and flower arrangements.

Companion planting: Tradition has it that rue should never be planted near basil, sage, or cabbage, but it might enhance the growth

of figs. Some gardeners recommend planting it with roses. No scientific evidence exists to support any claims for rue's effects.

CULTIVATION

Rue is grown in many herb gardens for its historical interest as well as its striking blue-green foliage. The herb is easily propagated by either seed, cuttings, or division. Supposedly, the rue stolen from a neighbor's garden will thrive best.

If planting seeds, start them indoors in February for May transplanting. The starts should be about 2 inches high before they are moved outdoors. Plant them in full sun in well-drained, not-too-rich soil, placing them about 18 inches apart. Cuttings should be rooted in the shade, then transplanted to a sunny location.

Rue makes an attractive pot plant; it'll thrive on a sunny windowsill in ordinary potting soil.

Pests and diseases: Root fungal problems may occur in areas with warmer climates. This can be prevented by providing good drainage.

Harvesting and storage: Rue can be harvested several times a year. After the first cutting, top-dress the plants with good compost to stimulate new growth. Harvest the leaves before the flowers form. Dry them in the shade and store in an airtight container.

GROWING CONDITIONS

- Plant hardiness zones 4–9.
- Soil pH 7.0.
- Well-drained, clay loam.
- Full sun.

SAFFLOWER

Carthamus tinctorius   Compositae

It's difficult to relate a bottle of cooking oil to a beautiful orange-yellow flower. But since the days of the ancient Egyptian pharaohs, the safflower has been the source of a cooking oil.

It is much easier to picture those orange-yellow flowers brightening foods (or a dress or a room). And so they have, for just as long as they have yielded their oil to the cook. Dried safflower is a popular food coloring agent and can be used to dye cloth or make cosmetics. Live safflower is a bright and colorful accent for an herb garden.

DESCRIPTION

Safflower is an annual plant with a smooth, erect, whitish stem that branches toward the top.

Flowers: Orange-yellow, compound, thistlelike, with several tubular florets; 1–1½ in. wide.

Leaves: Alternate, ovate, pointed at tips, minutely spiny toothed.

Fruit: Seedlike achenes; resemble tiny, pearly white shells; about ¼ in. long.

Height: 1–3 ft.

FLOWERING

Summer.

RANGE

Originally grew wild in Europe, Asia, and perhaps Egypt, although exact origin is unclear; cultivated commercially in California and Europe.

CHEF TIP

Heighten the flavor of safflower by crushing the flowers against a cutting board with the back of a spoon.

GROWING CONDITIONS

- Average to poor, dry soil.
- Full sun.

HISTORY

The use of safflower oil in cooking dates back to ancient Egypt. During the Middle Ages various medicinal uses were found for this flower. Those with constipation or respiratory problems drank the juice of the seed mixed with chicken stock or sweetened water.

Only relatively recently has the most significant aspect of the safflower been determined; it's the oil lowest in cholesterol of all contemporary vegetable oils.

USES

Culinary: Use dried safflower to enliven the hues of cream soups, marinades, pale sauces, salad dressings, basting liquids, flavored vinegars, pasta salads, and curries. The dried flowers produce a red color.

Dried safflower can be substituted for saffron, but its taste, in comparison, is simple and bland. You must use about five times the amount of safflower that you would of saffron, but you will get a slightly redder color.

Available commercially: Dried flowers and safflower oil.

Substitute: Saffron at about one-fifth the amount of safflower.

Dye: The flower heads yield yellow to red dyes for silk and wool. *(See the entry Dyes from Herbs.)*

Craft: Cuttings of safflower dry nicely and add bright color and interesting texture to dried herb and flower arrangements.

CULTIVATION

Sow seeds in early spring where they are to be grown, as they won't transplant well. Plants require full sun and will prosper in a dry, poor to average soil. Thin the seedlings to stand about 6 inches apart.

SAFFRON

Crocus sativus   Iridaceae

Many a gourmet gardener-cook plants a few of these crocuses with the hope of harvesting home-grown saffron. If that is your goal, you'd better plant several thousand corms: Some 35,000 flowers are needed to produce just 1 pound of the spice. Yet even if you aren't ready to start a crocus farm, don't ignore the plant. This pretty autumn flower is worth growing just for its beauty.

HISTORY

This jewel of a plant seems to date back to the very beginnings of civilization. Since antiquity, its yellow powder has been a kind of luxury item. The Greeks made a royal dye color with saffron, as did the Chinese. Hopefully they had dry cleaning back then because saffron dye is readily soluble in water. The gods, goddesses, heroes, and nymphs of Greek myths and poems wore robes dyed with saffron. Wealthy Romans perfumed their baths and homes with it. "The Scent was valued as much as the dye," wrote Maude Grieve in *A Modern Herbal;* "saffron water was sprinkled on the benches of the theatre, the floors of banqueting-halls were strewn with crocus leaves, and cushions were stuffed with it."

From the fourteenth to the eighteenth century, saffron was used as a medicine and spice in Europe. So widespread was its use at this time that any spice dealer was called a saffron grocer.

USES

Medicinal: Traditionally, saffron has been recommended against colds, tumors, smallpox, insomnia, and cancer. It is also considered an appetite stimulant and an aphrodisiac.

A volatile oil and two glycosides have been identified in saffron, but researchers have yet to learn whether these or any other saffron constituents have any therapeutic effects. We do know, however, that doses of one-third of an ounce or more can be toxic. Since saffron is so expensive, it is rarely used as a medicine, and overdose would be even rarer.

Culinary: Saffron's dark orange stigmata, called threads in the culinary world, have a rich, briny flavor. Traditionally, they have been used to flavor French bouillabaisse, Spanish paella, cakes, breads, cookies, and the cuisines of East India, the Middle East, and North Africa.

Saffron mingles well with mild cheeses, eggs, rice, lamb, fish,

DESCRIPTION

The saffron crocus resembles other true crocuses, and like other crocuses, the flower rises directly from the earth. This perennial has no true stem. What appears to be the stem is actually the tubular portion of the corolla.

Flowers: 6 tepals ("petals"); lavender, white, or reddish purple; 1½–2 in. long; reddish orange stigmata; fragrant.
Leaves: Linear, grasslike, 1– 1½ ft.
Fruit: Not produced.
Height: 18 in.

FLOWERING

September.

RANGE

Originated in Asia Minor; widely cultivated.

CHEF TIPS

- Use just a pinch in soups and stews that serve four to six. Too much saffron can give a medicinal taste.

- Soak saffron in hot water or stock before adding to recipes. Then add the saffron and the water. This allows the color to disperse throughout the food.

- Add a pinch of soaked saffron to cheese soufflés, savory cheese custards, tarts, and pies before baking.

- Add saffron threads to vinegars flavored with garlic and thyme. The combination is wonderful in fish salads and marinades.

437

Stigma

Foliage Stage

Flowering Stage

Leaf Cross Section

shellfish, poultry, pork, duck, cream, corn, sweet peppers, onions, shallots, garlic, and oranges.

Available commercially: Whole threads and ground, but whole threads are preferable. Don't mistake safflower for saffron, or you'll be disappointed in the taste.

Substitute: Safflower, for color only.

Ornamental: While spring crocuses appear after winter to cheer the heart, saffron opens its beautiful blooms in the autumn to lift the spirits after the pageantry of summer gardens has faded. Crocuses look stunning in rock gardens. Plant them in patches at the base of trees or along a shrub border.

Dye: Probably saffron's oldest use was as a dyestuff. It yields an unparalleled deep yellow dye; 1 part of crocin, saffron's major pigment, has the ability to color up to 150,000 parts of water a definite yellow. but in such small quantities that saffron yellow has always been associated with royalty and wealth. Four thousand blossoms are needed to produce 1 ounce of dye.

CULTIVATION

Plant corms in the fall or spring. Set them 3 to 4 inches deep, with the rooting side down. Allow about 6 inches between plants. They will propagate themselves, producing new clumps every year. If you must move them, do so in the summer after the foliage has died down, and immediately replant in the new location.

In areas with severe winters, a protective mulch is advised.

Harvesting and storage: The thin, dried stigmata of the flowers make up the true saffron of commerce, long recognized as the world's most expensive spice. Bought in bulk at the retail level, true saffron currently costs well over $4,500 a pound. Yet when you consider the backbreaking tediousness of the harvesting process, you wonder if that's return enough.

To obtain saffron, growers plunder the flowers daily during the relatively short blooming period. They remove the stigmata and sometimes part of the styles, and the work must be done by hand since no mechanical harvester has yet been developed. Thousands and thousands of flowers must be handled, even for a modest yield. The stigmata are placed beneath a weight on a special kiln. Under the pressure of the weight, the saffron dries to form a thick cake.

When you have just a few flowers to harvest, simply let individual stigmata dry on a piece of paper.

Store saffron in sealed glass vials in a cool, dry place.

GROWING CONDITIONS

- Plant hardiness zone 6.
- Full sun to light shade.
- Light, well-drained soil.

438

SAGE

Salvia officinalis   Labiatae

The silver-green sagebrush makes the high chaparral smell like one enormous Thanksgiving turkey. But if you tried to eat this native plant, you'd find it tasted a lot more like wormwood than like the clean-tasting herb you use in the kitchen. So, unlike cooks in the Mediterranean region, you can't pick sage from the wild but must grow it yourself.

HISTORY

To the ancients, including the Arabians, sage was associated with immortality, or at least longevity, and it was credited with increasing mental capacity. In the tenth century, the medical school at Salerno, Italy, coined the aphorism, "Why should a man die, when he can go to his garden for sage?" The genus name derives from the Latin for "salvation." Later, the plant was used to counteract snakebite. It was so prized for tea that the Chinese, of all people, were willing to trade their own fine green tea for it in a ratio of 4 to 1.

In Yugoslavia to this day, fields of sage are planted and harvested like wheat or hay, three crops a year, for cooking. American Indians, on the other hand, thought of it principally as a medicine, mixing it with bear grease for a salve they claimed would cure skin sores, as an infusion for rubdowns and baths, and as a sort of leafy, disposable toothbrush.

Americans of the 1800s said the herb cured warts. Claims have also been made for it as a cure for epilepsy, insomnia, measles, seasickness, and worms. It was thought to be especially good for stopping the flow of urine, milk, saliva, and, most of all, perspiration.

USES

Sage's culinary talent earns the herb a place in the garden and home. It also has medicinal and ornamental value.

Medicinal: The volatile oils and tannins in sage are thought to account for its reputation for drying up perspiration. A product made from it is marketed as an anhidrotic in Germany. The oils have antiseptic, astringent, and irritant properties. This makes sage useful in treating sore throats, mouth irritations, and possibly cuts and bruises. Experiments in 1939 showed it had estrogenic properties, which may have some connection to the herb's reputed ability to dry up milk. Research has shown it lowers blood sugar in diabetics.

Sage also contains terpene, camphor, and salvene. When fresh,

DESCRIPTION

Sage is a hardy perennial subshrub with woody, wiry stems that are square and covered with down. (See photos on pages 10, 238, 272, 511, and 514.)

Flowers: Grow in whorls of four to eight at axils; pink, purple, blue, or white; tubular, ½-¾ in. long; two-lipped; upper lip straight or arched; ring of hairs inside; purplish, bell-shaped calyx.

Leaves: Opposite; to 2 in. long; look pebbly and pucker-veined, as if made of wrinkled seersucker; grayish green, softly hairy or velvety; round-toothed margins; long stalked.

Fruit: An oval nutlet.

Height: 12–30 in.

FLOWERING

June.

RANGE

Sage is native to the northern Mediterranean coast. The widely cultivated herb is hardy north into Canada. The soil should be slightly alkaline, with little moisture needed once the plants are established.

SAGE SPECIES AND VARIETIES

Name	Growth	Habit	Comments
Salvia Clevelandii Blue sage	3 ft.	Blue flowers	Use in potpourris; recommended as a substitute for *S. officinalis* in cooking
S. elegans Pineapple sage	2–3 ft.	Pineapple scent, brilliant red flowers	Use for drinks, chicken, cheese, and in jams and jellies; grow indoors in good light
S. leucantha Mexican bush sage	4 ft.	Gray-green foliage with spikes of lavender flowers	Not winter hardy; flowers, which dry well, produced in abundance
S. officinalis 'Aurea' Golden sage	18 in.	Striking gold and green variegated leaves	Compact, dense growth makes a very showy border plant
S. officinalis 'Dwarf' Dwarf sage	18 in.	More compact grower, smaller leaf size	Makes a good border, rock garden, or container plant
S. officinalis 'Holt's Mammoth' Holt's mammoth sage	3 ft.	Larger, rounder leaves than garden sage	Grows quickly; good for cutting and drying bulk quantities
S. officinalis 'Purpurea' Purple sage	18 in.	Compact, aromatic, purple foliage	Use like garden sage in stuffings, sausage, omelets, soups, and stews
S. officinalis 'Tricolor' Tricolor sage	2–3 ft.	Variegated leaves in cream, purple, green	Very decorative
S. Sclarea Clary sage	3 ft.	Huge, pebbly gray leaves, spectacular lilac and pink flowers	A most unusual and showy sage (see the entry Clary)

the terpene predominates, but other aromatics gain ascendance as the plant dries, which may account for the stronger flavor of dry sage.

Culinary: Sage is lemony, camphorlike, and pleasantly bitter. Young leaves are eaten fresh in salads and cooked in omelets, fritters, soups, yeast breads and rolls, marinades, sausages, meat pies, and poultry stuffing. They are also cooked with liver, beef, pork, veal, fish, lamb, poultry, duck, goose, artichokes, tomatoes, asparagus, carrots, squash, corn, potatoes, eggplant, snap beans, leeks, onions, brussels sprouts, cabbage, oranges, lemons, garlic, cheese, lentils, and shell beans. Flavored sages, like clary and pineapple sage, can stand in for regular sage with almost any food.

SAGE—continued

Available commercially: Dried whole or dried crumbled leaves. Note that the taste of dried sage is different than fresh, often less lemony, and sometimes a bit musty.

Aromatic: Sage has been used as an ingredient of perfumes, soaps, and cosmetics. It is also used as an insect repellent, sending away flies and, in the garden, cabbage moths and carrot flies. It attracts bees, and the result is a splendidly aromatic honey. Some people say its fragrance induces sleep.

Ornamental: Sage adds a restful accent to the ornamental border and can serve as a beautiful backdrop for orange lilies or bright red roses. There are literally dozens of species of *Salvia,* and even more varieties and cultivars among these species. The species and varieties table accompanying this entry lists only a sampling.

Cosmetic: Sage infusions have been used to color silver hair. This homemade beauty aid works subtly—until you discontinue it; the colored hair may take on a greenish tint, if neglected.

Sage also stimulates the skin when used in skin lotions or herbal baths. It makes a soothing, astringent aftershave and is sometimes mixed with lavender for this purpose. (See the entries Lotions from Herbs and Bathing with Herbs for more information.)

Craft: The foliage of sage dries well and can be used in herb wreaths, especially a culinary wreath.

Garden Sage

Purple Sage

Variegated Sage

$SAGE$—continued

CHEF TIPS

- Use large sage leaves to wrap around quail and other small birds before roasting or grilling.

- Deep-fry sage sprigs and use as a garnish for roast meats.

- Lay fresh sage leaves on a pork roast before cooking. Or make slits in the roast and insert the fresh leaves.

- Mince fresh leaves and use them in the breading for fried chicken.

Dye: Sage tops yield a yellow-buff color to wool mordanted with alum; yellow to wool mordanted with chrome; and green-gray to iron-mordanted yarn.

Companion planting: Try planting sage with cabbages, carrots, strawberries, tomatoes, or marjoram to encourage their growth. According to seventeenth-century herbalist Nicholas Culpeper, sage and onions do not grow well near each other.

Preservative: Sage has antibacterial properties and can be used as a natural preservative for meats, poultry, fish, and condiments. Sage and rosemary together work better than either alone. Distilled sage extracts recently have been made into flavorless antioxidants to increase the shelf life of foods. An odorless and tasteless antioxidant prepared from sage and rosemary improved the stability of soy oil and potato chips.

Other: Sage has been smoked as a tobacco.

CULTIVATION

Sage seed stores poorly, and you should test its germination before planting a large amount. Fortunately, it germinates quickly, so you will soon know whether or not it is working. Sow in late spring and transplant to 20 inches apart when the seedlings reach 3 inches in height.

Some experts advise starting from plants or divisions because it takes two years to grow good-size plants from seed. When you do divide, use the outer, newer growth for replanting.

Sage can also be propagated from 4-inch cuttings taken in the fall for use the following spring, or from crown divisions.

Prune plants severely in the spring to keep them from setting seed, and replace them every three years or so, or they will become woody and less productive. Water sage well until it is established. For large plantations, you can also start it by layering. If the plants are new and you wish to hold them over the winter, the last fall harvest (in the first year the only harvest) should be no later than September and should be a light one. In subsequent years, two or three harvests are possible.

Pests and diseases: Sage is susceptible to wilt and root rot. The pests that might bother this plant include slugs, spider mites, and spittlebugs. (See the entry Growing Herbs for information on controlling pests and diseases.)

Harvesting and storage: To dry sage leaves, snip them from branches you have removed, discard the stems, and spread them on cloth or paper in the shade. Store when thoroughly dry in an airtight, colored glass or solid container. The dried herb has a stronger flavor, but a different taste, than the fresh sage.

Sweet Woodruff

Rue

Pineapple Sage

Rose Geranium

Tansy

Angelica

Labender
·FOAMING·
BATH SEEDS

Potpourri

Hyssop

Lavender

Lemon Balm

Bayberry

Scented Geranium

Lemon verbena

Hyssop

446

ST.-JOHN'S-WORT

Hypericum perforatum   **Hypericaceae**

Pinch the yellow flowers of this attractive perennial and—presto, the petals turn red. St.-John's-wort is a common roadside weed that is tied by both name and legend to religion and witchcraft. It was said on the Isle of Wight that if you stepped on the plant at twilight, you might be carried off on a magic fairy horse and not return until daylight.

HISTORY

For centuries this plant was thought to have the power to drive out devils. With the spread of Christianity, the plant was associated with St. John the Baptist. It was said to bloom first on his birthday, June 24, and to bleed red oil from its leaf glands on the day in August that he was beheaded. Moreover, the plant was believed to be most potent if harvested for medicinal purposes on St. John's Day.

The genus name comes from the Greek, meaning "above an ikon," and sprigs were once set above images to drive off malevolent spirits. Until the industrial era, Welsh families used it as a health test. Sprigs were named for each family member and were hung overnight from a rafter. The degree to which the sprig had shriveled by morning was said to suggest how soon a person would die.

The plant has the curious property of appearing to bleed when crushed, and this may explain why early Greek and Roman physicians used it to dress wounds. Seventeenth-century herbalist John Coles was an exponent of the Doctrine of Signatures. According to this doctrine, a plant's appearance should give some clue to its medicinal value. Coles, pointing out that the "little holes" (glands) in the St.-John's-wort leaves resembled pores, recommended the herb for skin problems of all sorts, including "hurts and wounds and inward bruises." It has also been used for nervous disorders, including bedwetting and urinary troubles, nervous coughs, gastric problems, uterine cramping, anemia, and worms. Like many other common herbs, it fell into disuse in the nineteenth century as a treatment. Just recently, however, it has seen a revival, especially in Europe, as a treatment principally for nervous complaints.

USES

We no longer burn St.-John's-wort to clear the air of evil spirits, but the plant still has several interesting uses.

Medicinal: The useful ingredients in St.-John's-wort are a volatile oil, a resin, a tannin, and a dye. The dye does double duty as an antidepressant in humans. The antibacterial and astringent properties probably come from the tannin and the oil.

UNSAFE

DESCRIPTION

St.-John's-wort is a hardy perennial that smells like turpentine or balsam. An erect plant, its round stems are distinguished by the two raised, lengthwise ridges each has. The creeping, tufted, yellow-brown roots send out runners.

Flowers: Bright yellow, borne in terminal, flat, leafy panicles, on branches, with opposite bracts at base of each pedicel; calyx and corolla marked with black dots and lines; five petals and sepals; three stamen bundles.

Leaves: Small, oblong; opposite, with each pair crossing those above and below; light green; transparent oil glands, especially near margins, look like holes.

Fruit: Three-celled capsule; numerous, small, black, round or oblong seeds.

Height: To 2 ft.

FLOWERING

July and August.

RANGE

Native to Europe; naturalized in North America.

HABITAT

Woods and meadows.

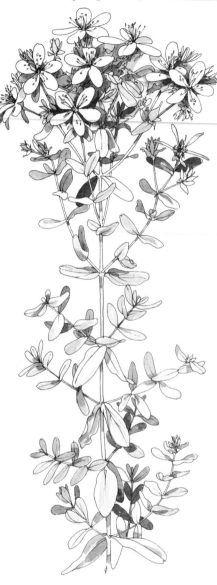

ST-JOHN'S-WORT—continued

The herb is said to soothe the digestive system. In particular, its ingredients were thought to relieve ulcers and gastritis, and the herb was called on as a folk medicine for diarrhea and nausea. Bruises and hemorrhoids are said to respond to it. It has served as a sedative, painkiller, and analgesic. The blossoms have been added to sweek oil (a refined olive oil used medicinally) for a soothing dressing for cuts. Herbalists credit it with increasing and inducing a sense of well-being. It has even been said to help repair nerve tissue after trauma.

Toxicity: Does this herb seem too good to be true? Well, it is. There's also a dangerous side to St.-John's-wort, and until more is learned about this side, the plant and its oil should be used with caution, if at all. In Australia, where St.-John's-wort is a rampant weed, it has killed pale-pigmented sheep and goats by inducing photosensitivity. If an animal or a light-skinned human eats the plant, exposure to direct sun may cause dermatitis, inflammation of mucous membranes, and more toxic reactions.

Pharmacognosist Varro Tyler, Ph.D., points out in *The Honest Herbal* that problems rarely result from normal doses. But he adds that "those who take the herb for extended periods should be aware of the possibility and discontinue usage if such symptoms occur."

Ornamental: Many *Hypericums* are more suited to the perennial bed, but St.-John's-wort is less sensitive to frost, and it does add cheer in the middle of summer when little else blooms.

Dye: Yellows and reds can be obtained from the flowering tops and stems of St.-John's-wort, depending on the mordant used. (See the entry Dyes from Herbs for more information.)

Other: Because of its antibiotic properties, the herb is now being investigated for use as a food preservative.

CULTIVATION

The herb grows wild. To transfer it to an herb garden or perennial bed, dig it intact. It may also be started from seed, cuttings, or division done in the fall. Even though it is a hardy perennial, St.-John's-wort is short-lived.

Despite the fact that it spreads by runners, St.-John's-wort is seldom invasive and can be controlled by pulling. Plants are commercially available and are often used in native gardens.

Harvesting and storage: For medicinal use, the leaves are either dried and stored in a dark place or pressed for the oil. The oil is added to olive or other vegetable oils, but it turns red with age. Kept in a dark container, the oil will keep for two years. The oil content of the plants is highest in the morning.

GROWING CONDITIONS

- Plant hardiness zone 5.
- Soil pH: acid or alkaline.
- Average to poor.
- Full sun to partial shade.

SALAD BURNET

Poterium Sanguisorba   **Rosaceae**

In trendy restaurants these days, a salad is likely to contain anything, even if it's a novel leaf with the bite of battery acid. Yet salad burnet, which tastes considerably better than battery acid, is known to only a few discriminating gardeners. Its flavor is often compared to cucumbers, and 400 years ago, it was as common in salads as cucumbers are today. It was a common addition to a glass of wine, much as a celery stick is used today to stir a tall drink.

In the garden it is valued for its handsome purple flowers and its adaptability to various soils. If you are designing an herb garden, consider burnet as an edging plant.

HISTORY

Burnet is one of the more venerable of forgotten herbs, used medicinally for at least 2,000 years. The Roman scholar Pliny discussed its medicinal powers in the first century A.D., although he may just have been recording older customs or even a different but closely related species. Later herbalists said that the great burnet *(Sanguisorba officinalis)* and the salad burnet have the same medicinal uses, so the confusion in Pliny's writing has not been worth untangling. (*Hortus Third* prefers *Poterium Sanguisorba* as the proper botanical name for salad burnet over a synonym, *S. minor,* which would put these two burnets in the same genus.)

That pinkish, rounded head of flowers must have reminded herbalists of blood; again and again, burnet is prescribed for something gory. The plant captured the interest of the great herbalists of the sixteenth and seventeeth centuries, a golden age for plant medicine; burnet moved sixteenth-century herbalist William Turner to remark in a medical text that the leaves reminded him of bird's wings, open in flight. Burnet could protect people from the plague, according to an eighteenth-century herbalist named Pechy, who described an antiplague recipe for 21 herbs, burnet among them, to be dissolved in white wine. Gerard described burnet as smelling like a melon or cucumber, but most noses miss the melon.

These traditions crossed the Atlantic, and burnet appears in American herbals. The Shakers mentioned using it in the 1820s for healing wounds.

Considering burnet's modest use as a medicine and salad ingredient, it is astonishing to note in Thomas Jefferson's letters that he once dispatched two boys to pick up 6 to 8 bushels of burnet seed. Based on his calculations, that would be enough to cover up to 16 acres with the perennial. He didn't have a salad bar or pharmaceuti

DESCRIPTION

This bushy perennial herb looks like a loose clump of divided leaves.

Flowers: Small and pinkish; borne in a rounded head; lower flowers have only male flowering parts; middle flowers have both male and female parts, and the upper rings of flowers have just female parts.

Leaves: Central stem with 7 to 11 plump, rounded leaflets. Basal leaves pinnate; 4–12 pairs of leaflets, 3/16–3/4 in. long, rounded to elliptical, toothed; upper leaves few, reduced.

Fruit: Achenes enclosed in the dried calyx tube.

Height: 3 ft. in flower; foliage forms 1-ft. basal rosette.

FLOWERING

May through June.

RANGE

Native to western Asia and Europe; naturalized in North America.

CHEF TIPS

- Add minced fresh burnet leaves to coleslaw.

- Toss fresh burnet leaves with thinly sliced beets, freshly snipped dill, and yogurt.

- Stuff burnet leaves and lemon slices onto the cavities of cornish hens before roasting. Remove before serving.

SALAD BURNET—continued

cal firm in mind, however, but used it for grazing livestock and
erosion control.

Burnet has a distinguished history as an ornamental in the garden, and it was championed by Sir Francis Bacon. He suggested that
gardeners cultivate plants that smell good when they're stepped on,
and he mentioned thyme and mint as well as burnet. Plant whole
paths of burnet, said Bacon.

USES

Medicinal: Burnet has long been associated with blood.
Sanguisorba means, literally, "drink up blood," and herbalists prepared a tea to stop hemorrhages and smoothed an ointment on
wounds. Various preparations were supposed to help women going
through a difficult menopause.

In the old view of wound healing, the medicine was supposed
to pucker up the tissues and draw the sides of the wound together to
heal. The same puckering or drying action could also help in other
ailments, the theory went. Thus an old herbal recommends burnet
for vaginal discharges and diarrhea.

The foliage contains vitamin C and tannins, but there is no
modern evidence that burnet is effective medicinally.

Culinary: Salad burnet tastes like cucumber. Only the tender
young leaves of the plant are used, because the older ones can taste
bitter. Use them in salads, flavored vinegars, herb butters, and iced
beverages (they were once placed in claret), and as garnishes. The
seeds are found in vinegars, marinades, and cheese spreads, and the
dusty pink flowers are used as garnishes and in salads.

Burnet blends well with dill, basil, thyme, garlic, oregano, marjoram, and tarragon.

Substitute: Young borage leaves.

Storage note: Burnet doesn't dry well. It becomes dark and loses
its cucumber taste.

Ornamental: Try burnet in a border of flowers for its delicate
foliage.

GROWING CONDITIONS

- Plant hardiness zone 3.
- Soil pH 6.8.
- Average, well-drained soil.
- Full sun to partial shade.

CULTIVATION

Propagate it by dividing in the spring. Burnet also grows readily
from seed and will reseed itself. Sow directly outside and thin to 12
to 15 inches. To stimulate new leaf growth, remove the flower stalks.
The plant is tolerant of a variety of soils, but it is partial to lime and
full sun. Once established, burnet needs little attention.

SASSAFRAS

Sassafras albidum   **Lauraceae**

This native American tree offers brilliant yellow, orange, and red foliage in the fall and three exotic sensations for the nose: The roots smell of root beer; the wood of athlete's-foot medicine; and the young leaves of citrus. The roots were once a valued flavoring agent in root beer, but safrole, a constituent of sassafras oil, has been identified as a carcinogen. There may not be enough oil in the sassafras tea to render it harmful, but prudence suggests making tea from other safer spices and herbs.

Sassafras bark was one of the first exports sent home from the New World. The soothing, aromatic tea was well-known to the Indians of the eastern woodlands and to the early settlers. It was recommended as a stimulant, feverfuge, antispasmodic, and even a cure for syphilis. After research in the 1960s showed that safrole causes liver cancer in rodents, the Food and Drug Administration outlawed the sale of flavorings containing it, including saffafras.

USES

In spite of the plant's status as a carcinogen, sassafras is still worth planting for the refreshing smell of its leaves and bark and for the colorful fall foliage. The wood looks something like ash or oak but is far lighter in weight and easier to work.

Medicinal: Although the plant's volatile oils are toxic, sassafras preparations are safe for external use. The root bark contains antiseptic constituents, making it an effective remedy for skin wounds and sores. It has been recommended for relief from the itching of poison ivy and poison oak. The gummy core of the branches was once used to soothe tired eyes.

Ornamental: Since only the smallest sassafras trees transplant successfully, this plant is seldom included in landscaping lists. Yet it is ideal for naturalizing in poor, rocky soils, damp spots, or just about any other location. Its fall color is spectacular, and the bright green leaves are a lovely background in the spring and summer.

Try growing very small trees in containers until they are large enough to move to their permanent location.

CULTIVATION

You can transplant young sassafras trees from the wild, but it is nearly impossible to move older ones since they have such long taproots. Sassafras trees are usually propagated by freshly ripened seed or by suckers, which the trees send forth freely. Root cuttings may also be used.

Pests and diseases: Gypsy moths eat the leaves, and sassafras is one of the favorite hosts of Japanese beetles. (See the entry Growing Herbs for information on controlling pests.)

EXTERNAL USE ONLY

DESCRIPTION

These small deciduous trees are immediately recognized by their aromatic, mitten-shaped leaves, which may have one or two "thumbs." The bark on the trunk is rough and gray, with deep channels.

Flowers: Pale, yellowish green, apetalous, in 2-in. racemes; male and female flowers usually on different trees.

Leaves: Alternate, downy; vary in form and size from ovate and entire to three-lobed, with most being three-lobed.

Fruit: Ovoid, one-seeded, pea-sized, blue drupe.

Height: 30–50 ft.

FLOWERING

Spring before the leaves appear.

RANGE

The United States from Michigan to Texas and east.

HABITAT

In sandy soils along the edge of woods.

GROWING CONDITIONS

- Plant hardiness zone 5.
- Any garden soil.

SAVORY

Satureja spp.   **Labiatae**

There are two savories: the annual summer savory (*Satureja hortensis*) and the woody perennial winter savory (*S. montana*). In almost every application except gardening, they are the same.

The primary use of savory is in cooking, and the two savories were among the strongest cooking herbs available to Europeans until world exploration and trade brought them tropical spices like black pepper. The savories have been used to enhance the flavor of food for over 2,000 years.

DESCRIPTION

The savories are members of the genus *Satureja*, which comprises about 30 species. Summer savory (*S. hortensis*) and winter savory (*S. montana*) are the best known. (See photos on pages 100 and 102.)

S. hortensis is an annual with a branching root system and bushy, finely hairy stems. The entire plant is highly aromatic.

S. montana is a hardy semievergreen perennial. It is woody at the base and forms a compact bush. It has a heavier aroma, while that of summer savory is sweeter and more delicate.

Flowers: S. hortensis: White or pale pink, two-lipped, to ¼ in. long, nearly stalkless; appear in upper leaf axils in groups of three to six. *S. montana:* White or lilac, lower lips spotted with purple; ⅓ in. long; grouped in terminal spikes.

Leaves: S. hortensis: Soft, hairless, linear, about 1 in. long, attached directly to the stem in pairs; grayish, turning purplish in late summer or early autumn. *S. montana:* Dark green, glossy, and lance-shaped, wider toward the tips, to 1 in. long.

Fruit: Four nutlets.

Height: S. hortensis: 1–1½ ft. *S. montana:* 6–12 in.

FLOWERING

S. hortensis: Midsummer through frost. *S. montana:* July through mid-September.

RANGE

Both species native to the Mediterranean region; naturalized in North America.

HISTORY

The genus's Latin name, *Satureja,* is attributed to the Roman writer Pliny and is a derivative of the word for "satyr," the half-man, half-goat creature that roamed the ancient mythological forests. According to legend, the savories belonged to the satyrs. The Romans used it extensively in their cooking, often flavoring vinegars with it. The poet Virgil suggested growing savory near beehives because of the pleasant-tasting honey it produced.

During Caesar's reign, it is believed that the Romans introduced savory to England, where it quickly became popular both as a medicine and a cooking herb. The Saxons named it savory for its spicy, pungent taste. According to some sources, it was not actually cultivated until the ninth century. The Italians may have been among the first to grow savory as a kitchen herb. It is still used extensively in their cooking and makes an especially good companion to green beans and lentils. Winter savory shrubs made popular hedges in Tudor herb and knot gardens and in shrub mazes.

For hundreds of years, both savories have had a reputation for regulating sex drive. Winter savory was thought to decrease sexual desire, while summer savory was said to be an aphrodisiac. Naturally, summer savory became the more popular of the two!

The seventeenth-century herbalist Nicholas Culpeper wrote that the savories were valuable for their "heating, drying and carminative [action], expelling wind from the stomach and bowels, and are good in asthma and other affections of the breast." It was regarded as a promoter of regular menstruation and as a tonic for the reproductive system. Culpeper said that "it is much commended for pregnant women to take inwardly and to smell often unto." He also recommended savory as a cure for deafness.

In *The Winter's Tale,* Shakespeare mentions it, together with lavender and marjoram. Winter savory is recommended by several old writers, in combination with other herbs, for dressing trout. Another seventeenth-century herbalist, John Parkinson, described how it was dried and powdered and mixed with bread crumbs, "to breade their meate, be it fish or flesh, to give it a quicker relish."

The early colonists brought both savories with them to the New World as trusted remedies for indigestion. American settler and writer John Josselyn listed its presence in the New England area in his book *New-England's Rarities,* published in 1672. Many of the old New England cookbooks discuss savory's varied uses.

As a medicine, savory has also been recommended as a general tonic, vermifuge, appetite stimulant, and treatment for diarrhea. A tea has been used as an expectorant and as a cough remedy. Mixed with flour and applied as a poultice, it eased the pain of sciatica and palsy. The crushed leaves were rubbed into insect stings for quick relief.

USES

The savories are cooking herbs almost exclusively today. But that doesn't mean they aren't useful home remedies.

Medicinal: Of the two, summer savory is most frequently specified for healing purposes. According to pharmacognosist Varro Tyler, Ph.D., it is fairly effective in treating several ailments. Its active constituents include carvacrol (carracol), p-cymene, and tannin, which give it mild antiseptic and astringent properties. A tea made from summer savory can be used for occasional diarrhea, minor stomach upsets, and mild sore throats. In Europe, it is sometimes

Summer Savory

Winter Savory

453

SAVORY—continued

taken by diabetics to alleviate excessive thirst. It is pleasant tasting and relatively harmless in moderate amounts.

Steep 2 to 4 tablespoons of the dried herb in 1 cup of hot water to make a medicinal infusion. Limit yourself to 1 cup per day.

Culinary: Both savories are used in cooking. The summer variety tastes like peppery thyme and blends well with most flavors, helping to bring them together. It's popular in teas, herb butters, flavored vinegars, and with shell beans, lentils, chicken soup, creamy soups, beef soup, eggs, snap beans, peas, rutabagas, eggplant, asparagus, parsnips, salsify, onions, cabbage, brussels sprouts, squash, garlic, liver, fish, and quince chutney. German cooking is famous for savory and beans, and there are many claims that savory is an antiflatulent.

Winter savory is stronger and tastes more piny. It is used with strong game meats and pâtés.

Available commercially: Dried leaves.

CULTIVATION

Both kinds of savory are easy to grow from seed or cuttings. Use fresh seed, as its viability decreases rapidly after one year.

Summer savory germinates quickly. Sow seeds no more than ⅛ inch deep in flats and transplant later, or plant directly into the garden. Space plants about 10 inches apart and keep them well weeded. If plants start to flop, mound soil slightly around the bases. Keep them well watered for best growth. Summer savory also makes a good subject for an indoor container garden.

Winter savory is somewhat slower to sprout; start it in a flat or purchase plants. Set plants in the garden 10 to 12 inches apart after the soil has warmed up. You can also grow it in a container, bringing it inside for the winter if you live in a cold climate. It grows in any well-drained soil of average to poor fertility and requires less water than its annual counterpart. In fact, too much moisture in the soil can cause winterkill. Winter savory is hardy as far north as New York City and can be harvested fresh all winter. However, it is a short-lived perennial and will probably need to be replaced with new plants (from seeds, cuttings, or divisions) every two or three years.

Harvesting and storage: You can begin harvesting summer savory as soon as the plants get about 6 inches tall. If you keep snipping the tops of the branches, you'll be able to extend the harvest. When the plants insist on flowering, cut the whole plants and lay them on screening or paper in a warm, shady place. When dry (in two days or so), strip the leaves from the stems and store in airtight jars. Collect the seeds as soon as they start to brown, place in an airtight jar with a desiccant added, and store in a cool, dry place.

CHEF TIPS

- Mince fresh summer savory leaves and combine with garlic, bay, and lemon juice as a marinade for fish.

- Cut baked potatoes into quarters lengthwise and scoop out the pulp. (Save pulp for another use.) Sprinkle the quarters with grated cheddar and minced fresh savory and bake at 475°F for about seven minutes, or until the cheese has melted.

- Cut mozzarella cheese into small squares and dip each into beaten egg. Dredge the dipped squares in a mixture of bread crumbs and minced fresh savory and bake at 450°F, until the cheese has just begun to melt and the crumbs have begun to crisp. Serve with tomato sauce that has been flavored with savory.

- Add minced fresh savory to mayonnaise and serve it as an accompaniment to poached fish.

GROWING CONDITIONS

Satureja hortensis:
- Soil pH 6.8.
- Average soil.
- Full sun.

S. montana:
- Plant hardiness zone 6.
- Soil pH 6.7.
- Light, dry, well-drained soil.
- Full sun.

SCENTED GERANIUM

Pelargonium spp.   **Geraniaceae**

Rose, apple, lemon, lime, apricot, strawberry, coconut, peppermint—they sound like the flavors of candy sticks you might find in apothecary jars on the sweetshop counter. But these are just a few fragrances in the amazing repertoire of scented geraniums. The unusual foliage, pretty blossoms, easy cultivation, and delightful aromatic properties of these herbs have endeared them to gardeners the world over. The genus name is Greek for "stork," and it describes the peculiarly shaped fruit.

HISTORY

Scented geraniums were probably enjoyed for centuries in South Africa before they were introduced to Europe by sailors who stopped off while rounding the Cape of Good Hope in the early 1600s. They quickly gained popularity throughout Europe as house plants, astringents for wounds, fragrant sachets, and aromatic teas.

Pelargoniums arrived in America during colonial days and caught on early in our country's history. Thomas Jefferson, in fact, brought several varieties to the White House with him.

Scented geraniums gained their greatest favor—and their most colorful history—in the mid-1800s. The French had discovered a way to substitute the oil derived from rose-scented geraniums for attar of roses in perfume making, introducing a very profitable commercial use for scented geraniums. Their popularity boomed.

Victorian gardeners and herbalists used them in bouquets and potpourris, ointments and poultices, teas, cakes, cookies, jams, and jellies—even wine! It's probably for this reason that they're often still associated with rosewood chairs, cabbage rose carpets, quaint little parlors, and other antique sentiments of that bygone era.

In recent decades, scented geraniums have fallen from favor. But there is now a renewed, nostalgic interest on the part of herb gardeners, and the plants are again prized by collectors. New scents continue to proliferate.

USES

These plants serve the imaginative herb grower in a variety of ways—from wound healers to cake sweeteners to spirit soothers.

Medicinal: Not much has been made of the medicinal properties of these plants. Folklore has it that scented geraniums work as excellent astringents, and some herbals profess that they are valuable in the treatment of dysentery and ulcers of the stomach and upper intestines. One headache remedy still in circulation is to bathe the

DESCRIPTION

Scented geraniums are not really geraniums at all, but pelargoniums. They do belong to the same botanical family as true geraniums, however, and their leaves look very similar. (See photos on pages 444 and 446.)

Flowers: A variety of shapes, sizes, and colors; most commonly in umbellate clusters; five sepals and petals; two upper petals often larger and colored differently from others; distinguished from true geraniums by calyx with a spur that extends backward from blossom and reattaches itself to flower stalk.

Leaves: Frilly, fernlike, and velvety soft, or crisp and round and almost sticky to the touch; typically grow opposite one another; well veined; distinctive fragrance discernible after brushing or rubbing leaves.

Fruit: Small, strangely elongated.

Height: To 3 ft.

FLOWERING

Varies depending on the variety.

RANGE

Native to South Africa; naturalized in the Eastern Mediterranean region, India, Australia, and New Zealand. Widely cultivated.

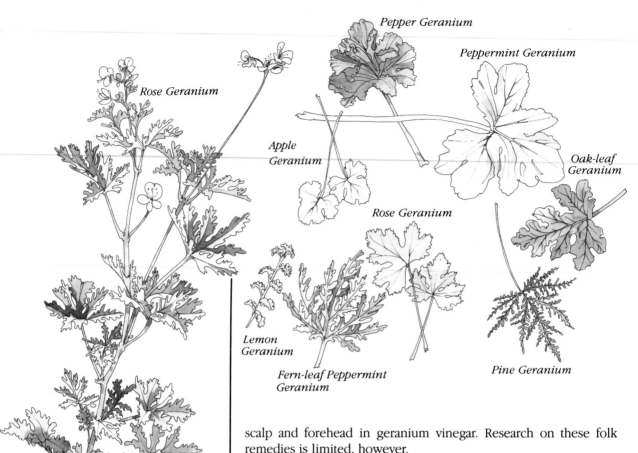

Pepper Geranium

Peppermint Geranium

Rose Geranium

Apple Geranium

Oak-leaf Geranium

Rose Geranium

Lemon Geranium

Fern-leaf Peppermint Geranium

Pine Geranium

scalp and forehead in geranium vinegar. Research on these folk remedies is limited, however.

Toxicity: Several studies have shown that scented geranium oil (the pure essential oil) can cause contact dermatitis, a rashlike condition of the skin, and it should probably be avoided by those with sensitive skin. This is true of most essential oils, of course.

Culinary: You can use the leaves of rose geraniums to flavor tea biscuits, jelly, and even sugar, as Cyrus Hyde of Well-Sweep Herb Farm in New Jersey explains. "Build up alternating layers of sugar and petals in a Mason jar, and place the jar where it will catch the sun for about two weeks. By that time, the leaves will have contributed their essence to the sugar and can be sifted out."

Peppermint and rose geraniums can be added to teas. A couple of rose geranium leaves will add a distinguished scent to that bland standard, apple jelly.

Aromatic: Today, as yesterday, the dried leaves and flowers of the various species of scented geraniums (rose, lemon, and apple in particular) make lovely sachets and potpourris. Try placing the leaves of lemon geranium in finger bowls. Certain scents also are used in the commercial perfume industry, particularly as men's colognes. Commercial geranium oils vary in their scent, depending on the country of origin. The best rose-scented oil is said to come from France. A pound of foliage yields roughly 1 grain of oil.

456

SCENTED GERANIUM SPECIES AND VARIETIES

Name	Scent	Leaf/ Flower	Comments
Pelargonium crispum Lemon geranium	Lemon	Small, crinkled leaf; lavender bloom	To 3 ft.; tall, narrow growth; traditionally used in finger bowls
P. denticulatum Pine-scented geranium	Pungent pine	Deeply cut, feathery leaf; pink flower	Compact plant
P. ×fragrans Nutmeg geranium	Nutmeg	Small gray leaf; white flower	Perfect basket plant
P. grossularioides Coconut geranium	Strong	Dark, rounded leaf on long petiole; tiny magenta flower	Everblooming
P. ×mellissinum Lemon balm geranium	Lemon	Large, lobed, leaf; lavender bloom	Fast, upright growth; used in jellies and cakes
P. ×nervosum Lime geranium	Lime	Toothed leaf; deep lavender bloom	Intense lime flavor; used in cakes and jellies
P. odoratissimum Apple geranium	Apple; very intense	Small, velvety leaf, white flower	To 1½ ft.; flowers grow on vinelike branches
P. tomentosum Peppermint geranium	Strong mint	Large, velvety leaf; white flower	To 3 ft.; prostrate grower; great basket plant
P. cv.'Attar of Rose' Attar of rose geranium	Rose	Fern-cut leaf; pink flower	To 3 ft.; used for jellies and pound cakes
P. cv. 'Rober's Lemon Rose' Rober's lemon rose geranium	Lemon-rose	Irregular, lobed leaf	To 3 ft.; used in jellies and cakes

The scents available include apple, apple cider, chocolate-mint (an olfactory imagination helps with that one), cinnamon, citronella, coconut, ginger, lime, musk, nutmeg, orange, rose-mint, pineapple, pink champagne (again, you have to let your nose enjoy the flight of fancy), and strawberry. Not all of the scents these little plants generate can be so neatly described. Others smell woodsy or spicy. Some aren't even pleasing to the average nose. One has been found to turn away the mosquito—*Pelargonium citrosum* 'Vanieenii'. Use it indoors or out. Some varieties contain oil of citronella.

Ornamental: If for no other reason than their fragrances, scented geraniums make lovely house and garden plants. But besides filling the air with lovely scents when brushed, these plants often offer striking foliage and blossoms, making them pleasing to look at as well. Where weather permits—they are very tender

457

SCENTED GERANIUM—continued

- Plant hardiness zone 10.
- Soil pH 6–7.
- Dry, well-drained, rich, loamy soil.
- Full sun.

perennials—they are lovely outdoor specimens and can be trained on trellises as well as potted in outdoor gardens and greenhouses. Of course, any scented plant is best placed where the foliage can be touched and the scent enjoyed.

For attractive, formal-looking potted plants, scented geraniums can be trained into standards.

Cosmetic: Scented geraniums are reported to be mildly astringent and stimulating. These qualities in addition to their pleasing fragrances make scented geraniums good choices for herbal facials and baths.

Companion planting: White-flowered varieties are said to work in the garden as a trap crop for Japanese beetles.

CULTIVATION

Scented geraniums are tender perennials. They are best started from cuttings. Take cuttings in spring or summer, using a sharp knife just below the node where a leaf grows from the stem. Place cuttings in clean sand, and allow enough space around them so that air can circulate freely. Water them, keep them shaded at first, and you should have little plants that can be transplanted in 2 or 3 weeks. Sow seeds indoors in the early spring, 10 to 12 weeks before planting outside. Expose plants to the elements only after all threat of frost is past. Keep the plants dry enough to prevent rot—never let potted geraniums sit long in water, but neither should you allow them to dry to the point that the leaves turn yellow. You can add regular doses of diluted fertilizer, but too rich a diet may diminish a plant's fragrance, especially if you overdo the nitrogen.

Container gardening: Indoors, scented geraniums need good air circulation and prefer daytime temperatures of 65° to 70°F with an evening drop of 10 degrees.

Take care when choosing containers. Scented geraniums shouldn't be confined to terribly tiny pots, but overpotting can result in improper growth and increase susceptibility to disease. The middle course is best. Keep the blooms pinched back to discourage overly rapid growth.

Pests and diseases: Scented geraniums are susceptible to bacterial wilt, botrytis, and blight and to infestation from whiteflies. But under optimal conditions, they are reasonably resistant to pests. (See the entry Growing Herbs for information on controlling pests and diseases.)

Harvesting and storage: For maximum oil content, pick leaves just as flowers begin to appear, and preferably do so early on a sunny, dry day. Dry leaves in the shade to preserve their fragrance.

SCENTS FROM HERBS

Fragrances can dazzle us with their immediate presence. Bring a bouquet of roses into the room, or brush by a bush of lemon verbena. Their scents instantly brighten your spirits and refresh the air. Fragrances can have a more subtle effect, too—the gentle but strong scent of bayberry candles warming the Christmas spirit; the allure of the dab of perfume behind the ear. They can evoke memories; they can re-create experiences long forgotten.

We delight in the aromas of herbs—pungent, sweet, spicy. Your nose's attention will be caught by a jar of potpourri or a sachet hidden in a dresser drawer. Potpourris, pomanders, sachets, aromatic waters—they are all easy to create and such a pleasure to enjoy.

POTPOURRIS

A potpourri is a mixture of coarsely broken bits of dried, aromatic herbs. The mixture usually is kept in a closed decorative container. When opened, the herbal mixture perfumes the air.

Potpourris are delightful to have around the home, and they are so simple to make. When concocting an original potpourri, first imagine the main scent that you want. This will come from the bulk of the herbs that you use. Then consider additives—seeds, spices, woods, roots, essential oils—that will blend with the main scent to enhance the fragrance.

Harvesting and drying herbs: Cut and collect your herbs on a sunny day, working in the early morning, just after the dew has dried. To capture them when their essential oils are at their peak, flowers should be gathered just after they have opened.

Gently pull off the petals, discarding any that are brown and wilted. You can place the petals on newspaper to dry, but spreading them on a screen exposes them more completely to the air and speeds drying (a shorter drying time helps to retain the volatile oils). Dry the flowers in a warm, dark, airy place, stirring the petals often.

The leaves can be stripped from the stem and dried in the same way, or you can hang bunches of herbs to dry.

When drying citrus peel, first scrape all the fruit pulp from the inner skin, then break the peel into small pieces, and allow it to dry until brittle in a warm place.

Check your herbs every day. The drying time varies depending on climate and weather conditions. Make sure your ingredients are perfectly dry or else mold will develop and ruin your potpourri.

You can gather herbs throughout the growing season, dry and store them in airtight containers, and keep them in a dark place until you are ready to make a potpourri.

MOIST POTPOURRIS

Many traditional potpourri recipes yield what are known as moist potpourris. They are pretty to look at, as are most dried potpourris, but they smell wonderful as well.

Rose petals are primary ingredients, but any fragrant flower petals will work. Many people partially dry the petals, though this is not essential. Add any oils or spices to the petals and layer them in a wide-mouthed jar with uniodized salt. Set the potpourri aside for several weeks, but do stir the mixture every day.

The traditional method of making a moist potpourri requires that you compress the potpourri under a weighted plate. Once fermentation of the mixture begins, let it sit for one to two weeks without stirring, until a cake is formed. Break the cake into small bits, and combine with spices, oils, and fixatives. Let it blend for a few more weeks, and then put it in a decorative container.

Since a moist potpourri isn't very attractive, put it in a porcelain or ceramic container, so it can be smelled but not seen.

Selecting herbs: Herbs used in a potpourri are chosen for both scent and color since the mixture should be attractive as well as fragrant.

For fragrance: acacia, allspice, angelica root, anise, basil, bay, beebalm, cardamom seeds, cinnamon, cloves, coriander seeds, costmary, frankincense, ginger, jasmine, lavender, lemon balm, lemon peel, lemongrass, lemon verbena, lilac, lily of the valley, marjoram, mint, myrrh, nutmeg, orange flowers or peel, patchouli, roses (choose from cabbage roses, *R. centifolia;* damasks, *R. damascena;* gallicas, *R. gallica;* moss roses, *R. centifolia* 'Muscosa'; and musk roses, *R. moschata*), rosemary, sage, sandalwood, santal (a soft, white wood), scented geraniums, sweet flag root, sweet woodruff, thyme, vetiver root, and violets.

For color: Any colorful garden flower that dries well can be added to the potpourri for its color. Add the petals or flowers of baby's breath, calendula, chamomile, delphinium, elecampane, goldenrod, hydrangea, larkspur, marigold, nasturtium, pansy, safflower, statice, tansy, yarrow, or zinnia.

Fixatives: A fixative is a plant or animal material that prevents the evaporation of essential oils and holds the fragrance in the potpourri.

The three common animal-derived fixatives are ambergris, civet, and musk. Although unpleasant smelling by themselves, these substances amplify, enrich, and set the beautiful fragrances of botanicals. All are fairly expensive, so you might want to use plant-derived fixatives, which work quite well and can be purchased from the pharmacist or made at home.

Orris root is the most commonly used of the plant-derived fixatives, and it complements lavender especially well. It is ground from the root of the Florentine iris, *Iris ✕ germanica* var. *florentina*. Though a very fine fixative, orris does cause allergic reactions in many people. If you, or the recipient of your potpourri is allergic, you may want to choose from among the other plant-derived fixatives: benzoin, rose attar, ground and dried rosemary, sandalwood, storax, sweet flag, tonka beans (vanilla scent), and vetiver root (nice with roses).

Add about 1 tablespoon of fixative per quart of herbs.

Oils: To enhance the scent of your potpourri or to add an accent, you can stir in just a touch of an essential oil. If you can't decide which oil to use, divide the mixture of herbs into portions and add a different oil to each to see which you like most. Be sure to label the potpourris before storing them.

Mixing: With the exception of the knife or scissors you clip your herbs with, it is best not to expose herbs to metal when drying or preparing. The metal can alter the fragrance somewhat. Instead, use wood, enamel, or ceramic utensils, and ceramic or glass bowls.

Crush or grind any seeds before adding. Stir together all dried ingredients, or if you really want to get into creating your potpourri, toss the leaves and petals with your hands. Your hands will be pleasantly scented afterward. If you want to add essential oils, stir in just a couple of drops—too much will overpower the fragrances of the herbs themselves and can make the potpourri overpowering. Remember, you simply want to enhance the scent.

When you've mixed the herbs thoroughly, pour them into a large wide-mouthed jar or ceramic pot, and cover tightly with a lid. Place the container in a cool, dark place for six weeks to allow all the fragrances to blend. About once a week, shake the contents or stir with a wooden spoon. At the end of the six weeks, you'll have a delightful potpourri to use in your home or to give as a gift.

Containers: Baskets, glass jars, glass bowls, porcelain or ceramic containers all work well. A glass container shows off the colors of your potpourri. If you have a lid, you can cover the potpourri on occasions when you will not be using or needing its fragrance. This helps preserve the fragrance.

SACHETS

Sachets differ only slightly from potpourris. The ingredients are the same. It's just that they are ground and crumbled rather than used whole, and they are stuffed inside decorative fabric bags or pillows. That's it! You can even take an existing potpourri, crumble the leaves and flowers, bundle it up in a handkerchief or piece of fabric, and tie a ribbon around it. Voila! It is ready to be tossed into the clothes drawer or the linen closet.

If you want to make sachets from scratch, follow the same procedures as you would for making potpourris. Be sure the herbs are completely dry, so they will not mildew. Crumble dried leaves and flowers almost to a powder and grind the roots and bark with a mortar and pestle. A little fixative helps to hold the scent.

You can choose from any number of fabrics, but you would be wise to choose one that has a tight weave. Silk is ideal.

Be creative with your sachet bags—embroider them, stitch on sequins or beads, or sew lace or fringe around the edges. Although most sachets are square, they don't have to be; heart-shaped sachets are nice for Valentine Day. The size is optional, too. Traditionally, sachets are rather small, about 2 inches on each side, but you can make them any size you like.

Toss small ones in clothes drawers. Place longer, flatter ones between linens. Stuff some sachets among the pillows of your sofa.

WOODSY/EARTHY SCENTS

bayberry
chamomile (applelike)
clary (spicy, haylike)
lady's bedstraw (grassy)
lavender cotton (musky, applelike)
marjoram (piny)
oakmoss
pine needles
rosemary
sandalwood
southernwood
sweet woodruff
thyme (piny, medicinal, refreshing)
vetiver
wormwood

SPICY SCENTS

allspice
angelica root (licorice)
anise
basil (clove-licorice scent)
bay
caraway
cardamom
cinnamon
cloves
coriander (fruity, sweet)
ginger
hyssop (like basil, geranium, thyme)
mint (refreshing)
nutmeg
pennyroyal (minty)
vanilla

SCENTS FROM HERBS—continued

EXOTIC/ORIENTAL SCENTS

frankincense (sharp, balsamic)
myrrh (woody, balsamic)
patchouli (musty, woody,
   sweet, balsamic)
sandalwood (woody,
   balsamic)
ylang-ylang (sweet, balsamic)

CITRUSY SCENTS

beebalm
lemon balm
lemongrass
lemon thyme
lemon verbena
orange peel

FLORAL SCENTS

acacia
carnation (spicy)
gardenia (very sweet, heavy)
geranium (rosy, blends well
   with roses, oriental notes)
hyacinth (delicate, smooth,
   sweet)
jasmine
lavender (heavy, strong)
lilac
lily of the valley (very sweet)
orange blossom
rose (range from violet to
   musklike scent)
scented geranium (scent will
   vary according to species)
sweet pea (light, sweet)
violet

Make larger, bulkier sachet bags to hang in clothes closets. You can even sprinkle some ground sachet powder in an envelope to scent a personal letter, or place a small sachet in a box of writing paper to add fragrance.

RECIPES

The fun of making potpourris and sachets is not just in working with colorful and fragrant herbs, but in blending and balancing scents to create your own favorite fragrance. You might want to start with one of the following recipes, but eventually, you'll want to experiment with different herbs. The possibilities are endless. Just remember to record your recipes and label your mixtures, so that if you create a fragrance that you especially enjoy or one that you particularly dislike, you will know how you made it.

In making a potpourri, mix all dried ingredients first, and then add any essential oils.

Spicy basils: Basil has a wonderful fragrance, and so do many of its spicy varieties. If you can spare some of this herb from your pesto or tomato sauce, add it to a potpourri. The following recipe is from Marilyn Hampstead's *The Basil Book:*

> 1 quart of licorice basil
> 1 quart of sweet basil
> 1 quart of French fine-leaf basil
> 2 cups of apple geranium leaves
> 2 cups of old spice or nutmeg geranium leaves
> 1 cup of thyme
> 2 cups of patchouli
> 1 cup of lemon eucalyptus or lemon verbena
> 1 cup of Clevelandii sage
> 3 ounces of vetiver root

Summer harvest: Created by Rosella Mathieu of Herb Garden Fragrances, this recipe is quite simple to prepare and can be varied in many ways.

> 1 cup of rose petals
> 1 cup of lavender
> 1 cup of lemon verbena
> 1 cup of mixed mints

Scentamental journey: Little girls often love to spend time at mother's dressing table looking at the makeup and smelling the perfumes. Barbara Remington, who created this recipe, finds its deep, heavy scent to be reminiscent of perfumes that once were on her mother's dressing table. Its name is a pun on one of her mother's favorite 1940s songs.

    2 quarts of rose petals
    1 cup of broken blue statice, blue bachelor's
       buttons, or delphiniums
    1½ of cups of patchouli
    3 tablespoons of orris root
    5 drops of oil of gardenia

Manly scent: A good recipe for a man's sachet.

    2 cups of lemon balm
    1 cup of thyme
    1 cup of nutmeg
    2 tablespoons of orris root

Herb garden: Culinary herbs do have uses outside the kitchen. Their fragrances blend wonderfully in potpourris.

    2 cups of thyme
    1 cup of rosemary
    ½ cup of lavender
    1 cup of mint
    ¼ cup of tansy
    ¼ cup of clove
    2 tablespoons of orris root

POMANDERS

Historically, pomanders were made from small balls of ambergris to which herbs and perfumes were added. The French originally called them *pomme d'ambre*—*pomme* meaning "apple" for its shape, and *d'ambre,* which means "ambergris." Men and women wore these *pomme d'ambres* to mask the stench of their unsanitary surroundings and also to protect them from disease and infection. Cases containing the *pomme d'ambres* hung on chains around their necks or from their belts. Members of royalty had exquisite cases made from gold, silver, ivory, and other materials. The name *pomme d'ambre* eventually came to mean the case as well as the ball of herbs.

Nowadays, pomanders are made from oranges and cloves. Actually, you can use any citrus fruit: oranges, lemons, or limes, although you probably don't want to be pushing hundreds of whole cloves into a grapefruit. For a medium-size orange, 2 ounces of cloves should suffice. Scatter the cloves all over the fruit, filling in the spaces

463

as you go along. When you are done, the fruit should be completely covered and the cloves touching each other. You might want to wear a thimble to protect your clove-pushing finger. Some pomander makers recommend the use of a darning needle, meat skewer, or ice pick to puncture the fruit's skin before inserting the cloves. Try what works for you.

To give your pomander a little more fragrance, you can dust it with powdered spices. Cinnamon, nutmeg, and ginger are nice individually, or use a combination. Either sift the spices over the pomander, or place them in a bowl and roll the pomander in them.

Dust the pomander with a powdered fixative to preserve the fragrance. Orris root is most commonly used.

When the cloves have all been pushed in and you've dusted it with spices and fixative, set your pomander in a dark, airy spot to age and dry. Leave it for about four weeks. Then you can decorate it with ribbon. To make a pomander to hang, run a string through it with a large needle. Place individual pomanders in dresser drawers, or display several in a decorative bowl. They make lovely gifts at Christmas. Anyway you use them, you will enjoy their spicy scent.

ROSE BEADS

If you love the scent of roses, one of the more interesting ways of capturing and enjoying the fragrance of roses is to make a beaded necklace from the petals.

Making these beads is simple and fun. You will need a lot of rose petals though—about a half a bushel—and considerable patience. It will take several weeks to prepare a paste from the rose petals, then several more to dry the beads formed of the paste.

To start, collect the petals early in the morning on a dry day. Use the fresh petals, discarding any that are brown or wilted. You can macerate them with a mortar and pestle as has been done traditionally, but pureeing them in a blender is easier. Rose beads have a very dull, ebony appearance. To acquire the color, simmer the paste gently for about an hour in an iron pot or skillet in just enough water to cover. Let the petals cool and simmer them again. The iron reacts with the roses to turn them black. Grind the petals each day for about two weeks, until a paste forms that is thick enough to roll into beads (it should be about the consistency of clay).

When your rose paste is ready, roll beads from it. Dipping your fingers into rose oil first or spreading some on the palms of your hands adds more fragrance as you roll the beads. Remember, when drying, the beads will shrink to about one-half their original size. Take a large needle and pierce a hole through the center of each bead. If you have several pins, you can leave the beads on the pins and stick them into cardboard to dry. Rosella Mathieu recommends stringing the beads onto No. 22 florist's wire and hanging them to dry. In either case, turn the beads every day, so they do not adhere to the pins or wire and then break when you remove them later. The beads should be dry in one to two weeks. Polish them with a soft cloth, string them, and wear them around your neck. Rose beads should last for years and years, and every time you wear them, the warmth of your body will help to release that lovely soothing fragrance of rose.

As with all organic products, rose beads might attract insects, so when you're not wearing them, be sure to store them in a closed jewelry box.

ESSENTIAL OILS

A lot of mystery is associated with distilling oils and blending perfumes. It seems such an exotic practice, but it is really quite simple.

What is difficult about extracting oils from herbs has nothing to do with the process—it is gathering all those herbs from your beautiful garden. Don't be intimidated by the huge quantities of flowers used commercially in making perfumes (12,000 pounds of jasmine flowers for 2 pounds of oil). Large amounts of flowers are needed to produce even an ounce of pure oil, but you can easily create fragrant waters and oils from herbs grown in the backyard.

Extracting oils with oil: One of the easiest ways to extract the fragrances of herbs is to soak them in oil. As strange as it may sound, oil attracts oil, bringing it out of the leaves and flowers.

Use a nonmetal container; a ceramic crock works well. Pour in pure olive oil or safflower oil to cover the fresh flowers or leaves. Set it aside for at least 24 hours. Strain the mixture, gently pressing the blossoms or leaves to release more fragrant oil. Add more blossoms to the already fragrant oil and repeat the process. Continue to repeat this procedure six or more times, and when you're done, you'll have a wonderfully fragrant oil that you can add to baths, lotions, potpourris, aromatic waters, soaps, candles, or whatever. Store the oil in a tightly sealed bottle.

Extracting oils with alcohol: Another simple method of obtaining herbal fragrances is by soaking the plant material in alcohol. You must use undenatured ethyl alcohol. If you have trouble finding it, you may use vodka. Just don't use rubbing alcohol. The procedure is identical to the one described above for extracting oils with oil. The fragrant alcohol that you create can be used as it is, or you can dilute

HERB PILLOWS

Herb pillows are very similar to sachets, only larger and flatter, and the herbs chosen to fill them should help you to sleep.

Hops is a good choice. Scientists have found that a substance in hops called lupulin acts as a natural sedative. As well as lupulin works to put you to sleep, unfortunately the scent of dried hops and their rustling inside the pillow work to keep you awake. To mask the fragrance, add some lemon verbena leaves or a lightly scented potpourri to the hops before stuffing the pillow. To muffle the noise, make the pillow from quilted fabric. Then you will be all ready to fall into a pleasant, fragrant slumber.

Stuff your pillow with any mixture of herbs that you find pleasing. Lavender has a reputation for soothing headaches, but its strong scent may not soothe you to sleep.

Your pillow can be any size. Don't stuff the pillow too full. It should be fairly flat. When you've finished sewing all the edges, lay it on top of your regular bed pillow, and let yourself fall asleep amid the fine fragrances of herbs.

SCENTS FROM HERBS—continued

SOURCES
OF ESSENTIAL OILS

Akwenasa Essentials
R.D. 2, Box 160A
Ghent, NY 12075
(518) 672-4519

Aroma Vera Co.
P.O. Box 3609
Culver City, CA 90231
(213) 675-8219

Aura Cacia
1 Executive Avenue, Suite 5
Rohnert Park, CA 94928
(707) 584-5115

Caswell-Massey Co. Ltd.
111 Eighth Avenue (catalog)
518 Lexington Avenue (shop)
21 Fulton Street (shop)
New York, NY 10011

Colin Ingram
207 Bohemian Highway
Freestone, CA 95472
(707) 823-1330

InterNatural
P.O. Box 580
Shaker Street
S. Sutton, NH 03273
(603) 927-4237

Original Swiss Aromatics
P.O. Box 606
San Rafael, CA 94915
(415) 459-3998

Weleda Inc.
841 S. Main St.
Spring Valley, NY 10977
(914) 352-6145

it with some water. It also makes a fine base for a perfume. Most perfumes contain a high percentage of alcohol because as it evaporates quickly from the skin, it sends out from you a blast of fragrance.

If you want to remove the oil from the alcohol, place it in the freezer. The alcohol does not freeze, but the oil solidifies and can be skimmed from the liquid.

This solvent method of extracting oils is particularly good for very delicate flowers like jasmine. It does not burn the petals as steam distillation does.

Pure essential oils: These are the most useful of the herbal oils. You can blend them in toilet waters or perfumes, scent soaps and lotions with them, or use them in other fragrant items. These oils are extracted by steam distillation. With the proper equipment, an incredible volume of herbs, and some persistence, you *can* distill your own pure essential oils. But it is much easier to buy them; a number of reputable companies (see the accompanying list of sources) sell them.

PERFUMES AND TOILET WATERS

To make simple perfumes and toilet waters, all you need are essential oils, alcohol (pure undenatured ethyl alcohol) or vodka, a fixative (such as storax oil, sandalwood oil, or orris root), and maybe some aromatic waters. As with potpourris, you should keep in mind the basic principles of blending. Create the perfume around a main scent, and then add secondary scents or contrasting fragrances that will work with the main fragrance to build on it or enhance it. This may seem a little abstract, but its meaning will become clear as you start experimenting.

The following perfumes and toilet waters are made by combining the ingredients in a glass bottle, shaking well, then setting them aside for several weeks to allow their fragrances to blend and fix.

Scent of roses: Let this perfume blend for at least four weeks before using.

> 1 cup of undenatured ethyl alcohol
> ¼ cup of rose water
> 1 tablespoon of rosemary oil
> 2 tablespoons of rose oil
> 1 tablespoon of storax oil

Herb scent: Occasional agitation during the setting period will improve the fragrance of this perfume.

> 1 cup of undenatured ethyl alcohol
> 1 teaspoon of basil oil

1 teaspoon of sage oil
1 teaspoon of dill oil
1 tablespoon of sandalwood oil

Lavender cologne: Combine and enjoy after several weeks.

1 pint of undenatured ethyl alcohol
½ cup of lavender water
2 tablespoons of lavender oil
1 tablespoon of storax oil

Lemon perfume: The lemon fragrance gets stronger with age.

1 cup of undenatured alcohol
2 tablespoons of lemon oil
1 tablespoon of citronella oil
1 tablespoon of lemon verbena oil
1 tablespoon of sandalwood oil

Spicy essence: Set aside for two months. Filter and store in a sterile glass perfume bottle.

1 cup of undenatured ethyl alcohol
1 tablespoon of clove oil
2 tablespoons of cinnamon oil
¼ cup of orris root

AND MORE USES FOR OILS

Those oils you've collected for perfumes can be used in many other ways, too.

Scents for candles: Scent your wax with additions of bayberry oil, clove oil, mint oil, rose oil, sage oil, lavender oil, lemon oil, or other aromatic herb oils. Various combinations of fragrant oils are often pleasing. Use about ½ ounce of oil for each pound of wax. Or you may add powdered herbs to the melted wax. Grind them with a mortar and pestle.

Scents for soaps: Just before pouring your soap into molds, add any of the following oils for a sweet-smelling aroma: lavender, citronella, rose, rose geranium, rosemary, cloves, cinnamon, sassafras, lemongrass, or lemon.

Perfumed ink: Calligraphy has become increasingly popular. More and more people learn this skill all the time. Envelopes, cards, and poems are being lettered in homes everywhere. To add a little surprise and interest to your pieces, use a fragrant ink. Simply make a strong infusion from dried herbs and add 2 or 3 teaspoons to a bottle of ink. The piny scent of rosemary would be nice for Christmas cards; use the sweet smell of rose at Valentine Day.

INCENSE

The thought of incense conjures up images of priests in dark and stony cathedrals, swinging smoking pots hung from chains or of persons speaking incantations over smoldering mixtures. We associate incense with the exotic, but historically its use was quite common and not just for religious or pagan rituals. People burned incense to scent their homes, to keep away disease, to perfume their clothing. Early doctors recommended that patients inhale incense for medicinal purposes. The word perfume means "through smoke," indicating that this is probably the first way men and women used fragrances.

Incense can be quite easy to make. The simplest recipes require that you mix together powdered herbs, then set them aside to age for several months. When you are ready to burn them, sprinkle them over hot charcoal.

SERPENTWOOD

Rauvolfia serpentina   **Apocynaceae**

DESCRIPTION

Serpentwoods are tropical shrubs or small trees. They contain a milky sap. The three primary species—*Rauvolfia serpentina* (serpentwood), *R. tetraphylla* (American serpentwood), and *R. vomitoria* (African serpentwood)—are more distinct geographically than in appearance.

Flowers: Numerous; in clusters; tubular; pink with five white lobes.

Leaves: Deciduous; in whorls of three to five; oval, pointed; 3–8 in. long.

Fruit: Fleshy, ovoid drupe; ¼ in. long; contains one or two seeds.

Height: 4½ ft; *R. vomitoria* to 15 ft.

RANGE

R. serpentina: moist forests in India, Indonesia, Burma, Thailand, and Ceylon; *R. tetraphylla:* southern Mexico to Colombia, including the West Indies; *R. vomitoria:* Senegal to Mozambique.

GROWING CONDITIONS

• Rich soil.

• Full sun to partial shade.

Serpentwood is one of the truly medicinal herbs. Its root is the source of the drug reserpine, which is widely prescribed for high blood pressure and as a tranquilizer.

Serpentwood has a 4,000-year history of use in India as a treatment for snake and insect bites, diarrhea, fever, and worms. It was used to stimulate uterine contractions in childbirth. But the most prominent use was "as a soother of the mind and an antidote to lunacy," according to William A. R. Thomson, M.D., author of *Herbs That Heal.* "It had become incorporated into the folklore of India to such an extent," wrote Thomson, "that it was regularly chewed by the holy men of the country seeking tranquillity for their meditations, and Gandhi is said to have been a regular drinker of a tea made from it."

The wide use in India, however, did not draw the attention of Western medical people, even when its active principles were isolated by Indian chemists, or when it was prescribed to lower blood pressure by Indian physicians. But in 1949, an Indian cardiologist, R. J. Vakil, M.D., wrote an article about serpentwood in the *British Heart Journal.* Within a few years, scouts for the pharmaceutical industry were scouring the tropics for *Rauvolfia serpentina* and its relatives. It has since been determined that a Central American species, *R. tetraphylla,* and an African species, *R. vomitoria,* are also pharmacologically potent.

USES

It's not ornamental, aromatic, or epicurean. The focus of serpentwood's utility has always been pharmaceutical.

Medicinal: Serpentwood is the source of 30 medically significant alkaloids, especially reserpine. Reserpine is primarily used in treating high blood pressure, but also for insomnia, hyperglycemia, hypochondria, mental disorders, and certain forms of insanity. "Its great value lies in its not requiring to be administered in critical dosages, rare side effects (recently stated to be carcinogenic and teratogenic), non-habit-forming, without withdrawal symptoms or contraindication," wrote botanist James Duke, Ph.D., in the *CRC Handbook of Medicinal Herbs.*

CULTIVATION

Serpentwood is an herb few North American gardeners will grow, simply because tropical conditions are required. Efforts to establish commercial plantings in Mexico and Puerto Rico in the 1950s were abandoned. Greenhouse culture is possible.

SOAPWORT

Saponaria officinalis   Caryophyllaceae

Boil the roots and leaves of soapwort and, true to its name, you'll get a sudsy solution that can be used to wash old and delicate fabrics. Herbalists have found internal uses for it as well, but it is toxic to both humans and animals and should not be ingested. Other common names include bouncing bet, bruisewort, latherwort, sheepweed, and wild sweet william.

In the Middle Ages, soapwort was called *Herba fullonis,* referring to its use to "full" or clean and thicken woolen cloth. It has also been found to clean kid gloves without damaging them. As a medicinal herb, soapwort was known to medieval Arabs and to the early Chinese and Indians.

USES

Saponification is the process of making soap, and the main use of this *Saponaria* is as a soap. The viscous saponin in the plant is responsible for forming the lather.

Medicinal: Soapwort has been credited as a diuretic, laxative, expectorant, and skin treatment. A few herbalists have recommended drinking soapwort tea to treat coughs. However, saponin is such a strong purgative that the plant shouldn't be taken internally. On top of that, it tastes like soap.

Applied externally, it is safe. The juice extracted from the leaves or roots is said to stop the itching and irritation of acne and eczema.

Ornamental: This species of *Saponaria* is a familiar wildflower and is quite lovely when naturalized along a wood's edge or hedgerow, where it will bloom throughout much of the summer and early fall. However, it is an invasive plant that self-sows enthusiastically.

Several tamer varieties of *S. officinalis* have been specially bred for garden use; *S. officinalis* var. *flore-pleno, S. officinalis* var. *caucasica,* and *S. officinalis* var. *plena* are among the double-flowered varieties, with blossom colors ranging from white to purple.

Cosmetic: Mixed with water, soapwort forms a lather that can be used as soap to cleanse the skin.

CULTIVATION

Saponarias are among the easiest perennials to cultivate. They tolerate most soils and, although full sun is preferable, they won't object to some shade. Propagation is by seed or division. Plant seed in the spring or fall, or for earlier blooms, sow indoors in the late winter. Once established, the plants need little care and can actually be invasive. To keep them from self-sowing all over the garden, cut back the plants after the flowers have faded.

DESCRIPTION

Soapwort is a hardy perennial with a single, erect, leafy stem that branches slightly. (See photo on page 274.)

Flowers: Pink or whitish, 1 in. across, five petals, 10 stamens; resemble those of flax; borne in terminal clusters.

Leaves: Opposite, lanceolate, nonhairy; to 3 in. long; on short, broad leafstalk.

Fruit: Four-toothed capsule.

Height: 1–2 ft.

FLOWERING

July through September.

RANGE

This particular genus is a native of western Asia; has become naturalized in the sunny waste places of eastern North America.

GROWING CONDITIONS

- Plant hardiness zones 3–8.
- Average to poor, well-drained soil.
- Full sun to light shade.

SOUTHERNWOOD

Artemisia Abrotanum   **Compositae**

Known as the lovers' plant, lad's love, and maid's ruin, southernwood was once used in aphrodisiac potions and perfumes. The herb was thought to stimulate not only young men's passion but also the growth of their beards, so they rubbed the fresh, lemon-scented leaves on their faces.

Its reputation as a protective nosegay was such that southernwood was routinely used in courtrooms to ward off a disease known as prison fever. Nosegays and branches of it were also used in churches, but for another purpose—the sharp, acid scent helped to keep people awake during tedious sermons.

Medicinally, southernwood has been used as an emmenagogue, stimulant-tonic, diuretic, antiseptic, and, as a close relative of wormwood (*Artemisia Absinthium*), as a worming medicine. It has also been used against tumors and cancers.

DESCRIPTION

Southernwood is a hardy, many-branched perennial.

Flowers: Small, inconspicuous, yellowish white; in loose panicles; seldom present in plants grown in the North.

Leaves: Finely divided, feathery; segments filiform or linear; somewhat downy; gray-green.

Fruit: Seedlike achenes.

Height: 5 ft.

FLOWERING

August.

RANGE

Native of Spain and Italy; naturalized in the United States, especially the eastern half.

USES

Southernwood has an essential oil, absinthol, that is effective against insects, intestinal worms, and some germs. But first and foremost, southernwood is valued as an ornamental.

Aromatic: The leaves discourage moths and can be used in linen closets and where woolens are stored. Add the leaves to a bath; they are aromatic and soothing.

Ornamental: In spite of small flowers, southernwood is an important landscape shrub. The leaves have a fine, feathery texture, and their gray-green color serves as a splendid backdrop for bright-colored flowers. The foliage remains fresh through hot summers. It can be used in bouquets. Plant southernwood in the back of borders or as a hedge. Its odor is thought to repel bees.

Cosmetic: According to modern herbalist Jeanne Rose, a decoction made from southernwood and barley is a good wash to use on acne.

Craft: Southernwood works well as a base for herb wreaths and herb baskets (see the entry Crafts from Herbs). The foliage can be used in any dried herb and flower arrangement.

Dye: Branches are used to make a yellow dye for wool. (See the entry Dyes from Herbs for more information.)

GROWING CONDITIONS

- Plant hardiness zones 4–8.
- Soil pH 6.7.
- Average, well-drained soil.
- Full sun.

CULTIVATION

Southernwood is best propagated from division in the spring or fall. Cuttings root easily. Plant them 2 feet apart. Southernwood will do well in an average soil and requires little care. It does need rigorous pruning in the spring to keep it in good shape.

STINGING NETTLE

Urtica dioica   Urticaceae

The nettle seemed a very powerful plant to our ancestors—a handful of the leaves stung like a handful of bees—and for centuries the human race has tried to figure out ways to harness that power.

Stinging nettles often look bushy, but that's because each plant can send out underground roots that generate new stalks, resulting in a very dense cluster. An individual stalk often has no branches, just a central stem that can reach 5 feet. The stalk sprouts pairs of dark green, opposite leaves that are vaguely heart-shaped with a saw-toothed edge.

Small, hollow hairs cover the stems and undersides of the leaves. When an animal or person brushes against the plant, the tips of the hairs break off, and the hair acts like a hypodermic needle, injecting a stinging venom into the skin. The plant's name comes from the Anglo-Saxon word for "needle." Figuring out exactly what causes the sting has preoccupied several researchers. Just extracting enough fluid from the hairs to study is a serious problem. A hundred hairs weigh only 1 milligram; in one study, extracting just 40 grams of the toxic principle required 100 kilograms of fresh nettles. Researchers found that the hairs contain formic acid, which causes some of the pain, but this did not explain the other effects. Other ingredients in the natural defense system include acetylcholine and histamine. If injected into the skin alone, the histamine causes only reddening, and the acetylcholine does little. However, when injected together, the chemicals caused that familiar burning pain after 15 to 25 seconds and itching about 30 seconds later. One hair alone does not pack the sting of a bee, but the collective effect of brushing against a leaf-ful of hairs is a close approximation.

Stinging nettles do bloom, although the average observer may discount the flowers at first as just so much irrelevant botanical fluff. The flowers are wind-pollinated so they have no showy petals with which to attract bees. Look for dangling clusters of tiny greenish tufts in the axils of upper leaves. The flowers are either male or female.

The sexuality of the plant as a whole seems to be a matter of dispute. The specific term *dioica* means "two houses," suggesting that the sexes each have an individual "house" on a separate plant. However, several American botanists say that each plant has both male and female flowers, but more of one than the other.

HISTORY

A modern gardener may want to keep his or her skin as far from stinging nettles as possible, but one of the plant's earliest uses was as cloth. Archaeologists found nettle fabric wrapped around a body in a

DESCRIPTION

This single-stalked perennial may form clusters and so appear bushy. Small stinging hairs cover the stem and undersides of the leaves. They contain irritating chemicals.

Flowers: Tiny, greenish; in clusters, in loose racemes, or in panicles.

Leaves: Opposite, heart-shaped, with saw-toothed edges; dark green above, paler beneath; covered with bristly hairs.

Fruit: Ovoid nut containing one seed.

Height: To 5 ft.

FLOWERING

July through September.

RANGE

Native to Europe and Asia; widely naturalized from Newfoundland to Ontario, as far west as Colorado, and south to the Carolinas.

HABITAT

Weedy places, often near water.

471

STINGING NETTLE—continued

NETTLE FERTILIZERS

Nettles are quite high in nitrogen, and practical gardeners everywhere have found ways to put this nitrogen to work for them in their gardens.

One technique is to make a liquid fertilizer or manure tea using nettles. Cover a bucketful of nettles with water. Set it aside to "brew" for one to three weeks. Then water your favorite plants with the resulting tea.

Biodynamic gardeners use nettle—along with dandelion, yarrow, valerian, chamomile, and oak bark—in a special additive in making compost.

Bronze Age burial site in Denmark. Nettle cloth again became common during World War I when the Germans were stretching their cotton supply; in 1916 they collected 5.9 million pounds of nettles.

The nettle's medicinal use also goes back to ancient times, with the curious practice of urtication, or slapping a paralyzed limb with bunches of stinging nettles. The Romans knew stinging nettles. In a variation on this original cure, Petronius wrote that a man could be thrashed on the kidneys and below the navel to improve his virility.

The plant's history as a wretched nuisance and enemy of gardeners goes back centuries, too. One of the oldest gardening books known in the West, written by the Swiss monk Strabo at his monastery on Lake Constance in the ninth century, laments digging nettles out of the garden.

The nettle found an important place in medieval medicine. In an Anglo-Saxon herbal of the tenth century, it was one of nine powerful herbs assigned the job of combating "evils." Stinging nettle was a good counterpoison, wrote the sixteenth-century authority Gerard, herbalist to King James I of England. He recommended it as an antidote to the poisonous herb henbane, among other things.

Nettle continued to be an important medicinal herb, and strange as it may seem today, the plant may have been brought to this country intentionally. Not that North America really needed another nettle species, already having several natives.

Both the seeds and flowers once figured in a wine-based tonic that was taken to combat fevers accompanied by chills. The seeds were used to treat all sorts of poisons, from bat bites to heavy metal toxicity.

Nettle tea was credited with many uses. It was combined with a sweetener to make an expectorant. In the spring, it was taken as a tonic. The tea was said to stimulate the kidneys, rid the body of worms, cure diarrhea, stop internal bleeding, and purify the blood. The crushed leaves themselves were stuck up the nose to staunch a nosebleed and were applied to the skin as a rubefacient.

A plant that combines virtues with stings has been the subject of proverbs: "Though you stroke the nettle ever so kindly, yet it will sting you," and "He that handles a nettle tenderly is soonest stung."

It also appears in a variety of folk customs. For example, Tyroleans caught in a thunderstorm would toss stinging nettle into a fire to protect themselves from lightning.

USES

Medicinal: The plant, collected before flowering and made into tea, has been used to treat asthma. Fresh nettle juice was rubbed into the scalp to make the hair grow, a custom that may be traced to the belief that plants were marked with clues to their medicinal virtues. A hairy plant was thought to be good for promoting hair growth. But although the sting might make someone's hair stand on end, there's no evidence that nettle juice will make it grow more profusely.

Nettles are high in vitamin C, which may account for their centuries-old reputation as a spring tonic.

Culinary: Stinging nettles offer vitamins to anyone brave or careful enough to collect and eat them. The young shoots won't sting, and some herb fanciers consume them raw, tossed into a lettuce salad. The greens can be cooked much like kale or spinach. Once boiled, the leaves lose their sting.

A tea from the leaves has been used to curdle milk in making cheese.

Cosmetic: Stinging nettles stimulate the skin and improve circulation. Use them in herbal baths.

Dye: The aboveground portion of the plant makes a green dye, while the roots create a yellow shade. (See the entry Dyes from Herbs for more information.)

Companion planting: Plant stinging nettles in the garden? Most people would pull them, but some gardeners do recommend growing them around vegetables and herbs. They are said to stimulate plant growth and increase essential oils in herbs. In addition, nettles host several beneficial insects that prey on harmful pests.

Other: Nettles were once mowed and served dried to horses and cows. Powdered leaves have been slipped into chicken feed to boost the nutritional value of their eggs.

If you have a place on your property where nettles thrive, consider putting a garden there; nettles flourish in fertile soil.

CULTIVATION

The stinging nettle grows easily from seed or division. Dividing may be a painful experience for the gardener; dress carefully and move cautiously.

Put the plant in rich soil that tends to be on the moist side. (In the wild, the plant often grows on stream banks.) It should tolerate part of the day in shade.

A practical bit of folk wisdom for gardeners is "Nettle in, dock out": If you are stung by a nettle, try treating the injury with the juice of curly or yellow dock. Mullein will also work, and even the nettle's own juice is said to be an antidote.

GROWING CONDITIONS

- Plant hardiness zone 3.
- Rich, moist soil.
- Full sun to partial shade.

473

SWEET CICELY

Myrrhis odorata   **Umbelliferae**

Here's an herb that seems to have made it onto everyone's "Most Often Overlooked" list, but not into very many gardens. Although some gardeners have found it difficult to propagate, it will reward the persistent with a beautiful ornamental form, a sweet anise taste, and a few medicinal uses.

Although the plant has been in use in cooking and medicine at least since Roman times, little seems to have been written about it. Indeed, the old herbalists spent most of their words in comparing it to other plants like hemlock, chervil, lovage, and anise. It was used as a preventative in time of plague, as a tonic for young girls and old people, an aromatic, a stomachic, a carminative, and an expectorant.

USES

Medicinal: Sweet cicely is employed in folk medicine in some parts of the world, but its uses have not been tested scientifically. It does seem to increase appetite and decrease flatulence, and we know that the roots are antiseptic. All seem to agree that it is harmless, which in a way seems to be damning it with faint praise.

Culinary: Sweet cicely's flavor is a combination of celery and anise. The leaves of the plant are used fresh as garnishes, in salads, or in recipes where a sweet touch is needed. The root is steamed, simmered, or cooked and pureed like a parsnip, and the seeds are used in candy, syrups, cakes, and liqueurs.

Sweet cicely cooperates with carrots, parsnips, potatoes, turnips, brussels sprouts, cabbage, cream soups and sauces, and fish, and in fruit soups, stewed fruit, fruit salads, pies, and tarts.

Substitute: Anise.

Ornamental: The lacy foliage and large white blossoms that bloom in spring make it a good plant for mixed flower beds. The seeds are decorative enough for winter bouquets.

CULTIVATION

If possible, start from purchased or dug seedling plants, or divide the plant in the fall. The seed needs to have undergone rather mysterious patterns of freeze and thaw and is notoriously slow and finicky about germinating. If you do use it, use fresh seed and sow in the fall.

Harvesting and storage: Harvest leaves throughout their growing season. One plant will yield 4 cups of leaves and ½ cup of seeds in a season. Plant parts are seldom dried.

DESCRIPTION

Sweet cicely is a hardy perennial with a scent like lovage. (See photo on page 102.)

Flowers: White, numerous, 2 in. across; in compound umbels of 5–10 smaller umbels; inner blooms male, outer blooms bisexual.

Leaves: Fernlike; two or three times pinnately divided; toothed or finely lobed leaflets; whitish, downy, and spotted underneath; leafstalks wrap around the stem.

Fruit: Shiny, dark brown, sharply ridged seeds; to 1 in. long; spicy, licoricelike flavor.

Height: 3 ft.

FLOWERING

May and June.

RANGE

Native to Europe; naturalized in North America.

CHEF TIPS

- Substitute sweet cicely for caraway seeds in baking.
- Press fresh sweet cicely leaves firmly into bluefish before grilling.
- Grate the root and add to quick breads and muffins.

GROWING CONDITIONS

- Plant hardiness zone 3.
- Moist, well-drained, humusy soil. Partial shade.

SWEET FLAG

Acorus Calamus   **Araceae**

These grassy-looking plants provide one of the ancient remedies that modern science has judged physiologically active. Ironically, modern science has also judged it too dangerous to use.

HISTORY

Both Western and Asian doctors have used sweet flag for centuries. Its short-term effects seemed beneficial; only in recent years have we been able to evaluate statistically the long-term effects.

The ancient Greeks and Arabians and doctors in India knew the plant and used it in remedies. Its Latin generic name is a modification of the one used by Dioscorides, the great Greek herbalist of the first century A.D. Calamus is mentioned in the Bible, but that may not necessarily be the same plant.

For a while, sweet flag was a botanist's one-up-manship plant. In the sixteenth century, the master botanist Clusius obtained a root from Asia Minor, grew it in Vienna, and distributed it to other European botanists. Late in the same century, the great English herbalist John Gerard wrangled a plant from an apothecary in Lyons, France, and he thus may have been the person to have introduced it to England.

There it found a welcome reception for its medicinal properties and its ornamental ones. In England, it quickly escaped from cultivation, and before long, the banks of the Thames River were lined with the plant the British call sweet sedge. The circle nearly closed when the demands of perfumers and wig powderers for rootstock resulted in overharvesting, which virtually eradicated the plant.

The pleasant scent of the plant encouraged its use as a strewing herb. Its rushes were strewn on the floors of churches to scent the air, as people crunched the stems underfoot. Even as recently as the 1920s, certain cathedrals clung to the tradition during festivals.

In America, it has had a long history, too. Apparently, it is indigenous to North America. The Plains Indians used the plant medicinally. In later years, the Shakers did, too. It was produced commercially for fragrance and flavoring, and until the late 1960s it could be found in hair and tooth powders as well as bitters, tonics, liqueurs, cordials, and beer.

USES

Contemporary uses of sweet flag have been restricted by recent

UNSAFE

DESCRIPTION

Sweet flag looks like an iris or a broad-leaved grass, but it's actually a relative of philodendrons and calla lilies. You may be able to feel warmth coming from the flowers; they give off considerable heat. (It's a family trait. Skunk cabbages, which are botanically related, can melt snow.)

Flowers: In 2-inch cylindrical spadix at top of flower stem; tiny, greenish yellow, six truncated petals, no calyx.

Leaves: Long, narrow, sword-shaped; ¾ in. wide; prominent midrib; arise from rhizome; clustered at bases.

Fruit: Oblong capsule.

Height: To 3 ft.

FLOWERING

Midsummer.

RANGE

Quebec to Minnesota, to Florida and Texas.

HABITAT

Wet meadows or river and pond banks.

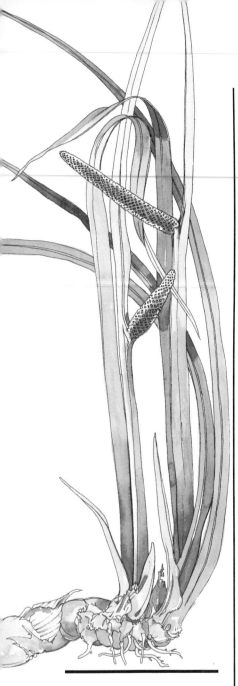

findings questioning its safety. Although it has long been a stock medicinal and culinary herb, such uses are now actively discouraged. But the plant has uses beyond these and shouldn't be ignored.

Medicinal: Long-term feeding studies in rats show oil of calamus to be quite carcinogenic. After 18 weeks, the animals exhibited depressed growth and abnormalities of the liver and heart. After 59 weeks, malignant intestinal tumors appeared. Rats developed tumors on diets with a variety of concentrations of the oil, from 500 to 5,000 parts per million, but control rats showed no tumors. Acting on this information, the Food and Drug Administration (FDA) disapproved sweet flag's use in foodstuffs in 1968.

Pharmacognosist Varro Tyler, Ph.D., author of *The Honest Herbal,* feels that calamus shows no benefit that cannot be provided more safely by other drugs. Its use, he says, "is no longer rational."

Herb writer Michael Weiner, while not disputing the research findings or the FDA's action, points out, nevertheless, that only one variety of sweet flag's oil—the Jammu variety from India—was tested and that other varieties are known to be different in chemical composition.

Culinary: Although sweet flag is still available commercially and many recipes still call for its use, you are far wiser to forego its cinnamonlike taste.

Substitute: Ground cinnamon.

Aromatic: Sheets, pillowcases, and underwear have shown no ill effects from exposure to sweet flag. The rhizome has a sweetish, slightly spicy scent and can be added to potpourris and sachets.

Ornamental: Though its flower is not attractive, its leaves are. Sweet flag is an excellent addition to a water garden.

CULTIVATION

The plant is hardy as long as it is in a moist spot. Some plants tolerate being an inch or two underwater. Semishade or sun will do. Just provide plenty of organic matter to hold water.

Sweet flag is best propagated by division in the spring or fall. It's also possible to grow the plant from seed. Sow them immediately after collecting and cleaning off the pulp. Don't let seeds dry out before, or after, planting.

Harvesting and storage: To use the plant for scenting clothes, collect the rhizome in the early spring or late autumn of its second or third year, a mucky operation but not a difficult one. Soak off the mud and dry the rhizome.

GROWING CONDITIONS

- Plant hardiness zones 3–10.
- Rich, marshy soil.
- Sun or shade.

SWEET WOODRUFF

Galium odoratum   **Rubiaceae**

Here is an attractive ground cover that broadcasts its aroma each May. Consider growing it as a low-maintenance carpet in a shaded spot in your yard.

The plant is unusual among aromatic herbs in that the leaves develop a distinctive scent of fresh-cut hay and vanilla only as they dry. The vanilla scent is lent by coumarin, a constituent of woodruff, as well as tonka beans and the herb melilot. Coumarin is widely used in perfumes and was the first natural scent to be synthesized from coal tars.

HISTORY

Medieval churches were prepared for religious holidays by hanging woodruff. People in Elizabethan England made wreaths, garlands, sachets, and tussie-mussies from these fragrant dried leaves.

In Germany, where sweet woodruff is known as the *Waldmeister* (master of the forest), it is used to flavor May wine as a traditional way to greet this spring month. The practice originated in the thirteenth century, and Germans still serve the *Mai Bowle* each day of the month. May Day celebrations have long marked the passage of winter, dating back to ancient Druid rituals. Adding herbs to a young wine has another practical purpose—it improves the taste of an otherwise thin and harsh-tasting wine.

In herbal folklore, sweet woodruff is said to signify humility because it grows—shyly—so close to the ground. The name derives from the French *rovelle,* or "wheel," which is descriptive of the way the leaves radiate from the stem, like spokes from an axle.

Listed here as a member of the *Galium* genus, sweet woodruff actually has roots in two genera: *Galium* (the bedstraws) and *Asperula* (the woodruffs). The distinction between the genera is a fine one—only the length of the corolla tube separates the *Asperula*s from the *Galium*s. *A. odorata* thus is a synonym for *G. odoratum.*

USES

Medicinal: Sweet woodruff has been used as a calmative, diuretic, diaphoretic, and antispasmodic. It was thought to be beneficial to the heart and liver. A medicinal tea can be made by infusing 2 teaspoons of the dried herb in 1 cup of water. It is said to soothe the stomach. Fresh leaves were applied to wounds.

In folk medicine, the herb had a reputation for combating jaundice and nervousness, healing wounds, and regulating the activity of

DESCRIPTION

This perennial member of the madder family is a fragrant, shade-loving ground cover. (See photos on pages 236 and 444.)

Flowers: Small, funnel-shaped, white, four petals; in loose branching cymes.

Leaves: Narrow and lanceolate; rough-edged; successive whorls of six or eight around the stem; dark green in color.

Fruit: ½ in. long, bristly, longitudinally ribbed.

Height: 8 in.

FLOWERING

May and June.

RANGE

Native to Europe, North Africa, and Asia; widely cultivated.

HABITAT

Moist, wooded locations.

SWEET WOODRUFF—continued

the heart. It was also added to other medicinal formulations to improve their taste.

Toxicity: Sweet woodruff is considered by the Food and Drug Administration to be safe only for use in alcoholic beverages. Large quantities have been reported to cause vomiting and dizziness. James Duke reported in the *CRC Handbook of Medicinal Herbs* that test animals suffered "extensive liver damage, growth retardation, and testicular atrophy" when fed coumarin as a part of their diet.

Culinary: The flowers and leaves make a delicious tea and found their way into Scandinavian cordials in the Middle Ages. To lend a subtle, grassy, vanilla bouquet to white wine, place fresh sprigs in the bottle for a day or so. To make the traditional German *Mai Bowle,* allow fresh sprigs of the herb to stand in Rhine wine overnight, then float fresh strawberries in the bowl before serving.

Aromatic: Sweet woodruff can be used in potpourris and perfumes, for scenting linens (it is said to repel insects), and to stuff mattresses. The plant makes an aromatic backing for the herb wreaths crafted at Well-Sweep Herb Farm in New Jersey. Its scent was once thought to impart a coolness to warm, stuffy rooms.

Ornamental: Sweet woodruff is a classic woodland resident, a white-flowered shade lover that springs up in the understory of trees and shrubs and skirts woodland paths. A natural or woodland garden would be incomplete without sweet woodruff.

A related species, *A. orientalis,* is grown as a carpetlike ground cover with blue flowers.

Dye: From the stems and leaves, a tan dye can be produced in wool mordanted with alum. The roots yield a red dye.

CULTIVATION

Sweet woodruff can be propagated by seeds in the fall to produce plants the following spring; cold weather encourages them to germinate. However, you'll be better off purchasing your first plants from a commercial grower or local herb gardener because woodruff is very difficult to start from seed; germination may take as long as 200 days.

Whatever your choice, provide a slightly acidic soil, rich in nutrients and high in humus; a leaf mold compost is the best medium. If you use a hoe, take care to avoid damaging the spreading root system. Keep the soil moist and the weeds at bay.

Harvesting and storage: Harvest sweet woodruff foliage whenever needed. The stems may be cut close to the ground. Either hand-tie sprigs and hang them in a warm, airy place, or chop the herb immediately after harvesting and dry in a warm, shady place.

GROWING CONDITIONS

- Plant hardiness zone 3.
- Soil pH 5.0.
- Moist, well-drained, humusy soil.
- Shade.

478

TANSY

Tanacetum vulgare   **Compositae**

Stay clear of traditional cures involving this potent herb. Tansy is still used sparingly in salads and in cooking, but larger, medicinally effective amounts can cause violent reactions and death.

That said, tansy is an attractive, easily grown plant for use in the garden or natural landscape.

HISTORY

Tansy takes its name from the Greek word *athanasia,* which means "immortality," and the plant was the critical ingredient in a potion that conferred immortality upon a handsome Greek boy named Ganymede, who became the eternal cupbearer for the god Zeus. According to the sixteenth-century herbalist Gerard, the connection with immortality was inferred by tansy's flowers, which do not wilt easily. Other authors have proposed less-romantic explanations. For example, the herb was put in coffins, perhaps because of its power as an insect repellent. Another herbalist has suggested that tansy's strong smell was a relief during funeral rites in an era without air conditioning.

The plant was also supposed to prolong mortal life through its numerous medicinal properties. Gerard prescribed it as a spring tonic and gout remedy and advised his readers that they could rid themselves of worms by chewing the seeds. The seventeenth-century British herbalist Nicholas Culpeper mentioned tansy as an aid in treating freckles, sunburn, and pimples. He even recommended holding bruised tansy leaves on women's navels to prevent miscarriages.

Tansy figured in the beauty aids of bygone days. Tansy was steeped in buttermilk for nine days to make a potion that was supposed to whiten the skin. (Perhaps it was the smell of nine-day-old buttermilk that made people turn pale.)

The smell of tansy was well-known in the English homes of the sixteenth and seventeenth centuries. It was one of the common strewing herbs—tossed on floors to release its scent when crushed underfoot. King James II had a royal herb strewer, and at James's coronation, the strewer and several assistants distributed 6 bushels of tansy and other herbs along the half-mile approach to the throne.

Tansy has a culinary history as well as a medicinal one. In England, the chopped leaves flavored various little cakes and puddings, particularly those served around Easter. Perhaps this was the cousin of the custom of including tansy as one of the so-called bitter herbs of the Passover seder. That strong kick of a flavor, or "domi-

TOXIC

DESCRIPTION

Given half a chance, tansy forms an ever-widening mass of slim stalks and dark green, fern-like leaves. The leaves of ornamental varieties are fine and feathery. This perennial spreads by sending out vigorous underground stems called rhizomes. When the plants are brushed or their leaves are crushed, they release an odor reminiscent of pine. (See photos on pages 32 and 444.)

Flowers: In loose clusters of yellow flower heads, ⅓–½ in. across; each flower head comprised of tightly packed tiny flowers; flowers in outer ring are female; those in center are bisexual.

Leaves: Fernlike; pinnately divided into about 12 oblong or lanceolate leaflets; leaflets pinnately lobed or toothed; lower leaves have stalks; upper leaves are stalkless.

Fruit: Ribbed achenes.

Height: 3–4 ft.

FLOWERING

July through September.

RANGE

Native to Europe; naturalized in North America from Nova Scotia and Ontario to Minnesota, Missouri, and North Carolina, as well as Oregon and Nevada.

HABITAT

Along roadsides and in other weedy places.

TANSY—continued

neering relish" as the seventeenth-century writer John Evelyn put it, could be pleasant in a salad if "sparingly mixt" (Evelyn again). He preferred his tansy cooked, however, and suggested this interesting spring stir fry: Brown tansy along with other herbs and spinach, green corn, violets, and primrose leaves, then serve hot with a dressing of orange juice and sugar. Izaak Walton, the seventeenth-century father of angling literature, used tansy in a recipe for cooked minnows. And according to rumor, tansy is one of the many herbs in the secret formula for Chartreuse liqueur, a recipe perfected in 1757. But considering that some 130 herbs are thought to be included, tansy's contribution likely would be a modest one.

The leaves have continued to appear in the kitchen, though not always for cooking. Colonial cooks rubbed tansy into their tabletops to discourage bugs. Even today, little tufts of tansy swing in windows here and there to repel flies. Fairman Jayne of Sandy Mush Herb Farm in North Carolina has tried it without success, but says the technique works for one of his neighbors.

USES

Medicinal: Tansy's use as a folk medicine is on hold because of questions of its safety. Certainly, it is not one for the amateur pharmacist. Tansy was used by American Indians to induce abortion, and this treatment was potentially fatal. The signs of poisoning include a fast, weak pulse, spasm, and foaming at the mouth. The leaves were used externally to encourage the fertility of the sexual organs and to relieve sprains and headaches. Added to bathwater, the herb was thought to ease sore limbs and reduce fevers.

The danger comes from thujone, a relatively toxic substance also found in wormwood. Tansy plants vary in their thujone content. The extracted oil of some contains none, while the oil of others approaches 95 percent thujone. Growing conditions do not seem to be a factor, and the thujone level appears to be genetically determined. Thujone is also the likely agent for whatever medicinal properties tansy may possess, so the plant's danger is inbred. The flavor, however, is not dependent on the oil.

Fortunately, sidelining tansy as a medicinal herb has not been much of a loss, according to pharmacognosist Varro Tyler, Ph.D. He believes that tansy's replacements are safer and more effective.

Culinary: Tansy's leaves are peppery and strong. They have been used as a substitute for pepper when that exotic spice was unavailable. Use them fresh and minced in pancakes, waffles, cookies, pudding, cakes, teas, liqueurs, salad dressings, and marinades. They are particularly well-known for adding zip to scrambled eggs, omelets, frittatas, herb butters, and stuffing for poultry and fish. Use the plant in moderation, not only because of its assertive taste but also because it is potentially toxic.

Ornamental: Tansy grows very lush foliage—almost tropical in appearance, says Fairman Jayne. He recommends the fernleaf tansy for its more delicate foliage. One of the best ways to grow the plant, he says, is in a container by a path so that passersby will brush against the leaves and release the fragrance.

A few of the small species native to the American West make good plants for the rock garden. *Tanacetum capitatum* creates a cushion of the characteristic feathery leaves less than 6 inches high. The flowers appear above cushion level. A similar species, though perhaps not producing as dense a cushion, is *T. nuttallii*.

Cosmetic: Tansy lotions have been highly recommended for their cleansing and soothing properties. They are especially helpful in controlling acne.

Craft: Dried tansy flowers aren't quite as bright as the fresh flowers, but they still retain a strong golden color. Use them in dried herb and flower arrangements.

Dye: The young leaves and flowering tops will produce yellows and greens in wool. (See the entry Dyes from Herbs for more information.)

Companion planting: Gardeners recommend planting tansy among blackberries, raspberries, and roses to enhance their growth. It also reportedly repels ants, Colorado potato beetles, flea beetles, imported cabbageworms, Japanese beetles, and squash bugs. However, if you want to try companion planting with tansy, you must be willing to spend time and effort controlling its growth. It can be invasive.

Other: This herb is also known as ant fern, and sprigs have been used to keep ants from raiding kitchen cabinets. You might try the old-time practice of planting tansy near the doorway to discourage flies from entering.

CULTIVATION

Tansy can be propagated by division or by seeds sown in the spring or fall.

The plant does well in a variety of garden soils, which explains tansy's phenomenal success as a weed. The richer the soil, the lusher the tansy, finds Fairman Jayne. The only trouble he has had with the plant is checking its relentless spread.

The very short species of tansy that form little cushions in rock gardens may not be as forgiving as the tall tansy. Give the smaller plants good drainage.

CHEF TIPS

- Use 1 tablespoon of minced fresh tansy in a marinade for 1 pound of beef.

- Toss a bit of minced fresh tansy into a green salad and dress with lemon vinaigrette.

- Add minced fresh tansy to egg salad and serve on crisp rye toast.

- When mulling ciders and wines, add a few fresh tansy leaves. Remove before serving.

GROWING CONDITIONS

- Plant hardiness zone 4.
- Soil pH 6.3.
- Average soil.
- Full sun to partial shade.

TARRAGON

Artemisia Dracunculus   Compositae

Among cooks, this herb is popularly associated with vinegar and fish. Its aniselike character is particularly suited to both, but tarragon deserves a wider role in the kitchen. Food writer Craig Claiborne has called it "seductive and satisfying." Tarragon has a somewhat mysterious property as well; chew on a leaf, and you may notice a numb feeling on your tongue.

HISTORY

The plant's name is derived from the French *esdragon,* meaning "little dragon." The dragonlike roots may strangle the plant if it is not divided often. In medicinal lore and legend, any plant with a serpentine root system is given credit for treating snakebite, and tarragon is no exception. The Roman scholar Pliny said it could prevent fatigue. Indeed, pilgrims of the Middle Ages put sprigs of it in their shoes before beginning long trips on foot.

Thomas Jefferson was an early distributor of tarragon in the fledgling United States. In a letter to the President, written in 1809, General John Mason reported that the plant Jefferson had given him "has flourished well in the open air—and will in Spring afford plenty of slips."

USES

Although chiefly a culinary herb, tarragon has been used to stimulate the appetite, relieve flatulence and colic, and cure rheumatism. It has been used to relieve toothache as a sort of local anesthetic. There appears to be no scientific basis for any of these practices, but tarragon can protect foodstuffs as an antioxidant. Tarragon is also used in perfumes, soaps, and cosmetics, and in condiments and liqueurs. It may be useful as an antifungal as well.

Culinary: Although it is one of the French fines herbes, tarragon can be dominating and overshadow or fight with other flavors. Use the leaves fresh in salads, as garnishes, or in such classic applications as remoulade sauce, tartar sauce, béarnaise sauce, French dressing, and veal Marengo. In general, don't add this herb with a heavy hand, and avoid bringing out its bitter side by cooking it too long.

Tarragon enhances fish, shellfish, pork, beef, lamb, game, poultry, pâtés, leeks, potatoes, tomatoes, carrots, onions, artichokes, asparagus, mushrooms, cauliflower, broccoli, beets, peas, parsley, chervil, garlic, chives, lemons, oranges, rice, and barley. Use it in flavored vinegars, herbed mayonnaise, herbed butters, cream sauces, and soups, and with cheeses, eggs, sour cream, and yogurt.

Available commercially: Dried or in tarragon-flavored vinegar.

DESCRIPTION

This aromatic perennial is grown for its distinctively flavored leaves. (See photo on page 101.)

Flowers: Yellow or greenish white; small, globe-shaped; in terminal panicles; rarely fully open and usually sterile.

Leaves: Linear to lanceolate, undivided; 1–4 in. long; borne singly at top of plant, in groups of three below.

Fruit: Achenes.

Height: 2 ft.

FLOWERING

Should not flower.

RANGE

Native to the Caspian Sea area and Siberia; widely cultivated in Europe, Asia, and the United States.

CHEF TIPS

- For maximum flavor, add tarragon to long-cooking soups and stews during the last 15 minutes only.

- Sauté boneless chicken breasts with walnuts and toss in chives and tarragon about 5 minutes before the chicken is done.

- Before roasting a chicken, stuff tarragon and garlic slivers under the breast and leg skin.

- Create a fish salad by combining poached haddock, crumbled feta cheese, pitted green olives, and fresh tarragon. Dress with a garlic vinaigrette.

Storage note: Frozen tarragon and tarragon stored in vinegar are superior in flavor to the dried.

Companion planting: Tarragon is supposed to enhance the growth of most vegetables when planted among them.

CULTIVATION

Although not a visually stunning plant, tarragon was at one time restricted to the formal gardens of the European nobility. Take note before buying tarragon seeds: They are apt to be of the less-versatile Russian tarragon, a variety that lacks the aromatic oils of the classical French tarragon (*Artemisia Dracunculus* var. *sativa*). Most gardeners acquire tarragon as seedlings, divisions, or cuttings. Take divisions in the early spring as the new growth comes up. Take cuttings in autumn or, in the North, preferably in the spring. Set plants 2 feet apart. Tarragon must be mulched in the winter to protect it from frost. You can bring it inside for a potted winter vacation, but it may transplant poorly and does require lots of light.

Even in warm climates, the plants should be divided every two or three years to assure vigor and flavor. Tarragon most often fails from having been planted in a wet or acid soil. It needs well-drained loam. The clump will always be larger in the second year, with shoots appearing in the late spring. All flower stems should be removed to keep the plant productive.

Container gardening: You can have fresh tarragon year-round by placing plants in pots for the sunny windowsill. See that the roots get good drainage. You can even force tarragon in the winter. In the summer, place a mature plant in a good-size pot, cut it down to the base, wrap the pot in plastic, and place it in the refrigerator until fall to bring the tarragon into dormancy. Then unwrap the pot and place it in a south-facing window to break dormancy and cause the plant to sprout. Take a sprig or two as needed throughout the cold months. A popular stand-in as a potted herb is the mint marigold (*Tagetes lucida*) from Mexico.

Pests and diseases: Check your plants occasionally for root rot or mildew. (See the entry Growing Herbs for information on controlling diseases.)

Harvesting and storage: Two harvests can generally be made each year, the first six to eight weeks after setting out. When harvesting, handle the leaves gently, as they bruise easily. Tarragon is best frozen or preserved in white vinegar, but it can be dried as well. Hang the plants upside down in bunches in a warm, dry place out of the sun. It will brown some in drying. Store in an airtight container.

GROWING CONDITIONS

- Plant hardiness zone 4.
- Soil pH 6.9.
- Rich, sandy, well-drained loam.
- Full to partial shade.

TEAS FROM HERBS

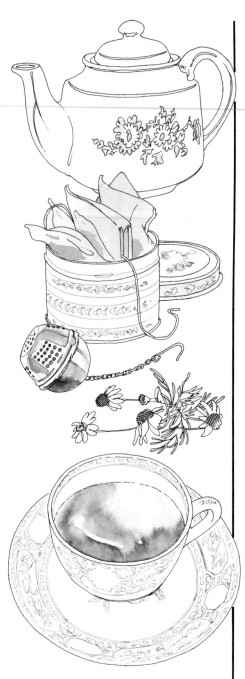

Of all the uses that herbs have—as crafts, dyes, seasonings, aromatics—the one that more people enjoy is the making and drinking of herb teas.

Herb teas were first used as medicines, and as such they are still brewed and consumed today. But they are also consumed simply as beverages. For some people, herb tea is the beverage of choice. A meal can't go by without a cup of herb tea.

CULINARY TEAS

The custom of "taking tea" began in the early 1600s when the East India Company first offered the loose leaves for sale. Rich Brits in London's Belgravia area enjoyed it daily at four-ish, and it soon became the thing to do. A single serving cost about the equivalent of one dollar then, so the rich filtered their used tea down to the servants who thought it was a great treat.

Taking tea continues today in snazzier London hotels, but because of life-style and diet, the custom is not practiced frequently in contemporary homes. In fact, taking tea is more of a formal affair in places like India and Hong Kong than it is in Great Britain.

High tea is the most formal kind and is served using silver and china with cream and lemon to add. An accompaniment of scones, strawberry jam, and thick Devonshire cream for spreading is expected. One or two types of petits fours, pastries, or tiny crustless cucumber sandwiches are also proper fare.

Scottish high tea is served between 5:00 and 6:00 in the afternoon and replaces dinner. Here, meats are offered, especially sausage and egg pie.

Herb teas are becoming more popular at traditional London establishments as well as in the United States. People are meeting for tea, rather than cocktails, and as caffeine drinks dwindle as popular late-in-the-day beverages, herb teas will continue to take their place.

How to make a proper pot of herb tea: First, bring fresh, cool water to a rolling boil. Then rinse a china, pottery, or other nonmetal teapot with some of the water. (Nonmetal pots help keep the tea pure in flavor and hot while it brews.) Next, toss in the herbs (roots, seeds, pods, leaves), using 2 tablespoons of fresh or 1 tablespoon of dried for each cup of water you'll be using, plus an extra 2 tablespoons of fresh or 1 tablespoon of dried "for the pot." (In other words, if you're brewing 4 cups of tea, use 10 tablespoons of fresh herbs or 5 tablespoons of dried.) Pour in the boiling water and let the tea steep for about five minutes. Keep the pot or teapot covered to retain heat. Steeping time will vary, depending on what herbs you're using, so do taste checks at intervals until you're sure. Strain the herbs out as soon as the tea has reached the desired strength. Serve herb tea with honey, lemon, orange slices, or fresh herb sprigs.

To make iced tea, follow the same procedure, except use 3 tablespoons of fresh herbs or 2 tablespoons of dried herbs. The extra amount allows for melting ice.

Herb teas can be frozen in ice cube trays and used to chill refreshing summer beverages. You can also freeze sprigs of herbs, like mint, in ice cubes for flavoring and decorating beverages.

Ideas for tea blends: Try any of the combinations below to find your favorite:

- spearmint, elderberry, and lemon balm
- tansy, sage, and rosehips
- marjoram, anise, and lemon verbena
- angelica, clove, orange peel, and nutmeg
- anise, chamomile, and costmary
- lemon verbena and borage
- blueberry leaf, beebalm, and ginger
- savory, lemongrass, and scented geranium
- thyme, sassafras, and strawberry leaf
- lemongrass, rosemary, and thyme
- rose petals, rosehips, and raspberry leaf
- nettle, ginger, and hyssop
- horehound and chamomile
- jasmine, orange peel, and sage
- fennel and goldenrod
- chicory, ginseng, and cinnamon
- elderberry, rosehips, and bay
- chamomile and valerian
- basil, lemon verbena, lemongrass, and lemon thyme
- pennyroyal, peppermint, and ginger
- chamomile and apple mint

MEDICINAL TEAS

Creating an herb tea for medicinal purposes is not a whole lot different than preparing one for culinary enjoyment. If you are out of sorts, just the ritual of brewing an herb tea can be soothing. Heating the water, holding the warm cup in your hands, feeling the steam rise up can be tremendously comforting.

The tea, usually an infusion (sometimes called a tisane), can be prepared in the same way a beverage tea is prepared. Toss a quantity of the herb in a nonmetallic container, pour in boiling water, and

TIMED BREW

The hot water is to remain upon it [the tea] no longer than whiles you can say the Miserere Psalm [Psalm 51] very leisurely.
Sir Kenelm Digby
The Closet Opened

CHEF TIPS

- Chamomile tea, made from the flower heads of the plant, is a good aid for digestion and upset stomachs. It has also been reported to improve one's disposition.

- Lemon verbena, lemon balm, and lemongrass are three lemon-scented herbs that make pleasant-tasting tea, whether served hot or cold. Use each alone, in combination, or with other herbs. Use one of them to replace the slice of lemon often served with tea.

- Borage leaves used in either hot or iced tea are known for giving a "lift" after a hard day. The pretty blue flowers add interest to iced tea and improve the flavor.

- Rosemary tea helps cure headaches and colds. Use it alone or in combination with other herbs.

- Sage produces a full-bodied tea useful for colds and fever or as a tonic.

- Catnip tea and catnip and fennel tea have long been used to help alleviate colic in babies.

485

TEAS FROM HERBS—continued

CAUTIONS

Not all herbs are suitable for making tea.

If you are interested in a pleasurable tea, obviously taste will be a guiding factor. But if you are brewing a medicinal tea, there's more to it than good taste.

You must know about the herb you are dealing with. Many herbs make wonderful healing teas, but some will make you ill.

A good approach is to try herbs one at a time. Read the individual herb entries in this book, judging for yourself their merits and deficiencies. Note especially what pharmacognosists have to say about them. Quite a number of herbs with long histories of use in folk medicine are only now being exposed as carcinogenic, for example.

Pay attention to what contemporary herbalists have to say. Sixteenth- and seventeenth-century herbalists like Gerard and Culpeper are fun to read, but they are not reliable sources of information.

Follow instructions for brewing the tea, and follow dosage guidelines.

Use your common sense. In her book *Herbal Medicine,* Dian Dincin Buchman quoted one of her grandmother's favorite dictums: "If the tea smells bad and tastes bad, it isn't right; but if it smells quite pleasant and possibly tastes bad, it can be tried out."

allow the herb to steep for 10 to 20 minutes. Most herbalists don't make too much of the process.

The quantity of herbal material doesn't vary much. Most herbalists prescribe an ounce of the dried herb—which would amount to about 2 cups—in a pint of water. Sometimes the recipes are worded in terms of a tablespoon of dried herb to a cup of water. Almost invariably, the amount of the fresh herb specified is double the amount of dried herb.

The part of the herb being used plays a role in how the tea is prepared. Most leaves and flowers will yield their healing virtues in an infusion. But roots and bark, along with leathery leaves, require more than a steeping. A decoction must be made. In this process, the roots, bark, or tough leaves are actually boiled in the water for a short time—two to five minutes—then steeped an additional 10 to 15 minutes.

In either case, strain the herb parts out of the tea before it is drunk.

It is particularly important with a medicinal tea to insure that as much of the active principle of the herb as possible be captured in the tea. One way to do this is to cover the tea to prevent the aromatic oils from evaporating into the air.

"If you're making an herbal preparation and you can walk into the room and say, 'Umm, doesn't that smell nice?' " explained California herbalist Nan Koehler in *The Woman's Encyclopedia of Health and Natural Healing,* "the chemicals are escaping and won't do *you* any good. So always use a lid so that the steam rises and then condenses back into the water."

And how should the medicinal tea be drunk?

Quite often, the tea is consumed at room temperature. In *The Herb Book,* herbalist John Lust recommended drinking the tea hot only if the goal is to induce a sweat or to break up a cough or cold. The tea is seldom bolted down. Rather, it is sipped throughout the day, perhaps a spoonful at a time. The cumulative dose would be 1 to 4 cups a day, depending upon the herb.

And how long should the regimen be followed?

Herbs, unlike prescription medicines that you may be used to, do not work overnight. "If you don't notice an improvement in your condition, then do it again a second day," said Koehler. "You should feel better by the third day."

"Herbs are not one-shot wonder drugs in the modern sense," Lust explained; "rather, their effectiveness is based on gradual action to restore the natural balance of bodily functions that constitutes health. Very few plant remedies produce lasting beneficial effects after one or a few doses."

THYME

Thymus vulgaris   **Labiatae**

"When in doubt, use thyme." That's the herbal rule of thumb offered for confused cooks by the *Grass Roots Herb Society Newsletter*. Thyme collaborates with dozens of foods, and you can grow thymes that taste and smell uncannily like other herbs. The essential oil that gives thyme its personality has a long list of medicinal uses. Bees love the tiny blossoms. It makes an ideal edging plant, and it is available in varieties with pink, lavender, crimson, or white flowers. It is one of the first choices for a windowsill herb.

"Thyme is very nearly the perfect useful herb," sums up the newsletter.

It's difficult to discern whether the thyme that has intrigued people since the days of old is *Thymus vulgaris,* the common thyme, or *T. praecox* subsp. *arcticus,* known as creeping thyme, mountain thyme, wild thyme, and mother-of-thyme. Old herbals make reference to both. The latter is generally smaller than common thyme but shares the shape and color of both inflorescence and leaf. With its creeping habit of growth, *T. praecox* subsp. *arcticus* is particularly suited for chinks and crevices between paving or rocks on a terrace garden.

HISTORY

The herb's name has been traced to a couple of possible sources, one impressive and one quite homely. *Thymus* was Greek for "courage," as might be considered appropriate for an herb that is invigorating to the senses. But the name may also derive from the Greek's term "to fumigate," and again this would be fitting, as the herb was burned to chase stinging insects from the house. A bed of thyme was thought to be a home to fairies, and gardeners once set aside a patch of the herb for them, much as we provide birdhouses.

The little plant has been a symbol for several societies, representing style and elegance to the early Greeks, chivalry in the Middle Ages, and the Republican spirit in France. On a practical level, thyme was used to flavor liqueurs and cheese. A caraway-flavored variety, *T. Herba-barona,* was imported from Sicily and Corsica to the Continent, where it was the choice for seasoning beef.

The plant's medicinal reputation grew over the centuries. Thyme pillows were thought to relieve both epilepsy and melancholy. From the fifteenth through the seventeenth centuries, thyme was used to combat the plagues that swept over Europe, and as recently as World War I, the essential oil served as a battlefield antiseptic.

The herb was thought to have a psychological effect on people. A soup of beer and thyme was an antidote to shyness; a range of

DESCRIPTION

A perennial, thyme is a small, many-branched, aromatic shrub. (See photos on pages 99, 237, and 273.)

Flowers: Numerous, tubular, lilac to pink; under ¼ in. long; in small terminal clusters.

Leaves: Opposite, oblong-lanceolate, stalkless or nearly stalkless, ¼–½ in. long; edges rolled under; undersides pale, hairy.

Fruit: Four, tiny, seedlike nutlets.

Height: 1 ft.

FLOWERING

June and July.

RANGE

Native to the western Mediterranean region and widely cultivated. The plant is said to grow wild in an area of the Catskill Mountains of New York State, where it was introduced in the fleece of sheep imported from Greece. Naturalized patches have also been sighted in western Massachusetts.

THYME—continued

CHEF TIPS

- Serve sprigs of fresh thyme on iced beet borsht that has been topped with plain yogurt.

- Sauté strips of roasted pepper in olive oil, minced garlic, and thyme. Serve over pasta or rice.

- Marinate artichoke bottoms in olive oil, lemon juice, and fresh thyme. Arrange on an appetizer platter with sprigs of fresh thyme.

- Add sprigs of fresh thyme to olives in their brine.

- Halve cherry tomatoes and scoop out the seeds. Then combine yogurt, minced fresh thyme, basil, and a touch of Dijon mustard. Fill the tomato halves with the mixture and garnish with fresh thyme sprigs.

nervous disorders, including nightmares, was said to respond to thyme tea.

Thyme sailed to the New World with the first European settlers, and today it grows wild in a few areas of North America.

USES

Medicinal: Thyme takes its place in herbal medicine with other old-fashioned "simples," like sage and lavender, as a treatment for a variety of ailments. You may have noticed its flavor in cough medicines. It has also served as a carminative, vermifuge, rubefacient, and antiseptic. Thyme is particularly beneficial in quieting gastrointestinal complaints, and it was boiled in wine for a digestive drink. A tea has been prescribed for shortness of breath and congested lungs.

The Greeks used thyme for nervous conditions, as an antiseptic, and as a fumigator. Apparently, the herb has antispasmodic qualities that make it effective in relieving asthma, whooping cough, and stomach cramps. Herbalists have prescribed a cold infusion of the entire plant for dyspepsia; a warm infusion was recommended for hysteria, flatulence, colic, headache, and dysmenorrhea. Inflammations and sores may be soothed by a poultice made by mashing the leaves into a paste.

Toxicity: The essential oil of thyme is thymol. If taken in pure form, it can cause such adverse symptoms as dizziness, diarrhea, nausea, headache, vomiting, and muscular weakness. It can also have a depressing effect on the heart, respiration, and body temperature, and it can overstimulate the thyroid gland. While thyme once was used as a vermifuge, particularly to cure hookworms, the strong dose needed to expel the worms can be fatal. For internal use take thyme-based preparations in moderation. The oil may even irritate sensitive skin, so proceed cautiously if you apply a poultice of the leaves.

Culinary: Thyme tastes delicately green with a faint clove after-taste. It ranks as one of the fines herbes of French cuisine. Leaves and sprigs are used in salads as garnishes and most famously in clam chowder, bouquets garnis, and French, Creole, and Cajun cuisines.

Thyme works well with veal, lamb, beef, poultry, fish, poultry stuffing, pâtés, sausages, stews, soups, stocks, bread, herbed butters, herbed mayonnaise, flavored vinegars, mustard, and bean and lentil casseroles. Use it with tomatoes, onions, cucumbers, carrots, eggplant, parsnips, leeks, mushrooms, asparagus, green beans, broccoli, sweet peppers, potatoes, spinach, corn, peas, cheese, eggs, and rice. Its flavor blends well with those of lemon, garlic, and basil. For a different taste, try flavored varieties such as lemon thyme and oregano thyme. Gourmet shops and Greek groceries may stock thyme-flavored honey; try it when formulating honey-based cough remedies. Thyme is one of the flavorings in Benedictine liqueur.

Available commercially: Dried leaves.

Aromatic: The dried flowers of thyme, like lavender, have been used to preserve linen from insects. The leaves and flowering tops are an ingredient in sachets. Thymol is used in making colognes, aftershave lotions, soaps, and detergents.

Cosmetic: Thyme has antiseptic and stimulating properties that make it useful in herbal lotions and baths. (See the entries Lotions from Herbs and Bathing with Herbs for more information.)

Companion planting: Thyme reportedly benefits eggplant, po-

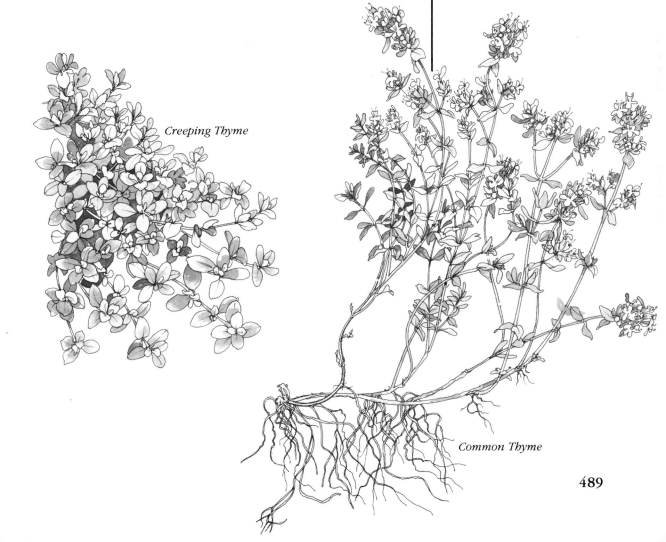

Creeping Thyme

Common Thyme

THYME—continued

GROWING CONDITIONS

- Plant hardiness zones 5–9.
- Soil pH 6.3.
- Light, dry, well-drained soil.
- Full sun to partial shade.

tatoes, and tomatoes, when planted near them. In addition, gardeners recommend plantings of thyme to repel imported cabbageworms and whiteflies.

CULTIVATION

If you are a beginning gardener, try growing common thyme before trying more finicky species. Plants grown from seed are best sown indoors, as they need a temperature of around 70°F to germinate. Sal Gilbertie of Gilbertie's Herb Farm recommends cluster sowing, in which plants are set outside in a clump to produce a stronger, quicker-growing crop. To do this, simply sow about 20 seeds in a 4-inch clay pot filled with a mixture of sand, peat moss, loam, and perlite, topped with a covering of fine sand. He recommends a daily misting until the seeds germinate, which should take less than a week. Thereafter, water at the base of the plants when the soil is dry to the touch. Two weeks after germination, he says, feed the plants either fish emulsion or skim milk. The plants can be placed in a sheltered, sunny outdoor spot once they stand 4 inches high, and they can then be moved out into the garden a week later.

You can divide or take cuttings from established plants anytime from midspring to early summer, but preferably in spring. Plants also may be propagated by layering.

Division is a simple matter of uprooting the plant, being careful not to harm the roots, and separating it into two or three sections for transplanting into new spots.

To propagate from cuttings, snip 3-inch pieces from stems with new green growth, not from the old woody growth. Place the cuttings in wet sand and keep them moist for two weeks, or until the roots appear. You will know the cuttings have rooted because they will resist a gentle tug and will show new top growth. At this time they can be transplanted to small individual pots or into the garden.

Thyme requires relatively little care. Without well-drained soil, however, the plant is susceptible to fungal diseases. Avoid wetting the leaves when watering, as this reduces their fragrance. In the North, plants must be protected from a deep frost with mulch. The low, creeping thymes used as ground covers withstand winters better than the bushy varieties, but they are vulnerable to poor soil drainage. They will do best in relatively poor soil. Culinary varieties are usually replaced every two or three years because they become woody and straggly.

Pests and diseases: Thyme is susceptible to fungal diseases and root rot and can become infested with spider mites. (See the entry Growing Herbs for information on controlling pests and diseases.)

Harvesting and storage: Bees have as deep an affection for

THYME SPECIES AND VARIETIES

Name	Height	Leaves/ Flowers	Comments
Thymus Broussonetii Broussonetii thyme	5–12 in.	Lavender-pink flowers	Grows as a many-branched shrublet; pine scent
T. camphoratus Camphor thyme	6–12 in.	Compact, dark green leaves	Camphor scent; requires mild, dry climate
T. ×citriodorus Lemon thyme	4–12 in.	Dark green, glossy leaves	Small bush; strong lemon scent; used in cooking fish or chicken, also in tea
T. × citriodorus 'Argenteus' Silver thyme	10 in.	White-edged leaves	Shrublike; good for hanging baskets and as an accent plant
T. Herba-barona Caraway thyme	2–5 in.	Shiny, dark green leaves; lavender blooms	Caraway scent; nice ground cover, good in rock gardens and hanging baskets; good for flavoring meat, soup, vegetables, and poultry
T. Herba-barona 'Nutmeg' Nutmeg thyme	4 in.	Short, fat stalks; pink flowers	Spicy scent; fast creeper; very similar to caraway thyme
T. nummularius	8–12 in.	Smooth, glossy, green leaves; bright pink flowers	Suitable as a hedge
T. praecox subsp. *arcticus* Mother-of-thyme	to 4 in.	Dark green leaves	Forms thick, dense mat; traditional ground cover
T. praecox sub. *arcticus* 'Coccineus' Creeping red-flowered thyme	4 in.	Tiny rose-colored blooms	Forms dense, dark green mat; good as ground cover or between stones
T. pseudolanuginosus Woolly thyme	2 in.	Minute, silver-gray leaves; tiny, rose-pink flowers	At home in the rock garden, among paving stones, or along walkways
T. vulgaris Common thyme	6–15 in.	Oval, gray-green leaves; tiny white to lilac flowers	Small, upright shrub; variety most often used in cooking

thyme as humans do. If you don't care to have these creatures invade your garden, harvest the leaves before the fragrant blossoms open in midsummer. You can take small amounts for immediate use, as needed, or harvest the entire plant by cutting it back about 2 inches from the ground. The plant will grow back again before the season ends, but if you take this second harvest, which many people do, the plant will be less hardy in the winter. The harvested stems can be tied in bunches and hung to dry in a warm, airy place, or, you can strip the leaves and place them on a thin screen to dry before storing. You can also freeze the herbs in an airtight container.

TROPICAL PERIWINKLE

Catharanthus roseus   **Apocynaceae**

Tropical periwinkle is a pharmaceutically gifted plant, but as herbs go, it is highly powerful and should not be used as a home cure. Enjoy it as a ground cover, edging plant, or cut flower. It is particularly popular where summers are intensely hot and humid.

DESCRIPTION

Tropical periwinkle grows as either an annual or perennial. It is a deciduous non-woody plant, erect, and many branched. The stems contain a milky latex. (See photo on page 274.)

Flowers: Showy; magenta or rose-purple; appear in twos and threes in leaf axils; tubular with five corolla lobes that spread out horizontally; 1–1½ in. across, flaring to 2 in.; mouth of corolla tube closed with bristlelike hairs.

Leaves: Opposite, paired, smooth, oblong, and narrowing at base; spinelike point at tip; 1–3 in. long; short leafstalks.

Fruit: Two paired pods; 1 in. long; containing up to 15 cylindrical seeds.

Height: 1–2 ft.

FLOWERING

May through October.

RANGE

Native to Madagascar; naturalized throughout the tropical world.

HISTORY

Tropical periwinkle received official status as a medicinal plant only in recent years. Researchers at Eli Lilly and Company, in search of a cancer cure, began a general survey of folk remedy plants, and they found that extracts of *Catharanthus roseus* leaves could prolong the lives of mice with chemically induced leukemia. This led to the development of two anticancer drugs, vinblastine sulfate (formerly called vincaleukoblastine) and vincristine sulfate (formerly called leurocristine), both of which are now available world-wide under the registered trade names of Velban and Oncovin, respectively. The Lilly survey also turned up an amazing variety of uses to which this single plant has been placed.

USES

This great variety of medicinal uses for tropical periwinkle would alone attest to its value, even if the plant lacked further attraction as an ornamental.

Medicinal: Vinblastine sulfate, made from tropical periwinkle, is used to treat Hodgkin's disease and choriocarcinoma, a type of skin or lymph cancer. An alkaloid in the plant, vincristine, is employed in childhood leukemias and breast cancer. Administered together in a test, the two substances produced beneficial results in 43 percent of patients with malignant lymphoma. In addition, a vinblastine sulfate ointment has been used to treat psoriasis.

Evidence on tropical periwinkle's usefulness in treating diabetes and hypoglycemia is contradictory. Most experiments show it has no effect on blood sugar levels in rabbits, but it has produced the desired effect in cats and abated some symptoms in humans. The plant's astringent and antiseptic tannins are probably responsible for cures of hemorrhaging and eye troubles. Control of menstrual hemorrhaging is probably due to the presence of vincamine, an indole alkaloid that contracts uterine muscles. However, little scientific work has been done on these properties.

Toxicity: Vincristine and vinblastine sulfates are both very potent drugs. The former is neurotoxic, damaging the nervous system, while the latter decreases the number of white blood cells. Tropical periwinkle should never be used without medical supervision. An

overdose can be fatal. The plant has caused poisoning in grazing animals, and the extracts, even in small doses, cause platelet damage when used in cancer therapy.

Both vinblastine and vincristine sulfates, but principally the former, cause blurred vision, hair loss, nausea, vomiting, stomach cramps, phlebitis, rashes, temporary mental depression, loss of tendon reflexes, headache, nosebleed, loss of appetite, diarrhea, and numbness. All are side effects of cancer chemotherapy.

Excessive doses can lead to liver damage, convulsions, and harm to the nervous system, including psychosis, coma, and hallucinations. The chemicals also impair bone marrow function and suppress the immune system.

Ornamental: Tropical periwinkle is a beautiful ornamental garden plant. It can also be used for indoor bouquets and arrangements. It is suited for window boxes, beds, and borders and is attractive as a potted plant in a greenhouse or window garden.

CULTIVATION

The members of the *Catharanthus* genus, which are natives of Madagascar (with the exception of one species, *C. pusillus,* which is from India), now grows wild throughout the entire tropical world. It can be cultivated if granted hot summers and a very long growing season. It favors arid coastal plains but can be found up to 1,600 feet above sea level. Seed for *C. roseus,* the most useful species, usually comes from Japan. The plant is grown commercially for medicinal purposes in Africa, India, Australia, and Hungary.

In the United States, *C. roseus* is the only *Catharanthus* that is cultivated. It has become naturalized in parts of the South, where high temperatures are coupled with high humidity. It is extremely sensitive to frost.

Start tropical periwinkle from seed indoors in February, or take cuttings in the fall and keep them over the winter in a greenhouse or other warm, humid place. When the seedlings are 3 or 4 inches tall, pinch the tips to promote branching. Set them in the garden only when the soil is thoroughly warm, hardening them first in a sunny cold frame. Space them 10 to 12 inches apart.

In dry weather, water the plants frequently, making sure the soil is both constantly moist and well drained. Mist the plants, if possible. Soil fertility is not important. Keep tropical periwinkle bushy by occasionally cutting back or pruning. It tends to become scraggly after several years.

Tropical periwinkle is usually not bothered by pests or disease.

GROWING CONDITIONS

- Plant hardiness zone 10.
- Average, well-drained soil.
- Full sun to partial shade.

UVA-URSI

Arctostaphylos Uva-ursi   **Ericaceae**

Marco Polo discovered this herb's uses when in China, and Kublai Khan learned of it during his invasions. By the thirteenth century, European herbalists recognized uva-ursi as an important medicinal herb.

The tiny shrub's berries are said to appeal to bears, and it is even known in some quarters as bearberry. But the bright red berries—attractive to look at—are boring to the human tongue.

DESCRIPTION

A delicate, perennial ground cover, uva-ursi has short, dark stems, and long fibrous roots. (See photo on page 170.)

Flowers: White, tinged with red; ¼ in. long; in small clusters at ends of branches.

Leaves: Leathery, oblong, tapering to leafstalk; undivided; green on upper surface, pale and veined on underside; 1 in. long; on short leafstalks.

Fruit: Small, round, smooth, glossy red berries.

Height: 3 in.

FLOWERING

April and May.

RANGE

Throughout the northern hemisphere, particularly in dry, rocky areas.

USES

Uva-ursi is primarily a healing herb.

Medicinal: Uva-ursi's leaves and berries contain tannic and other acids and the glycoside arbutin, all of which give the herb its astringent and antiseptic properties. The plant's traditional uses make sense in light of its chemical makeup. The Chinese, Europeans, and American natives all considered it a kidney herb. They prescribed the leaves and fresh berries for treating kidney stones, bladder infections, incontinence, and similar ailments.

For a tea low in tannic acid, use cold water, not hot, and allow the leaves to steep for 12 to 24 hours. Drink too much, and you are in line for a stomachache; ongoing use may lead to poisoning.

Externally, the herb may be used to soothe sprains and swellings. American Indians rubbed wet leaves on sore muscles, or made a poultice from the crushed, boiled plant. Old-timers say washing with an infusion of the leaves keeps poison-ivy rash from spreading.

Ornamental: Arbutus is a more decorative ground cover, but uva-ursi comes into its own on rocky hillsides and sandy banks, where it resists erosion. Consider horticultural varieties specially bred for their bright berries or dense foliage.

Dye: Unmordanted wool can be dyed camel using the leaves of uva-ursi. The whole plant produces a green in wool mordanted with alum and iron.

CULTIVATION

With a bit of luck, you can transplant uva-ursi from the wild into the garden. Try layering by planting one of the plant's runners in a clay pot and leaving the runner attached to the mother plant until it has rooted. It is also possible to start new plants from green stem cuttings or seeds.

Uva-ursi needs little care aside from watering when dry. Occasionally pinch back young plants to encourage compact growth. Generally, it grows free of pests and diseases.

GROWING CONDITIONS

- Plant hardiness zone 2.
- Peaty, moist soil.
- Full sun to partial shade.

VALERIAN

Valeriana officinalis   **Valerianaceae**

The Pied Piper of Hamelin may have used more than music in luring the rats out of town. Legend suggests that he also employed valerian, an herb known to both intoxicate cats and attract rats. However he did it, in ridding the village of Hamelin of its rats, the Pied Piper certainly calmed its citizens.

And today the best-known use of valerian is as a natural tranquilizer. Valerian-based teas and drugs have a long history of safe and efficacious use, and in Europe, valerian-derived pharmaceuticals are widely available. Don't look for them in the United States, however.

HISTORY

Some botanists think that the spikenard referred to in the Bible as a perfume brought in from the East was actually a species of valerian. This species had to be quite unlike the valerian we know today, for our valerian, when dried, is distinctly unpleasant to smell. American herbalist Michael Moore says it is "the precise smell of dirty socks."

Cats don't agree, of course. They go crazy with the odor and will roll in your garden if you plant valerian there. Herb writer Jeanne Rose suggests you make a valerian-stuffed pillow for your feline friend.

Valerian has long been used as a stomachic, antispasmodic, carminative, and antidote to the plague. It has also been used since ancient times in the treatment of epilepsy. The British herbalists Gerard and Culpeper both recommended valerian for the latter condition. Combined with cinchona, valerian yielded a medicine to treat fevers.

The use of valerian that dominates all others, however, is that of a tranquilizer. Throughout history, such has been its use. It was listed in the *U.S. Pharmacopoeia* from 1820 to 1942 and in the *U.S. National Formulary* from 1942 to 1950. But after centuries of use throughout the world, valerian-based drugs are effectively not available in the United States. Current drug laws require proof of efficacy, and no drug company will invest the millions that such testing costs in a drug that cannot be protected by patent. "Plant" drugs cannot be so protected.

In contrast, more than 100 proprietary drugs based on valerian and its derivatives are marketed in West Germany. The evidence there suggests the drug is both safe and effective.

USES

Medicinal: A number of scientific studies have shown that active

DESCRIPTION

The valerian family contains about 200 species, one of which smells bad enough to be named Phu. *Valeriana officinalis* is an herbaceous perennial. The whole plant, with the exception of the flower, has a fetid smell. Its stem is erect, grooved, hollow, hairy, near the base, and sometimes branched above. It bears four to eight pairs of leaves. (See photo on page 272.)

Flowers: Small, tubular, five-lobed, pink-tinged, three stamens; in 4-in.-wide panicles that expand as they open.

Leaves: Dark green, opposite, simple, pinnately lobed, sometimes divided more than once; pairs, united at the base and at right angles to those above or below them on the stem; terminal leaflet, with 7–10 pairs of lateral toothed leaflets; upper leaves more pointed than lower; all hairy along veins on underside.

Fruit: Seedlike achenes.

Height: 3½–5 ft.

FLOWERING

June.

RANGE

Native to Europe and Asia.

HABITAT

Grasslands, damp meadowland, and stream sides, but also in high, dry places up to 6,600 ft.

VALERIAN—continued

ingredients of valerian, the valepotriates, do act as tranquilizers in small animals and in humans. They produce fewer side effects than diazepam, a tranquilizer much better known as Valium. And they can be taken with alcohol without the synergistic effects, including depression, which are usually associated with the simultaneous use of alcohol and tranquilizers. One recent study showed that valerian preparations could halve the time it took human subjects to fall asleep, but they also reduced the performance and mobility of the subjects.

Valerian may work by affecting the central nervous system; thus it is more a psychological drug than a physiological one.

In preparing a calming tea, only the fresh rootstock should be used, says contemporary herbalist John Lust. He recommends an infusion of 1 teaspoon of the root in 1 pint of water. It should be drunk cold, 1 cup during the course of a day or at bedtime. The tea is particularly bitter.

Toxicity: Valerian does have its negative side. Large doses may cause vomiting, stupor, and dizziness, and continued use may lead to depression.

Aromatic: Valerian has been used to perfume soap. Oil from the root is used to flavor tobacco and beverages.

Ornamental: Also known as garden heliotrope, valerian is an old-time favorite. You can buy cultivars of several colors, and its blooming period and appearance recommend the plant as an addition to flower beds and herb gardens. Routine care is minimal, but beds must be redug and thinned periodically. Once established, the plant can naturalize itself.

Cosmetic: A soothing herbal bath can be prepared using valerian. (See the entry Bathing with Herbs for more information.)

CULTIVATION

Valerian grows wild in North America and is regarded as an ornamental plant, but it is grown commercially in parts of Europe. It can be propagated by crown or runner division in the spring or fall, and daughter plants can be collected at the end of the summer. Set plants at least a foot apart. Give them rich soil and plenty of water and weed frequently. Seeds may also be sown in a cold frame in April and transplanted in May, but they germinate poorly. The whole planting should be dug and renewed by division every three years, or overcrowding will decrease its vitality.

Harvesting and storage: The roots are harvested in the fall or spring before the shoots come. Wash them, then dry quickly and thoroughly at 120°F until brittle. Store free of moisture. The roots keep their odor and flavor for a long time.

GROWING CONDITIONS

- Plant hardiness zone 4.
- Soil pH: tolerates a wide range of pH.
- Rich, moist, humusy soil.
- Full sun to partial shade.

VERVAIN

Verbena officinalis   **Verbenaceae**

Vervain is a very old companion of the human race.

Even the Egyptians considered it ancient, originating from the tears of the goddess Isis as she wept for the dead god Osiris. Vervain was sacred to the Romans; the Latin name of the genus comes from the classical name for "sacred boughs." It is associated with the crucifixion: Reportedly the herb was pressed on Christ's wounds to stop the bleeding. It was sacred, too, to the Persians and the Druids.

Vervain appeared in medieval medicine. The court physician to Theodosius I, for example, described how vervain cures tumors of the throat. Cut the root in two pieces, he said. Tie one around the patient's throat and hang the other over a fire. As the heat and smoke dry out one part of the root, the tumor will shrivel, too. To get rid of pimples the medieval way, stand outside with a handful of vervain in a handkerchief. When a shooting star is streaking by, rub the vervain over the pimple, and the blemish will disappear. Don't use your bare hands, or you'll simply transfer the pimple to your hands.

Vervain was still valued in the seventeenth century when London herbalist Nicholas Culpeper praised it. Among vervain's many virtues, Culpeper reported that "used with lard it helps pain in the secret parts."

USES

Medicinal: Vervain has been reported to have broad healing powers: astringent, antispasmodic, diaphoretic, emmenagogue, febrifuge, and on for dozens more. There does not seem to be any modern scientific evidence to support the claims, however.

Toxicity: Vervain is certainly not sacred to modern scientists. They report that a glycoside in vervain causes vomiting, even in moderate doses.

Cosmetic: A bath prepared from vervain is said to be quite soothing. (See the entry Bathing with Herbs for more information.)

CULTIVATION

Vervain grows very easily from seed, says Holly Shimizu, curator of the National Herb Garden in Washington, D.C. Though it seems rather short-lived, it reseeds itself readily.

Harvesting and storage: According to the Druids, who used a lot of vervain and were entitled to an opinion, the plant should be collected when neither the sun nor the moon is in the sky. And in exchange for removing such a valuable plant from the earth, honeycombs should be left on the ground.

DESCRIPTION

A spiky-looking plant, vervain should not be confused with blue vervain (*Verbena hastata*), although it probably will be since even botanists disagree about vervain identification.

Flowers: Tiny, purplish white; tubular with five spreading lobes; four stamens; in rings on tall spikes at top of plant.

Leaves: Opposite, oblong to lanceolate, deeply divided; upper leaves attached, lower on leafstalks.

Fruit: Nutlets.

Height: 1–3 ft.

FLOWERING

Throughout summer.

RANGE

Native to Europe; naturalized in North America.

GROWING CONDITIONS

• Rich, moist loam.

• Full sun.

VIOLET

Viola odorata   **Violaceae**

"Sweet violet, sweeter than all the roses."

In the seasonal soap opera of the garden, the violet plays the part of the ingenue. Its understated beauty, down-turned head, subtle, sorrowful color, fleeting fragrance, and general air of artless innocence make us ever fearful that the violet may be overlooked, and therefore we seldom overlook it. We can also use the violet in cooking and medicine, although there it goes in and out of favor, the more sentimental of ages prizing it most.

DESCRIPTION

The violet is a low-growing perennial herb. It grows from a short rootstock that sends out stolons. Sparsely covered with down, the stolons arise from rosette tufts of foliage. They substitute for stems and produce flowers in the second year. The stolons root at their tips to produce new plants.

Flowers: Fragrant, solitary, on stalks arising from leaf axils, with five sepals and five unequal petals; lower petal becomes a hollow spur containing spurred anthers; upper petals have hairy center lines; other anthers unite into a tube around the capsule; purple, violet, occasionally white or pink; slightly over ½ in. wide.

Leaves: Oval to kidney-shaped or heart-shaped, bluntly toothed with short leafstalks, downy; to 2½ in. wide.

Fruit: Spring flowers sterile in temperate areas. Fall flowers yield small capsules containing up to 60 seeds.

Height: 4–6 in.

FLOWERING

April and May.

RANGE

Native to Europe, Asia, and North Africa; naturalized throughout the temperate zone.

HABITAT

Damp places, wooded clearings, and limy soil.

HISTORY

Legends about the violet go back at least to the ancient Greeks. When the goddess Io was turned into a heifer by her lusty lover Zeus, in an attempt to protect her from the jealous Hera, Zeus gave her pastures of violets to eat. Violets also sprang where Orpheus slept. The flower was a symbol for Athens.

Modern legends are no less romantic. The posy was a love token between Napoléon Bonaparte and Josephine and later his political emblem.

The ancient writers Herodotus and Pliny wrote of the medicinal virtues of the violet, the latter prescribing it for gout and spleen disorders. In the seventeenth century, a violet conserve called "plate" was used in lozenges against bronchitis.

In Toulouse, France, during troubadour times, violets were given as a poetry prize, and in southern Germany in the Middle Ages, the finding of the first spring violet was celebrated with dancing.

USES

Medicinal: The leaves and flowers have antiseptic and expectorant properties, and one experiment carried out in 1960 showed that a violet extract damaged tumors on mice. Not enough scientific work has been done, however, for anyone to know how the constituents of the violet work. It is known that the plant contains myrosin and other glycosides and saponins. It serves as an emetic in quantity, and it has been used to treat respiratory disorders, as a gargle, in cough mixtures, and as a diuretic. The flower is healthful if only because it contains an abundance of vitamins A and C. An aspirinlike substance has also been obtained from the plant.

In China, violets are burned under abscesses to cure them and are used in poultices.

Toxicity: It appears that something in the violet irritates the mucous membrane, causing catharsis and expectorant action. Eating the seeds may cause vomiting. Otherwise, the plant is not toxic. The flowers are used to color medications.

Culinary: Violet flowers and leaves are softly fragrant and are used as garnishes in chilled soups and punches. The petals are often candied and used to garnish cakes, pastries, and poached fruit.

Violets add verve to jams, jellies, liqueurs, puddings, flans, gelatins, fruit salads, and green salads. Violet water, made by weighting and steeping leaves and petals in water until fragrant, is used in tea breads, cupcakes, puddings, ices, fruit compotes, and chilled soups.

Available commercially: Candied violets or violet water.

Aromatic: The flower used to be widely used in the perfume industry, but it has largely been replaced by synthetics. It is still highly prized for perfume of the highest quality. Violets are used in potpourris and in nosegays, although the odor is not long lasting. An interesting, if unproven, theory is that the flower affects the sense of smell, so that unpleasant odors smell less strong after violets have been smelled. This is what made the flowers useful as strewing herbs and nosegays.

Ornamental: The violet is humble and inconspicuous, but it's a welcome addition to the ornamental bed or herb or rock garden.

Violaceae is a family composed of pansies, garden violas, and violets; nothing more. One would think the internal classification would be easy, but, instead, it is quite complex, and for the most unexpected of reasons: Our ingenue of the garden is quite promiscuous. One expert estimates that there are more hybrid varieties of violet than there are pure ones. The ancestor violet, *Viola odorata,* has been cultivated in its original form for 2,000 years.

CULTIVATION

Propagate from division or runner in late winter to early spring, setting 1 foot apart. Some species will grow from seed sown in outdoor boxes in autumn and covered with burlap. The seed must freeze to be viable. Mulch the plants with leaf mold in the winter.

In transplanting a violet plant from the wild, try to match the original environment. Keep the plant moist if it originally grew near water, and in shade if it is used to that. Violets self-sow readily and also spread by runner. They may need to be thinned, and runners should be cut off to allow the crowns to flourish.

Pests and diseases: Violets are susceptible to red spider mites. (See the entry Growing Herbs for information on controlling pests.)

Harvesting and storage: The flowers are occasionally dried for culinary or medicinal use. They lose their odor quickly and will also lose their color if not dried slowly and well. Store out of light. The blue coloring matter turns green in water storage.

GROWING CONDITIONS

- Plant hardiness zones 5–8.
- Soil pH: acid to neutral.
- Rich, moist, humusy soil.
- Partial shade.

VIRGINIA SNAKEROOT

Aristolochia Serpentaria   **Aristolochiaceae**

The Virginia snakeroot has some of the funniest-looking, or most interesting, flowers in the herb garden. It's easy to see how our ancestors recognized its relationship to other members of the birth-wort family. It immediately acquired virtue by association.

UNSAFE

DESCRIPTION

This plant grows some-what upside down with the flowers appearing at the bottom on the stems. In a vague, flowery way, the blossom looks like a snake opening its mouth to strike.

The rest of the plant is anticlimatic after the flowers. The stems are sparse in foliage. It's a perennial herb.

Flowers: Plump, brownish purple; no petals, S-shaped tube formed from calyx that flares open at the base; ½ in. long; each blossom borne on separate 1–2-in. stalk.

Leaves: Heart-shaped and pointed, 1½–4½ in. long.

Fruit: Angled capsules.

Height: 2 ft.

FLOWERING

Early summer.

RANGE

South from the mid-Atlantic states and southern Illinois.

HABITAT

Woodlands with moist, rich soil.

HISTORY

"Best birthing" was the name given to the genus of plants containing the Virginia snakeroot and its odd-flowered relatives (from the Greek *Aristos,* which means "best," plus *locchia,* which means "delivery"). It may have been an application of the Doctrine of Signatures, which indicated that all plants were marked in code, indicating their benefit to the human race. To apply the doctrine to the *Aristolochias,* you would have had to have been pregnant in an era when death in childbirth was common and anything hinting at comfort was welcome. But the flowers of this group of plants do look (perhaps somewhat) like a pregnant uterus with the birth canal opening up below it.

Centuries before the Virginia snakeroot was discovered by Europeans, the connection between the genus and childbirth had been firmly established. The earliest complete herbal in Western medicine describes a birthwort as useful in childbirth. The author was the Greek physician Dioscorides, who lived in the first century A.D.

The other theme that runs through the history of the *Aristolochias* is its ability to cure snakebite. It has been reported that Egyptian snake handlers partially anesthetized the animals with some species closely related to *Aristolochia* before doing daring tricks. In Europe, the tradition was old. One herbal includes a wood-cut of a snake cringing back in terror as a man holds out an *Aristolochia.*

The Virginia snakeroot entered Western medicine with the exploration of North America. The Indians were supposed to have used the Virginia snakeroot as an antivenom, and Europeans quickly adopted it. It was "the much-admired snakeweed of Virginia" when it was included in Thomas Johnson's 1633 revision and expansion of John Gerard's sixteenth-century state-of-the-art herbal. It was a long tradition that seems to be coming to an end in our day. Now Virginia snakeroot seems most widely recommended for those who want an authentic air for reconstructed colonial herb gardens.

USES

Medicinal: Unless you have years of experience with this herb, stay away from it. In fact, some herbalists suggest staying away from it, period. The wrong dose can cause vomiting, intense bowel pain,

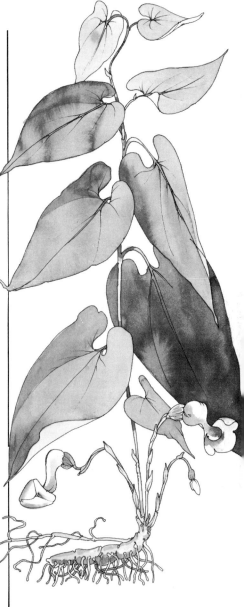

dizziness, and death by respiratory paralysis.

In the interests of preserving herbal lore, the Virginia snakeroot's traditional uses are discussed here. But this does not constitute an invitation to be reckless.

The dried rhizome (underground part of the stem) and roots, known as serpentaria, were listed in the *U.S. Pharmacopoeia* from 1820 to 1942. This material contained 0.5 to 2 percent volatile oil, of which borneol was the important part, as was a bitter substance called aristolochin and an alkaloid called aristolochine.

Much of the plant's reputation came from its alleged ability to treat snakebite. This property expanded into protection from all sorts of poisons, including the bites of mad dogs. Now herbalists hesitate in this recommendation. British herbalist Maude Grieve put it delicately in *A Modern Herbal:* "... though there is much direct testimony, the claim is not considered to be authoritatively proved."

It has also been used to treat malaria, to stimulate the appetite, to increase perspiration, and to cure a host of other maladies.

Ornamental: In the search for that Early American look or for landscapes of native plants, the Virginia snakeroot may find a place. It will have to overcome centuries of prejudice. It belongs "only in the gardens of the Curious" for it "is of no great Beauty," sniffed the *Useful Family Herbal* in 1754. Even the great twentieth-century horticulturist Liberty Hyde Bailey dismissed the plant as "occasionally cultivated." He was hardly a fan of the birthwort genus with their "irregular and grotesque flowers ... usually fetid in odor, often very disagreeable."

But Holly Shimizu, curator of the National Herb Garden in Washington, D.C., admires the plant, despite its somewhat hesitant growth: "... beautiful S-shaped flower, beautiful leaves ... lovely plant."

CULTIVATION

According to Shimizu, Virginia snakeroot is slow to establish itself, but eventually it grows well, and without pest problems. Shimizu suggests starting a plant from root divisions. She planted hers in average garden soil, although she noticed improved growth after enriching the soil. Her plant is thriving in full sun, although she says Virginia snakeroot would also grow in shade. She supported the plant with a trellis, but it's not racing up the supports and creating a bushy arbor. It dies back every winter.

Harvesting and storage: Dig the roots in the fall, trimming off the aboveground stem. (No more than 10 percent of the stem was allowed when the plant was sold as a drug.) Dry the roots and store them in a tightly closed container.

GROWING CONDITIONS

- Plant hardiness zone 5.
- Moist, fertile, well-drained soil.
- Full sun to partial shade.

501

WAHOO

UNSAFE

Euonymus atropurpurea   **Celastraceae**

Christened "wahoo" by American Indians, this plant was long used internally as a physic and also on facial sores. But wahoo is extremely toxic and has fallen from favor as a medicinal plant.

The *Euonymus* genus takes its name from the Greek goddess Euonyme, the mother of the Furies; the connection apparently is that the shrub has irritating properties. Wahoo was frequently called skewerwood, prickwood, or spindle tree because the hard wood was used to make toothpicks, spindles, and skewers. Pipe stems were once whittled from it, and shoots were converted into an excellent, easily erased charcoal for artists.

DESCRIPTION

Wahoo is a deciduous shrub or tree.

Flowers: Small, dark purple; clustered in loose cymes; sepals and petals in fours.

Leaves: Opposite, elliptical and pointed, finely toothed; hairy underneath; 2 to 5 in. long; on short stalks; turn pale yellow in fall.

Fruit: Smooth capsules; pink to scarlet; deeply lobed; over 1/2 in. across; contain brown, scarlet-coated seeds.

Height: To 25 ft.

RANGE

Native from New York to Florida and Texas; naturalized as far west as Montana.

HABITAT

Near streams, in ravines and damp glades, and in the woods. It is not particular about soil or location, but it will not do well in the extreme North.

USES

Medicinal: All parts of the plant have been used sporadically in folk medicine. The seed oil was employed as an emetic and purgative. The fruits were said to be diuretic. The dried root bark was used as a stimulant and a laxative and in the treatment of dropsy.

The American Indians used a bark decoction for uterine troubles and eye ailments, a poultice for facial sores, and an infusion as a physic.

A 1917 report claimed the plant affected the heart much like digitalis, and its popularity as a heart medicine jumped. But only four years later, wahoo was dropped as an official drug plant, although it remained in the *U.S. National Formulary* until 1947.

Toxicity: The bark, leaves, and fruit are all dangerously emetic and purgative. The bright-colored berries may attract children, and eating as few as three or four can prove fatal. Wahoo appears on the Food and Drug Administration's unsafe herb list. This plant is emphatically not recommended for home medicinal use.

Ornamental: Plants of the *Euonymus* genus in general are attractive as border shrubs, hedgerows, espaliers, screens, foundation plantings, and single subjects. Their red berries draw more attention than their small flowers. Wahoo itself is usually dismissed as a poor representative of the genus's ornamental qualities.

CULTIVATION

Since wahoo has no specific soil requirements and is adaptable to most any location, it is very easy to grow. It can be propagated by seeds sown in the spring. New shrubs are also easily started in the fall by placing a 3-inch branch tip into a fine, sandy loam. The roots of the new plantings must be kept damp, and the top should be sprayed regularly.

GROWING CONDITIONS

- Plant hardiness zone 5.
- Any gardening soil.
- Full sun to partial shade.

WILLOW

Salix spp.   **Salicaceae**

The willows are one of the big success stories of herbal medicine. They are fever fighters and painkillers without question. But more than that, the willows are rich in lore and in practicality, serving mankind in the landscape and the home shop.

HISTORY

Throughout history, people have appreciated the graceful form of the willow in the landscape. During his exile on Saint Helena, Napoléon's favorite spot was beneath the boughs of a weeping willow. The first weeping willows in America were grown by an Anglican clergyman, Samuel Johnson, from cuttings taken from a tree growing beside the house in Twickenham, England, once occupied by the great British poet Alexander Pope. From Johnson's plantings along the Housatonic River in Connecticut, the willows spread far and wide. George Washington planted them at Mt. Vernon, and James Madison at his home, Montpelier.

Dioscorides, that herbal genius of the first century A.D., may have been one of the first to recognize the ultimate healing virtue of the willow. He prescribed willow preparations for pain and inflammation. These prescriptions were dutifully passed from herbalist to herbalist for centuries, as were all of Dioscorides' prescriptions.

In another place, at another time, the Hottentots, who certainly hadn't read Dioscorides, used willow preparations to treat rheumatic fever. Likewise, the American Indians discovered similar uses for the willow, which they passed along to the white settlers.

Perhaps the most interesting bit of willow lore is the story of its relationship to aspirin, today's commonplace, everyday fever fighter and painkiller.

Around the time that Johnson was planting America's first weeping willows, Europeans were searching for an economical substitute for quinine, the fabulous South American, malarial-fighting bark. More than a few herb-oriented doctors felt that willow was that substitute.

One of the willow's active principles is salicin. It is a principle the willow shares with a number of other plants, and it was from one of those other plants—queen of the meadow (now *Filipendula Ulmaria* but at the time a part of the *Spiraea* genus)—that salicin was first isolated in the 1820s. The name given to the substance once it had been isolated, however, came from the willow's genus name, *Salix*. For another 30 years, European chemists fiddled with salicin: An Italian produced salicylic acid from it, and a German took that and synthesized acetylsalicylic acid.

DESCRIPTION

There are about 500 willows, from tall trees to arctic plants barely 2 inches high. Several species are used medicinally.

Flowers: Tiny, petal-less; in dense cylindrical catkins.

Leaves: Alternate, undivided, narrow, lanceolate.

Fruit: Small capsules; downy seeds.

Height: Depends on species: *Salix alba* to 75 ft.; *S. nigra* to 35 ft.

FLOWERING

Midspring.

RANGE

Temperate regions of the Northern hemisphere.

503

EVOLUTION
AND THE WILLOW

Willow flowers, those fuzzy, yellowish catkins, illustrate a stage in evolution.

They show that willows are evolving from being insect-pollinated to being wind-pollinated. Petals, which serve no purpose on a plant that doesn't need the services of pollinating creatures, interfere with breezes; they don't exist on a willow flower. The male parts of the flowers, the stamens, are bunched together in a tight catkin, exposed to the wind. The female flowers also are grouped together in catkins, free from petals and exposed to the pollen-bearing wind.

That the willows aren't fully free of insect help in pollination is attested to by the fact that the female flowers still produce nectar to attract insects.

WILLOW—continued

It was then put on the shelf and forgotten until the late 1890s, when Felix Hoffman, a chemist at Fredrich Bayer & Company in Germany, embarked on a search for a drug to alleviate his father's rheumatoid arthritis. He came upon information about this acetylsalicylic acid, prepared some, his father loved it . . . but his superiors at Bayer hated it. Of course, the Bayer executives later relented and, after contriving the name aspirin from *Spiraea*—who would buy a drug with the tongue-twisting name acetylsalicylic acid?—put it on the market.

USES

Today, Americans take aspirin far more readily than their ancestors could down a tea of willow bark. But they love the willow in the landscape as much as Washington and Madison did.

Medicinal: Willow bark is used by herbalists as an anodyne, antipyretic, astringent, detergent, tonic, antiperiodic, and antiseptic. It is useful for headache, neuralgia, hay fever, fever, and pain and inflammation of joints (just like aspirin).

In *Weiner's Herbal,* herbalist Michael Weiner recommended a decoction of 1 teaspoon of white willow bark slowly boiled in 1½ pints of water in a covered container for 30 minutes. After slowly cooling, it should be drunk a mouthful or tablespoonful at a time, "as needed to promote sweating in chills and fever."

Ornamental: The willows are highly valued as ornamentals. The graceful form, lovely foliage, and on some varieties, decorative silvery catkins or "pussies" make them an important feature of the garden design. A weeping willow, drooping near a pool, makes an artistic setting.

But willows have practical contributions to make in the landscape. As lovers of wet ground, they have been used to good effect in marshy areas and to hold stream banks.

Cosmetic: Decoctions of white willow bark are used in facial lotions and in herbal baths for their astringent properties. (See the entries Lotions from Herbs and Bathing with Herbs for information on preparing herbal lotions and baths.)

Other: Willow wood has a variety of uses. Though not easily worked, it is quite resilient and has been used to make tool handles and fencing. The American Indians used it for poles for teepees. Today, it is a staple in the making of artificial limbs.

Basketmakers prize the pliant young willow shoots. They have given rise to a whole genre of baskets.

CULTIVATION

Willow trees can be started by unconventional techniques. In fact, a willow once was propagated by tossing a willow basket into a pit in the yard of a house in Philadelphia. Eventually someone noticed that the basket was growing into a tree.

You can root leafless, several-foot-long branches of first-year wood in moist soil. And 9- to 12-inch hardwood cuttings, taken in the spring or fall, will root if left in water. Even leafy summer cuttings will root.

The trees, however, are difficult to transplant. Prune them back considerably at planting time, and brace yourself; the tree will recover slowly.

Willows are associated with soggy soil and indeed thrive in it. However, they grow in almost any soil that is not extremely dry. Once established, they grow fast and must be pruned to keep their good looks. The shrubby species can be seriously chopped back; they may look pathetic for several months but will burst forth into even bushier growth.

Pests and diseases: Willows are very susceptible to damage from insects. Particularly troublesome pests include imported willow leaf beetles, willow flea weevils, gypsy moths, fall webworms, aphids, and scale. Willows are also susceptible to fungal diseases, willow blight, and willow scab. (See the entry Growing Herbs for information on controlling pests and diseases.)

GROWING CONDITIONS

- Any moist gardening soil.
- Full sun.

Flowers   *Fruit*

505

WINTERGREEN

Gaultheria procumbens   Ericaceae

Anyone who has ever sought relief from a muscle ache and reached for the Ben-Gay has experienced the soothing qualities of wintergreen's active constituent. Even more familiar is the refreshing minty taste of oil of wintergreen, a popular flavoring for gum, candy, toothpaste, and birch beer.

Penobscot, Sioux, Nez Percé, and other Indian tribes used a tea made from the leaves for a variety of ailments, as did the early settlers. Crushed into a poultice, the leaves were an important Indian remedy for aching, arthritic, or overexerted muscles and joints. Poultices also relieved swellings, wounds, rashes, inflammations—even toothaches. Internally, wintergreen tea was taken to relieve fever, gonorrhea symptoms, sore throats, upset stomachs, and ulcers.

During the American Revolution, the colonists often substituted wintergreen for the heavily taxed imported tea. Although the familiar wintergreen flavor is now produced synthetically, it was once the reason for gathering, drying, and shipping large bales of the plants to distilleries where the volatile oil was extracted.

DESCRIPTION

This low, glossy-leaved, woody perennial forms an attractive ground cover in acid woods from Canada to Georgia. It is especially striking in the fall, when the plants are dotted with festive red, edible berries.

Flowers: Solitary, nodding, white, ¼ in. long; five petals fused together, except at tips, forming a bell- or urn-shaped flower.

Leaves: Evergreen, leathery, shiny on top and paler beneath; elliptical to obovate; to 2 in. long.

Fruit: Round, red berrylike capsule, ¼ in. in diameter; appears late summer through early winter.

Height: 4 in., creeping.

FLOWERING

July.

RANGE

Native to North America; common east of the Mississippi from Canada south to Georgia.

HABITAT

In wooded areas and clearings.

USES

Medicinal: Wintergreen's active constituent is methyl salicylate. It is found in both the leaves and the berries. A cloth soaked in oil of wintergreen can relieve body aches and pains, but the pure oil can irritate the skin and should be used cautiously. Do not take the oil internally, as it may cause inflammation of the stomach lining. To make a tea, add 1 teaspoon of chopped fresh leaves to 1 cup of boiling water, and steep for 5 to 20 minutes.

Culinary: Nibble on the shiny leaves for a natural chewing gum—but only for half a minute or so because the sweet, aromatic taste soon turns bitter. In some parts of the country, a wintergreen-flavored teaberry ice cream is available, and teaberry gum has been popular for decades.

Cosmetic: Because of the methyl salicylate in wintergreen, a decoction can help heal external skin problems, provided you are not allergic to the herb. Use it in lotions or baths. (See the entries Lotions from Herbs and Bathing with Herbs for more information.)

GROWING CONDITIONS

- Plant hardiness zone 4.
- Soil pH 5.0–6.0.
- Moist, humusy, peaty, or sandy soil.
- Partial shade.

CULTIVATION

The propagation of wintergreen can be accomplished by suckers, layering, division, cuttings, or seed. It grows well in an acidic soil in a partially shaded location. Mulch the plants with pine needles.

Harvesting and storage: Harvest the leaves anytime. Pick the fruit as soon as it turns bright scarlet. Use either plant part as soon as possible because the volatile oil dissipates quickly.

WITCH HAZEL

Hamamelis virginiana   Hamamelidaceae

Does it work, or doesn't it? Millions of gallons of distilled witch-hazel extract are sold yearly as a health and beauty aid, yet few authorities assign it any therapeutic value beyond mild astringency.

A tea steeped from the leaves and bark has long been employed for ulcers and hemorrhoids. The Indians drank the tea as a general tonic and used it as a rinse for mouth and throat irritations. They also found relief from feverish colds, coughing, and heavy phlegm in witch-hazel steam baths. Witch-hazel compresses were used to treat headaches, inflamed eyes, skin irritations, insect bites, burns, and infections. An extract was applied to strained muscles and arthritic joints.

Witch hazel's spooky name, by the way, has nothing to do with witches. The name instead derives from the Old English word for "pliant," and in fact the limber branches were used as archery bows.

USES

Medicinal: The leaves, twigs, and bark all contain tannic acid, gallic acid, and volatile oils. The *U.S. Dispensatory* lists the liquid or dry extract of witch-hazel leaves as a treatment for hemorrhoids, suggesting that the tannin is the formulation's active principle.

Cosmetic: The distillation process used to prepare the familiar "witch-hazel water" removes the astringent tannins, leaving only the volatile oil. The dispensatory comments that "exactly how it functions and to what degree are not clearly established."

Nevertheless, this witch-hazel product is sold in great quantity for external use, as an astringent skin cleanser, body lotion, aftershave, massage liquid for body and scalp, and an aid in setting hair. The extract is also used for insect bites and sunburn.

CULTIVATION

Witch hazel is striking in the winter landscape, especially in the North, where it is the only hardy winter-blooming shrub. *Hamamelis virginiana* flowers in October and November; the vernal witch hazel (*H. vernalis*) may display its blossoms as early as January or February, even in New England. Witch hazels grow best in partial shade, in moist, peaty, or sandy soil. Seeds should be stratified: Give them warmth for the first five months, then expose them to a temperature of 40° F for three more months. Then they should germinate. Seed is available from nurseries. Witch hazel may also be propagated by cuttings or layering.

DESCRIPTION

These are deciduous shrubs or small trees, with twisting stems, long, forking branches, and smooth, gray to brown bark.

Flowers: Four bright yellow, threadlike petals, ½–¾ in. long; calyx dull yellow on inner side.

Leaves: Obovate or elliptical with rounded to heart-shaped bases; coarsely toothed; hairy on undersides; 3–6 in. long; five to seven pairs of veins; turn bright yellow in fall.

Fruit: Urnlike, woody seed capsule; matures the following fall; forcefully ejects two hard, black seeds as far as 20 ft.

Height: 8–15 ft.

FLOWERING

September and October.

RANGE

Indigenous throughout most of North America except the far West, especially from the Maritimes and Quebec south to Florida and west to Minnesota and Texas.

HABITAT

Grows in moist, light woods and along rocky streams.

GROWING CONDITIONS

- Plant hardiness zone 5.
- Soil pH: neutral to acid.
- Moist, rich soil.
- Full sun to partial shade.

WOAD

Isatis tinctoria   **Cruciferae**

Blue-skinned warriors once fought in the British Isles. They used a blue paste prepared from fermented woad leaves as both a styptic for wounds and a war paint. Their use is just one of many woad has had. Grown as a dyestuff for nearly 2,000 years, it was replaced by chemicals only in this century. Its medicinal use has waned also, for its toxicity makes it unsuitable in home remedies.

DESCRIPTION

Woad is a biennial that puts out large bluish green leaves the first year and 3-ft. flower stalks the next year.

Flowers: Yellow, ¼ in. wide; in terminal panicles.

Leaves: Oblong to lanceolate, entire or toothed, bluish green; to 4 in. long; attached to stem; smaller at top of stem.

Fruit: Black seedpods, ½–1 in. long.

Height: 3–5 ft.

FLOWERING

May.

RANGE

Native to central Europe and the Mediterranean region to central Asia; naturalized in parts of Britain, northern Europe, and North America.

HISTORY

Woad was the principal blue dye in Europe until indigo was imported from the Far East. As a healing herb, woad was known to the ancient Greeks and Romans, and it was used as a skin colorant in battles and in religious ceremonies in Britain. Commercial cultivation of woad came to an end with World War II.

USES

Most gardeners prefer just to look at the herb, rather than put it to a practical use, although home dyers still color wool with woad.

Medicinal: The herb is too poisonous to be used internally, but it once was applied externally as an astringent. A poultice of leaves was placed on an open wound to stop bleeding.

Ornamental: Woad puts forth profuse yellow blossoms and is attractive enough to be grown in the perennial flower bed or the natural landscape.

Dye: Traditionally, woad is used to dye yarns and fabrics blue, but pinks can be obtained from the young leaves when an alum mordant is used. Extracting dye from woad is a complicated process. However, if you enjoy creating herbal dyes and are interested in the challenge, instructions on using woad can be found in any good book on natural dyes (see the Bibliography).

CULTIVATION

Start woad from seed in the spring or late summer. Germination takes about 10 days. The following spring, thin the seedlings to about 8 inches apart. Once established, the plants will self-sow freely each year.

Pest and diseases: Like other members of the mustard family, woad is susceptible to club root, cabbage maggot, and other maladies. Plant the herb well away from related crops, and you'll have fewer pest problems. (See the entry Growing Herbs for information on controlling pests and diseases.)

Harvesting and storage: To make dye, the leaves are gathered in the second season, just before the plant blossoms.

GROWING CONDITIONS

- Plant hardiness zone 5.
- Rich, well-drained loam.
- Full sun.

WORMWOOD

Artemisia Absinthium   **Compositae**

Of all the artemisias—there are about 400 of them—wormwood is one of the very best known. It has long been recognized for the task its name implies, but it may be best known as the active ingredient in the alcoholic drink absinthe. If you want to see what that beverage did to people, you need look no farther than the nearest reproduction of Edgar Degas's painting *The Absinthe Drinkers.*

HISTORY

The earliest known description of wormwood is found on an Egyptian papyrus from 1600 B.C. Even then it was used to rid the body of worms.

According to legend, wormwood grew up in the trail left by the serpent's tail as it slithered out of the Garden of Eden. Wormwood is one of the bitter herbs of the Bible.

Mexican women, according to Maude Grieve's *A Modern Herbal,* used to wear wormwood garlands on their heads when they celebrated the festival of the goddess of salt with dancing. The bitter herb has long been used as an insect repellent. Wormwood was once used as a strewing herb. The Germans made a wine with it, and it continues to be used as a flavoring agent in liqueurs.

A whole history could be written about the rise and fall of absinthe as an addicting and deteriorating drink that led to serious mental disturbance, to seizures, and sometimes to death. Absinthe was made using the leaves and flowering tops of wormwood, together with many other aromatic plants. The result was a green-colored liqueur, described—while it was still legal—as "one of the favorite drinks for those who love stimulating beverages."

Among the lovers of stimulating beverages was impressionist painter Vincent van Gogh. Allegedly, van Gogh was whacked out on absinthe when he cut off his ear to send to a lady friend.

In his book *American Medicinal Plants,* published in 1892, Charles Millspaugh reported that "the effects prominent in absinthe drinkers are: Derangement of the digestive organs, intense thirst, restlessness, vertigo, tingling in the ears, and illusions of sight and hearing. These are followed by tremblings in the arms, hands, and legs, numbness of the extremities, loss of muscular power, delirium, loss of intellect, general paralysis, and death." He added that "peculiar epileptic attacks," which came to be called "absinthe epilepsy," resulted.

It is no wonder then that absinthe is illegal in most countries of the world, including the United States and Canada. France, which was the leading producer of absinthe, was also one of the last coun-

UNSAFE

DESCRIPTION

By late autumn, wormwood is at the height of its glory in appearance. A hardy perennial, it is unharmed by frost. It is spreading in habit. (See photos on pages 31 and 33.)

Flowers: On an erect panicle; small, round, greenish yellow in floret form.

Leaves: Round-to-oval, long stalked, 1½–4 in. long, deeply divided pinnately into blunt, fingerlike segments, smaller and less divided higher on the stalk, gray-green in color; covered with fine silky hairs; distinct acid odor.

Fruit: Simple seeds.

Height: To 2½ ft.

FLOWERING

July and August.

RANGE

Native to the Mediterranean region; naturalized throughout the temperate world; widely cultivated.

WORMWOOD—continued

tries to ban it, that in 1915. Wormwood, however, is still used to flavor alcoholic beverages, including vermouth and Campari.

USES

Wormwood, with rue the most bitter of all herbs, has never been used much in cooking for obvious reasons, but it is useful in many other ways.

Medicinal: For centuries wormwood has been used as a worming medicine for men and animals. In the 1950 edition of *The Standard Cyclopedia of Horticulture,* botanist Liberty Hyde Bailey noted, "Wormwood tea is an odorous memory with every person who was reared in the country."

It was also used as an antiseptic, antispasmodic, carminative, sedative, stomachic, tonic, and stimulant. It has been given to those suffering from poor circulation, rheumatism, fever, colds, and jaundice, and to women in labor.

The active principle of wormwood is thujone, which in large amounts is a convulsant poison and narcotic. Citing striking similarities between thujone and THC (tetrahydrocannabinol), the active principle of marijuana, scientists have speculated that thujone produces its mind-altering effects by "reacting with the same receptor sites in the brain as those which interact with THC." Pharmacognosist Varro Tyler, Ph.D., writing in *The Honest Herbal,* concluded, "The theory requires experimental verification, but it does explain why absinthe, even when consumed in relatively small amounts, could cause such profound mental and physical changes in habitual or even casual users."

Tyler does not "endorse" the use of wormwood, and most herbalists stress that caution is necessary in its use. Michael Weiner, noted in *Weiner's Herbal,* however, that "thujone has a very low water-solubility; thus it would be difficult to experience the adverse effects of absinthe when the plant is used in the form of a normally brewed herbal tea."

External uses seem less problematic. Compresses soaked in wormwood tea are recommended for irritations, bruises, and sprains. According to herbalist John Lust, "The oil acts as a local anesthetic when applied to relieve pains of rheumatism, neuralgia, and arthritis." Used in this way, the oil exerts antifungal and antibacterial activity. It may, however, cause dermatitis in some people. It is used in some antiseptic lotions, including Absorbine, Jr.

Toxicity: The essential oil of wormwood is especially dangerous.

(continued on page 515)

Tricolor Sage

Lavender Cotton

English Lavender

Spearmint

512

Borage

Corsican Rue

Foxglove

Costmary

513

Sage

Red Emperor Sage

Golden Sage

514

WORMWOOD—continued

Almost a century ago, Millspaugh reported: "A druggist's clerk took about half an ounce of the oil; he was found on the floor perfectly insensible, convulsed, and foaming at the mouth; shortly afterward the convulsions ceased, the patient remained insensible with the jaws locked, pupils dilated, pulse weak, and stomach retching. After causing free emesis and applying stimulants, the man recovered, but could not remember how or when he had taken the drug."

This account is often cited, as are the sad history of absinthe and the dangerous effects of thujone, in warning against the use of wormwood.

Aromatic: Wormwood is recognized as an effective insect repellent. It is used in sachets to keep moths away and is planted in gardens to discourage pests such as black flea beetles, cabbageworm butterfly, and slugs. Tea made of it will repel aphids.

In making a sachet with it, you can add mint, tansy, thyme, cinnamon sticks, and cloves to improve the effectiveness and the odor.

Ornamental: The attractive green-gray foliage makes wormwood a good bedding shrub, foundation plant, and addition to the herb garden.

Branches can be used in winter bouquets, dried or fresh.

CULTIVATION

Wormwood can be grown in any garden, even in one with poor soil. Routine care can be limited to weeding thoroughly and adding compost occasionally.

Seed is small but easy to germinate. It can be sown in the garden in the fall or started in flats in late winter. When transplanting, it can be set 15 inches apart the first year, then thinned to 30 inches apart in later years to allow for spreading. Wormwood can also be propagated from ripened cuttings taken in March or October or by plant division in the fall.

Wormwood is not a good companion in the garden, however. It contains large amounts of absinthin, a substance toxic to other plants. Absinthin is water-soluble and will wash off the leaves and into the soil. There it will inhibit the growth of nearby plants.

Harvesting and storage: Gather the top parts of stalks only when in flower after July. Discard damaged leaves. Pick on a dry day, and dry hanging in bundles in a shady place at around 70°F. Pack in airtight containers. Plantings will last seven years, but their production will peak in the second or third year. In these years, the plant can be harvested twice.

AN OLD LOVE CHARM

On St. Luke's Day, take marigold flowers, a sprig of marjoram, thyme, and a little *Wormwood;* dry them before a fire, rub them to powder; then sift it through a fine piece of lawn, and simmer it over a slow fire, adding a small quantity of virgin honey, and vinegar. Anoint yourself with this when you go to bed, saying the following lines three times, and you will dream of your partner "that is to be":

"St. Luke, St. Luke, be kind to me,
In dreams let me my true-love see."

Mrs. M. Grieve
A Modern Herbal

GROWING CONDITIONS

- Plant hardiness zone 4.
- Soil pH 6.6.
- Well-drained clay loam.
- Full sun to partial shade.

YARROW

Achillea Millefolium   **Compositae**

Yarrow is a European native that has taken famously to the United States. It grows nearly everywhere as a weed. Distinctive in both aroma and appearance, it is popular in perennial flower beds.

DESCRIPTION

Yarrow is an erect perennial herb with lovely fernlike foliage. It is covered with silky or wooly hairs. (See photos on pages 169 and 377.)

Flowers: Numerous white flower heads composed of disk florets surrounded by five ray florets; resemble miniature daisies; flower heads borne on broad, terminal, flat-topped clusters.

Leaves: Fernlike; pinnately divided into many tiny, fine leaflets; up to 6 in. long, 1 in. wide; upper leaves stalkless, lower leaves stalked.

Fruit: Achenes.

Height: 3 ft.

FLOWERING

June through September.

RANGE

Native to Europe; naturalized in North America.

HABITAT

Roadsides, waste places, and fields.

HISTORY

Thanks to modern, high-tech archaeology, fossils of yarrow pollen have been identified in Neanderthal burial caves, suggesting that its association with the human race is some 60,000 years old.

Yarrow is an old herb, regardless. The most authentic way of casting the I Ching, an ancient Chinese method of answering questions about the future, involves 50 dried yarrow stalks. And yarrow figured in the Trojan war some 3,000 years ago, when Achilles packed it on his comrades' wounds to stop the bleeding. Some botanists say yarrow's scientific generic name, *Achillea,* came from this story. But others attribute the name to the discoverer of the plant, who also happened to be named Achilles.

Whether or not yarrow was in the field hospitals at Troy, the plant developed a reputation for wound healing and was part of the battle paraphernalia right up through the American Civil War. The Chinese used a relative, *A. sibirica,* to treat bleeding and inflammation. Among native American Indians, the Blackfoot, Illinois, Miami, Micmac, and Ute applied yarrow to injuries and sores. Yarrow was an important plant in native American medicine. At least 46 tribes used yarrow, and they found 28 ailments that responded to the herb.

A list of yarrow's admirers reads like Who's Who of herbal medicine through the ages. In the first century A.D., the Greek physician Dioscorides smeared yarrow on ulcers to prevent inflammation. In the 1500s, the British herbalist John Gerard recommended yarrow for relieving "swelling of those secret parts" and told about an anonymous friend of his, who may have been embarrassed to have all of Europe reading the story, who "lightly bruised the leaves of common yarrow with Hog's grease, and applied it warm unto the privie parts, and thereby did divers times help himself and others of his fellows, when he was a student and a single man living in Cambridge." Nicholas Culpeper, the seventeenth-century British herbalist, recommended yarrow for wounds. A British shopkeeper named Abraham How wrote that he combined yarrow with brandy and gunpowder, plus comfrey or borage, for back pain.

The Shakers knew yarrow and included it in treatments for a variety of complaints from hemorrhages to flatulence. The herb was prescribed commonly enough to be included in the *U.S. Pharmacopoeia* from 1836 to 1882. As of 1982, yarrow still appeared in the pharmacopoeias of Austria, Hungary, Poland, and Switzerland. The

Rumanian pharmacopoeia still listed the volatile oil.

One of the less-glorious wounds yarrow was supposed to heal was a nosebleed, and the plant was in fact called nosebleed in the sixteenth century. The leaves were supposed to be crushed and packed into the nostrils.

In some accounts, however, the plant was supposed to *cause* nosebleeds. Why would anyone want to *cause* a nosebleed? Well, it was an old treatment for a headache. And it was a peculiar alternative to pulling the petals from a daisy. According to the British herbalist Maude Grieve, some folks believed you could determine the devotion of a lover by poking a yarrow leaf up your nostril and twitching the leaf while saying, "Yarroway, Yarroway, bear a white blow; if my love love me, my nose will bleed now."

Other peculiar customs appear in yarrow's long history as a magic herb (which can't really be disentangled from its medicinal history). Yarrow was one of the herbs packed into Saxon amulets. There were amulets for protection from just about everything— blindness, robbers, even the barking of dogs. Witches used yarrows in making incantations, an association that may be the source for the common names devil's nettle, devil's plaything, and bad man's plaything.

Yarrow was sewn up in flannel and put under the pillow to make the sleeper dream a vision of his or her true love. However, if the sleeper dreamed of cabbages—not so remote a possibility given yarrow's leafy fragrance—then death or other serious misfortune was about to strike.

USES

Medicinal: Yarrows have been prescribed for just about every ailment at one time or another, but certain medicinal uses recur throughout history. And chemical analysis has detected some compounds that might explain, and validate, these applications.

For centuries, yarrows have been used on wounds, and in the 1950s an alkaloid from the plant was found to have some ability to make blood clot faster.

As far as yarrow's alleged ability to keep wounds from becoming inflamed, a volatile oil called azulene and related compounds have shown anti-inflammatory activity. Previous experimenters had produced conflicting results, perhaps because they used extracts from what are now classified as different species. *A. Millefolium* may be azulene-free and hence lacking anti-inflammatory properties. *A. Millefolium* var. *lanulosa* and *A. collina,* on the other hand, are supposed to contain azulene. Even within azulene-containing spe-

AMERICAN INDIAN USES FOR YARROW

abortive
analgesic
bloody urine
bowel complaints
bruises and sprains
burns
common cold
cramps in neck
dermatological aid
earache
emmenagogue
eyewash
febrifuge
headache
hemorrhage
indigestion
kidney aid
laxative
liver aid
sleep aid
sore throat
spiritual aid
spitting blood
stimulant and tonic
swollen tissues
tea for sickness
toothache
wounds and sores

517

YARROW—continued

acrid
alterative
aromatic
astringent
cathartic
detergent
diuretic
stimulant and tonic
stomachic
tonic

cies, the chemical content varies with part of the plant, its age, the season, and environmental conditions. Newly classified species have different percentages of volatile oils, and it could be that this variation accounts for the wide variety of uses to which yarrow has been put throughout history.

Research from the 1960s indicates that yarrow shows some antispasmodic effects, perhaps because of substances called flavonoids. The plant also has salicylic acid derivatives (salicylic acid is aspirin), and these may account for its use in treating fevers and reducing pain. Finally, the plant contains some thujone, which in sufficient quantities can cause abortions. Perhaps this explains the plant's use in treating various women's complaints.

Toxicity: Yarrow is not generally considered toxic, but some people seem to be allergic to it, breaking out when in contact with the plant or showing positive patch test reactions. Its effect may be cumulative: An exposure that is too slight to cause a reaction may nevertheless increase a person's sensitivity.

Ornamental: At any time during the late spring and summer, there's at least one kind of yarrow blooming in herb grower Fairman Jayne's North Carolina garden. He grows six varieties at his Sandy Mush Herb Farm.

Yarrows can be especially attractive when mixed into a perennial border with other plants, says Jayne. Varieties offer a range of effects, from the airy, white, open flower heads of Angel's Breath to the tight, flat heads of the pink varieties (Jayne describes their color as "cerise"). Pick faded blossoms to extend blooming.

Cosmetic: Astringent and cleansing, yarrow is recommended for use in skin lotions. (See the entry Lotions from Herbs for more information.)

Craft: Yarrow dries beautifully. Try either the pink or the yellow cultivars in herb and flower arrangements.

Dye: The flowers yield a yellow dye to wool mordanted with alum. Using the whole plant, olive is obtained in iron-mordanted wool.

Companion planting: Gardeners will tell you that yarrow increases the essential oils of other herbs when planted among them. Research hasn't confirmed or denied this claim. Yarrow does benefit the garden by attracting beneficial insects, including predatory wasps and lady beetles.

CULTIVATION

Yarrows can be divided in the spring or fall, and most can be grown easily from seed. They appreciate full sun and adapt to a variety of soils, perhaps excluding soggy ground. The plants' roots

GROWING CONDITIONS

- Plant hardiness zone 2.

- Soil pH 6.1.

- Moderately rich, well-drained soil.

- Full sun.

will help hold the soil on steep banks. Ground covers of yarrow can be mowed once a year.

The only yarrow likely to give anyone trouble is the creeping wooly yarrow (*A. tomentosa* 'Nana'), says Fairman Jayne. The creeping plant will rot unless it has good drainage. He places his plants on top of a rock wall where they can bask in full, hot sun. Wall-less gardeners could build up a mound for the plant, he suggests, letting it creep downward and find its natural boundary where soil conditions no longer suit it.

As for invasiveness, Jayne says that the white and pink yarrows will spread, though not relentlessly. He just pulls out the runners when he's nearby and thus easily manages to keep them under control. In his experience, the other kinds "stay put."

The old, original yarrow, *A. Millefolium,* is by far the most widespread species in Europe. It was introduced to North America, where it spread across Canada and the northern United States. In these areas in particular, what looks like yarrow may indeed be the European plant. However, it may also be a native American species, *A. Millefolium* var. *lanulosa,* which looks almost exactly like it but has 36 instead of 54 chromosomes. Both species grow in sunny, open places like roadsides or weedy meadows.

Pests and diseases: Yarrows suffer few problems but may occasionally be bothered by powdery mildew, rust, or stem rot. (See the entry Growing Herbs for information on controlling diseases.)

519

YOHIMBE

Pausinystalia johimbe   **Rubiaceae**

The bark of this tropical tree has been ingested, sniffed, smoked, and rubbed on the body for its effect on sexual interest and performance. Like many aphrodisiacs, however, yohimbe bark is not all that it's cracked up to be. It may cause temporary impotence—certainly a step in the wrong direction—and other far more serious side effects.

HISTORY

The bark has long been valued as an aphrodisiac, in demand the world over. Strangely, there has been little scientific work on just how it works. The bark is taken as a sweetened tea, or smoked, or sniffed as a hallucinogen. The plant yields yohimbine, which in the form of an alkaloidal salt, yohimbine hydrochloride, has been used in prescription formulas intended to improve sexual performance. Scientific papers discuss the effects of such yohimbe extracts on animals, but there has been no reported study of the bark extracts.

USES

Medicinal: The drug yohimbine dilates the blood vessels of the skin and mucous membranes, thus bringing the blood closer to the surface of the sex organs and simultaneously lowering blood pressure. The problem with yohimbe as an aphrodisiac is that if the blood pressure is normally low, fatigue may produce temporary impotence instead of vigorous performance. It also increases the reflex excitability of the lower region of the spinal cord. Its local anesthetic effect is said to be equal to cocaine, but it is longer lasting.

Yohimbe has been used to lower blood pressure, as an antidiuretic, for angina pectoris, and for treatment of atherosclerosis and impotence, but there is no proof it is effective in these uses.

There are many cautions to exercise in considering the use of yohimbe. It should never be taken at the same time as foods or substances containing tyramine, an amino acid. Liver, cheese, and red wine are in this category, as are certain diet aids and decongestants. People should avoid it if suffering from any of several problems: hypotension; diabetes; heart, liver, or kidney disease; and nervous disorders, especially schizophrenia. Anxiety reactions, and in severe cases, psychosis, have been produced by yohimbine.

Symptoms of overdose include weakness, nervous stimulation followed by paralysis, fatigue, stomach disorders, and ultimately, death. The Food and Drug Administration considers yohimbine an unsafe drug.

DESCRIPTION

Yohimbe is a tree of tropical West Africa.

RANGE

Yohimbe grows wild in Cameroon, Gabon, and Zaire.

ZATAR

Thymbra spicata   Labiatae

When an Arabic-speaking person utters the name of this herb, it sounds, to an English-speaking person, as though it had three syllables, za-a-tar, although it has only two. Zatar has an exotic name because it is exotic. You won't find too many herb farms that sell it (although Cyrus Hyde grows it at Well-Sweep Herb Farm in Port Murray, New Jersey). Most of the zatar plants grown in North America have been brought here from the Middle East, particularly Lebanon and Syria, where, though it is sometimes grown in gardens, it is usually collected from the wild. As foreign as this herb is, however, you can find it in backyard gardens in Middle Eastern neighborhoods.

USES

The name zatar refers to the species *Thymbra spicata,* but it has also been used to describe varieties of thyme and oregano. When you purchase zatar, be certain you are getting the herb you want.

Culinary: Zatar tastes like hearty thyme and is famous in Arabic and North African cooking. It can be used with chicken, fish, and beef; on cheeses; in breads, breadsticks, rice, cracked wheat, and couscous; and with yogurt sauces and soups.

Zatar zips up eggplant, cucumbers, summer squash, carrots, onions, tomatoes, snap beans, potatoes, peas, parsley, chilies, sweet peppers, scallions, spinach, shell beans, and lentils.

Joe Vallan, the owner of Soumaya and Sons Bakery in Allentown, Pennsylvania, describes a recipe that calls for blending zatar with sesame seeds, sumac (*Rhus coriaria,* which can be purchased in Middle Eastern groceries and bakeries), salt, and olive oil. The mixture is used as a dip for bread or is spread on bread and baked in the oven. A variation of the recipe substitutes ground *Origanum syriacum* for salt and is spread over flat loaves of bread. This savory treat is the national snack of Lebanon.

Available commercially: Dried, often with sesame seeds. It can be found in shops and bakeries that specialize in Middle Eastern foods.

Substitute: Dried thyme.

CULTIVATION

According to Cyrus Hyde, zatar can be propagated from cuttings as well as seed. He grows his in a fertile, well-drained soil in a sunny location. Cy brings his zatar in for the winter. Kim Kuebel, who grows zatar in Boerne, Texas, supports this. The herb overwinters in Texas, but he recommends protecting it from a hard freeze in areas that experience harsh winters.

DESCRIPTION

A low-growing shrub of the mint family, zatar possesses the characteristic square stem. The branches are erect and slightly hairy. (See photo on page 99.)

Flowers: Pink, tubular corolla to ⅝ in. long; hairs on inner surface of corolla; upper lip larger than lower lip; in headlike cluster or spike 1–4 in. long.

Leaves: Smooth, entire, sessile, linear, ¼–⅝ in. long.

Fruit: Four nutlets.

Height: To 22 in.

FLOWERING

Summer.

RANGE

Native from Greece to Israel.

GROWING CONDITIONS

- Soil pH: alkaline to neutral.
- Fertile, well-drained soil.
- Full sun.

BIBLIOGRAPHY

BOOKS

Angier, Bradford. *Field Guide to Medicinal Wild Plants.* Harrisburg, Pa.: Stackpole Books, 1978.

Audubon Society. *The Audubon Society Field Guide to North American Wildflowers.* New York: Alfred A. Knopf, 1979.

Bacon, Richard M. *The Forgotten Arts. Growing, Gardening and Cooking with Herbs.* Dublin, N.H.: Yankee Books, 1972.

Bailey, L. H. *The Standard Cyclopedia of Horticulture.* 3 vols. New York: Macmillan Co., 1950.

Balsam, M. S., and Edward Sagarin. *Cosmetics: Science and Technology.* New York: Wiley-Interscience, 1972.

Bayard, Tania. *Sweet Herbs and Sundry Flowers: Medieval Gardens and the Gardens of the Cloisters.* New York: Metropolitan Museum of Art, 1985.

Beston, Henry. *Herbs and the Earth.* Garden City, N.Y.: Doubleday, Doran and Co., 1935.

Blunt, Wilfrid, and Sandra Raphael. *The Illustrated Herbal.* New York: Thames and Hudson, 1979.

Bonar, Ann. *The Macmillan Treasury of Herbs.* New York: Macmillan Co., 1985.

Boxer, Arabella, and Philippa Back. *The Herb Book.* London: Octopus Books, 1980.

Bricklin, Mark. *The Practical Encyclopedia of Natural Healing.* Emmaus, Pa.: Rodale Press, 1983.

————. *Rodale's Encyclopedia of Natural Home Remedies: Hundreds of Simple Healing Techniques for Everyday Illness and Emergencies.* Emmaus, Pa.: Rodale Press, 1982.

Buchman, Dian Dincin. *Feed Your Face.* London: Duckworth, 1973.

————. *Herbal Medicine: The Natural Way to Get Well and Stay Well.* New York: David McKay Co., 1979.

Bush-Brown, James and Louise. *America's Garden Book.* New York: Charles Scribner's Sons, 1980.

Carr, Anna. *Good Neighbors: Companion Planting for Gardeners.* Emmaus, Pa.: Rodale Press, 1985.

Clarkson, Rosetta E. *Green Enchantment: The Magic Spell of Gardens.* New York: Macmillan Co., 1940.

————. *Herbs and Savory Seeds: Culinaries, Simples, Sachets, Decoratives.* New York: Dover Publications, 1972.

Craker, Lyle E., and James E. Simon, eds. *Herbs, Spices and Medicinal Plants: Recent Advances in Botany, Horticulture and Pharmacology,* Vol. 1. Phoenix, Ariz.: Oryx Press, 1986.

de Bray, Lys. *The Wild Garden: An Illustrated Guide to Weeds.* New York: Mayflower Books, 1978.

Duke, James A. *CRC Handbook of Medicinal Herbs.* Boca Raton, Fla.: CRC Press, 1985.

Dye Plants and Dyeing—A Handbook. New York: Brooklyn Botanic Garden, 1976.

Dyer, T. F. Thiselton. *The Folk-lore of Plants.* New York, D. Appleton and Co., 1889.

Everett, Thomas H. *The New York Botanical Garden Illustrated Encyclopedia of Horticulture.* New York: Garland Publishing, 1981.

Fernald, Merritt Lyndon, ed. *Gray's Manual of Botany.* 8th ed. New York: D. Van Nostrand Co., 1950.

Fettner, Ann Tucker. *Potpourri, Incense and Other Fragrant Concoctions.* New York: Workman Publishing Co., 1977.

Foster, Gertrude B. *Park's Success with Herbs.* Greenwood, S.C.: George W. Park Seed Co., 1980.

Foster, Steven. *Herbal Bounty.* Salt Lake City, Utah: Gibbs M. Smith/ Peregrine Smith Books, 1984.

Freethy, Ron. *From Agar to Zenry: A Book of Plant Uses, Names and Folklore.* Dover, N.H.: Tanager Books, 1985.

Garland, Sarah. *The Herb Garden.* New York: Penguin Books, 1984.

Gibbons, Euell. *Stalking the Healthful Herbs.* New York: David McKay Co., 1966.

Goodwin, Jill. *A Dyer's Manual.* London: Pelham Books, 1982.

Gouzil, Dezerina. *Mother Nature's Herbs and Teas.* Willits, Calif.: Oliver Press, 1975.

Grae, Ida. *Nature's Colors: Dyes from Plants.* New York: Collier Books, 1979.

Grieve, Mrs. M. *A Modern Herbal.* 2 vols. New York: Dover Publications, 1971.

Griggs, Barbara. *Green Pharmacy: A History of Herbal Medicine.* New York: Viking Press, 1981.

Hampstead, Marilyn. *The Basil Book.* New York: Pocket Books, Division of Simon and Schuster, 1984.

Hancock, Ken. *Feverfew: Your Headache May Be Over.* New Canaan, Conn.: Keats Publishing, 1986.

Harris, Ben Charles. *Ben Charles Harris's Comfrey: What You Need to Know.* New Canaan, Conn.: Keats Publishing, 1982.

Heiser, Charles B., Jr. *Nightshades.* San Francisco: W. H. Freeman and Co. 1969.

Hemphill, John and Rosemary. *Herbs Their Cultivation and Usage.* New York: Sterling Publishing Co., 1983.

Hériteau, Jacqueline. *Potpourris and Other Fragrant Delights.* New York: Simon and Schuster, 1973.

Hills, Lawrence D. *Comfrey: Fodder, Food and Remedy.* New York: Universe Books, 1976.

———. *Comfrey the Herbal Healer.* Bocking, Braintree, Essex, England: Henry Doubleday Research Association, n.d.

———. *Comfrey Report: The Story of the World's Fastest Protein Builder.* Bocking, Braintree, Essex, England: Henry Doubleday Research Association, 1974.

Hobbs, Christopher. *Milk Thistle: The Liver Herb.* Capitola, Calif.: Native Herb Co., 1984.

Jacobs, Betty E. M. *Growing and Using Herbs Successfully.* Charlotte, Vt.: Garden Way Publishing, 1981.

———. *Growing Herbs and Plants for Dyeing.* Tarzana, Calif.: Select Books, 1977.

Keller, Mitzie. *Mysterious Herbs and Roots: Ancient Secrets for Beautie Health, Magick, Prevention and Youth.* Culver City, Calif.: Peace Press, 1978.

Keys, John D. *Chinese Herbs.* Rutland, Vt.: Charles E. Tuttle Co., 1976.

Krochmal, Connie. *A Guide to Natural Cosmetics.* New York: Quadrangle/New York Times Book Co., 1973.

Krochmal, Arnold, and Connie Krochmal. *A Field Guide to Medicinal Plants.* New York: Time Books, 1984.

Lampe, Kenneth, M.D. *AMA Handbook of Poisonous and Injurious Plants.* Chicago: American Medical Association, 1985.

Lees-Milne, Alvilde, and Rosemary Verey, eds. *The Englishman's Garden.* Boston: David R. Godine, 1983.

———. *The Englishwoman's Garden.* London: Chatto and Windus, 1983.

Leighton, Ann. *Early American Gardens: "For Meate or Medicine."* Boston: Houghton Mifflin Co., 1970.

Lesch, Alma. *Vegetable Dyeing: 151 Color Recipes for Dyeing Yarns and Fabrics with Natural Materials.* New York: Watson-Guptill Publications, 1970.

Le Strange, Richard. *A History of Herbal Plants.* New York: Arco Publishing Co., 1977.

Lewis, Walter H., et al. *Plants Affecting Man's Health.* New York: John Wiley & Sons, 1977.

Lust, John. *The Herb Book.* New York: B. Lust Publications, 1974.

McLean, Teresa. *Medieval English Gardens.* New York: Viking Press, 1980.

Miller, Amy Bess. *Shaker Herbs: A History and a Compendium.* New York: Clarkson N. Potter, 1976.

Mills, Simon, M.A., M.N.I.M.H. *The Dictionary of Modern Herbalism: A Comprehensive Guide to Practical Herbal Therapy.* New York: Thorsons Publishers, 1985.

Moore, Michael. *Medicinal Plants of the Mountain West.* Santa Fe: Museum of New Mexico Press, 1979.

Moring, Stephen E. *Echinacea: A Natural Immune Stimulant and Treatment for Viral Infection.* Sunnyvale, Calif.: Botica Analyticum, 1984.

Morton, Julia F., D.Sc., F.L.S. *Major Medicinal Plants: Botany, Culture and Uses.* Springfield, Ill.: Charles C. Thomas, 1977.

Natural Plant Dyeing—A Handbook. New York: Brooklyn Botanic Garden, 1973.

Ohrbach, Barbara M. *Scented Room: Cherchez's Book of Dried Flowers, Fragrance, and Potpourri.* New York: Clarkson N. Potter, 1986.

Oliver, Paula. *The Herb Gardener's Resource Guide.* 2d ed. Shevlin, Minn.: Northwind Farm, 1985.

Paterson, Wilma. *A Country Cup: Old and New Recipes for Drinks of All Kinds Made from Wild Plants and Herbs.* London: Pelham Books, 1980.

Peterson, Roger Tory and Margaret McKenny. *A Field Guide to Wildflowers of Northeastern and Northcentral North America.* Boston: Houghton Mifflin Co., 1968.

Potterton, David, ed. *Culpeper's Color Herbal.* New York: Sterling Publishing Co., 1983.

Robertson, Seonaid. *Dyes from Plants.* New York: Van Nostrand Reinhold, 1973.

Rogers, Jean. *Cooking with the Healthful Herbs.* Emmaus, Pa.: Rodale Press, 1983.

Rose, Jeanne. *Ask Jeanne Rose about Herbs.* New Canaan, Conn.: Keats Publishing, 1984.

———. *The Herbal Body Book.* New York: Grosset & Dunlap, 1976.

———. *Herbs and Things: Jeanne Rose's Herbal.* New York: Grosset & Dunlap, 1972.

———. *Jeanne Rose's Herbal Guide to Inner Health.* New York: Grosset & Dunlap, 1979.

———. *Kitchen Cosmetics.* San Francisco: Panjandrum/Aris Books, 1978.

Rosengarten, Frederic, Jr. *The Book of Spices.* New York: Jove Publications, 1973.

Sanderson, Liz. *How To Make Your Own Herbal Cosmetics: The Natural Way to Beauty.* New Canaan, Conn.: Keats Publishing, 1979.

Santillo, Humbart, B.S., M.H. *Natural Healing with Herbs.* Prescott Valley, Ariz.: Hohm Press, 1984.

Schultes, Richard Evans, and Albert Hofmann. *Plants of the Gods: Origins of Hallucinogenic Use.* New York: McGraw-Hill, 1979.

Seymour, John. *Gardener's Delight.* New York: Harmony Books, 1979.

Shaudys, Phyllis V. *The Pleasure of Herbs: A Month-by-Month Guide to Growing, Using, and Enjoying Herbs.* Charlotte, Vt.: Garden Way Publishing, 1986.

Simmons, Adelma Grenier. *Herb Gardening in Five Seasons.* New York: Hawthorn Books, 1964.

Simon, James E., Alena F. Chadwick, and Lyle E. Craker. *Herbs: An Indexed Bibliography 1971-1980.* Hamden, Conn.: Shoe String Press, 1984.

Spoerke, David G., Jr. *Herbal Medications.* Santa Barbara: Woodbridge Press, 1980.

Stuart, Malcolm, ed. *VNR Color Dictionary of Herbs and Herbalism.* New York: Van Nostrand Reinhold, 1979.

Swanson, Faith H., and Virginia B. Rady. *Herb Garden Design.* Hanover, N.H.: University Press of New England, 1984.

Thomson, William A. R., M.D. *Herbs That Heal.* New York: Charles Scribner's Sons, 1976.

———. *Medicines from the Earth: A Guide to Healing Plants.* San Francisco: Harper & Row, 1983.

Thorpe, Patricia. *Everlastings: The Complete Book of Dried Flowers.* New York: Facts on File Publications, 1985.

Tisserand, Robert B. *The Art of Aromatherapy.* New York: Inner Traditions International, 1979.

Tolley, Emelie, and Chris Mead. *Herbs: Gardens, Decorations, and Recipes.* New York: Clarkson N. Potter, 1986.

Tyler, Varro E., Ph.D. *The Honest Herbal.* Philadelphia: George F. Stickley Co., 1982.

———. *Hoosier Home Remedies*. West Lafayette, Ind.: Purdue University Press, 1985.

Verey, Rosemary. *Classic Garden Design*. New York: Congdon and Weed, distributed by St. Martin's Press, 1984.

———. *The Scented Garden*. New York: Van Nostrand Reinhold, 1981.

Weiner, Michael A., M.S., M.A., Ph.D., with Janet Weiner. *Weiner's Herbal*. Briarcliff Manor, N.Y.: Stein and Day, 1980.

Weiss, Gaea, and Shandor Weiss. *Growing and Using the Healing Herbs*. Emmaus, Pa.: Rodale Press, 1985.

Wheelwright, Edith Grey. *Medicinal Plants and Their History*. New York: Dover Publications, 1974.

NEWSLETTERS AND PERIODICALS

The American Herb Association Quarterly Newsletter. The American Herb Association, P.O. Box 353, Rescue, CA 95672 (quarterly).

The Business of Herbs. Blue Ridge Press, P.O. Box 559, Madison, VA 22727 (bimonthly).

Coltsfoot. Rte. 1, Box 3BA, Shipman, VA 22971 (quarterly).

Foster's Herb Business Bulletin. P.O. Box 32, Berryville, AR 72616 (four times a year).

The Herbal Gazette. Box 491, Mt. Kisco, NY 10549 (bimonthly).

Herbalgram. Herb News, P.O. Box 12602, Austin, TX 78711 (quarterly).

The Herbalist Almanac. Indiana Botanic Gardens, Hammond, IN 46325 (annually).

The Herbal Technologist. 6739 W. 44th Ave., Wheatridge, CO 80023 (monthly).

Herbal Thymes. 39 Reed St., Marcellus, NY 13101 (quarterly).

Herban Greenhouse News. Herban Greenhouse, Rte. 1, Box 130, New Hartford, CT 06057 (8 issues annually).

The Herbarist. The Herb Society of America, 2 Independence Ct., Concord, MA 01742 (annually).

The Herb Basket. P.O. Box 1773, Brattleboro, VT 05301 (bimonthly).

Herb Blerbs. Pike's Peak Herb Association, P.O. Box 38264, Colorado Springs, CO 80937 (quarterly).

Herbletter. 4974 Riverdale Rd. S., Salem, OR 97302 (quarterly).

The Herb Magazine. P.O. Box 722, Boulder, CO 80830 (bimonthly).

Herb Market Report. Organization for the Advancement of Knowledge, 1305 Vista Dr., Grants Pass, OR 97527 (monthly).

The Herb Newsletter. P.O. Box 42236, Tacoma, WA 98442 (10 issues annually).

Herb of the Month Club. Berry Patch Herbs, Box 1000, Atkinson, NH 03811 (monthly).

The Herb Quarterly. Uphill Press, Inc., West St., P.O. Box 275, Newfane, VT 05345-0275.

The Herb Report. P.O. Box 95-3333, Stuart, FL 33495 (monthly).

The Herb, Spice, and Medicinal Plant Digest. L. E. Craker, Department of Plant and Soil Sciences, Stockbridge Hall, University of Massachusetts, Amherst, MA 01003 (quarterly).

HortIdeas, Gregory and Patricia Y. Williams, Rte. 1, Box 302, Black Lick Road, Gravel Switch, KY 40328 (monthly).

Living with Herbs. 71 Little Fresh Pond Rd., Southampton, NY 11968 (monthly).

Plant Lore. 16 Oak St., Geneseo, NY 14454 (semi-annually).

Potpourri from Herbal Acres. Pine Row Publications, Box 428, Washington Crossing, PA 18977 (quarterly).

Southern Herbs. P.O. Box 3722, Winter Springs, FL 32708 (quarterly).

Today's Herbs. BiWorld, P.O. Box 1143, Orem, UT 84057 (monthly).

The Tymes. 2219 Long Hill Rd., Guilford, CT 06437 (monthly).

INDEX

Page numbers for illustrations and photographs appear in **boldface** type; page numbers for tables and lists appear in *italics*.

526

539

543

INDEX – continued